The Hamlyn Guide to
HOME
MAINTENANCE

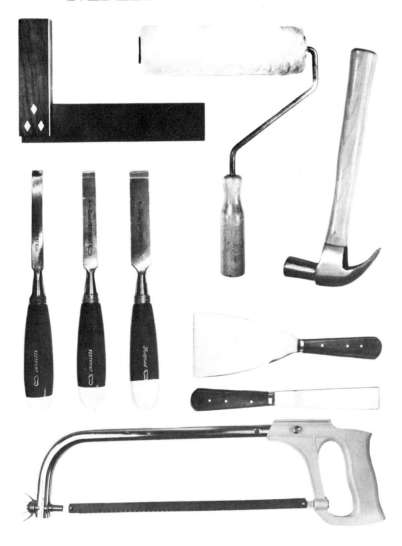

Home Repair and Maintenance
Tony Wilkins

Home Building Work
Bill Goodson

Home Plumbing
Ernest Hall FRSH

Home Electrics
Geoffrey Burdett

Home Decorating
Tony Wilkins

The Hamlyn Guide to
HOME
MAINTENANCE

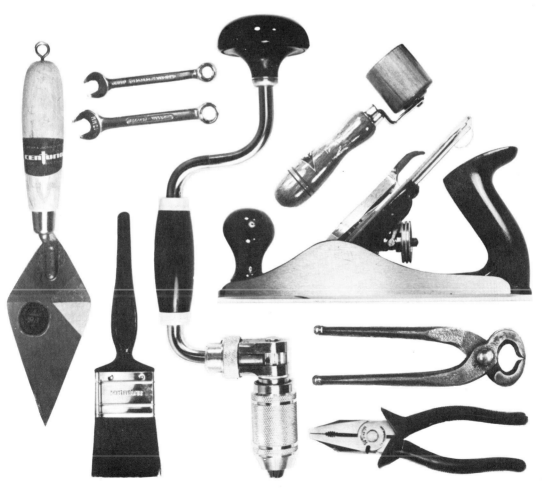

HAMLYN

This edition first
published 1979 by
Hamlyn Publishing
Bridge House, London Road, Twickenham, Middlesex

7th impression 1986

ISBN 0 600 36393 7

Printed in Spain

D. L. TF. 644-1984

Preface

For most people, the purchase of a home of one's own is the biggest financial investment we will make in a lifetime, and we are likely to spend most of our working life paying for it. Even so, there are few who regret the decision to get a place of their very own. A place you can call home; where you can shut the door on the world.

Unfortunately, beneath the sentiment lies the hard reality. All property, from the most humble up to the palatial, depreciates with the passing of time. Wood tries to rot away; metal rusts; masonry flakes and cracks; colours fade. When taking on the responsibility of a home of your own, accept the fact that unless you spend time and money on maintenance, your asset will quickly depreciate in value. The more the neglect, the faster the process of breakdown will move.

Regular periods of maintenance and redecoration are of far more value than infrequent purges. The costs are less; the work is easier, and the chances of the weather really getting into the actual fabric of the house are reduced.

Maintenance is also part of the investment programme, because when you come to sell your property you can be sure it will hold its value, and that it will stand up to the private survey.

This book has been planned in five main sections: 1 Home Repair and Maintenance; 2 Home Building Work; 3 Home Plumbing; 4 Home Electrics; 5 Home Decorating; and provides comprehensive information on all aspects of home maintenance and home improvements.

The purpose of Section 1 is twofold. First to point out the many areas where repair work and maintenance may be necessary, and second to introduce to you the tools and materials you will need to carry out the work.

In the latter respect we are very privileged. There is now a whole d-i-y industry geared to meeting our needs in both excellent tools and materials. Processes have been very much simplified, and products are designed to be effective and easy to use. In many cases throughout the text you will find that detailed instructions on the use of particular tools and materials are not given in full. This is because clear instructions are given with the products when purchased, and it is a waste of space to repeat them here. It is vital that instructions given are studied carefully and carried out faithfully, for it is in this area that so much d-i-y work founders. Poor preparation, careless application, the use of the wrong tools, all add up to an inferior job.

When you come to the larger jobs once looked upon as the preserve of the tradesman, the hire shop comes into its own. These shops will offer you the same facilities that they offer to the professional, giving clear instructions on equipment you would not want to buy, but which can take the strain out of the work and speed it up very considerably.

Section 2 gives basic information on the main building crafts, including carpentry and joinery. Provided you are reasonably handy with ordinary tools, you should have no difficulty in making a satisfactory job of those building additions and improvements to the house and garden which you have long desired.

The construction of brick, timber and precast buildings is fully described, and the projects covered in detail include sheds, a home workshop, a brick garage and a small conservatory, as well as many simple indoor improvements such as built-in cupboards and wardrobes. The basic requirements of the Planning Regulations and Building Regulations (both of which often cause confusion to the amateur) are also explained.

Section 3 has been written for the householder who would like to know how his plumbing system works, how it can be improved and how to diagnose and remedy faults. The information given will prove invaluable whether you are a d-i-y enthusiast or a home owner who wishes to do no more than to discuss intelligently with your builder aspects of domestic hot and cold water supply or drainage.

If you wish to convert your lavatory suite from high level to low level, to provide an extra washbasin or shower, or even to install a complete hot water system, you will find the best way to set about these tasks in Section 3. On the other hand, if you are unlikely to attempt anything more ambitious than rewashering a tap, silencing a noisy ball-valve or protecting your plumbing system from frost, you will also find the answers to these simple problems.

In every home, at one time or another, some electrical job has to be done. It may be only replacing a light bulb, fitting a plug on the flex of a new electrical appliance or table lamp, or mending a fuse when part of the lighting is blacked out. Or you may suspect the wiring of your house needs renewing or you wish to install lighting and heating in a new extension, or lighting points and sockets need to be moved. Section 4 tells you in simple language how to go about these tasks and many others, safely and competently.

Home decorating can be a very personal matter as far as colour, pattern texture and finish are concerned, but there are essential basic techniques which must be mastered in order to get the very best from the available materials. Preparation is 90 per cent of the battle, and if this work is not done well, everything following will be second-best.

Section 5 has been written to help you get to know the surfaces you will encounter; how to clean them, strip them, or, if necessary, replace them. You can also learn what tools to use for which job, which paints go where, plus some useful short cuts which will save much time.

Contents

Section 1

Home Repair and Maintenance

FOR YOUR REFERENCE

Below is listed a good basic tool kit which will see you through most repair jobs about the house. But you will find many others which can be added as you progress in certain fields. All those mentioned here are referred to in the following chapter.

Work bench, fixed or portable
Steel rule
Steel tape
Try square
Tenon saw
Hacksaw and blades
General purpose saw
Cross cut saw
Plane with disposable blades
Shaping tools
Wheel brace and set of twist drills
Screwdrivers, for single slot, Phillips and Pozidriv screws
Bench vice—can be clamp-on
Wrench
Pincers
Pliers, large and fine nose
Claw hammer
Pin hammer
Chisels
Craft knife
Masonry drills
Adjustable spanner
Soldering iron
Wire brush
Safety glasses
Files
Spirit level
Marking knife
Marking gauge
Chain wrench
Tinsnips
Putty knife
Nail punch
Bevel
Smooth plane
Brace and set of bits

Spiral ratchet screwdriver
G cramps
Club hammer
Glass cutter
Tile cutter
Trowels, large and small
Soft face hammer
Tape—surveyor's
Grindstone
Blowtorch
Welder
Nut splitter
Riveting kit
Case opener
Power drill
— plus the following attachments:
    Sander
    Saw—circular
    Saw—jig
    Vertical drill stand
    Spray gun
    Rasps
    Flexible drive
    Speed reducer
    Right-angle drive

Integral power tools include:
    Jigsaw
    Circular saw
    Band saw
    Router
    Belt sander
    Grinder
    Floor sander
    Orbital sander
    Planer

Chapter 1
The tools you will need

A good selection of tools is essential for repair and maintenance work. If you are just setting up a kit, aim to get into good habits and use your tools for the job they were designed. A good chisel is not a screwdriver or a tyre lever. A coal hammer is not designed to drive nails, and pliers won't undo nuts very well. I have seen all these tools used in the ways described!

Buy the very best tools you can afford— even if it means buying less. A good tool will last more than a lifetime if looked after properly, and it will do a job well. Cheap, bargain-price tools may range from inefficient to dangerous, and in the long run they save no money as they will need replacing.

Store your tools so that they are easy to find. Ensure that they do not bang against each other and become dull or blunt, and keep them dry so that they do not rust. Keep edge tools sharp at all times, for apart from cutting badly, a blunt tool is dangerous in that it is much more prone to slipping.

If you are unable to sharpen your own saws and drills, take them to a good tool shop and have the job done properly. It makes an incredible difference to the efficiency. Remember that some tools, like chisels and plane irons, still come needing a final sharpening. For this you will need a stone, and a simple sharpening jig which holds a blade at the correct angle while it is rubbed on the stone.

Tool safety

When using tools, it is absolutely vital to cultivate the right attitude, for if used thoughtlessly or carelessly they can be dangerous. Make sure all tools are kept out of the reach of small children. Do not allow children in your working area unless under supervision.

Any tools connected to the electricity supply should be disconnected if left, even if for a few moments. Small children are inquisitive, and this could lead to dreadful accidents. Keep soldering irons out of reach while cooling; they are extremely hot even when they appear cold.

Some of the tools you will need. Buy the best you can afford

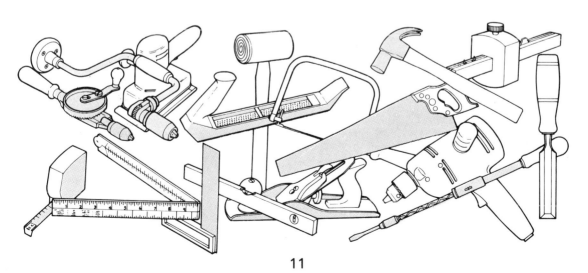

Where a tool is held in one hand—for example a knife or chisel—always cut *away* from your other hand. This means siting it behind the direction of cut. Never ignore or remove guards, and when using a tool like a power saw, use scrap wood to push short pieces past the blade. Take extreme care with abrasive cutting discs, these are as lethal as any saw blade, yet there is no form of guard supplied when used in a power tool.

Always wear protective glasses when doing such jobs as wire-brushing metal or masonry or when using a grinding wheel. Similarly protect your eyes when using chemicals such as paint stripper or rust remover. Special safety goggles are sold by good tool shops which are light and easy to wear, yet which give excellent protection.

Never use chisels or files without a correct handle. The tang will drive into your hand very easily.

Always have adequate ventilation when using adhesives with heavy vapours, and never use petrol for cleaning. Take great care with blowtorches and never leave inflammable materials lying around.

One moment's thoughtfulness can save a lifetime of remorse.

Left, a rigid workbench for general repair work. Right, a useful folding workbench

Workbench

If you have room in a workshop or a large garage, a good solid workbench with a woodworker's vice and a small metalworker's vice will prove invaluable as a base for repair jobs. It should have a clear uncluttered top and stout legs which hold it firm when you are sawing or planing.

The great problem with a fixed bench is that it is often difficult to handle or turn long strips of material because of the proximity of the walls. It will help if there is room to pull the bench away from the wall.

Light is also important, and if daylight is not available, adequate artificial light is necessary. As well as fixed lights, adjustable lights are an asset so that you can lose awkward shadows.

In recent years the attitude towards the workbench has been transformed by the introduction of a portable bench. Adjustable to one of two heights, this has two large wood jaws which act as both powerful vice and working surface. Grooves in the jaws make it possible to hold bars or tubes, and special plastic stops can be positioned to hold sheet materials.

The beauty of this new approach is that the bench folds flat—small enough to be housed in the boot of a car, or hung out of the way on a garage wall. This means it

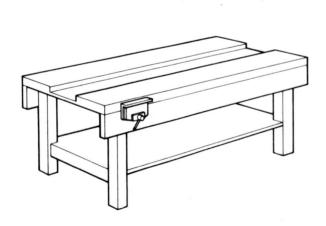

can be taken to the job in very many instances, whether indoors or out, to tackle anything from pipe threading to holding a door while it is trimmed to size.

As well as normal uses, various power tool equipment can be firmly held by making up suitable blocks of wood to be gripped in the jaws. For example, a vertical drill stand can be mounted on the bench top in this way, giving a very secure mounting.

Basic tools

Steel rule

This will be useful for accurate measurements over short distances, and it will offer a true edge for marking with a knife or cutting. Keep this blade slightly oiled to avoid rusting. A wood ruler is no substitute for this tool.

Steel tape

Choose a tape at least 3 m long, and preferably with both imperial and metric markings. One with a lock is useful so that the blade can be held extended with no hand on the other end. A dressmaking cloth tape is no substitute for a steel tape.

Try square

A try square will enable you to mark accurate right angles, provided it has a true surface to be positioned against. It is also useful for checking items like picture frames, table legs and shelf brackets before finally fixing in place. A try square with sliding metal rule is useful as this combines the services of square, depth gauge and 45° angle marking.

Tenon saw

This has fine teeth set in a blade strengthened by a special metal strip running along its back. Choose one about 25 cm long. It is ideal for cutting small wood sections and for joint cutting. It is not suited to cutting sheet materials as the stiffened back gets in the way.

Hacksaw

Frame sizes vary and it would pay you to invest in two. A small frame with blades to match for fine metal cutting work, and a larger frame and blades for heavier work and sheet cutting. Apart from the usual frames, simple grip handles are available which will hold a piece of hacksaw blade. Such a tool is very useful in confined areas where a normal frame would get in the way. Note that a blade mounted in this way is always fixed so the cut is made on the *pull* stroke and not the push. A push cut would bend the blade. When fixing blades in a hacksaw frame always obey the instructions with regard to blade tensioning.

Apart from standard blades, graduated blades, ranging from coarse to fine, are available. This simplifies starting a cut prior to rapid cutting of material.

Multi-purpose saw

This is a very useful new saw for d-i-y use, as it has a blade designed for cutting wood or metal. Most saws can be adjusted to any one of a number of blade angles in relation to the handle.

The saw is ideal for reducing second-hand timber which may well contain old nails. It is also useful for cutting sheet materials where the accuracy of a tenon saw is not required.

14

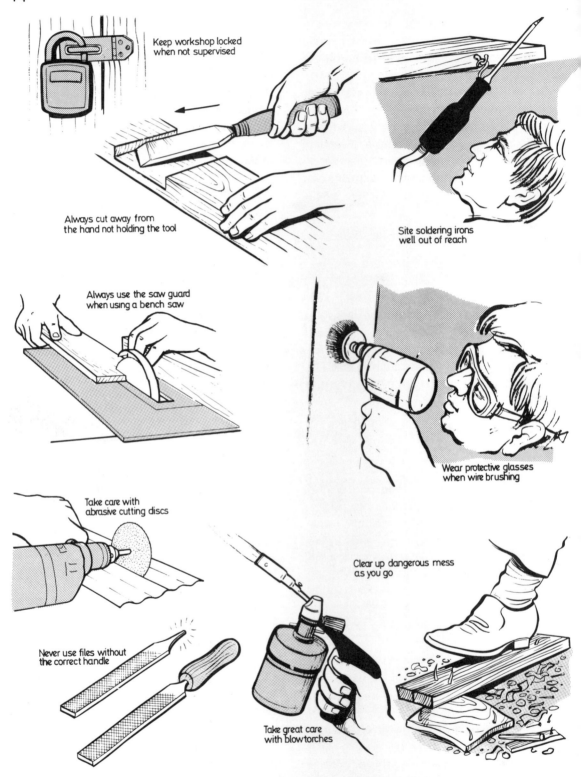

Keep workshop locked when not supervised

Always cut away from the hand not holding the tool

Site soldering irons well out of reach

Always use the saw guard when using a bench saw

Wear protective glasses when wire brushing

Take care with abrasive cutting discs

Never use files without the correct handle

Take great care with blow torches

Clear up dangerous mess as you go

Care and safety is important. Here are a few tips to keep you accident-free

Cross-cut saw

This saw, about 60 cm long, is designed for general wood cutting mainly across the grain of the wood. Its teeth are designed to cut through the wood fibres; it does not work very efficiently along the wood grain. If you plan to do along-grain cutting quite often, a rip saw should be added to your kit. It should not be used on timber containing nails as the teeth will be very easily blunted or damaged.

Disposable blade plane

Another tool designed for the d-i-y enthusiast, this plane has blades rather resembling tough razor blades. It is easily adjusted, needs no sharpening, and as soon as a blade is blunted, it may be removed and a new one inserted.

For many d-i-y projects, prepared timber is accurate enough to make frames, without planing. But the plane comes into its own for fine cutting to size and making things fit accurately.

Shaping tools

Closely allied to the plane is the shaping tool which, without the finesse of a plane will remove timber quickly and accurately. It may also act as a rasp, shaping wood to any contour. If you examine the blade closely you will see the perforated blade has dozens of fine chisel-like blades which cut in turn into the wood. A special blade is produced for metal cutting.

Various sizes and shapes are available, and two or three will prove invaluable.

One type, with a rasp-like blade has a handle which swivels to form either a plane or file. The blade can also be tensioned to form a curve.

Wheel brace

When fixing timber, it is wise to pre-drill it so that no pressure is exerted by screws causing it to split. This rule also applies in hardwoods when nailing. For this drilling you need a wheel brace and a set of twist drills, which may also be used for drilling metal. Add a rose countersink bit so that the heads of countersunk screws can be taken flush with the surface of the wood.

Be gentle when drilling with very fine twist drills. They snap easily if the drill is moved out of vertical while drilling.

Screwdrivers

A collection of screwdrivers will be needed for various repair work, and the general rule is that the screwdriver tip should fit neatly into the slot and wherever possible fit the width of the slot. If the tip is too wide, it could damage the surrounding area and if too narrow, the tip will be strained and twisted. The tip should be square, with sharply defined edges.

For electrical work you will find drivers with insulated handles tested up to high voltages—but at no time should you use this as an excuse to touch live equipment. It is purely a safety measure. You will encounter three main slot designs today:

Single slot. The standard screw slot requiring a standard screwdriver.

Phillips cross slot. The screwdriver tip has a cruciform shape which fits into the slot, giving a far more positive location with no danger of slipping. These have been in use for many years.

Pozidriv screws. This has a more sophisticated cruciform slot with sloping sides and is gradually replacing the Phillips slot. If used with the best Pozidriv drivers, there is the considerable advantage that a

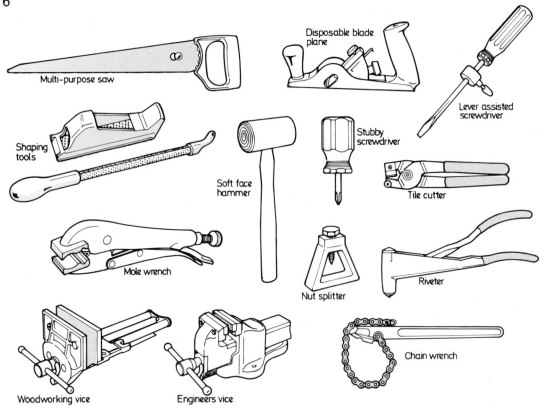

Multi-purpose saw

Disposable blade plane

Lever assisted screwdriver

Shaping tools

Stubby screwdriver

Soft face hammer

Tile cutter

Mole wrench

Nut splitter

Riveter

Woodworking vice

Engineers vice

Chain wrench

screw can be held locked on the end of the driver. This makes it possible to insert screws in awkward places, and apply pressure without holding the screw in your hand until it is started. Cheap Pozidriv drivers should be avoided as they lose this advantage through their poor fit.

You will need three drivers to cover the range of screw sizes in the Pozidriv range, and you will find a really fine tip invaluable when you encounter items like fine piano hinges and certain modern domestic appliances held by the smallest Pozidriv screws.

Back to drivers generally, a long blade helps with good driving, but there will be occasions when there is no room to manoeuvre a long blade. Add a stubby screwdriver or two to your kit to meet these circumstances—and a couple of right-angle driver blades for the really difficult locations.

If you need extra leverage to undo screws,

drivers are available which have a lever which can be slipped over the screwdriver blade. Undue force should never be used to do up screws. You can turn a head off a screw in this way.

Vice

Apart from a vice fixed to a workbench, it helps to have a clamp-on vice which can be fixed to any firm surface, such as a kitchen table. This will be useful for smaller indoor repair jobs. It is worth investing in a vice with interchangeable jaws, for when dealing with soft metals or plastics, rubber jaws are far kinder. Such a unit is not really designed for heavy jobs like sawing and planing, for the clamp cannot hold it firm enough.

Snap-on wrench

This type of wrench can be adjusted by means of a screw so that it will snap firmly on to any object, holding it in a vice-like grip. This has the advantage of leaving one hand free to hold the wrench without applying pressure while the other hand uses file or spanner. You can also buy a simple clamp into which the wrench drops, converting it into a miniature vice, ideal for holding small items while they are worked on.

It is not wise to use such a wrench as a spanner, as the hardened jaws can easily damage the flats of nuts.

Pincers

Pincers are very useful for pulling nails and tacks. Where you encounter large nails, use the claw of a claw hammer instead.

Pliers

You will need a heavy duty pair of pliers for gripping and pulling. The pliers will also have two keen cutting edges for cutting wire, plus two aligning slots which cut wire with a shearing action.

You should add a pair of fine-nose pliers for dealing with more delicate work. Never over-strain the nose section or they lose their effective grip.

Claw hammer

This combines a good striking face with a well-shaped claw with a vee slot. The slot should be sharp enough to grip a nail firmly while it is pulled. There is a choice of wood handle or hollow metal handle with rubber grip. The latter is the more comfortable tool to use.

Pin hammer

Designed to drive small nails, pins and tacks, this is a much lighter tool to handle. It should be kept for the lighter jobs and not abused. The flat end is called a pein, and it is designed to tap into place small nails and pins held between the fingers.

There is also a simple device called a pin push. This consists of a handle to which is attached a hollow tube in which a small nail can be held by magnetic attraction. A smart push on the handle is all that is required to drive the pin home.

Chisels

These do not get so much use as they used to when most things in wood were held together by joints cut with saw and chisel. Even so it will pay to have a set of three or four. Choose the bevel edge type in 6 mm, 12 mm, 19 mm and 25 mm sizes. Also buy plastic caps to protect the tips.

As mentioned earlier, chisels do not come sharpened, and you will need a stone and a honing gauge to get them in working order and to keep them really keen.

Buy a mallet with which to hit the chisel handle. Never use an ordinary hammer for this job.

Craft knife

Choose a type with interchangeable blades, and buy some spares. Take extreme care as such a knife is razor-sharp. Special blades for carpet and vinyl cutting, and for scoring laminates are available.

The carpet blade is curved and has a blunt tip so it cuts without touching the floor. A laminate blade scratches more than cuts, after which the laminate is snapped.

Masonry drills

When drilling into walls, you need to use special drills with a hardened tip. It is very easy to recognise the difference if you compare the tip with a standard twist drill. Buy good masonry drills, and get them sharpened as soon as they start to 'whistle' in a hole without cutting. You will find that the drills relate to wall plug and screw sizes, and you should always match drill, plug and screws when fixing.

Adjustable spanner

It is wise to buy two spanners. One for fine work and one for heavy work. Buy good spanners with no 'play' in the jaws and which need little effort to open and close.

If you plan to tackle plumbing work, you will need to invest in a much larger spanner or wrench, as most adjustable types do not open far enough to take the nuts on sanitary ware.

Soldering iron

A pencil-tip type of iron will cope with most domestic work, but it will not retain enough heat for dealing with large sheets of metal where there is considerable heat dissipation. Similarly, for really fine electronic work you will need a much smaller iron or you risk spoiling components and circuits.

Buy a roll of cored solder which has a flux inbuilt. The flux is necessary to ensure sound joints.

Wire brush

This is invaluable for removing scale from rust or brushing off surplus mortar, and it should always be used in conjunction with a pair of safety goggles or glasses. These protect the eyes against flying particles. Good goggles are shatterproof, even when struck quite hard.

Files

It will pay you to make a collection of files—from coarse to fine, flat, half-round, triangular and circular. These will prove invaluable for small adjustments to metal components. Never use files without a proper handle as the tangs can be very dangerous.

Files are for metalwork and have little effect on wood. The wood equivalent is the rasp, which has coarser teeth which are easier to clear. A couple of rasps are a good investment for fine shaping areas where a plane would be difficult to use. See also 'shaping tools' described earlier.

Spirit level

An invaluable tool for many jobs such as: checking that shelves are level; that wall tiles start horizontal; checking the fall on guttering and paths and that posts are set truly vertical. Choose a type with both horizontal and vertical checks and, for a little extra, you can have one with a bubble which can be set to any chosen angle. For checking over longer distances, you need a dead true batten on which to stand the level.

Marking knife

When working to fine tolerances, a pencil is not all that accurate. A marking knife is better—and it gives a start for things like the chisel and saw. Keep it for marking.

One or two woodworking pencils are an asset too. These have flat heads which can be sharpened to a fine spade-like point.

Additional tools

The tools mentioned so far will see you through most jobs, but there are others you will probably wish to add as your scope of work increases. Here are a few.

Marking gauge

If you plan to make joints, however simple, you will benefit from an adjustable marking gauge. The body can be adjusted, then a steel pin does the actual marking on the wood. There is a more elaborate model called the mortise gauge which has two pins, and as its name implies it is designed for marking out mortise and tenon joints.

Chain wrench

This is invaluable if you tackle any pipework, whether plumbing or central heating. It will grip or turn pipes of a wide range of diameters far more effectively than a wrench.

Tinsnips

Designed for cutting and trimming sheet metals, tinsnips are invaluable in many repair jobs where metal sheet or perforated materials are used.

Putty knife

The ideal tool for cutting and smoothing putty to the correct angle. There are variations on a theme now for amateur use to ensure the correct finishing angle, and one of these could be added if you do not have much success with a knife.

Nail punch

This is for setting nails below a surface without bruising the wood. It can be used wherever the nail heads are to be hidden by a wood stopping or filler.

Adjustable bevel

This tool is useful for fine woodworking where angles need to be accurately marked.

Smooth plane

Again, this is a tool for the woodworker who wants accurate surfaces. It is worth investing in a smooth plane 20 to 25 cm long. This is the shortest of the woodworking planes, and the enthusiast may wish to invest in a jack plane and a jointer plane. The general rule is that the longer the plane base, the more accurately it cuts flat surfaces.

Brace and bits

This is the tool that will be used for boring holes larger than can be tackled with twist drills. Its chuck is designed to take bits with square shanks, and bits come in a variety of sizes. Alternatively you can invest in one or two expansive bits, where the cutter can be adjusted to give holes of different sizes.

You can also buy screwdriver bits to fit the brace, and these are invaluable for turning large screws which have been over-tightened. Be warned when using such a driver to tighten screws that you can very easily turn the head off a screw with this tool.

Spiral ratchet screwdriver

The action used with this screwdriver is to pump the handle to and fro, which in turn causes the driver blade to rotate, either driving in or loosening the screw. It is ideal for repetition work with prepared holes. You have a choice of bits, including a small range of drills for fine hole making.

G cramps

Two or three of these will prove useful for holding components firmly to a base while being worked on. They offer a simple way of holding sheet materials while using a power drill to make holes or cut shapes. They will also kill vibration when using a power jig saw, and can be used to prevent a cut closing when sawing sheet material.

Club hammer

This hammer has a heavy, solid head designed to exert considerable force on steel chisels. Used with a steel chisel, it is the tool used for cutting paving slabs, splitting and channeling concrete or making holes in brickwork. Again, when using this tool, it is wise to wear safety glasses to avoid flying pieces damaging your eyes. For accurate cutting of paving slabs, there is a wide version of the steel chisel called a bolster, and it is a worthwhile investment for garden work.

Glass cutter

Buy a good wheel cutter. It is far easier for the amateur to use than the more expensive diamond cutter, and just as effective when used properly. You can buy one with inter-changeable wheels if you plan to do a lot of glasscutting, but a single wheel model is adequate for most people. The notches on the cutter are for nibbling away narrow areas of glass.

Tile cutter

The easiest type to use rather resembles a very thin, pointed pencil, and the hardened tip will score the surface of a tile very easily. A more sophisticated type has a wheel cutter and a pliers action clamp which will hold and snap a tile along the cut. Yet another type offers a base with a wheel cutter projecting upwards over which the tile is run.

Trowels

Invest in both a small and a large trowel. The large trowel for handling mixed mortar and concrete, when tackling repairs, and the small trowel for finer repair work and for re-pointing brickwork and mortar. If you do repair work to rendering and plaster-work, you will need to add a hawk for carrying your mix, and a float for spreading it. The float is not an easy tool to use, and plastering requires very considerable expertise.

Soft-face hammer

Choose a hammer with interchangeable heads, or at least with a hard and a soft face. This hammer, or mallet, is invaluable for dismantling items which would bruise if hit with a steel hammer. For example, it will undo chromium-plated wing nuts without marking them, and a larger version will hammer out a car bodywork without further marking the metal.

Surveyor's tape

This is a really long tape which comes into its own when checking large measurements or marking out for paths and patios.

Grindstone

This is useful for re-sharpening steel chisels or removing damaged metal on edge tools prior to re-sharpening on a stone. You would be wise to wear safety glasses when using the grindstone.

Some of the attachments available for a power tool

Tools for specific jobs

Once you start, the collection of tools seems endless, and you will add items needed for specific jobs.

A *bottled gas blowtorch* is useful for paint removal, soldering and light brazing work. This is easier to use than the old blow-lamp which needed priming and heating before it would light. Nowadays you can get the added refinement of automatic crystal ignition. This is useful when working outside on ladders or scaffolding as it means ignition is a one-handed job.

If you tackle metalwork, such as wrought iron work or car body repairs, a simple *welding outfit* will be an invaluable addition to the kit. This can be mains operated, or for smaller jobs, battery-operated.

Where rusted nuts and bolts are encountered, a *nut splitter* is useful. This has a wedge which can be tightened against the face of a nut until it cuts through to the thread, making it possible to lift the nut away.

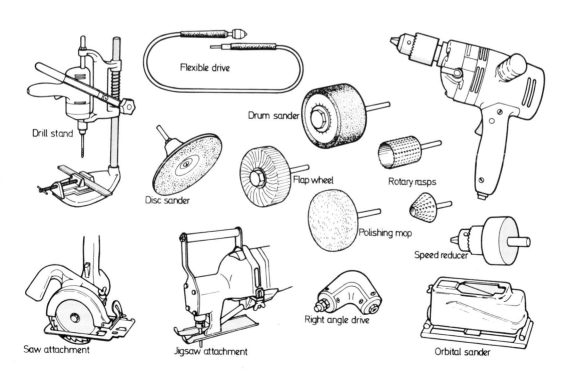

Drill stand
Flexible drive
Drum sander
Disc sander
Flap wheel
Rotary rasps
Polishing mop
Speed reducer
Saw attachment
Jigsaw attachment
Right angle drive
Orbital sander

Stud rivet kits are useful for many repair jobs. The riveter rather resembles a pair of pliers into which is fed a special hollow rivet. Pressure on the handles expands the rivet until a special pin breaks away, leaving a neat repair.

A *case opener* is a tough metal lever with a shaped end which is used for opening packing cases. It is ideal for lifting stubborn floorboard nails and for levering up boards when access below is required.

Power tools

So far, we have reviewed a considerable number of hand tools, and while it is possible to get by with just these, the introduction of power tools will help considerably. It will take the hard work out of many jobs; speed up your work very noticeably and, in many cases, produce far more accurate work.

It is worth a little thought before investing in power tool equipment, for there are two approaches to the subject. First, you can buy a basic power tool to which you plan to affix various attachments made for that tool. Or second, you can buy a power tool for drilling, then buy individually powered tools designed to do specific jobs.

The first approach is the cheapest, but you will be limited because a drill has not the ideal speed for actions such as sawing. You may find that the way you hold the tool has to be a compromise because the attachment protrudes from the chuck of the drill. There is also the disadvantage that you may be for ever changing attachments—though work can often be planned to change as little as possible.

The second approach is the most expensive, but it has the advantage that each tool is designed for a specific job, and that it is ready for use whenever you pick it up. There is a trend towards integral units—certainly as a person gains experience—and has the money for the investment.

Power drills

You will find these come in a wide price range, from a small single speed unit designed basically for drilling, through to a powerful variable speed model incorporating hammer action. The variable speed is useful as it enables you to make a slow, deliberate start when drilling items like ceramic tiles or glass, increasing speed as the drill tip bites. You can also adjust from slow for drilling to fast for sawing and fine sanding.

Hammer action is invaluable when drilling in tough surfaces like dense paving slabs and reinforced concrete lintels. When hammering, special masonry drills should be used.

Sanding

The most common attachment is the disc sander, which fits into the chuck of a power drill. It should only be used for coarse working as the circular action tends to make score marks which are difficult to lose. Various grades of abrasive are available, from coarse to fine.

The more effective tool is the drum sander. This again fits in the chuck, but it has a drum of foam around which is fitted a belt of abrasive. Belts are available from very fine to coarse, and they are held in place by a heat-softened wax. Because the rotation is in one direction, it can be worked with the grain of a piece of wood, making no scratch marks. Also, because of its size, the drum is self-cooling, which means the abrasive is less likely to clog with melted paint when sanding down painted surfaces.

The latest addition to the range of sanders is the flap wheel. This is made up of strips of abrasive mounted on a central core. Flap wheels come in a range of sizes, and are effective for work like reducing rust or smoothing awkward sections of timber.

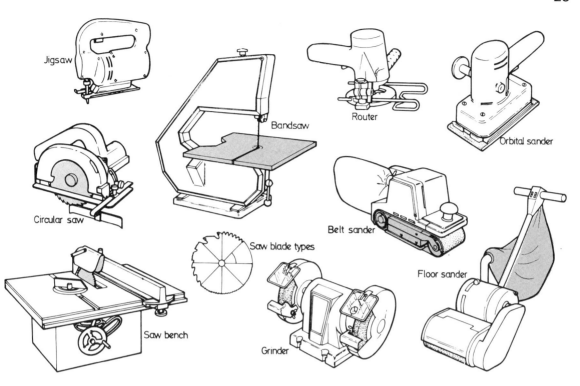

Jigsaw

Bandsaw

Router

Orbital sander

Circular saw

Belt sander

Saw blade types

Floor sander

Saw bench

Grinder

Integral motor power tools—designed to do one job efficiently

For fine surface finishing over large areas the orbital sander is useful. This is best bought as an integral power unit, and if you watch it closely you will see it makes very fine circular passes—so fine that the wood is not marked.

For larger jobs where a lot of sanding is to be done, you can get a belt sander, and for even larger projects such as floor re-surfacing there is a belt floor sander with vacuum cleaner action for collecting the dust. The two latter sanders are best hired when required.

Sawing

Attachments are available for fitting to many power tools, but the depth of cut and the actual cutting power is limited. Sawing is also a two-handed operation. One hand for the power tool and the other for the handle of the saw attachment. For regular cutting work the integral saw is a good investment. It cuts at the right speed; is balanced for one-hand operation, and gives a greater depth of cut. Various circular saw blades are available, and the illustration shows the main tooth forms. Say what the blade is for when buying. Such blades must be sharp if they are to cut without imposing a strain on the power source.

Apart from straight cutting, you can cut curves and awkward shapes with a jig saw. This is available as an attachment or as an integral unit, and it does take a little practice to be able to cut to a line without wavering.

For those wishing to do considerable cutting to shape, and wishing to tackle thicker materials, there is the more expensive bandsaw. Here, the saw blade is in a continuous strip, turning in one direction.

Where finer control is required when cutting, the ideal is to use a saw bench.

Here the blade is set below the work, protruding through it, and the work is fed to the blade. It is vital that great care is taken to keep the hands away from the blade, and the guard fitted should be used at all times. The simplest table will be set at right angles to the blade, but a useful refinement is to have a tilting table so that angled cuts can be made to a very fine wheel setting.

I would include with the cutting tools the now well established abrasive cutting discs which will cut through materials as varied as brickwork and corrugated iron sheeting. Very great care must be used with such discs. No guard is used, yet the disc will cut more rapidly than a circular saw blade. Wear safety glasses to protect your eyes from flying particles.

Just a few of the tools it would pay you to hire rather than buy. These will only be needed occasionally for specific jobs and it is not worth buying your own. Remember to contact the hire shop in good time as these large tools are in great demand. Especially in the summer!

Routing

The router is a more specialised shaping and cutting tool running at very high speeds and using specially shaped cutting heads for different jobs. This is an integral tool because of the high speed, and it is useful for reproducing mouldings, edgings, rebates and other shapes not easily produced in any other way.

The router may be a hand-held tool offered to the job, or it may be bench-mounted and the work offered to it.

Drilling

Apart from normal hand-held drilling operations, a vertical drill stand which holds a drill firmly in place is ideal for fine drilling work—such as repairs to metalwork or dowel hole drilling. The base may be fixed at right angles to the drill, or tilted to a given angle.

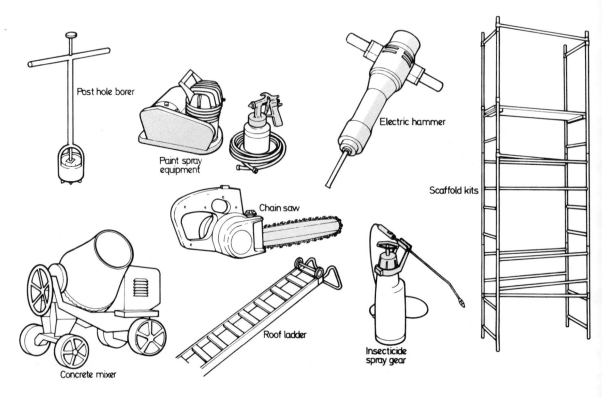

Post hole borer

Paint spray equipment

Electric hammer

Scaffold kits

Chain saw

Concrete mixer

Roof ladder

Insecticide spray gear

Spray painting

Attachments are available for some power tools to convert the drill into a spray gun, but the best guns are again integral units with a powered feed. This may take the form of air pressure which forces the paint from a nozzle, or it may be pumped liquid forced through the nozzle. The latter is the most effective method of painting as there is far less movement of air-borne spray. Even so, it is wise to mask all areas nearby which are not to be painted. Use masking tape, not clear adhesive tape. With small items, make a booth of cardboard to contain any over-spray.

Rotary rasps

These have the same action as the router, except they are coarser in action. A set of rasps which will fit in the chuck of a power tool are a useful addition to the kit for shaping and boring.

Flexible drive

This is a means of transmitting the rotary action of the drill through a flexible cable to a secondary chuck; it can be very useful for fine drilling and shaping work in awkward spots. Care should be taken not to overload the cable.

Speed reducer

If you have a power tool with a set speed, it is possible to buy a speed reducer designed to fit into the chuck of the tool. By holding the knurled wheel, considerable reduction in speed can be obtained, making the tool more suited to starting a drill tip on smooth surfaces such as tile or metal.

Right-angle drive

A special angle attachment is available which turns the drive from a power tool chuck through 90° to a secondary chuck. This device is very useful when working in confined spaces or up against a wall, such as when drilling holes for new plumbing pipes as close to a corner as possible.

Tool hire

As mentioned earlier, there will be occasions when specialist equipment would be of assistance, yet it is not worth buying it outright. This is where a good hire shop will prove extremely useful. Just about every professional tool is available on loan, including chain saws, electric and petrol concrete mixers, pneumatic drills, steam wallpaper strippers, rotary cultivators, scaffold kits, woodworm treatment sprays and ancillary equipment, extra ladders and scaffold boards, paint spray guns and industrial size power tool equipment.

Delivery and collection by your own transport will save on costs, as will careful planning of work so that you do not keep hired items any longer than necessary.

Find your local hire shop and get a catalogue. This will show you the range of gear available, and the current prices for hire either by the day or the week.

Access equipment

Apart from the tools listed, it is vital that you have the correct means of reaching your work, whether it be just to the ceiling or up to the roof ridge. Never take chances on make-do equipment!

For interior work you need a sturdy pair of steps with wide base and preferably a grip handle at the top so that you have a grip to steady yourself. Make sure you have non-slip treads.

For exterior jobs, an extension ladder is necessary. It should extend at least three rungs above gutter level at the highest wall height, have comfortable treads and be easy to handle. You have a choice of timber or alloy, both now being similar in price. The alloy will last longest without signs of deterioration, but timber is much warmer on the hands in really cold weather. Metal also tends to get grubbier than wood, but it is considerably lighter. The choice is yours!

This is the correct way to raise a ladder. This way you will not lose control over it

Cord-operation to raise a ladder section is useful, but unless you are experienced, it pays to have help when raising and lowering. The illustration shows the safe way of raising an extending ladder. Where a three-section ladder is needed, you definitely need help, for when extended such a ladder can be very difficult to control.

Where you need to reach the roof ridge or a chimney stack, it is wise to hire a roof ladder which hooks securely over the ridge. The wheels are so you can get the ladder in place easily—then you merely turn the ladder over.

Where walls are to be repaired or painted a scaffold kit designed specially for d-i-y use is invaluable. This comes in easy-to-assemble sections, and once erected to the required height provides a safe, comfortable working platform. The tower should always be climbed from the inside to avoid tipping. If such a tower proves too much of a financial outlay, you can hire one. But plan your work carefully so you do not keep it too long. Modest charges soon add up.

An alternative working platform can be made using two ladders, a pair of builder's cripples and scaffold boards. The cripples are supports on to which the boards can be laid to provide a walkway. A simple guard rail will make working that much safer. This can be behind you just below waist height.

Chapter 2
Materials for repairs

The range of materials now available for d-i-y use is now quite bewildering, and the difficulty nowadays is not finding a remedy, but of knowing out of the scores of types available which is best suited to the job in hand. Whatever the material, it must be stressed at the outset that new material must go on to clean, dry, firm surfaces. You cannot expect even the best filler to grip loose rust, flaking paint or rotting wood.

Basic materials and how to deal with them will be covered in following chapters, so for the time being we will have a look at some of the products at your disposal and their applications.

Fillers

Papier mâché

I make no excuse for starting with probably the oldest and best tried filler whose history, I would guess, goes back thousands of years. It is made by shredding newspaper, adding water to thoroughly soften it, squeezing out, then adding a quantity of glue size powder dissolved in water. Mix to the consistency of putty, and it becomes a good filler for stopping gaps in floorboards. It will set hard in time and can be sanded down as necessary.

To match stained boards, merely add water stain, a little at a time, until you get the right colour. The material is also extremely cheap to produce!

Cellulose filler

This is of far more recent origin and the cellulose filler has proved invaluable for sealing cracks in plaster and wood. Because of its adhesive nature, it does not shrink out of a crack like the old fillers, and, once set, it can be sanded, scraped or drilled.

Plaster fillers

A number of plaster-based materials are still available, and if bought in bulk they can prove cheaper to use for the larger repair jobs. One of the most useful materials is Keenes cement, which is cheap and easy to use. It does set quite fast, so only small

Mastics are available in a number of forms. Here are some of them. Right, to add adhesion to a mix, use pva adhesive in the mixing water

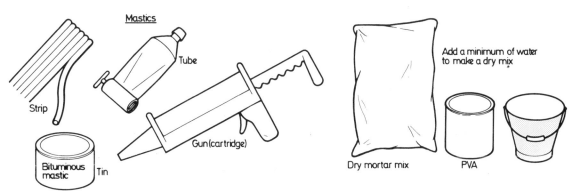

Mastics

Strip

Tube

Gun (cartridge)

Bituminous mastic Tin

Add a minimum of water to make a dry mix

Dry mortar mix PVA

amounts should be mixed at a time. Deep holes should be filled in a number of layers rather than in one go, and the minimum of water should be added.

Plaster of Paris is not really suitable for d-i-y use because it goes off far too quickly. It could be used as a deep gap filler for filling the hole three quarters full, as it will set almost immediately. You could then finish off with cellulose or Keenes cement with no delay.

Swedish putty

This is another old but effective way of repairing or filling where a water-resistant surface is required. Cellulose filler is made up with water in the normal way but keeping the mix very dry, then a quantity of oil-based paint is added and worked in until a creamy mix is produced. It is ideal for sealing gaps behind areas like old stoneware sinks where there is no expansion and contraction movement.

Fine surface filler

Another relative newcomer, sometimes called spachtel, this is supplied as a ready-mixed paste. It has a very fine finish, and is ideal for filling cracks in timber prior to painting. It is supplied either in tubs or in plastic tubes. The tubed material lasts better because the air cannot get at the filler.

Stoppings

These are well-established products well known by woodworkers as first-rate fillers. Smooth in texture and adhesive by nature they fill without cracking away as they dry. A number of colours are available

to match major timbers, making them suitable for filling timbers which are then to be finished with varnish or seal. You can also buy an exterior grade for use out of doors.

Most fillers are affected by damp, so for items like filling cracks in garden furniture, use an exterior filler. Like the fine surface fillers, stopping comes ready-mixed.

Putty

One of the traditional fillers and sealers, putty still may be used as long as it is well protected by paint. It will harden as it dries, so it is not suitable for areas where there is likely to be movement, as it merely cracks away, leaving a gap into which damp can seep.

Remember there are two types. Standard linseed oil putty, which dries by the absorption of the oils into the wood, and metal casement putty which will dry even though the metal to which it adheres is non-porous. Be sure you specify which is needed when tackling window repairs.

Mastics

These may resemble putty, but they have the advantage of remaining flexible even after the surface has dried. This is a big advantage when dealing with materials which may move, if only slightly—for example, when sealing a gap between brick and a timber frame.

Mastic comes in a number of forms. One type takes the form of thin strips rather resembling rolled Plasticine, ready to be pressed into small gaps. It is also available in tubes to be dispensed rather like toothpaste, and in cartons which fit in a special mastic gun. The gun is ideal for larger sealing jobs, and the tube nozzle can be cut to whatever diameter is required.

A bituminous mastic is also available, usually supplied in a tin, and this is ideal for sealing gaps in bituminous roofing sheets or for filling cracks in rainwater goods. Added strength can be achieved by working hessian strip into the repair, then laying bitumen over it. This helps particularly where there may be slight movement, likely to open up a repaired joint.

Mortar mix

Cement-based mortar consisting of sand and cement is suitable for repairing cracks in concrete, but it needs to be reinforced by the addition of pva adhesive. This can be added to the water used to make up the mortar, and it can also be brushed liberally into cracks and gaps, using the adhesive neat, prior to applying mortar. If you do not add the adhesive, the mortar will tend to crack away unless laid very thick.

You can buy the ingredients to make your own mortar or, for smaller projects, you can buy dry mixes at the builders merchants. All you need do is add water. If you do not finish a bag, seal it in a polythene bag and store in a dry place or the whole lot will go off.

The simple way to level an uneven solid floor

Screeding compound

This is more than a gap filler. It is a resurfacing material and can be used for levelling uneven concrete floors prior to putting down floorcovering. When mixed to the right consistency, it pours rather like syrup, finding its own level. This saves the skilled operation of trowelling out to get a smooth surface that used to be necessary.

Read the instructions carefully so you do not mix more than can be used in a stipulated time. All cement-based materials go off quicker in warm weather.

Two-part fillers

Epoxy resin fillers are now very well established, particularly for car body repair work, though they can be used for many repairs such as sealing cracks in guttering or building up sections of damaged metalwork.

The filler is usually grey in colour and it consists of two parts. When mixed at the recommended quantities, the filler immediately starts to harden by chemical action—and nothing will stop it, even if the material is submerged in water. For this reason it is important to mix only enough for the job in hand, or you can end up with a lot of waste which cannot be re-softened.

With large gaps, it is wise to reinforce the repair with wire gauge or perforated zinc over which the filler is spread. Alternatively, the filler can be reinforced with glass fibre

Using screeding compound

Remove dust from floor

Mix the powder with water as directed

Pour slurry on to the floor and spread with an old broom

Leave to set
The material is self-levelling

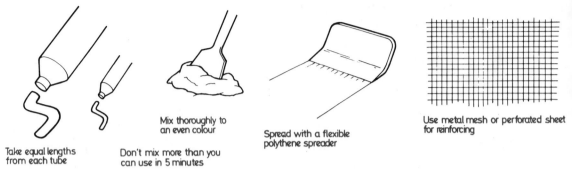

Take equal lengths
from each tube

Don't mix more than you
can use in 5 minutes

Mix thoroughly to
an even colour

Spread with a flexible
polythene spreader

Use metal mesh or perforated sheet
for reinforcing

How to use an epoxy-based repair material

bandage built up sandwich-fashion and then coated with filler, working it well into the bandage.

Ceramic putty

Another material closely related to the epoxy filler is an epoxy putty. Here, a material closely resembling putty is supplied in two parts. Both parts remain reasonably soft and pliable until equal parts are mixed together, after which the material sets rock hard. Once set, it is impervious to water, grease and most chemicals.

Ceramic putty is ideal for repairs to sanitary ware, sealing gaps, encasing wires. It is best kept for smallish jobs as epoxies tend to be on the expensive side for large projects.

Sealants

A tubed sealant based upon silicone rubber is now available to be used mainly as a gap sealer. Designed to be squeezed from a nozzle, it becomes tough-dry in a matter of minutes, setting to a rubbery yet flexible consistency which maintains its high adhesion even in damp conditions.

There is a real art in spreading it—pushing forward, nozzle first. Read the instructions carefully and do a test run before tackling anything too ambitious!

Adhesives

Nothing in the d-i-y field has changed more than the range of adhesives. From a basic one or two types we now have a vast

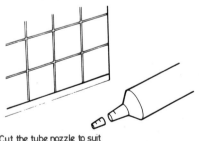

Cut the tube nozzle to suit
the gap to be sealed

Feed sealant into the gap,
pushing the nozzle ahead of you

Smooth minor irregularites
immediately with a wet finger

Using a sealant to fill a gap such as is found between a tiled wall and a bath

number, and I think it fair to say that there is not one which will deal with all materials. Each type has its advantages and limitations, so it is wise to read very carefully any pack or packet before buying. Here are the most common ones you will encounter.

Animal glue

This is the good old Seccotine or Croid-type material which served us so faithfully over the years. It is still around in tubes, and it has a place for simple repairs where the wood can be held while the adhesive sets; where slight staining does not matter, and where no damp is likely to be present. It has no real advantages over more modern materials.

Resin adhesive

This is usually supplied as a powder designed to be mixed with water as required, and is resistant to damp, making it suitable for exterior repairs. It is a strong, reliable woodworking adhesive.

PVA adhesive

Supplied as a liquid with the consistency and appearance of single cream, this is one of the most versatile adhesives introduced in recent years. It gives strong joints, is resistant to damp and it keeps well.

It has many applications—from the ideal card adhesive for the nursery to woodworking. It can be used as an additive for concrete to increase its general adhesion and it can be used as a surface coating for concrete to stop it dusting. You will also find it supplied for fixing expanded polystyrene wall veneers and ceiling tiles. Remember to buy it in the most economic

way possible for the job in hand. A tub used for wall veneer fixing will keep a nursery school in adhesive for a whole term!

When using rubberised adhesives, make a disposable brush from a piece of tubing and coarse string. Pull through and cut off as used

Rather than ruin good brushes, make your own which can be disposed of after use

Clear resin

This has become the most popular household adhesive for general repair work. It has a strong solvent which dries off quickly, so you get strong joints in a short time. Coat both surfaces, allow to go touch dry and then press together. It is best suited to flexible surfaces, and is not designed for woodworking joints.

Rubber resin

This is the popular impact type adhesive used widely for securing laminated plastics. It is applied to both surfaces, allowed to become touch-dry, then the two surfaces pressed together.

If the surface area is fairly large, it will secure timber to a flat surface such as plaster. I have fixed pelmet battens in place over plaster hiding a concrete lintel with complete success. It will fix most flexible materials, but is not really suitable for woodworking joints.

Latex

This rather resembles the rubber resin, but it is milky in colour with a strongish smell. It is designed for carpet and fabric binding and it gives a quick clean joint. Another advantage is that it rubs easily from the fingers—something you cannot do with rubber resin.

Epoxy resin

This is a two-part material, resin and hardener, and once equal parts have been mixed together, setting is by chemical action which nothing can stop. It is ideal for repairs to metal, china and glass, and, once set, being unaffected by heat, damp or most chemicals.

Two basic types are now available. A standard adhesive which sets over some 12 hours, faster if the material is warmed, and a fast setting adhesive which is set in about 5 minutes. The latter is extremely useful where it is hard to hold pieces in place while the adhesive sets. In extreme circumstances it is now possible to hold the pieces in place until the resin sets. Polythene gloves help here as some people are allergic to epoxy resins.

Using an epoxy resin adhesive for repair work

Cyanoacrylate

This is a most remarkable material which gives the benefits of almost instantaneous repairs to hard materials like metal and glass and flexible materials like synthetic rubbers. It resembles water to look at, but there the resemblance ends, for one small drop is all that is needed to give an immediate bond between surfaces. For this reason, extreme caution is called for. Take care not to get it on fingers or eyelids. It will stick these together with equal speed and is then very difficult indeed to get them unstuck! It is also expensive, so keep it for small jobs which need speed.

I have found it has the disadvantage that, because of the speed of setting, there is little time to position awkward pieces, say, of a broken vase or piece of pottery. If fitting together is tricky, use an epoxy resin material where you have more time.

PVC

For sticking pvc materials such as plastic raincoats, paddling pools and beach balls, you need special pvc adhesive which has a solvent content to soften and weld the pvc together. Some materials seem suitable, but when dry they can be peeled away because there has been no solvent

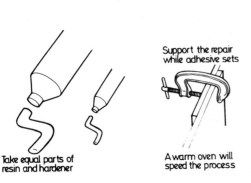

Take equal parts of resin and hardener

Support the repair while adhesive sets

A warm oven will speed the process

For awkward or rapid repairs, use a quick set adhesive -the repair could be held; as setting time is 5-10 minutes

action. When in doubt, experiment on a small area before tackling a major repair.

You can also buy a pvc repair tape which has the same action. This is useful for emergency repairs.

Polystyrene cement

This too has a solvent action, and is now widely used for model kits where the basic plastic used is polystyrene. As it has a solvent effect, keep surplus adhesive off the face of the plastic as it will mark it.

Choice of adhesive

Because of the complexity of materials available today—especially among the plastics—it may be necessary to find the right adhesive by experiment, perhaps because you cannot find out what the material is you wish to repair. Try your adhesion tests on scrap materials if possible, and make sure the joint is really dry before testing for adhesion.

Problem areas include expanded polystyrene. Do not use adhesive with a heavy solvent—such as rubber resin. It will completely dissolve the plastic. Do not try to stick polythene; it has a wax-like surface which rejects all known adhesives. Polythene will have to be heat-welded. Nylon has the same nature and I know of no adhesive which will hold it.

Do not use hard-setting materials like resin adhesives on flexible surfaces; they will crack up when flexed. The reverse also applies. Do not use flexible adhesives such as rubber resins on small joint areas where strain may be applied; the flexible adhesive will not take the strain.

Tapes

Adhesives are being backed up by a whole range of adhesive tapes which very often simplify a job. Double-sided adhesive pads can be used for fixing metal tiles to walls, and bathroom fittings and hooks to walls or doors. Double-sided tapes can be used for securing floorcoverings of all kinds, and heavier duty adhesive pads are now used for holding wall panelling to a wall.

As with all fixing jobs, it is important that the surfaces to be fixed are clean, dry and free from grease. Carpet tape will prevent carpet fraying at the edges. pvc tape will repair rips in pvc items, masking adhesive tape will protect areas you do not wish to paint, and insulating tape will protect electrical wiring.

Nails

You are sure to need nails at some time, so it pays to keep a good selection, classified according to size and shape. Here are the most common ones together with a rough guide as to their use.

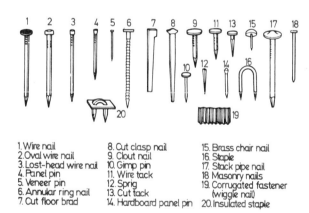

1. Wire nail	8. Cut clasp nail
2. Oval wire nail	9. Clout nail
3. Lost-head wire nail	10. Gimp pin
4. Panel pin	11. Wire tack
5. Veneer pin	12. Sprig
6. Annular ring nail	13. Cut tack
7. Cut floor brad	14. Hardboard panel pin

15. Brass chair nail	
16. Staple	
17. Stack pipe nail	
18. Masonry nails	
19. Corrugated fastener (wiggle nail)	
20. Insulated staple	

Make sure you choose the right nail for the job. There are plenty to choose from

Bear in mind that it is possible to get rust-resistant nails, and these should be used wherever there is the chance of rusting. The traditional rustless nail was galvanised, and this is still quite adequate for many exterior jobs. But you can also get aluminium alloy nails which have a far smoother finish. I would choose these wherever possible.

Wire nail

This is the common round nail with a flat head, useful for all framing jobs where fairly large sections of softwood are being used. If the round nail has to be used in thin section timber or with hardwoods, always drill a hole to prevent the wood splitting.

Oval wire nail

As the name suggests, the body is oval, making it less prone to splitting wood. Use it with its narrowest profile along the wood grain. You will see it has a different shape head too, which makes it possible to sink the head below the wood surface. A nail punch can be used to do this, after which the remaining small hole can be filled.

Lost head wire nail

This is the nail to use for carpentry repair work. It makes a smaller hole; is far less likely to split the wood, and its head is designed to be sunk below the surface of the wood.

The remaining hole can then be filled.

When used with hardwood, it is still wise to drill holes first to prevent the nail splitting the wood.

Panel pin

You will find these useful for cabinet and furniture repairs—especially for securing moulding. The fine body will not split the wood, and the head will sink easily below the surface.

Veneer pin

Not such a common item these days, but if you have to make repairs to veneered surfaces, they are designed to hold veneer in place while your glue sets—then they are pulled out.

Ring nail

The serrated body of this nail drives home easily enough, but it resists being drawn. This makes it ideal for holding materials firm where a normal nail might slip. For example, it will hold hardboard to a timber floor when there is slight spring in the floor. Also, it will hold firm in woods like red cedar where normal nails can often be drawn with the fingers, the wood is so soft.

Cut floor brad

This is the crudest form of nail, being cut from sheet metal. Its rough rectangular form affords a very good grip, and you will find it used in house construction for jobs like securing floorboards.

Cut clasp nail

Another nail cut from sheet metal and used in building for rough joinery work where a good grip is needed. This nail was also widely used for fixing into masonry before the hardened masonry nail became available.

Clout nail

This has a short body and large head, designed for holding sheet materials such as roofing felt. Serrations on the nail body help to give it a better grip in timber. Choose galvanised nails for all exterior work.

Gimp pin

With a square body and flat head, this nail is designed for holding material to a framework in upholstering.

Wire tack

This has a shorter body and larger head than the gimp pin, and this also is used in upholstering, mainly where frame sections are thicker.

Sprig

A very useful little headless tack with a sharp point. It is used for holding glass in place prior to applying putty to a timber frame. Also useful for holding glass, picture and backing in place when picture framing.

Cut tack

This tack has a large head and a heavily tapered body, making it easy to drive and to withdraw. It is used for securing materials such as underfelt and upholstery fabric to timber.

Panel pin

The type shown is called a deep drive pin, as the diamond-shape head is automatically driven below the surface as it is hammered home. It is ideal for fixing plywood and hardboard where the heads are to be hidden with filler. Because of the head shape, panel pins are a little harder to hit with a hammer! Shanks may be round or square.

Chair nails

Usually brass, chair nails resemble a drawing pin with domed head. You will need them for upholstery repairs, for holding the covering fabric in place. They may also be used to disguise tack heads and also as a decorative finish.

Staples

You will find these in upholstered furniture, holding the springs in place. They are also widely used for fencing, wherever wire or netting has to be held.

Insulated staples

Used for holding electrical wiring in place, insulated staples usually comprise a square section staple with a small piece of insulating material at the head. This prevents the staple cutting into the wire or cable.

Stack pipe nails

You will not encounter many of these, but they are used for securing pipe brackets to masonry. The large head is designed to sit neatly on the bracket.

Masonry nails

These are especially hardened nails designed to be driven straight into masonry to hold battening in place. Check on the recommended sizes for given types, for it is important that not too much nail is driven into the masonry. A long nail will merely act as a metal wedge, splitting a brick or block, and giving no grip at all.

Corrugated fasteners

These are useful for securing frame sections prior to covering with plywood or hardboard, and for joining boards together. The fastener pulls the two components together as it is driven home. Sometimes called wiggle nails.

Screws

Although a seemingly simple device, the screw is a most misunderstood piece of hardware. Through abuse and mis-use, simple fixing jobs become sheer hard work. The most important lesson to learn is that the holding power of a screw does not depend on the force used to drive it. In fact too much force can split wood or turn the head off the screw. The secret is to make start holes into which a screw can be driven with the minimum of force. Work is easier, and the holding power is in no way affected.

The illustration shows the holes you need to make. First, a clearance hole in the item to be fixed into which the shank of the screw just fits. Second, if the head of the screw is designed to be flush with the surface, you need a countersunk hole into which the head will recess. Third, you need a smaller diameter hole in the lower piece of wood into which the thread will not quite go, so it bites into the surrounding timber. A little grease or Vaseline on the screw thread will make driving even easier, and it will ensure that the screw comes out easily should it ever be necessary.

Screws are sold by gauge sizes, e.g. number 8 or number 10. This refers to the diameter of the screw shank and it is calculated by measuring across the head in $\frac{1}{16}$ ths, doubling this figure and subtracting two. So, if the head measures $\frac{5}{16}$ in, doubling gives you 10; minus 2 equals 8. You have a number 8 screw. All you then need add is the length, so you would order a 2 in. number 8.

You will find that head shapes vary, but the most common are described below.

Countersunk screws

Here the head is designed to be recessed so that it ends up flush with the surface—or it could be taken lower and the remaining recess filled.

Raised countersunk screws

The head is recessed into the wood, but a slight dome remains proud of the surface.

Round head screws

The screw sits on the surface, and is the type which would be used in conjunction with washers, or to hold metal brackets in place.

Slot types

You will encounter three slot types which were mentioned earlier in this chapter under screwdrivers. These are:

Single slot. This is the traditional slot into which a standard screwdriver fits, and it is important that the driver chosen fits the screw head correctly. Too large a screwdriver will mean the tip slips from the slot. Too small a driver will twist the screwdriver blade.

Phillips cross slot. The cross has a simple cross section into which fits the tip of a special Phillips screwdriver. The big advantage is that the tip can't slip from the slot— an important point when screwing into a decorative surface.

Pozidriv slot. This is a more sophisticated cross slot where a specially shaped screwdriver tip fits so well into the slot that you can in fact pick up the screws on the tip. This is useful for starting screws in awkward to get at spots, and again you have the advantage that the driver does not slip out. Pozidriv screws come in a wide range of sizes, and it is essential to ensure that the screwdriver fits the head perfectly.

A relatively new screw design is available called the Twinfast. This has a special double thread which allows a screw to be driven much faster than normal.

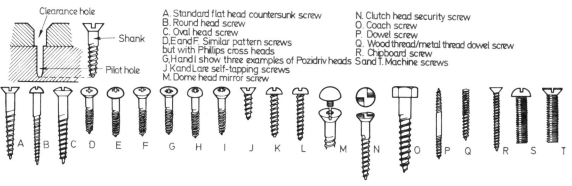

Clearance hole

Shank

Pilot hole

A. Standard flat head countersunk screw
B. Round head screw
C. Oval head screw
D, E and F. Similar pattern screws
but with Phillips cross heads
G, H and I show three examples of Pozidriv heads
J, K and L are self-tapping screws
M. Dome head mirror screw

N. Clutch head security screw
O. Coach screw
P. Dowel screw
Q. Wood thread/metal thread dowel screw
R. Chipboard screw
S and T. Machine screws

A B C D E F G H I J K L M N O P Q R S T

These are the most common screws you will encounter in repair work

Special screws

Apart from the normal range, there are all kinds of specials. Here are a few examples.

Chipboard screws

The shank and body of this screw are very similar in thickness so there is no wedge action when driving into chipboard. This helps prevent splitting. Even so it is wise to make start-holes to avoid splitting the board. Most chipboards split more readily than timber.

Self-tapping screws

Designed to be used for fixing metal sheet, they will drive into a prepared hole, cutting a way in for the thread to grip. They are widely used in cars for fixing items to the metalwork of the car. They are also used for cutting their own thread when driven into plastics. A start hole is necessary, then the thread cuts into the surrounding plastic.

Coach screws

A heavy screw with a head designed to be turned by spanner rather than screwdriver. Used for heavy woodworking.

Dome-head screws

Also called mirror screws, a special screw has a slot and a threaded hole into which a special dome head can be screwed after the screw is in place. This gives a decorative finish. There are now modern alternatives, including small plastic inserts which will press into the recess in a Pozidriv screw. Also, a dome and nylon collar which can be used press stud fashion when used in conjunction with dome head screws.

Machine screws

More of an engineering screw, this is designed to be used with threaded inserts or nuts. It is not designed to be driven into timber.

Clutch head screws

A special security screw which has an unusually designed head. There are faces upon which a screwdriver can bear to tighten the screw, but there are none for loosening the screw. Sloping surfaces deflect the screwdriver. Ideal for fixing padlock hasps and staples and any other item of hardware which you do not want anyone to interfere with.

While the standard screw is of steel, rust-resisting screws are available. Brass can be used for boatbuilding. Aluminium alloy can be used anywhere you are likely to encounter damp conditions which could cause corrosion.

Chapter 3 Timberwork

The first point to establish with timber is that it will not last for ever. In its natural state in the wood or forest, once a tree dies it starts to decay. It is attacked by the weather, many types of fungi, and wood boring insects until eventually the timber is broken down completely and absorbed into the soil.

When timber is used for construction work, you will find that the same processes will try to continue. If damp can get into it, it will rot and if left unprotected, it will be attacked by woodboring insects. Let us look at these enemies of timber in a little more detail.

Wet rot

This is quite a common form of rot, though it is the least serious as it will not spread from the area under attack. Timber has to be wet to start with, and the causes may range from rainwater gathering around the stump of a fence post, to an area of floorboards soaked by water leaking from a radiator or pipe.

Where do rot spores come from to start the infection? Well, the answer is that they are always in the air in vast quantities. For example a mushroom of 3 in diameter will produce in the region of 1,800 million spores. They are so small that they blow away in the wind, awaiting the day when they encounter damp wood on which they can start to grow.

Wet rot appears as whitish strands spreading over the timber surface; a rather dank and musty smell, and cracks running along the grain of the wood. It will also noticeably darken the wood.

When dealing with wet rot, the first step is to locate the source of dampness and stop it. As suggested above, this may mean draining a hole in which a post stands; repairing a leaking pipe joint or sealing a hole in a radiator. Whatever the cause, once the wood can start to dry out, the rot will die off. Unfortunately you may find that some of the timber has softened and decayed. This timber must be cut back to sound wood, then a new piece of wood inserted. It is a waste of time trying to patch up damaged wood with fillers. The immediate effect may look good, but soon the filler will work loose as it has nothing firm to hold on to.

Having made good the repair, treat the timber with a good wood preservative, putting it on generously, and if possible soaking the ends of timber sections in preservative. In locations where damp may

What to do if you encounter wet rot

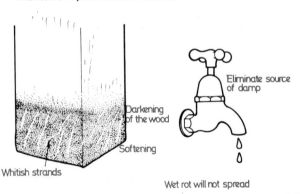

Whitish strands

Darkening of the wood

Softening

Eliminate source of damp

Wet rot will not spread

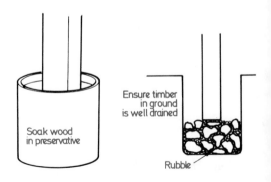

Soak wood in preservative

Ensure timber in ground is well drained

Rubble

be encountered, it will pay you to buy pressure-impregnated timber for replacement work. It costs a little more than normal timber, and you can be sure that nothing will affect it. Alternatively, for fencing work, make up a single trough with bricks and heavy gauge polythene sheeting, pour in your preservative, then lay the timber in the preservative and leave it to soak. This has far more effect than brush coating.

When you come to erect fence posts, stand the base of each post on rubble before filling in. This will ensure good drainage and prevent water accumulating at the base.

Dry rot

The name here is misleading, because the dryness refers to the wood after it has been attacked. It too must be wet if an attack is to develop—but under different circumstances from wet rot.

If timber is dry, it will not be attacked, even though there may be millions of spores in the air. However, given poor ventilation, and a moisture content above 20% (25% is ideal) the dry rot spores can start to germinate. The attack may take place just about anywhere in a house where the right conditions prevail. These may be under a floor where the ventilation has been reduced or cut off, behind a skirting board, in a cupboard or under built-in units.

The first signs are a musty smell in the room and perhaps the warping or cracking of timber. You will see cracks across the wood, rather resembling the crazed effect you see on soil suffering drought. This is the effect of the fungus feeding off the cellulose in the timber, and it results in a severe weakening and softening of the wood. You will be able to push a knife point into the affected areas.

If you lift the affected wood, you will somewhere find what is called a fruiting body—a mushroom-like growth, probably surrounded by a whitish mass of strands rather resembling dirty cotton wool. From here on it gets nasty, for behind the thin strands come thicker ones capable of carrying water. These transfer water to dry areas of timber, thus ensuring that the rot can continue to spread. It is not unknown for an attack in a cellar to reach very quickly to the roof timbers—even passing through brickwork on the way!

Obviously this type of rot is a far greater threat than the wet rot as it is not contained within the original damp area. For this reason, if you do find an attack, deal with it as quickly as possible. If you do suspect an attack, but would like it verifying, call in one of the specialist companies who deal with timber preservation and have a free survey.

Treating dry rot

The first job, having located the dry rot fruit, is to cut away timber and plaster until the full area of attack has been exposed. It is vital not to miss anything, or you may have the rot continuing elsewhere.

Having ascertained the extent of the attack, deal with the cause of the damp. It could well be a leaking drain or gulley; air bricks covered with board to 'prevent draughts'; a defective damp proof course; missing or damaged roof tiles; gutters leaking water on to the wall, defective plumbing or leaking radiators. Unfortunately—unlike wet rot—when you have cured the trouble, the job is not finished. All infected timber must be cut out and burned, and all surrounding brickwork, plaster and timber treated with a powerful fungicide or dry rot fluid.

Masonry can be sterilised by playing a

40

How to recognise and deal with dry rot

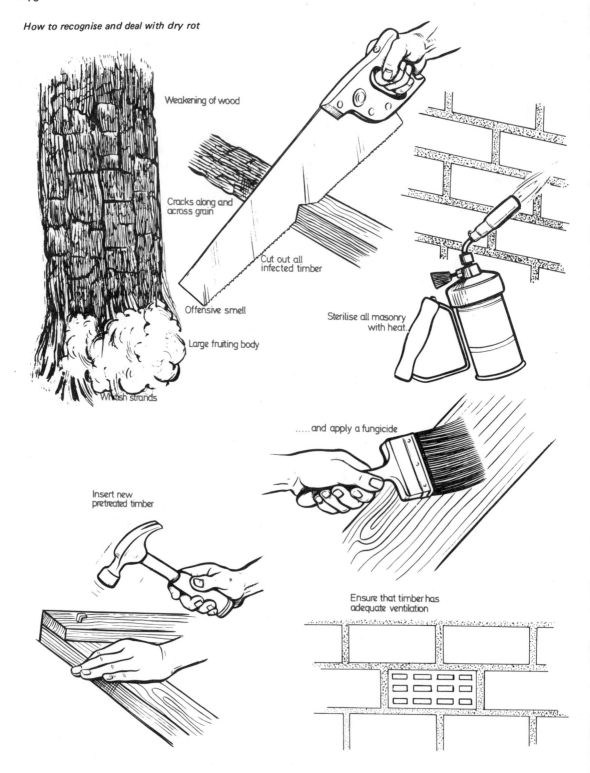

Weakening of wood

Cracks along and across grain

Cut out all infected timber

Offensive smell

Large fruiting body

Whitish strands

Sterilise all masonry with heat...

.....and apply a fungicide

Insert new pretreated timber

Ensure that timber has adequate ventilation

blowtorch over it, but great care must be taken not to start a fire.

Having cut out all infected wood, it should be replaced with either pre-treated timber, or with timber well soaked in preservative. It is far better to be over liberal with preservative — just in case an area should have been missed.

If you feel this job is too much for you, there are specialist companies who will do it, and offer a 20 or 30 year guarantee. This is certainly worth keeping against the day when you have to sell the property.

Of course it will cost considerably less to do the job yourself, but unfortunately there are still building societies who insist on the work being done by a specialist company before they will grant a mortgage. This is despite the fact that there are materials available to the d-i-y man which would do the job just as effectively.

With the repair work complete, make sure that the timber stays dry and well ventilated. Never block air bricks under the house. They are there to ensure adequate underfloor ventilation, and, as already stated, if the air is flowing freely, this keeps the moisture content low—and you will get no rot.

Insect attack

The beetle you are most likely to encounter is the common furniture beetle (or wood-worm as it is better known). Its presence is usually detected by tiny holes in a piece of timber and a fine dust, which if you look very closely resembles tiny cigar-shaped pellets. Unfortunately, these are signs that your beetles have flown, for these are the holes they make as they leave the timber—so let us go back to the start of the life cycle.

A female beetle will lay·from 20 to 40 eggs in crevices in rough timber, perhaps in the loft, or perhaps in the plywood backs of furniture. After about a month, the eggs hatch, and small grubs emerge which immediately start to burrow into the wood by eating it at one end and excreting it as pellets at the other. They continue tunnelling for about three years, after which each turns into a chrysalis; just under the surface of the wood. In four to eight weeks, it will turn into an adult beetle, and once the transformation is complete the beetle bites its way out of the wood, leaving behind that tell-tale little hole. The beetle will fly off to mate and then the whole cycle will be repeated.

I don't think the woodworm is really an insect to fear, for I have never heard of a house collapsing from its efforts. Even so, as soon as you discover an attack, it is wise to take steps to stop it. There are a number of ways you can do this, ranging from a simple local injection to large area timber treatment.

For a small area, you can get an aerosol can of fluid together with a tube and nozzle. Fit the tube to the can, insert the nozzle in a hole, and press. Protect your eyes against spray-back, and it pays to hold a cloth around the nozzle if you are near decorations, in case you splash them. Move from hole to hole injecting the fluid, and you can be assured that all the tunnels in that area will have been flooded, killing off any grubs inside, and making the wood unpleasant to eat.

For larger areas, the woodworm fluid can be brush applied, working it well into cracks and crevices where eggs are most likely to have been laid.

For difficult areas like loft spaces, you can hire a professional spray gun with lance and nozzle, and this will enable you to reach awkward places which are difficult to reach by hand. Use adequate fluid, but not too much. If you flood the area, you could have it soaking through your ceilings and making

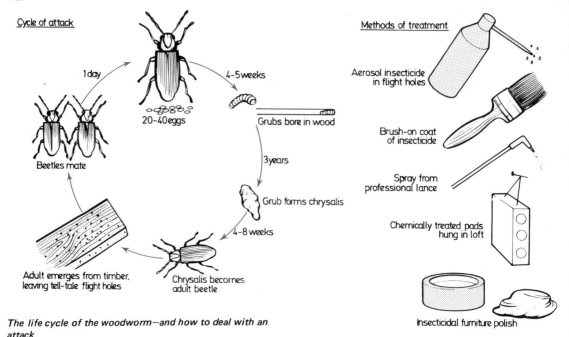

Cycle of attack

1 day

4-5 weeks

20-40 eggs

Grubs bore in wood

Beetles mate

3 years

Grub forms chrysalis

4-8 weeks

Adult emerges from timber, leaving tell-tale flight holes

Chrysalis becomes adult beetle

Methods of treatment

Aerosol insecticide in flight holes

Brush-on coat of insecticide

Spray from professional lance

Chemically treated pads hung in loft

Insecticidal furniture polish

The life cycle of the woodworm—and how to deal with an attack

marks. It is also wise to hire an industrial face mask to keep the fumes away. I would also add safety glasses to keep spray away from the eyes.

This is another job where you can get a free professional survey if you have doubts about whether or not you have an attack. The company will either quote for doing the job, or for supplying you with the necessary materials to do it yourself. This is yet another area where some building societies insist the job is done by a specialist company before they will grant the loan. (Often hitting a young couple by giving them expense at a time they could well do without it!)

There are other beetles which cause trouble, but the only one which poses a serious threat in certain definable areas is the House Longhorn beetle. This really is a menace, because the beetle is 12—25 mm long (½—1 in) and it makes a hole up to 9 mm (³⁄₈ in) across. It is found in roof timbers of attics where it attacks the softwood in a way which will in a very short

time weaken the whole roof structure. Fortunately it is confined to the South of England, mainly in the west of Surrey. Should you find any largish holes with an elongated opening, filled with wood dust call in an expert company for a diagnosis. If it is the longhorn beetle, he must be dealt with quickly!

If you live in the area likely to be affected, make periodic checks in the loft for attack. Dig the point of a knife into structural timbers to see if there are tunnelways just below the surface.

The Death Watch beetle is not a domestic problem, although it is the bane of preservers of historic buildings where it will attack hardwoods which are old and damp. It practically never attacks sound, dry, ventilated timbers.

Apart from the action already described, it is possible to take precautionary measures to avoid beetle attack. One method is to buy special packs of chemical impregnated strips. A strip is hung in its container in the loft space, where fumes given off will kill off flying beetles. The strip needs renewing periodically, and details of the renewal times will be found on the pack.

Furniture may also be protected by using a special insecticidal furniture polish. The polish will contaminate cracks and gaps, killing off any beetles or eggs which come into contact with the timber. As has already been mentioned, the ideal protection is to use pre-treated timbers wherever new work is done, or replacement timbers are installed. Such timber, because it is pressure-impregnated, will be immune to insect attack throughout its life, and in view of the benefits, it is incredible to think that new housing is still constructed with un-treated timbers.

Exterior timbers also need protection, and you will find this dealt with in chapter 5. Now let us move to some other specific areas where timber may come under attack.

Doors which are painted

The front door is often affected in a number of ways, and because it is usually the first part of your house which greets the visitor it is worth keeping it looking good.

A timber panelled door which is painted may suffer from a breakdown of the paint film, and this is usually associated with slight shrinkage of the panelling—perhaps through excessive sun. This creates fine cracks in the paint film into which rain can get, and this will soak into the timber and eventually push off the paint.

The remedy is to attend to the door when it is really dry. Strip off the paint with a blowtorch, rub smooth, then fill all cracks with a fine surface filler or a stopping. A chemical stripper is not ideal here, as both the liquid used, and the neutraliser can damp down the timber. Using a blow-torch will, if anything, dry the timber even further.

Be sure to prime the bare wood, working it well into crevices. If you encounter knots which have resin seeping from them, cover the area of the knot with a patent knotting to seal in the resin. Otherwise when the sun gets on the door, it may continue to exude resin, pushing off any new paint coating.

Paint may also be pushed off by blistering. This is often caused by paint being applied when the moisture content of the wood is

Weak spots in your defences where damp will attack

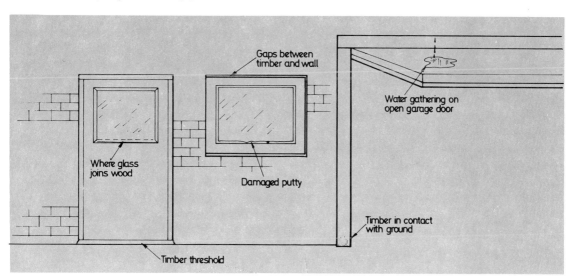

Gaps between timber and wall

Water gathering on open garage door

Where glass joins wood

Damaged putty

Timber in contact with ground

Timber threshold

high. Moisture is trapped in and when the sun gets on the door, the moisture turns to vapour under sufficient pressure to push up the paint surface. The only remedy is to strip off the paint with a blowtorch and re-paint the wood when it is dry.

This is something to bear in mind when painting timber during the autumn and winter months. You will find that early and late in the day there may be condensation on the exterior of the house. Let this condensation dry off before painting.

Paint in sound condition may just have bleached out in the sun, making it look rather drab. Here, there is no need to strip it off, as it can form the foundation of a new coat. Rub the surface with a damp pumice stripping block to remove the glaze from the paint. This gives the surface a key ready for the new coat.

Wipe the surface clean with a lint-free rag and clean water, allow to dry, and the surface is ready for re-painting. If the colour is similar, you may get away with a straight coat of gloss paint, but bear in mind that a top coat has very little obliter-ative power; it resembles a coloured varnish. To hide a colour, you should use a matching undercoat which will obliterate, then follow this by the gloss coat.

Exposed front and back doors may be attacked by wet rot, particularly where a poor quality, badly seasoned timber has been used for a back door. On my quite modern estate, all the houses in our road suffered from rot in the back door after about nine years. This was caused by the reeded glass being inserted reed-side out, so that the retaining beading was not in close contact with the glass. In consequence, water could drain down into the door timber where it caused rotting.

The only remedy is to remove the glass, cut out all damaged timber and replace it with new, treated timber. Then re-glaze, making sure that the glass is well bedded into putty so there is no chance of water getting in. When you re-paint, take the new paint just on to the glass so you give a positive seal between putty and glass, or beading and glass.

Garage doors

A similar problem may be encountered with timber garage doors, where the part-glazing has weak points where moisture can get in. You will also get trouble with older tongue and groove panel doors where the wood has shrunk, forming cracks between panels and frames. Where there is the chance of slight movement, providing the wood is sound, you can seal the cracks with a flexible epoxy filler. This will give a tough but elastic surface which will adhere firmly to the timber, after which you can rub it down and re-paint. It is wise to put such fillers on to bare wood, for if they are put over paint, the only adhesion to the wood is via the paint film. If this loses its hold, obviously the filler must flake away.

Rot in the framework of a timber garage door will have to be cut away and new treated timber inserted. Do not try to fill gaps in the rotten wood with filler—it will not last.

If bolts work loose in timber doors, remove the bolts, drill out any soft wood, fill the holes with an epoxy filler and then when set, re-drill for new bolts. If you have difficulty undoing the rusted bolts, see chapter 4 which deals with metalwork, including the problems of rusting.

Timber doors may also sag with age because of their considerable size and weight. A metal bar used as a brace as shown in the illustration can pull the door back into place. Alternatively, you can use a straining wire as used for tensioning fencing; the screw-tightening device will allow you to tension the cable until it lifts the door the required amount. Obviously such jobs need the removal of the door and the door laying flat. As a further measure to remove the strain from a large door, fit a wheel castor so that the castor takes the weight when the door is open and closed. The illustration shows where to position this.

The up-and-over timber door can also present problems, very often because of bad design. On the same estate I referred to earlier, the timber up-and-over doors rotted away in the bottom panel because when the door was in the open position, the door panels were horizontal and the bottom one projected from the garage opening about 150 mm. If it were left open during rain, water dripped from the wall on to the panel, where it soon found its way into the timber, eventually causing rotting.

Again, such damage calls for the rotten wood to be cut away and new timber inserted. Then all cracks should be sealed with a mastic or flexible epoxy filler prior to re-painting.

Three ways of preventing a door sagging

Doors with natural finish

So far we have dealt with painted timber doors, but some of the trickier problems concern natural finishes where an attractive timber has been treated with a transparent coating so the wood grain shows through. By far the greatest problem is caused by the use of an unsuitable material in the past and the worst offender is linseed oil.

This looks attractive when first applied to bare hardwood, but given some months, it becomes sticky, attracts dust and loses its sheen. As far as I am concerned it is a material of the past, like whitewash, and it should not be used merely because it has been used previously.

It is best to use a chemical paint stripper, a scraper and fine wire wool to remove the old material down to bare wood, always working with the grain of the wood to avoid scratches. With the old oil off, rub down the wood with a fine grade glass-paper until the surface is really smooth—again be sure to work only with the wood grain. Scratches across the grain are practically impossible to lose and when you re-coat the timber, even the smallest scratches will show up.

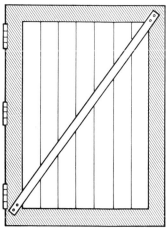

Metal bar as door brace on garage door

Straining wire to lift door from floor

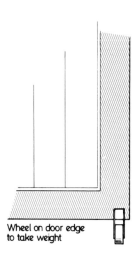

Wheel on door edge to take weight

If you want a glossy appearance to the door, there is still nothing to beat a good quality exterior varnish. The type of varnish supplied by a ship's chandler for use on boats is very durable. The first coat needs working well into the surface of the timber, then, when dry, it can be followed by two further coats.

An alternative is to use an exterior grade polyurethane varnish, but with this material, it is essential to ensure that no water can creep round the back of it and attack the finish from behind. Once it does this the varnish will peel.

Apart from glossy finishes, you have a choice of sheens. There are new preservative stain finishes in a number of attractive colours which soak into the wood giving complete protection against the weather, but without imparting a gloss. Then there are exterior grade teak oils for darker woods, siliconised to resist moisture penetration. These too impart a sheen rather than a gloss, and they allow the beauty of the wood grain to show through.

If you are planning to fit a new hardwood door, ask at the time of purchase what finish is recommended. Having installed the door, get the finish on as quickly as possible before dirt and grease get a hold.

Should you encounter cracks and gaps to fill during renovation, it will be necessary to use a stopping of the appropriate colour. Standard fillers would of course show up against the natural timber—even when coated with the new finish.

Unfortunately, timber is not a very stable material. It expands and contracts according to the moisture content, so that in winter a door may stick tight, while in the warm summer months it is an easy fit. The simplest way of dealing with this problem is to trim the door back on the sticking edge with a shaping tool or plane, then fit a flexible draught strip to seal the slight gap formed. The seal will take up the gap in summer and winter—with no more sticking. If the treatment has been applied to a front door exposed to the weather, it will also kill draughts.

Warping is another problem with older poor quality doors. This can be caused by facing one side of the door with hardboard or plywood so you get uneven expansion. You may solve the problem by facing the other side to act as a balancer. Failing that, you can try exerting pressure at one point. Note where the door closed first and put a wedge in at this point to stop the door closing all the way. Now force the door closed where it is not shutting properly, and keep it closed under pressure. This will help take the 'wind' out of the door.

Where a door is badly warped, it will pay you to discard it and fit a new one. Internal doors, which give most trouble, are still very reasonably priced.

Window frames

Timber frames give little trouble until the weather gets in. Then it is a question of steady deterioration as the paint is pushed off and more damp gets in. Very often an older frame will shrink away from the surrounding brickwork, forming a gap into which rain can be driven. Then the damp will attack from behind, with serious results.

Check for such gaps, and fill these with a mastic to keep the weather out. Never use putty or mortar as these set hard and if there should be any movement, they will crack away, letting in the damp once more. A mastic will stay flexible throughout its life; except on the surface, where it will harden off enough for you to be able to paint over it within a few days.

If sections of frame have become damp, wait until the timber dries out then examine it. If it hardens up, but just has fine cracks, fill these with a fine surface filler or exterior grade stopping before rubbing down and priming prior to painting. If the wood has become soft, so that you can dig a knife point in, you must cut back the damaged wood until you reach sound material, then insert a new piece. This can be glued in place using a waterproof resin adhesive, then fine gaps can be filled with fine surface filler or stopping.

Window frames tend to expand and contract with the moisture content, so these too may stick in the winter and work free in the summer. Very often a build-up of many coats of paint is the cause, and stripping back to the bare wood and starting the decoration again will solve the problem. If there is a sticking problem, use a shaping tool or plane to trim the frame, then fit flexible draught excluding strip to seal the resultant gap. This will make the window easy to operate, and it will ensure it is draught-proof during the winter months.

Where frames are in very poor condition, you can now buy special replacement frames in metal which are designed for the handyman. Or you can get standard joinery frames from a good timber merchant which will fit the cavities. Before choosing new frames consider very carefully whether they will be in character with the house. Modern picture window type frames may not suit your cottage style home.

Warped timber frames are a real problem, for it is not possible to apply any pressure to the frame without the risk of breaking the glass. You will have to take the frame out completely, remove the glass, then examine the twist. Damp the frame and apply a counter-twist, weighting the frame and holding it until it dries out. With a little experimentation you may get it back into shape—after which you can re-glaze and re-paint.

Never leave bare wood any longer than you can help. Get the priming coat on as quickly as possible, and keep the frame in the dry.

This is why it is wise to plan your decorating in manageable stages. Wood need never be left bare from one decorating session to another.

How to treat an oak sill prior to painting

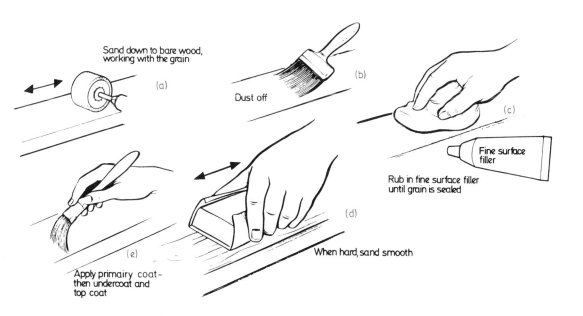

Sand down to bare wood, working with the grain

(a)

Dust off

(b)

(c)

Rub in fine surface filler until grain is sealed

Fine surface filler

(d)

When hard, sand smooth

(e)

Apply primary coat—then undercoat and top coat

Window sills

Window sills often present a problem, because it is a surface over which water runs regularly during the winter months. Very often, part of the problem is that oak sills have been fitted to make them weather better—but oak and paint do not go well together! The reason for this is that air is trapped in the grain of the oak and when the sun shines on it, the air expands enough to push off the paint.

If you encounter oak, strip it down to bare wood, then work fine surface filler into the grain, pressing it in with a rag. Larger cracks can be sealed with an epoxy resin filler, then once set, it should be rubbed smooth and primed in the usual way.

Softwood sills are not so weather-resistant and, in this case, a damaged sill should be stripped to the bare wood. Check with a pointed knife for soft, rotten wood. If you find any, it must be cut out and new timber inserted. If sound, fill cracks with an epoxy filler or fine surface filler; rub smooth when hard, then prime as soon as possible. Do not neglect the end grain, for this is where the damp gets in fastest. Also examine the underside of the sill. There should be what is called a drip groove which encourages water to drip off rather than reach the wall surface.

Very often this groove becomes filled in with coats of paint. If this has occurred, strip off the paint to bare wood, gouge out the drip groove, then prime and re-paint.

If the sill has no groove, it will pay to pin a fine strip of hardwood beading to the underside of the sill before you paint. This will have the same effect as a groove. If you find gaps between the sill and the wall, fill them with a mastic. This is another point of entry for damp.

With your timberwork once more in good shape, it is vital to ensure that the weather cannot find a way in. Make sure that the putty in frames is sound and not cracking away. If pieces can be prised out, remove all loose material, brush out any dirt or dust, and apply a coat of priming paint before you re-putty (see chapter 8 for re-glazing tips). When you re-paint the putty (after allowing a week for the surface to harden) take the paint just on to the glass so you get a seal between putty and glass. Once the water finds an entry point here, you can get frames rotting from inside.

Main timbers

Where you encounter trouble with main structural timbers, such as floor joists, ceiling joists and rafters, you would be wise to seek professional guidance before cutting them out and replacing.

The borough surveyor, contacted through the town hall or municipal offices will advise you—and this may be an area where it will pay to sub-contract the work.

Floorboards

Many people who buy older properties encounter problems with the floors. These are subjected to considerable punishment, and as timber moves and shrinks with the years, you may have anything from irregular surfaces, to actual movement. Let us look at some of the problems you may meet.

Gaps

Some old floors had boards butted together, and as the boards have shrunk—particularly with the introduction of central heating—quite large gaps may appear.

If the floor is sound and well secured, large gaps can be filled by cutting a batten to a slight wedge shape, and tapping the batten into the gap after coating with adhesive (a pva adhesive would do). When the adhesive has set, plane down the strips as near the floor as you can, then finish off with a drum sander.

Smaller gaps can be filled with papier mâché. This is pressed into the cracks, working it well down; allowed to set hard, then rubbed smooth. It is a very old remedy, but still as effective as ever. Both battens and papier mâché can be stained if necessary to match surrounding boards. It is best to experiment, erring on the light side, as stains tend to dry darker than you expect.

If gaps appear in a poorly laid tongued and grooved floor, you have a bigger problem. It is not practicable to fill the gaps. The professional approach would be to lift the boards and re-lay them, tightening them up and filling the final gap with a new board. This is possible if you have the house empty and you have time to work on the house. If this is not possible you can cover the whole floor with hardboard, providing the floor is sound and well fixed. This will provide a good surface for floorcoverings of any kind.

You can fix the board with deep drive panel pins, or for insurance against the pins springing out, with small ring nails. Bear in mind that a board floor gives no access underneath. If you need to get at gas points or junction boxes, it will pay you to make removable panels, fixing them in place with small countersunk screws.

Wear

Where boards are slightly worn, forming hollows, hire a floor sanding machine and take the boards down to form a new surface. Do be sure to remove all old tacks and pins, and hammer down any proud floor nails, or you will ruin the belt on the sander.

Where boards are badly worn but still sound, if you have the opportunity to lift the boards you could turn them, to give you a brand new surface on the top. Obviously this is a long job, and it is not easy to lift the boards. The illustration overleaf shows you how this is done. Obstinate nails may have to be hammered down rather than drawn.

Removing and replacing damaged timber

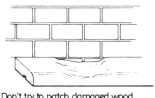
Don't try to patch damaged wood

Cut it out, leaving only sound timber

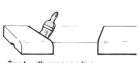
Treat with preservative

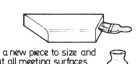
Cut a new piece to size and coat all meeting surfaces with weatherproof adhesive

Tap into place and wipe off surplus adhesive

Sand smooth, Fill any gaps with fine surface filler

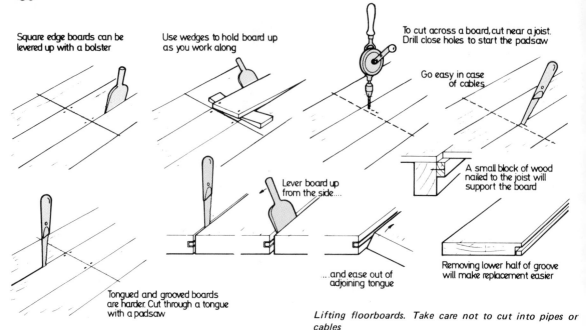

Square edge boards can be levered up with a bolster

Use wedges to hold board up as you work along

To cut across a board, cut near a joist. Drill close holes to start the padsaw

Go easy in case of cables

A small block of wood nailed to the joist will support the board

Lever board up from the side....

...and ease out of adjoining tongue

Removing lower half of groove will make replacement easier

Tongued and grooved boards are harder. Cut through a tongue with a padsaw

Lifting floorboards. Take care not to cut into pipes or cables

When dealing with an upper floor of an older house, hammering may be out of the question as it would bring the ceiling plaster down. This is another case for covering the floor with hardboard to give a new surface.

If floorboards are in bad shape, and springing badly, it will be necessary to form a tougher surface than hardboard. In this case, flooring grade chipboard could be laid over the old floor, screwing it in place with countersunk screws. This too presents problems, because it will raise floor levels. It may not affect the skirtings too much, but you may have to saw a strip off all the doors and you will need a chamfered beading to lose the little steps you will have formed.

Where the floor has to be removed because of serious rot, it will be simpler to lay flooring grade chipboard instead of floorboards. Far less fixing is necessary, and you will have a far smoother surface than you would get with floorboards, however carefully laid.

For fixing, drill clearance holes for screw heads at joist positions, countersink the holes with a rose countersink bit, then secure with countersunk head screws.

Movement

In an older house, you may find that the whole floor is moving on the joists. This is a more difficult problem to cure because it probably means that the joists are loose in the holes in which they rest, or the wall plates holding them have failed.

It will be necessary to gain access to the joist ends by lifting the floor, then you will have to re-anchor the joist ends by wedging them firm. If you find this job too difficult, you may be able to compromise by opening up the floor for a tradesman to get at the fault, allowing him to do the repair work, then leaving you to put the boards back. In this way you could considerably reduce labour charges.

Whenever you do expose joists or other supporting timber, it will pay you to treat the exposed timber with a preservative. Look upon it as an insurance policy against any future trouble.

Parquet flooring

If you inherit parquet or strip flooring, this may have been neglected over the years, leaving it looking very rough and scuffed. This is another situation where it will pay you to hire a floor sanding machine for a full day or weekend. The sander can be used to take off the top surface of the timber, exposing new wood, and it can look as new as the day it was first put down. Having got it clean and smooth, it is vital to get the wood sealed immediately before dirt and scuff marks can ruin it again.

Apply a polyurethane seal with a lint-free rag such as an old handkerchief wrapped around a ball of cotton wool. Work the sealer well into the wood and leave it to dry. When hard, give it a light rub with very fine glasspaper—not hard enough to scratch the wood surface. Then dust free and apply one or two more coats of seal, this time with a brush. If you want a glossy finish you can buy seal to give this. If you prefer it there is a seal which produces a matt sheen.

If the floor is in a reasonable condition which does not warrant sanding, but where scuff marks are spoiling the appearance, remove the marks and any accumulated dirt with fine wire wool dipped in turps substitute. Always rub with the wood grain—never across. This is to ensure you do not make scratches which cannot be removed. When the floor is clear of marks, give a light rub over with fine glasspaper, dust clean, then seal with one or two coats of polyurethane seal.

If you find loose blocks, prise them up, clean out all traces of accumulated dirt from underneath, and dig out any hard adhesive. Then use a bitumen-base adhesive or a black rubber adhesive to stick the blocks back. Try to keep adhesive off the face of the flooring blocks; such materials are not easy to remove. Where you find small gaps remaining, smooth down matching wood stopping to fill them. When set, smooth down with fine glasspaper, working only with the grain of the surrounding wood.

Skirting boards

The skirting board is designed to hide the joint between a wall and a floor, usually being fixed to the wall so the floor can move under it. Where a board has pulled away, you will find that it is nailed to plugs in the wall, and either the nails or the plugs have worked loose. Prise the board away, clean out all loose material from behind, plug the wall where necessary using a modern wall plug to match up with new countersunk holes in the board.

If you plan to add extra power socket outlets, this is the ideal time to run your new cable. It is not often you can gain access to the wall behind a skirting board.

Where you have the chance to re-site the boards it is a good idea to lift the board about 6–8 mm ($\frac{1}{4}$–$\frac{5}{16}$ in) from the floor then re-fix it. This forms a gap into which carpet can be pushed when you are laying it, giving a very neat finish.

Where a skirting board has rotted, replace it with new treated timber. If you are working on an exterior wall where you feel damp may have struck through, treat the wall area with a damp repelling liquid of the type which soaks deep into the masonry. Then fix the new board with aluminium alloy countersunk screws.

Chapter 4
Metalwork

As timber is attacked by insect and rot, so iron and steel are under constant threat by rust and corrosion. All that is required is damp air in contact with bare metal, and it is just a matter of time before you have a heap of useless oxide of iron. Translate this problem into damaged window frames, rusting car bodywork, seized nuts and bolts and sagging gutters, and it represents destruction measured in hundreds of millions of pounds a year—to say nothing of the inconvenience caused.

The basic point to remember is that if you exclude air from the metal in some way, no rusting will take place. Therefore, dealing with the problem of rust falls into two main categories; prevention and elimination.

Protecting metal

Oils and greases

A fairly recent method of rust prevention is to use a fine protective oil in aerosol form. If the oil is sprayed on to all the exposed metal parts of, say, a lawnmover, it will form a fine, unbroken film which actually pushes water off and keeps the air away. It will evaporate after a while, so regular repeat coating is advisable. During the winter months, after a good spray, one coat should see you through to spring.

Oil spray applied to the undersides of mudguards and car wings will discourage a build-up of dirt. It will also ensure good electrical contact where wiring is exposed to the elements.

Metal garden and hand tools will benefit from a coating of oil, especially if stored out of doors. Keep an oily rag in a screw-top jam jar, and as you finish with tools like saws and chisels, given them a rub over with the rag before putting away. When you come to use them, it only takes a second to rub off the oil film with an old towel, and your tools will be in perfect condition.

Items like bolt threads, gate mechanisms and pulley wheels which are exposed to the elements need something heavier than fine oil, as this evaporates too quickly. A grease is more effective, but make sure that this does not come into contact with hands or clothes. Keep a pot of grease handy and an old paintbrush to spread it. Always make a regular check on metalwork that needs protecting.

Chemical protection

Special papers which are chemically impregnated are available; the idea being that fumes are given off which prevent metal rusting. Obviously the chemical is most effective in a confined space, so you can use it in drawers, boxes, and glass containers housing metal objects. If a strip of this paper is kept with screws and nails in a screw-top jar, they will stay bright. If you wish to store spare ironmongery in plastic bags, slip a piece of paper in each bag before sealing.

While on the subject of storing, never store metal items in jars or plastic bags without some protection. You could be sealing moist air in the bag, which could cause more rusting than if they had been left in the fresh air.

An alternative to the paper is silica gel crystals. These crystals have the ability to absorb considerable quantities of water, so if placed in a container they will keep

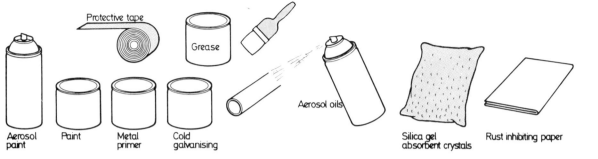

Aerosol paint | Paint | Metal primer | Cold galvanising | Protective tape | Grease | Aerosol oils | Silica gel absorbent crystals | Rust inhibiting paper

Ways of treating metal to prevent rust and corrosion

the air inside dry—until the crystals are saturated. Once this point is reached, you merely place the crystals in the oven and dry out the water. The crystals are then ready for use again. You can buy tell-tale crystals which change colour as they become overloaded with water. This can be useful, especially during a winter storage period when the items are not in use.

Do not wrap tools in old rags or newspapers to protect them; both these absorb moisture from the air until quite damp, and you will be merely holding the damp in contact with the metal. Rag is suitable as long as it is well soaked in a protective oil.

Tapes

Although used mainly in industry, special tapes are available for covering metal or for winding round pipes, where they are to be perhaps buried in the ground. Again, the simple principle applies. The tape keeps air and moisture away from the metal, so there is no corrosion.

Paints

There is nothing new about rust-resisting paint, and it should be used where items are to be handled, making oils and greases impractical. The metal must be clean and grease-free, then it should be painted with a metal primer, followed by a good quality exterior grade paint. For durability choose a polyurethane paint. Ensure that all of the metal is treated. Gaps in the system can allow localised rusting which can soon spread. If you accidentally scratch or chip the paint coating, deal with it as soon as possible before the surface rusts.

A cold galvanising paint gives excellent protection to a metal surface. This is a zinc-rich paint with the zinc held in a binding agent. Stir the paint well to mix the two together before applying to a clean, dry surface. The zinc coating will resist rusting, and once it has set, it can be painted in the normal way.

Alternatives to metal

A different approach to prevention is to consider what alternatives there are to metal when constructing or repairing. There are many materials now available which will not corrode or rust; if you can choose from these you have a distinct advantage.

Nails and screws are available in aluminium alloy and some are galvanised. Hinges are available in nylon; gutters, downpipes and waste systems made in pvc are quite common; and even chromium plating can be imitated in acrylic plastics. It is obviously sensible to choose materials which do not corrode and which need little or no maintenance.

Dealing with rust

Where you encounter rust, all loose material must be removed down to sound metal. For this you can use a hand-held wire brush, or a wheel or cup brush mounted in a power tool. Whichever you choose, be sure to wear protective goggles as you can suffer eye damage from the flying particles. Special toughened plastic safety glasses are not expensive, and they will allow you to work in complete safety.

If dealing with a rusted metal window frame, be sure you get to the source of the rust, even if you have to strip off a lot of extra paint. It is no use at all painting over rust, as the action will continue under the paint and eventually push your new coating off.

When you are back to sound metal, rub over with fine emery paper to smooth the metal, then dust off and apply a cold galvanising paint or a chemical rust inhibitor.

How to remove rust—and how to protect the clean metal

This is a special liquid which either converts the iron oxide to iron phosphate, or forms an inert tannate film. Read the instructions carefully before you use it, both to see how it is applied, and also whether it needs neutralising after use. Once the rust killer has done its work, you can apply a metal primer, followed by the normal paint coating.

When using these chemicals, be sure to protect your eyes against splashing. The safety glasses will protect you.

In severe cases, you may find the metal eaten away to form a hollow—or at the worst a hole right through. It is best to be ruthless and file away all loose and flaking metal until you are back to solid material, rub clean and dust off. Then mix an epoxy resin filler—as much as you can use in about ten minutes (five in hot weather) and fill in the cavity proud of the surface. If there is a smallish hole, cover the far side with a piece of wood or hardboard covered in polythene. The polythene will ensure that the filler lets go when set.

When hard, you can rub back the filler until it is flush with the surrounding metal. Apply rust inhibitor to the surrounding metal, then prime and paint.

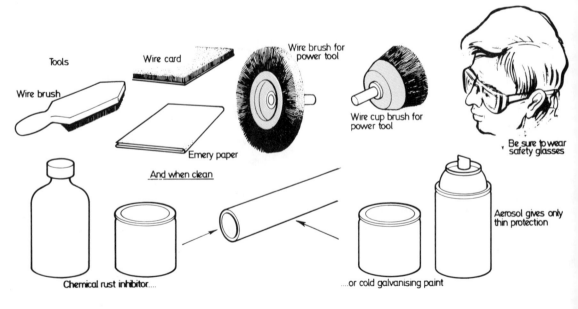

Tools

Wire brush

Wire card

Wire brush for power tool

Wire cup brush for power tool

Emery paper

Be sure to wear safety glasses

And when clean

Chemical rust inhibitor....

....or cold galvanising paint

Aerosol gives only thin protection

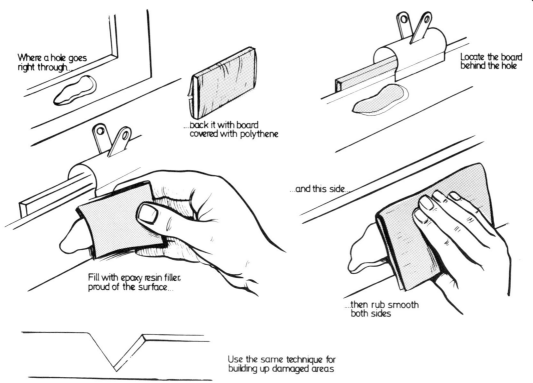

Where a hole goes right through...

...back it with board covered with polythene

Locate the board behind the hole

...and this side...

Fill with epoxy resin filler, proud of the surface...

...then rub smooth both sides

Use the same technique for building up damaged areas

Filling holes in metalwork

Where you encounter a large hole, the filler will need support. You can give this by backing the hole with perforated metal sheeting sold for this purpose. Anchor the sheet in place with a little epoxy filler, then fill the hole as previously described. Allow to set, and rub smooth.

The epoxy filler can be used to build up damaged areas, such as where a cast iron gutter has a piece broken away. The area to be repaired must be clean and dry so that the filler can get a good grip, then you mould the filler to the required shape and let it set. Once hard it can be filed, drilled and sanded as for metal.

Where metal is badly rusted and no longer has any strength, it will be necessary to remove the damaged section completely and insert new metal. This job has been greatly simplified by the introduction of d-i-y welding equipment.

It pays to keep a selection of pieces of metal in your repair kit; these should be of various gauges (thicknesses) and types. A typical selection might be tinplate cut from old cans, thin sheet steel, brass and alloy. You can cut the thin material with tinsnips or with the pliers-type nibbling tool which has changeable cutting blades. Thicker materials need a hacksaw and a selection of small files for cleaning up.

If you intend to do much metalwork it will be necessary to add a heavy metal-working vice to your tool kit so that you have a firm and heavy surface in which to grip and work your metal. You will also need a set of high speed steel twist drills for drilling holes, and it will help considerably if you invest in a vertical drill stand. You will get much more accurate holes with less fear of breaking your drills.

When drilling metal, never hold the material in your fingers. If the twist drill snags up, it will rotate the metal violently, and you can get a very nasty cut. Treat all metal sheet with respect; it can be very sharp, and it would be wise to wear your leather gardening gloves if you are not used to metalworking.

Dismantling metalwork

One of the greatest time wasters in repair work is trying to dismantle rusted or corroded components. If you cannot separate the components you have little chance of repairing. If the trouble is minor, applying easing oil to the area to be stripped, or, if possible and you are sure no harm will be done, submerse the components in de-rusting fluid. Eventually the corrosion will dissolve and you will be able to apply a spanner or screwdriver.

However, there are situations where it is not possible to apply this technique, such as where the bolts holding the sections of a shed have rusted badly, but the nut and bolt are tight against the wood. Very often the bolt head has no slot, relying on a square on the shank to stop it turning. So if you force the nut, the whole unit revolves in the wood.

Tips to make metalworking easier and safer

Where corrosion is not too severe, apply easing oil to the bolt thread where visible, then use a small hacksaw and file a slot in the bolt head. This will allow you to hold a screwdriver in the slot while you try to turn the nut. Hold the driver still by gripping its blade in a grip wrench.

If this fails, you can drill down into the bolt head, using a twist drill as near the size of the bolt shank as possible. It is a slow job, but eventually the head of the bolt will drop away and you will be able to withdraw the whole thing from the wood. Yet another alternative is to use a special nut splitting tool. This is applied to one flat of the nut and, as the splitter is tightened, it forces a sharp wedge into the metal, which it eventually splits, releasing the nut from the thread. Using this latter method, you can use the bolt again, merely finding a nut to fit it.

Before reassembling nuts and bolts, treat the thread with a special oil available which makes any future dismantling easy. Alternatively, you can use grease or Vaseline. Never use soap as this can encourage rusting and it certainly does not work as well as oil or grease.

On more delicate work where you do not wish to saw or drill, try applying the hot tip of a soldering iron to the bolt end.

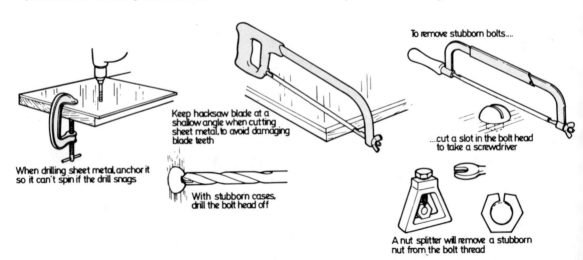

When drilling sheet metal, anchor it so it can't spin if the drill snags

Keep hacksaw blade at a shallow angle when cutting sheet metal, to avoid damaging blade teeth

With stubborn cases, drill the bolt head off

To remove stubborn bolts....

...cut a slot in the bolt head to take a screwdriver

A nut splitter will remove a stubborn nut from the bolt thread

The heat will expand the metal, very often breaking the grip of the rust. When applying the spanner, force the nut just a shade tighter before trying to loosen. A trick which often succeeds where all else fails!

In some cases you may not want a nut to be loose, or it may vibrate loose when the equipment to which it is fixed vibrates.

Where a nut must be secure, you can apply a second nut as a lock nut, or you can buy special nuts with a plastic insert which acts as a damper and a lock. You can also buy a special compound which, when applied to the thread, will ensure the nut does not work loose. This will not stop you undoing it with a spanner at some future date.

Chapter 5
Walls and ceilings

It is not so easy to write about walls nowadays, for building methods have changed quite considerably in recent years. At one time houses had solid walls or cavity walls mainly of brick, then lightweight blocks were introduced mainly for use on the interior wall. Today we have an increasing use of timber frame construction where only a decorative skin of brick is applied to the exterior after the main construction is complete.

Before you take on the job of wall repair or maintenance it will pay you to find out how your walls are constructed. Is the outer wall, for example, a structural part of the house? Is the stone or brick facing mainly decorative?

Settlement cracks

Settlement or movement can be a problem, and this is quite common, especially when we have long, dry summers. Soil can shrink and expand according to its water content, and this is most noticeable with clay soils.

Unfortunately, if a house is standing on soil which moves, something has to give. This may only be the joints in a room between walls and ceiling; it may be a long but not very wide crack running across a large wall surface such as that on the stair well, or it may be the joint between a garage and the house wall to which it is attached.

Such seasonal movement is very difficult to hide. Indoors it can take the form of a cove cornice which can move the crack, and outside it may be a flashing which can move enough to disguise the crack. On inside decorated walls hiding the crack is not so easy. Most cellulose fillers used to fill cracks when they are open cannot withstand the tremendous pressure exerted when the crack closes during the winter months. They merely get crushed out so the gap is back next year. If the wall plaster is hard and strong, an epoxy type filler stands a better chance of survival, but you may merely get a new crack nearby.

Hessian type wallcoverings, grasscloth and similar materials disguise cracks by moving with them and, of course, sheet or strip wall panelling will also be effective. Anaglyptas are not normally successful as they have little shear strength.

Seasonal movement is nothing to worry about, apart from appearance, but what is far more serious is subsidence. This is

Settlement cracks—very common in dry weather

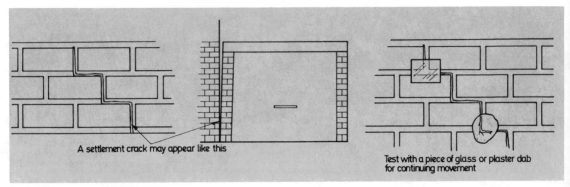

A settlement crack may appear like this

Test with a piece of glass or plaster dab for continuing movement

where the ground actually sinks, and it may be caused by building on land which has not settled sufficiently, for example putting new estates on covered rubbish tips. Worse still, the subsidence may be the after-effects of old mine workings where vibration or flooding has caused ground to collapse.

If you discover cracks which seem to continue widening rather than opening and shutting with the seasons, test the area by securing a piece of glass across the crack with epoxy resin adhesive. Make sure the adhesive gets a good grip on the brick. Alternatively, build up a flat blob of plaster of paris across the gap at a couple of points. Now wait to see what happens; as the structure moves, the glass will crack or the plaster break,and you will get a very clear picture of how much movement is involved.

Settlement is not the kind of problem you can deal with on your own, and if you suspect this trouble, call in to see your local borough surveyor and discuss the matter. He will know the area and the condition of the land upon which your home is built. If there is a serious settlement, then it may be necessary to have the foundations strengthened by underpinning. This can be an expensive process as considerable digging is involved down to and below foundation level.

Dealing with cracked mortar and damaged brickwork

If your house is fairly new, slight settlement cracks are quite commonplace. You will find that these usually follow the mortar joints and do not continue to expand. In such cases, all you need do is rake out any loose mortar, and fill with a new mortar mix. Damp the existing work first to cut suction, and be sure to use a very dry mix

for filling so that you do not mark the surrounding brickwork. For smaller jobs, mortar supplied as a dry mix in paper sacks is the most economical. Merely add the minimum of water as required.

In older properties, you may find that the mortar pointing is crumbling. This needs replacing, so rake out the old mortar to a depth of about 12 mm (½ in). (The drawing overleaf shows a tool which can be made from a piece of scrap metal to do this job.) Then brush out the joints to remove dust, damp the gaps with water, then apply a dryish mix of mortar. The trickiest part of the job is getting a good finish to the joints. There are three basic finishes as illustrated, the hollow joint being the simplest.

Soft bricks which have become porous are often affected by the frost, causing flaking of the surface. Use a steel chisel and club hammer to cut into the brick about 25 mm (1 in), then you need to find a matching brick. Split this with a club hammer and bolster to give you a piece which can be inset over the damaged area, sticking it in place with mortar. Then re-point as for the rest of the wall. Having restored the area, apply a liberal coating of silicone water repellent to the bricks and pointing. This will ensure that the frost will not cause damage in future.

Cleaning brickwork

Where brickwork has become dirty, scrub it with a stiff brush and plenty of water. Do not use detergent or soap or you will get a whitish staining of the bricks which is impossible to lose.

A textured brick can often be improved by wire brushing, but be sure to protect your eyes. Another 'wrinkle' is to find a piece of matching brick, break it, and use a piece as a pumice block, scrubbing the

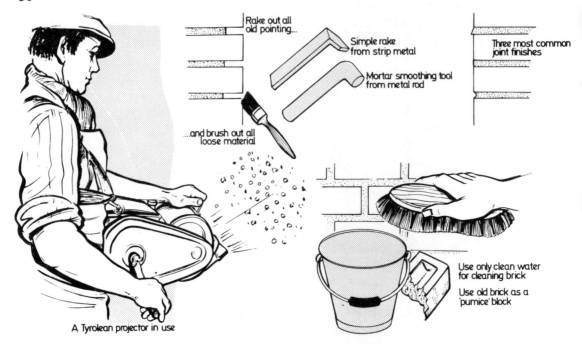

Rake out all old pointing....

Simple rake from strip metal

Mortar smoothing tool from metal rod

Three most common joint finishes

...and brush out all loose material

Use only clean water for cleaning brick

Use old brick as a 'pumice' block

A Tyrolean projector in use

brickwork with it. This will rub away the grime without affecting the colouring of the brick in any way.

Very often grubby mortar can make a wall look dull. You can improve the appearance by raking back the mortar by about 19 mm (¾ in) and re-pointing with a lighter coloured mortar. You can order white cement for special jobs like this, which will lighten the mix. Again, keep the mix as dry as possible, so it does not mark the bricks, and damp the brickwork before adding the new material.

Wherever possible, avoid painting brickwork. It never looks good and once painted there is no way of getting the paint out of the pores of the brickwork. If the wall really looks dull, it is better to consider adding a new surface. The simplest method is to use what is called a Tyrolean projector. This is a special tool which can be used to fling a thin mortar mix on to the wall to produce an interesting textured surface. This tool can be borrowed from most hire shops, together with full details on how to make suitable mixes.

Ways of dealing with jaded walls

The advantage of this system is that it fills all the brick joints, giving a smooth but textured surface. This can then be painted with any of the exterior paints, from emulsion to stone paint.

Repairing rendered surfaces

Rendered wall surfaces can be painted with masonry paint. Do not worry about hair line cracks as a full bodied masonry paint will lose these. Large cracks should be cleaned and sealed with mortar. If some pva adhesive is added to the mixing water this will ensure good adhesion; then, when dry, you can paint.

Where rendered surfaces have been stained by mould growth, buy a special primer sealer to sterilise the wall and to prepare it for the new paint. With some cement-based paints you will be advised to use a sealer anyway, so be sure to check just what you need when buying your materials.

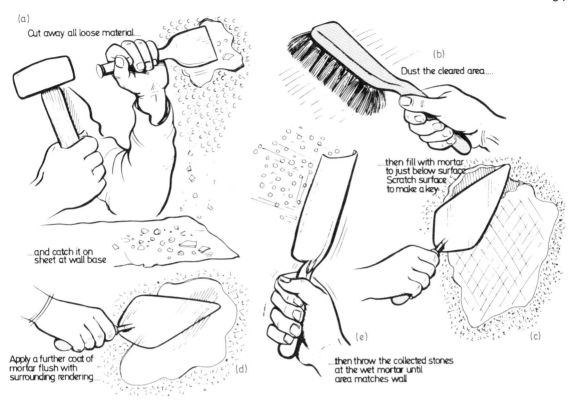

(a) Cut away all loose material....

...and catch it on sheet at wall base

(b) Dust the cleared area....

....then fill with mortar to just below surface. Scratch surface to make a key·

(c)

(e) ...then throw the collected stones at the wet mortar until area matches wall

(d) Apply a further coat of mortar flush with surrounding rendering....

How to repair damaged pebbledash

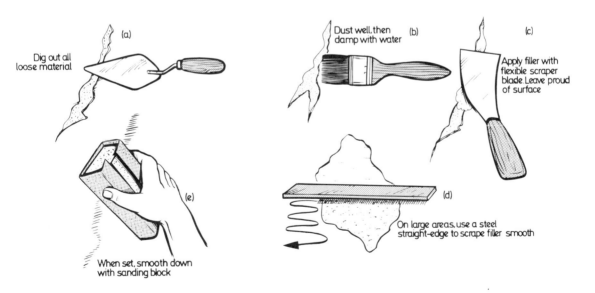

(a) Dig out all loose material

(b) Dust well, then damp with water

(c) Apply filler with flexible scraper blade. Leave proud of surface

(d) On large areas, use a steel straight-edge to scrape filler smooth

(e) When set, smooth down with sanding block

Repairing damaged wall rendering

Pebbledash and spar dash can be painted, and the best tool to use is the shaggy hair exterior grade nylon paint roller. If you prefer a brush, use one at least 127 mm (5 in) wide, or use a sweeping brush of the type you use with a dustpan. You will find the handle of this type of brush very comfortable to use.

Unfortunately, the layer of mortar holding the stones can bulge away from the wall with age, and this is far too unstable a surface to redecorate. Spread sacking or sheet polythene along the wall, then hack off the damaged areas using a bolster and club hammer, protecting your eyes. When the damaged areas are clear, sort out the rubbish and rescue all the old stones, place these in water to clean and wet them. This is a better idea than buying new stones, as new ones will be far brighter and cleaner, and the repair will be very noticeable.

Brush clean the bare areas, damp with water, then add a layer of cement mortar. If the repair is shallow, only one application is necessary. If the holes are deep, apply one layer to within 6 mm (¼ in) of the surface, allow it to start to harden, say half an hour, then scratch the surface with a trowel point to form a key for the next coat. With the top coat in place, throw the stones on to the wet mortar, pressing them lightly with a piece of board to ensure they are anchored and that they match the surrounding area.

Where the dash is in a really bad state, it will be necessary to pull the lot off, in which case the simplest way of redecorating is to use the Tyrolean projector already described.

Treatment of outside timbers

If your home is part-faced with timber, this should be treated as for the rest of the paintwork if already painted. If treated with a natural finish, give it a liberal coat of matching wood preservative. If you have red cedar timbering, there is a special grade of preservative; which includes stain, designed to re-colour the cedar to its approximate original colouring. Cedar shingles should be treated in a similar way, and it is wise to give them a regular coating so the wood does not dry right out and curl. Be sure to fix loose timberwork with alloy or galvanised nails so you do not get staining.

Plastic boarding is quite common, and this should need no treatment other than a good wash down with water and detergent to remove grime. Do not use abrasives as you will merely roughen the surface and encourage dirt to stick. Do not use chemical solvents as these will soften and mark the plastic. Of course never, ever, use a blow-torch!

Repairing interior plaster walls

Interior walls where the plaster is in good condition usually need little treatment. You may encounter minor cracks, plus holes where fitments have been put up in the past. These should be cleaned of loose material, damped with water and filled with cellulose filler. Always fill just proud of the surface, then rub back with glass-paper until level with the surrounding wall.

Where pieces of plaster have dropped out, tap the wall and listen for a hollow sound. If it does sound hollow, you will need to cut back the plaster until you reach solid material. Dust clean, then damp and apply some filler such as Keene's cement to within 5 mm (¼ in) of the surface. Allow the filler to start to set, then scratch the surface to give a key for new material, then apply a top coat, smoothing it just proud of the surface. When hard, use glasspaper to get a really smooth surface.

In some older properties you may find the plaster is in very poor shape, perhaps pulling away with the old wallpaper. In this case there is no point in patching. The whole lot needs to be hacked off to the brickwork—this is a really messy job! There will be a lot of dust, and to keep it down it is a good idea to damp the plaster thoroughly before hacking it away. Replastering is not a job for the inexperienced, and it will pay you to get a plasterer to resurface the wall. The alternative is to dry line the wall, using sheet plasterboard—and this you can do yourself.

Lining walls

The standard way of lining used to be to fix timber battens to the wall to which the plasterboard could be nailed. With the introduction of new adhesive plasters, it is now possible to apply blobs of special plaster to the cleaned wall, then press the sheet plasterboard in place. Jointing is the most difficult of the fixing operations, and this is done with a special jointing tape and finishing plaster, full details of which can be obtained when buying the boards.

An advantage of dry lining is, as the name implies, that there is no water to dry out after the job is done, as there is with wet plastering. So, once joints are dry, you can start redecorating.

If you plan to do any rewiring, such as fixing wall lights, remember the ideal time to do it is before putting on the sheet plasterboard. You can channel the wall to recess the cables to the lights, then lose the lot under the board. You will, of course, need holes in the plasterboard large enough to feed the cable through.

You may also have to remove skirting boards before lining and then replace them over the top of your new wall surface. This is the ideal time for the fixing of new socket outlets as you can arrange the wiring behind the plasterboard, then merely fix your new sockets when the new wall is finished.

Filling gaps between walls and ceiling

We have already considered slight movement of the house on its foundations, and a weak spot for cracking is the joint between the walls of a room and the ceiling. Filling at this point has little effect, so the best solution is to fit a coving to bridge the gap. The simplest type is made of expanded polystyrene, but this has problems in that it comes in short lengths which have to be butt jointed. Losing the joints is very difficult as polystyrene is hard to smooth. It tends to rough up as you rub it.

The best coving is made of gypsum plaster. This is far heavier to handle, but very attractive when fixed. Again, the introduction of adhesive plasters makes it possible to stick it in place with no other support necessary. It can be obtained in long lengths if you wish to have the minimum of joints; shorter lengths are available if you find them easier to handle. Cutting is simple enough, but making the mitres for internal and external corners calls for a little practice. You can get some very odd shapes, even though a template is supplied.

Ceiling faults

This brings us to the ceiling, and here it is the older property which will give us most trouble. The old system of making a ceiling was to fix laths to the ceiling joists with a small gap between each lath. Then a special fibrous plaster was pressed on the laths so that is squeezed up between them and keyed itself in. Then a finishing coat was applied. Old age, plus severe vibration over the years may have broken the keying and, in consequence, you can get sagging in places.

Where the damage is slight, it is possible to use alloy screws to screw the plaster back to the laths. Or, if you can gain access to the underfloor above, such as in the loft, you can press the ceiling back into place with a length of timber and piece of board. Then pour a fairly wet mix of Keene's cement, or even plaster of Paris over the damaged section to form a new key.

Where the ceiling is in a bad way, it will have to come down, and this is an extremely messy job, because of the dust. As with stripping walls, it is wise to damp down the ceiling plaster to reduce the dust while you pull it and the laths away from the ceiling. You can then replace the laths with ceiling plasterboard, nailed with special plasterboard nails to the joints. The joints will have to be sealed with a special jointing tape and finishing plaster.

If you want a simpler solution, leave the joints and cover the whole ceiling with one of the plastic compounds designed for

texturing. By the time it is stippled or combed you will not see the joists and you will have hidden the nails.

The modern plasterboard ceiling does not present such drastic problems. The most common one is slight cracking at the joints. This is often caused in bedrooms by loading too much in the loft and these cracks are not easy to lose. A lining paper often helps, or you can use one of the plastic compounds already referred to.

Where a ceiling looks in poor condition through cracking, but is holding up well, the simplest disguise is to use one of the many designs of expanded polystyrene or fibreboard ceiling tiles. If you choose expanded polystyrene, remember you must apply adhesive over the whole ceiling area, *not in blobs.* This is to ensure that, should there be a fire, no burning pieces of expanded polystyrene will drop away. If you prefer something with more fire resistance, there are fibreboard and textured plasterboard tiles. They are more expensive, and considerably heavier than plastic tiles, but are still well within the scope of the d-i-y enthusiast.

Ceiling types—and how to apply expanded polystyrene tiles

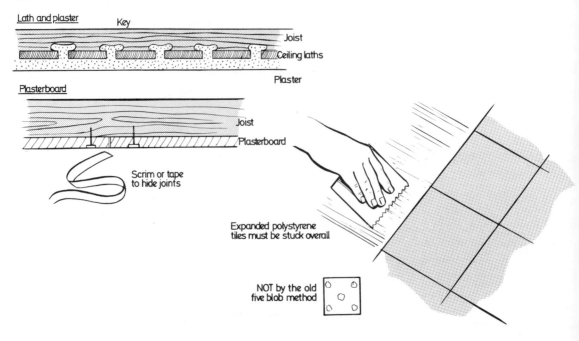

Lath and plaster — Key — Joist — Ceiling laths — Plaster

Plasterboard — Joist — Plasterboard — Scrim or tape to hide joints

Expanded polystyrene tiles must be stuck overall

NOT by the old five blob method

Stains may also be a nuisance. The cause may be a burst pipe or leaking tank some time in the past which carried rust into the ceiling which may bleed through your paint. It may also have been caused by an over-zealous operator applying older type wood-worm killers and letting the fluid seep through the ceiling. Before decorating, and assuming the stains are dry, apply a liberal coat of aluminium primer sealer to the stained area. This has a scale-like construction which effectively seals off the stain and, once dry, you can decorate over it. Do not confuse this material with aluminium paint which has not the same qualities. The aluminium in the latter is finely ground and does not have the same sealing properties.

Failure of new decorations to stick firmly to the ceiling can be most annoying, and the most common reason for this is that in the past distemper was used for decoration.

This has a chalky quality, and nothing will adhere to it. The only treatment is to remove it by rubbing with a coarse rag and plenty of water until you get down to bare plaster. Thick areas can be damaged then scraped off, holding a dustpan underneath to catch the mess. Hard deposits can be sealed with a special distemper sealer.

Mould growth

Both walls and ceilings which become damp can encourage the growth of mould spores. These are harmless, but they do ruin decoration, staining areas with brownish spots.

Such trouble must be dealt with by removing the wall covering and treating the bare plaster with a fungicide. This will kill off the spores. As an extra precaution, use a paste containing a fungicide when re-papering.

Chapter 6
Damp

Damp, in all its forms, does very serious damage to most building materials; it will rot timbers, rust metal and ruin all forms of decoration. Damp should be treated very seriously, and for this reason, we have a chapter solely devoted to it, even though it is mentioned in other chapters. Wherever damp is encountered, the rule is to deal with it as soon as possible, for the longer it is left, the more serious will be the problems of repair. This, in turn, means more expense.

There are three main sources of damp; rain penetration, moisture rising from the soil, and moisture-laden air which leads to condensation. All three are considered in this chapter.

The roof

This is the area which receives the brunt of any rainfall, so it must be in good condition. Unfortunately it is the most difficult area to check and to repair. You should make it a rule that no roof work is attempted without the correct means of access. This means a ladder extending at least three rungs above gutter height; then a correct roof ladder which is designed to hook firmly over the roof ridge. This combination will ensure that you have a safe means of getting to the roof, and something firm to hang on while you work. Make sure you erect the ladder at the correct angle—1 metre out for every 4 metres up (or 3 ft for every 12 ft). Also make sure that the base of the ladder is anchored so it cannot slip.

Examine the ridge tiles. They should all be firmly anchored in place, but frost may have attacked the mortar and broken the bond. If you have deeply profiled tiles, you may find that gaps are also filled with mortar; this is termed pargeting. This mortar too may work loose, or you may find that if it is on the soft side the birds will peck it out to gain access to the loft for nesting. Any mortar in this condition should be replaced.

Damaged or displaced tiles need replacing or putting back. If you live in an older house with a slate roof, check that the nails are still in good condition. A common fault is that the nails corrode away, allowing the slates to slide. It is wise to remove any moss growth as you proceed. Remove the moss with a small trowel, then brush with moss killer.

Now move over to the chimney stack and see that the general condition of the brickwork is good. In older properties where there has been damp in the flue lining, and perhaps deposits of corrosive chemicals from fuel burned, you may find the mortar has been badly damaged, and it could be that the stack is unsafe. This is a job where you should get professional advice, for the sheer weight of this brickwork makes it quite unmanageable unless you have roof scaffolding and the correct equipment.

If the stack is sound, check the mortar holding any chimney pots. This is called the flaunching and any damage needs putting right. If the fireplaces below are no longer in use, cover the unused pots with a half round tile, fixing each in place with cement mortar. This will prevent rain getting down the flue and perhaps causing damp patches on bedroom walls.

In an older property where this is a stack for a boiler, check to see that the flue has a liner between the boiler and the chimney pot. When inefficient stoves were used in the past a lot of heat went up the flue. This did not matter too much

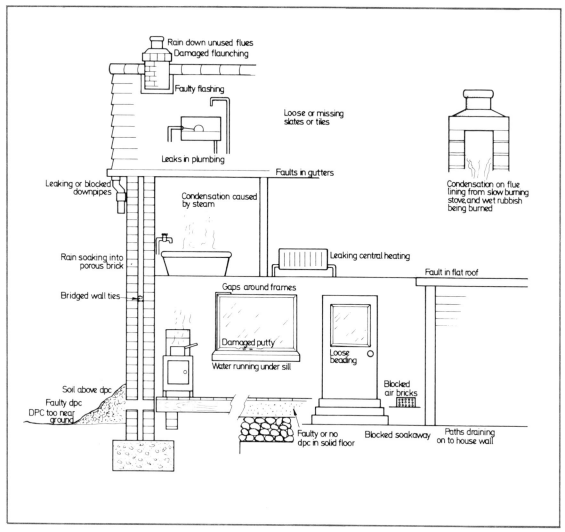

Where damp is most likely to attack your home

then, as the lost heat kept the flue warm. Nowadays, when boilers are far more efficient and therefore lose far less heat up the chimney, you can get gases condensing on the cold flue, causing staining and damage to the flue lining.

The simplest way of adding a lining is to use a flexible metal tube connected between boiler and chimney pot. However, there are certain fuels which attack even this type of lining, so it is wise to check before ordering. If a flexible liner is not suitable,

you will have to use salt glazed pipes, but these are far more difficult to fix in an already completed flue.

At the base of a chimney stack you will find sheet material has been used to seal the joint between the roof and the stack. This is called a flashing, and it is important that it is in good condition. The most common material used is lead but, in some modern houses, you may find a fibrous sheeting has been used instead. Very often the mortar holding the flashing cracks away. This, of course, needs making good, and any gaps in the flashing need sealing with a mastic.

Now move down to gutter level. Again, you will often find that mortar is used to seal the gaps at the tile ends. Birds very often dig this out so they can nest in the eaves, so loose and crumbling material should be removed and new mortar applied.

Gutters and down pipes

We are now in a position to examine the state of the gutters. This will vary considerably according to the age of the house and its location. Ensure that there are no holes in the gutter, and that water can flow freely to the down pipes. You can test these points by taking a can of water to the point farthest from a down pipe and feeding the water into the gutter, and watching how it flows.

The water may flow sluggishly due to silt off the tiles, and in rural areas the gutters can soon become choked with leaves, old nests and other debris. All this must, of course be removed, and it pays to have regular checking sessions, with the most important one after the leaves have fallen off the trees.

To discourage birds, fit a wire or plastic cage in the top of each down pipe. If you are troubled with leaves, fit a plastic mesh guard over the gutter to keep them out.

If water finds a way out of the gutter other than the down pipe, it may saturate a wall area. If you are unlucky, this may find a way to the internal leaf of the wall and you will find damp patches in the adjacent bedroom.

You may also have noticed when doing the water check that water gathers in certain spots, indicating that the gutter has sagged at this point. The usual cause is a faulty gutter bracket. The actual bracket may be damaged, or the holding screws may have rusted in the board into which they are screwed.

Down pipes rarely give trouble, though they may become blocked if birds are given the chance to nest in the tops. With the old cast iron type, you will see that there are gaps between each pipe section where one pipe fits into another. It is wise not to seal these gaps, as they give you a clear indication if the pipe becomes blocked; it will always overflow at the joint immediately above the blockage. If the joints are sealed, the water must overflow at gutter level.

Very often you can clear nest debris by feeding a garden hose in the top of the pipe, turning on the water and pushing the hose down. A note of warning, however—do not wear your best clothes for this job! If the blockage really is serious, you can hire a flexible drain clearing tool of the type operated by a hand drill. It is easy to use and very effective.

Checking rainwater gutters. Do it regularly

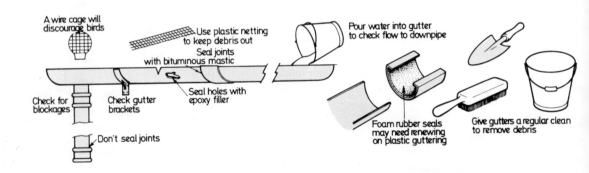

A wire cage will discourage birds

Use plastic netting to keep debris out

Seal joints with bituminous mastic

Seal holes with epoxy filler

Check for blockages

Check gutter brackets

Don't seal joints

Pour water into gutter to check flow to downpipe

Foam rubber seals may need renewing on plastic guttering

Give gutters a regular clean to remove debris

Walls

Next, examine the walls. It is not often realised that brick walls are designed to absorb a certain amount of water without any ill effects. This latter evaporates as the weather dries. Where the bricks are too porous, or where the pointing between them is crumbling, rain may penetrate too far.

With a properly constructed cavity wall, this penetration may still have little effect other than to cool down the wall too much. If any of the wall ties are bridged by mortar, due to poor workmanship, the moisture will pass across into the inner leaf of the wall and appear as damp patches indoors. You cannot reach the wall ties, but you can seal the outer brick wall to prevent damp getting in.

First you need to re-point the brickwork wherever you find the mortar soft and crumbling. Then treat the wall with a silicone water repellent fluid, flooding it on to the wall so that it completely coats the outer face of the brick. Try to keep it off window frames, porch roofs and glass, for although transparent, it forms a skin of silicone which is just about impossible to move. Cracks and gaps in any wall rendering need to be sealed, and you can find details of this in chapter 5.

About 150 mm (6 in) up from the ground, at the base of your walls, you should find a horizontal layer set in the brickwork. This is the damp-proof course, and it may take the form of a bitumen strip, pieces of slate or special impervious bricks, all of which will be referred to as the dpc. This is designed to prevent damp climbing up into the brickwork from the earth below, and to do this it must of course be continuous and unbroken. Should the dpc become bridged in any way water may find its way into the house at skirting board level, resulting in damp patches, ruined decorations, and possibly wood rot.

In an old house, there may be no damp proof course, but just a very thick wall, relying on its sheer bulk to keep the damp at bay. Very often it can, but where paths have been built up close against the wall, or earth is piled against it, you may find that the wall shows signs of retaining the damp.

Putting in a damp-proof course (dpc)

Where a damp-proof course is faulty, or does not exist, there are two courses of action. First, you can employ a reputable company to do the work of inserting a damp-proof barrier, or, second, you can tackle the job yourself. Let us look at these options.

One professional treatment is called electro-osmosis, and it calls for specialists. The work involves setting a copper strip in the wall, then connecting it to a special earthing terminal sunk deep into the ground. The effect is to earth out the electrical potential inherent in each droplet of water rising by capillary action in the wall. For some reason which no one seems to understand, it reverses the flow of droplets and water is in fact driven down, not up. Given time, the wall will dry out. With this method you receive a guarantee assuring you that the trouble will not recur.

Another approach is to sink tubes into the wall, to which are connected bottles containing a damp-resisting liquid. The liquid is gravity-fed into the wall, where it forms a barrier against rising damp. Yet another system consists of small drainage tubes set into the wall, angled down so that moisture drains off with a syphonic action. There are also firms who saw through a horizontal mortar joint, inserting a new damp-proof course membrane as they go.

If you have the work done professionally, be sure to keep the guarantee against the

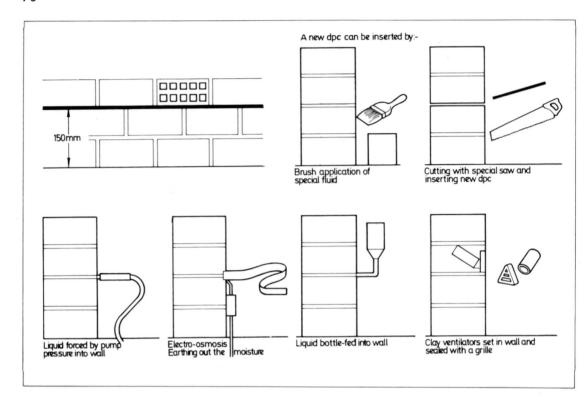

A new dpc can be inserted by:-

Brush application of special fluid

Cutting with special saw and inserting new dpc

Liquid forced by pump pressure into wall

Electro-osmosis Earthing out the moisture

Liquid bottle-fed into wall

Clay ventilators set in wall and sealed with a grille

150mm

day you may wish to sell. If your house has had a reputation for damp, you need to have proof that the matter has been effectively dealt with.

The second option is to tackle the work yourself, and this is possible without too much trouble. There is a specialist company willing to supply the know-how and the necessary damp resisting liquid to anyone willing to do the actual work. The fluid is gravity-fed into the walls through holes bored in them, and it will form a barrier through which the damp cannot pass. Once completed, the company offer a 20 year guarantee against further trouble in the area treated.

I think this is the ideal solution for young couples with limited financial resources buying their first home where they have to put right damp problems. If you are involved with a building society, check

Different ways of providing a wall with a damp proof course (dpc)

first that they accept the system. I have found at least one society which will not.

A second system involves the use of a special damp-resisting fluid which has to be brushed on to the wall. There is an interior and exterior grade which, when used correctly, will give a barrier in depth. The makers state that the liquid can penetrate up to 230 mm (9 in) in masonry. Obviously the ideal time to apply such a liquid is while the wall is dry, as once a wall is damp, its ability to absorb liquid is reduced. At the time of writing, no guarantee is offered with this process, but the company has been operating successfully for many years in the industrial field, before coming on to the d-i-y market.

Hire shops can give assistance, as certain shops now stock a unit which dispenses damp-resisting liquid under pressure so that it can be forced into the wall. This greatly speeds up the process, as gravity-feed is a slow business.

The damp-resisting liquid which is brush-applied can also be used for sealing off areas affected by damp—other than defective damp proof courses. The liquid is useful around window frames, and particularly window ledges, to make the masonry impervious to water. This process should not be confused with a silicone water repellent which is a surface treatment only. The latter does not protect in depth.

Flat roofs

Flat roofs to porches, garages or extensions can be a real headache as far as damp penetration is concerned, for moisture lying on a flat surface has an excellent chance of percolating through at some weak point. Treatments for flat roof areas can be found in chapter 7.

Door and window frames

However well door and window frames fit when first installed, wood tends to shrink with age, allowing gaps to form between the frame and the adjoining masonry. This will allow water to get in—especially on aspects where the wind plays on the wall. Water may then be under pressure, and it will seep in. The damage it may do to timberwork has already been mentioned in chapter 3, but if it penetrates to the inner surface of the wall, it can also cause stains on your wallcoverings—or it may actually push them off. The use of vinyl will have little effect against attack from the rear—except perhaps to hide the trouble until a more advanced stage of attack.

Seal all gaps in the frames with mastic. You can use strips for small gaps, or a tubed mastic or mastic from a cartridge for the larger gaps. Do not use cement mortar or putty, as both these materials harden with age, in which case the cracks will open again.

Do not ignore damaged putty in frames, as damp may seep into the frame, causing rot in timber and rust in metal. Both of these problems are dealt with in chapters 3 and 4. Also check the bases of exterior doors, as rain may be driven in under wind pressure, soaking mats or carpets. The simplest solution here is to fit a weather bar which will keep the water out. There are a number of designs, but basically you have interlocking mouldings which come together when the door is closed, directing water into an outer groove from which it can drain away. Choose a type which offers the least obstruction at floor level to avoid the possibility of someone tripping over it.

Drainage from paths and drives

The only exterior damp problem worth mentioning is that of drainage from paths and drives and, in severe cases, from land. This will depend entirely on the location of the house, but if the house is situated in a hollow, it must be well drained. If water tends to drain off the land, seek the advice of your borough surveyor concerning the possibility of land drains—porous piping which can collect and lead away surface water.

Ensure that paths drain away from house walls and that any new paths are cambered with a convex surface to drain off water. Patios should have drainage holes if all the joints have been pointed. Down pipes which are not connected to a drainage system should have a suitable soakaway nearby to absorb excessive amounts of water. In most areas you are not permitted to drain rainwater into the normal drainage system; it is just not built to cope with floodwater, and in freak storms you can end up with water pressure lifting manholes and distributing sewage into gardens and roads.

Check to see the little walls around gulleys are unbroken. These allow for a degree of back-flooding without the water coming over the top. If you remove the little wall, there can be flooding if the drains block.

Interior damp

You will encounter two main forms of internal damp and many people still find it hard to distinguish one from the other. First there is structural damp, where you will see the effects internally of some of the problems we discussed outside—blocked gutters and down pipes, damage to the roof, porous walls, gaps around windows and doors, faulty dpc.

All of these problems appear during spells of wet weather and this is really the time to hunt for weak spots in the defences.

Check the roof when the rain is really coming down heavily. Look for tell-tale rivulets down rafters, wet patches on the loft floor, and damp patches on the chimney breast where it goes out through the roof. The noise of soot dropping in blocked fireplaces, suggests that water is coming down the flue. Check also for signs of water dripping from gutters or cascading out of down pipes. With all these problems, the first priority is to seal off the entrance points from the outside. Only then can you set to and repair the inside.

The second form of damp is far more subtle, and it is caused by condensation. The general rule is that it does not occur on mild damp days; watch for it on cold, dry days. The first signs are usually on single glazed windows, where you will see the glass has steamed up. This is caused by moisture-laden air coming into contact with a cold surface and the effect is for the moisture in the air to be deposited as tiny droplets of water.

Warm air can hold considerable amounts of water vapour, which is why you may see no sign of trouble in the warmer rooms. However, when this warm air encounters a

How to clear water from paths and drives

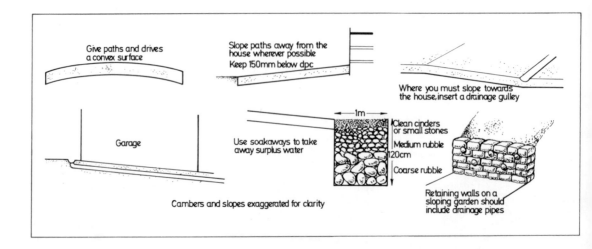

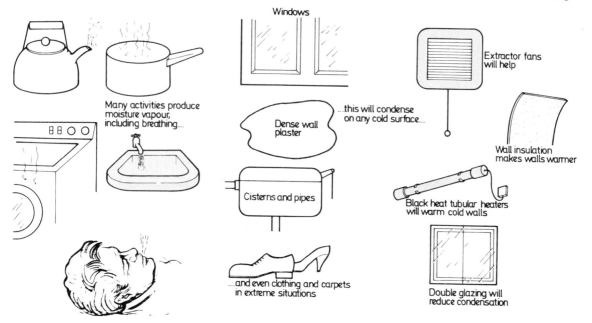

Many activities produce moisture vapour, including breathing....

Windows

...this will condense on any cold surface....

Dense wall plaster

Extractor fans will help

Wall insulation makes walls warmer

Cisterns and pipes

Black heat tubular heaters will warm cold walls

...and even clothing and carpets in extreme situations

Double glazing will reduce condensation

The causes and cures for condensation in the home

colder surface, then it loses the ability to hold the water vapour and you have condensation. Unfortunately glass is not the only surface affected. A cold wall will encourage condensation, which will appear as a damp patch on your decorations. North facing walls, or walls exposed to winds will be most affected and also areas which are badly ventilated, such as behind a wardrobe or chest of drawers.

These patches are often mistaken for structural damp, so if you spot them on a cold, dry day—suspect condensation!

Preventing damp by double-glazing

Double glazing helps cure the problem on windows, for the air trapped between the two panes of glass keeps the inner face warm and less likely to encourage condensation. With some d-i-y systems, condensation forms between the panes of glass. This does not happen with factory-sealed units, because a dry gas is inserted during manufacture, but it may apply to some home-installed systems.

For this reason it is wise to install a system where you can get at the interior in some way for an occasional wipe over of the surfaces. You can make frames removable; to hinge open or to slide. It does not really matter as long as you have access. Do not seal the frames with putty or mastic, for you may well trap enough damp air between frames to give misting when the sun comes out. This time you will not be able to get at it!

One trick for reducing the problem is to drill fine holes from the centre air gap through to the outside air, angling the holes down so no water can pass up. The theory is that outside cold air during winter is far drier than the air inside your house, so the gap will keep dry through fine ventilation.

Making walls warmer

Walls can be made warmer by cavity infill—the system done by professional operators

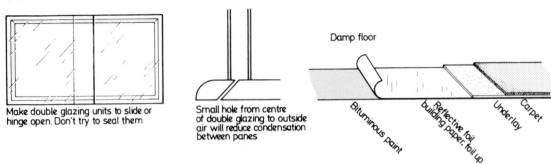

Make double glazing units to slide or hinge open. Don't try to seal them

Small hole from centre of double glazing to outside air will reduce condensation between panes

Damp floor

Bituminous paint

Reflective foil building paper, foil up

Underlay

Carpet

Centre, how to reduce condensation in your double glazing. Right, a way of stopping damp rising through a floor

to improve the wall insulation. Once a house has been treated, it is rare that condensation appears on the wall. Note, however, that if the air is still full of moisture it will try to find somewhere to condense. If only windows are double glazed, you may then find more damp on exposed walls. If the walls are cavity filled, you may, in severe cases, find moisture on carpets situated on cold floors; on shoes and clothing in wardrobes, and on cold lavatory cisterns and basins. It seems impossible to win!

Another way of treating walls is to line the inside face with an expanded poly-styrene veneer stuck on with a special adhesive. You can then decorate over the top. The wall will be warmer to the touch after treatment and far less likely to encourage condensation.

Added warmth can be achieved by fitting a black heat tubular heater on particularly cold wall surfaces. Fix the heater at the base of the wall and it will give just enough warmth to keep the chill off the surface. Rated at only 60 to 80 watts to the foot it is not expensive to run.

Where damp is actually striking through a wall from outside, the expanded poly-styrene material is of no value. In fact it will be pushed off the wall as the damp attacks the adhesive holding it. The best treatment is to seal off the wall from out-side, but where this proves impossible due

to access—as with a basement area—you can buy special damp-resisting lining material by the roll which will hold back the damp. This is stuck to the wall. There is also a damp-resisting coating which can be brush applied, and this too forms a damp-resisting skin which holds back the moisture. It in no way cures the fault.

The above methods are not, in my opinion, the ideal solutions, for there is always the danger that damp, when it is unable to escape, may climb higher up the house and come out in rooms so far not affected.

Treating damp walls

In basement areas, and other areas where the walls are in poor condition due to damp, you can buy a special corrugated wall surfacing material called a lath. This is fixed to the wall, after which its corrugated surface forms the ideal surface for replas-tering. Once treated, no further damp can get through. Such treatment can make a damp basement habitable in a very short time.

When it comes to decorating walls in potentially damp areas, there are special anti-condensation paints available. These resemble emulsion paint, but they have the ability to absorb a certain amount of moisture, allowing it to evaporate off later. These paints also contain a fungicide which discourages mould growth. Remember that ceiling tiles of expanded polystyrene or fibre board will make the surface warmer, discouraging condensation. If you wish to decorate such tiles, the ideal time is before you put them up; it is much easier.

We have touched on remedial measures, but by far the best action is to find ways of reducing the moisture content of the air. Extractor fans in kitchen and bathroom will help—coupled with keeping these doors closed while steam is being produced. Invisible steam in a warm room will quickly pass to colder rooms, given the chance, so steam from a warm bathroom may appear as damp patches on the wall of the spare bedroom.

One of the results of condensation on paintwork and wallcoverings is the growth of fine moulds which cause staining. This problem has been dealt with at the end of chapter 5.

Dampness in floors

Floors may also suffer from damp. The timber floor is normally no problem, though you should make sure that air bricks on exterior walls are kept free at all times. Never allow these to be blocked during winter months, or you may get trouble with dry rot (see chapter 3).

The main trouble comes from solid floors where the concrete is actually sitting on the ground. If the floor is properly constructed it should include a horizontal damp-proof course which prevents moisture rising through. If this is the case, and you experience damp in cold weather, this too may be a simple case of condensation.

You can test it by building a little wall of putty or Plasticine to form a box, then pressing a piece of glass on to the wall. Press it fairly close to the floor, but not touching it. If moisture gathers on the top of the glass, this is condensation—moisture being deposited from the room. If you find

moisture on the underside of the glass, this is moisture coming up through the floor—rising damp.

In most cases, the problem can be solved by treating the floor with a damp-resisting sealer. This may be an epoxy-based material or it may be bitumen-rubber based. An ideal combination is to coat the floor with a bitumen based coating, then place on it a waterproof building paper with a reflective foil face. Fix it with the foil surface up, and you have a surface which is ready to cover with underlay and carpet, or vinyl. The foil acts as a reflector, preventing room warmth being absorbed by the concrete.

There are a few severe cases where, due to the location of the house in a hollow, water comes up under pressure. This has been known to lift wood-block floors and no simple coating will prevent it. If you find you have persistent damp in a floor and you live in an area with high ground around you, seek the advice of your borough surveyor. You may need land drainage to take the water away.

If the moisture is a case of condensation, a reflective building paper, followed by underlay and carpet, or a foam-backed vinyl, should solve the problem. A solid sheet vinyl on its own may not be enough and you may find moisture from condensation between floor and vinyl.

Another offender is the old quarry tiled floor. This can be very cold to the touch, and you may find condensation on floorcoverings. A simple solution, if you do not mind losing the tiles, is to cover the floor with a screeding compound. This is a self-levelling cement-based material which will produce a new surface on which to lay your covering, and it will not be so prone to condensation. It is also an ideal way of levelling uneven floors such as old quarries. No floorcovering will last long on a rough, uneven floor.

Checking for water leakage

Apart from the two main causes of damp already discussed, it is wise to keep a regular check on all areas where water is involved in one way or another.

Look for leaking pipes under sinks and basins where a joint may have loosened. Feel around the points where pipes go below floorcoverings—especially where you have vinyl on the floor. The old linoleum floorcoverings used to break up if subjected to continuous damp, and that in itself was an indication of trouble. Today, vinyls, being impervious to water, will show no external signs of damp though the floorboards below may be saturated.

Check on water closets, especially the seal between the basin and the soil pipe. As mentioned earlier, slight damp may just be condensation, but a bad seal can cause more permanent damage. Make sure central heating pipes are tight at the joints. Capillary soldered joints do not give trouble, but compression joints may need occasional tightening.

See that pressed steel radiators are not leaking. The old cast iron radiators were ugly, but would last for ever. Modern steel ones are very thin and can be attacked from within. You can combat this by inserting an anti-corrosion fluid in the system either as soon as the central heating is installed or after draining down and re-filling. The liquid can be inserted by pouring into the expansion tank, then draining water off at the drain cock on the boiler so the water in the tank is drawn into the system.

If you find small pinhole leaks, there is a liquid sealer which can be added to the central heating system to seal off the holes from inside. It is important to catch trouble early or you will have to replace the radiators.

Check the hot water cylinder in the airing cupboard and see that there are no leaks. The older type tanks of galvanised iron with the circular inspection plate should be checked externally for signs of rusting or leaking at joints. The water storage tank (or tanks) in the loft should be examined for corrosion. If you have the galvanised iron type of tank, drain it off every three or four years and examine the inside for rusting. A coat of special tasteless bituminous paint every few years will ensure that the tank stays in good condition.

If you are replacing a tank, a polythene one will give far less trouble as it is unaffected by rust or corrosion. The only point to remember is that it is a more delicate piece of equipment. Never hoist yourself into the loft by pipes connected to the tank—or you may get very wet!

Frost-protection is of course a precautionary measure against damp and it is wise to ensure that all exposed pipes are well lagged, including expansion pipes and waste pipes. This is particularly important when a roof area has been well insulated, because the waste heat from downstairs which used to keep the chill off the loft is no longer available, so the loft space will be that much colder.

Chapter 7 Repairs at roof level

The roof is without doubt the most difficult area you will have to deal with, and if you are in any way worried by heights, keep off it. If you do venture on, be sure to use the proper means of access. As previously mentioned you will need a ladder which extends at least three rungs above gutter height at the point at which you are working, and a roof ladder of the type which hooks over the ridge.

Make sure the ladder cannot slip, and be particularly careful when resting it on plastic guttering. This is far more slippery than metal. It is quite strong enough to take the weight, but it would be wise to put a ring bolt into the fascia board (to which the gutters are fixed) and then run a cord from the ring to the ladder rung. This will give you a sound footing when stepping back on the ladder from the roof ladder.

The main thing to check for on the roof is weak points where the rain could find a way into the house. The effects of damp have already been dealt with in detail in chapter 6. As suggested in that chapter, it is a good idea to check from inside during heavy rain. This will give you a guide as to where exterior repairs may be needed. It is not always easy to pinpoint the source of trouble, for water may trickle in rivulets down a rafter or along the roof felting before dripping off and becoming visible.

Tiles

Start at the top of the roof with the ridge tiles; these may be loose due to frost action. Lift off loose ones and chip away all loose or soft mortar, then make up a new mortar of 1 cement to 7 or 8 soft sand plus a plasticiser.

Dealing with gaps in roofing

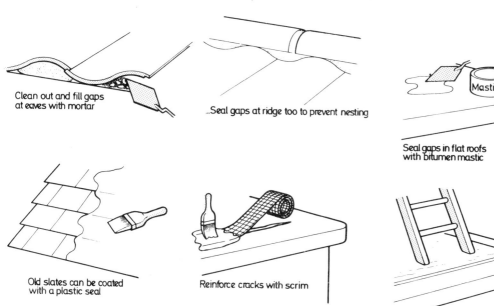

Clean out and fill gaps at eaves with mortar

...Seal gaps at ridge too to prevent nesting

Mastic

Seal gaps in flat roofs with bitumen mastic

Old slates can be coated with a plastic seal

Reinforce cracks with scrim

Use a board to protect flat roof from ladder feet

Keep the mortar mix as dry as possible so that it does not slop about and mark your tiles. Damp the ridge tiles in water and drain off before putting them back. This reduces the suction of the tiles so that they will not remove water from the mortar. Bed the tiles on the mortar and make a neat joint with a small trowel.

The same mortar mix can be used for sealing any gaps at the tile ends. Frost, and the action of birds looking for good nesting points may have removed the old mortar. Clean out any remaining mortar and brush the tiles clean with an old paintbrush kept for dusting. Then damp the holes with water and apply your dryish mix, trowelling it smooth. If birds really are a nuisance, add a little black pepper to your mix and they will not be so keen on pecking it out.

Cracks in tiles can be sealed with mortar, and to improve adhesion, you could add a little pva adhesive to the mixing water, or seal the holes with an epoxy filler. A touch of tile paint can be used to disguise the repair.

If a tile has slipped, and this is a rare occurrence unless you are dealing with an older property, it means it has lost its nibs, or the tiling batten underneath has rotted away. Very often it is a combination of rusted nails which lose a hold on the tile, plus the weight of snow or ice during a cold spell. If you find loose ones, clean the meeting faces and use an epoxy filler as an adhesive. This will bond the loose one to its neighbours.

Slates

Small cracks in slates can be sealed with the same filler, but where you meet serious gaps or breaks, use glass fibre bandage to reinforce the repair. Spread a thin layer of filler over the damaged area, lay down some bandage and press it into the filler with an old brush. Then spread another layer of filler over the top. This will give a strong repair which, even if the slate moves slightly, will not crack.

If the slates are in a generally poor condition, i.e. flaking away and slipping, you can now buy an excellent plastic coating which, when spread over the slates, forms an unbroken flexible plastic skin over the whole roof area. Where money is short, this offers an ideal alternative to having the roof stripped and re-covered. The secret is to lay the material on thick—do not try to spread it like paint.

Gutters

When you reach gutter level you may find another series of gaps in a heavily profiled roof, where the birds have pulled out the mortar and nested. Dig out all old and flaking material and re-point with the same mortar mix we used further up the roof. Again, your black pepper will discourage birds.

Check that the gutter brackets are anchored securely to the fascia boards. In older houses, the board may have become soft through rot so that screws lose their grip; or the screws themselves may have rusted away until they no longer grip. In the first case it will be necessary to remove the guttering and brackets from the damaged area, take down the fascia board and put up new board. As you have the opportunity, prime and paint the new board before you put it up. It is much easier.

Be warned that if you are taking down cast iron guttering it is extremely heavy—you will need some help. A simple pulley and rope system with the rope lashed to the guttering will make lowering easier. Never take a chance on your own!

If only the screws have failed, remove the gutter sections, plug the holes in the fascia board with mastic or exterior grade stopping and re-position the brackets. Remember that your gutter must have a steady fall towards the down pipe, at least 25 mm (1 in) in every 3 m (10 ft). This is best marked out with a string line and pins before you start fixing brackets, or you may find you run out of fascia board before you get to the end!

Check the gutter lengths for rusting, or for gaps between sections. Rust should be removed back to bright metal, then the area treated with a rust inhibitor before you fill the damage with epoxy filler. Get it to a nice smooth finish by rubbing with emery when hard to ensure there are no snags to hold debris. Joints, where there may be slight movement, can be sealed with a bitumen mastic trowelled into the gap. Again make sure it has a smooth finish.

Where guttering is in a bad way and is not strong enough to refit, get one of the modern plastic systems. They are far easier to handle because the sections are so much lighter; one person can fit a full length. Once installed, plastic gutters are self-cleaning and need no painting. By the way, remember to paint your fascia boards before putting up new guttering. You can't use a blowlamp near plastic gutter brackets, gutters or down pipes.

You will find sections of guttering merely clip together, bedding down on a special foam gasket. Down pipe sections are usually welded together with a special cement.

Chimney stacks

Before leaving roof level, have a look at the chimney stacks. Any pots should be bedded on mortar, called 'flaunching', and if this is damaged, the old mortar should be chipped away and new mortar applied. Cracks and gaps in otherwise sound mortar can be filled with a mortar mix to which has been added some pva adhesive to increase adhesion.

Check also the pointing between the bricks. If this is crumbling, dig it out to a depth of about 12 mm (½ in), brush the joints clean and re-point with a mortar. You can buy this as a dry mix in bags, and

Dealing with a chimney stack—and how to get to it safely

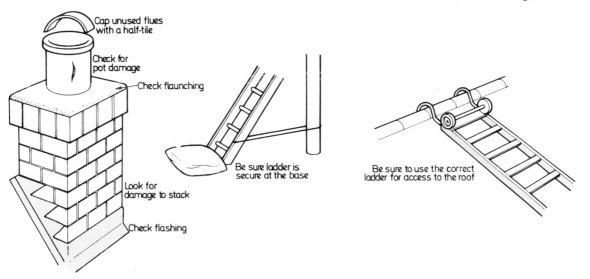

Cap unused flues with a half-tile

Check for pot damage

Check flaunching

Look for damage to stack

Check flashing

Be sure ladder is secure at the base

Be sure to use the correct ladder for access to the roof

all you need is to add water. Again, be sure to keep the mix really dry or you will mark your brickwork. Damp the joints before you fill them with clean water applied with an old paintbrush. This stops the bricks sucking water from your new mortar and weakening it.

If you find the stack is in poor shape, with bad cracking and perhaps deformation of the stack, this is probably caused by damage coming through from the inside. For this job you would be wise to call in professional help because of the weight of material involved. A scaffold will have to be erected around the stack while it is dismantled and rebuilt.

At the base of the stack you will find the joint between stack and roof slates or tiles. This is called the 'flashing', and it should be examined to see there are no gaps or cracks. Sometimes the flashing works away from the joints in the stack, in which case you need to dig out the old mortar, brush the gaps clean, push the flashing back in place and secure it with scraps of lead used as wedges. Then re-point as with the rest of the stack. If it is loose at the roof side, lift the flashing, brush on a liberal coat of bituminous mastic and press the flashing on to it.

Flat roofs

Flat roof areas often create a problem because water frequently seems to find a way in. Basically this is because the water may not drain off, but just lies on the roofing in pools, seeping into the smallest cracks.

The most common covering material is bituminous sheeting, very often covered with a layer of fine stones. If you can find definite cracks, clean them out, then fill the cracks with bituminous mastic applied with a small trowel. Where there are tears, or the cracking is quite severe, strengthen the repair with a hessian bandage. Apply a layer of mastic, press the hessian into it until well bedded down, then apply a further layer of bitumen.

Where a roof is in bad shape, brush it clean, then apply a plastic roofing compound, laying it on thick. This will set to a tough unbroken skin, giving you a brand new surface. Pay particular attention to flashings, where they are set into brickwork and then taken on to the roof. This is a very weak spot, and mastic should be used in preference to mortar. Should there be slight movement, the mastic can take it.

Lean-to glass roofs

Lean-to roofs always present a problem—first of access, then of keeping clean, for dirt and moss growth soon spoil a clear surface. Where possible it is a good idea to have an opening panel in the roof so that a ladder can be put through. Failing this you will need scaffold boards rested across the joists to give you safe access. Never risk walking across the glass, even when wired.

A weak solution of caustic soda will remove most glass grime, but protect your hands with rubber gloves, and your eyes with safety glasses. Where you think water may be getting in at the glazing bars, clean off any dust and dirt, then seal the bars with mastic glazing tape, pressing it well into the corners. The easiest to handle has a foil face and this also looks neater and prevents the mastic drying out.

Corrugated plastic sheeting is best cleaned with water and liquid detergent. Do not use an abrasive. If grime has got between sheets, you will have to remove the sheets and scrub them clean with a soft scrubbing brush and detergent. There is a transparent glazing tape available which is useful for sealing gaps likely to collect dirt. The tape is waterproof, providing it is applied to a clean, dust-free, dry surface.

Chapter 8
Outside jobs

The two main materials encountered on outside work are timber and concrete, and you will find it useful to refer to chapter 3 in addition to the information given in this chapter. Timber will be affected by damp, and concrete, while durable, is weakened by the attack of frost during winter months. Water seeps into cracks, freezes and expands, applying very considerable pressure to the concrete, causing flaking and splitting.

Fence and gate posts

Timber posts are the most vulnerable, particularly the section below ground level where perhaps water has gathered and rotted the bases. A common culprit is a concrete housing; this is where a post has been positioned, then the hole filled with concrete.

This certainly gives an initially strong support, but when the post shrinks slightly, water can seep down into the concrete where it is held in contact with the timber. This inevitably leads to rotting and loosening of the post and then you have a real job releasing it. The illustration shows a way of applying leverage to lift the post free—after which the concrete will have to be removed.

If new timber posts are to be put into the ground, be sure they are well soaked in preservative—especially into the end grain. Then stand the base on rubble to ensure good drainage and fill in with earth. You will get far less trouble this way and it is not so hard to get the post out should the need arise.

By far the best way to erect timber posts is to use concrete spurs. The spur is cemented into the ground and the timber post bolted to it. This means that the timber never comes into contact with the ground at all. It is also a good idea to cap the top of each post with a piece of zinc or aluminium. Angle the top to shed the water, then pin the sheeting in place with alloy nails. Very often you will find that the end of a post is the first to begin to rot as water seeps into it.

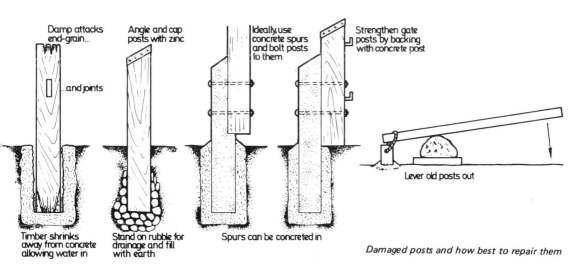

Damp attacks end-grain...

...and joints

Angle and cap posts with zinc

Ideally, use concrete spurs and bolt posts to them

Strengthen gate posts by backing with concrete post

Lever old posts out

Timber shrinks away from concrete allowing water in

Stand on rubble for drainage and fill with earth

Spurs can be concreted in

Damaged posts and how best to repair them

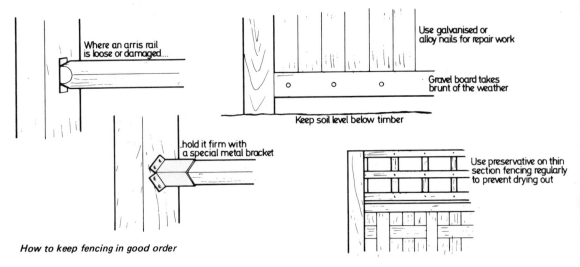

Where an arris rail is loose or damaged....

Use galvanised or alloy nails for repair work

Gravel board takes brunt of the weather

Keep soil level below timber

hold it firm with a special metal bracket

Use preservative on thin section fencing regularly to prevent drying out

How to keep fencing in good order

As has been mentioned for other timber-work, it pays to buy pressure-impregnated wood which will be unaffected by damp or insect attack. You will see it widely used for motorway fencing.

Gate posts also present a problem because of the strain on the post holding the gate; especially if children use the gate as a swing! Where a post is loose, try to sink a concrete post behind it then bolt the timber post to it. The concrete post can then be set in concrete to give maximum support. You can get a permanent concrete stain to tone down the post to match the adjacent timber.

Timber gates also suffer from shrinkage, loosening up the joints. If you encounter this problem, take off the gate and, after numbering the joints, tap the gate apart using a rubber hammer. Clean off all the old glue, then re-assemble using a water-proof resin adhesive. Where there are gaps to fill you can use an epoxy filler, forcing the joint into a surplus of filler, then trimming off what is not needed. If you have to use screws or nails, use aluminium alloy which does not rust or stain your timber. Never try to re-assemble rotting sections; cut out all rotting timber and replace it with new.

Fencing

Arris rails, supporting fencing boards, often rot where the rail enters the recess in the timber or concrete post. The simplest way of tackling this problem is to buy special rail repair brackets which act as supports for the damaged rail. The bracket can be screwed to the timber post, but with concrete ones you will need to drill and plug. If you find drilling into the post heavy going with a standard power tool and masonry drill, borrow a hammer action drill. It will make the job much easier.

When repairing fencing, make sure that the soil level is well below your fencing boards, otherwise damp will climb into the wood, probably rotting it. Some fences incorporate a special rail along the base of the fence which takes the brunt of any wetting or build-up of soil. If it becomes damaged, it can be removed and a new rail fixed in place, preferably with rustless screws.

If feather-edge boards are neglected, the thinnest sections will tend to curl, causing gaps to open in the fencing. To improve matters, choose a period of dry weather and thoroughly soak the fencing with water until the boards are pliable enough to be eased flat. Now use alloy nails to nail the boards flat. If you have to work near the edges of boards, use oval nails, or take the trouble to drill holes through the boards into which the nails can be driven. It may sound a lot of extra trouble, but it will ensure that you do not split your boards.

When the fence has dried out, give it two liberal coats of a good wood preservative. Then repeat the treatment whenever the wood starts to look dry and 'thirsty'. Choose a dry period to apply the preservative with an old paintbrush, it will not soak far into wet timber.

The thinner the sections of timber, the more treatment they seem to need—as with woven fencing panels and trellis. Give these regular treatment with a wood preservative to keep them in good condition. The wood should never be allowed to really dry out. Where material like trellis comes into close contact with greenery, there is a special grade of preservative which will not harm plant life. Many normal grades of preservative will kill plants if they come into contact before the timber has really dried off.

Putting new felt on a shed roof

Sheds, garages and workshops

Timber sheds, garages and workshops also need regular treatment if the wood is to stay in good condition. Gloss paint can be used, but I always feel this is the last resort because it hides the natural beauty of the wood. If you inherit a painted structure, then treat it as any other painted surface and keep it in good condition. The important point is to ensure that the paint gets into all cracks and joints, for these are the weak points in the system. If the damp can get behind a paint film, it will soon push it off.

The normal method of decorating is to use a wood preservative, and while the accepted colour is light or dark brown, you can now get a whole range of colours, from yellow through to black. These pigmented preservatives can look most attractive, and there is no reason now why a garden room should not have orange walls with a green door—yet, with the grain of the wood showing through.

If you have a western red cedar building, then you will want to maintain the golden colour for which it is noted. Unfortunately the colour bleaches out with time, and you end up with a far less attractive grey. You can buy special preservatives designed to restore the colour by staining and this is

Battens will help secure felt

Use only short clout nails

Use bitumen adhesive for extra strong joints

The order for fixing roofing felt

the kind to choose for cedar. It is advisable not to wait until the timber is grey but to give regular coats while it is still golden and it will look more natural.

The garden workshop is not the cosiest of places during the winter months, and if you want to use it for storing tools and appliances, it is worth considering adding a weatherproof inner lining. You can do this very simply with a reflective foil building paper stapled or drawing-pinned between internal timbers. Have the reflective foil in, then cover over the timbers with fibre building board. Far less damp will get in after such treatment. As an alternative material, 500 gauge polythene sheeting could be used, stapled or pinned.

Western red cedar is a very soft wood, and nails will not get a good grip. So if you find beading or cladding coming away, replace the pieces with ring nails. These get a far better hold on the timber, and they will not pull out.

While checking outbuildings, examine the roof covering. It is probably bitumen roofing felt held with large head clout nails and perhaps reinforced with battens to hold it firm in high winds. Small tears can be sealed with a bituminous mastic and overlapped joints which are lifting can be stuck down using the mastic as an adhesive.

Where the roof covering has hardened with age and is cracking, it needs replacing. Rip it all off and burn it. Examine the roof timbers to see they are sound, then treat them with a liberal coating of preservative and allow it to dry out. You will find that modern preservatives are much faster drying than the older creosotes.

Buy a good heavy gauge roofing felt and unroll it before use. Let it stretch and flatten before you fix it. Then start at the eaves, lay strips horizontally and secure with clout nails. Place the nails so that a generous overlap of felt covers them when the next piece goes down. To get a really good seal, use bituminous mastic as an adhesive between pieces of felt. Continue until you reach the ridge, then tackle the other side if you have two sloping faces. The last piece to go on is a ridge piece—preferably stuck down.

Battens can be added to anchor the roof, but do not use too heavy gauge nails, as obviously these will be making a hole in your new covering. Treat the battens with preservative before fixing and allow them to dry before nailing in place. Put a spot of mastic over each nail head to seal it to the timber.

If yours is virtually a flat roof, start at lowest point of the roof and work up. This ensures the water runs over the joints and not into them.

Concrete surrounds and paths

Now let us have a look at the concrete surrounding the house. As mentioned earlier the main problem will be caused by the action of frost causing cracking and flaking. All loose material should be chipped away then the area wire brushed (do not forget to protect your eyes).

You can buy epoxy-based repair materials for concrete, but they tend to be expensive so, for most repairs, use a mortar mix of say 1 of cement to 6 of sand, plus the addition of some pva adhesive to the mixing water. Before you apply the mix, damp the area to be repaired, allow the water to soak in, then apply a neat brush coat of pva adhesive to the cracks. Then fill with mortar.

As has already been suggested, work with a dryish mortar mix of about sand-pie consistency. A sloppy mortar will mark the surrounding concrete and be difficult to clean off. When the repair has been made and the mortar wiped level with the rest of the concrete, cover it with damp rag or sacking for a few days so that the mortar dries out slowly. Fast drying mortar will give a very weak repair.

Where the edge of a path or step has been broken away, make up a simple mould around the damaged area into which you can pour concrete. Again, the addition of pva and the brushing of the area with neat pva will ensure a good bond. Off-cuts of laminate are ideal for moulds, shiny side to the concrete. Alternatively, you can use hardboard brushed with oil or covered with polythene so the concrete will not stick. Allow three or four hours before easing the mould away, then cover the area with damp sacking and protect it for a couple of weeks until the repair is really mature.

Where paving slabs have been used for steps, and these have been damaged on corners, it may be possible to ease the slabs out and turn them so the damage is to the rear and hidden by the risers. The same applies to brick edgings. Once the damage has been repaired, a liberal coating of silicone water repellent will discourage water from soaking in. This in turn can reduce frost damage. I once stopped the disentegration of rockery stones with silicone repellent—with no effect on the plants growing around them.

Stained areas of concrete, such as the oily marks left by a parked car on a drive, can look a mess. The worst of the oil can be removed with an oil and tar remover brushed into the stain, then washed away, but you may still be left with a mark. You can disguise this by using a concrete stain over the whole drive area. A reasonable black stain is available. Also have a simple drip tray which can be slid under the car when it is left standing.

To enhance the appearance of dull concrete, you can now buy cold macadam materials with which to re-surface the concrete. First, after cleaning the area, a bitumen priming coat is used to ensure good adhesion, then the cold bitumen is tipped from the bag and spread with a rake. It is then rolled, keeping the roller drum wet so that it does not stick to the bitumen and pull it up. Then after rolling, fine chippings can be thrown on and rolled.

For areas of shingle, a special cold bitumen liquid is available which can be sprayed over the shingle, binding it together. The latest approach to laying bitumen and stones is to buy it by the roll ready for laying on to any clean, firm surface. A priming coat is put down to ensure good adhesion, then a backing paper is removed from the roll, and the material pressed into place, producing an instant macadam surface.

Patios and paving slabs

Patios can present a problem, especially after periods of prolonged dry weather, for paving slabs may start to rock or even subside. To re-bed a slab, lift it by carefully levering it up with a spade, tamp down hard the material underneath to form a foundation. If you find soft spots, put rubble down and tamp it into the ground, then lay five blobs of new mortar slightly higher than you know will be needed. Damp the underside of the slab and lower it back in place, keeping the pressure as even as possible. Then tap down the slab using a rubber hammer or a baulk of timber until the slab is flush with its neighbours.

Always tap around the edges of a slab. A hard knock in the centre could break it. Never use a metal hammer—the handle of a club hammer is a reasonable substitute for a rubber mallet.

While on the subject of subsidence, you may occasionally find an area of path has sunk at the joint between sections, forming a ledge over which people could trip. Thin

Brush area free of all loose material, ...and fill holes with rubble

Apply priming coat

Then tip and spread cold macadam

Roll with wet roller

Add chippings

Then give a final roll

The sequence for laying cold macadam on a path or drive

layers of concrete are not the easiest of repairs, but you can put down a thin screed if you use the method already described, of adding pva adhesive to the water of the mortar mix, then applying a liberal coating of neat pva to the concrete to be covered.

If the surface of the conrete is very smooth, it would be wise to roughen it up with a steel chisel and club hammer before putting down your pva. Protect your eyes, and sweep up all the dust and loose material before applying the adhesive. Nothing sticks well to dust. With the surface prepared, apply your new mortar, trowelling it out and feathering it so you lose the step. You may need to tap it over with a piece of board to add light ridges so that it matches the surrounding area.

Chapter 9
Twenty
common
problems

Not all the problems you are likely to encounter are easily classifiable. So here are some of the most common ones. I have omitted problems concerning plumbing and electrics as these are dealt with in section 3 (Home Plumbing) and 4 (Home Electrics).

Removing a cracked ceramic tile

The problem is to get the tile out without spoiling surrounding tiles. Drill a hole in the centre of the tile with a glass or masonry drill. Protect your eyes with safety glasses, then lever the tile away through the centre hole, using an old screwdriver blade. Work from the centre outwards.

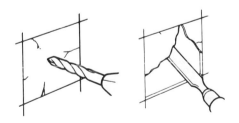

If yours is an old tile, it will be set in mortar, and it will be quite hard to move. The remaining mortar will have to be chipped away with a steel chisel and club hammer. Then apply new tile cement and stick the new tile in place.

The newer thin ceramic tiles stuck in place should be easier to move. Scrape

away the remaining tile cement with an old chisel blade. If stubborn, heat the blade to soften the cement. Then apply new adhesive and fix the replacement tile. Fill the gaps with new grouting. Allow to dry, then rub away the surplus with a screwed up piece of newspaper.

Lifting damaged vinyl tiles

There is no way to get solvents at the underside of a vinyl tile, so the best approach is to use heat. Place a piece of cooking foil over the damaged tile and apply a hot iron to the foil. Keep the heat in contact until it has had time to get through to the underside, then prise up a corner of the tile and pull. It should strip away. If you are experienced with a blowtorch, this can be used as an alternative to the iron. But do be sure to keep the flame on the move so that the plastic is warmed but not melted.

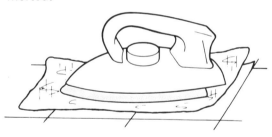

There will be a residue of adhesive, so heat a scraper and apply it to the adhesive. This should soften the adhesive enough to make it lose its grip on the floor. Solvents such as petrol very often do little more than make the adhesive very sticky, and there is a danger of fire from the fumes given off.

Having removed the old adhesive, apply fresh adhesive and fit a new matching tile. Be careful not to slide the new tile in place or you will force adhesive up between the tiles.

Easing a door lock

If a rim lock gets hard to turn, do not be tempted to squirt oil into the key hole. This can act as a collector of dust, and in a short time make the trouble even worse. Apply a little fine oil—such as you get in an aerosol spray can to the key, then place the key in the lock and turn it a few times. The oil will be sufficient to lubricate without gumming up.

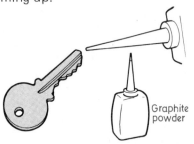

Graphite powder

A good alternative is to use a graphite powder from a puffer pack. This is a dry lubricant which will not cause clogging. For mortice type locks, a keyhole cover is a good investment. It will prevent a through flow of air, which during dry summer months can carry a fair amount of gritty dust.

Latches and bolts which will not engage

Where a latch fails to enter a latch plate, or a bolt will not go into the securing plate, it usually means the door has dropped a shade, so the parts no longer line up. First

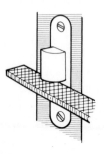

check the door hinge at the top. A slight looseness here is sufficient to cause the trouble. If this fails, slip a piece of carbon paper between latch and plate so that when the door is closed a mark is made on the plate. Now you have the choice of filing a little from the bottom edge of the latch, or the latch plate opening—or both. Remove a little metal at a time until the door closes correctly.

You cannot do this with a bolt. You will have to remove one part or the other—depending upon which is most convenient, plug the existing screw holes with an epoxy filler, then re-drill and screw into place. A slight tapering of the bolt tip will help to locate the tip and make it easier to close.

When you have to fit new latches or bolts, bear this problem in mind and err on the high side when fixing so that a slight drop of the door does not matter.

Loose knobs

Furniture and drawers and doors can come in for quite a bit of rough handling, and it is often the knobs which suffer. The knobs may work loose, or even pull out completely. If a timber knob pulls out, it may only be a question of applying adhesive to the wood and pressing it back in. If it is a good fit, cut a V-notch in the dowel to let the air escape; this saves all the adhesive being pushed out of the hole.

Sometimes a screw is inserted from the inside to go into the end of the dowel knob and the screw pulls away. Usually a little adhesive on a matchstick, broken in the hole and left to set is sufficient. If this is not strong enough, fill the hole with epoxy filler and push the screw into it while soft.

Where a knob has become a loose fit in a hole, line the hole with epoxy filler, cut a V-nick in the dowel of the handle and

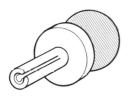

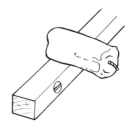

push the knob in place. Trim away surplus before it sets hard and leave to set.

In the case of ceramic knobs which have a simple screw as a means of fixing and where the hole has become enlarged, increase the hole size slightly to take a small gauge plastic wall plug. Press this in the hole and trim it flush with a craft knife, then screw the handle back in place.

Some knobs have a long bolt passing right through the drawer front and held by a nut at the rear. If the wood has worn at the rear of the drawer, remove the holding nut and slip on one or two washers, then replace and tighten the nut.

Where a wood handle has pulled away, drill holes for screws from the rear of the front piece; push in screws and press the handle against the tips to mark the exact location, then drill smaller start holes in the handle. This is essential to stop the hardwood of the handle splitting. Now screw up from the rear, after putting a touch of adhesive on the back of the handle.

Sticking drawers

This is not so much of a problem on modern furniture since the introduction of plastic slides. If you encounter older units with wood to wood slides, you may find some jamming. Examine the slides for damage. If they are badly worn it will be necessary to unscrew them and replace with new hardwood strips but, if in good condition, rub lightly with glasspaper to remove any roughness. Then rub the runners with the stub of a candle which acts as an effective lubricant. You can also buy a special aerosol wood lubricant which siliconises the surface. Whichever process you choose, open drawers with care after treatment!

If you are making up new runners, line the meeting faces with off-cuts of laminate. This provides a good, hardwearing running surface. If making up new drawer systems, try to obtain the all-plastic glide systems which run much more freely.

Squeaking stairs

This can happen on both old and new properties, particularly after the installation of central heating. As timbers dry out, wedges and glues lose their hold and allow timber to move and rub against an adjoining timber area. The result is a squeak.

If you can get at the underside of the staircase, the problem is far easier to deal with. Look for the wedges holding the treads and risers in place and if loose, pull them free and remove any hardened glue. Apply new glue to the wedges and drive them back in place. When set, the squeak

Wedge

should have gone for good. A little epoxy filler pressed into gaps and cracks will be an insurance against further trouble.

Where you cannot get under the stairs, try to locate where the movement is. Cracks can be filled with epoxy filler, and treads and risers can be locked together by drilling and screwing down from tread into the riser below. Pre-drill for screws and countersink the tread so that screws go well below the wood surface. Then fill with wood stopping.

Slight squeaks can often be cured by puffing talc between gaps. This acts as a lubricant, stopping the rubbing which causes the noise.

Squeaking floorboards

Here we have the same basic problem as with the stairs, often caused by timber drying out and causing gaps. Press on the floor until you find the exact location of the squeak, then find the nearest adjoining joist. Drill the board to take the shank of a screw, countersink the board, make a start hole in the joint, then drive the screw home really tight. You should hear the board groan for the last time as the screw pulls it down tight to the joist.

Where there is no joist to screw in to, locate the exact spot where the squeak occurs, then drive a chipboard screw down between the boards. This type of screw has no plain shank, and the serrations formed by the thread tend to prevent any movement of the board. Again, a puff of talc

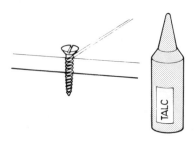

between boards will often lubricate the area well enough to stop noise.

If you do encounter squeaks, deal with them before covering the floor with hardboard or plywood. These materials will not cure the trouble—in fact they could magnify the noise.

Replacing broken glass

Unfortunately there is no way of repairing cracked glass. It has to come out and be replaced by new. Assuming a pane is broken, wear thick leather gardening gloves while removing glass from a frame and use pincers to wiggle loose any obstinate pieces. With the glass out, chisel out all old putty, including the bedding putty. Use an old chisel, kept for such rough jobs, and a mallet.

A timber frame should be rubbed smooth with glasspaper, then the wood sealed with primer. A metal frame should be checked for signs of rust. Any rusted areas must be rubbed down with emery paper to remove deposits of rust, then treated with a rust inhibitor.

Measure very carefully for your new piece of glass, checking the diagonals to ensure that the pane is square. If you encounter an odd shape, such as in a front door, make a stiff paper pattern and take this with you when you order your glass. Deduct 3 mm ($\frac{1}{8}$ in) from each dimension so there is air around the glass when placed in the frame. For fairly small panes of glass, up to about 1 m (3 ft) square, use glass 3 mm thick. For larger panes of the modern picture window size, use 4 mm ($\frac{3}{16}$ in) and 6 mm (¼ in) for anything above this.

There are locations, such as doors and low windows, where it would be wise to install safety glass. You can now buy a laminated glass which has tremendous resistance to impact; it will shatter, but the whole piece will stay together offering no jagged edges. You would merely bounce off instead of going through! Such glass is about three times more expensive than normal glass, but the additional expenditure does offer safety and security. No thief will shatter this glass and put a hand through to release a catch.

If you wish to cut your own glass, you need a good wheel-type cutter, a straight edge and an accurate rule. Be sure to use fresh glass, because old glass will often break other than along the line. An ordinary sheet of newspaper is another excellent aid, for the rules used between columns and any horizontal lines will be extremely accurate. You can mark a very good straight line or right angle merely by laying the glass on the paper.

Experiment with your cutter before attempting to cut an accurate piece. The cutting wheel must just whisper over the glass leaving a clear score line; it must not judder or slide. With a score line made, position the glass over two or three matchsticks so the sticks run under the score, then press down either side. The glass should break clean along the cut. Small slivers can be nipped away with the square recesses on the cutter, or with pliers.

With your glass, you need linseed oil putty for timber frames, or metal casement putty for metal frames. The latter is designed to be able to harden off without any of the oil being absorbed. Linseed oil putty on metal would never harden; certainly not within a reasonable time.

Lay a bed of fresh putty in the recess of the frame upon which the glass is pressed until it squeezes around the glass to cushion it against shock. Always press around the edges of a piece of glass—never in the centre. Secure the glass in a timber frame with headless tacks or sprigs. A couple each side is sufficient. The side of a chisel is the ideal hammer for this job, sliding it across the glass. On metal frames you will find small slots for wire clips and it is wise to use about two clips a side. You do not need to occupy all available holes.

With the glass secure, apply your finishing putty, angling it with a putty knife. This is not an easy job and it takes practice to get a good mitre at the corners. There are small glazing tools available which simplify the job for the beginner, but it is never easy the first time.

Make sure the putty does not come above the frame when viewed from inside. If it does, reduce the height of the putty with your knife. Allow your putty to harden for about a week before painting. When painting make sure the paint goes just on to the glass to seal the joint between glass and putty.

Loose glass in a leaded light

A true leaded light is quite a complicated structure. It is not easy to effect repairs as each piece of glass is actually set into an H-section of lead. Where panes rattle in the lead, buy a tube of lead adhesive of the type sold with imitation leaded light materials. This is a waterproof, transparent material, which is not visible when set.

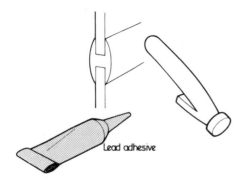

Lead adhesive

Squeeze a little into cracks in the window lead, then cut a clothes peg (as illustrated) to form a pressing tool. Press the lead gently back into place, where the adhesive will hold it.

If a pane is broken, after easing out the broken glass it will be necessary to cut and open three sides of the lead frame so that you can put in the new piece of glass. Then use the adhesive and your peg tool to get the lead back into place. Should the broken glass have been coloured, you can buy special glass colouring paints which are transparent and weather resistant.

Where a leaded light pane has completely deteriorated, put in a piece of plain glass, then build up the pattern using special lead strip sold for imitation leaded lights. This is either stuck in place with the special adhesive, or there is a new self-adhesive type ready to be stuck straight into place after removing a backing paper. The finished effect is quite good, but obviously if you can afford a replacement leaded light (custom built) this will still look better when closely examined.

The kits can be used to very good effect for changing the appearance of an existing set of windows. The simple diamond pattern will add character to the older house, and if you wish the upper lights could be coloured in a simple pattern.

Sticking doors

If a door does not close properly, assume that it did so at some time. Check first at the hinge side of the door. Tighten the screws as tight as they will go and very often this solves the problem. If this is not enough, and, if there is a reasonable gap at the hinge side, remove the door and deepen the hinge recesses slightly. This will widen the gap on the catch side by an equivalent amount.

Where there is no room to make this adjustment, then you may have to take some wood away at the catch edge. The tightness may be through a build-up of too many coats of paint. If you are not sure just where the door is sticking, slip a piece of carbon paper in the gap and shut the door. A mark will be left wherever the door catches and this is where you have to remove material.

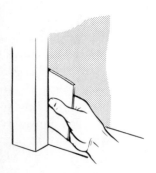

Very often the application of a drum sander is sufficient to ease the door. Failing this, use a shaping tool or, to take off a larger amount, a plane. If you have to plane, take the door off and secure it so that you can do the job properly.

The same advice applies where wood must be taken off the base of a door—perhaps because you have to put down underlay and carpet. Mark the door base where you wish to cut, and score through the paint with a knife. This helps prevent hard paint chipping away when you use a saw.

Use a fairly fine toothed hand saw working without applying too much pressure. The vertical stiles will cut easily, but the horizontal run of timber where you are cutting with the wood grain is never easy.

If only a small amount of wood needs to be removed, a plane would prove the easier tool to use. Work from each end when planing the vertical stiles, or you will split the wood when you come to the end.

Broken sash cords

Broken cords should never be ignored as a falling sash can be dangerous. As soon as one cord goes, it is advisable to replace them all. The cords are connected to weights which run in special pockets built into the window frames. It is these weights which counterbalance the weight of the window sash and make it easy to move.

To get at the cords, you remove the beading which is holding the sashes in place. These will be pinned, so prise them away with an old chisel. Now you will be able to pull the sash away. Cut the cord near the sash, and gently lower the weight down into the box. Remove the other sash in the same way, after taking out the centre beading which holds it in place.

You will see each box has a wood cover. Prise off the covers, then ease out the weights, lifting them clear of the boxes. Clean up the sashes by removing the staples holding the old sash cord in place, then put them aside. Now comes the tricky job of feeding new cord over the pulley wheels and down into the boxes. Tie a length of string to some poppet beads. Feed the beads over the wheels, then tie the new sash cord to the end of the string and feed it through. Remove the string and tie the new cord to the weight in the same way as the old cord was secured. Make sure that

it cannot come loose! Now lower the weight back into its box.

Replace the box covers, oil the pulley wheels, and you are ready to fix the sash cords in place. The bottom sash will be using the inner pulleys, and the top sash the outer pulleys. For the top sash, allow the weights to rest on the bottom. Hold the sash in place at the top and mark where the pulley wheels come in relation to the sash. Hold the cord against the sash, and pull it out as you remove the sash. Fix the

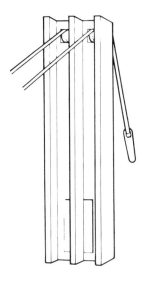

cord about 300 mm below the mark. Repeat for the other side. Trim off any surplus cord.

The lower sash needs the cords pulling down so that the weights rise to the top. Wedge the cords with the weights up to the top, then secure the cords to the top of the lower sash frame. The old marks will show you where to secure them. Trim off surplus cord. Test that the sash moves freely, then replace all the beadings.

The job sounds complicated, but it is one of those where you should note carefully how you dismantle the beadings and remove the cords. You can then merely work in reverse order when replacing everything.

Sticking curtain rails

If your home is fitted with old brass runners, it will pay you to strip them out and put in new plastic ones. These systems have improved tremendously in recent years.

To make the curtains run easier, remove the curtains, then apply a fine spray of aerosol lubricating and cleaning oil. Wipe off any surplus before putting curtains back.

Wax polish

If you have more modern rails and these do not run freely, apply a little clear furniture polish to the runners and wipe off surplus. The same treatment can be used for curtain slides.

Ugly pipe runs

In older properties, pipes tend to run on the surface of walls, where they are an eyesore. In the larger kitchen where timber panelling would not be out of place, they could be lost in the gap between wall and new panelling fixed to timber battens a shade deeper than the pipes.

If you use this method, it is advisable to leave a slight gap top and bottom so that warm air can flow through during winter months. This, of course, applies where pipes are fixed on outer house walls. Interior partition walls will not get cold during winter.

Where it is not practicable to use panelling, the pipes can be boxed in, making a simple box of fibre board or hardboard

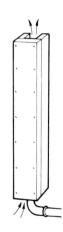

on a simple timber frame. Again, when working on outer walls, be sure to leave an air gap top and bottom. If the pipes are isolated from the room, they could freeze.

Hollow wall fixing

Modern methods of partitioning may be easy to build, but they can be tricky to fix things on to because they have a hollow core. To fix heavy cabinets you need to find the vertical timber studding in the wall and use this for anchor points. A horizontal batten fixed to the studding can be used to rest a cabinet on, then you only need screws to hold the unit to the wall.

To make these fixings you need special hollow fixing anchors. These come in a number of types, but the basic principle

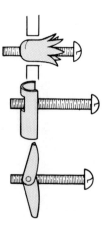

is the same. Part of the fixing is fed into the cavity of the partition, where it is anchored, forming a good grip when the screw is tightened. Most ordinary wall plugs are not suitable as they can get little grip on the partition, and will probably disappear into the cavity.

Similar cavity fixings will have to be employed when securing items like new wall sockets. If you are about to put up new partitioning, it would pay you to knock pieces of timber into the cavity of the partition at points likely to be used for fixing. The timber will give you a far stronger anchorage than any fixing device.

Resurfacing laminates

Where you encounter laminate worktops or table tops which you would like to replace, wherever possible leave the old laminate in place and put a new one over the top. Score the old laminate thoroughly with a coarse abrasive pad to give a good key for the next sheet, then apply adhesive to both surfaces as you would for any contact fixing. Allow the surfaces to become touch-dry, then bring the two surfaces together.

Door slamming

In modern homes particularly, lightweight flush doors tend to swing open and slam shut very easily. This is accentuated during fine weather when doors are left open and winds are quite strong—with the potential danger to the smaller members of

the family and the danger of glass doors being damaged.

Small but efficient door closers are available which will effectively control movement of the door and prevent it swinging free. These modern closers are small and unobtrusive.

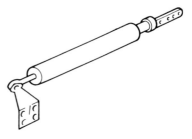

To stop a door banging when it shuts, fit a small rubber dome of silence to the door frame so that the door hits the rubber first. If there is little clearance available, you may have to trim the dome down. Where there is the minimum of room use a small strip of foam rubber draught excluder as a buffer.

Damaged plaster mouldings

In some older properties, ornate mouldings are used both as cornices and as ceiling decoration. If pieces have become damaged, small areas can be built up with cellulose filler, then when set rubbed down with glasspaper and rasp to match the surrounding area.

Where a shaped cornice is involved, fill the damaged area with cellulose filler proud of the surface, then make up a simple template cut from sheet metal. Pull the template over the filler so that it scrapes away the surplus material until the repair matches the surrounding moulding.

If the damaged area is intricate—e.g. flowers or leaves—you can buy a special rubber moulding material which can be melted then used to make a female mould

from an existing piece of decoration. When set, the mould can be pulled away, then the mould filled with casting powder mixed to a creamy consistency with water. This will reproduce a perfect replica of the decoration and it can then be cut into the damaged area and stuck in place. Very accurate repairs can be made in this way.

Post pulling from the wall

Very often the weight of a gate will pull the post away from a supporting wall. This is usually because the builder merely used a wedge of wood as a wall plug into which the securing screw or screws were driven. When the wood shrinks or rots, the post comes away.

Buy an anchor bolt long enough to pass through the post and at least 40 mm (1½ in) into the wall. You may have to buy a star drill to make a hole in the wall to take the

bolt, as the bolt will be bigger than the average large masonry drill. The bolt is inserted into the wall then, as the unit is tightened, a cone in the bolt is pulled up, spreading the bolt sections and jamming it firmly in the wall. The post will then have a very firm anchorage point. In normal circumstances, two such bolts are all that is needed.

Noise through a window

Even double glazing will not completely cut out noise from outside, as the panes are too close together. To cut down noise you need to add another pane of glass at least 75 mm (3 in) away from the existing one. This new glass should be of different weight to ensure that the pane does not vibrate in sympathy with the existing one.

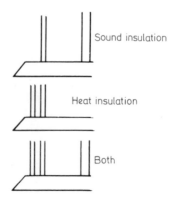

Sound insulation

Heat insulation

Both

Make sure there are no gaps around the frame and, of course, opening a window immediately cancels out the effect of insulation.

Chapter 10
Seventy
repair tips

In tackling the many repair jobs around your home, it is possible to waste valuable materials and time through quite small mistakes. The following tips are designed to make you wise to some of the pitfalls and positive wrinkles. They are based on many years of experience. The tips are subdivided to make reference easier.

Timber and boards

If you have to nail into hardwood, such as is used for beadings, drill fine holes through the wood to take the nails. This will greatly reduce the risk of splitting. Do not nail too near edges, and try to avoid lining nails along wood grain. A staggered row will help prevent splitting. When using screws a similar rule applies. You should use slightly larger start holes for hardwood than for soft woods to avoid splitting. Never overtighten screws—especially when using brass or alloy ones. You can easily turn the heads off when a dense timber cannot give.

Where timber used for fence boards has warped badly, remove each board and nail a piece of scrap wood on each end to act as a handle. Soak the board until saturated with water, then move it over a garden fire, forcing a twist into it, counter to the direction of the warp. The steam produced will make the board pliable and you will be able to get the board straight. Weight the board until quite dry, then replace in the fence.

Where a number of boards are involved, the steam generated by a steam wallpaper stripping machine will make the job easier. Wear leather gloves to avoid scalding.

Dowelled joints are ideal for making strong joins in timber, and they are particularly good for strengthening joints in veneered chipboards. There are a number of dowelling jigs on the market which simplify accurate alignment.

You can make your own dowels from lengths of dowel rod, and a simple way to reduce the size of a dowel is to drill a suitably sized hole in a piece of mild steel sheet. Anchor the sheet, then tap the dowel

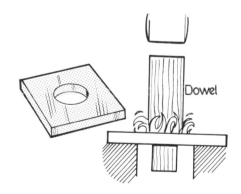

through the hole using a wood or rubber mallet. To reduce from large to quite small, use a number of holes and work down from one to the other until the required size is obtained.

It is possible to shape plywood by cutting through the laminates to a set depth. This is best done with a power saw where the depth of cut can be accurately set on the depth gauge. The amount of bend will be governed by the spacing of the cuts, and it is well worthwhile experimenting with scrap material before moving on to an actual job.

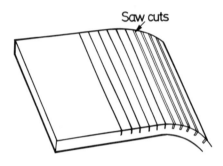

Saw cuts

It is also important that the cuts made are truly parallel with each other so that your curve is true. A saw bench, where the wood is run over the saw blade, and where an accurate fence guide can be used, will produce the best work.

When shaping or cutting sections of timber, there is always the danger of splitting or breaking. You can reduce the risk by clamping up your piece alongside one or two pieces of scrap timber, then working all together. In this way, the good material is protected and held firm. The same rule applies when planing or shaping across end grain where there is a real danger of splitting an edge. Where a piece of wood has to be shaped along its length, if possible leave a spare area of wood at each end by which the work can be held. Then cut this off when shaping is complete.

Making a timber joint by drilling into end grain may be a simple way of putting pieces together, but it does not give much strength. You can produce a far better job by inserting a dowel, positioned so that

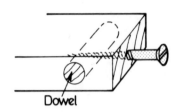

Dowel

when you screw into the end grain, the screw will be anchored in the dowel. A start-hole in the dowel will ensure the screw enters properly without splitting the wood. Don't rely only on screws. Apply a wood glue to the meeting pieces before screwing-up — applying extra to the end grain to allow for absorption.

Where the hole in a screwed joint has become enlarged — perhaps through movement — remove the screw, then enlarge the hole to take a ribbed plastic wall plug, tapping it in flush with the wood. Now you can use the same size screw as previously, but it will anchor far better in the plug. If the plug is of the expanding type, make sure it expands into the widest section of the timber — not across the narrowest dimension. With large holes — such as in fencing — it is possible to push one wall plug into another to get a good grip.

With timber prices so high these days, quality is sometimes questionable. For carcase repair work, the occasional knot — or even missing knot — may cause little trouble. But where timber is to be used decoratively, and particularly where it will get warm, avoid all but really sound knots. They may work loose after you have decorated the timber. Patent knotting will seal a knot so that no resin is exuded after painting.

An exception to the rule is where timber is to be used for decorative interior panelling. Here, knots can look attractive, and polyurethane wood seal can be used to anchor them in place.

For most timber repair jobs where new timber is to be inserted, plan to make your insert over-size so that it stands proud of the timber surface. When the adhesive is hard, use a shaping tool or rasp to rough shape the wood to the surrounding area, then finish off with a sander, working only with the wood grain, until the whole area is smooth. Where there are slight gaps, work a fine surface filler into them, allow to set and finally sand smooth. Always prime bare wood before redecorating. If fine nails were used to hold the new wood, punch them below the wood surface, fill the holes and smooth before priming.

Where timber is to be used indoors, bring it inside a week or two before use. This applies particularly during the wet winter months where the moisture content between outdoors and in a centrally heated home may be very considerable. Leaving it indoors will allow the timber to adjust its content while it can still move freely. To prevent hardboard buckling indoors, sprinkle the back of sheets with water and store back to back for a few days before using. This will allow the board to adapt to its surroundings.

Glass

Wherever you have to handle glass, it pays to wear a pair of leather gardening gloves as edges can be very sharp. If glass has to be handled quite a bit, use the edge of a carborundum stone to rub down and remove sharpness. Even a few minute's work will make the glass safe to handle. Where plate glass is to be used for replacement sliding doors perhaps to a cupboard, it is worth paying the extra at the glaziers to have the edges ground to shape. This will ensure that the doors run smoothly. Carry large pieces of glass vertically, protected by paper. Carrying it flat may cause it to break merely through its own weight.

Do not store old glass against the day when it can be used again. For some reason it ages and becomes very hard to cut accurately. Wherever possible buy fresh glass as you need it. Unless you have considerable experience, choose a wheel glass cutter — not a diamond-tipped cutter. The diamond works very well in the hands of an expert. Good wheel cutters are provided with extra wheels, so move the cutter on as a wheel becomes dulled. You should hear the cutter whispering over the glass if it is cutting well.

Glazed panels in doors — and particularly exterior doors — always present an accident hazard. A door may slam violently in the wind, or a person may fall against it. Wherever there is a risk it will pay to fit a toughened glass. You can now buy a special laminated glass which has a tough plastic film sandwiched between two pieces of glass. This makes it tremendously tough, and while it will craze, it will not break or form dangerous splinters. It costs more than standard glass, but the investment is worth the extra.

Wherever an awkward shaped piece of glass has to be replaced, don't rely on measurements alone. Make an accurate template from stiff brown paper or thin card — allowing about 1½ mm all round so that putty can cushion the glass in its frame. Where such a piece was leaded, a good imitation leaded light can be made using self-adhesive lead strip and special glass stains. You need to make a patterned template, then lay the glass on this while the lead is added. Use coloured stains on the inside. A slightly irregular application of glass stain colours will look more like real stained glass.

There is no satisfactory way of repairing cracked glass, but the crack can be sealed by applying a special waterproof transparent adhesive tape. It is best to apply this as soon as possible, before dirt has time to get into the cracks. Look upon the seal as a temporary repair only.

Where patterned glass is used in exterior doors or windows, insert new glass with the pattern side in so that the smoothest face can be sealed against the weather. This is particularly important where glass is held in place by a timber beading, for it is vital that no rain can get down behind the beading. Rain entering at this point is one of the commonest causes of door frame rot. Another advantage of having the pattern side in is that there is nothing on the outside to collect dirt and grime, and window cleaning will be easier.

Use plenty of bedding putty with patterned glass so that all gaps are adequately sealed between frame and glass.

To temporarily obscure glass, whiting or window cleaning liquid left to dry on the window will do. But where you wish to obscure the glass to give permanent privacy, there are self-adhesive plastic sheets available in a number of decorative patterns. Clean the glass thoroughly, strip off just a little of the backing paper, position the sheet, then pull away the rest of the backing paper. Press edges well down to prevent moisture getting under and lifting the sheet.

If you prefer to do the job with patterned glass, a good variety is available from most glaziers.

If you wish to drill a hole in glass, use a special glass drill either in a wheel brace, or in a power tool of the type which has a good speed reducer. High speed is a distinct disadvantage. A small piece of transparent adhesive tape will help you position the tip of the drill, and it pays to make a little 'well' around the mark with Plasticine, into which a little oil or turps can be poured to act as a lubricant. As the drill tip breaks

through, turn the glass over and finish off from the other side to avoid splintering the edges of the hole as the drill breaks through. Apply the very minimum of pressure at all times and don't try to rush the job.

This is really a non-tip, but it is one that crops up very regularly. There is no easy or cheap way to re-silver mirror glass. Once the mirror deteriorates, it is wise to replace it, or take it to a glaziers for re-silvering. The materials needed are not easy to obtain and some are dangerous to handle. Producing a good mirror finish is still a job for the experts!

When using mirror clips to hold a mirror to a wall, it is always wise to use soft washers between wall and mirror back. This is to absorb any minor irregularities in wall surface which could otherwise impose a severe strain on the mirror. Never overtighten holding screws — in fact err on the loose side for safety.

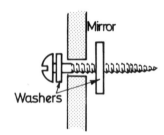

Lightweight mirrors or mirror tiles can be held by special double-sided adhesive pads, but they must always be applied to clean, dry, grease-free surfaces. You can stick on to tile, plaster or well adhering paint. You cannot stick to wallpaper or vinyl wallcoverings.

Brick

Unless you are experienced at using a bricklaying trowel, cut a brick by using a bolster and club hammer. Place the brick on a bed of sand to absorb the impact, then tap a line with bolster and hammer, leaving a clear vee nick in the brick. When there is a clear mark, increase the impact and give one sharp blow along the line. The brick should break clean. The same technique can be used for shaping or cleaning up. The rough face of a brick can be smoothed with an abrasive cutting wheel used in a power tool, but take great care. Wear protective gloves — and safety specs.

Cleaning decorative brickwork is not easy, as soaps and detergents leave stains. A scrubbing brush and clean water are best, with a wire brush used for obstinate marks. Where you encounter mortar stains, perhaps through careless bricklaying, the mortar marks can be removed by using a special chemical cleaner used by builders for cleaning their tools. It dissolves cement mortar without affecting the bricks. Ask at your largest builders merchants for details.

Drilling holes in brick is best done with a special masonry drill. This should be of a size to match the wall plugs and screws you plan to use. The masonry drill can be used in a hand wheel brace, but it is easier to use if mounted in the chuck of a power drill. Use the lowest speed you can. Ease the drill from the wall occasionally to clear the brick dust and to allow the tip to cool. Always drill under applied pressure, and never let the tip just skate over the surface.

Where larger holes are needed — such as when fixing a post to a wall with anchor bolts — use a special star drill, which is made in sizes to match bolts. This is tapped smartly with a hammer, and slowly rotated as the drill bites.

Special long drills and extension drills are available where extra deep holes are required.

Brick and briquette fireplaces can discolour with age, and cleaning is not easy. Use the technique already mentioned for brick cleaning, plus the addition of a rub with a piece of matching brick. When clean, colour can often be restored by using special brick stains, available in a limited range of colours. These restore the brick colours without affecting the surface. It is never wise to use coloured seals as these block the pores of the brick and add an unnatural sheen.

If an open fire is used, a stainless steel surround fitted in the fireplace opening is a good investment. It will prevent sooting up of brickwork.

Where exterior bricks are over-porous, they can be sealed with a silicone water repellent which prevents the ingress of moisture while still allowing the brickwork to 'breathe'. It should be applied liberally so it flows over the surface — but keep it off woodwork and window glass. It is very hard to remove from such surfaces.

Cement/Concrete

It is always wise to buy fresh cement as you need it, for it is not an easy material to store. If you must store it for a while, place the opened bag in a tough polythene bag or sack and seal the top. Store the pack in the dry, and don't rest it on a floor likely to get wet. For small repair jobs buy a small pack of ready-mix, and don't open any more than you can use. Cover sand and aggregates, especially during wet weather, as the moisture content can change dramatically. It is not possible to use cement which has hardened in the bag. Don't be tempted to powder it down and use it. Throw it out.

Cement works best with the minimum of moisture, so always err on the dry side when mixing concrete. Apart from strength, a sloppy mix is likely to stain surrounding areas; it will be hard to place and it won't hold its shape. So that a dry mix retains its strength while setting, damp the surfaces to which it is to be applied. This applies also to mortar, for the joints should be damped with a paint brush and water so that moisture is not drawn from the mortar mix.

There are times when plain concrete can look rather stark, and it is now possible to stain concrete, toning it down to match other surfaces or applying a decorative colour. Applications include staining concrete spurs holding fencing so the spurs are less conspicuous, and painting plain paths and patios to give the appearance of crazy paving. Stains are permanent and need no protective coating.

Where paths and patios are used during icy weather, it is wise to consider making them non-slip. This can be done during building by ridging the concrete just before it sets, or by including an aggregate and brushing away the top cement before it sets to expose stones. Paving slabs can be made with a layer of stones as a top dressing, or fine stones can be embedded into concrete before it sets. Don't go to the other extreme and make the surface a danger to small children if they fall!

A reasonable non-slip surface can be produced by adding silver sand to a good quality exterior grade emulsion paint. It needs regular stirring to keep the sand suspended, and it must be applied to clean surfaces.

Concrete will lose strength if it dries too rapidly after laying. The damper it can be kept, the better. Old sacking damped with water is ideal during warm weather, or failing that use polythene sheeting. Rain will rarely affect drying concrete. In fact it will prolong the curing period. Don't lay concrete during periods of frost. Wait until the weather improves.

It is essential to clean off all tools used for concrete work — particularly those you may have hired, such as a concrete mixer. Most can be washed off with water, but obstinate layers can be removed while 'green' (not yet hardened) with a coarse wire brush. Really hard concrete should be dissolved with a special chemical cleaner available from builders merchants.

Clean up splashes on paths and walls as they occur. Don't wait until the concrete hardens. The chemical referred to will remove stains from brick without affecting the brickwork.

Make sure you get the right sand for the job in hand. Sharp sand, which is clean but gritty, is fine for paths and drives. But for mortar mixes choose a soft sand which gives a soft, buttery mix — but which stains the hands. When ordering, clearly specify the purpose for which the sand is going to be used.

When filling a childrens' sand pit, always choose a sharp sand — never a soft builders sand. As already mentioned, the soft sand will stain. Put a cover over your sand pit to keep off animals and to prevent debris blowing in.

Where concrete tends to flake or pull away from an under-layer of concrete, use a pva adhesive to bond them together. The adhesive can be used as an additive to the water in the actual mix, and also it can be brush-applied to the surface to be covered just before the new material is laid. In this way, concrete can be feathered down to nothing and still not flake.

The pva can also be used to coat dusting concrete. Brush the surface clean, apply a layer of pva with a brush, and it will effectively seal the surface.

Making fixings to concrete can be tackled in the same way as for brick, using a masonry drill or star drill. When plugging, make sure the plugs are suitable for outdoor use. Dense concrete with a sharp aggregate is very hard to drill, and it may be necessary

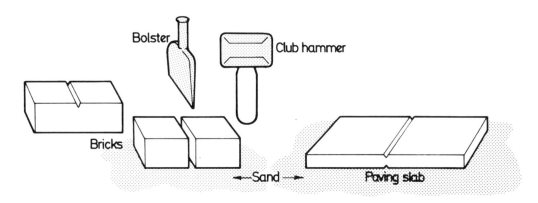

to use a hammer and jumping tool to break stones. A good alternative is to use a power tool with hammer action — combining the best of drilling and hammering. Where items like sheds and greenhouses have to be secured to concrete, always choose an expanding type anchor rather than a normal plug. They give far better anchorage.

Cutting slabs calls for practice, so try out your technique on broken pieces before cutting good slabs.

Lay the slab on a bed of sand to cushion the impact, then tap a line on the slab using bolster and club hammer until a clear vee nick is formed. Turn the slab over and repeat the operation. Now place the bolster on the slab, in the cut, and tap smartly. The slab should break clean along the mark. When you are experienced, you should be able to split a slab without turning it over.

Taking off narrow strips is quite hard, and it calls for care in making the initial vee nick. It may be safer to nibble the waste away with two or three cuts with the bolster, rather than trying to remove the strip in one piece.

Electrics

While the subject of home electrics is covered in section 4, a few tips on electrical repairs will not be amiss here.

While the rigid plastic used for plugs and sockets can usually be repaired with an epoxy resin adhesive, it is very good practice to remove and replace all damaged fittings. Never get into the habit of making 'temporary' repairs with adhesive tape, whether insulating or not. If plugs or connectors are likely to get knocked about, choose rubber replacements which are unbreakable. Where lampholders are subject to considerable heat — as in enclosed shades — use brass lampholders rather than plastic. Make sure the flex used is also heat-resistant.

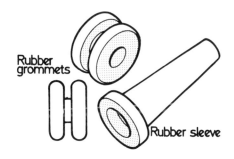

Wherever flex passes through metal or thin section plastic, be sure to fit a rubber grommet. This ensures that the flex cannot be damaged by sharp edges constantly rubbing. Where flex is constantly on the move — as with an electric iron flex — fit a rubber sleeve close to the iron so that it takes the brunt of any wear. Replace it when it becomes worn. Whenever flex shows sign of fatigue, replace it before any real damage is done. Replace the whole length. Don't connect in a new piece of flex.

If a socket is loose on the wall, and the screws fail to tighten, the problem may be that the wall is hollow. Switch off the electricity supply; remove the socket from the wall and check. If the wall is solid, new wall plugs may be all that is necessary. If you encounter a hollow wall, you need special cavity wall anchors designed to grip on the inside of the partition. These take various forms, from those operated by a gravity toggle, to a type which splays out as tightened. Don't tighten holding screws more than is necessary or you may damage the partition.

Where a surface-mounted switch is loose, you will need to get at the base plate. Disconnect the power, remove the switch cover and try to tighten the two holding screws in the base plate. They may just have worked loose. If they won't tighten, release the wires to the switch, remove the screws and pull the plate away — having noted which wires go where. You may need to put in new wall plugs before replacing the plate. If the plate is damaged, replace the switch.

If a flush mounted switch is loose, even with the two screws tight, it is likely that the box housed in the wall is loose. Switch off the power, remove the cover and ease it and the connected wires away from the wall. Check to see if the screws holding the box are tight. If not, tighten. If they will not tighten, you must disconnect the wiring taking note of which wire goes where. Take out the box; re-plug the wall and replace, making sure none of the wiring is trapped by the box. Re-wire the switch.

Where a ceiling rose is loose, switch off the power, remove the cover by unscrewing,

to expose the pattress (that section of the rose connected to the ceiling). Check whether the retaining screws have worked loose. If they will not tighten it may be that the screws were merely driven into the ceiling plaster — which is not adequate for mounting. Ideally you need to get into the space above the fitting by lifting a floorboard, then place a piece of wood between the ceiling joists so that the screws can be driven into this wood through the plaster. If this is not possible, you may be able to use cavity fixings as mentioned for hollow walls.

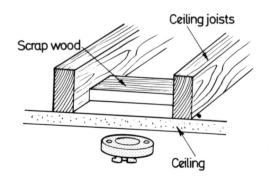

If outside wiring to sheds or garages does not work, it is essential to check it very carefully. Disconnect the cable from the mains supply then check the cable run. It must either be carried overhead, supported by a steel cable capable of supporting it, or it must be connected by means of a special underground cable. On no account can power be carried by a cable draped along a fence or laid in earth. If in any doubt, refer to section 4—Home Electrics.

If flex must be joined, be sure to use proper flex connectors so that a good screwed joint is produced. Wherever wires are to branch off, use a connector box with screwed terminals. Do not accept taped joints. Where flex is to be used out of doors, and it needs to be extended, use the correct three terminal male and female connectors, with the female always on the live end of the extension. Another safe way of extending is to use an extension cable reel. Taped joints are never acceptable for outdoor extensions.

Where you find flex is run under carpets or rugs, remove it and find a safer route. This is the most common cause of flex failure leading to a short circuit and perhaps a fire. Flex is not designed to be constantly trodden on. Pin the flex to the skirting board with insulated staples, or tuck under the skirting board if there is a gap. Ideally fit new socket outlets so that flex does not need a long run to standard and table lamps. New socket outlets must be correctly wired to cable — never to flex.

In an older property, where you encounter rubber-sheathed cables where the sheath is hardening, it is a clear indication that the property is ready for re-wiring. Don't be tempted to patch it up (refer to section 4—Home Electrics). Perished cables are a real danger and they greatly add to the risk of fire.

Plumbing

As the subject of home plumbing is dealt with in section 3, only a few minor repairs are mentioned here.

If the overflow in the loft is dripping water, suspect the ball valve in the cold water storage tank. You may need a new valve seating, or the ball may have failed. As an emergency repair for a punctured ball float, empty out the water, then slip a polythene bag over the ball and secure with an elastic band. Modern ball floats made of plastic have a far better chance of survival — and they will not corrode. Plastic valves

are also available which make far less noise than older patterns.

If a tap continues to drip after fitting a new washer, the valve seating may be damaged. It is possible to grind a new flat surface on the valve, but if you are unable to do this, buy a new plastic valve seating designed to be pushed on top of the old one. This will give the tap a new lease of life. A nylon jumper unit is also available to go with the new seating.

A damaged water pipe can be repaired with a modern resin-hardener paste, but it needs to be reinforced by glass fibre tape. The paste on its own has not sufficient strength. Apply paste, wind on a turn of bandage and apply a further layer of paste, then another wind of bandage. An extremely strong repair can be made in this way. After a freezing spell, check exposed compression joints, as pressure may have forced them loose.

Take great care when loosening or tightening nuts on basins, for it is very easy to crack the basin. The secret is to apply an equal force to, for example, a tap as to the nut you are trying to undo, thus cancelling out any strain on the basin itself. If you must try to tap any part loose, use a rubber faced hammer which will not cause any damage. Wherever nuts will not move, apply easing oil, then give the oil chance to work. This often works where force fails.

If you encounter water hammer — a severe knocking in pipes when a cistern is filling — suspect the ball valve vibrating up and down as the valve starts to close. You can buy a special paddle designed to damp the movement which clips to the ball arm. Or, make a damper from a plastic beaker suspended from the ball arm by wire, and completely submerged in the water.

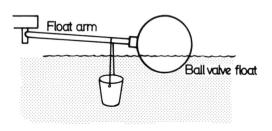

Another cause of hammer is the jumper of the tap washer moving up and down. A captive jumper will often cure this trouble.

Gaps around baths and basins are a problem, as the gap can vary in size according to movement. So a flexible seal of some kind is necessary. A silicone rubber sealant applied to clean, dry surfaces will give a good flexible seal — but it takes practice to get a really smooth finish. If you are applying new tiles, you can buy quadrant tile sets designed to hide the gap and blend with your tiling. This joint is not flexible, so the quadrant must extend far enough over the bath or basin to ensure that water drains off.

Where you encounter leaking pipe joints which will not respond to tightening, there is a tape available (called ptfe tape) which will ensure a good seal. It is easier and less messy to use than the old boss white paste. The joint is opened, tape wound around the thread, then the joint re-made. Where a compression joint will not tighten, suspect the cone or the olive, which is designed to make a seal without undue pressure. If damaged or deformed, replace it. Capillary joints which leak must be heated to separate, then the joint re-made. The joint cannot be patched from the outside.

If the joint between the lavatory pan and the waste pipe is leaking, empty the pan as far as possible and allow the joint time to dry. Now dig out any crumbling filling from the joint, then fill with glazing cord or tape. This is a mastic-like material applied to cord or bandage, and when tamped well home, it will give a good watertight joint. Give a final smooth with your finger. The surface will become touch-dry, but the joint will remain flexible.

A chip in a basin is not easy to disguise, but it can be built up using a liquid porcelain paint. This should be applied one coat at a time, then left to harden before the next layer is applied. Repeat the process until the paint is flush with the surrounding material. If done well, the repair will be hard to spot. For repairs out of sight, a ceramic putty is ideal. This comes as two parts which, as required are mixed together, after which hardening is by chemical action. Once set, the putty can be painted to match the unit.

Ideally a central heating system should contain an inhibitor liquid to prevent corrosion or the formation of sludge. If you find a pinhole in a radiator with water weeping out, buy a radiator sealing liquid and feed it into the sealed system by way of the small expansion tank in the loft. This will seal off minor leaks. Systems not containing an inhibitor are best drained off, re-filled with clean water, then an inhibitor added via the small expansion tank.

Plastics

Thermosetting plastics — those unaffected by heating — can usually be repaired using an epoxy resin adhesive or the cyanoacrylate type adhesive. As already mentioned, don't make a habit of mending broken electrical appliances; replace them. Assemble broken pieces dry first to ensure where they fit, before coating with adhesive. A quick-setting epoxy will enable you to hold the repair. It will harden in five minutes. A cyanoacrylate sets in about ten seconds! Don't get it on your fingers!

Polythenes cannot be bonded with adhesives. They seem to grip while wet, but once dry, drop away. Polythene can be welded by using a warm soldering iron over a piece of aluminium foil. Or sheet polythene can be welded using a special welding wheel — rather like a soldering iron with a wheel at the end — or by using the edge of a warm domestic iron applied over a piece of foil. Never apply the iron direct to the polythene. It may melt on the sole plate of the iron and be very hard to remove! Polythene can be held temporarily by self-adhesive plastic tape.

Polystyrene can be repaired with a special polystyrene adhesive of the type used for assembling plastic toy kits. The adhesive contains a solvent which softens the polystyrene, so make sure you do not spill it on decorative surfaces. This adhesive is not designed for expanded polystyrene.

Expanded polystyrene can be stuck with one of the adhesives sold for fixing ceiling tiles or holding wall veneer. It should never be used with an adhesive containing powerful solvents, as the solvent destroys the structure of the foam. For a good waterproof joint between expanded polystyrene and other materials, use a black exterior grade rubber adhesive. The solvent is mild enough not to damage the foam.

Synthetic rubbers such as used for pulley belts and drive belts can be very rapidly stuck using cyanoacrylate adhesive. Providing the surfaces meet well, bonding time is measured in seconds, though full strength may take an hour or so. Bear in mind that a belt which shows signs of deterioration is best replaced as soon as possible. The adhesive may well keep the appliance in use until a new belt can be obtained.

Plastic trims where the material is flexible are best secured with a rubber based adhesive. Items such as car trims where the weather is an enemy can be stuck in place with a silicone rubber sealing compound, which also acts as a very effective adhesive. Surfaces to be stuck must of course be clean, free from dust and loose rust — and they must be dry.

Scratches on acrylic plastic surfaces — such as on an acrylic bath — can be polished out using metal polish wadding. It takes time, and care should be taken to blend in the area with its surrounding plastic. Acrylics are easily scratched, so avoid scouring powders. Keep paint strippers and hot cigarettes away too!

Most thermoplastics can be handled easier when warmed. If shaping is possible, the plastic needs to be heated. Use hot water for mild warming, or a hair dryer for greater heat. The hair dryer, for example, is ideal for softening a vinyl floor tile which has lifted. When warmed, it will go down on to new adhesive much more readily. Thermosetting plastics do not respond to warming.

Most plastics can be drilled. Hard materials can be drilled at speed, but the plastics which soften with heat are best hand drilled at the lowest possible speed. Otherwise you can soften the plastic enough for it to melt on to the twist drill.

Plastic laminates can be cut with a knife fitted with a special laminate cutting blade. The surface of the laminate is scored, then the sheet bent *up* (not down) with the pattern side up. It can also be cut with a fine tooth saw, and the edges smoothed with a cabinet scraper, a fine rasp or very fine glasspaper. It can be drilled with normal twist drills, and stuck in place with rubber-based adhesive.

Floorcoverings

If a small area of carpet is damaged —perhaps by a burn — cut out a square just taking in the damaged area and insert a matching square. It can be held in place with a small square of hessian soaked with latex adhesive, or by using a square of carpet binding tape. If any tufts stand proud, press down, then trim lightly with scissors.

Where carpet is fraying at the edges, turn back the edge and secure with latex carpet adhesive or with carpet tape. Trim off any loose strands. To prevent fraying of other sections, coat the back of the carpet for a width of about 50 mm to bind all the threads together. This helps particularly with some of the cheaper grade carpets where fraying starts as soon as the carpet is cut to size.

Where carpet or vinyl is lifting at doorways, it pays to buy an edging strip to

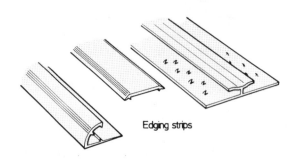

Edging strips

hold it down. These are available in various types, to secure either one edge of carpet; two edges, or an edge of carpet one side and vinyl the other. The strip is designed to be screwed in place, and if correctly fitted it will offer no obstruction to a door.

Where a vinyl floorcovering has been scuffed by shoe marks, rub the area with a pad of fine wire wool lubricated with turps. This will remove the marks without damaging the floor. Ideally, areas like parquet and decorative vinyl should be protected by runners — or outdoor shoes should be barred from the house!

Where a rug tends to creep, or where a runner slides, secure it with small squares of self-adhesive Velcro tape. This has fine hooks and loops which hold firmly, but which can very easily be separated when necessary.

Alternatively, use carpet press studs for runners where it does not matter if you screw into the floor. If it does matter, use rubberised netting under the runner. This very effectively anchors a carpet.

Section 2

Home Building Work

A BASIC TOOL KIT

Below is listed a good basic kit which will see you through most home building work. But you will find many other things which can be added as you progress in certain fields. All those mentioned here are referred to in the following chapter.

Surveyor's tape
Builder's line
Builder's square
Wooden pegs
Trowels, large and small
Spade
Ladder
Work bench, fixed or portable
Steel rule
Steel tape
Try square
Tenon saw
Hacksaw and blades
General purpose saw
Cross cut saw
Shaping tools
Wheel brace and set of twist drills
Screwdrivers
Bench vice—can be clamp-on
Wrench
Pincers
Pliers, large and fine nose
Spirit level
Chisels
Masonry drills
Files
Marking knife
Marking gauge
Chain wrench
Putty knife

Nail punch
Bevel
Smooth plane
Brace and set of bits
Spiral ratchet screwdriver
G cramps
Club hammer
Glass cutter
Soft face hammer
Power drill
— plus the following attachments:
   Sander
   Saw—circular
   Saw—jig
   Vertical drill stand
   Rasps
   Flexible drive
   Speed reducer
   Right-angle drive

Integral power tools include:
   Jigsaw
   Circular saw
   Band saw
   Router
   Belt sander
   Grinder
   Floor sander
   Orbital sander
   Planer

Introduction to Section 2

Whether you are a house owner-occupier or a tenant you should be interested in the construction of your house. If you can use tools correctly and care to study the elements of building, it is possible for you to undertake the small building projects which are described in this section.

The information given is concerned with simple foundation work, concreting, bricklaying, masonry, carpentry, joinery and roofing, as applied in house building. What use you can make of it depends upon your willingness to learn and the skills you can develop with practice.

Always start with something small and simple. Do not be discouraged by false starts. Have another go. Don't tackle more ambitious jobs until you have developed sufficient skill.

Building work which is part of the house and any structural alteration needs official approval before you start. So does any separate structure such as a garage, car port and garden buildings larger than a shed.

The Building Regulations, which specify requirements for safe and proper construction state that plans must be submitted for approval to the local Council (Surveyor's office).

If in doubt, call at the council surveyor's office. The staff will tell you whether plans and application forms are required. You can discuss the proposal with them, and also ask if planning permission is needed—a separate matter from the Building Regulations.

Usually planning permission is not required for small extensions or garden buildings which do not project in front of the building line and which are required only for normal domestic use. The Planning Regulations are rather complex and it is advisable to consult the Council's surveyor.

The designs and details in this section are generally in accordance with the Building Regulations but there are factors which in some cases may call for modification. Here again the council surveyor will advise you.

You can buy a copy of the Building Regulations and any current amendments from Her Majesty's Stationery Office, 49 High Holborn, London WC1V 6HB. There are branches in several provincial cities. Any bookseller can obtain a copy for you. They are not easy to understand but I have explained in this section as much as is necessary for small home projects.

NOTE

Most of the drawings in this section are dimensioned in Imperial units as they are likely to be better understood than metric units for some years to come. However in the text both Imperial units and approximate metric equivalents are quoted.

It is useful to remember that approximate equivalents are as follows:

$$25mm = 1 \text{ in}$$
$$100mm = 4 \text{ in}$$
$$300mm = 1 \text{ ft}$$
$$1m = 3 \text{ ft } 3 \text{ in}$$
$$1000mm = 1 \text{ m}$$

Showing how part of the back garden can be improved by laying a mixture of plain and coloured paving slabs (Edwin H. Bradley & Sons Ltd)

Chapter 11
Foundations, solid floors and pavings

In this chapter we deal mainly with the use of concrete for floors and foundations of garages and other small buildings. The last part of the chapter details the methods of laying paving slabs for paths, terraces and patios.

Tools for setting out

The basic tools for setting out are as given in the following list.

A builder's line (or long length of strong string) wound on a pair of pointed wood pegs or short steel rods;

A builder's square. This can be 'home-made' of planed wood battens to form a right angled triangle (one side 3 units, the other 4 units and the diagonal 5 units—the units can be feet or metres in the 3:4:5 proportions;

A few wood pegs to drive into the ground when marking lengths or corners.

Other useful tools

In addition to the above you will need the following.

A garden fork and spade for removing surface soil and trenching;

A pickaxe for very hard ground;

A strong wheelbarrow;

A bucket and a watering can with rose outlet;

A long spirit level and a straightedge of planed wood about 100 x 38 x 1800 mm (4 in x 1½ in x 6 ft).

Materials

Concrete can be obtained ready mixed, either wet in a mobile mixer, ready for placing, or as a dry mix in bags for mixing with water as required. Both these types are more convenient than buying separate ingredients—Portland cement, sand and gravel aggregate.

Ready-mix (wet) concrete can be ordered from depots in most towns. If you state the dimensions of the work and the purpose and date required, the supplier will quote for the quantity needed. Take care not to order more at a time that you can place in an hour or two, as cement mixes start setting within an hour.

Dry mix concrete (dry cement, sand and gravel aggregate) can be bought in paper bags from most DIY shops, for mixing with water on the site. This is especially convenient for small jobs or for larger jobs which cannot be finished within a few hours as you can mix the material with water as and when needed. There are several brands which are readily available. A suitable type is Marley mix No. 2.

If desired separate ingredients can be bought. This is the cheapest way if you can obtain supplies of suitable washed sand and washed gravel or crushed stone in your district as well as Portland cement.

Always state the purpose when ordering, as sands and aggregates vary in the range of small and coarse particles. For foundations under walls a high proportion of coarse material is suitable. For thin pavings or slabs, finer material is needed. Specify all sand and aggregates for building purposes to be 'washed' as dirty materials can cause trouble.

Garden stones (flints) and broken bricks, washed, can be used in foundation concrete. Clinkers and ashes should not be used.

Mixing concrete

Concrete suitable for foundations, garage and other thick solid floors and drives may consist of

1 part Portland cement;
2½ parts clean sand (of normal damp-ness but not saturated);
4 parts coarse aggregate.

The above measured by volume, using a clean bucket or bottomless 'box' which can stand on a clean paving stone or platform.

All-in aggregate or ballast is a cheaper alternative to separate sand and gravel. It consists of both materials as the aggregate is taken from a quarry of sandy gravel. It can be used in ordinary foundations and as over-site concrete under timber floors but it is not suitable for work needing consistent strength. For paths, pools, steps and slabs less than 73 mm (3 in) thick use a fairly strong concrete:

1 part Portland cement;
2 parts clean sand of normal dampness;
3 parts clean coarse aggregate of maxi-mum size 10 mm (⅜ in).

If you want a smooth surface, for screeding (surfacing) concrete floors and paths, or for making thin slabs use a mix of cement and sand only:

1 part Portland cement;
3 or 4 parts clean sand, graded from fine to coarse.

Mixing the ingredients for concrete is important as improper mixing may result in loss of strength. The sand and coarse aggregate should first be thoroughly mixed in the dry state on a clean surface, turning it over repeatedly with the spade to make an even distribution of the two materials. Then add the correct proportion of Portland cement and again mix thoroughly in the dry state.

Form a hollow in the top of the heap and add clean water through the rose of a watering can, rather slowly, stopping to occasionally turn the heap with the spade to ensure even absorption of the water. If you add all the water at one go without mixing it in, the cement will be washed out. The aim of mixing is to coat each piece of aggregate or ballast with a coat of cement-sand.

Most beginners tend to add too much water and this makes a weak concrete tending to uneven mixing and causing excessive shrinkage when the concrete is placed. Mixing should be thorough to give a rather stiff concrete.

Another common fault is to use too much cement under the impression that it will make a very strong concrete. The richer the cement in concrete the greater the tendency to crazing and cracking through excessive shrinkage. The propor-tions already given are adequate for the purposes stated.

For most purposes ordinary Portland cement is suitable. It should be fresh and if stored, should be in a dry place. If a bag is opened and left for some time the cement will absorb atmospheric moisture and will partly set into lumps. If it is in this state, it should be discarded.

Foundations

Any building, even a garden shed, needs a firm foundation. The type of foundation depends on the load and the nature of the ground or subsoil.

Strip foundations consist of concrete placed in a strip at the bottom of a trench. The strips must be deep enough to be beyond the disturbance through shrinkage and swelling which may be caused by drying out and cracking of the subsoil in a drought, or by uneven bearing value of the subsoil which may be strong in one place and weak in another.

Subsoils vary widely in strength and resistance to weather changes. Compact gravel or sandy gravel is well drained by its nature and if it is not on a steep hill a minimum trench depth of 450 mm (18 in) is usually sufficient for small houses. Chalky ground varies but if it is well drained a depth of 600 mm (2 ft) may be sufficient. Where the ground is liable to saturation greater depth may be necessary.

Clays are variable in nature. but they are all liable to shrinkage in drought. Local practice is the best guide—trench depths of between 600 mm (2 ft) and 1000 mm (3 ft 3 in) may be regarded as a normal range according to the depth to which shrinkage

fissures may open in a drought. In some cases even greater depths may be needed. The local council surveyor can tell you what depths are suitable.

You may wonder if such depths are necessary for small buildings such as garden sheds, summer houses, home workshops and prefabricated room extensions and conservatories. For garden sheds or similar structures you can afford to take a slight risk. A trench depth of 300 mm (1 ft) may be sufficient on compact, well-drained ground. However, if a solid floor is also required it is economical to form this as a raft, as described later. This forms a foundation and floor combined.

You can make a rough investigation of your subsoil by digging a few trial holes. The surface soil is usually loose garden soil and this should be removed from the whole area of the building. It may be anything

The string line is passed around the corner pegs—it must be kept level. The square corners can be formed by the 3:4:5 method, using any convenient units of measurement or by using a large wooden square

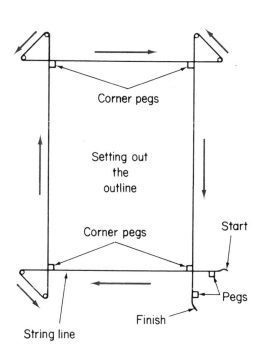

Corner pegs

Setting out
the
outline

Corner pegs

Start

Pegs

Finish

String line

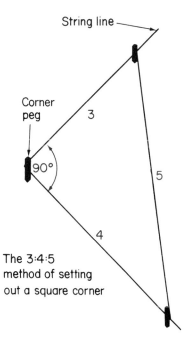

String line

Corner
peg

3

90°

5

4

The 3:4:5
method of setting
out a square corner

from about 75 mm (3 in) to 300 mm (12 in) deep and if it is rich soil it can be spread over the garden. Then, excavate the trench until you have a firm undisturbed bottom. You can test for firmness by dropping a heavy post on it, which should make only a slight impression.

If you take out several trial holes, notice whether there is any variation in the nature and type of subsoil. Some sites have been partly filled with surplus soil or rubbish and may contain weak parts which call for deeper foundations than the main part.

If, from this or any other cause, as on a sloping site, the foundations have to be stepped the concrete should be continuous, forming a riser or step from the lower to the higher level.

Setting out

Before the excavation begins, the outline of the walls should be set out on the ground. Start by stretching a string line across the front building line. Secure to a peg at each corner and then stretch it along one side. Here you must place the wooden square at the corner and adjust the line to make a right-angled (90 deg) corner, unless for some unusual reason a skew angle is needed. Each side must of course be carefully measured, preferably with a long tape measure.

To check for squareness of the corners and trueness of the lengths, measure the diagonals from opposite corners. Both should be the same length. This applies to a plain rectangle and does not include any projections.

I am assuming that you have a plan of the building, even if it is only a shed. If no scale plan is available make a sketch plan and mark the dimensions in figures. This will prevent mistakes or careless guesswork.

By the foregoing method you will have in position the four corner pegs of the building. But you must remove them before you start excavating as they would be in the way. Before removing the pegs set up a

Profiles set up clear of the trench position. Lines can then be stretched to guide the trench and foundation positions. The first bricks can be levelled as bottom section

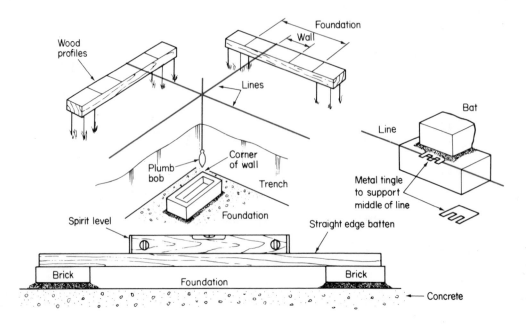

profile at each corner. This can be a horizontal batten marked with trench and wall widths, and fixed on pegs opposite each wall and corner as shown in the diagram. Then, to set out the trenches, lines can be stretched from profile to profile. Each pair of lines allow the trench width for one side to be marked on the ground and trenching can then begin.

When setting out on sloping ground, the tape measure must be held level to give correct wall lengths. If it is held on the slope the wall length will be short. As the level tape will be held some distance above the ground at the lower end of the slope a batten or plumb line should be held truly upright at that end, so that the true measurement can be transferred to the ground.

Levelling

The trench bottom must be levelled. A long spirit level can be used, or a short one placed on a long straightedge (see diagram). If any part of the trench has been carelessly excavated deeper than required, the depression should be left to be filled with the foundation concrete and *not* filled with earth as this would form a soft spot.

If you come across a weak patch in part of the trench you should excavate deeper, if it is definitely soft. But if there are several soft patches of limited extent it is advisable

to reinforce the concrete foundation with a pair of 10 mm ($^3/_8$ in) mild steel rods.

If on sloping ground, the strip foundation must be stepped, as already mentioned. The trench bottoms should be stepped so that the minimum depth of the foundation will be as specified. It follows that most of the foundation must be deeper than specified.

Wood pegs should be driven into the trench bottom at intervals of about 1800 mm (6 ft), with the peg tops levelled above the trench bottom by thickness of the concrete required. By placing a long straightedge batten from peg to peg the concrete can be finished level as it proceeds.

Shallow trenches in reasonably firm ground do not need side support. But in soft ground or fine sand it may be necessary to support the sides by placing thick boards and wedging stout cross timbers across the trench to hold the boards against the pressure of the earth. Deep trenches should be carefully timbered and shored; so should excavations for basements.

A strip foundation in a trench, and the sequence of building up the foundation to dampproof course level are shown in the diagrams.

The concrete which should be rather stiff, should be finished level by spading the surface and then left for a few days.

Forming a concrete strip foundation. If the site slopes the foundation must be stepped as shown left. Depth can be measured as shown right

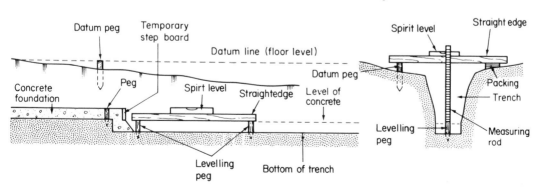

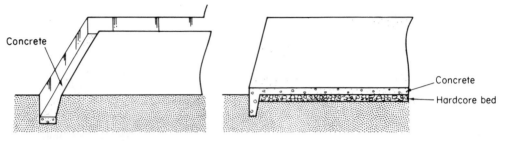

Concrete

This is a strip foundation in a trench

Concrete

Hardcore bed

This is a raft foundation on the surface

Left, the concrete strip foundation is suitable for most walls. Right, the raft foundation is suitable where a solid floor is required or where the ground is soft

Below, the sequence of levelling the foundation and starting a single brick wall

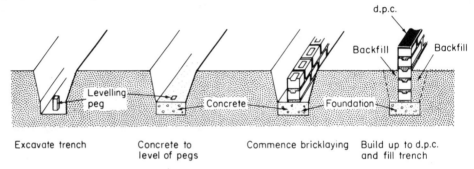

d.p.c.

Backfill   Backfill

Levelling peg

Concrete

Foundation

Excavate trench | Concrete to level of pegs | Commence bricklaying | Build up to d.p.c. and fill trench

Raft foundations

Concrete raft foundations are economic where solid floors are required, as the raft also provides a floor as a bonus. It also allows load bearing walls to be built directly on the raft. A raft foundation is suitable also for rather weak ground or ground of unequal bearing value.

The surface soil should be excavated down to the firm subsoil. If the raft must be laid on a site which has been filled (the fill material must be well consolidated) the subsoil cannot be reached. A heavy roller should be run over the site to make sure that the fill is well settled.

Where surface soil is removed it will be necessary to fill up with hardcore (broken stone or clean broken brick—but not shale, ashes or rubbish as chemical action from such materials may disrupt the concrete). The hardcore will allow the concrete to be placed at the required level.

The fill should be well consolidated by ramming or rolling. For a deep fill it should be placed in layers or about 250 mm (10 in); each layer being consolidated before adding the next.

To prevent damp rising through the concrete it is advisable to place a damp-proof membrane of thick polythene over the hardcore. If the hardcore is uneven or of sharp edged material, the surface should be smoothed by adding sand or fine grit. If the raft is to serve also as a floor, the surface of the hardcore fill should be carefully levelled so that concrete of even thickness can be added. The perimeter of a raft should be finished with a rib placed in a trench (see diagram) so that the hardcore fill cannot be squeezed out or rainwater allowed to penetrate under the raft.

Concrete rafts are sometimes reinforced with steel wire fabric or expanded metal. This is only necessary if the bearing value of the ground is very unequal.

The thickness of the raft depends upon load and subsoil strength but 100 mm (4 in) is sufficient for light single floor buildings, conservatories and ground floor room extensions. For houses, 150 mm (6 in) to 225 mm (9 in) according to the nature of the subsoil may be required.

Where there is several feet of weak ground overlaying strong subsoil, piling may be necessary for supporting beam or raft foundations for a house. Short bored piles are suitable. Holes about 225 mm (9 in) diameter are bored through the weak ground, with a special type of earth auger, at intervals of up to 3 m (10 ft), and concrete is poured in and consolidated.

On steeply sloping sites buildings can be built on columns of brickwork, steel or concrete, leaving an open space underneath, if this is convenient. Each column must have a square foundation of suitable size to spread the load and to anchor it firmly. The tops of the columns are joined by beams on which the superstructure is erected.

For small garden buildings on sloping sites short piers or columns are often the most economical form of foundation. A datum peg or post should be driven into the ground with the top at the required level so that by using a straightedge batten and spirit level the piers can be built to comply with it.

Concrete floors

A concrete ground floor is similar to the concrete foundation raft previously described. The surface soil must be removed and a bed of consolidated hardcore laid to an appropriate level. The concrete mix should be as shown in the table below.

The concrete should not be less than 100 mm (4 in) finished thickness. In a domestic building, as well as in most others, a solid floor on the ground must be damp-proofed. This can be done by sandwiching a membrane of hot bitumen or tar pitch not less than 3 mm thick, or three coats of bitumen or bitumen-rubber emulsion between the concrete base and a fine concrete topping 50 mm (2 in) thick. These bitumen coatings are available as proprietary brands (a typical make is 'Synthaprufe').

Where timber blocks, parquet or wood panels are to be laid on fine concrete topping the dampproof membrane may consist of asphaltic or pitchmastic material in which the wood flooring is bedded.

The dampproof membrane should be placed at a level not lower than the level of the ground or paving adjoining any external wall of the building. It must be joined and sealed to the dampproof course (see page 134) in the walls. The fine concrete topping on the base concrete should consist of the 1:2:3 mix previously described.

	Cubic ft of aggregate per 1 cwt of Portland cement	
	Damp sand*	Course aggregate†
Ordinary for most purposes, nominal mix 1:2:4	2½	5
For extra strength or thin sections, nominal mix 1:1½:3	$1^7/_8$	3¾

*Dry sand increases in bulk when damp—the figures allow for this.

†E.g., washed gravel, shingle or strong broken stone or brick.

All-in aggregate (sand and gravel mixed) can be bought from some quarries. The purpose should be stated when ordering.

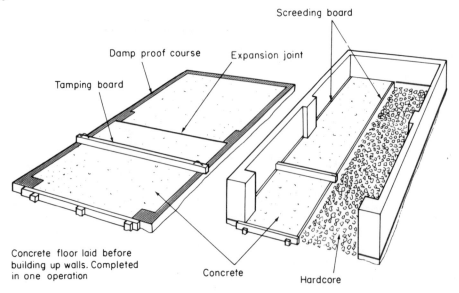

Screeding board

Damp proof course   Expansion joint

Tamping board

Concrete floor laid before
building up walls. Completed
in one operation

Concrete

Hardcore

Two ways of laying a concrete floor. Left, at dampproof course level. Right, walls built up first and floor laid in two sections

For a garage or other small floor it is convenient to level off the concrete at dampproof course level.

The base concrete should be swept and if it is dirty it should be thoroughly washed. It should be slightly damp when the topping is applied. If the topping is to be added to an existing smooth surfaced concrete floor a proprietary adhesive bonding liquid should be mixed with a 1 to 4 cement-sand mix, after cleaning the old surface.

To produce a level and even surface, wood battens or boards, the thickness of the required topping, as shown in the diagram should be laid along opposite sides of the floor. Except for a very narrow room, intermediate battens should be laid at intervals of about 1500 mm (5 ft). The trade name for these battens is screeds or screeding battens.

The topping mix should be fairly stiff but must be thoroughly mixed and should be placed within one hour of wet mixing. After spreading about one square metre (slightly more than 1 sq. yd.) a length of

straight batten or board should be placed to span the screeds and worked along them to level the surface. A slight tamping action should accompany the movement.

A wide floor, divided by screeds, should have the topping applied in sections, leaving the final section to be completed when the adjoining section has hardened sufficiently to allow you to stand on it. Alternatively, it may be possible to finish the final section by standing on a plank placed over the screeds.

After a few hours, when setting has just commenced, each section can be trowelled with a rectangular steel trowel but this should be lightly done. Too much trowelling draws neat cement to the surface which shrinks when dry and scales off.

The screeding battens should be gently removed before the topping sets hard and, of course, the gaps made good by filling with topping mix and levelling with the flooring trowel.

The topping should not be allowed to dry out during the first ten days. It should be covered with polythene sheeting or other suitable material so that the chemical action of setting and hardening, which can only take place in the presence of water, can continue. It takes about a month for Portland cement mixes to reach nearly maximum strength. Rapid drying results on crazing and dusting up.

Car drives and paths

A concrete car drive may be laid in two widths with a gap between for economy, or in full width. Both these drives are shown in the diagrams. The two-width or strip method, each strip not less than 750 mm (2 ft 6 in) with a gap between of about 500 mm (20 in), can be formed by excavating the surface soil in the strip widths to a depth of at least 150 mm (6 in) and laying a bed of hardcore, well rammed, in preparation for concreting.

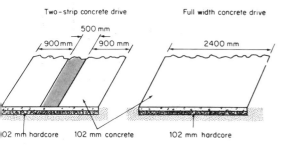

Two-strip concrete drive   Full width concrete drive

500 mm

900 mm / 900 mm   2400 mm

102 mm hardcore   102 mm concrete   102 mm hardcore

The cross section can be straight on sloping ground. On level ground the drive should be cross-cambered for drainage

The concrete should be a nominal mix of 1 cement, 2 sand, 4 coarse aggregate, parts by volume (see page 114) laid to a finished thickness of not less than 100 mm (4 in). The sides should be set out with string lines on pegs.

Side forms of boards on edge secured with wood pegs should be placed to form support for the edges. These should, of course, be removed when the concrete has set.

A thick wood tamping board can be worked along the surface to give an even finish. A perfectly smooth finish may be obtained by trowelling, as already described, but on a slope it is better to have a slightly rough surface to prevent skidding. Finishing by tamping with the board will then be sufficient.

A full width concrete drive can be formed in the same way. A width of 1800 mm (6 ft) is a reasonable minimum.

As some shrinkage of the concrete is inevitable, long drives should be laid in sections about 3 m (10 ft) apart. A temporary board can be placed to divide the sections—it should be lightly oiled to prevent adhesion. When the board is removed the gap can be filled with sand or cold asphaltic material. In effect this forms an expansion-contraction joint and prevents the formation of unsightly irregular cracks which often occur in extensive continuous areas of concrete.

The concrete should be covered with polythene sheeting, as described for topping, to prevent rapid drying out.

Bituminous and asphaltic surfacing

Bitumen is used to coat gravel or stone chippings for surfacing drives and paths. Asphalt is a bituminous material used as a mix with crushed limestone or grit. Both are obtainable in hot and cold forms. The hot form must be heated shortly before application and is not really convenient for d.i.y. use.

Bituminous mixtures in cold form can be bought and are easily applied. As shown in the illustration a firm foundation or base is essential. This may consist of a bed of hardcore, not less than 100 mm (4 in) thick for a car drive, well consolidated and with the surface covered with coarse sand to fill the gaps between the larger pieces. As the tracks or car wheels tend to form depressions in any but a very firm surface, consolidation

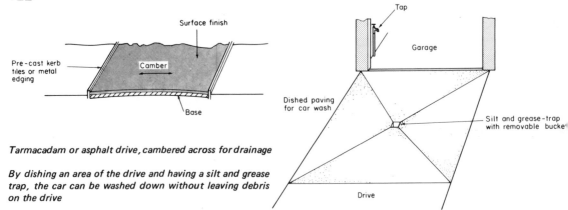

Tarmacadam or asphalt drive, cambered across for drainage

By dishing an area of the drive and having a silt and grease trap, the car can be washed down without leaving debris on the drive

of the subsoil and base by tamping or rolling is essential.

The proprietary surfacing materials of this type are supplied in bags and are simply spread with a rake and then rolled. The manufacturers enclose printed instructions.

A more laborious method is to use cold bitumen, sold in drums, spreading it with a broom over the base and then applying gravel. This is then rolled in and a sprinkling of sand given to cover any exposed bitumen. For a more durable finish a second coat of bitumen followed by an application of finer gravel or grit can be given, finishing with a roller.

For draining water when washing the car on the drive, a drain gully trap in a slightly dished part of the drive, is advisable. This should be fitted with a removable bucket to catch debris.

Paths and pavings

Pavings for paths, terraces, patios and yards can be of poured concrete or asphaltic materials, as already described for drives. On firm subsoil poured concrete 75 mm (3 in) thick is generally sufficient and this can be laid directly on ground which has had the top soil removed and the base well rolled or rammed, but it is better to cover the ground with a layer of sand.

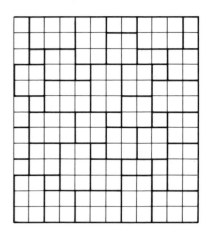

Using 225 × 225, 225 × 500, 500 × 500, 500 × 685 mm

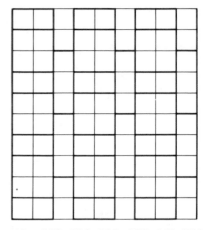

Using 600 × 600, 600 × 300, 915 × 300 mm

Paving slabs set out on a 300 mm (12 in) module, using various sizes to produce interesting patternrs. Two or more colours add to the variety. Standard metric sizes are figured here

Bituminous or asphaltic materials should be laid on a firm base of small hardcore or furnace ashes (*not* domestic fire ashes) at least 2 in thick.

The paths or other areas should be set out with string lines and pegs. If a curved path is wanted use a rope or clothes line and adjust it until you are satisfied with the curve as viewed from various angles. Then the two edge lines can be incised on the ground with a pointed rod or a spade.

Paving slabs or flags of pre-cast concrete or natural stone are more attractive than poured concrete or asphaltic materials in a garden. They also have the advantage of allowing easy removal if alterations are required later.

As the natural grey colour of ordinary concrete slabs is rather monotonous it is advisable to buy slabs of two or more colours. These are made by adding special pigments to the mix.

Two or more sizes of slabs allow various attractive patterns to be formed as shown. The following are stock sizes, the larger ones 50 mm (2 in) thick and the smaller 38 mm (1½ in):

Large 915 mm x 600 mm	(3 ft x 2 ft)
600 x 600	(2 ft x 2 ft)
600 x 458	(2 ft x 1 ft 6 in)
Small 300 x 300	(12 in x 12 in)
300 x 150	(12 in x 6 in)

Laying paving slabs

There are several methods of laying paving slabs. With all methods a firm base is essential to prevent uneven settlement. Soft surface soil should be excavated, and the excavation should be levelled, or graded to an even slope. With a wide area such as a patio, surface drainage is important, especially if the area adjoins the house

wall. A slight even fall away from the house wall of, say, 25 mm (1 in) in 3 m (10 ft) is sufficient. Use a straightedge batten and a spirit level and drive a few wood pegs along the outer edge, with the tops lower than the wall edge by the required amount. You can either drive a line of pegs at the higher (wall) edge or mark the higher level along the wall.

After excavating the top soil, a bed of boiler ashes or small gravel about 50 mm thick should be raked to an even surface and then tamped or rolled, if you have rather weak subsoil. Even if you have firm clay this bed will give drainage for any rainwater penetrating the joints as well as providing a suitable bed for laying the slabs.

On a subsoil, such as firm but fine earth or sandy gravel, it is sufficient to spread about 25 mm of sharp sand or ashes, raked evenly, over the excavation. Really fine earth, riddled to eliminate stones, will serve the same purpose.

On such a prepared bed the larger slabs can be laid directly, tapping each slab down over the centre. It is advisable to use the mortar dab method—placing a large dab of mortar to support the corners of the slabs. The larger slabs should also have a dab under the middle. Each slab should be tapped down, using a wood mallet. This should be lightly done—heavy blows might crack the slabs or prevent even surfacing.

It is essential to keep the surface to an even plane. A straightedge should be placed over each slab as it is laid to check that it conforms to the surface of adjoining slabs.

The mortar should not be very strong. A cement-lime-sand mortar of 1 part Portland cement, 2 parts hydrated powder lime and 5 parts sand is suitable. This will allow even settlement and avoid the excessive shrinkage which is inevitable with a strong cement mortar.

The joints may be tightly butted, without

mortar between the slabs. If you prefer a mortared joint make it about 10 mm ($\frac{3}{8}$ in) wide so that it can be easily filled with mortar. Pointing mortar should be stronger than the bedding—a mix of 1 part Portland cement, 4 parts washed builders' sand is suitable. It should be rammed down the open joint and finished flush.

Narrow joints of about 3 mm ($\frac{1}{8}$ in) are difficult to point with ordinary stiff mortar —hence the preference for wider joints. Narrow joints are best filled with slurry, which is cement mortar with sufficient water added to allow it to flow.

Mortar smears should be cleaned off the surface of slabs, especially coloured slabs, before they set. For this, use rags soaked in clean water.

Natural stone slabs should be laid by the methods just described for concrete slabs. But care should be taken to select a stone which will not readily laminate (i.e. break away in thin layers) under wear and frost action. You can make a rough test by first examining it closely—prominent layering or laminations at the edges will be obvious and if the stones are struck with a hammer the surface laminations may break off. Feint laminations and a dense grain indicate a suitable stone.

For paving, natural stone should be about 50 mm (2 in) thick or little more with a fairly regular surface. Large sizes, although attractive, are very heavy to handle.

Large slabs, whether of stone or concrete, are best 'walked' along by lifting one edge and then allowing one corner to stand on the ground while the other is lifted and moved, repeating the movement with opposite corners. On reaching the laying position the lower edge can be adjusted to the required position and the slab then gently lowered. Slight adjustment can be made by levering. By this method you need not lift and carry the whole slab.

Brick paths

Bricks are excellent for paths and pavings provided they are of dense hard texture. Common bricks and the cheaper facings are not suitable as they tend to flake and crumble under frost action. Bricks can be laid on edge, or flat if they have no frog (depression), in any kind of bond or pattern, in square or herringbone arrangements.

As bricks are small units they should be laid on a bed of thick mortar—at least 25 mm (1 in)— of 1 part Portland cement to 4 parts builders' sand. If the ground under is soft or liable to shrinkage it is advisable to lay a

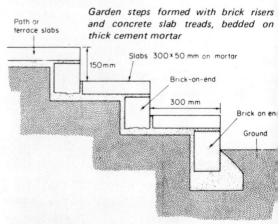

Garden steps formed with brick risers and concrete slab treads, bedded on thick cement mortar

Path or terrace slabs

150mm

Slabs 300 x 50 mm on mortar

Brick-on-end

300 mm

Brick on end

Ground

concrete foundation at least 50 mm (2 in) thick. The bricks can then be bedded in mortar, both bed and side joints about 10 mm ($\frac{3}{8}$ in) thick. The mortar should be rather stiff but thoroughly mixed. Care should be taken to avoid smearing the bricks; if this occurs it should be cleaned off without delay.

Steps for terraces and paths can be formed with half-brick courses for risers, set on end, and concrete slabs for treads, as shown in the diagram. A mortar of 1 cement to 3 washed sand should be used for bedding and the joints pointed. The bricks for risers should be hard, well burnt. Common bricks tend to flake in frosty weather.

Chapter 12 Brickwork and blockwork

In this chapter we cover building walls with bricks and also with solid and cavity blocks. Although the information given assumes you are building a garage or small outbuilding or extension, the principles outlined are equally applicable if you are rebuilding a house or bungalow.

Tools

In addition to the setting out tools—the square, lines and pegs, described in Chapter 11—the following basic outfit is needed.

A long spirit level cum plumb rule (bricklayers' level) with both horizontal and cross levels, at least 600 mm (2 ft) long.

This can be used horizontally for checking the levels of foundations and brickwork or blockwork courses or vertically for checking that walls are plumb upright, as indicated by the cross levels.

For plumbing vertical surfaces you can use a string plumb line. A plumb bob costs little but any small weight will serve. A snag about using a plumb line is that it is difficult to use in a strong wind. It is easier to use if suspended in a plumb rule with a hole to accommodate the bob.

A bricklayers' line wound on a pair of steel pins is needed to keep courses straight and level. The pins have blades which are inserted into joints at the wall corners and the line is then stretched tight and level just clear of the wall face. Check the line with the spirit level and take care that it does not sag. The bricks or blocks are laid level with this line. If bricklayers' line and pins are not available you can manage with a thin string line and two 150 mm (6 in) nails.

Essential tools for brickwork and blockwork—for setting out, laying, cutting and pointing. A mortar board and bucket for mixing water is also needed. The wooden square can be set out in metric units, if desired, in any 3:4:5 proportions

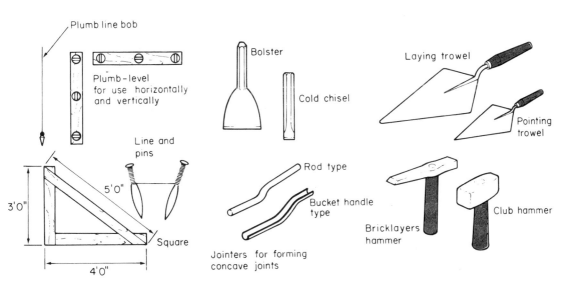

Plumb line bob

Plumb-level for use horizontally and vertically

Bolster

Cold chisel

Laying trowel

Pointing trowel

Line and pins

5'0"

3'0"

Square

4'0"

Rod type

Bucket handle type

Jointers for forming concave joints

Bricklayers hammer

Club hammer

A laying trowel, about 200 mm (8 in) or little more, and a pointing trowel about 100 mm (4 in), a bricklayers' hammer with a flat hammer end and a chisel end, useful for rough cutting; a bolster chisel with a 100 mm (4 in) blade and club hammer complete the essential kit. The pointing trowel is for flat finished joints but it is easier to use a round jointer, producing a hollow finish. You can make one out of a short length of old bucket handle or 10 mm ($^3/_8$ in) mild steel rod, cranked or bent to form a handle.

Scaffolds

Unless you are building a house you will not need ordinary scaffolding, but if you are it may be cheaper to hire than to buy. Scaffolding is of two main types—galvanised steel tubes erected with special clips or joints, and galvanised tubular frames.

The ordinary tubular type consists of standards (uprights), ledgers (horizontal) and putlogs (cross pieces which are supported at the outer end on the ledgers and the inner wall under construction). The frame type is independent of wall support.

Light platform scaffolds for home use are advertised by several firms. These are sectional and are easily assembled and taken apart. They can be used at various heights. The platform is about 1.2 m (4 ft) × 900 mm (3 ft) and is protected by handrails and toe boards. Properly fixed and used these are very safe and although the lateral range is small from a single position, they can be easily moved along.

Ladders in wood and aluminium alloy are made in various grades of strength. Builders' ladders are very heavy to stand up to rough use. Light ladders are sufficient for normal house heights but should be placed on a non-slip surface and, the top should be secured if possible by tying to a window frame. The angle of the ladder should be such that the base distance from the wall is one-quarter the vertical height ground to ladder top—i.e., as measured up the wall. If you are working at a considerable height a helper should stand on the lowest rung as an extra precaution against the ladder slipping.

Extendable ladders in two or three sections are the most convenient and the sections can be used separately for short heights. Wood ladders must be stored under cover to prevent deterioration, but metal (aluminium) ladders can be left in the open, although some people find the treads harder on the feet. All ladders should be stored horizontally, perferably on stout wall hooks.

A pair of steps is essential for reaching moderate heights. Here again the choice is between wood and metal. With two pairs of steps of similar rise and a wide scaffold plank supported on the steps at the ends you have a short scaffold though not a really safe one. It is, however, convenient for heights of only a few feet—but 'mind your step'.

Never lean sidewards from a ladder, steps or scaffold. This is particularly dangerous on a ladder as it may slip sideways.

Brick shapes and facings

Bricks are made in a wide range of types, textures and colours, so care must be taken to select the kind suitable for the purpose.

Common bricks, such as fletton commons, are of medium density, suitable for foundation walls, and for outer walls of dwellings provided the exposed surface is finished with rendering or a cement paint or other coloured or white paint. Common

Frog
Standard brick

Plinth bricks

Double bullnose brick

Some bricks have frogs—some not. There are many 'specials'

bricks are not suitable for extreme exposure on both sides, such as retaining walls and garden walls as they may be flaked or crumbled by frost action.

Facing bricks range from mass produced medium density bricks of fletton clay surfaced with coloured mineral granules burnt on to the face to hand-made bricks using specially prepared coloured clays.

The mass produced facings, as made by the London Brick Co. (LBC Bricks), are produced in a range of colours and textures. They are very good facings at an economical price, and are readily available.

Wire cut facings made from coloured clays have a crimped texture and are very good and medium priced. Lime-sand (calcium silicate) bricks are of light colours —cream, pink, white—with several strength grades, some for use in place of clay common bricks and the superior grades for facings. They are smooth and of precise shapes. Concrete bricks are pre-cast and incorporate coloured pigments for facings —they are good bricks but rather heavy.

A range of special shapes is stocked by most leading manufacturers. Examples are: bullnose (one or more edges rounded); bevelled plinths; squints for corner angles of 45, 30 and 60 degrees; sills; copings (half-round and saddleback).

Engineering bricks are very dense and strong. Generally the colours are blues, purples and reds. They are useful for chimney tops and copings and for retaining walls or wherever great strength and weather resistance are required. Some are used for facings but the regular colours and smooth face gives a rather hard appearance.

Brick sizes

The standard brick size in metric units is 215 x 102.5 x 65 mm. In calculating the heights and lengths of brickwork courses the joints must be included. A joint of 9 mm (about ⅜ in) gives a 74 mm (or 2.95 in) height for one course and bed joint. There is tendency to increase the joint thickness slightly to accommodate slight unevenness in bricks to about 12 mm (approximately ⁷⁄₁₆ in) which gives a height for one course and bed joint of 77 mm (3 in).

The old standard format for brickwork was taken as, to include joints, 9 in x 4½ in x 3 in. The metric format corresponds very nearly to this.

Non-standard bricks are made for special purposes. Small bricks are available for building brick fireplace surrounds. These are hand-made and of various colours and textures. These bricks are also used in ready-made 'slabbed' surrounds.

Blocks

Blocks for walls are of three main materials: dense concrete for external use; medium and light-weight concrete for internal use, and some of medium weight are suitable for external use; clay blocks for internal and external use.

There are several standard sizes of concrete blocks but the most common is 440 mm x 215 mm (17½ in x 8½ in) on the face and with thicknesses of 75 mm (3 in), 90 mm (3½ in), 100 mm (4 in), 140 mm (5½ in), 190 mm (7½ in), 215 mm (8½ in).

The 100 mm (4 in) thickness is widely used for the inner section of cavity walls and for internal load bearing walls, usually in lightweight concrete (load bearing grade).

For the above purposes aerated concrete blocks, of proprietary brands (e.g. Thermalite, Celcon) are now often used instead of the older clinker concrete blocks. Blocks of this type have superior thermal insulation, better dimensional stability and are easier to cut by sawing. If rendered or tile hung they can be used externally. Although the standard type of block is usually plastered inside, a special faced type is made to be left for direct decoration.

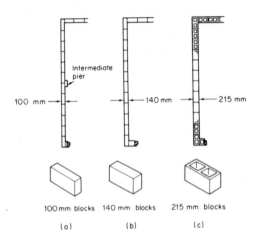

Intermediate pier

100 mm — 140 mm — 215 mm

100 mm blocks   140 mm blocks   215 mm blocks

(a)   (b)   (c)

Walling blocks are made in several thicknesses—some solid, some hollow. They take less mortar than bricks but most are rather heavy

Hollow clay blocks are made in standard sizes of 290 mm (11½ in) x 215 mm (8½ in) x thicknesses of 75 mm (3 in) and 100 mm (4 in). Plain face for self finish and keyed or grooved for plastering or rendering. There are several proprietary types with special characteristics.

The advantage of concrete and hollow clay blocks over brickwork, at least for interior use where light- or medium-weight blocks are normally used, is that a given area can be laid in a smaller time and less mortar is used.

Stone blocks

Natural stone varies widely in colour, density and durability. As quarried it may be produced in rough irregular lumps called rough rubble. These may look quite attractive in walling but they are laborious to lay and take a lot of mortar.

Regular rubble may be of several sizes but of roughly rectangular shapes and are easier to lay.

Sawn stone blocks are of regular rectangular shapes and assorted sizes. Regular courses can be laid, although each course may be of different thickness.

Before buying natural stone it is advisable to see some walls built of similar material—notice how it looks and how it has weathered. Stone which crumbles or flakes when weathered should be avoided.

Reconstructed stone

Blocks of reconstructed stone incorporate crushed natural stone as the main aggregate, with white or coloured cement. Several firms advertise such material for walling. Durability is usually better than natural stone. There is a range of sizes but for home use it is advisable to use the smaller —brick size or a little larger—as it is heavy material. Both smooth and textured surfaces are available.

Coloured concrete blocks are made of ordinary concrete coloured with pigments. They are inferior in appearance to reconstructed stone but their durability is good.

Split concrete blocks, made with stone aggregates, have an attractive outer irregular surface with the aggregate exposed.

Pierced ornamental blocks or pre-cast coloured concrete are made by several firms for building garden walls and screen walls. The manufacturer's printed instructions should be followed regarding laying, maximum heights, lengths and where piers are necessary.

Mortars

There are several mortar mixes but for home use only two need be considered.

Cement mortar of 1 part Portland cement to 3 or 4 parts builders' washed sand makes a strong mortar suitable for retaining walls and for garden walls if they are of strong dense facing bricks. The admixture of a little plasticising liquid is advisable as it will make the mortar easier to work. For a small job you can use washing-up liquid, but plasticising liquid can be bought from builders' merchants.

Strong cement mortar should not be used for house walls or any buildings of soft or medium density bricks as it has rather high shrinkage which may cause crazing or cracking of the bricks or joints.

Cement-lime mortar of 1 part Portland cement, 1 part hydrated powder lime and 5 or 6 parts of washed builders' sand is strong enough for ordinary brickwork.

Dry mix mortars in bags can be bought at d.i.y. shops and builders' merchants. There are two types—cement mortar and bricklaying mortar (this is a cement-lime-sand mix). For most home jobs, dry mixes are the most convenient buy as the contents are ready for mixing with water and are of consistent proportions. There are several proprietary brands, including Marleymix No. 3 cement mortar and No. 4 bricklaying mortar. As the ingredients tend to separate in the bag they should be well mixed in the dry state before adding water.

Mixing mortar

If separate ingredients are bought, the proportions can be measured by volume, as previously specified, using a bucket or box. The sand should be placed on clean dry paving or, better, a clean boarded platform. Add the cement, for a mortar without lime, and mix dry. Hollow the mound and add clean water through a rose, mixing thoroughly with the spade. Beware of adding too much water. You want a fairly stiff but workable mix. A sloppy mortar will spill down the wall and also tend to crack.

Separate ingredients for a cement-lime-sand mortar should be mixed as follows. The hydrated powder lime should first be soaked in a bucket overnight. Next day the surplus water should be poured away leaving soft lime putty. Mix this with the sand in the proportions already specified to make what is called coarse stuff. Then take enough coarse stuff and mix with the proportion of cement, add just sufficient water to give a workable but fairly stiff mortar when thoroughly mixed.

A cement-lime-sand mortar is 'buttery' and easy to work off the trowel. The strength depends almost solely upon the cement, so it is essential to use fresh Portland cement which has not absorbed atmospheric moisture.

For stonework masonry a similar 1:1:6 cement-lime-sand mortar is suitable for work exposed outside. For interior work a weaker, 1:2:9 mix, is often recommended. If a dry ready mix is ordered it should be 'masonry grade'.

A cement mortar of 1 part cement to 5 or 6 parts sand can be used for external work but with the addition of a plasticiser, as mentioned for brickwork mortar. For internal work a 1:7 mix is suitable.

Brickwork bonds

Stretcher bond is generally used for walls of single brick thickness. The bricks are laid lengthwise (stretchers) with each vertical joint over the centre line of the stretcher below.

The brick outer section of house cavity walls is usually of single thickness stretcher bond, but sometimes snap headers are used with the stretchers to give a more interesting bond appearance.

Headers are bricks laid across a wall, usually a wall of double thickness—215 mm (8½ in) thick—to bond both thicknesses together. They are used in the following bonds.

English Bond. One course of stretchers alternating with one course of headers.

English Garden Wall Bond. One course of headers to three courses of stretchers.

Flemish Bond. A header-stretcher sequence in every course, the header centred over the stretcher in the course below.

Flemish Garden Wall Bond. A header to every three stretchers in each course, the header centred over the middle of the three stretchers below.

Header Bond. Headers only, used on curved walls where the radius is too short to allow stretchers to be used.

In the above bonds bricks overlap those below by a quarter of a brick length 53 mm (2⅛ in).

Corners and stopped ends of walls must have this quarter taken up by a brick bat 53 mm (2⅛ in) called a closer placed next to the corner (quoin) header. This must be carefully cut by placing the brick on a firm surface, scribing a line, then placing the blade of a bolster chisel on the line and striking it with a club hammer.

The splayed corner of a wall supporting a bay window is formed by laying squint bricks of appropriate angle.

Care should be taken to avoid straight vertical joints through sucessive courses—hence the need to overlap or bond the bricks.

How to build a single brick wall in stretcher bond. The corners should rise in advance of the main part. Keep the line level as a guide

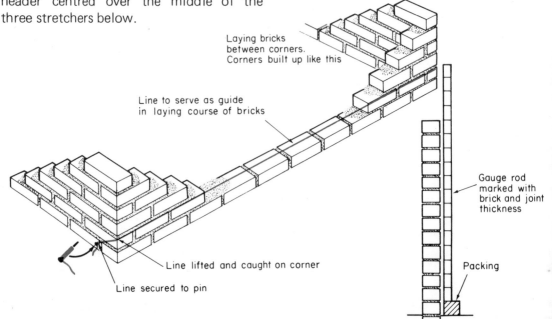

Laying bricks between corners. Corners built up like this

Line to serve as guide in laying course of bricks

Gauge rod marked with brick and joint thickness

Line lifted and caught on corner

Packing

Line secured to pin

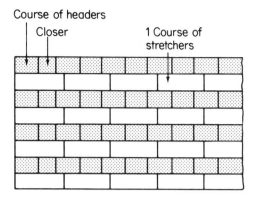

ENGLISH BOND

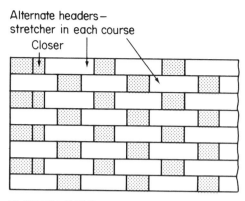

FLEMISH BOND

These diagrams show three different types of bond—English bond, Flemish bond and English Garden Wall Bond

Left, one course of headers in one course stretchers. Right, stretchers alternate with headers in each course Below, one course of headers to three course of stretchers. Notice the closer next to the corner header

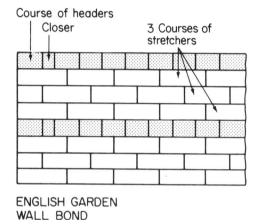

ENGLISH GARDEN WALL BOND

Building brick walls

Brickwork walls for most ancillary home buildings, such as garages, fuel stores, garden buildings and support walls for conservatories and greenhouses, are usually of single brick thickness—102.5 mm (4¼ in) laid in stretcher bond.

With the foundation concrete laid, as described in Chapter 11, place a brick at each corner while you check the lengths of walls. It is advisable to lay a course of bricks dry with a joint gap of about 12 mm ($^{7}/_{1 6}$ in) between them. Then you can see if the length of the wall can be formed without having to cut a brick bat to fit an exact measurement. A slight adjustment of the joint width can be made if the overall fit is not exact. It is useful to plane a piece of wood to the required joint width for use as a gauge.

A gauge rod can also be made by marking a batten with the course heights—brick height plus one bed joint. Four courses to 300 mm (12 in) is generally suitable.

Commence bricklaying by building up the corners a few courses, then complete the first course along the foundation. Build up the corners again, keeping them a few courses higher than the main part of the wall until you reach the top.

The courses must be kept level. Use the string line, secured at each corner by inserting the pins into a mortar joint, and carefully checking with the spirit level. The spirit level should also be placed on the brickwork occasionally and, if it has cross levels, it can be held upright against the face of the wall at intervals to test for being plumb (truly vertical). Alternatively, use a plumb bob and line.

If you are a beginner it pays to check the work frequently at first and also to

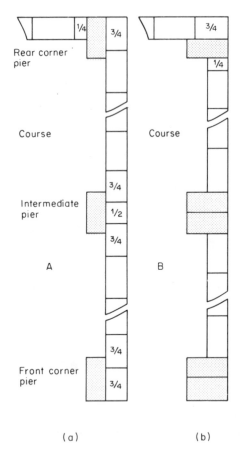

Rear corner pier

Course

Intermediate pier

A

Front corner pier

(a)

B

Course

(b)

Bonding plans for a single brick stretcher bond wall with piers, suitable for a garage of average size. Course (a) alternates with course (b)

Checking a brickwork corner with a bricklayer's spirit level-cum-plumb rule

stand well back at one end and look along the wall. Any faults in level or plumb will then be apparent and you can correct the work you have done fairly simply. It is only too easy to build a long stretch of wall and then to find that it leans dangerously.

Openings for doors and windows must be left. It is advisable to build-in the frames, placing them in position at sill level and nailing raking struts of timber to hold them upright. Galvanised metal lugs should be screwed to the frame sides at intervals of about 900 mm (3 ft) at suitable levels for building into the bed joints of the brickwork.

Building Regulations

Under the Building Regulations a wall of single brick or block thickness (not less than 100 mm (4 in), must not exceed 3 m (10 ft) high from the foundation. The wall must be bonded at each end and intermediately with piers or butressing walls not less than 200 mm square (8 in x 8 in) including the wall thickness, so that the wall is divided into lengths not exceeding 3 m.

An exception to this rule is where the wall is less than 2.5 m (8 ft) high from the foundation and less than that distance in length. A short garden wall is an example;

Bricklaying to a line stretched and levelled

in such case piers are not essential for strength but may be required for the sake of appearance.

Double-brick walls

Walls of double brick thickness—215 mm (8½ in)—are of course stronger and look better than those of single brick. For work such as domestic garages and long or high garden walls piers are not needed. The English or Flemish bonds, as described earlier in this chapter are suitable—either the full bonds or the garden wall types.

Where facing bricks are used outside and common bricks inside, the garden wall types are economical in facings and of adequate strength. The outside face should be the 'fair' face (perfectly flush) and the inside will inevitably be uneven.

Protecting from weather

Brickwork and blockwork should be protected from hot sun and dry winds to allow moisture to remain in the mortar for at least a week as the setting and hardening action depends upon this.

In very dry weather cover the work with any kind of sheeting as you go along.

In frosty weather, the work must be covered to prevent the mortar freezing and crumbling. The top course should be covered with a plank when left overnight.

Dampproof courses

To prevent damp rising upwards through porous walling materials a dampproof course (d.p.c.) must be built into the wall. This should be at least 150 mm (6 in) above the highest part of the adjoining ground or paving and below the level of the surface of the ground floor (see illustration).

D.p.c. materials of bitumen, suitable plastic, bitumen impregnated felt, or a combination of bitumen and lead, copper or aluminium strip, are flexible and supplied in rolls of various wall widths. They should be laid on a bed of mortar and covered with a second bed of mortar to prevent penetration by sharp corners or grit and to give good adhesion.

In old houses the dampproof course usually consists of two courses of slates in strong mortar. Houses older than about mid-nineteenth century may not have a dampproof course.

Where the ground floor is below the ground level or the 150 mm (6 in) clearance described above cannot be achieved, a

Typical small scale cross section, left; with enlarged detail, right; as for a house. Height of rooms figures are usual but are more than the minimum of 2.3 m (7 ft 6½ in) laid down in the Building Regulations

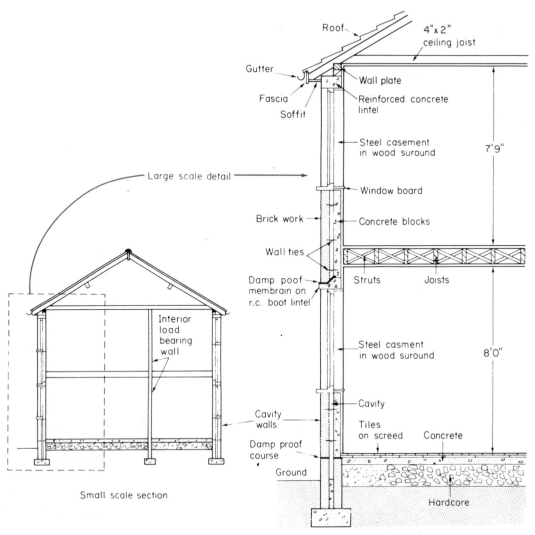

Roof

4"x 2" ceiling joist

Gutter

Wall plate

Fascia

Reinforced concrete lintel

Soffit

Steel casement in wood suround

7'9"

Large scale detail

Window board

Brick work

Concrete blocks

Wall ties

Struts   Joists

Damp poof membrain on r.c. boot lintel

Steel casment in wood suround

8'0"

Interior load bearing wall

Cavity

Cavity walls

Tiles on screed   Concrete

Damp proof course

Ground

Hardcore

Small scale section

vertical membrane must be placed on the inside face and this must be sealed to the level dampproof course. Three coats of bitumen or bitumen-rubber emulsion can be used for this purpose.

With a solid concrete ground floor incorporating a dampproof membrane, as described on page 119, the membrane must be sealed to the level of the d.p.c. by turning it up if necessary.

Cavity walls

The bricks and blocks used in the outer walls of houses are porous. So solid walls may absorb an amount of rainwater to admit damp to the inside surfaces. The horizontal d.p.c. described above prevents damp rising from wet ground but cannot prevent it passing through the wall.

The most widely used modern method of preventing damp penetration is the cavity wall as illustrated. Normally, this consists of an inner section of 100 mm (4 in) load bearing lightweight blocks separated from the outer single brick wall by a cavity 50 mm (2 in) wide. But structurally the two sections are connected across the cavity by galvanised steel ties built into the bed joints, one per square metre.

Floor joists and roof plates bearing the roof loads are supported on the inner wall section but as this is tied to the outer section stability is assured.

To prevent damp penetration the cavity must not be bridged except by suitable ties and at the top of the wall where it is protected by a projecting roof. In the case of a parapet there must be a d.p.c. in the parapet and joined to the roof covering.

The d.p.c. placed horizontally above ground must be in two separate parts and the cavity must be extended not less than 150 mm (6 in) below the d.p.c. level. Below that, the lower cavity should be filled with mortar or fine concrete.

Building with shell-bedding hollow blocks. The vertical joints should be mortared on the inner and outer edges only. The block should be given several sharp taps with a trowel to settle the mortar and make it stick (Cement & Concrete Association)

The struck joint (Cement & Concrete Association)

As the cavity walls are built mortar droppings may collect on the metal ties and form a porous bridge for water, allowing damp to penetrate to the inside wall face. This can be avoided by placing a batten across the ties immediately below as you lay further courses. The batten can be lifted easily if a string loop is tied to each end, or from corners. It can be withdrawn horizontally if a brick is temporarily left out opposite the end of the batten.

(a) *Reinforced concrete lintel—depth and reinforcement varies with load and span*

(b) *Wide spands should be remporarily supported with a prop until the brickwork above has set*

(c) *Reinforced concrete lintels. Left, for single brick wall. Right, for cavity wall*

(d) *Galvanised steel lintel—made for various spans*

Building cavity walls

When building cavity walls both sections, outer brickwork and inner blockwork, should be built up together. It is risky to build up the single brick outer wall first—although some bricklayers do—as a strong wind may blow it down before the mortar has set.

Care must be taken at door and window openings to avoid bridging the cavity with solid brick or block work. The jambs (sides) of the openings should be protected by placing a vertical dampproof strip of bituminous or plastic material sandwiched between the solid wall sections.

The head over openings should be protected by placing a tray flashing of lead or bituminous sheet over the head, turned up

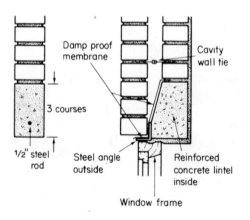

(a)

Clear span

2 courses

3/8" steel rod

Mild steel reinforcement

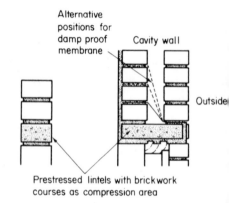

Alternative positions for damp proof membrane

Cavity wall

Outside

Prestressed lintels with brickwork courses as compression area

(b)

Damp proof membrane

Cavity wall tie

3 courses

1/2" steel rod

Steel angle outside

Reinforced concrete lintel inside

Window frame

(c)

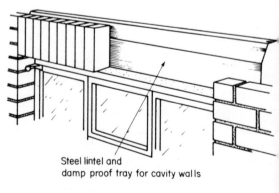

Steel lintel and damp proof tray for cavity walls

(d)

in the cavity and turned at the back into the bed joint of the inner wall section. The tray should project 150 mm (6 in) beyond the opening at each end.

A dampproof strip may be needed under the sill, but where a window frame has a wood sill placed over the cavity this strip may not be needed.

Lintels

Where galvanised pressed steel lintels (beams) are used over door and window openings they form a dampproof tray. Pre-formed plastic extrusions are made for attaching to the jambs of wood or metal windows for making a dampproof closure to the cavity as well as a firm fixing for the frame, so that strip dampproofing is not needed.

Suspended floors

Timber suspended ground floors need under-floor ventilation, usually provided by building in air bricks which also ventilate the cavity. This also reduces the thermal insulation of the wall by admitting cold air to the cavity. It is better to use proprietary plastic extruded floor vents which bridge the cavity but are shaped to prevent water creeping across.

Garden walls

Brick walls for garden boundaries are built in the bonds already described. The illustration shows other typical examples.

Garden walls. Top left, single brick stretcher bond with terminal pier. Top right, double brick in Flemish garden wall bond. Bottom left, double brick wall in English garden wall bond. Bottom right, plans of courses

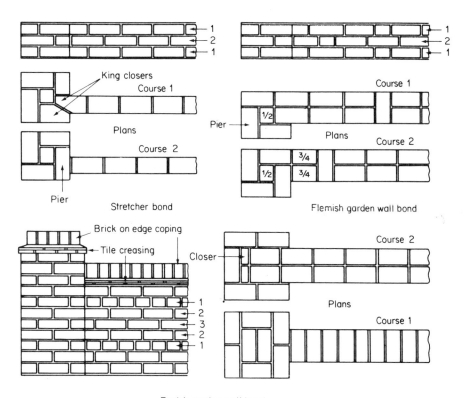

Stretcher bond

Flemish garden wall bond

English garden wall bond

Building stone walls

The methods of building stone walls depend on the shapes and sizes of the blocks, whether rough rubble, regular rubble, large or small squared blocks, one size only or two or more sizes.

If rectangular blocks of a single size not much larger than standard bricks are used, they can be laid as already described for brickwork. Use a level line and pins, and raise it every course, or every two or three courses will do as you gain experience.

Remember that the line must be stretched level and the work checked both for level courses and for plumb upright faces and corners. The corners should be stepped up a few courses in advance of the main length of wall. Two or more sizes can be bonded as shown.

Blocks of a regular thickness, not less than 100 mm (4 in) thick, can be built in single thickness. If all are of the same size, including length, they can be laid in stretcher bond, as described for single brickwork walls. Walls of double or more thickness, including rubble walls, must be bonded across at intervals of three or four courses. With rough rubble, single bond stones, the thicknesses of the wall should be placed at intervals of not more than 1 metre (3 ft 3 in) horizontally and vertically.

Dry stone walling for garden walls, consists of assorted sizes of rubble. The stones need to be fairly thick, 500 mm (about 20 in), at least for low walls and thicker for high walls. There is an art in laying; the main point is to lay each stone so that it is held tightly by adjoining stones. Gaps can be wedged with small bits. Although no mortar is used in traditional dry stone walling, it is advisable in garden walling to finish the top course or coping in medium strength mortar. Using rough rubble a coping can be formed by 'laying the top course with the stones upright.

Copings for stone walls of rectangular blocks in mortar are special blocks with a sloping top or saddleback, projecting on one or both sides to shed rainwater. But flat paving slabs, slightly wider than the wall, cost less and are satisfactory on a garden wall.

For parapet walls above flat roofs, as sometimes used around garage roofs, the coping can be of pre-cast concrete saddleback section. Alternatively, you can use a proprietary type of heavy duty plastic or of aluminium alloy, fixed with special clips or brackets. All types are made in various widths.

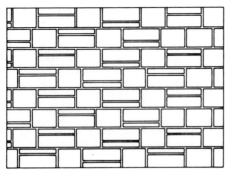

Regular courses

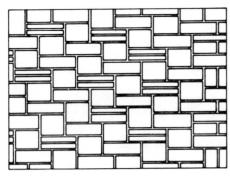

Irregular courses

Stone walls. Pre-cast reconstructed stone blocks can be laid in various patterns—these are two examples

Sills

If a wood window frame has a sill, as part of the frame, which projects 25 mm (1 in) or more beyond the wall face, no separate wall sill is needed. Some wood frames and also steel frames do not have projecting sills; in these cases a wall sill is necessary.

A wall sill can be formed in several ways, using flat clay roofing tiles or concrete tiles, or standard bricks. Roofing tiles—265 mm (10½ in) x 165 mm (6½ in)—bedded in cement mortar to an outward slope, two courses to break side joints and neatly pointed, are often used. Facing bricks on edge, preferably a dense type, also bedded in cement mortar to an outward slope and projecting slightly, look attractive and the projecting edge is not so vulnerable to damage as is the tiled type. But there are also special thick sill tiles of clay with a bullnose edge which are bedded as a single course.

Pre-cast concrete sills are made in a range of sizes and sections, all with an outward slope. One type is made for standard wood windows and another for standard metal windows.

All wall sills should have an outward slope to shed rainwater and preferably a projection and a drip groove underneath. The window frame should stand on the sill and it is advisable to seal it with a non-hardening mastic, frame sill to wall sill.

Piers and columns

Attached piers are projections from a wall and serve a variety of purposes. They are intended to strengthen the wall, as for single thickness walls described on page 131; to take a concentrated load, as a bearing for a steel joist; or for architectural effect. These piers must be bonded into the wall.

Columns or independent piers are free-standing and used either for supporting porch roofs; for beam foundations on a sloping site; or for garden pergolas.

Piers and columns may be built of standard brickwork, concrete blocks, or natural stone blocks. The foundation for an attached pier should project from the wall to give even bearing on the ground. For a column, the foundation should project all round, generally to double the width of the column.

Columns or stanchions of tubular steel can be used to support porch, canopy and car port roofs. The base should be anchored into a concrete foundation. For most purposes concrete 300 mm (12 in) square X 200 mm (8 in) thick, deep enough to rest on firm subsoil beyond shrinkage movements, will be sufficient.

Bungalow. Detail at eaves level showing piers at sides of front doorway and wall plate ready for rafters

Chapter 13

Fireplaces, flues and chimneys

A fireplace recess in or against a wall must comply with certain Building Regulations.

On an internal wall the back of the recess must be of solid brick or block not less than 200 mm (8 in) thick, extending to the full height of the recess. Above that level the flue is formed and the solid walls of the flue and chimney must not be less than 100 mm (4 in) thick.

On an external wall the back may be less than 200 mm (8 in) but not less than 100 mm (4 in) thick. The greater thickness is desirable to reduce heat loss through the wall. The thickness of the fireback and any filling behind it must be additional to the above thicknesses.

The jambs (sides) of the recess must be of solid brick or block not less than 200 mm (8 in) thick.

Hearths

The constructional hearth, usually of concrete, must not be less than 125 mm (5 in) thick, extending not less than 500 mm (1 ft 8 in) in front of the jambs and not less than 150 mm (6 in) beyond each side of the opening. A heating appliance for solid fuel or oil which is not placed in a brick or block recess must stand on a solid hearth with sides not less than 840 mm (2 ft 9 in).

An ash pit can be formed in a solid hearth, to hold an ash bucket. This is provided that the solid non-combustible bottom and sides are not less than 50 mm (2 in) thick and no combustible materials, such as timber joists, are built into a wall below or beside the ash pit within 225 mm (9 in) of the inner surface of the pit. Floor joists passing near the ash pit must have a clear air space of at least 50 mm (2 in) between the joists and the outer surface of the pit.

The above paragraph applies especially to solid fuel appliances with under-floor draught.

Brickwork and blockwork for fireplaces flues and chimneys must be properly bonded and laid in mortar, as described in Chapter 12.

Flues and chimneys

Flues formed in brickwork or blockwork are usually of a nominal 200 mm (8 in) square section for a solid fuel appliance. The Building Regulations require the flue section to be such that it will contain a diameter not less than 175 mm (nearly 7 in).

The gathering which is formed over an open fireplace recess slopes inward from the sides and a throat not less than 100 mm (4 in), but not much more, front to back, leads into the flue proper. The surfaces should be smooth so that the smoke and fumes have an easy run up the flue.

The flue walls should not be less than 200 mm (4 in) thick, exclusive of lining.

Lining

A brick or block flue must be lined with rebated and socketed clay flue linings (or flue linings made from kiln-burnt aggregate and high alumina cement). An alternative

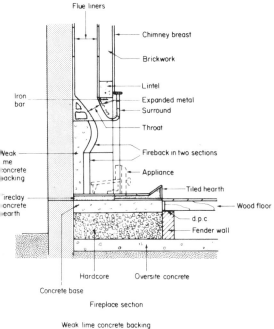

Fireplace section

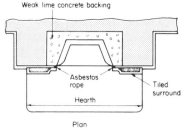

Plan

Fireplaces with open grate and tiled surround. Manufacturers issue illustrated instructions for fixing

Lead flashing to chimney during construction. The lead is tucked into joints in the brickwork which are then pointed

s glazed clay pipes, with spigot and socket ends, socket uppermost. All these linings should be jointed in cement mortar.

There are also proprietary flue blocks of high alumina concrete from which the entire flue and chimney can be constructed. One type is designed for fixing to an existing exterior wall which is convenient when a fireplace is added to a room.

Proprietary flexible flue liners of various types are made for adding to existing flues. These are particularly useful where old flue linings have decayed or where gas or oil burning appliances are fixed in a converted fireplace. The flexible linings can be threaded

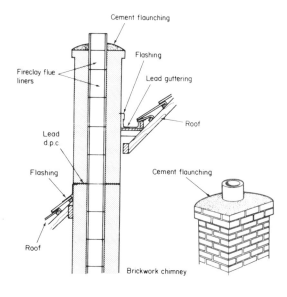

Typical brickwork chimney lined with fireclay liners. The cement flaunching at the top protects the chimney from rain absorption

through from the chimney top. Suitable terminals of asbestos-cement are made for fixing to gas and oil flues at the chimney head.

Outlet

Where a closed stove or boiler of the independent type, whether fixed in an open recess or standing on an open hearth, has the flue outlet connected to a brick or block flue, there must be a small chamber formed at the bottom of the flue. This should be preferably fitted with a small bucket, to collect condensate or debris, and an access cover to allow the bucket to be emptied.

A straight vertical flue is better than one with a bend. If a bend is unavoidable it should be at an angle to the horizontal of not less than 45 degrees. Where flue liners are used with a flue bend, the special bend fittings should be used.

Chimneys

The head or outlet of a flue serving a solid fuel or oil burning appliance must be not less than 1 m (3 ft 3 in) above the highest point of contact between the chimney or flue pipe and the roof, with the following exception.

Where a chimney or flue pipe passes through a pitched roof (a roof with an angle of not less than 10 degrees) at the ridge, or within 600 mm (24 in) of the ridge, the top of the flue (excluding the chimney pot or terminal) may be less than 1 m (3 ft 3 in) but not less than 600 mm (2 ft 2 in) above the ridge.

The top must also be at least 1 m (3 ft 3 in) above the top of any part of any window or skylight capable of being opened, or of any ventilator.

Flues or gas appliances

The Building Regulations relating to domestic gas fires and other appliances are complex. Generally, the printed fixing instructions issued by the manufacturers of a particular appliance should be carefully followed.

Special flue blocks and pipes are made for gas appliances fixed in new houses but flues and chimneys of normal brick or block construction can be used. Adequate air supply is essential for any gas consuming appliance.

The flue outlet must be fitted with a terminal designed to allow free discharge to minimise downdraught and to protect the flue from debris, and so situated that air can freely pass across it at all times.

The outlet from a gas appliance must be at least 600 mm (2 ft) away from any openable window, skylight or ventilator in any external wall or roof.

A brick or block chimney head should be protected by rendering with cement mortar sloped outwards to throw off rain water. This is called 'flaunching'. It helps drainage if the two top courses project about 50 mm (2 in).

Flues for solid fuel appliances

With flues for solid fuel appliances a chimney pot is not essential but it may help to prevent downdraught by raising the outlet above the area of air turbulence caused by wind striking the roof or near-by trees. When a strong wind strikes one side of a building it creates an area of pressure but on the opposite it creates suction. If the chimney rises from low down on the pressure side of the roof the top may sometimes be within the pressure area and downdraught may be caused.

If the flue is fitted with clay liners, the

top liner usually projects and, in effect, forms a pot. Round clay pots with square bases are made in several heights. The usual fixing is by bedding in the flaunching mortar but in areas exposed to strong winds it is better to bed the base one or two courses down. With a tall pot this is essential.

Anti-downdraught pots may be necessary in some situations. There are several types but it is advisable to try a metal type which can be clipped into an existing pot if downdraught occurs. A new house in a district exposed to strong winds may have louvred clay pots fitted as the chimneys are built.

Where an open fireplace is to be closed or bricked up, perhaps with an electric panel fire inserted, the chimney top should be protected against rain by fitting a half-round edge tile or a special pot with a ventilated cap. This allows the flue to be ventilated but prevents rainwater soaking down it.

Open fires

The fireplace recess is normally 342 mm (13½ in) deep, front to back and from 685 mm (2 ft 3 in) to 915 mm (3 ft) wide. If an open fire appliance is to be fitted, a firebrick back must be fixed first. This is made of refractory clays which will not readily crack, and there are three standard widths— 355 mm (14 in), 406 mm (16 in) and 457 mm (18 in). The 406 mm (16 in) is most widely used for small rooms. The standard height is 600 mm (24 in).

Standard firebrick backs, which are shaped to include the sides, are usually made in two sections; the upper section having a projecting bulge. This makes fixing and removal easier and also reduces the risk of cracking.

The fireback should be built-in with a weak lime mortar or weak concrete filling,

which will yield to expansion and ease future replacement. A mix of 1 part hydrated lime, 2 parts sand and 4 parts crushed brick, by volume, is suitable. This has very little setting strength but good thermal insulation.

Most builders usually support the head of the fireplace opening with a reinforced concrete lintel placed higher up than is needed. It is then necessary to fix a lintel beneath it so that the level of the opening is about 25 mm (1 in) below the top of the fireback, and the back of this lintel should be sloped to form the throat which has already been described. Special refractory throat hoods are made which are better for this purpose, especially where a surround of slabbed tile or facing bricks projects much in front of the fireplace breast.

An alternative to the above methods is to fix a wrought iron bar 75 mm (3 in) x 10 mm ($^3/_8$ in) at a suitable level under the builder's lintel and make up the space above with shaped brickwork. This is not a sound method as the brickwork filling may crack.

The fireback should be set so that a gap of about 6 mm (¼ in) is left behind the edges of the fireback and the back of the surround. This is filled with a weak mortar which gradually cracks and drops out. It is better to seal it with asbestos rope.

A tiled slab hearth and surround may be fixed with the hearth slab tight against the wall and the surround slab standing on the hearth or with the surround slab standing on the concrete hearth (a wide surround may overlap on to the floor), depending on the design. An inspection will indicate which method is suitable.

The hearth slab should be bedded in a lime-cement-sand mortar (see page 129). The surround slab should be fixed to the wall with round-head screws into wallplugs through the projecting metal lugs which are cast into the back of the slab in manufacture. The slab should be placed against the bare brickwork or blockwork and the wall plaster made good to it on completion.

Fires incorporating boilers

There are numerous appliances incorporating boilers both for domestic water supply and for central heating through radiators. Most are totally enclosed—some for building into a fireplace recess and some free-standing. Fixing instructions are issued by the manufacturers.

Fires, open and enclosed, can be obtained with under-floor draught supply and deep ash buckets. These allow better control over combustion and the ash bucket needs emptying only after several days' use. The pipe supplying under-floor air to the base of the fire is connected to an air brick in an outer wall. It is advisable to have two air pipes; for example, one in the front wall, the other in a side wall. This allows for the effect of a strong wind on one wall.

Chapter 14
Small brick buildings

The main part of this chapter is concerned with building a brick garage. First of all, though, we will devote a few paragraphs to constructing a fuel bunker.

Constructing a fuel bunker

With efficient modern appliances and fires for space heating and hot water supply, and the fact that coal and smokeless fuels are again competitive with oil, gas and electricity, the problem of solid fuel storage is still important in many homes.

Fuel bunkers of pre-fabricated concrete sections can be bought and are easy to bolt together, on a slab or concrete base, but the sections are heavy to handle. If you can tackle simple bricklaying, a brick walled bunker may be preferable, and you can choose the size and capacity.

The example is of single brick thickness with a wood top and lid. Inside measurements are: 1 m (3 ft 4½ in) square on plan, average height 1.3 m (4 ft). Solid fuels vary in weight from light coke to heavy coal. This bunker should hold about ½ ton of the heaviest and ⅜ ton of the lightest (the Imperial ton is roughly equal to the metric tonne).

A bunker of similar construction could be larger. If the width is increased by half this would increase the capacity by half. If you use two kinds of solid fuel, a double bunker would be suitable—twice the width but with a dividing wall in the middle.

The walls in brickwork or blockwork, at least 100 mm (4 in) thick, should be laid in stretcher bond, building up the corners slightly in advance of the main part, and taking care to level the courses and plumb

A coal bunker with walls of single brick in stretcher bond. For two kinds of solid fuel a pair could be built, semi-detached

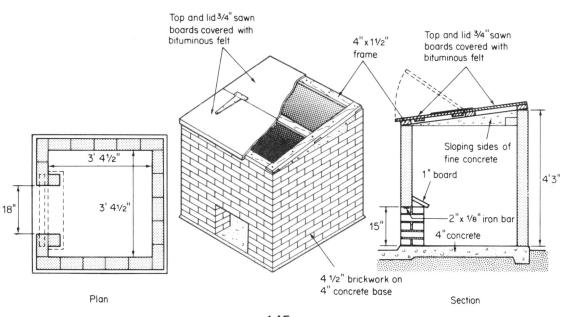

Top and lid ¾" sawn boards covered with bituminous felt

4" x 1½" frame

Top and lid ¾" sawn boards covered with bituminous felt

3' 4½"

3' 4½"

18"

Sloping sides of fine concrete

1" board

4'3"

15"

2" x ⅛" iron bar

4" concrete

4½" brickwork on 4" concrete base

Plan

Section

the surfaces, as described on page 131. A cement-sand mortar; 1 part Portland cement to 4 parts washed builders sand, with a little plasticising liquid added to make it easy to work—as mentioned in an earlier chapter, for a small job like this washing-up liquid will serve.

The sides should be finished to a slope along the top edge so that the roof can slope for shedding rainwater. The top course of bricks can be cut and the roughness rendered smooth with mortar. Alternatively, the top can be formed in cement mortar or fine concrete by fixing two boards on opposite sides, to the required slope, and pouring the mortar or concrete between the boards, finishing by tamping it and finally smoothing the top with the trowel.

When set the top should be drilled to take wallplugs to allow the roof frame to be screwed down.

An opening must be left in the brickwork or blockwork front to allow the fuel to be shovelled out. The brickwork should be returned to form a short pier each side of this opening. Then a 25 mm (1 in) thick board should be fixed on top, sloping a little, so that the fuel is prevented from spilling through the opening. This is preferable to a vertical sliding door.

The roof

The roof frame consists of 75 mm (3 in) x 38 mm (1½ in) timber, fixed with 8 gauge galvanised screws. The frame should be halved (jointed) at the corners, and covered with 20 mm (¾ in) boards. The lower part should be framed as a full width lid, hinged to the upper part with 450 mm (18 in) tee hinges. Roof and lid should be covered with bituminous roofing felt, with the edge of the felt on the fixed roof overlapping the lid felt by about 20 mm (¾ in).

The full width lid can be pushed back to give an ample opening when fuel is delivered in bags.

The timber roof should be brush treated with preservative before fixing the felt.

Building a garage

A home garage with walls of bricks or blocks is within the capacity of an experienced d.i.y. family. I say 'family' because if the job is to be done in a reasonable time, you need some help even if it is only fetching and carrying tools and materials. In fact this is the best kind of help because you can then get on with the skilled work.

You should have had some bricklaying and carpentry experience first, if it is only building a low wall in the garden or a timber shed.

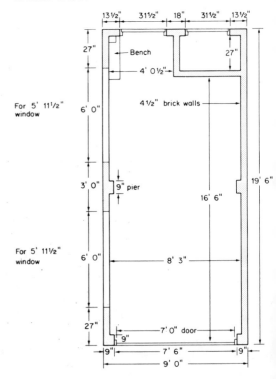

Plan of a garage with a rear compartment for solid fuel, tools, or as a boiler house; single brick walls (or blocks) with piers

The garage can be attached to the side of the house or detached with a passage between, whichever is most convenient.

Plans must first be submitted to the local council (Surveyor's Office) and an approval notice obtained before you start work (see Introduction, page 111).

A detached garage

The diagrams show the plan, elevations and sections, as required by the council's surveyor and also as working drawings on the job. In addition the surveyor must have a block plan showing the position of the site.

The plan shown includes a fuel or tool store at the rear Alternatively, an oil fired boiler for central heating could be accommodated here.

The inside length of the garage is 5 m (16 ft 6 in), inside width 2.5 m (8 ft 3 in). If you have the space it is an advantage to make the garage so that the car doors can be opened fairly wide on one side at least.

The walls are of single brick thickness (or standard 100 mm (4 in) concrete blocks can be used). Projecting piers bonded to the wall must be placed at the front, rear and mid-way along the sides. The front piers should allow for a standard entrance door at least 2.1 m (7 ft) wide. Standard windows of wood or metal can be used. Two wide windows are better than one as you need plenty of daylight if you do any servicing of the car.

The roof is flat in cross section (see diagram), but a fall for drainage is necessary. The roof fall can be lengthwise, as shown, or sideways; not less than 50 mm (2 in) in 3 m (10 ft) is advisable. The floor to ceiling height in the middle should not be less than 2.28 m (7 ft 6 in).

Assuming that the council have approved your plans (in writing) and have supplied notice forms for you to complete and send to the surveyor at various stages of the work (work commenced; foundations ready for inspection; walls completed; roof completed; building completed), you can order the materials and start work.

The job should be done in the following sequence.

Front section of garage, with single brick (or block) walls and flat roof with back fall for drainage. See also plan and side elevation on pages 146 and 148

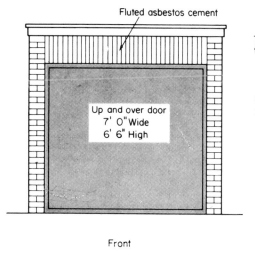

Fluted asbestos cement

Up and over door
7' 0" Wide
6' 6" High

Front

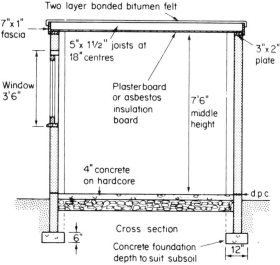

Two layer bonded bitumen felt

7" x 1" fascia

5" x 1½" joists at 18" centres

3" x 2" plate

Window 3'6"

Plasterboard or asbestos insulation board

7'6" middle height

4" concrete on hardcore

d p c

Cross section

6"

Concrete foundation depth to suit subsoil

12"

Setting out

Strip the top soil and roughly level it over an area extending about 300 mm (1 ft) beyond the outer line of the walls. Set out the outline with string line and corner pegs, squaring the angles. Fix wood profiles at each corner well clear of the wall corners. Stretch lines all round to give the trench lines— score these on the ground and excavate the trenches to a firm bottom (the council surveyor will advise what minimum depth is required).

The strip foundation concrete can be placed as soon as the trench bottom has been levelled. In most cases a width of 300 mm (12 in) and thickness of 150 mm (6 in) may be sufficient, with projections to take the piers.

If the ground has been filled to a depth of several feet or is rather weak it will be better to have a concrete combined foundation and floor (see page 118). Although the concrete can be prepared by any of the methods described in Chapter 11, the easiest is to buy ready-mix (wet) and prepare for placing it as soon as delivered.

Top, side elevation of garage, with two standard windows (a single window or any suitable type if preferred). Roof joists should be tilted slightly to allow for back fall to roof. Below, cross-section of the garage. See also pages 146 and 147

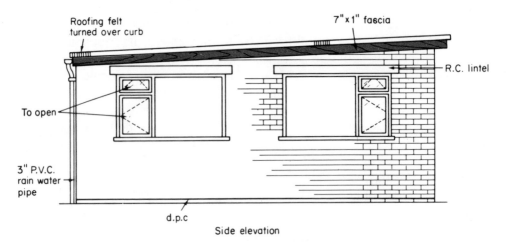

Side elevation

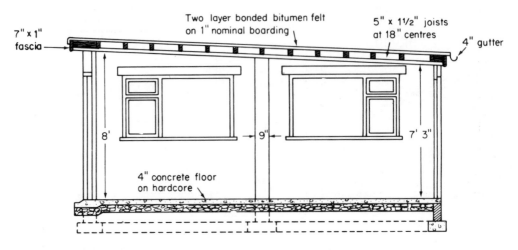

Cross section

Laying the bricks

Assuming that strip foundations have been placed in a trench, the next step is to stretch lines from the corner profiles to the outline of the walls. Hold a plumb line at the corner intersection of the lines to give you the first corner mark on the foundation. Repeat at each corner.

Check the length of walls with a tape measure. Lay a brick at each corner, bedding it in mortar, but then lay one course loose to check if you can fit whole bricks within the length, allowing for joints. Make any slight adjustment necessary. Then the first course can be laid, advancing the corners first, as already described.

The front piers are two bricks square, including the wall thickness. Whole bricks are used in one course but to allow the next course to overlap, three-quarter bats must be cut with the bolster chisel and club hammer. With the intermediate piers, a pair of whole bricks are laid as headers in one course but a half bat and a stretcher must be laid in the next course (see page 132 for details of bonding).

On reaching ground level you must consider where the dampproof course should be placed. It should be at least two courses above the finished ground level or paving but this will bring it above the floor level. Some builders place the dampproof course of a garage at floor level, which may be less than one course above ground. It is better to place the d.p.c. two courses up and then give the inside face of the wall two or three coats of a bituminous emulsion from under the floor level to d.p.c. level.

The door frames

When the d.p.c. has been placed, the door frames should be erected. They can be left until the walling is finished but it is better to build them in as the bricklaying proceeds, so that galvanised steel ties screwed to the frame sides can be built into wall bed joints. The feet of the frame should have metal dowels fitted for securing them to the floor concrete.

Before fixing wood frames clean them up with medium sandpaper, even if this rubs off some of the priming paint. Then give them an undercoat of paint. Also paint the sides, which will be in contact with the wall jambs and the end grain at the feet, with a coat of gloss paint. This treatment will prevent rot starting when these surfaces are concealed.

Take care to plumb the frames upright and to provide temporary struts to prevent accidental movement while the walls are built.

It is usual for the rear or side door of a small garage to be hung to open outwards so that the car can be driven close to it. But if you have enough length it is better to hang it to open inwards as with outward opening the door blows about in a strong wind if left open. So bear this in mind when fixing the frame as the rebate for the door must suit the direction of opening.

For the front entrance door you must have a rebated frame for hinged side hung doors, opening outwards. But most people now prefer an up-and-over door of wood, metal or fibreglass. For this type a plain frame 100 mm (4 in) x 75 mm (3 in) is usually suitable. The manufacturers of this type of door issue illustrated fixing instructions which should be carefully followed.

The concrete floor can be placed either when the brickwork reaches floor level or after completion of the walls. The former is the most convenient as the work can be done partly from outside.

The concrete should be covered with polythene or other sheeting to retard drying out, for at least one week.

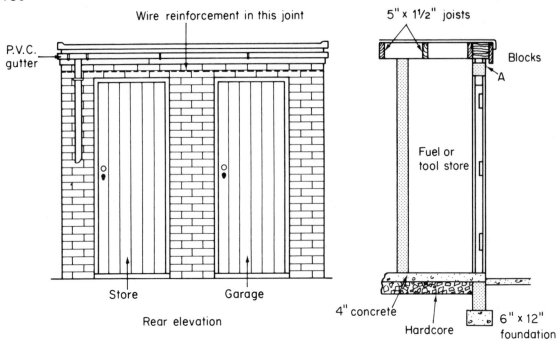

Wire reinforcement in this joint

5" x 1½" joists

P.V.C. gutter

Blocks

A

Fuel or tool store

Store   Garage

Rear elevation

4" concrete

Hardcore

6" x 12" foundation

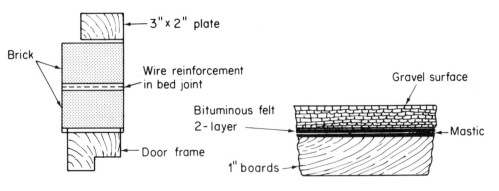

3" x 2" plate

Brick

Wire reinforcement in bed joint

Door frame

Detail of doorway head at A

Gravel surface

Bituminous felt 2-layer

Mastic

1" boards

Detail of roofing

The window frames

Take care not to go on building complete courses beyond window sill level. As soon as this level is reached place the window frames in position. A galvanised steel tie should be screwed to the frame sides and built into the brickwork, and the projecting ends of the wood sill also built-in.

The front frame can be extended over the entrance doorway so that the space over can be boarded or covered with flat asbestos-cement sheet.

Garage; top, rear elevation and section. Bottom left, detail over rear doors. Bottom right, detail of felt covered roofing with gravel finish

If you prefer brickwork over the front opening it will be necessary to fix a reinforced concrete beam. This can be formed by erecting timber shuttering of thick boards, at least 30 mm (1⅛ in). The bottom board should be supported on stout struts and metal G cramps or short battens nailed across the top edge of the boards. The shuttering must be secure and should not bend when the concrete is poured in.

A 1:2:3 mix, Portland cement—washed sand—coarse aggregate of small chippings (see page 114) is suitable. The timber shuttering should be lined with thin oil or polythene sheeting to prevent adhesion. After placing 38 mm (1½ in) of concrete, the steel reinforcing rods should be placed. Two rods of mild steel, not less than 10 mm (³⁄₈ in) diameter for a span not exceeding 2.4 m (8 ft) with the ends bent upwards will be sufficient. The concrete should be filled up to make a beam depth not less than three courses of brickwork, 230 mm (9 in).

Alternatively, you can buy a pre-stressed concrete lintel which is only 75 mm (3 in) deep but this type must be temporarily propped underneath while at least three

Garage; details of front with overhang of roof. Top left, wall plate bolted down to brickwork. Roof joists are nailed to plates

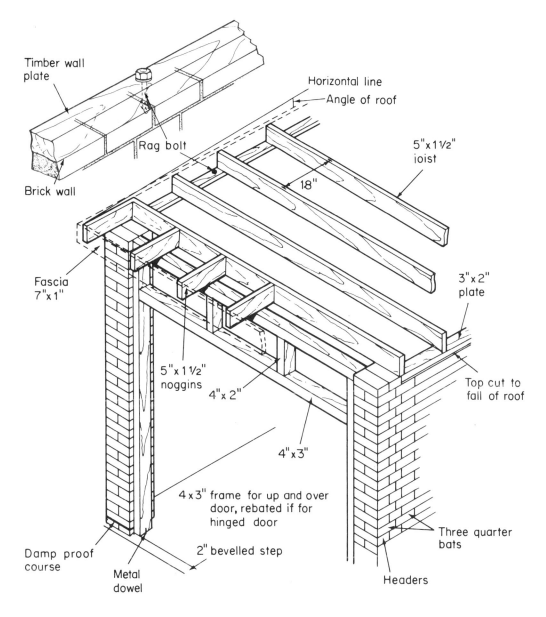

courses of brickwork are built on it. In fact the brickwork forms part of the beam by taking the compressive stress while the lintel takes the tensile stress.

The side windows should also have reinforced concrete lintels if brickwork is built over them. Some builders place a garage window high up and merely nail a timber place over the head. This will serve if no brickwork is built over the opening, though the roof joists must bear on the plate so it should be not less than 75 mm (3 in) thick.

The roof

The roof, as illustrated, projects at the front. As the roof joists are placed across the side walls the front projection is formed by placing noggins (short lengths of offcuts from the joists) and nailing them to the first joist and also to the top frame or plate.

The roof has a fall of about 228 mm (9 in) from front to rear end, as already explained, the side walls must be finished to this slope. The timber plate should be bolted to the wall with three 10 mm ($\frac{3}{8}$ in) 150 mm (6 in) bolts, preferably anchor or rag bolts, built into the brickwork. Builders often neglect to do this but unsecured flat roofs have been known to sail away in a very strong gale.

The roof joists are spaced 450 mm (18 in) centres, nailed to the wall plates. Ends are flush with the outer wall face and are covered by nailing on a fascia board. The projecting front and rear are also covered with a fascia board. Roof construction and coverings are further described in Chapter 16.

The ceiling may be covered with 10 mm ($\frac{3}{8}$ in) plasterboard or with asbestos insulating board, using 2.4 mm (8 ft) long sheets, the length crossing the joists. A proprietary filler can be used for filling the joints, using a putty knife or small trowel.

An alternative to a flat roof is a pitched centre ridge roof, covered either with concrete tiles or asbestos-cement sheeting, as described in Chapter 16.

A rainwater gutter, 100 mm (4 in) half round or rectangular section, fixed on brackets, with one stopped end and one stopped end with outlet spigot, and a 3 in downpipe are needed to drain the roof. The gutter should be laid to a slight fall towards the outlet. A string line should be stretched as a guide when fixing the brackets to the fascia. Plastic p.v.c. gutters and pipes are available in most d.i.y. shops.

Chapter 15
Carpentry-floors and joists

Carpentry is the craft of building construction in timber—mainly sawn timber (not planed). In the case of houses this includes timber floors and roofs. Partitions, conservatories, garden buildings and fences may also be framed in timber.

Several firms offer prefabricated houses and bungalows which include timber framed walls. These are made in sections for erection on prepared foundations by a builder or a reasonably skilled d.i.y. team.

Tools

For cutting and fixing sawn timbers few tools are needed. More tools will be required for joinery, see Chapter 17. All woodcutting tools must be of good quality and maintained in good condition for ease and accuracy in working.

These are the tools you will require:

Handsaw, 600 mm (24 in), medium teeth for ripping and cross cutting.
Backed saw, 300 mm (12 in) for cutting joints and accurate trimming.
Portable electric saw (optional). Useful on a big job.
Sawing horse or trestle, preferably two for supporting long lengths of timber.
Claw hammer, large.
Try square, for marking off lengths with square ends.

Rules, folding boxwood, also a long tape measure or flexible steel rule.
Brace, preferably ratchet type, with set of bits or drills.
Electric drill (optional), preferably two-speed type.
Screwdriver, large and small.
Pincers.
Hasp or shaper plane, coarse, for trimming.
Carpenters' pencil.
G clamps, one medium size, one large, for holding timbers in position while sawing or fixing.
Plane, large, required if sawn timbers need to be planed to required thickness.
String line, for setting out and alignment.
Spirit level, large.

Materials

Timber

Most of the timbers used in carpentry are softwoods. Timbers *imported* into the UK are: Douglas Fir, Western Hemlock, Pitch Pine, Redwood and Spruce. Timbers *grown* in the UK include: Douglas Fir, Larch and Scots Pine.

Western Red Cedar is sometimes used for framing conservatories and garden sheds where high resistance to decay is desirable, but this timber is not as strong as the above softwoods. It is usually planed for use and makes very durable exterior boarding, but the natural brown colour tends to fade in sunlight. Wood preservative dyes can be applied to renew the colour.

Hardwoods are not much used in carpentry but where ceiling joists are exposed, oak or one of the imported hardwoods may be used for the good appearance, at considerable extra cost.

153

Carpentry timbers should be straight and free from large defects such as loose knots, shakes or deep fissures. Although as sent from the timber conversion yards they may be properly seasoned, hardwoods may absorb excessive moisture if left in the open. They should be stored under cover but well ventilated by separating them with slips of thin wood.

Softwoods can be impregnated with chemicals to give high resistance against dry rot, insect attack and fire. Hardwoods such as oak and iroko have some natural resistance to fire. Impregnated timber can be ordered through most main timber suppliers at an extra cost of about 15 per cent.

Brush application of preservatives, such as creosote, gives temporary protection to softwoods. However penetration is not deep and the treatment must be renewed every two years or so if the timber is exposed to damp conditions.

In some areas in the south of England, preservative treatment of structural softwoods is compulsory owing to the prevalence there of wood-boring insects. The local council surveyor will give advice on this.

To avoid dry rot, structural timbers must be continuously ventilated and protected from damp. Hence, air bricks are used to ventilate the under-floor space of ground floors of timber and it is necessary to protect joists from rising damp by placing them above a dampproof course.

In damp stagnant air the fungus spores of dry rot quickly develop and destroy the timber. Such timber should be removed and burnt.

Nails

In carpentry, steel round wire or oval nails are generally used for fixing one timber to another. The round-head wire nail is used for most work but the oval nail has a neater head which can be punched in if desired. The lost-head nail is easier still to punch in.

For fixing joints and roof timbers, wire nails 100 mm (4 in), 125 mm (5 in) .and 150 mm (6 in) are suitable, but smaller sizes are made. All are sold by weight.

Screw nails have a spiral twist running the full length. They have superior holding power against withdrawal stresses.

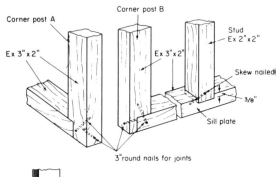

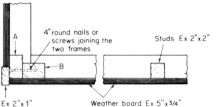

Simple framing joints. These joints are suitable for substantial sheds and conservatories. The frames can be sectional, the corners being joined A to B by screwing or nailing

Screws

Although not much used in carpentry, screws are sometimes an advantage for superior holding power or where in an existing structure heavy hammering might damage ceilings. A hole should be drilled slightly smaller than the maximum diameter of the screw thread.

Nails and screws used in exterior positions exposed to the weather should be galvanised or of rustproof metal to avoid rapid corrosion.

Simple framing joints, secured by nailing, are illustrated.

For heavy loads, bolts can be used, either alone or with timber connectors. There are several types. The coach screw-bolt is a stout screw, one end pointed and the other square headed so that it can be screwed into a hole of appropriate diameter with a spanner. This type is used where it would not be possible to pass a bolt right through the two timbers.

The ordinary coach bolt has a square nut and a round head. It is made in a range of sizes but, for most carpentry uses 10 mm ($^3/_8$ in) diameter bolts are adequate. A washer should be placed behind the nut.

The stress transmitted to the timber fibres by a bolt is concentrated on a rather small area. So for heavy loads a timber connector, square or round, is placed between the two timbers and the bolt then tightens the connector which transmits much of the stress over a wider area. Bolts and timber connectors are often used in roof trusses to joint overlapping timbers.

Jointing plates

Nail plates form another type of joining device for light roof trusses and frames. They consist of steel plate with a series of nail holes to take comparatively small 50 mm (2 in) nails.

Spiked plates have integral spikes similar to nails but they cannot be hammered in. They are forced in with a special compression tool and are used mainly in the manufacture of prefabricated roof trusses.

Timber floors

Timber floors consist of floor joists and floorboards or panels. A ground floor of this type is called a suspended floor because it is supported at the ends; and, for a wide floor, at intermediate positions, usually on sleeper walls with timber plates placed on a dampproof course (see illustrations).

The Building Regulations require a space height from the over-site concrete to the underside of the floor joists of not less than 125 mm (5 in). This space must be clear of debris and ventilated (usually by air bricks in the outer walls and honeycomb construction in the sleeper walls).

As a precaution against rot it is advisable to give a generous brush coating of preservative to the ends of the floor joists. This treatment should extend 300 mm (1 ft) from each end of the joist.

A timber joist ground floor must be ventilated underneath through air bricks. Where a timber joist floor adjoins a solid concrete floor, pipes must be laid to allow through ventilation

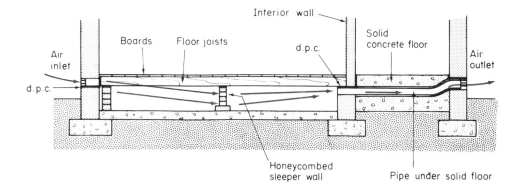

Interior wall

Boards   Floor joists   d.p.c.   Solid concrete floor

Air inlet   Air outlet

d.p.c.

Honeycombed sleeper wall   Pipe under solid floor

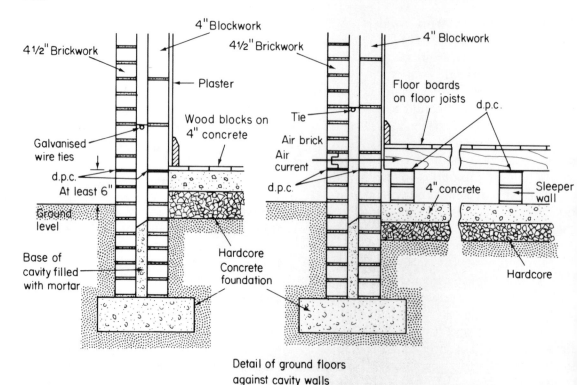

Detail of ground floors
against cavity walls

Upper floors of timber joist construction also serve as ceiling joists. In small houses these joists span between opposite load-bearing walls—from an outer wall to an inner dividing wall, or between two inner dividing walls. For exceptionally wide spans it is economical to use rolled steel

Detail of ground floors against cavity walls. Left, solid floor. Right, timber joist floor. Notice positions of dampproof courses and the dampproof membrane in the solid floor

Galvanised steel joist hangers. Left, hooked over a timber beam. Right, built into brickwork bed joint

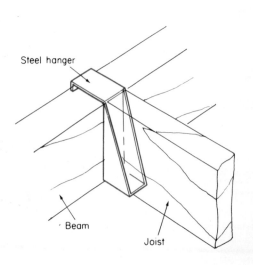

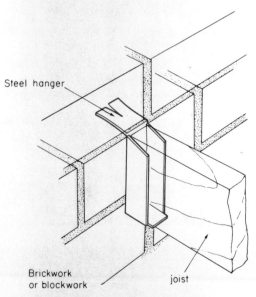

beams to give intermediate support to the floor joists. The steel beams must be cased in incombustible material, such as plaster-board.

With cavity outer walls, the joist end is built into the inner section of the wall. It should not project into the cavity as, if it does, mortar droppings might lodge there and form a bridge for moisture to cross the cavity (see page 135).

Steel joist hangers are convenient for supporting upper floor joists on beams or walls.

Floor joist sizes

Timber floor joists for domestic buildings must be selected for size according to the spacing and floor load. This data is tabulated in the Building Regulations. Depths of joists range from 75 mm (3 in) to 225 mm (9 in); thicknesses from 38 mm (1½ in) to 75 mm (3 in). These are nominal standard sizes, as sawn.

Standard spacings, centre to centre, are 400 mm (16 in) and 450 mm (18 in), for tongued and grooved floorboards of not less than finished thickness 16 mm (approximately $2\frac{1}{32}$ in).

The table shows standard spacings for the 38 mm (1½ in) thickness, usually the most economical to use.

This table applies only to normal domestic floor loads and where the dead loads (weight of flooring excluding the joists) and any partitions or other structural loads supported on the floor do not exceed 25 kilogrammes per square metre (5lb per sq. ft.) The Building Regulations should be consulted for dead loads exceeding this figure.

Where a heavy partition, such as concrete blockwork, is built on a timber floor it may be sufficient to place two floor joists together if the partition runs parallel with the joists. If it runs across the joists it may

| Floor | | Joist spacing | |
Joist size mm	Joist size in.	400 mm (16 in)	450 mm (18 in)
38 x 75	(1½ x 3)	1.03 m (3 ft 3 in)	0.93 m (3 ft)
38 x 100	(1½ x 4)	1.74 m (5 ft 6 in)	1.57 (5 ft 2 in)
38 x 125	(1½ x 5)	2.50 (8 ft 2 in)	2.31 (7 ft 6 in)
38 x 150	(1½ x 6)	2.99 (9 ft 9 in)	2.83 (9 ft 2 in)
38 x 175	(1½ x 7)	3.48 11 ft 5 in)	3.29 (10 ft 9 in)
38 x 200	(1½ x 8)	3.96 (12 ft 9 in)	3.75 (12 ft 1 in)
38 x 225	(1½ x 9)	4.44 (14 ft 3 in)	4.20 (13 ft 9 in)

be necessary to use joists of greater size than the foregoing table.

Furniture counts as live load and normally no extra joist strength is required.

In the case of old cottages it is advisable to check the condition and sizes of floor joists as they may not be of adequate strength or have been weakened by settlement or decay.

Ceiling joists

Ceiling joists under a pitched roof are usually a structural part of the roof as they serve as ties secured to the rafters and wall plates at the ends. They prevent the thrust of the rafters spreading the roof or exerting outward thrust on the walls.

The Building Regulations give tables for the various spans and for ceiling joists of 38 mm (1½ in), 44 mm (1¾ in) and 50 mm (2 in) thickness and depths ranging in similar sizes to those mentioned for floor joists. Where there is no floor load to be carried, ceiling joists for small houses are usually either 38 mm (1½ in) x 75 mm (3 in) or x 100 mm (4 in). In some cases the 44 mm (1¾ in) thickness is preferred and in fewer cases the 50 mm (2 in).

The Building Regulations give tabulated data for all sizes but the data given here is for the most economical thickness—38 mm (1½ in).

Ceiling Joist size mm	Joist size in.	Joist spacing 400 mm (16 in)	450 mm (18 in)	
38 x 75	(1½ x 3)	1.8 m (6 ft)	1.74 m (5 ft 7 in)	
38 x 100	(1½ x 4)	2.39 m (7 ft 9 in)	2.31 m (7 ft 7 in)	
38 x 125	(1½ x 5)	2.98 m (9 ft 7 in)	2.87 m (9 ft 3 in)	Maximum span of joists
38 x 150	(1½ x 6)	3.57 m (11 ft 6 in)	3.44 m (11 ft 2 in)	
38 x 175	(1½ x 7)	4.14 m (13 ft 6 in)	4.00 m (13 ft)	
38 x 200	(1½ x 8)	4.72 m (15 ft 5 in)	4.55 m (14 ft 9 in)	

The span across the full width of a house or bungalow roof is not necessarily the span of the ceiling joists as specified in the table. If intermediate support is provided on interior load-bearing walls or on strong timbers called binders, (which are placed over the joists at right angles to them and nailed from below), the tabular span is taken between the points of support. For example if a room is 3.7 m (12 ft) wide between outer and inner loadbearing walls, and a binder is placed mid-way between the two, the tabular span can be taken as 1.8 m (6 ft). From the table, ceiling joists 38 mm (1½ in) x 75 mm (3 in) spaced at 400 mm (16 in) centres are suitable.

An alternative to placing binders above the ceiling joists is to place a beam below. This may be of timber, steel or reinforced concrete.

Chapter 16
Roofing
and roof
construction

Pitched roofs may be of any angle over ten degrees to the horizontal. The pitch must be suitable for the type of roof covering to ensure weathertightness. Below ten degrees a roof is regarded as flat, though a slope is necessary for drainage.

Tiled roofs

Most house roofs are now covered with tiles of pre-cast concrete with a coloured surface. Clay tiles and natural slates are still used to a less extent but are more costly.

Pre-cast concrete tiles are made in a wide range of shapes and sizes, from traditional plain tiles, 265 mm x 165 mm (10½ in x 6½ in) to the largest tiles which are approximately 430 mm x 380 mm (17 in x 15 in). All patterns are illustrated in manufacturers catalogues which can be seen at any builders merchants.

Plain tiles have a double end lap and are hung to battens by the projecting nibs at the rear head.

Single-lap tiles include traditional profiles, such as pantiles and Roman tiles, but with interlocking side laps which form positive weather stops. Pantiles have a roll-and-trough cross section. Roman tiles have a double roll separated by a flat section. Both produce interesting shadow lines. The largest tiles are flat and some resemble large slates.

Ridge and hip tiles and valley tiles are made. Alternatively, valleys can be lined with sheet lead.

Most modern tiles are of the single lap type, including the pantile profile. The head lap is adjustable but as the side edges interlock this lap is fixed.

The minimum recommended roof pitch for most single lap tiles is 30 degrees, with reinforced underfelt draped over the rafters and tiling battens nailed over the underfelt. If the rafters are boarded or covered with insulating sheeting, and underfelt on top with tiling battens on counter-battens, the pitch may be lower.

Plain tiles should have a roof pitch of not less than 35 degrees, with reinforced underfelt. In a position exposed to very strong gales 40 degrees or more is recommended.

There are several patterns of large pre-cast concrete tiles which are suitable for very low pitches — 17½ degrees down to 12½ degrees, with underfelt. The manufacturers' recommendations should be followed for pitch and other details.

Roof construction

There are two types of pitched roof construction. The traditional method, still used, is to build it up on the site with rafters, ridges, purlins and ties — the latter serving also as ceiling joists. A modern method, which is increasingly used, is to obtain prefabricated trussed rafters which can be quickly erected — of these, more later.

A timber pitched roof consists of sloping rafters cut at the lower end to fit over horizontal wall plates and at the top bevelled against a ridge board.

For small span roofs, except a lean-to, a centre ridge with a collar (see diagram) are suitable.

With the ceiling joists the pitched roof

159

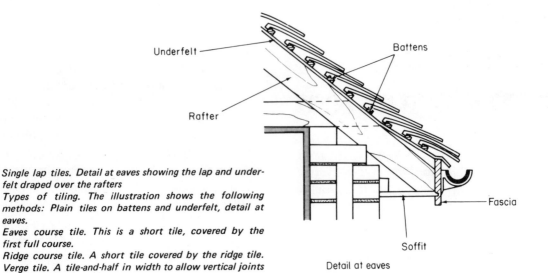

Underfelt

Battens

Rafter

Single lap tiles. Detail at eaves showing the lap and under-felt draped over the rafters
Types of tiling. The illustration shows the following methods: Plain tiles on battens and underfelt, detail at eaves.
Eaves course tile. This is a short tile, covered by the first full course.
Ridge course tile. A short tile covered by the ridge tile.
Verge tile. A tile-and-half in width to allow vertical joints to be staggered

Fascia

Soffit

Detail at eaves

Plain tile

Eaves course

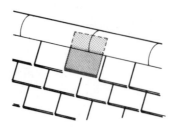

Ridge course

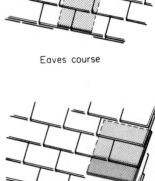

Verge tile

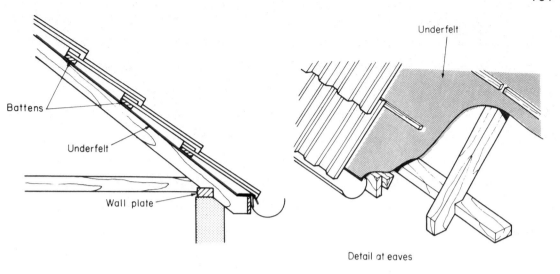

Battens

Underfelt

Wall plate

Underfelt

Detail at eaves

Pitched roofs of small spans. The collar and the tie strengthen the roof frames and prevent the rafters thrusting the walls outwards

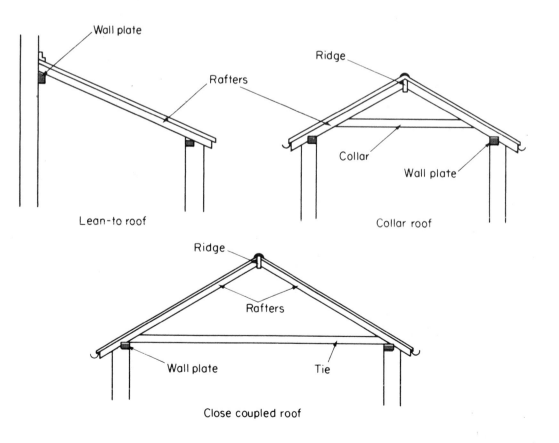

Wall plate

Rafters

Lean-to roof

Ridge

Collar

Wall plate

Collar roof

Ridge

Rafters

Wall plate

Tie

Close coupled roof

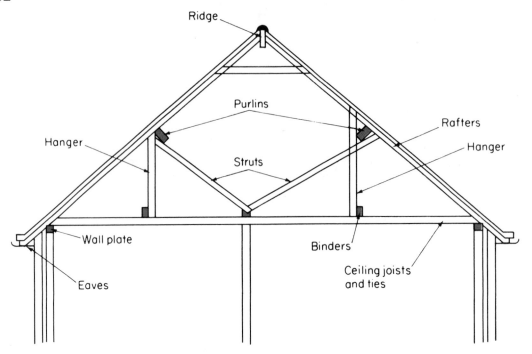

Traditional framed roof. Rafters with intermediate support on purlins and struts. The hangers and binders give intermediate support to the ceiling joist

forms a triangle — a strong form of frame. Intermediate support to the rafters may be given by fixing purlins, which are placed under and at right angles to the rafters and are usually supported at the ends on walls with intermediate support on struts resting on partition walls.

The ceiling joists or ties may be nailed at wall plate level to form a flat ceiling across the full span of the roof. Alternatively they may be raised some distance above the wall plates and nailed to the sides of the rafters so that they give extra head room.

A pitched roof may have gable ends or hipped ends. The gable roof is the simpler as the common rafters are all of equal length, given an equal span. The purlin ends can be built into the gable walls.

A hipped roof is more complicated as a series of shortened rafters, called jack rafters, must be cut to a double bevel against the hip rafters. The hip rafters

must be cut to fit over the wall plates and against the ridge end. Purlins must be supported on struts of trusses.

Where a loft room is placed within a roof windows may be arranged in the gable ends. Windows can also be placed in the roof, as illustrated. This is, of course essential with a hipped roof. The rafters must be trimmed to form a suitable opening either for a dormer window or a rooflight.

Rafter sizes

The size of the rafters depends upon the pitch of the roof and the span between points of support. A table of sizes is given in the Building Regulations for rafters having a pitch of more than 10 degrees but not more than 22½ degrees. Another

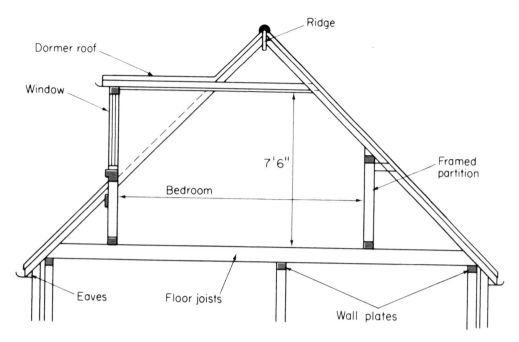

Roof room and dormer. The dormer extends the area of headroom as well as providing a window. The side frames are supported on the floor joists

table is for a pitch more than 22½ degrees but not more than 30 degrees. A third for pitches between 30 degrees and 42½ degrees.

The rafters should be normally spaced at 400 mm (16 in) or 450 mm (18 in), whichever spacing is adopted for the ceiling joists. This is so that the rafters can be nailed alongside the ceiling joists.

The lower the pitch, the deeper the dimension of the rafters, as the bending stresses are greater than at high pitches. For example, for pitches of 22½ degrees and lower the maximum span for 38 mm x 100 mm (1½ in x 4 in) rafters spaced at 400 mm (16 in) centres is 2.39 m (7 ft 10 in) but for pitches between 30 degrees and 42½ degrees for this size rafters the maximum span is 2.81 m (9 ft 2 in). These figures are for tiles of normal light weights. The Building Regulations provide data for all pitches and weights.

Prefabricated timber trussed rafters are manufactured for erection on site at 600 mm (2 ft) centres, as illustrated.

Pitched roofs for covering with corrugated sheets of asbestos-cement, aluminium alloy, galvanised steel or plastic, can be of low pitch — not less than 10 degrees. The manufacturer's instructions should be followed regarding the necessary supporting timbers for these sheets as sizes and strengths vary with the pattern and material.

The construction of timber roofs for sheeting is different from that described for tiles. Horizontal purlins are fixed parallel to the wall plates and ridge, spaced so that they support the head and tail of the sheets where they overlap and also with intermediate support for the longer sheets. The purlins must be supported at the ends and, if necessary at intermediate positions.

Fixing corrugated and plastic sheeting

Driving screws, galvanised, with plastic cup washers should be used for fixing corrugated sheets. Holes should be drilled in the sheets, not punched. Suitable fixings can be obtained when buying the sheets. For an example of a structure with a roof covered with corrugated translucent plastic sheeting see page 197.

The laps of translucent plastic sheeting should be sealed with sealing tape to prevent dust and fine debris accumulating within the lap.

Corrugated sheeting tends to collect condensed moisture on the underside in a damp cold atmosphere. Sheeting of asbestos-cement or of metal can be insulated underneath by first covering the roof structure with insulation board. This will also reduce heat loss in winter and excessive solar heating in summer.

Purlin joined to beam with a metal framing anchor. These anchors are fixed with special nails provided

Flat roofs

A flat roof is any roof from level up to 10 degrees slope. For draining rainwater a fall of not less than 38 mm (1½ in) in 3 m (10 ft) is necessary. Where the roof is for access only for maintenance or repair, and for boarding and covering with bituminous felt, the timber joist of structural grade softwoods, spaced at 400 mm (16 in) or at 450 mm (18 in) centres should be of the sizes specified for ceiling joists (page 158).

If a flat roof is to be used as a balcony or sun roof stronger joists are required. The sizes specified for floor joists (see page 157) may be suitable with a slight reduction in the span.

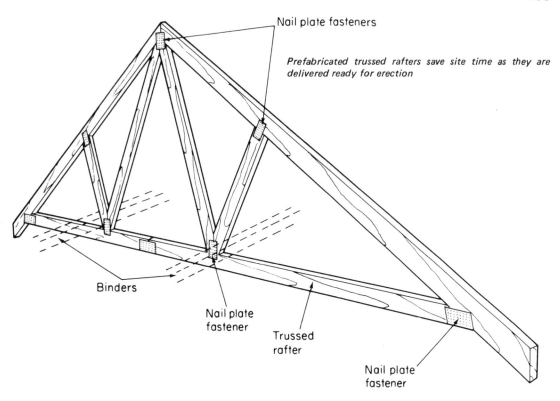

Nail plate fasteners

Prefabricated trussed rafters save site time as they are delivered ready for erection

Binders

Nail plate fastener

Trussed rafter

Nail plate fastener

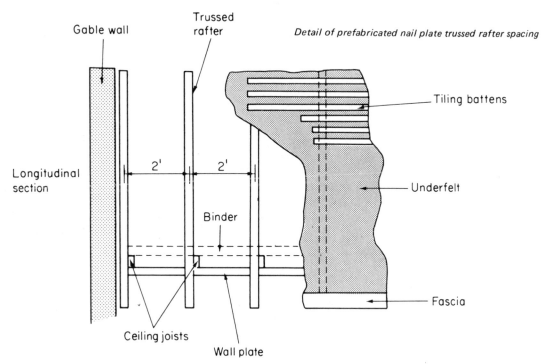

Gable wall

Trussed rafter

Detail of prefabricated nail plate trussed rafter spacing

Tiling battens

Longitudinal section

2' 2'

Underfelt

Binder

Ceiling joists

Wall plate

Fascia

Prefabricated trussed rafters

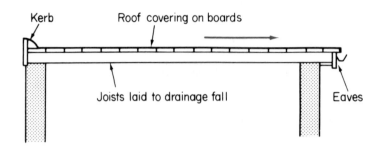

Kerb Roof covering on boards

Joists laid to drainage fall

Eaves

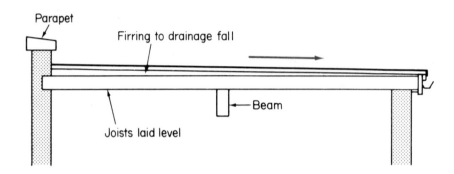

Parapet

Firring to drainage fall

Beam

Joists laid level

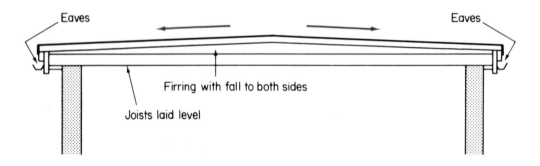

Eaves Eaves

Firring with fall to both sides

Joists laid level

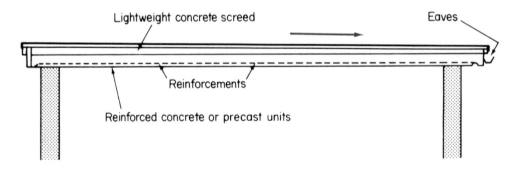

Lightweight concrete screed Eaves

Reinforcements

Reinforced concrete or precast units

Flat roofs, but with a slight fall for drainage. Thermal insulation should be added for dwellings. A concrete flat roof needs temporary shuttering or pre-cast concrete beam units

Garden shed roofs are usually of light construction. In some cases, however they may be too light with consequent sagging. Snow and wind loads must be considered and it is advisable to comply with the table on page 158 even for light sheds. The exception is that for spans not exceeding 1.5 m (5 ft) 38 mm x 50 mm (1½ in x 2 in), joists are suitable.

The fall for drainage may be obtained by fixing the roof joists at the required slope but, for a level ceiling, the joists should be fixed level and tapered firring pieces nailed on top. Most timber suppliers will cut these firrings to order — machine sawing two tapered pieces out of one length of timber.

If on brick or block walls, flat roof joists should be securely nailed to the wall plate timbers. The wall plates should be fixed to the wall top with anchor bolts. Failure to fix securely may result in the roof being lifted by wind suction in a gale.

Corrugated asbestos-cement sheets and translucent plastic sheets are sometimes used on flat roofs. These are not very satisfactory at very low pitches. If they are so used it should be noted that they will not support any extra load and you should not stand or kneel on them. Accidents have been caused by standing on asbestos-cement roofs. Where access for repairs is necessary, scaffold boards should be placed and secured over the roof sheets.

Chapter 17 Joinery-tools, materials, joints

Joinery differs from carpentry as it calls for planed and well finished surfaces, accurate dimensions and preparation of joints. So, in addition to the tools used in carpentry (see page 153), further tools are needed. There are numerous joinery tools but the following is a basic collection which will serve for most home joinery, including simple built-ins and furniture.

Tools

Tools must be kept in good condition if satisfactory work is to be done. Plane and chisel blades must be frequently sharpened. Saws must be re-set and sharpened as the teeth wear (most tool shops will undertake this rather tricky job). All tools must be protected from damp.

Benches

A bench is essential but it need not be an elaborate or expensive one. You can knock up a useful bench using softwood, at least 50 mm x 50 mm (2 in x 2 in) for the legs and 20 mm x 75 mm (¾ in x 3 in) for the rails. Fix rails all round the top and also about half way down the legs by nailing or screwing. The top should be covered with planed boards about 20 mm (¾ in) thick nailed or screwed to the rails. Punch the nail heads down, using oval wire nails, and countersink screw heads slightly below the surface.

A woodworker's vice (of moderate size) should be fixed to one side of the bench. A quick release mechanism is useful but not essential. Line the cheeks with pieces of 12 mm (½ in) planed wood. For light jobs, a portable vice, which is simply clamped to the bench or even a kitchen table, is sufficient.

Planes and saws

You will need a general purpose plane, preferably of steel, at least 230 mm (9 in). A grooving or fillister plane is necessary if you want to make built-ins or furniture. This enables rebates and grooves to be made for doors, frames and jointing.

A general purpose, 600 mm (24 in) saw, medium teeth, and a tenon saw for fine cutting are sufficient for most jobs, but a hacksaw or frame saw is useful for a variety of small jobs. A coping saw is similar but has a fine blade and the frame shape allows curves to be cut in boards or plywood.

A spokeshave is useful for rounding off ends of small sections of wood. A shaper plane or tool with serrated blades which are interchangeable (there are several proprietary makes), is useful for various shaping jobs.

Electric tools

A portable electric drill saves time and labour if you have much drilling to do. There are various accessories, such as circular saws and drill stands, which can be fitted to it.

If you want to make much joinery – for example some furniture – an electric woodworking machine in your workshop will enable sawing, drilling, turning, planing, rebating, grooving, sanding and most jointing jobs to be done speedily. But a good universal machine costs a few hundred pounds and is hardly justified for occasional woodworking.

Small hand tools

In addition to the large claw hammer, mentioned under carpentry, a smaller Warrington hammer for driving small nails and panel pins is essential.

A gimlet for boring small holes, a bradawl for smaller holes, and a brace and set of bits will serve for most drilling jobs. A geared hand drill with a set of twist drills is more convenient than a brace for some jobs. For drilling holes in walls for wall-plugs a masonry drill is necessary.

A try square and a marking gauge are necessary for setting out joints and lengths. A 600 mm (24 in) folding rule and a flexible steel rule 1.8 m (6 ft) long will be useful for measuring.

You will need screwdrivers, small and large, or a ratchet type with a set of driver bits and small diameter drill bits. This should include a star driver for fixing screws with star shaped 'Posidriv' slots. Pincers are required for removing nails.

Chisels, narrow, medium and up to 25 mm (1 in) for cutting. Use gouge chisels if you want to cut concave grooves. If you are going in for wood carving buy a good set of wood carving tools — these have various shapes and are better adapted than ordinary chisels for the purpose.

Scrapers are required for removing paint and varnish; but it is advisable to apply a paint removing paste on thick finishes to soften them. A blowlamp or blowtorch is an alternative but take care if working on delicate woods—the flame can mark them. The blowtorch is more convenient than a blowlamp and is finding increasing favour with the d.i.y. enthusiast.

Finally, you will need a carborundum stone and an oil can. You can hone chisels and plane blades accurately if you use a honing gauge which holds the blade at the correct angle.

Materials

Timbers are divided into softwoods and hardwoods but the densities in both classes vary and in this matter the terms are misleading. Softwoods come from the conifer group — fir, pines, redwood, spruce, red cedar, larch and hemlock. Hardwoods come from the broad-leaf trees — including oak, mahogany, teak and many African, and Asian timbers now widely used, including abura, afara, African walnut, iroko, makore, obeche, sapele, utile, and padauk.

Softwoods are used for standard mass produced joinery including window and door frames, floorboards, built-ins and porches, for paint or preservative stain finishes.

Parana pine is a superior softwood which is recommended for good quality joinery and furniture. It is close grained and works well. For interior work it looks attractive if finished with a transparent sealer or varnish.

Wood with large or loose knots is not good for general joinery but knotty pine boards look attractive on walls and ceilings and for cottage type built-ins.

Hardwoods are generally denser and more costly than softwoods. In most cases the appearance is good and the surface is merely sealed. Densities and working qualities vary. Teak and iroko, for example, are very hard. Mahogany varies but Honduras mahogony works and finishes well.

Plywoods and blockboards

The thinner plywoods are three-ply and one face is usually superior in appearance than the other. The core is at right angles to the face veneers. Multiply has a core of two, three or more plies.

Standard plywood thicknesses are

mm	in
3.2	1/8
5.0	3/16
6.5	1/4
9.5	3/8
12.5	1/2
16.0	5/8
19.0	3/4

Blockboard is made with blocks up to 25 mm (1 in) wide as the core with facing veneers. Some types have decorative veneer or hardwood, on ply backing.

Laminboard has a core of narrow strips of wood, faced with veneer, as with blockboard, on ply backing.

Standard thicknesses are

mm	in
12.5	1/2
16.0	5/8
19.0	3/4
22.0	7/8

Composite boards

These are plywoods faced with plastics or with sheet metal and are made under proprietary names.

Composite boards with cores of insulating material faced with plywood are available for use as thermal insulating partitions or linings.

There are several grades of plywood, blockboard and laminboard according to the quality of the veneers.

Ordinary plywoods are made with water soluble adhesives and are only suitable for interior use in normal dry conditions. Exterior grade plywoods are made with synthetic resin adhesives which have high resistance to damp and superior strength.

Chipboard or particle boards

This may be either boards or panels made of wood chips processed with synthetic resin binder and compressed. There are several types but the most widely used are of medium density.

These boards or panels are free from warping and can be used for large jointless surfaces such as wardrobes, cupboard doors and table tops

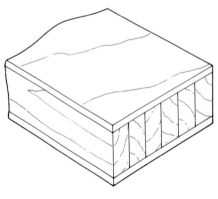

Laminboard

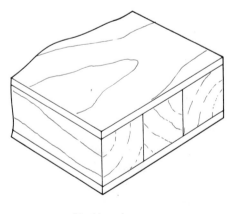

Blockboard

The boards do not warp under normal conditions and cost less than natural wood. They can be used for built-ins, partitions, and there are proprietary types with special surfaces and veneers. For shelves and making furniture, the boards are obtainable in a range of widths and lengths with the edges also veneered.

A special grade of chipboard, 19 mm (¾ in), is made for flooring panels. Ordinary chipboards are not suitable for exterior damp conditions but a special damp-resisting type is made. All types are easily sawn and can be fixed by nailing or screwing.

Hardboards

Dense boards of wood fibre are called hardboards. Ordinary hardboards are generally used for such work as backing cupboards but with suitable framing can be used for many purposes, including built-ins.

Tempered hardboard is a superior grade of high damp resistance and strength, and is intended mainly for exterior use. For outside use, however, it needs protecting with paint.

It can be used to form a new floor surface over an existing boarded floor. Ordinary hardboard is suitable for this purpose if the floor is to be covered with wall-to-wall carpet, vinyl, or for cork or other flooring tiles.

Decorated hardboards have a variety of special finishes — enamelled or lacquered; plastic faced; printed wood grain effects with a plastic finish; and veneered with natural wood.

Perforated and slotted hardboards are used for ventilation panels, decorative effects and to provide wall panels with demountable hooks for hanging tools, clips and pictures.

Insulating boards

Low density fibreboards are in this class, in thicknesses of 12 mm (½ in), 18 mm (¾ in) and 25 mm (1 in). They are suitable for lining walls partitions and ceilings, but generally the fire retardant grade should be used where the surface of the board is exposed.

The thermal insulation of walls and partitions can be improved by lining with insulation board on wood battens spaced 400 mm (16 in) centres. The boards can also be nailed to ceiling joists. Wood boarded floors on open joists can be insulated by laying insulation board between the joists and the floor boards. Timber flat roofs can be insulated in the same way and concrete flat roofs may have bitumen impregnated insulation board bedded in bitumen on the concrete.

Laminated plastic sheets, 1.5 mm thick, which have a dense non-absorbent surface, are made in a wide range of colours and decorative patterns. They must be stuck to a rigid base, such as blockboard, with an impact adhesive.

Plasterboard is an excellent material for lining partitions, walls and ceilings.

For thermal insulation foil-backed plasterboard should be used, as the bright aluminium backing reflects heat rays. But the backing must face an air space, so this type of board must be nailed either to timber frames or battens.

Weather boards

Wood boards for external cladding may be of a good quality softwood (preferably impregnated by the timber supplier with preservative), or of Western red cedar which has high resistance to decay, or a suitable hardwood.

Horizontal boarding should have rebated (overlapping) edges. The 'shiplap' pattern is generally favoured as it has an attractive curved upper edge.

Vertical boarding should be grooved and tongued with a chamfered vee or curved edge. Some wide boards are made which are moulded to appear as two or three boards of varying width.

Weather boards should be nailed, with galvanised steel or aluminum oval or lost head nails, to supporting battens or timber framing, spaced not more than 450 mm (18 in) centres. They should not be tightly cramped at the joints but allow freedom of swelling and shrinkage, which is inevitable even with painted boards. If tightly cramped they will corrugate when swollen by damp absorption. The edge joint should be barely a touch fit. In very dry weather a slight clearance should be left at the edges.

Softwood weather boards may be finished by oil painting—primer, undercoat and gloss coat (two gloss coats are better than one to start with). Alternatively, a preservative stain finish may be applied. But this should be renewed every three years.

Hardwood boards may be sealed with a polyurethane sealer or a high quality transparent varnish. But these, too, need renewal at intervals of a few years. To do this, first scrape and rub down with sandpaper to remove the old finish, and then apply two coats of the new finish.

Care should be taken to seal the ends of weather boards, with paint or sealer, as damp is readily drawn through the end grain. This is where rot usually starts.

Generally, horizontal weather boarding is better than vertical as rainwater is less likely to enter the joints. It is easier to remove a horizontal defective board and replace with new.

Joints

Joints can be cut with a tenon saw or, if dowelled, with a drill. They may be glued, nailed or screwed together. Some of the most useful and simple joints are illustrated.

Boarding for external and internal use. These boards can be used for cladding sheds, workshops and garden buildings or for interior decorative use on walls and ceilings

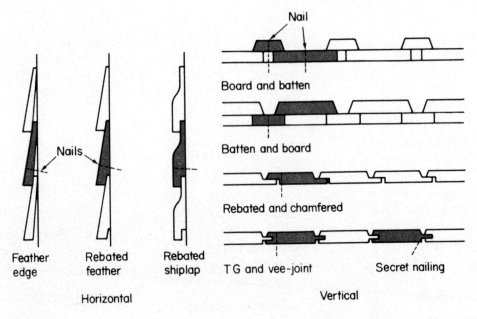

Feather edge | Rebated feather | Rebated shiplap

Horizontal

Nail — Board and batten — Batten and board — Rebated and chamfered — TG and vee-joint — Secret nailing

Vertical

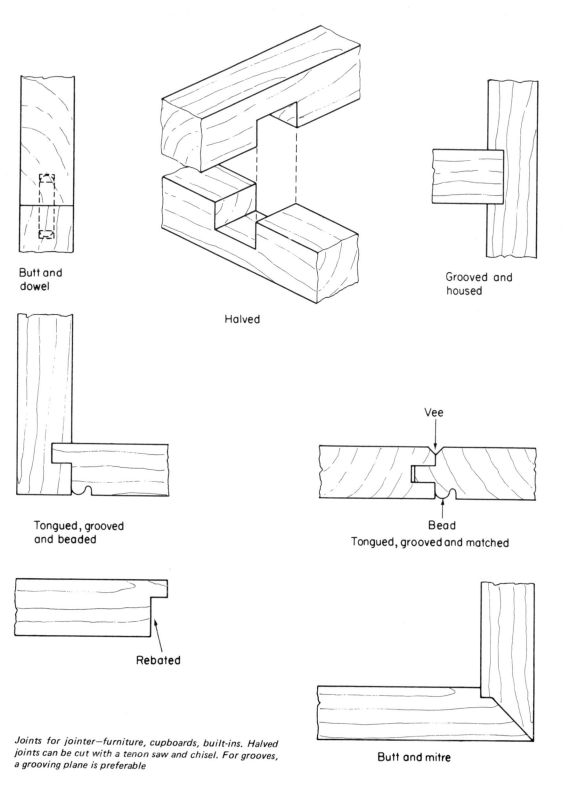

Butt and
dowel

Halved

Grooved and
housed

Tongued, grooved
and beaded

Vee

Bead

Tongued, grooved and matched

Rebated

Butt and mitre

*Joints for jointer—furniture, cupboards, built-ins. Halved
joints can be cut with a tenon saw and chisel. For grooves,
a grooving plane is preferable*

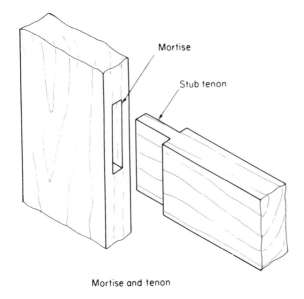

Mortise

Stub tenon

Mortise and tenon

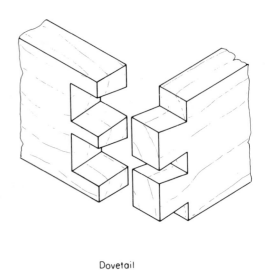

Dovetail

A butt joint can be secured by two or three wood dowels glued in. The holes drilled in each piece of wood must correspond exactly. For this purpose a dowelling jig should be used.

A halved (half lap) joint is simple to form by making two saw cuts at the end of each piece of wood, for a corner joint, or two saw cuts and then cutting the waste out with a chisel for a cross halved joint.

A simple corner joint for rails is the rabbet (rebated joint), with the end of one piece rebated to allow the plain end of the other piece to be glued into it.

A grooved joint is formed by cutting a groove across the grain of one piece so that the plain end of the other piece can be glued into it. A good simple joint for joining a shelf to a side support. To conceal the joint the groove can be stopped about 18 mm (¾ in) short of the front edge though this needs extra care in chiselling.

A dovetail joint makes a strong fixing but needs careful setting out and exact cutting. There are several forms of this.

A mitre joint for a corner consists of the ends of both pieces bevelled at 45 degrees.

A mortise slot can be cut by drilling and chiselling. The tenon cut with a tenon saw, also used for cutting dovetails. Electric woodworking appliances simplify this sort of work

It has no strength in itself but can be made secure by glueing a triangular corner block into the corner.

Multiple dovetailed joists, as used in making drawers, are for the skilled and patient woodworker. The combed joint is similar except that the joint projections and recesses are not of dovetail shape. These joints are easier to make if a machine saw with a special attachment is used.

Mortise and tenon joints are used chiefly for joining rails to stiles (horizontals to verticals) in panelled doors. They are cut by drilling and chiselling to remove the waste for the mortise recess and by cutting with the tenon saw to form the tenon.

Another type of mortise and tenon is for joining corners of frames for built-ins and furniture. This is a tenon at the end of one piece fitted into an open slot in the other piece.

Joint fittings

In many cases cut joints can be avoided by using proprietary fittings or devices of metal or nylon plastic. A very useful type consists of a pair of blocks, with holes for screwing to the inside corner of a frame, such as the rails of a cupboard, with integral dowel projections on one block which engage with corresponding holes in the other. This has the advantage of being easily demountable.

Steel corner brackets for screw fixing can be used for supporting shelves and for securing an internal corner in a frame.

Chapter 18

Windows, doors and staircases

Windows and doors come in a variety of types and sizes and all are described in this chapter. Patio doors (or french windows) are also covered. Unless you are building a house or reconstructing a very old one, you will probably never need to construct a staircase. However, a few notes on staircases are given at the end of this chapter.

Types of window

Windows are made in a range of standard sizes, suitable for houses and bungalows, but there are special types which can be made to order.

The four materials used for windows are:

1. **Wood.** Softwood for painting; hardwood for sealing or varnishing.

2. **Steel.** Galvanised, for painting.

3. **Aluminium alloy.** Usually fitted in a hardwood surround. No painting needed.

4. **Plastics** in extruded sections.

Wood casement windows

Mass produced wood casement windows, manufactured by members of the British Woodwork Manufacturers Association under their EJMA mark, are good low-cost windows. It is essential to keep them well protected by painting, especially by good initial painting when they are clean and dry. They can be obtained ready treated with a preservative which will take a paint finish. The various types of casement windows are as follows.

Casements, side hung (some with top hung vents), traditional in design, single frames 438 mm (1 ft 5¼ in) wide and multiple frames with two, three and four lights divided by mullions. These come in two types, plain lights for single panes of glass and divided lights with glazing bars for small panes.

Casements, landscape or sunshine types, with a fixed single wide pane and some with side hung openable casements, others with top hung openable vent lights.

Casements, pivot range. These have square shaped panes, with centre pivoted casements and single, double or treble frames. Pivot windows are reversible—which is a considerable advantage for cleaning especially upstairs windows—and with suitable fittings they can be set open in any position.

Feature windows are based on the landscape or sunshine large pane windows. The jambs are extended from floor level with a middle rail which forms a panel below for glazing or filling with boarding or exterior grade plywood. Some types are made in combination with a door frame, one type for inward opening door, another for outward opening.

A typical section through a casement window, as fixed in a cavity wall, is shown.

Sash windows

Sash windows, double hung for vertical sliding, of traditional appearance, but with spring balance fittings, in place of the old sash cords and balance weights, are made for plain panes or with glazing bars for small panes.

Sash windows are associated architecturally with Georgian houses.

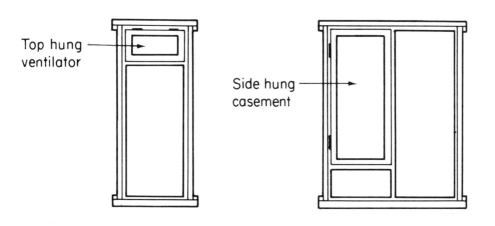

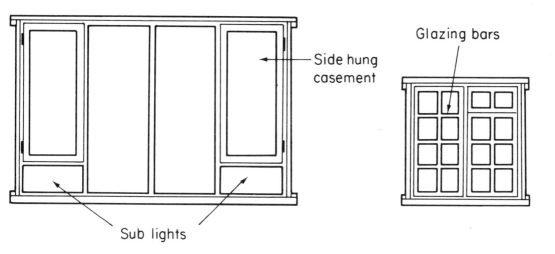

Top hung ventilator

Side hung casement

Side hung casement

Glazing bars

Sub lights

Standard wood casement windows

hese are some of the many standard windows available a wide range of sizes. They can be treated with a ecial preservative which can be painted over

ow windows

ow windows, with glazing bars for small anes, are also made in several standard zes and these, too, are suitable for eorgian style houses.

A moulded glass fibre roof and fascia is applied as an extra by the makers. This akes installation easier, but a flat boarded oof, lead covered, can be built on the bow ame if preferred.

Bay windows

There are four standard plan shapes of bay windows. Square bays have returns at 90 degrees; splayed bays have returns at 30–45 and 60 degrees; curved bays are of two radii – 1.6 m (5 ft 2 in) and 3.7 m (12 ft 2 in) – the former with a bold projection, the latter with a shallow projection.

Square and splayed bays are also made with a single return, right hand or left hand, for fitting into a wall corner.

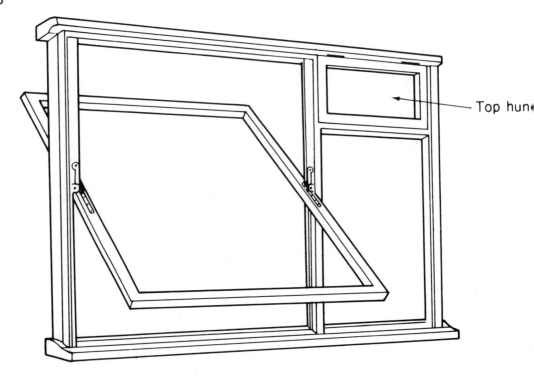

Top hun◦

Wood pivoted windows

Standard windows with wide panes give a better view. The pivot type is convenient as it can be reversed for cleaning

Fixed

Fixed

Standard wood landscape windows

Plastics windows

Rigid PVC extruded sections are used for making window frames by several well-known manufactures. These originated on the Continent and this is sometimes evident from some of the styles which are available.

The weathering and other characteristic appear to be satisfactory. They are fitte◦ with clip-on glazing beads.

PVC plastics are also used by som◦ manufacturers as a sheathing over a woo◦ or metal core which is thus protected fro◦ damp and needs no painting.

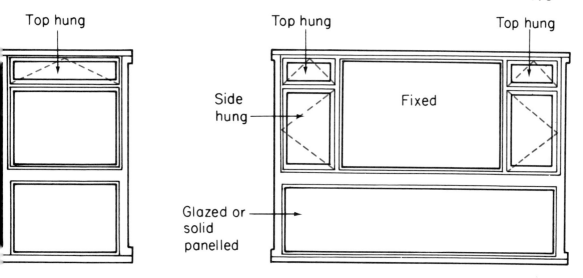

Feature windows

Feature windows have the sill at floor level. The combined window/door frame is convenient for a narrow hall

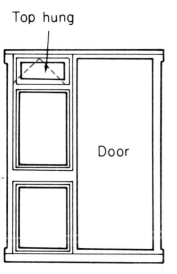

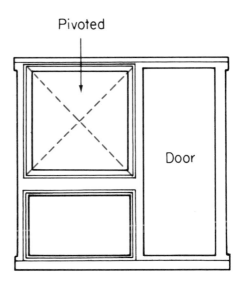

Combined window/door frame

Steel windows

These windows are made of steel sections with hinged casements fitting into a fixed frame. The wide range of sizes and types approximate to the range for standard wood windows. The windows are galvanised which protects against corrosion, provided the galvanising is not damaged by rough usage. Painting on the galvanised surface gives additional protection. Side hung, top hung and pivot casements are available.

Steel windows should be set in a wood surround which gives a better appearance

180

and also protects the steel frame during transport and fixing.

Aluminium windows

Aluminium alloy in extruded sections is used for many types of windows and there are several proprietary ranges and types. The lighter sections are suitable for domestic

use. Most aluminium windows are horizontal sliding fitted with nylon draught stripping.

In addition to the normal ranges, some manufacturers offer an interior range for fixing inside existing windows to form a double window for thermal insulation and draught proofing. Most are easy to fix with simple tools. The glass is usually fixed in plastic channels, and no putty is required.

For the exterior windows, the metal frame should be set in a hardwood surround which protects the window against damage in handling and adds to the appearance.

Aluminium windows do not corrode in normal atmospheres where atmospheric pollution is low. The surface needs only occasional cleaning with soapy water. Anodised transparent finish gives a slightly better appearance but is not necessary for protection. Some manufacturers offer acrylic plastic finishes in various colours.

If you wish to paint aluminium frames a zinc chromate primer should be used. Ordinary lead based primer does not take well.

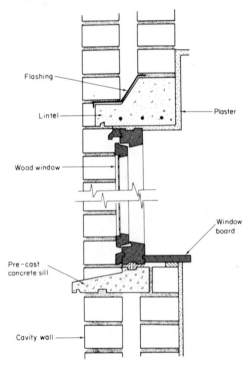

Left, detail of a standard wood window set in a cavity wall. Other types of lintel and sill are optional

Balanced sash windows are suitable for Georgian style houses. Modern standard types are usually spring balanced

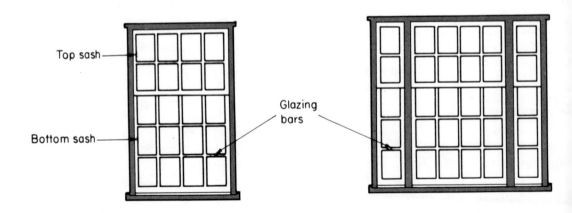

Glazing

Clear sheet glass, as normally used for house windows, has blemishes which slightly distort vision. The 3 mm thickness (24 oz per sq. ft.) is used for small to moderate size panes and the 4 mm (32 oz per sq. ft) for larger panes not exceeding 2 m x 1.25 m (6 ft 6 in x 4 ft).

Float glass is now widely used in place of sheet, as the surfaces are perfectly flat and give undistorted vision. The 3 mm thickness up to 1.27 m x 1.27 m (4 ft x 4 ft) panes and the 5 mm up to 2.5 m x 2.25 m (8 ft x 7 ft) for positions of normal

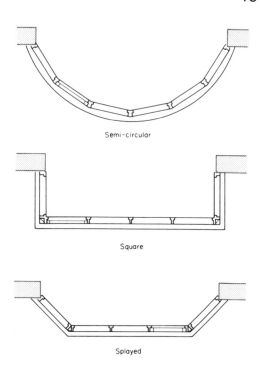

Semi-circular

Square

Splayed

Right, standard bay windows are made in a range of widths and projections. They add floor area and extend the view

Galvanised steel windows of a variety of types and sizes are made. They look better set in a wood surround

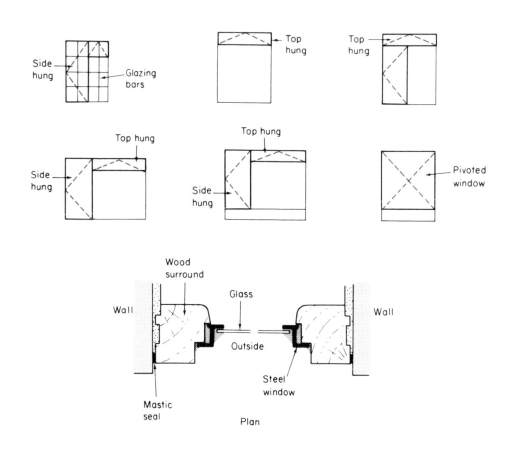

Side hung — Glazing bars

Top hung

Top hung

Side hung — Top hung

Top hung — Side hung

Pivoted window

Wall — Wood surround — Glass — Wall

Outside

Steel window

Mastic seal

Plan

exposure. Greater thicknesses are made for larger areas. These are used mainly for shop windows in place of the more costly plate glass.

Solar control glass, tinted bronze or green for reducing solar energy in hot weather, is useful in large glass areas, particularly south facing. Rolled translucent glass with a pattern on one side, flat on the other, used where vision obscuration is required.

Wired glass, with wire mesh embedded, is used where fire resistance is required. The transparent wired (Georgian) glass gives clear vision and the translucent wired cast glass obscured vision.

Glazing methods

Linseed oil putty is the traditional glazing material for wood windows. It is not suitable for metal windows, for which a special metal glazing putty is available. There are also proprietary multi-purpose putty materials for use with wood or metal frames.

Linseed oil putty should not be painted until it has started to harden, which generally means waiting about a fortnight. But it should be painted before it dries out; otherwise it will crack.

Before placing the glass in position the rebate into which it fits should be back puttied, applying the putty with thumb and finger. Smooth it slightly with the putty knife, then place the glass and press it gently all round. A few steel glazing sprigs should be tapped in each side, top and bottom to secure the glass. Puttying should then be completed with the knife (or a small trowel). The edges should be trimmed straight and the excess putty squeezed out at the back of the rebate cut straight and flush.

Double glazing

There are two types of double glazing. First, the fixing of a second pane of glass to an existing single glazed frame. Second, the sealed glazing unit (or insulating glass) which is manufactured by separating two sheets of glass to form an air gap and sealing the edges.

Most new windows for double glazing are fitted with insulating glass in a rebate deeper than is normal for single glazing. One type of insulating unit is made with the inside and outside glasses fused together at the edge to form a single unit. Two thicknesses are made, with air gap of 5 mm and 7 mm. The depth of the rebate should be not less than 11 mm for the 5 mm air space units and 13 mm for the 7 mm air space type. The units are made in standard sizes to fit modern standard frames. The manufacturers of double glazing units supply printed fixing instructions which should be carefully followed.

Sealed double glazing units have the air gap dehydrated in manufacture so that internal condensation (within the air gap) should not occur.

Double glazing by fixing a second sheet of glass in a light plastic or metal frame to an existing single glazed window reduces the tendency to condensation of moisture from the room atmosphere but cannot completely prevent it. If this form of double glazing is in a hinged or horizontal sliding frame it is an easy matter to open it and wipe off any condensed moisture.

Sound resistant double glazing must have an air space of not less than 100 mm (4 in) to be effective. The two sheets of glass must be fixed in a double frame, or a deep frame with inner and outer rebates. Special double casement windows are made for this purpose.

Doors

Doors for houses may be of wood, metal, or plastic.

Wood doors are of three distinct types; flush doors consisting of a wood core faced both sides either with plywood or hardboard; panelled doors consisting of framed vertical stiles and horizontal rails grooved to accommodate panels, and ledged boarded doors.

All types are made in softwood and hardwood; the latter are more costly though of superior quality. Softwood doors are for painting, whilst hardwood doors are for finishing with polish or a sealing varnish to enhance the natural colour and grain and also to provide an easily cleaned surface.

Fire resisting doors are made to comply with the Building Regulations for use where a house garage has a communicating door with the hall or other house space. These are flush doors with sheets of plasterboard or asbestos insulation board behind the facing sheets. For this purpose the door should be fitted with a self-closing fitting.

Doors to outbuildings are usually matchboarded, with boards grooved, tongued and vee jointed, nailed to horizontal ledges and braced with diagonal members. Such doors should be hung with the bottom of the brace on the hinged side so that the brace resists the tendency of the boards to sag.

Doors may have a glazed upper panel or a full length glazed panel, with or without glazing bars.

Exterior doors should have joints put together with a water resistant resin adhesive. Flush doors are made with water soluble adhesives for interior use and water resistant adhesives for exterior use—an important point when ordering.

Some of the door patterns available in softwood, hardwood, plastics and metal

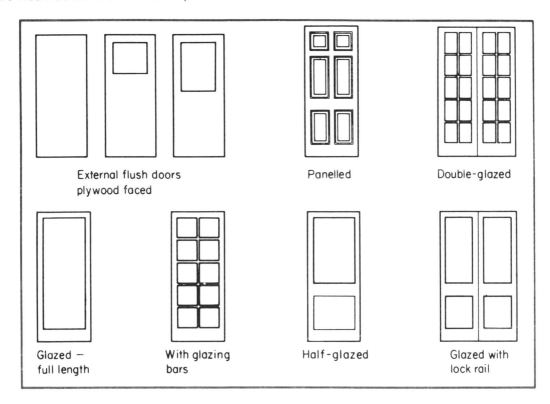

External flush doors plywood faced

Panelled

Double-glazed

Glazed — full length

With glazing bars

Half-glazed

Glazed with lock rail

Aluminium and plastics doors

Aluminium and steel doors are made for houses. Exterior doors of aluminium alloy, with a glazed panel, and complete with an aluminium frame incorporating draught-proof features, are finding favour, but they are costly.

Flush doors faced with plastic, white, coloured or imitation wood grained, are easy to clean and need no painting.

Sliding doors

Where free floor space is limited near a doorway, a sliding door is an advantage. Sliding door gear suitable for light house doors is supplied in packs by several manufacturers, with printed fixing instructions.

Similar gear is suitable for wardrobes. For small cupboard doors there are plastic channels with nylon runners which are easily fixed.

Patio doors and french windows

The traditional French window is inward opening, but most so called French windows in Britain are outward opening and are really glazed casement doors. They may be single or in pairs. If outward opening, metal hooks or friction stays should be fitted to hold them in the open position.

Patio doors, glazed full length and horizontal sliding, are now often preferred to side hung traditional casement doors. Most patio doors advertised are of aluminium alloy framing and track, but they can be of suitable hardwood, specially made. Most local joinery firms will make them to order and they can be hung with suitable sliding door gear.

The aluminium alloy sliding patio doors and windows are weather and draught-proof and need no maintenance other than

Sliding windows and patio doors can be easily adjusted for ventilation, they are draught proof and as they do not swing open they do not obstruct space

 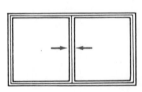 

Horizontal sliding aluminium windows

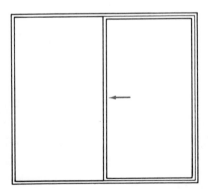 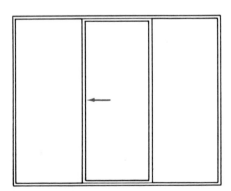

Aluminium patio door/windows

occasional cleaning with soapy water. The full length glass is usually of double glazed insulating units, though single glass doors are also made.

A disadvantage of any full length glazing, from a few inches above floor level upwards, is the risk of injury through accidental collision. It is possible to walk into the glass under the mistaken impression that the door is open. This risk can be diminished by fixing a strip of coloured adhesive tape (the type used for binding carpet and other materials) across the glass at a height of about 900 mm (3 ft) above the floor.

Safety glass, of the type used in car windscreens, has been suggested as the best way to reduce accidental injuries. Some firms supply patio doors fitted with this type of glass.

Door locks and bolts

Locks are of two main types. Mortise locks which are fixed into a mortise or slot cut in the stile of the door (with flush doors which have a hollow core, a lock block is included in manufacture so that a mortise can be cut). Rim locks which are fixed to the inside face of the door. Mortise locks are neater as they are concealed and also give greater security.

There is a wide variety of locks in addition to ordinary types and many have features which greatly improve the strength and resistance to breaking-in. Cylinder locks are fitted partly in a hole drilled through the door but they are essentially rim locks with the main case screwed to the inside and edge of the door.

Bolts are of two main kinds. Most are screwed to the inside face of the door, but there is a mortise type which is fixed into a slot cut in the door and this gives better security as well as a neater appearance.

Cupboards and built-ins

The leading joinery manufacturers stock a standard range of whitewood kitchen units—cupboards, sink units—and also full height cupboard fronts which can be used as door and frame fronts for built-in wardrobes and store cupboards. There is a range of sizes and types and as the cost is relatively low it is hardly worth while making a unit as a one off job, provided you only want plain whitewood for painting.

There are various proprietary ranges of such units in decorative hardwoods and plastic sheet fronts. These are more costly but have a superior finish, which needs little maintenance beyond cleaning.

Where built-ins are to be constructed in the house they can either be made as independent units to fit a given space or,

Using a spirit level-cum-plumb rule to test a vertical surface, preparing for a built-in wardrobe

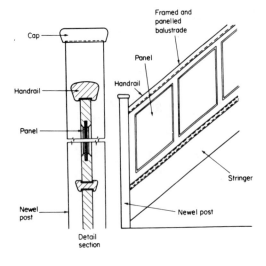

Detail section

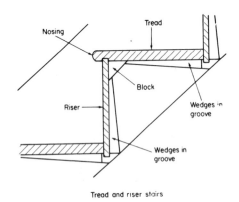

Tread and riser stairs

Detail of stair balustrade panelling, handrail and newel
post is shown on the left
The treads are supported at the ends in grooves cut in
the side stringers, the front of the treads are grooved to take the
riser

Below, a typical example of open riser stairs as standardised
by one manufacturer. The treads are supported on bracket
blocks set into the stringer bearers

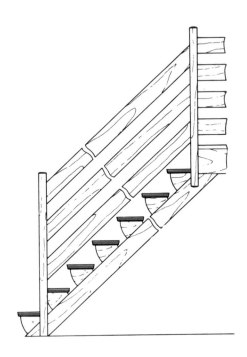

where there is an existing wall recess or corner, they can be built piece by piece, using the walls as part of the built-in unit.

Generally, frames 50 mm (2 in) x 38 mm (1½ in) are suitable, with halved joints glued together or plain butt joints secured with proprietary screw blocks (see page 175). Doors can be of blockboard, laminboard or veneered chipboard, cut from a single sheet. Hardboard or plywood on a thin frame can be used but the framing must be sheeted both sides to prevent warping. Alternatively, panelled doors with plywood panels in grooved framing can be used.

Care should be taken to keep all corners truly square. Where a unit is built into a wall recess it may be found that the walls are not perfectly plumb and square, so some packing may be needed.

Staircases

Staircases may be of softwood, hardwood or metal. There are three main types for houses: the tread and riser type with the steps supported at each end on a stringer (a strong board set at the angle of the stairs); the open riser type, with no riser but with a thicker tread to span between the stringers; the spiral type which is usually built around a central newel post.

The standard whitewood staircase made by leading joinery firms for small houses, to suit normal ground floor to ceiling height of 2.43 m (8 ft) plus an additional step formed by the landing, is a tread and riser type. The stringers and balustrades are supported top and bottom of the stairs by jointing to newel posts. Treads and risers are housed in grooves cut in the stringers and are glued and wedged, as illustrated.

The bottom step projects beyond the newel post and the exposed end is curved.

A staircase may be in one straight flight or in two shorter flights with an intermediate landing, turning through 90 degrees or 180 degrees. Where space is restricted winders or tapered steps may be introduced, but these must comply with Building Regulations regarding size and shape.

Open riser staircases are also produced by some joinery firms to their standard design. A typical example is illustrated. They are usually made of hardwood with each tread supported on brackets joined to stout carriage timbers (instead of stringers).

The design of staircases is subject to the requirements of the Building Regulations. The most important are summarised as follows. These are for domestic stairs in a single dwelling.

The pitch angle of the stairs is not more than 42 degrees to the horizontal.

The headroom is not less than 2 m (6 ft 6 in) measured vertically above the pitch line, with a clearance of not less than 1.5 m (5 ft) measured at right angles to the pitch line.

The rise of a step is not more than 220 mm (8½ in); and the going of a step, measured on plan from the nosing of its tread and the nosing of the tread next above it, is not less than 220 mm (8½ in). Obviously you cannot have both the same or the pitch angle would be 45 degrees, whereas the permitted limit is 42 degrees.

In practice a rise of 200 mm (8 in) with a tread of 220 mm (8½ in) is suitable.

With open riser stairs the nosing of the tread of one step must overlap on plan the back edge of the tread of the step below it by not less than 16 mm ($^5/_8$ in).

The stairway must be guarded on each side either by a wall, a secure balustrade, screen or railing not less than 840 mm (2 ft 9 in) measured vertically above the pitch line. For a landing this height must be not less than 900 mm (2 ft 11½ in).

Wood trim and mouldings

Skirtings, architraves or mouldings for trimming doorways or windows, cover strips, picture rails, and small mouldings are called wood trim. They are stocked in a range of patterns and sizes.

Wood trim, such as architraves and small mouldings, is usually fixed to wood backing with small oval or lost head nails. These are punched down and stopped with a filler, then rubbed smooth so that the head is concealed when the work is painted.

Where mouldings or wood strips are fixed direct to block or brick walls, hardened masonry nails or screws and wallplugs may be used.

Skirtings on plastered walls should be supported at the back with wood grounds of the plaster thickness which can be fixed to the wall with masonry nails. The skirting boards can then be nailed to the grounds.

A shrinkage gap may develop between the bottom of a skirting board and a boarded floor. This can be covered with a small quadrant (quarter round) moulding nailed to the floor only—not to the skirting. This leaves it free to move slightly with any further shrinkage.

Chapter 19
Garage doors, fences and gates

After 20 years or so, a close-boarded fence will probably have to be replaced or, at the least, some boards and the arris rails may need renewing. This chapter includes information on close-boarded fences, palings and chain-link fences together with notes on types of post and construction and hanging of gates.

However, we will first start with some brief notes on garage doors.

Garage doors

Garage doors are of two distinct types—wood doors side hung on strap hinges and up-and-over doors of wood, metal or glass fibre reinforced plastic. In addition there are horizontal sliding and folding doors but these are not now much used for domestic garages. Generally, the up-and-over doors are preferred.

Standard wood doors for garages are of two types—boarded on ledged and braced framing, and framed and panelled. They are made in a standard width of 2.134 m (7 ft) and two heights, 2.134 m (7 ft) and 1.981 m (6 ft 6 in). The doors may be completely boarded or panelled or the upper third may be framed and glazed.

Suitable wood frames are supplied to match, of 75 mm x 100 mm (3 in x 4 in) softwood. The feet are fitted with metal dowels for building into the concrete floor.

Up-and-over doors are usually of galvanised steel or aluminium alloy but also of wood and glass-fibre plastic. There are several proprietary types and manufacturers catalogues should be consulted. If possible a visit should be made to the nearest stockist where the doors can be demonstrated. Some doors are spring balanced and some weight balanced. There is a range of widths for single or double car garages. Wider doors are rather heavy and need a strong pull to open and push to close. For a double car garage there is something to be said in favour of two separate single doors with a centre pier or column.

The gear for up-and-over doors is fixed to the side jambs and head of the opening in some cases and to the jamb and roof joists in others. So the type should be chosen to suit the garage construction.

Up-and-over doors of glass fibre reinforced plastic are made in panelled patterns. The mechanism is similar to the metal doors of this type. The material is strong and durable—similar to the plastic material used for moulded boats—and does not need painting.

Door frames

Frames for exterior doors are rebated inside for inward opening and outside for outward opening. Some are made with a sill which may incorporate a steel weather bar, but proprietary metal or plastic weather-tight thresholds are better.

The frame is usually of softwood but hardwood should be used with a hardwood or an aluminium alloy door. The fixing is by ties or lugs screwed to the sides and

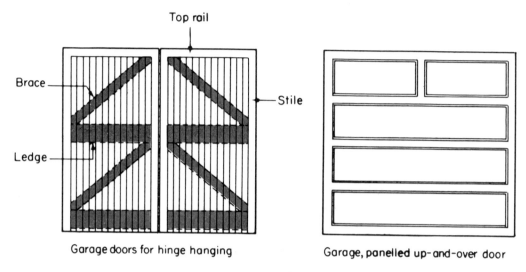

Garage doors for hinge hanging

Garage, panelled up-and-over door

Garage doors are made in various patterns and materials—in wood, metal and plastics. The up-and-over type is generally preferred

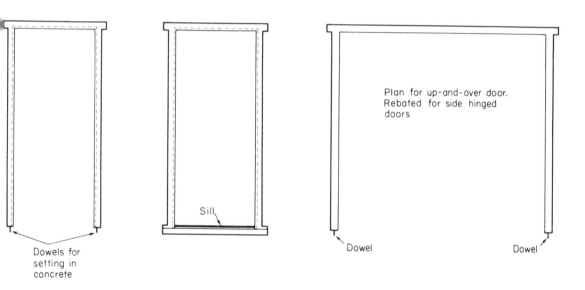

Wood door frames are rebated for side hinged doors. Draught strip material can be fixed to the rebate and a weatherproof threshold fixed to the sill. Wood sills should be of hardwood

built into the wall jambs. If the frame has no sill the feet are dowelled into the concrete or step.

Interior doors are usually hung to a lining on which a thin strip of wood is nailed to form a door stop. In light partitions rebated frames may be used or linings fixed to timber partition studs (uprights)

Side hung doors may be hung with butt hinges; 100 mm (4 in) for exterior doors, 75 mm (3 in) for interior doors. Each hinge leaf is sunk into the door or frame and fixed with countersunk screws. But there is

Feather edge boards

Feather edge
close boarding

Plan

3"x 3" arris rail

Cap

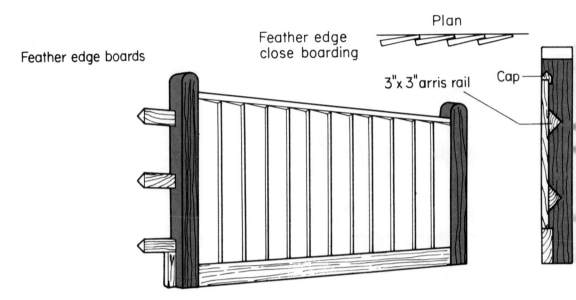

Boarded fence. The feather edged boards overlap. Rails can be triangular as shown, or rectangular. The ground board keeps the vertical boarding clear of the ground and helps preservation

a type for which cutting into the door or frame is not required.

Rising hinges can be used to lift the door as it opens and so to clear an adjoining floor covering.

Fences

Fences may be ornamental or protective, or both. If you want to keep out dogs and cats you need either close boarding or close chain link. The fence should be fairly high to prevent animals jumping over it. If you want to keep out intruders you need a high strong fence, but it need not be close boarded. A fence of either palings, rails or strong chain link mesh is perhaps better than close boarding which conceals the intruder.

Under Planning Regulations the height of front fences—those in front of the building line—is limited to 1.2 m (4 ft) and to 2.1 m (7 ft) for side and rear fences. In order to make the rear of the premises difficult for intruders to enter you must have a high fence and side gate to close the gaps at the side or sides of a semi-detached or detached house. If you feel there are special reasons why you should be allowed to have higher fences than mentioned above you can apply for planning permission.

There is a very wide range of materials, patterns and systems of fencing and gates, in timber, steel, plastic and pre-cast concrete.

Post and wire fences are suitable if you intend growing a hedge. Wired cleft chestnut fences give better protection against animals.

Interwoven softwood slat fences in panels for fixing between posts are cheaper than boarded fences but less durable. They are rather easily damaged and then tend to go to pieces.

A better type of panelled fence is that of thin larch weatherboarding on a light framing. Larch has good resistance to decay. These panels are prefabricated, like the interwoven type, and are fixed between posts simply by nailing.

Boarded fencing of the traditional type consists of posts, rails and vertical boards, which are feather edged for nailing to the rails. The fencing can be sawn to length from suitable timber or bought in kit form.

ready for erection. The boards are fixed to overlap slightly.

Durability is an important factor in fencing, so it is worth some extra cost to choose decay resistant timbers—oak, larch or Western red cedar.

If a softwood—a fir or pine wood—is used, it must be obtained pressure impregnated with preservative if it is to last any length of time. Brush treatment with a preservative is effective for a year or two but must be renewed regularly to prevent decay.

Protection

The most vulnerable parts of a timber fence are those in or close to the ground. Post stumps especially need protection. Softwood posts should have a few holes drilled diagonally from a few inches above ground level downwards. These should be filled with preservative, using a funnel, and refilled when the first dose has soaked into the timber. The holes can then be plugged with cork or piece of wood. The treatment can be renewed every few years.

Vertical boarding should not be allowed to touch the ground. A horizontal ground board should be fixed to the posts, nailing it to wood fillets at the post sides. The vertical boarding then terminates on top of the ground board. If the ground board rots it can easily be removed and replaced with new.

Posts

Pre-cast concrete posts are the best for durability. They can be obtained slotted to take timber rails. Short concrete stumps are also available for repairs to decayed timber posts. The decayed stump is sawn off above ground and holes drilled higher up so that the concrete stump can be bolted to the timber.

In soft ground posts should be concreted into the ground, with about 12 mm (6 in) of concrete all round and underneath, and the top of the concrete brought above ground and finished by trowelling to an outward slope. A 1:2:4 cement-sand-ballast mix is quite strong enough.

In strong ground, such as sandy gravel, the posts can be wedged in at the bottom with a few bricks and the hole then filled with the soil, well rammed.

High boarded fences should have extra support against strong winds by fixing diagonal struts to every second or third post.

A saddleback capping on top of the boards is advisable to protect them from rain and also to add to appearance. The wood posts, too, should be capped, either with bevelled wood caps or metal (lead, zinc, aluminium). These caps should be cut at the corners and turned down about 25 mm (1 in) and nailed along the edges with rustless nails.

All nails used in fencing should be galvanised steel or, better still, aluminium alloy.

Horizontal boarding can be used instead of vertical and if thick enough—not less than 16 mm ($^5/_8$ in)—horizontal rails are not needed. The boards can be nailed to wood fillets on the sides of the posts. Alternatively the boards can be nailed on the face of the posts but it is then desirable to have boards long enough to span two bays, with the ends staggered on alternate posts.

Palings

Rail and pale fences look good and are particularly suitable for front boundary

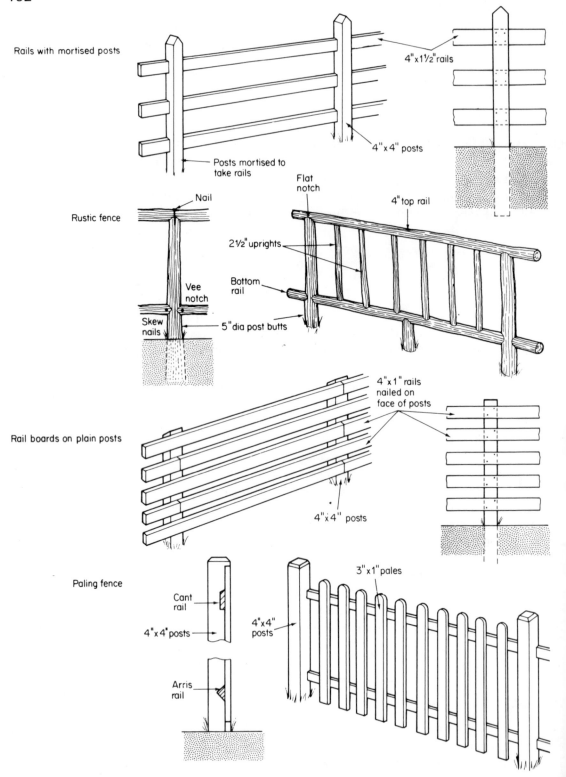

Rails with mortised posts

4"x1½"rails

4"x4" posts

Posts mortised to take rails

Rustic fence

Nail

Vee notch

Skew nails

5"dia post butts

Flat notch

4" top rail

2½" uprights

Bottom rail

Rail boards on plain posts

4"x1" rails nailed on face of posts

4"x4" posts

Paling fence

Cant rail

4"x4" posts

Arris rail

3"x1" pales

4"x4" posts

Fences of open types with railings and palings. Posts should preferably be of oak, or larch. If rustic material is used the bark should be stripped

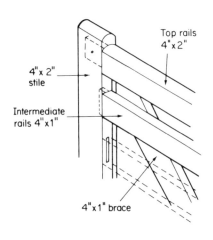

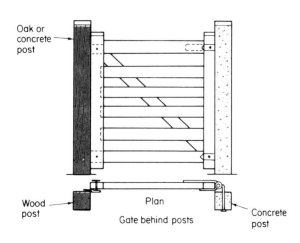

A typical garden gate of wood—preferably of hardwood. The rails are tenoned into the vertical stiles. Posts preferably of oak or pre-cast concrete

encing, using either sawn timber treated with preservative or planed and painted wood. Several types are available.

The pales should be 75 mm x 18 mm (3 in x ¾ in), with 75 mm (3 in) spaces between. With posts spaced at 2 m (6 ft 6 in) centres the rails can be 100 mm x 50 mm (4 in x 2 in) fixed through mortise slots cut in the posts.

Post and rail fence

This is a rural type fence, usually of oak or elm. Posts are usually 100 mm x 100 mm (4 in x 4 in) with 100 mm x 50 mm (4 in x 2 in) rails fixed through mortise slots in the posts.

Fencing kits, as already mentioned, are offered by several firms. These include some special types, such as louvred fences in which boards are fixed, either vertically or horizontally at 45 degrees. This forms a screen which allows air to pass through but obstructs vision.

Metal railings

There are many types of metal railings from the severely practical chain link mesh, attached to posts of pre-cast reinforced concrete or of tubular steel, to ornamental fencing of straight and curved mild steel bars and rods.

Ornamental metal fences are best set on a low brick or block wall. The fences are supplied in sections with lugs for building into the supporting wall and also at the sides for building into piers.

Plastics fencing

Sectional fencing is made in durable plastic material, with posts and rails of box or hollow section. They are rot proof and do not need decorating.

With reasonable treatment this type of fence may be expected to last well, but any damage may be difficult to repair.

Gates

Gates may be of either wood or metal. The wood types include close-boarded with feather edged boards overlapping. Rail and pale with open spaces between the pales and various ornamental patterns. The gates are framed with mortise and tenon joints.

The joints should be put together either in thick gloss paint or a water resistant adhesive, and the tenons should be secured with pegs. A simple type of gate is illustrated on page 193.

Gates of rot resistant woods—oak, larch, Western red cedar, elm—or one of the more durable imported hardwoods, should be treated with a preservative of suitable colour to maintain the appearance as well as to give extra protection.

Metal gates are made in a wide variety. Manufacturers issue illustrated catalogues and fixing instructions.

Strong posts, fixed into the ground by concreting, are essential to prevent the post on the hanging side from moving by the pull of the gate. Oak or other durable hardwood or concrete posts 150 mm x 150 mm (6 in x 6 in) is recommended.

Brick or block piers can be used instead of posts. They should be at least a brick and-half square for single gates and two brick square for double gates.

Care should be taken to set out a straight line of fencing by stretching a string line end to end. Intermediate post positions should be marked with pegs. Rail ends should meet at posts.

On sloping ground the fence sections should be stepped and each section levelled

Gate posts should be positioned to give the correct clearances for hinges and fastener.

Chapter 20

Small timber buildings

Small timber sheds, home workshops, conservatories, verandahs and porches are made by many firms in prefabricated sections for erection on a concrete or paved base/foundation. They are simple to erect, but if you prefer to build from basic materials there is nothing difficult about the construction. Follow the jointing methods described in Chapters 17 and 18.

Constructing a shed/workshop

The design for a shed or workshop (which could have a variety of uses) illustrated is 2.35 m (7 ft 9 in) wide over the frames. It may be of any reasonable length but for most purposes 3 m (10 ft) will be suitable.

The construction is substantial, of timber, preferably planed, with horizontal shiplap boards on 50 mm x 50 mm (2 in x 2 in) upright studs and horizontal rails with 75 mm x 38 mm (3 in x 1½ in) rafters and 75 mm x 50 mm (3 in x 2 in) sill plates and corner posts.

A standard wood casement window and a ledged, braced and boarded door can be

Shed/workshop/playroom/summer house. The construction is fairly simple. Weather boards or asbestos-cement sheets for exterior cladding. Any suitable standard window and door can be used (see page 196 for plan)

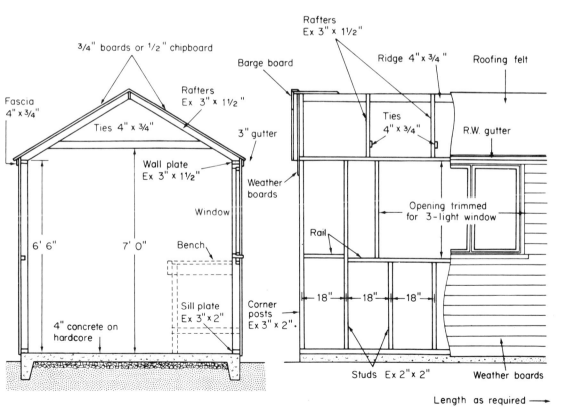

Cross section

Side

195

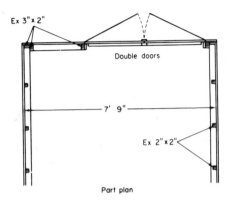

Ex 3" x 2"

Double doors

7' 9"

Ex 2" x 2"

Part plan

The shed/workshop shown in the previous illustration in section and elevation is here in part plan. Sides and front and back can be made in sections. See page 172 for simple joints

nailed to the frames. Any suitable size and pattern of window and door can be selected. It is advisable to coat the sides of the window and door frames with thick gloss paint shortly before fixing them. This will seal the junction and prevent interior decay.

The base floor can be of concrete 100 mm (4 in) thick on a level bed of hardcore, with the perimeter trenched down below ground level. The overall size of the base should be the same as that of the bare framing, so that the lower edge of the boards will stand clear of the concrete base and allow rainwater to run off.

The framing consists of studs (uprights) and rails (horizontals). You can make halved joints where they meet, but nailing with 50 mm (2 in) nails will stiffen the whole structure. The boards should be 12 mm (½ in) rebated shiplap section for horizontal fixing. For vertical fixing, tongued and grooved vee jointed section of the same thickness can be used.

An alternative to boards of natural wood is tempered hardboard (see page 171); ordinary hardboard is not suitable. Tempered hardboard is denser and better resistant to damp but it must be protected by painting. Alternatively, you can use flat asbestos-cement sheets, but these are brittle and will not stand hard knocks.

The roof can be boarded with sawn boards 12 mm (½ in) thick or with 19 mm (¾ in) chipboard. This should be covered with a good quality mineral-surfaced bituminous roofing felt.

A fascia board should be nailed all along each end of the roof and a plastic rainwater gutter and downpipe fixed along the front. The pipe can terminate above a rainwater butt or be connected to an underground pitch fibre pipe leading into a soak-away sump (a hole in the ground filled with rubble).

The boarding can be painted—primer, undercoat and gloss coat. Alternatively, a preservative can be brushed on, with a renewal coat every two or three years.

To prevent damp rising through the concrete base-floor, a layer of thick polythene should be laid over the hardcore before placing the concrete. The timber bottom rail of the framing should be given two coats of bitumen paint or emulsion before fixing as this will inevitably be in a damp position in wet weather.

A structure of this kind makes a substantial shed for storage, a home workshop, a playroom, or, with a pair of casement doors, a summer house.

If you want it to be used in winter with some form of heating it should be insulated. The simplest way to do this is to back the boarding between the frames with 12 mm (½ in) expanded polystyrene sheets. Alternatively, nail foil-backed plasterboard sheets on to the inside face of the frame.

Building a conservatory

A conservatory can be added to a house or bungalow without interfering much with the existing structure. There are many prefabricated types advertised and these are fairly simple to erect on a prepared concrete base-floor. If you prefer to build from basic

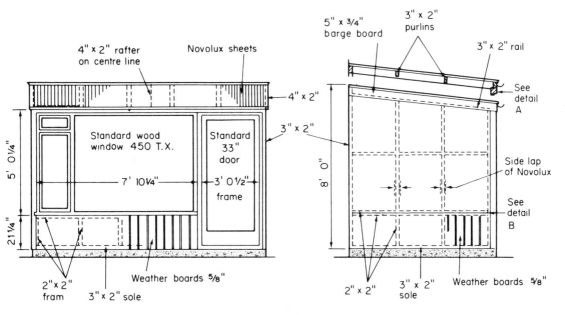

A conservatory using a large standard window, door and frame for the front with corrugated plastic sheeting on a wood frame for the sides. (Where one side is close to a boundary it must be of brickwork or blockwork to comply with Building Regulations)

materials, the design illustrated is suitable. The construction is simplified by making use of a standard wood window and casement door.

The plinth wall can be of 75 mm x 50 mm (3 in x 2 in) planed softwood framing, with external horizontal shiplap or vertical tongued and grooved boarding, as described for the shed-workshop. The inside of this framing can be lined with foil-backed plasterboard.

The plinth frame should be bolted down to the concrete base/floor, which should be 100 mm (4 in) thick.

Anchor bolts are best but coach bolts are suitable if a large washer is placed against the round head so that it gives a good hold in the concrete. The bolts can be cast into the concrete at intervals of about 600 mm (2 ft), with the bottom plate drilled to correspond.

The finished floor should be at least 100 mm (4 in) above the ground level. The surface soil should be stripped first and a bed of hardcore levelled and consolidated, then blinded with sand to provide a smooth surface for a dampproof membrane of thick polythene.

The underside of the frame plate should be given two coats of bituminous paint before fixing. Alternatively, a strip of bituminous felt can be laid as a dampproof course.

The front of the conservatory consists of a standard wood casement window (a choice can be made of the many patterns and sizes available), with a glazed door and frame placed against the frame and screwed to it.

The sides of the structure may be framed and clad with Novolux corrugated sheets, or with weather boarding.

Corner posts are 75 mm x 50 mm (3 in x 2 in) nominal, but planed down to the same depth as the window and door frames. A door strip can be nailed to the posts each side of the door to form a rebated frame. Alternatively, a standard door frame can be used, extending it at the top to form a fixed light over the doorway.

The roof can be framed with purlins and supporting rafters to be covered with corrugated translucent plastic sheets. The

standard sheets with 75 mm (3 in) corrugations, such as Novolux, can be fixed with
the drive screws and plastic washers to
purlins spaced up to 900 mm (3 ft) centres.
The cheaper plastic sheets with small
corrugations are not recommended for
permanent roofing.

The window frame can be screwed to the
posts and the sills screwed to the timber
plinth. (A brick or block plinth wall can be
built if preferred; in this case the window
frames should be secured to the wall with
anchor bolts set in cement mortar.)

A boarded and felted roof, similar to
that described for the shed-workshop, with
the addition of a plasterboard or insulating
board ceiling, will give much better thermal
insulation. If the conservatory is mainly for
plants it should be remembered that this
type of roof will, of course, reduce the
daylight.

Verandahs

A verandah may be open or enclosed. The
open type consists of a flat or lean-to
roof supported on posts. It may extend the
full width of the rear wall of the house or
bungalow. Where a corner space exists
between the back of the garage and the
house, it may cover the corner and so give
shelter between the rear garage door and
the kitchen door.

The construction is mainly similar to the
conservatory described above.

The posts for an open verandah should
be secured to the concrete foundation (or,
in the case of a verandah on a raised terrace,
to the brick retaining wall) by a galvanised
steel or a copper dowel inserted in the foot
of the post and set in a concrete base.

To prevent rot attacking the foot of the
post the end grain should be coated with
two coats gloss or bituminous paint—one

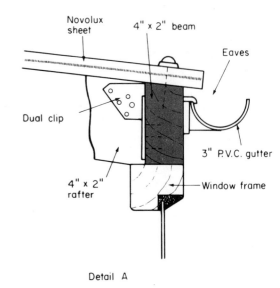

Detail A

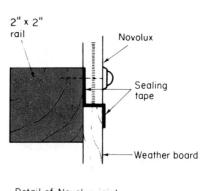

Detail of Novolux joint
to timber

Detail B

Detail of fixings for the Novolux sheeting to roof and side
for the conservatory shown in the illustration on page 19.

coat before the dowel is fixed and anothe
after, including the dowel.

The raised base or stool should be of
fine concrete with small grit aggregate of
a stiff mix. It can be built up in layers,
allowing the inner layer to partly set and
then applying the final layer. This can be
done after the post has been erected and
temporarily supported with struts.

The front beam can then be bolted to

the post heads. The roof frame can be constructed with purlins supported on main rafters. In the section shown in the diagram the main rafters are supported against the house wall on a timber plate fixed to the wall with expanding shell bolts (Rawlbolts). The front ends are cut to fit over the front beam and then skew nailed.

Small section fillets are screwed to the sides of the rafters and the purlin ends are cut to fit over these. Alternatively, metal fastening plates can be used.

With purlins at not more than 900 mm (3 ft) centres the roof can be covered with corrugated sheets—the large 75 mm (3 in) profile, as described for the conservatory.

Chapter 21
Plastering and rendering

The term plastering is confined to interior work on walls and ceilings. Rendering is the usual term describing external cement mixes applied as a finish to walls of common bricks or blocks.

Plastering is not an easy craft for a beginner and for most purposes it is advisable to line walls and ceilings with a dry finish—plasterboard or other wallboard. These are briefly described in Chapter 17.

Plastering on walls

Modern plasters are produced from gypsum. There are several types, from plaster of Paris which sets within a minute or so and is useless except for spot repairs, to the general purpose gypsum plasters which are retarded in setting to give you time to apply and finish the surface.

For most purposes two-coat plastering on brick or block walls is sufficient, though a better finish is obtainable with three coats, especially if the wall has a very irregular surface. Any depressions in the wall can be filled with a mix of cement-lime-sand in the proportions of 1:2:9. A strong cement mix is not suitable for this as it would shrink and crack.

The equipment needed consists of a mixing board about 1 m (3 ft 3 in) square, a clean bucket, a trestle or table, a plumb line and bob, a straightedge batten 2 m (7 ft)

long, and a hawk. The latter is a piece of board about 250 mm (10 in) square with a handle underneath. You can carry a small supply of plaster on it, holding the hawk in one hand while you apply the plaster with the other.

Plaster is applied with a rectangular steel or aluminium plastering trowel about 225 mm × 100 mm (9 in × 4 in).

For small jobs it is advisable to buy general purpose plaster, but ask for a copy of the manufacturer's printed instructions. The plaster must be kept dry while stored.

Mixing

Place the dry plaster powder on a board about 1 m (3 ft) square, scoop a hollow in the middle of the heap and apply water through the rose of a watering can, while a helper mixes it with a trowel.

Take up some plaster on the hawk, tilt it towards you as you work so that you can take it up a trowelfull at a time.

Start plastering at the bottom of the wall and sweep it upwards with the trowel, to a thickness of about 12 mm (½ in) for the undercoat. The surface should be left fairly straight but not perfectly smoothed.

On a wall you should first nail wood screeding battens of 1.8 m (6 ft), plumbing them vertically up the wall. Alternatively, you can form the screeds in plaster, using a straightedge to true the surface.

Whichever method is used, when the plaster has been applied between the screeds, and whilst it is still soft, the straightedge must be moved over the screeds to level off the plaster. When this has nearly set the screed battens (if you used these) can be removed and the gaps made good with plaster.

Before the undercoat sets, but has firmed, it must be scratched to form a good key for the finishing coat. A scratcher can be made with a short length of wood batten, with a handle nailed to one side, and six 2 in nails driven through the batten piece. Scratch the surface of the plaster, but not deeply.

When the undercoat has set and dried, the finishing coat can be applied with the trowel, starting at the bottom and sweeping upwards. It should finish about 2 mm thick. The surface should be ironed smooth but this must be done before final setting of the plaster.

Ceilings

The traditional method of lathing ceiling joists was to nail wood laths with small gaps between to the joints. This method is now obsolete.

Gypsum lathboard—a type of plasterboard—is nailed on with 38 mm (1½ in) rustless nails, leaving a gap between the sides of the boards. A strip of scrim fabric should be set in plaster at the angle between the wall and the lathboard, as reinforcement to prevent cracking at this point.

It will be understood that the ceilings should be done before the wall plastering and the scrim set at the corner before the ceiling undercoat is applied.

Plastering, especially on ceilings, is hard, as well as skilled, work. Try your hand on a small area before tackling a full-size room.

Thermal insulation of ceilings

For ceilings under the roof of a bungalow or the top rooms of a house, a high degree of thermal insulation is required. At least 76 mm (3 in) of glass fibre quilting is required, or other material with equivalent thermal insulation. Official regulations may increase this thickness in the near future. Experts advise 100 mm (4 in) at least, but in Northern Europe at least 177 mm (7 in) is standard.

There are two types of glass fibre and mineral wool, one 450 mm (18 in) wide, in rolls, for placing between ceiling joists; the other 1.8 m (6 ft) blanket material for draping over the joists.

Mineral wool loose fill, supplied in bags, can be poured into the space between the joists.

External rendering

Renderings of cement mixes on external walls should be of moderate strength or, for sheltered positions, of rather low strength. Very strong mixes, such as 1 cement to 3 sand by volume, are liable to shrink and crack on large areas.

For ordinary brickwork or blockwork a mix of 1 cement, 1 hydrated powder lime and 5 to 6 parts washed sand is suitable. The wall surface should be clean and, if smooth, the joints should be raked out and smooth faced blocks should be punched or hacked to afford a key for the rendering.

Although one-coat rendering may suffice, it is liable to allow the joint lines to show through. Two-coat work which consists of an undercoat 12 mm (½ in) thick and a finishing coat 7 mm to 9 mm (average ¼ in or a little more) is advisable.

The finish should be scraped with the edge of the trowel or textured by dabbing with a coarse cloth or by using a wood comb or one of the special tools made for the purpose.

A smoothly trowelled finish is undesirable as it tends to show fine crazing or cracks.

Roughcast and pebbledash

Roughcast finish consists of a wet mix of the same proportion as the undercoat with the addition of sand and crushed stone or gravel, about 7 mm to 12 mm, (average about $\frac{3}{8}$ in). It is thrown on with a scoop and makes a durable finish.

Pebbledash consists of small pebbles or crushed stone, graded in sizes as for rough-cast, but thrown on dry to be embedded in the undercoat while this is still soft. It is advisable to add pressure with a trowel or wood block to make sure of good adhesion. This makes a very durable finish which sheds rainwater easily.

Special coloured mixes are obtainable for application with a hand machine—the Tyrolean finish is one. This throws the wet mix on by turning a handle.

Section 3

Home Plumbing

Acknowledgements

I gratefully acknowledge the help and encouragement that I have received in the preparation of this book from the following firms and organisations and also from my friend and colleague, Charles Burley, who read through the typescript in the light of his 45 years practical experience in the building trade.

Armitage Shanks Ltd., Armitage
Barking Brassware Co Ltd., Barking
Conex Sanbra Ltd., Tipton
Deltaflow Ltd., Crawley
Do-it-yourself Editorial Staff
The Electricity Council
Fordham Pressings Ltd.,
    Wolverhampton
Glynwed, Bathroom and Kitchen
    Products Ltd., Long Eaton
Ideal Standard Ltd., Hull
IMI Range Ltd., Stalybridge
Ingol Precast Ltd., Preston
Kay & Co Ltd., Bolton
Key Terrain Ltd., Maidstone
Marley Extrusions Ltd., Lenham
Osma Plastics Ltd., Hayes
Peglers Ltd., Doncaster
Rokcrete Ltd., Clacton-on-sea
Sofnol Ltd., Thaxted
Twyfords Ltd., Stoke-on-Trent
Walker Crossweller Ltd., Cheltenham
Wednesbury Tubes Ltd., Bilston

Note on metrication

The progress of metrication has not, at the time of writing, reached completion as far as plumbing equipment is concerned.

I suspect that, for many years after this process has been completed, a great many British householders—and plumbers—will continue to *think* in terms of feet, inches and gallons rather than in terms of metres, millimetres and litres.

Because of this I have, throughout this section, attempted to supply both metric and imperial measurements where both seemed to be of value. The figure given in brackets, whether metric or imperial is the one that at the time of writing seemed to me to be of lesser importance.

It should be noted that the metric *equivalent* is not necessarily a straight translation of the imperial value. For instance the 15mm metric copper tube is the equivalent of the ½ in imperial copper tube—but 15mm does not equal ½ in. The reason for this apparent disparity is that the imperial measurement is of the internal diameter of the tube, the metric measurement is of the external diameter.

Ernest Hall

Introduction to Section 3

The scope of home plumbing

Plumbing has not quite the same meaning for the tradesman plumber as it has for the householder. To the man in the trade it means the ability to work skilfully in lead, zinc and copper. It means knowledge and experience of solders and fluxes, of stocks and dies, tank shears and Stillson wrenches and pipe bending machines.

To the householder, for whom this section is intended, *plumbing* really means his domestic water services. It means the hot and cold water taps, the hot water system, the sink, the wash basin and the bath. It means the lavatory and the underground drains. The householder's interest in plumbing begins with the service pipe bringing water into his home from the main. It ends with the final length of drain connecting the the manhole inside his front garden with the public sewer.

It is this difference in outlook that makes the tradesman plumber suspicious of the

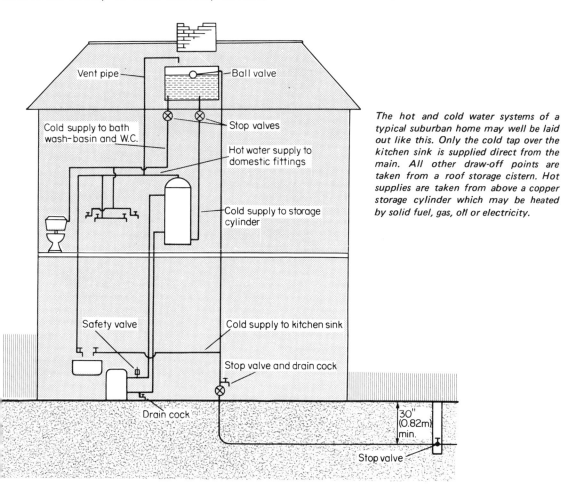

The hot and cold water systems of a typical suburban home may well be laid out like this. Only the cold tap over the kitchen sink is supplied direct from the main. All other draw-off points are taken from a roof storage cistern. Hot supplies are taken from above a copper storage cylinder which may be heated by solid fuel, gas, oil or electricity.

Vent pipe

Ball valve

Cold supply to bath wash-basin and W.C.

Stop valves

Hot water supply to domestic fittings

Cold supply to storage cylinder

Safety valve

Cold supply to kitchen sink

Stop valve and drain cock

Drain cock

30" (0.82m) min.

Stop valve

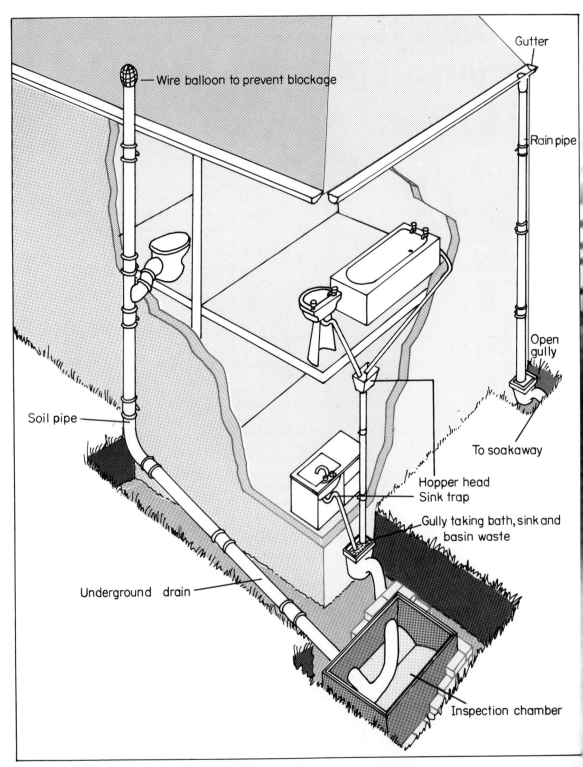

Gutter

Wire balloon to prevent blockage

Rain pipe

Open gully

Soil pipe

To soakaway

Hopper head
Sink trap

Gully taking bath, sink and
basin waste

Underground drain

Inspection chamber

A house built over a decade ago will probably have a 'two pipe' drainage system. 'Soil fittings' w.c.s and urinals—were connected directly to the drain via a main soil and vent pipe. 'Waste fittings'—baths, basins, bidets and sinks—discharged over trapped yard gullies.

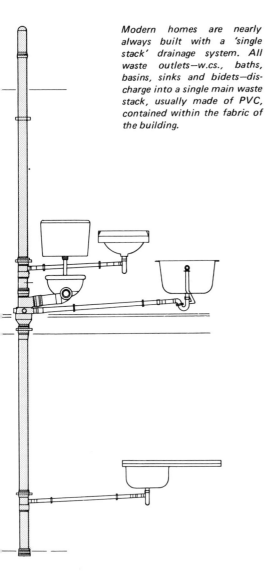

Modern homes are nearly always built with a 'single stack' drainage system. All waste outlets—w.cs., baths, basins, sinks and bidets—discharge into a single main waste stack, usually made of PVC, contained within the fabric of the building.

Over a decade of replying to plumbing queries sent in to the readers' problems service of Do-it-Yourself magazine; has taught me that intelligent and determined householders can do far more than simply carry out emergency repairs. Readers have written to tell me how, using the materials and techniques now available to the handyman, they have converted their lavatory suites from high to low level, have renewed baths, sinks and wash basins and have installed complete hot water and central heating systems. For d.i.y. enthusiasts planning projects of this kind, this section will prove to be of value.

I hope too, that it will also interest the householder who is unlikely to attempt on his own accord anything more ambitious than curing a dripping tap or overflow pipe; the man who would like to stop the ball-valve of his cold water storage tank making *quite* so much noise in the middle of the night, or who wishes that he had known what was involved when the plumber shook his head solemnly and said, 'you'll really have to have an indirect system, sir'.

I would like to prove to him that his plumbing system need not be the noisy, metallic monster of his imagination, threatening simultaneously to engulf his possessions in scalding—or icy—water, and his family in debt.

Finally, as a former local authority Public Health Inspector and Housing Manager, I hope that this section may be of some value to trainees in these and similar professions who need to be thoroughly familiar with domestic plumbing and drainage but who do not need to acquire many of the professional plumber's practical skills.

An efficient, unobtrusive plumbing system is the mark of a really comfortable home. This section will tell you how your plumbing system measures up to modern standards, and how easy it would be to bring it up to date.

do-it-yourself enthusiast. How can a householder—a bank or insurance official, a civil servant, a doctor or a lawyer—possibly acquire, in his spare time, skills to which the tradesman has devoted a life's work?

The householder neither wants, nor needs, to acquire these skills. He does want to know how his domestic plumbing system works and how to protect it from frost and corrosion, how to identify faults and how to carry out emergency repairs. How many professional plumbers welcome an urgent call to clear a sink waste pipe or to renew the washer on a tap?

Chapter 22

Cold water services and the cold water storage cistern

Home plumbing begins with the service pipe bringing water into the home from the main. The householder's responsibility for this pipe extends from the Water Authority's stop-cock which will be in a purpose-made pit in the footpath or roadway. This will probably have a specially shaped shank which can be turned only by means of one of the Water Authority's turn-keys.

Pre 1939 the service pipe would have been of lead. In a more recently built home it will be of 15 mm (½ in) copper tubing or, just possibly, of polythene tubing. It must be at least 0.82 m (2 ft 6 in) below the surface of the ground and, in order to permit any air in the pipe to escape, it should rise slightly towards the house.

It is very important, as a frost precaution, that the minimum depth of 0.82 m is maintained throughout the length of the pipe. It sometimes happens that an enthusiastic landscape gardener creates a sunken garden above the service pipe, reducing its effective depth by half. This could be disastrous during a period of severe frost.

Where the service pipe is taken through the foundations of the house it should be threaded through a length of drain pipe to protect it from being crushed as a result of any slight settlement that may take place. The kitchen floor, through which the pipe will rise into the house, is most likely to be of solid construction. If the service pipe has to enter the house through the open under-floor space of a boarded floor, it should be very carefully lagged against frost.

One way to do this is to take it up through the centre of a 100 mm (4 in) or 150 mm (6 in) drain pipe and to fill the space between the service pipe and the sides of the drain pipe with vermiculite chips.

The service pipe—now often called the 'rising main'—should rise into the house against an internal wall in the kitchen. Immediately above the floor should be the householder's own stop-cock with, just above it, a drain-cock.

These two fittings enable the water supply to the house to be cut off and the rising main drained when required. You should make sure that every member of the household knows where this stop-cock is situated

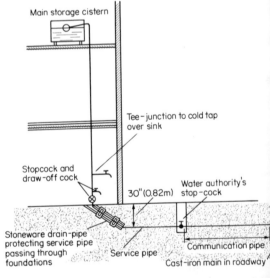

As a frost precaution the service pipe bringing water into the home from the water authority's main must be at least 0.82 mm (2 ft 6 in) below ground level throughout its length. It should always be taken up to the main storage cistern against an internal wall of the house.

Where the service pipe or 'rising main' enters the house through a hollow boarded floor, special precautions are necessary to protect it from icy underfloor draughts. It is best threaded through a 150 mm (6 in) stoneware drain pipe packed with vermiculite chips or similar insulating material.

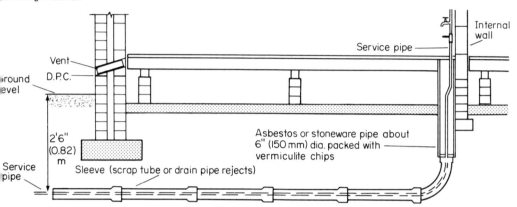

nd how to use it. In an emergency—a burst pipe, a leaking cold water storage tank or a jammed ball valve—turning off this stop-cock will immediately stop any further flow of water into the house and will limit any damage which might occur.

It is a good idea too, to turn this stop-cock on and off two or three times at inter-vals of six months or so. A stop-cock long disused, can jam and prove to be useless when most needed.

From this stop-cock and drain-cock, the pipe will rise vertically to discharge by means of a ball valve into the main cold water storage tank or cistern. In some house-holds, the lavatory flushing cistern and the bathroom cold taps will be supplied direct from the rising main. Many Water Autho-rities however require these draw-off points to be supplied from a storage tank. Only the cold tap over the kitchen sink—supplying water for drinking and cooking—and perhaps a garden supply, are permitted to be taken direct from the main.

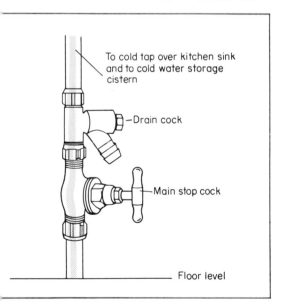

The householder's main stop-cock which is often to be found under the kitchen sink, enables the water supply to the house to be cut off at will. The drain-cock immediately above it makes it possible to drain the rising main.

Cold water storage cistern

The main cold water storage cistern prob-ably causes more anxiety to the householder than any other piece of plumbing equip-ment. It is out of sight, and usually in a spot where it cannot be readily inspected. If it leaks or overflows, the resultant flood may do hundreds of pounds worth of damage to ceilings, furnishings and carpets.

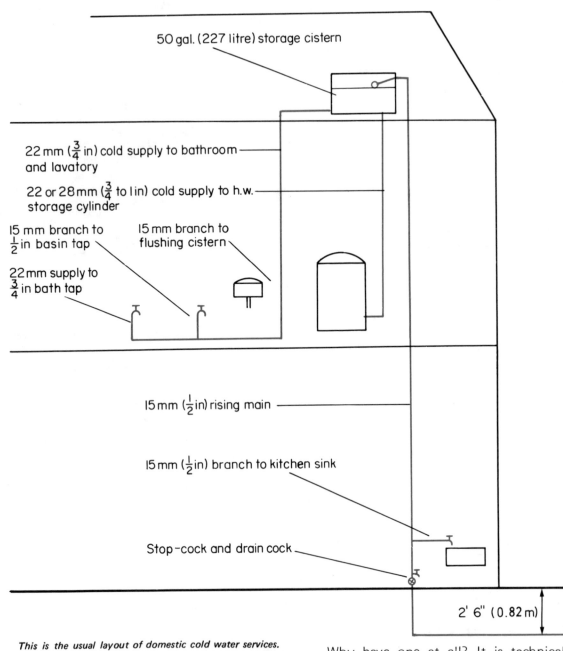

50 gal. (227 litre) storage cistern

22 mm ($\frac{3}{4}$ in) cold supply to bathroom and lavatory

22 or 28 mm ($\frac{3}{4}$ to 1 in) cold supply to h.w. storage cylinder

15 mm branch to $\frac{1}{2}$ in basin tap

15 mm branch to flushing cistern

22 mm supply to $\frac{3}{4}$ in bath tap

15 mm ($\frac{1}{2}$ in) rising main

15 mm ($\frac{1}{2}$ in) branch to kitchen sink

Stop-cock and drain cock

2' 6" (0.82 m)

This is the usual layout of domestic cold water services. The only connections made directly to the rising main are the cold tap over the kitchen sink and the ball-valve connection to the cold water storage cistern. With the permission of the Water Authority a garden or garage supply might also be taken from the rising main. No branch cold supply pipe must be taken from the 22 mm or 28 mm (¾ in or 1 in) cold supply pipe from the cold water storage cistern to the hot water cylinder. Distribution pipes are connected to the storage cistern at points 2 in above the cistern's base to reduce the risk of grit or debris being drawn into the plumbing system.

Why have one at all? It is technicall possible to connect all cold water service direct to the rising main. There are als gas and electric hot water appliances d signed for mains connection.

However most Water Authorities requir the provision of a substantial storage cister in each home to act as a buffer betwee hemselves and consumers at times of peak demand.

The storage cistern has advantages for the householder too. It provides a substantial reserve of water against breakdown of the mains supply. It also provides a supply of water at constant, relatively low, pressure to feed hot water supply apparatus. Most hot water systems demand a storage cistern. Although it is sometimes possible to incorporate such a cistern in the hot water system itself, it is generally more convenient to replenish the hot water system from a main cold water storage tank.

Where should the main cold water storage cistern be situated? The traditional site, up in the roof space, has come in for a good deal of criticism in recent years. It is argued that, by keeping the cistern out of the roof space it is more accessible for inspection, the risk of contamination is reduced and, above all, there is far less risk of frost damage to the cistern itself or to the pipes connected to it.

All this is perfectly true. Yet if the cistern is brought out of the roof space it must be placed in the upper part of an airing cupboard or in a special cupboard in the bathroom or bedroom. Here, since no cistern is entirely silent, it will make its presence known by its noise; and it will attract condensation.

Its relatively low level will mean a poor flow of water from bath and basin taps and a slow refill to the lavatory flushing cistern. It will make it much more difficult and expensive to install a shower.

On balance I feel that the roof space is still the best position for the storage cistern. It should be situated against a chimney breast taking a flue in constant use, lengths of pipe in the roof space should be kept as short as possible and these pipes, and the cistern itself, should be thoroughly protected against frost. Methods of doing this will be discussed in a later chapter.

Wherever the cistern is situated it must be properly supported, preferably above one of the dividing walls of the house. A gallon of water weighs 10 lb so that a cistern with a capacity of 50 gal (227 litres) will contain over 4 cwt of water quite apart from the weight of the cistern itself.

Most Water Authorities require that storage cisterns of this kind should have an *actual* capacity of 50 gal (227 litres). This is the capacity to a water level 112mm (4½ in) from the cistern's rim.

Galvanised steel storage cisterns

Galvanised mild steel is the traditional material of which storage cisterns are made. Tens of thousands of cisterns of this material are in use and are giving trouble-free service.

They have disadvantages though. They are heavy and generally need two men to manhandle them up into the roof space. Cutting the holes for pipe tappings is best done with special tools made for the purpose. The biggest disadvantage of galvanised steel cisterns, however, is their liability to corrosion. This drawback has increased with the, nowadays, almost universal use of copper tubing for plumbing.

It is well known that if connecting rods of zinc and copper are immersed in a weak acid—an electrolyte—the conditions of a simple electric cell are produced. Electric current will pass from one rod to the other, bubbles will form in the electrolyte and the zinc will dissolve away.

Something like this may happen when copper tubing is connected to a galvanised steel storage cistern. The water in the cistern will, if slightly acid, act as the electrolyte. The zinc coating of the galvanised steel may dissolve away and permit water to attack the steel underneath. This process is called electrolytic corrosion.

Asbestos cement cisterns

Asbestos cement cisterns cannot corrode. They have rounded internal angles and smooth jointless walls which make for easy cleaning. Once installed and protected from frost they should last forever.

These cisterns are rather heavy. A typical asbestos cement cistern with an actual capacity of 50 gal weighs 104 lb. They are also liable to damage both during installation and from frost. They must be handled with care. Holes should not be bored nearer than 4 in to the base of the cistern. Tappings should be sealed off with two washers on each side of the cistern wall. One of these washers, the one against the cistern wall, should be of soft material.

As the cistern walls are ½ in thick, making holes for tappings can present difficulties. One manufacturer recommends the following procedure: Mark out the circumference of the hole and drill a complete circle of small holes inside this circumference. Use an ordinary brace and bit but with the bit ground to an angle of 20° instead of the usual 59°. When all the holes have been drilled, the piece in the centre can be pushed out and the hole finished with a half-round rasp.

This technique can be adopted by those with a minimal tool kit for cutting holes of any size in any storage cistern, tank or cylinder.

Plastic cisterns

Cisterns of plastic materials have advantages over both galvanised steel and asbestos cement. As well as being proof against corrosion, they are light, tough and easily fitted.

Plastic cisterns may be rectangular or circular in shape. The black polythene circular cisterns have the advantage that they can be flexed to pass through a relatively small trap-door into the roof space. A 50 gal capacity circular cistern will be 3 ft in diameter and almost 2 ft high. It can however be flexed to pass through any opening 2 ft square.

Plastic cisterns must always be supported on a flat, level platform. A piece of chip board spiked to the rafters will meet this requirement.

Since they do not offer the same support as steel or asbestos cisterns, the rising main when connected to a plastic cistern, must be firmly secured to the roof timbers. All pipes connected to such a cistern must join it squarely so as not to strain the cistern walls. Soft, plastic, washers must be used in direct contact with the cistern walls and no boss white or other sealing material.

The makers of one brand of asbestos cement cistern recommend that holes for tappings should be made in this way. The householder with a minimal tool kit can use the same method for making circular holes in any material.

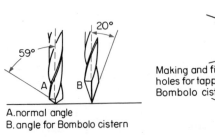

59°

20°

A.normal angle
B. angle for Bombolo cistern

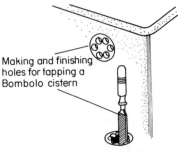

Making and finishing holes for tapping a Bombolo cistern

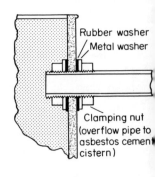

Rubber washer

Metal washer

Clamping nut (overflow pipe to asbestos cement cistern)

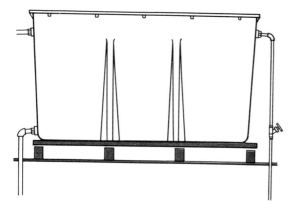

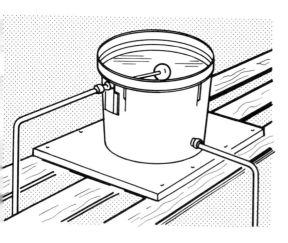

Plastic cisterns may be rectangular or round. They must rest on a flat, level base — not just on the ceiling joists — and care must be taken to ensure that all pipes connect squarely to the cistern walls. The great advantages of plastic cisterns are their lightness and their immunity to corrosion.

should be allowed to come into contact with the plastic.

Irrespective of the material from which the cistern is made, it should be provided with a dust-proof, but not air-tight, cover. Makers of asbestos cement and plastic cisterns often manufacture purpose-made covers that can be bought as an extra. It is however perfectly easy to make a lid of hardboard, plywood or asbestos board cut to size and provided with a 25 mm (1 in) wood strip fastened round its edges.

Connecting pipes

All cold water storage cisterns are supplied with water through a ball valve, usually fitted 37 mm (1½ in) below the cistern rim. The overflow or warning pipe must be fitted below the level of the ball valve inlet and about 25 mm (1 in) above the full water level of the cistern. This pipe will be a minimum of 22 mm (¾ in) in diameter.

There will normally be at least two pipes connected to the lower part of the cistern: a 22 mm (¾ in) diameter pipe supplying the bath cold tap with 15 mm (½ in) branches taken from it to the wash basin and the lavatory flushing cistern, and another 22 mm (¾ in) or 28 mm (1 in) pipe supplying cold water to the hot water storage cylinder.

These pipes should be connected to the cistern at a point at least 50 mm (2 in) above its base to reduce the risk of sediment from the mains being drawn into the pipes.

Faults in the cold water system

1. *Poor flow or poor pressure through draw-off points from the main* (cold tap over kitchen sink or ball-valve to storage cistern):

Check that the main stop-cock is fully open.

Check that the tap and ball-valve are functioning properly. See taps and ball-valves (Chapter 25).

2. *Poor flow or poor pressure through draw-off points from storage cistern* (bathroom cold taps or ball-valve to lavatory cistern):

Check that taps and ball-valve are functioning properly and that a low pressure ball-valve is installed in the lavatory cistern.

Try treatment suggested for air-locks in 'Faults in Hot Water Systems'.

3. *Corrosion in cold water storage cistern* (evident as a 'dusting' of rust on cistern walls, rust patches, particularly round tappings or warty outgrowths of rust and scale):

Drain and dry cistern thoroughly. Remove every trace of rust by wire brushing (use goggles to protect the eyes) or abrasive paper. Fill in any deep pit marks left by this process with an epoxy resin filler. Apply two coats of a *tasteless and odourless* bituminous paint. This treatment will give protection for two or three years and can be repeated as often as required.

A galvanised steel cistern not yet showing signs of rust can be protected from corrosion by means of a sacrificial anode. This is a block of magnesium immersed in the water and in electrical contact with the cistern walls. Magnesium has a high potential and electrolytic action will take place between the magnesium and the zinc coating of the cistern—to the advantage of the zinc. The magnesium block will slowly dissolve away—will be sacrificed—and the galvanised steel protected. This method has proved to be most effective in hard water areas.

4. *A leaking cold water storage cistern* (first indication may be water dripping through the ceiling of room below):

Immediately turn off main stop-cock and open up bathroom taps. This will drain the cistern and limit the damage.

Only after doing this should you climb into the roof space to investigate and to mop up between the rafters.

A leaking cistern will generally need replacement but the trouble could be due to a jammed or otherwise faulty ball-valve. See 'ball-valves'.

5. *Water hammer* (heavy drumming noise in the pipes, especially when a tap is turned off or on):

Usually due to a faulty tap or inefficient ball-valve. See 'taps' and 'ball-valves'.

Chapter 23

Domestic hot water supply-cylinder storage systems

t is difficult to recall that less than three decades ago the hot water system in most British homes consisted of a kettle on a gas ing, supplemented perhaps by a temperamental 'geyser' in the bathroom and a solid fuel, gas or electric clothes boiler.

Nowadays an efficient supply of hot water on tap is regarded as essential in every home. This has been recognised by successive governments who have included a hot water system among the basic amenities towards the installation of which any home owner can claim, as a right, a cash grant from his local Council.

The cylinder storage system of hot water supply is one of the most versatile and popular means of obtaining domestic hot water on tap. Originally used always in conjunction with a solid fuel boiler, perhaps supplemented by an electric immersion heater in the summer, it can be used with any fuel and can be adapted both to supply hot water and to provide a central heating system.

A simple 'direct cylinder' system is illustrated. The cold water storage cistern, hot water storage cylinder and boiler are ideally situated in a vertical column. This arrangement cuts down lengths of pipework and also means that any waste heat from boiler and cylinder rises to give the cold water cistern a measure of protection against frost.

The cold water supply to the cylinder is taken from a point 50 mm (2 in) above the base of the cold water storage cistern to a tapping near the base of the cylinder by means of a supply pipe at least 22 mm (¾ in) in diameter. The flow pipe from the boiler—probably 28 mm (1 in) in diameter—is taken from the upper tapping of the boiler to the higher of two tappings provided in the cylinder wall. From the lower tapping in this wall another 28 mm (1 in) return pipe is taken to the lower or return tapping of the boiler.

A 22 mm (¾ in) vent pipe rises from the apex of the cylinder dome to terminate open-ended over the cold water storage cistern. From this vent pipe is taken the 15 mm (½ in) hot water supply to the kitchen sink and a 22 mm (¾ in) supply pipe to the hot tap of the bath. From the latter pipe line a 15 mm (½ in) branch will be taken to supply the hot tap of the bathroom wash basin.

Since the hot water supplies to the kitchen and bathroom taps are taken from *above* the storage cylinder it will be obvious that the cylinder, boiler and flow and return pipes, cannot be drained from these taps. To enable the whole system to be drained when required, a drain-cock must be provided, close to the boiler, on the return pipe from cylinder to boiler. In addition, a spring-operated safety valve is often fitted close to the boiler. Traditionally this valve is fitted into the flow pipe from boiler to cylinder, though there is something to be said for locating it on the return pipe adjacent to the drain cock.

Most direct cylinders intended for use with solid fuel boilers are provided with an immersion heater boss in the dome. Into this can be screwed a long, vertically fixed immersion heater to provide hot water

—— Hot water (secondary)

—— Cold water

Supply pipes to hot water taps are taken from the vent pipe above the level of the cylinder. Thus the cylinder cannot be drained from the hot taps. Supply pipes should fall slightly away from the vent pipe to allow any air bubbles to escape. Flow and return pipes from boiler to cylinder should rise throughout their lengths.

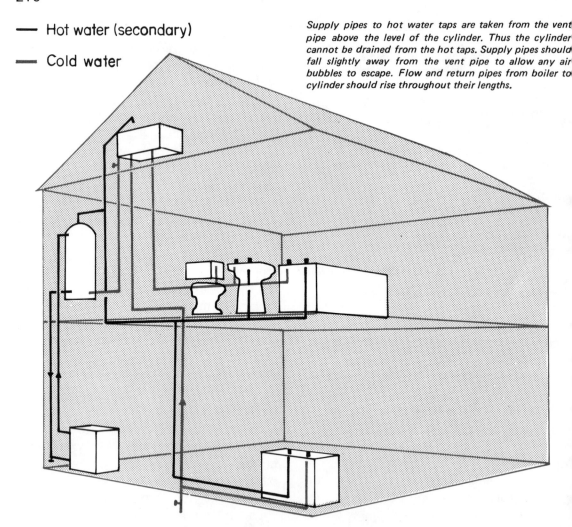

during the summer months when the boiler is not in operation.

This is how a simple cylinder storage system works:

The boiler fire, when lit, heats the water in the boiler. As water is heated it expands and pint for pint—or litre for litre—weighs less than it did when cold. Colder, denser and heavier water from the return pipe then flows into the boiler pushing the warmer, lighter water up the flow pipe into the cylinder. In other, rather less accurate but more familiar, words 'hot water rises' and is replaced by cold. Circulation has begun and will continue for so long as the boiler fire is alight.

The warm water enters the cylinder near its dome and, since it is lighter in weight that the other water in the cylinder, it will 'float on top of it', remaining at the top of the cylinder and gradually extending downwards as circulation continues.

Since the supply pipes to the hot taps are taken from above the cylinder it will always be the hottest stored water, from the upper part of the cylinder, that will be drawn off.

As water is drawn off from the hot taps, cold water will flow in to the lower part of the cylinder from the cold water storage cistern. This will, in its turn, pass down the return pipe to be heated in the boiler.

The demand for the speedy installation of compact hot water systems into homes that had previously lacked them, and into flats converted from older, larger houses, resulted in the production of packaged hot water systems. Some of these are advertised, with justification, as being complete 'packaged plumbing systems'.

The earliest on the market consisted of a copper hot water storage cylinder, usually of 25 gal capacity, with a small feed cistern—also cylindrical and made of copper, immediately above it. The small feed cylinder was sufficiently large to supply the hot water system, but not to provide a cold water supply to the bathroom and lavatory.

Systems of this kind could therefore only be installed in those areas where the Water Authority permitted bathroom and lavatory cold water draw-off points to be taken direct from the main.

(a) a small packaged or 'two-in-one' hot water system. The small cold water storage cistern of such a unit would be capable of supplying the hot water cylinder only. Supplies to all cold taps and flushing cisterns would have to be taken direct from the rising main.

(b) a complete 'packaged plumbing system' with full size 50 gal cold water storage cistern and 25 gal hot water cylinder. This needs only to be fitted with an immersion heater and connected to the rising main and distribution pipes to provide a complete hot and cold water service.

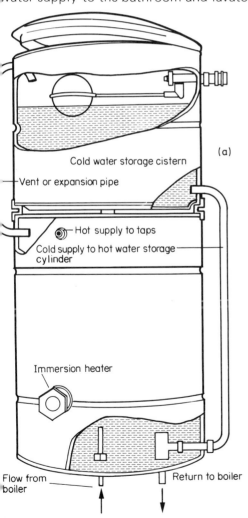

(a)

Cold water storage cistern

Vent or expansion pipe

Hot supply to taps

Cold supply to hot water storage cylinder

Immersion heater

Flow from boiler

Return to boiler

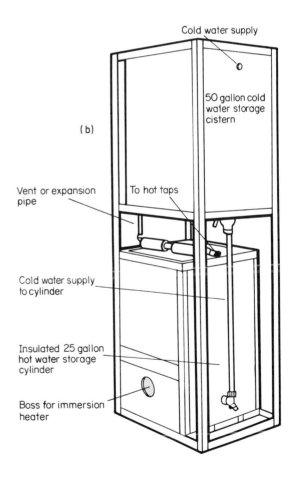

(b)

Cold water supply

50 gallon cold water storage cistern

Vent or expansion pipe

To hot taps

Cold water supply to cylinder

Insulated 25 gallon hot water storage cylinder

Boss for immersion heater

Later more sophisticated units were produced with a standard 50 gal cold water storage cistern. These could be placed in position, in a bathroom cupboard or airing cupboard, to provide a complete plumbing system, needing only the means of heating and the connection of the rising main and the hot and cold water distribution pipes.

Essentially these packaged or 'two-in-one' tanks are simple cylinder storage systems in which the cold water storage cistern and the hot water storage cylinder are brought into close proximity to form one unit. Pipe runs are accordingly shortened and, since the cold water cistern is immediately above the hot water cylinder, the risk of frost damage to the cistern is virtually eliminated.

The only disadvantage of the larger units of this kind is the fact that they normally have to be fitted at too low a level to provide sufficient pressure for a conventional shower.

Packaged or two-in-one systems—and some conventional systems—may dispense with a boiler of any kind and depend solely upon an electric immersion heater. In such cases the flow and return tappings will be blanked off. Provision must still be made for draining the cylinder when required. This is usually done by fitting a drain-cock on the cold water supply pipe, just before it enters the cylinder.

Faults in cylinder storage hot water systems

1. *Scale formation resulting from hard water*

When water containing dissolved bicarbonates of calcium or magnesium is heated to temperatures above about 140° F (60° C) carbon dioxide is driven off and the *bicarbonates* are changed into insoluble *carbonates* which form scale on internal boiler surfaces and on the elements of immersion heaters.

This results in delay in obtaining hot water and, with a boiler system, gurgling, hissing and knocking sounds from the boiler as overheated water forces its way through ever narrowing channels.

The scale insulates the metal of the boiler, and of the electric immersion heater, from the cooling effect of circulating water. Immersion heaters burn out and fail and, eventually, the metal of the boiler will burn through and a leak will develop.

Hot water systems can be descaled chemically by means of proprietory solutions introduced via the cold feed from the main cold water storage cistern. It is far better though, to prevent scale formation.

There are several ways in which this can be done. In hard water areas the immersion heater thermostat should be set at 140° F (60° C) and, where practicable, the boiler temperature maintained at this level. Water softening (see 'Hard Water Problems') or the introduction of chemical scale inhibitors into the cold water storage cistern are other means of controlling scale. It should be noted that chemical scale inhibitors, such as 'Micromet', do not *soften* water. Their action is to stabilise the chemicals causing hardness so that they do not precipitate out when heated.

Another method is to provide an *indirect* hot water system. An indirect cylinder storage system is illustrated. As can be seen an indirect system has a primary circulation, passing through the boiler, quite separate from the domestic hot water supply.

The primary circuit has a separate water supply from a small feed and expansion, or header, tank. Water in the storage cylinder is heated indirectly by a closed coil or heat exchanger from the primary circuit that passes through it.

In the primary circuit the same water is used over and over again, only the very small losses from evaporation being made up from the feed and expansion tank. Thus,

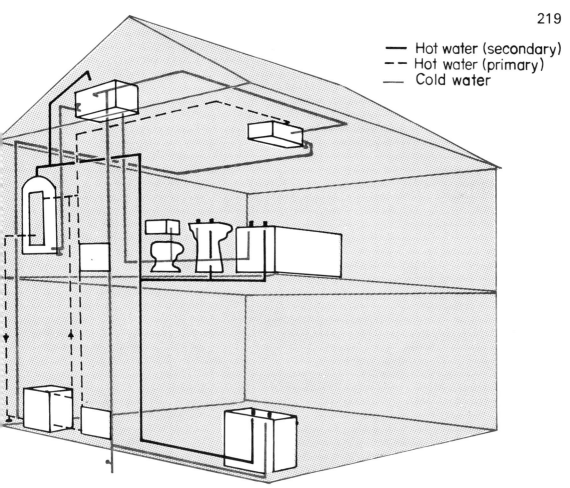

when it is first heated, a small amount of scale is precipitated onto boiler surfaces. After that no more scale formation will occur.

Scale formation in the domestic hot water circuit will be minimal because the water in the outer part of the cylinder will rarely reach the high temperature at which scale formation takes place.

An indirect system also offers relative freedom from internal corrosion since the dissolved air, on which corrosion depends, is driven off when the primary circuit is first heated. Small amounts of air will however continue to be taken into solution via the surface of the water in the feed and expansion tank. It is wise therefore to introduce a chemical corrosion inhibitor into this tank.

In an indirect hot water system, hot water for domestic use is heated by a closed heat exchanger or calorifier within the specially constructed indirect cylinder. The water in the 'primary circuit' — circulating between boiler and cylinder — is used repeatedly, only the very small losses resulting from evaporation being made up from the small feed and expansion tank.

Water within the indirect cylinder is heated for domestic use by heated water circulating through a coil connected to the primary circuit.

It should be noted that with a conventional indirect system of the kind illustrated the primary circuit must be supplied from its own feed and expansion tank—never from the main cold water storage cistern. If the primary circuit of such a system is fed from the main storage cistern, mixing of the primary and domestic water will occur whenever the water in the primary circuit expands and contracts on heating and cooling. Fresh, hard and corrosive water will be drawn into the primary circuit and the advantages of an indirect system will be destroyed.

There are, on the market, patent 'self-priming' indirect cylinders that need no feed and expansion tank.

These appliances have a specially designed inner cylinder which, when the system is first filled, permits water to spill over from the domestic hot water into the primary circuit to fill it. A large air bubble, or air lock, then forms to prevent the return of the primary water. Provision is also made for the accommodation of the expansion of the water in the primary circuit when heated.

Some doubt has been expressed about the effectiveness of these systems in separating the primary from the domestic hot water. My own experience suggests that they are effective enough for general purposes provided that the water in the primary circuit is never allowed to boil and that there is sufficient space within the inner cylinder to accomodate the expansion of the particular primary circuit when heated.

An indirect cylinder should *always* be provided where hot water supply is to be installed in conjunction with even the smallest central heating system. Even where hot water only is required, an indirect system is recommended in areas where the water supply is hard or corrosive.

2. *Rusty red water running from the hot water taps—particularly noticeable from the bath hot tap when a considerable volume of water has been drawn off.*

Check that the rust does not originate from the main cold water storage cistern. If it does, take appropriate action as suggested in Chapter 22.

If the cistern is free of rust the chances are that the rusty water results from corrosion within the boiler. The provision of an indirect system (see 1 above) is the only permanent answer but the use of a scale inhibitor such as Micromet in the cold water storage cistern may help.

3. *Air Locks*

The indications of an air-lock (poor and erratic flow from a hot tap, often accompanied by hissing and spluttering) are sometimes mistakenly attributed to scale formation in taps or supply pipes. Air locks result from bubbles of air, trapped in the supply pipe, preventing or restricting the free flow of water.

When a primatic system is filled for the first time water spills over from the outer cylinder into the primary circuit (1) but is prevented from returning by an air-lock that forms in the inner cylinder (2). On being heated, water in the primary circuit expands, pushing the air in the air-lock down into the lower hemisphere of the inner cylinder (3).

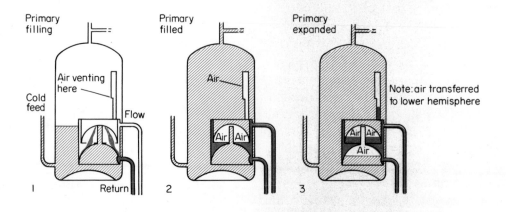

They can usually be cleared by connecting one end of a length of garden hose to the cold tap over the kitchen sink (this is supplied direct from the main) and the other end to the tap giving trouble. Turn both taps on full and the mains pressure should blow the air bubble out of the system.

Always seek the cause of recurring air locks. Perhaps the most common cause is having a pipe of too small a diameter taking cold water from the storage cistern to the hot water cylinder.

If this pipe is only 15 mm (½ in) in diameter it will be incapable of replacing water drawn off from the ¾ in bath hot tap. As a result the level of water will fall in the vent pipe and eventually, bubbles of air from the vent pipe will be drawn into the hot water supply pipe.

If the supply pipe *is* of the right diameter check that any control valve fitted into it is of the same size. A 15 mm control valve fitted into a 22 mm (¾ in) supply pipe will effectively reduce the diameter of the pipe to 15 mm. Check too that any such valve is fully open.

Other possible—though less probable—causes of air-lock are too small a cold water storage cistern or a sluggish ball-valve supplying this cistern.

'Horizontal' runs of pipe connected to the main vent pipe should always fall slightly away from the vent so that any air bubbles can escape.

4. *Loud bubbling noises, possibly accompanied by the sound of water pouring out of the vent pipe into the cold water storage cistern,*

This again, is the result of a form of air-lock. The flow pipe from the boiler should *rise* all the way to the cylinder flow tapping. The vent pipe from the dome of the cylinder should *rise* throughout its length.

If, in either of these pipes, there is a horizontal run or, worse still, a slight

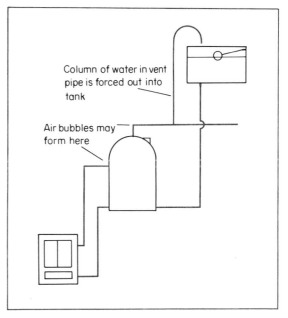

Column of water in vent pipe is forced out into tank

Air bubbles may form here

If the pipes indicated do not slope slightly upwards air bubbles will collect in the horizontal lengths. Pressure will eventually force these air bubbles out of these pipes and they will escape via the vent pipe, noisily pushing the column of water in the vent pipe in front of them.

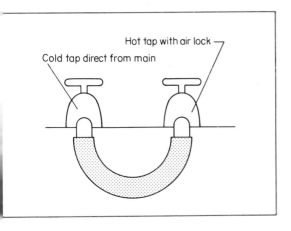

Hot tap with air lock

Cold tap direct from main

It is usually possible to clear an air-lock by connecting the tap giving trouble to the cold tap over the kitchen sink. When both taps are turned on, the water from the sink tap being under mains pressure forces the air bubble out of the system.

back fall, dissolved air—driven off in bubbles from the boiler—will collect at this point.

Pressure will build up behind this bubble until it is sufficient to drive it out of the pipe. It will then, if sufficiently large, push the water standing in the vent pipe out into the storage cistern.

5. Reversed Circulation

This may occur during the summer when the boiler is not in use and hot water is being supplied by immersion heater only. A wasteful—and very expensive—circulation may take place *down* the flow pipe to the boiler and back, via the return pipe, to the cylinder.

A probable cause is having the cylinder more or less on the same level as the boiler. The best position for the storage cylinder is close to the boiler but at a higher level.

If the cylinder cannot be raised the situation can be remedied by realigning the flow pipe so that it rises *inside* the cylinder insulation to the flow tapping.

An even more serious form of reversed circulation will occur when a door is interposed between boiler and cylinder and the flow pipe is taken, as indicated, over the door. When the boiler is out of use electrically heated water will inevitably rise up the vent pipe and, cooling, descend to the cold boiler.

Moving the position of the cylinder is the only really satisfactory solution to this problem. A second-best remedy is to extend the flow pipe so that it enters the cylinder below the level of the immersion heater. This involves the provision of an additional vent pipe. It will effectively prevent reversed circulation but will result in delay in the cylinder heating up when the boiler is in use.

(a) Reversed circulation can result in high electricity bills. The remedy in this case is to take the flow pipe to the cylinder within the cylinder insulation.

(b) Reversed circulation resulting from this layout is less easily cured. The best solution is to redesign the system so that there is no door interposed between boiler and cylinder but a 'second best' remedy in indicated.

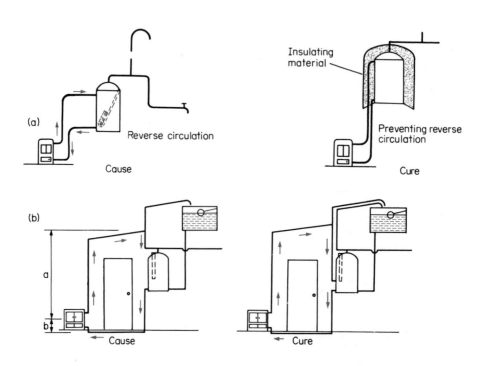

(a) Reverse circulation

Cause

Insulating material

Preventing reverse circulation

Cure

(b)

Cause

Cure

Chapter 24
Water heating by electricity and gas

In the previous chapter I mentioned that a cylinder storage hot water supply might be provided with an electric immersion heater, either to supplement a boiler using some other fuel, or as the sole source of hot water supply.

Water heating by electricity

Most manufacturers of electric appliances manufacture cylinders, complete with immersion heaters, designed as a sole source of domestic hot water. These are usually intended for installation under the draining board of the kitchen sink and, for this reason, are often called 'under draining board' or UDB heaters.

A feature of appliances of this kind is very heavy, built-in, insulation. They are most usually provided with two, horizontally aligned, electric immersion elements. These take advantage of the fact that hot water 'floats' on top of cold.

The upper element is kept permanently switched on to provide the relatively small amounts of water required for washing up, washing and shaving and so on. It heats only the water in the cylinder above the upper

(a) The upper immersion heater of this unit is switched on continuously to ensure that there is always sufficient hot water for personal washing, washing up etc. The lower heater is switched on an hour or so before a larger volume of water is required for, for instance, baths or domestic laundry.

(b) This off-peak water heater switches on at night, when electricity charges are lower, and switches off during the day. It has been estimated that 50 gal of hot water is sufficient for the daily needs of an average family. The tall, slim design ensures stratification of the heated water.

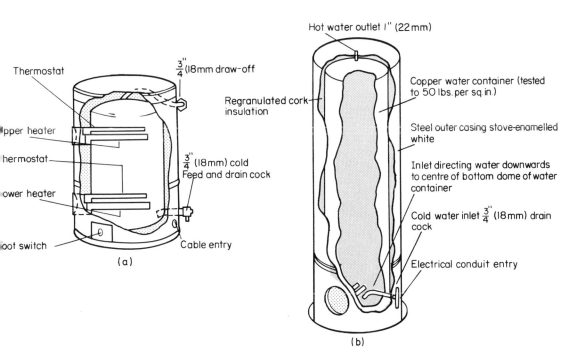

Thermostat
Upper heater
Thermostat
Lower heater
Foot switch

$\frac{3}{4}$" (18mm draw-off
$\frac{3}{4}$" (18mm) cold
Feed and drain cock
Cable entry

(a)

Hot water outlet 1" (22mm)
Regranulated cork insulation
Copper water container (tested to 50 lbs. per sq. in.)
Steel outer casing stove-enamelled white
Inlet directing water downwards to centre of bottom dome of water container
Cold water inlet $\frac{3}{4}$" (18mm) drain cock
Electrical conduit entry

(b)

element. The lower element is intended to be switched on an hour or so before greater volumes of hot water are required for baths or laundry purposes.

A variation on the same theme is the off-peak electric water heater designed to take advantage of the cheaper off-peak electricity charges. Typically a heater of this kind is tall and slim to encourage the stratification of the heated water. A special 'spreading' device is provided for the cold water inlet at the base to ensure that incoming cold water spreads evenly over the lower part of the cylinder, pushing the heated water upwards without mixing with it. These off-peak cylinders are also provided with very heavy built-in insulation.

They customarily have a capacity of 50 gal--twice that of the average UDB heater. It has been estimated that 50 gal of hot water meets the daily needs of a normal family. The heater is switched on overnight, to take advantage of the off-peak rates. During the day the electric element is switched off and the stored, heated water used by the family.

Essentially UDB and off-peak heaters of this kind are cylinder storage systems specially adapted to make the best use of electricity as a means of heating. Most of them need a separate cold water storage cistern but there are 'two-in-one' versions—usually called 'cistern heaters'—which incorporate their own small, cold water supply cistern in the upper part of the unit.

Such cistern heaters must be situated above the level of the highest hot water draw-off point. Their advantages and disadvantages are identical to those of the smaller two-in-one or packaged hot water systems described in Chapter 23.

Open-outlet electric water heaters, frequently installed over sinks and wash basins, operate on a rather different principle. These are designed for connection direct to the main and an essential part of their

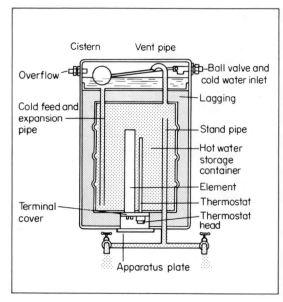

This is essentially a simple, cylinder hot water system especially designed for use with electricity as the sole source. The small cistern is, of course, not large enough to supply any cold water fitting. These must be supplied from another cistern or from the main.

The open-outlet electric water heater has the control valve on the inlet side of the heater. Cold water flowing into the appliance displaces heated water which overflows down a stand-pipe to the outlet spout. (courtesy of Heatrae Ltd)

design is the position of the control valve or tap. This must be on the inlet side—*not* on the outlet—of the appliance.

These units have a vertically aligned immersion heater inserted through the base. When hot water is required the inlet control is opened. Cold water flows in at the base and the hot water within the unit overflows through an internal stand-pipe connected to the outlet spout.

Modern variations of this appliance may be installed under, instead of over, the sink or wash basin. These must still comply with the essential requirement of a controlled inlet and a free outlet.

In recent years a number of electric 'instantaneous' water heaters have come on the market. These too are connected directly to the water main and have their control valve on the inlet side of the appliance. Used mainly for spray hand washing and for the

Instantaneous electric water heaters can be useful for the provision of a supply of hot water to a shower or a wash basin where a more conventional means of supply would be difficult or uneconomic. They can give trouble from scale formation in hard water areas.

provision of showers in situations where this would otherwise be impossible, they heat water 'instantaneously' as it passes through electrically heated channels within the appliance.

They have the advantage that electricity is used only to heat water actually drawn off and are therefore particularly economical in situations where use of hot water is occasional only.

Their disadvantages include a rather low rate of delivery, scale trouble in hard water areas and the fact that they have not yet received the universal approval of Water Authorities and Electricity Boards. The need for energy conservation may well lead to further development of this kind of appliance.

Water heating by gas

In the field of instantaneous water heating gas has, so far, all the advantages. Instantaneous gas water heaters are available for installation over baths, sinks and wash basins and larger 'multipoint' models can provide a whole-house domestic hot water supply. Normally supplied direct from the main they make it possible, where this is permitted, for the cold water storage cistern to be dispensed with entirely.

The problem of the disposal of the flue gases, which invested the Edwardian 'bathroom geyser' with its potentially lethal qualities, has been solved by the invention of the 'balanced flue'.

The combustion chamber of balanced flue gas appliances is completely sealed off from the room in which the appliance is situated. Air to support combustion is drawn from an inlet through the external wall behind the appliance. The flue outlet is immediately adjacent to this inlet.

Thus, the system is balanced. If a gale force wind is blowing against the wall in which the flue outlet is situated, it will

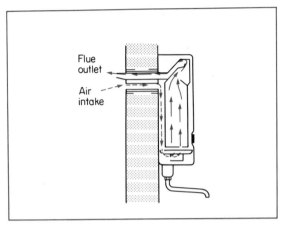

Flue outlet

Air intake

Balanced flue gas appliances are available for space or water heating and can be installed against any external wall. The combustion chamber is sealed off from the room in which the appliance is fitted. Air intake and flue outlet are adjacent and are therefore 'balanced'.

be blowing equally against the fresh air inlet. Normal combustion will be un-affected.

Instantaneous heaters are not, of course, the only means by which gas can be used to provide domestic hot water supply. There are gas over-sink storage heaters similar to electric free outlet heaters. Large gas-fired boilers, used in conjunction with indirect hot water systems (see previous chapter), can provide both hot water supply and central heating. Small gas boilers, or 'circulators', usually fitted closely to the walls of a storage cylinder, operate in the same way as a solid fuel boiler to provide hot water supply only.

Faults in electric and gas hot water systems

These systems are, on the whole, extremely efficient and trouble free. Complaints are more likely to relate to excessive fuel bills than to inefficient operation. If your bills are consistently higher than those of friends or neighbours with similar systems, consider the following points. Any one of them could be the cause.

1. Inadequate insulation of storage cylinder

An uninsulated copper cylinder 18 in in diameter and 36 in high (nominal capacity 30 gal) will lose 86 units of electricity per week if the air temperature is 60°F (15°C) and the temperature of the water in the cylinder is maintained at 140°F (60°C). If the water temperature is maintained at 160°F (71°C) it will lose 115 units per week.

Work out the money wasted each week at the current price of electricity per unit!

Efficient lagging is the answer. Thickness of lagging material is more important than the nature of the material used. Optimum thickness is 3 in. The cylinder above will lose only six units of electricity per week if maintained at 140°F (60°C) and lagged with a 3 in thickness of glass fibre. If the thickness is reduced to 2 in, 8.8 units will be lost each week.

Never strip off part of the lagging to heat an airing cupboard. It is cheaper to install a small low-output electric heater in the cupboard.

2. Long 'dead legs'

In most modern homes the bathroom and kitchen are in close proximity. In a two storey house the bathroom will probably be above the kitchen. In a bungalow it is likely to adjoin the kitchen.

This keeps pipe runs—'dead legs'—from the cylinder to the draw-off points, short Long dead legs waste heat. When the tap is turned off the dead leg is full of water that you have paid to heat. It will cool rapidly

A dead leg of 15 mm (½ in) copper tubing carrying water at 140°F (60°C) to a sink or basin tap will waste about 0.19 units per foot run per week. A similar 22 mm (¾ in) copper tube will waste 0.38 units per foot run per week.

Where the hot water storage cylinder is in, or adjacent to, the bathroom and the kitchen sink is more than, say 20 ft away, it is worth considering providing a separate

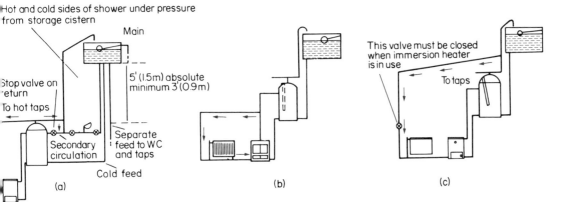

Hot and cold sides of shower under pressure from storage cistern

Main

Stop valve on return

To hot taps

5' (1.5m) absolute minimum 3' (0.9m)

Secondary circulation

Separate feed to WC and taps

Cold feed

(a)

(b)

This valve must be closed when immersion heater is in use

To taps

(c)

(a) A secondary circulation is sometimes provided on the hot water supply to — for instance — a shower, to reduce the delay in the arrival of the hot water. This secondary circulation must be stopped when the water is heated by electricity.

(b) Circulation of electrically-heated water through a towel rail or radiator will result in high electricity bills. Where such a circulation is provided it should either be wholly below the level of the immersion heater or, alternatively, a stop-valve (c) must be provided so that circulation can be stopped when the immersion heater is in use.

small water heater, over the kitchen sink.

3. Circulating piping

Electrically heated water should never be permitted to circulate. Sometimes, for instance, in order to speed up delivery of hot water to a shower some distance from the cylinder, a secondary circulation, as illustrated, is provided.

If you have a secondary circulation of this kind see that it is fitted with a stop-valve on the return run and that this valve is turned off when the water is being heated electrically.

In Chapter 23 we saw that even the smallest central heating system required the provision of an indirect cylinder. Yet it is quite permissible to run a single heated towel rail from a direct hot water system. This is, in fact, common practice.

Electrically heated water must never be permitted to circulate through such a towel rail.

Where practicable the towel rail circulation should be taken from the flow pipe from boiler to cylinder below the level of the immersion heater. Where this is impracticable fit a stop-valve into the towel rail circuit and see that it is turned fully off when the immersion heater is switched on.

Electrically heated water circulating through a 15 mm (½ in) copper tube at 140°F (60°C) will waste 1.36 units of electricity *per foot run* per week. If, as is possible with a towel rail circuit, the tubing is 28 mm (1 in) in diameter the wastage will be 2.33 units per foot run per week. (See also 'Reversed Circulation', Chapter 23).

4. One-pipe circulation

If the vent pipe from the cylinder rises vertically upwards throughout its length to the cold water storage cistern, there will be appreciable heat wastage from one-pipe circulation.

Currents of heated water will rise, by convection, up the centre of the 22 mm (¾ in) vent pipe. Cooling, they will descend against the inner walls of this tube.

One-pipe circulation can be prevented by taking the vent pipe *almost* horizontally from the dome of the cylinder for a distance of about 18 in before permitting it to rise vertically upwards to the cold water storage cistern.

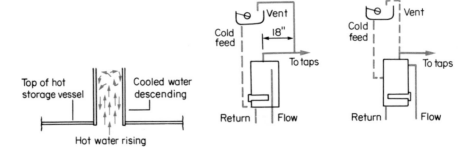

Heat wastage from 'single pipe' circulation will result if the vent pipe rises vertically from the dome of the hot water cylinder. This can be prevented by taking the vent pipe horizontally for 450 mm (18 in) before it rises to the storage cistern.

Other faults in electric and gas hot water systems

1. Faults common to all cylinder storage hot water systems

Cylinder storage hot water systems operated by gas or electricity are, of course, prone to air-locks and other faults affecting all cylinder storage systems (see Chapter 23).

2. Poor recovery period after hot water is drawn off from storage cylinder

Check that thermostat of electric immersion heater is correctly set—140°F (60°) in hard water area, 160°F (71°C) in soft water area.

Trouble could be due to build-up of scale on electric immersion heater. Electrically heated cylinder systems can be descaled chemically in the same way as simple cylinder systems operated by a boiler (See previous chapter). Aim at scale prevention —correct thermostat setting, use of scale inhibitor in cold water storage cistern, water softening (see Chapters 23 and 30).

3. Poor flow or inadequately heated water from an instantaneous gas water heater

This trouble could again be caused by scale formation in the water channels.

Descaling a large multi-point instant aneous heater is hardly a d.i.y. job bu smaller appliances can usually be descaled as follows.

Cut off the water and gas supply. Discon nect the water inlet to the heater. Connec a length of rubber hose or other rubbe tubing to the water inlet and insert a glas funnel in the other end of the tube. Rais funnel to above the level of the top of the heater and fix in position. Pour in descaling fluid. *Pour slowly and carefully,* looking out for foaming back up the tube.

When faced with a poor flow or inade quately heated water from an instantaneou water heater don't overlook the natura limitations of these appliances. They canno heat a given volume of water to a pre determined temperature. What they *can* d is to raise a given volume of water *through a predetermined range of temperatures.* Ir prolonged cold weather either outlet tem perature of the water, or flow, will be reduced.

5. Drip from spout of free outlet wate heater, particularly when heating up.

This trouble is usually assumed by th householder to be due to a faulty washer i the inlet control valve. It is however mor likely to be caused by scale formation ir the siphon device at the top of the stand pipe outlet inside the appliance.

The purpose of this siphon is to lowe the water level in the appliance to a leve ½ in or so below the rim of the stand-pip when the control valve is turned off

This ½ in is to accommodate the expansion of the water in the appliance as it heats up. If the siphon becomes clogged with scale it will fail to operate. The appliance will fill to the rim of the stand-pipe when cold. There will then be a constant drip, resulting from expansion, as the water heats up.

Once again, descaling is the remedy. Small open outlet appliances can be descaled as described in 3 above for small instantaneous heaters.

Chapter 25
Taps, stop-cocks and ball-valves

Taps, stop-cocks and ball valves—or float-valves as they are increasingly called—have in common the fact that they are all fittings designed to control the flow of water through pipes.

Taps

Looking through an illustrated catalogue of modern taps it is easy to forget that, despite the 'tomorrow's world' appearance of most of the taps displayed, they all—with

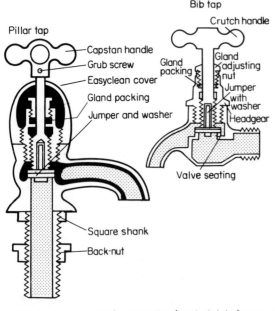

Bib (horizontal inlet) and pillar (vertical inlet) taps of this kind provide the basic design for practically all domestic taps, despite the vastly different appearance of some modern models.

one exception—operate on exactly the same principle as the old crutch-headed bib-cock familiar half a century ago. In fact, of course, even today straightforward 'crutch' or 'capstan' headed bib and pillar taps are manufactured and sold. The great majority of taps in British homes are still of this traditional pattern.

Bib-taps have a horizontal inlet. Twenty years ago this is the kind of tap that would have been found in any suburban home projecting from the tiled wall above the ceramic kitchen sink. The advent of the enamelled steel and stainless steel sink unit has relegated the more basic kinds of bib-tap to the outside wall, to provide a garden and garage water supply. Variation on the bib-tap theme are however still to be found over some wash basins and baths, particularly where space is limited or concealed plumbing it particularly required.

Pillar taps, with a vertical inlet, are nowadays fitted almost universally in the holes provided for them in modern sinks, wash basins and baths.

Both kinds of tap work in the same way. Turning the tap-handle clockwise forces the valve—or jumper—complete with its composition washer, down on to the valve seating to close the waterway. Turning the handle anti-clockwise frees the valve and allows water to pass out of the tap.

Bath, sink and basin mixers are simply two taps with a common spout. Sink mixers have a rather different design from bath and basin mixers because it is both illegal and impracticable to mix in any plumbing fitting, water from the main (the cold supply to the kitchen sink) and water from a storage cistern (the hot supply). This difficulty is overcome by providing separate channels for the hot and cold water within the spout of the mixer. Hot and cold streams of water mix *in the air* as they leave the nozzle.

The one exception in design to which I referred is Bourner's 'supatap'. The supatap, renowned for its rapid washer change without the need to cut off the water supply, gives a particularly smooth flow of water and has an appearance that many find attractive.

The tap is opened and closed by rotating its nozzle, provided with 'ears' for that purpose. A failing of early supataps was the fact that the metal ears of a hot tap became uncomfortably hot as the tap was used. Later models have ears of kemetal plastic which has excellent insulating qualities.

To connect a hose to a supatap a special hose adaptor is essential. This attaches to the ears of the tap to permit the nozzle of the adaptor to remain stationary while the body rotates with the tap nozzle.

Taps have not, at the time of writing, been subjected to the benefits, or otherwise, of metrication. They are still catalogued as ½ in or ¾ in. Bath taps are normally ¾ in and the ½ in size is used for sinks, basins and garden water supplies. ½ in taps are, of course, designed to connect to modern 15 mm copper tubing and ¾ in taps to the 22 mm size. It is probable that, when taps are metricated, these are the nominal metric sizes by which they will be designated.

How to fit a tap

To fit a pillar tap into a ceramic sink or basin, unscrew the back-nut and slip a plastic washer over the threaded 'tail'. Insert in the hole provided. Slip another plastic washer over the tail and tighten up the back nut. This nut should be tightened sufficiently to hold the tap securely but don't overtighten. Ceramic surfaces are easily damaged.

When fitting a pillar tap into a sink, bath or basin of stainless or enamelled steel or other thin material, the same procedure is adopted except that a special spacer or 'top hat' washer must be provided between the back-nut and the under surface of the fitting to accommodate the protruding shank of the tap.

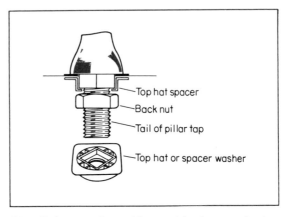

When fitting a tap into a thin material — for example, the stainless steel surface of a sink or vanity unit — a 'top hat' or spacer washer must be provided to accommodate the protruding shank of the tap.

Faults in taps

1. Dripping after the tap has been turned off

This is an indication that the washer needs to be renewed. Set about it this way:

With any tap other than a supatap, cut off the water supply. For the cold tap over the kitchen sink turn off the main stop-cock (see Chapter 21). Other taps *may* have stop-valves in the pipe-lines supplying them with water but the probability is that they will not.

To cut off the water supply to these taps you will therefore have to tie up the float arm of the ball-valve supplying the main cold water storage tank. This will prevent water flowing into this tank and permit you to drain it from the bathroom taps.

Provided that the bathroom cold taps are supplied from the main storage tank and not from the main you need not drain off the hot water stored in the cylinder, even if it is the washer of a hot tap that needs renewal. Open up the bathroom cold taps and leave open until water ceases to flow. Then open up the hot tap that needs to be rewashered. A pint or so of water will flow out of it and flow will then cease. This is because the supply to the hot taps is taken from *above* the storage cylinder.

Unscrew the easyclean cover of the tap. You should be able to do this by hand. If you are compelled to use a wrench, pad its jaws to protect the chromium plating.

Raise the easyclean cover and you will see the large hexagon nut with which the top-gear of the tap is screwed into the body. Hold the body of the tap firmly with one hand, or with a padded wrench, grasp the hexagon nut with another wrench and unscrew so as to remove the top-gear.

If you are dealing with the cold tap over the kitchen sink you will probably find the jumper with washer attached resting freely on the valve seating inside the tap body. Other taps will probably have the jumper pegged into the head-gear, so that it can be rotated but cannot be withdrawn.

To renew the washer you unscrew the small retaining nut, fit the washer and replace the nut.

This may be easier said than done. It is quite on the cards that the nut will have become so scaled up and corroded as to be all but unmoveable. With a free, un-pegged, jumper there is an easy answer. Fit a new jumper complete with washer. You can get these at any household or d.i.y. store.

If the jumper *is* pegged into the head-gear you have a more difficult problem. Make a real effort to unscrew that nut. apply a drop of penetrating oil and try again after fifteen minutes or so.

If the nut really cannot be moved, force the jumper out of the head-gear with the blade of a screw-driver, breaking the pegging. Fit a new jumper and washer

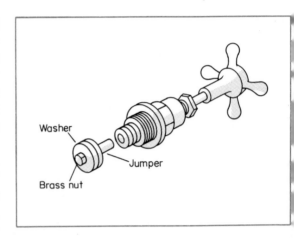

Some taps have the jumper 'pegged' into the headgear of the tap. The jumper will turn round and round but cannot readily be removed.

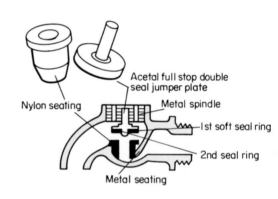

The 'Full Stop' tap washer and seating set provides a simple d-i-y method of 're-seating' a tap. The nylon seating is placed in position on the existing valve seating and the head-gear is then screwed down hard.

complete but, before you slip it into position, burr the stem of the jumper so that it fits fairly tightly into the headgear.

Continued dripping after rewashering indicates that the valve seating has become scored and damaged. It is no longer providing a watertight joint. The easiest solution to this problem is to fit one of the new plastic valve seating and jumper sets. These are forced down onto the existing valve seating to give a watertight connection.

My own experience suggests that a tap fitted with one of these plastic valve seatings may continue to drip for a time. This stops as the tap is used and screwed down hard so as to force the new seating tightly against the old one.

How about modern taps with shrouded heads? With these the handle and head-gear appear to comprise a single unit.

To dismantle these taps prize off the small plastic 'hot' or 'cold' indicator in the centre of the shrouded head. Under this you will find the head of a screw that keeps the head in position. Undo this screw and the head can be removed, revealing the interior of the tap to be little different from that of a conventional pillar or bib tap.

Nothing could be simpler than rewashering a Supatap. Don't turn off the water supply. Unscrew and release the retaining nut directly above the nozzle. Then turn the tap on—and on. At first the flow of water will increase but it will cease as the check-valve falls into position. Continue to unscrew until the nozzle comes off in your hand.

Tap the nozzle on a hard surface to loosen the anti-splash device. Then turn the nozzle upside down and this anti-splash, which holds the washer and jumper, will fall out.

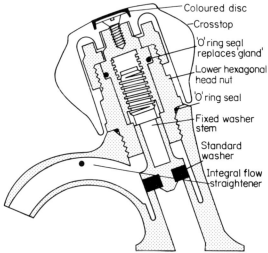

Opella 500 series pillar taps are suitable for standard baths, basins and sinks. They are of kemetal plastic construction and have an O-ring ring seal instead of the conventional gland.

Renew the washer and jumper, replace in the nozzle and screw the nozzle back on to the body of the tap. As you do this, don't forget that the nozzle has a *left-hand thread*. Turn anti-clockwise to replace it. Finally, reconnect the retaining nut to the top of the nozzle.

2. Water leaking past the spindle of the tap when the tap is turned on.

This is due to failure of the gland packing and is most likely to occur in older pattern taps with a traditional 'gland'. Connecting a hose to a kitchen tap may produce this trouble by creating back-pressure within the tap.

Another possible cause is detergent charged water dripping from the hands, running down the tap spindle, and washing the grease out of the gland packing. It was to prevent this—as much as for improved appearance—that the all-protecting 'shrouded head' was developed.

First of all try tightening the gland adjusting nut. This is the first nut through which the spindle of the tap passes. You will probably have to remove the crutch or capstan head and the easyclean cover to get at it.

To remove the head or handle unscrew and remove the tiny grub screw holding it in place. The head may then come off easily. If it does not, raise the easyclean cover as far as it will go and jam a piece of wood, or two clothes pegs, between the bottom of the cover and the body of the tap. Screw the tap down and the upwards pressure of the easyclean cover will force off the head.

Give the gland-adjusting nut half a turn or so in a clockwise direction. This may cure the trouble.

Eventually, of course, all the adjustment will be taken up and the gland will have to be repacked. To do this unscrew and remove the adjusting nut to reveal the gland

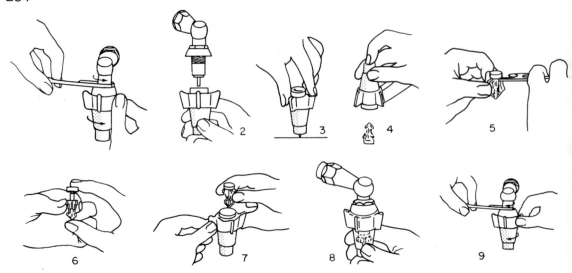

Supatap washer change

1. Partly open nozzle and undo tap nut completely (in direction of arrows). Water will commence to flow.
2. Continue opening nozzle until it is detached. Flow will be reduced to a trickle before nozzle is completely free.
3. The centre of the anti-splash protrudes below the nozzle. Press this against a hard surface (not the basin) to release the anti-splash from nozzle.
4. Press out the anti-splash and jumper from the nozzle.
5. The jumper may be fast in the anti-splash but can be levered out with a coin or a blade.
6. Replace a new washer-jumper into the anti-splash and make sure that the pin clicks into the top hole of the anti-splash.
7. Put anti-splash, complete with washer jumper into the nozzle with the washer uppermost.
8. Ensure the washer jumper is in position indicated by dotted lines and screw nozzle back into shank.
9. As the nozzle is being screwed onto the shank the water supply will again commence. Continue screwing until almost closed then tighten top retaining nut and close tap completely, turning in direction of arrows.

chamber. Pick out, with the point of a penknife, all existing packing material. Repack the gland with household wool steeped in petroleum jelly. Pack down tightly and screw the gland adjusting nut back into position.

3. Water hammer

Water hammer—heavy banging or vibration in the supply pipes—especially noticeable when a tap has been turned off, is due to shock waves resulting from the sudden stoppage of a flow of water.

Faulty gland packing is a common cause. As water escapes past the spindle the tap becomes easier and easier to turn. Eventually it may be possible to spin it on and off with a flick of the fingers.

This will inevitably produce water hammer. The remedy is as suggested in 2 above.

A faulty or unsuitable ball-valve (see 'ball-valves') is another common cause of water hammer.

Stop-cocks

Stop-cocks or stop-valves are essentially a form of screw-down bib tap, set in the run of water pipe, to stop or control the flow of water at will. They may be provided with compression joint inlets and outlets for connection to copper, stainless steel or polythene tubing, screwed inlets and outlets for connecting to steel tubing or plain ends for soldering to lead pipe.

When fitting a stop-cock it is essential to ensure that the arrow engraved on the body of the fitting points in the same direction as the flow of the water. If a stop-cock is fitted the wrong way round, water pressure will force the washer and jumper on to the valve seating and prevent the flow of water even when the valve is open.

There are now tiny and unobtrusive stop-cocks, operated by a screwdriver, that can be fitted into the water supply pipe-line immediately behind any tap or ball-valve. In this position they enable the water draw-off point to be isolated for washer changing or other servicing without the need to drain the system or to cut off the supply to any other plumbing fitting.

(a) A screw-down stop-cock resembles a bib-tap set into the run of a pipe. The arrow engraved on the body indicates the direction of water flow.

(b) The Markfram mini-stopcock is turned on and off by means of a screw driver. Fitted in a water supply pipe close to a tap or ball-valve it permits those fittings to be changed or serviced without interrupting water supply to other draw-off points.

Faults in stop-cocks

1. Washer failure and leakage past spindle
These troubles can occur in stop-cocks as well as in taps. Remedies are indicated above. Gland failure, indicated by leakage past the spindle, should receive immediate attention. Leakage on to a boarded floor, in the confined ill-ventilated spaces in which stop-cocks are frequently found will, almost inevitably, introduce dry rot into the home.

Where the water supply needs to be cut off to the main stop-cock it may be necessary to ask the Water Authority to turn off *their* stop-cock in the highway.

2. Stop-cock jammed through long disuse
This is a very common failing of stop-cocks. It is usually discovered only when a plumbing emergency occurs. The stop-cock is found to be immoveable.

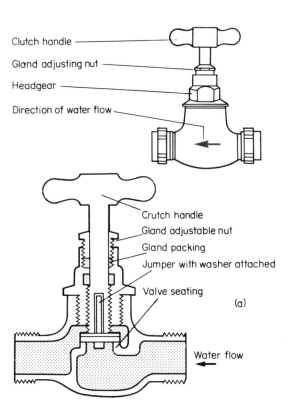

Clutch handle
Gland adjusting nut
Headgear
Direction of water flow

Crutch handle
Gland adjustable nut
Gland packing
Jumper with washer attached
Valve seating

(a)

Water flow

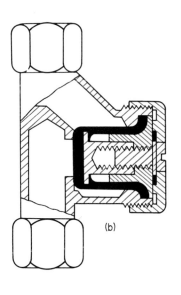

(b)

This is a trouble easier to prevent than to cure. It is a good idea to open and close all the household stop-cocks two or three times, at least twice a year. This will make sure that they are in working order when the need arises.

Ball-valves

A ball-valve, or float-valve, can be regarded as a tap with a float-operated control, designed to maintain water at a constant level in a water storage or lavatory flushing cistern.

There have been some interesting developments in ball-valve design in recent years and even in recent months. It seems at least possible that the diaphragm/equilibrium valve on the lines of the 'Torbeck' valve produced by Ideal Standard Ltd. during 1974, will set the pattern for the future.

Undoubtedly however, ball-valves of traditional pattern will be found in British homes for many years to come.

The simple, sturdy and straightforward Croydon pattern valve is nowadays more likely to be found serving a cattle trough or a municipal allotment storage cistern, than in the home. This valve has a washered plug that moves vertically up and down within the valve body as water level in the cistern rises and falls.

The body is so shaped as to permit water to gush out, in two noisy splashing streams, through channels on each side of the plug, as water level falls. Its noisiness makes it unsuitable for domestic use.

One or other of the variations on the Portsmouth pattern ball-valve is the one most likely to be installed in the cisterns of houses built more than a decade or so ago.

The washered plug of the Portsmouth ball valve moves horizontally within the valve body. A slot in the lower part of the plug accommodates the upturned end of the float arm. As water level falls, the movement of the float arm pulls the plug away from the valve nozzle and permits water to flow into the cistern.

It used to be the practice to screw a metal or plastic 'silencer tube' into the outlet of these ball valves. It reduced the noise of refilling by introducing incoming water at a point below the level of water already in the cistern. These silencers are now forbidden by Water Authorities because of the risk of back-siphonage from the cistern into the main in the event of a failure of mains pressure.

Within the past decade a different kind of ball valve—developed at the Government's Building Research Station at Garston and known as the Garston, the BRS or the diaphragm ball-valve—has become increasingly popular.

Garston valves may be made of either brass or plastic material. Their essential feature is a large rubber diaphragm, which presses against the nylon valve nozzle to close it, as water level rises. The only moving parts are the float arm itself and the tiny plunger that it presses against the diaphragm. These moving parts are pro-

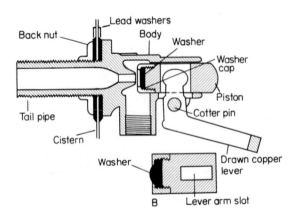

The Portsmouth pattern ball-valve is still the most common type in use. At the prompting of the float arm or lever, a brass plug into which the washer fits, moves horizontally in the valve body to open or close the valve. It used to be the practice to screw a 'silencer tube' into the outlet but this is now prohibited.

tected from water by the diaphragm and therefore cannot be affected by hard water scale or corrosion. The nylon nozzle ensures a smooth and relatively silent delivery of water.

Early models of these valves were provided with screw-in or push-on silencer tubes similar to those available for Portsmouth valves. Since these silencer tubes have been prohibited, the manufacturers have produced Garston valves with an overhead outlet incorporating a sprinkler device that delivers the water as a gentle shower, rather than as a noisy stream.

Ball-valves are described either as 'high pressure', 'low pressure' or 'full way' depending upon the size of the nozzle orifice. Valves connected directly to the rising main are normally 'high pressure'; those supplied from a storage cistern in the roof space 'low pressure'. Where, as in the case of a flushing cistern supplied from a packaged plumbing system, the main cistern is only a few feet above the level of the flushing cistern, a full-way valve may be required.

In some areas water pressure in the mains fluctuates considerably. A high pressure valve will deliver water unacceptably slowly during the day. On the other hand, during the night when pressure is higher, a low pressure valve will let water pass and produce a dripping overflow pipe.

The answer, under such circumstances, is to fix an equilibrium ball valve. The Portsmouth version of an equilibrium valve has a channel passing through the plug to admit water into a chamber behind it. Thus, there is equal pressure in front of and behind the valve. It is in a state of equilibrium and is activated solely by up and down movement of the float arm; not by the pressure of water trying to force it open.

These valves also eliminate the 'bounce' on the valve seating as the valve closes. This is a frequent cause of water hammer and other ball-valve noise.

Until recently equilibrium valves have been available only in the Croydon and Portsmouth patterns. Now however we have the Torbeck diaphragm/equilibrium valve to which I referred earlier. This incorporates features of the Garston and the conventional equilibrium valve.

The Torbeck

The Torbeck, like a conventional equilibrium ball valve, has a water chamber—the 'servo chamber'—behind the diaphragm closing the nozzle aperture. Water flows into this chamber via the metering pin opening but is prevented from passing through into the cistern, when this is full of water, by the sealing washer on the float arm. This closes the pilot hole.

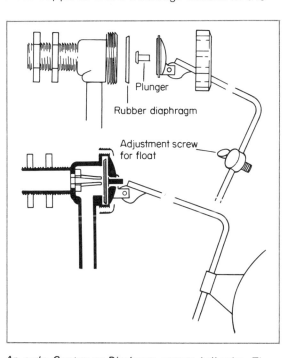

An early Garston or Diaphragm pattern ball valve. The end of the float arm pushes a small plunger against a large rubber diaphragm to close the valve. Design points are easy dismantling, moving parts protected from the water by the rubber diaphragm, detachable nylon nozzle and means of adjusting water level by moving the float up or down the vertical end section of the float arm. The silencer tube shown is now prohibited.

Plunger

Rubber diaphragm

Adjustment screw for float

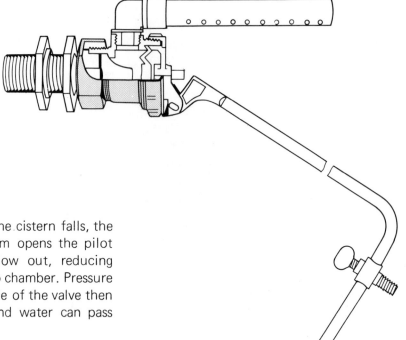

When water level in the cistern falls, the descent of the float arm opens the pilot hole and water can flow out, reducing the pressure in the servo chamber. Pressure of water on the inlet side of the valve then opens the diaphragm and water can pass through into the outlet.

The Torbeck has an overhead outlet like a modern Garston valve. This is fitted with a collapsible plastic silencer tube, which reduces the noise of water delivery but is immune to the risk of back siphonage.

The design of the valve has permitted the use of a very small float and short float arm—an important consideration when replacing the ball-valve of a lavatory flushing cistern.

A modern diaphragm ball valve by Peglers. Note the overhead outlet with spray delivery tube and the readily demountable nylon nozzle which permits rapid conversion of the ball valve from high to low pressure.

The plug of an equilibrium ball valve of this type has a channel drilled through it to permit water to pass through to a space behind the plug. Thus water pressure on either side of the plug is equal and water pressure is not continually trying to force the valve open.

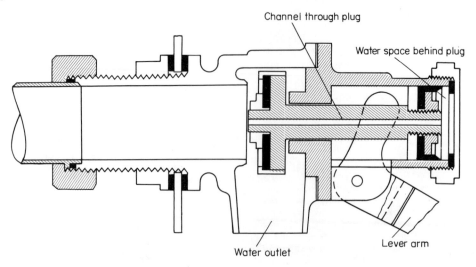

Channel through plug

Water space behind plug

Water outlet

Lever arm

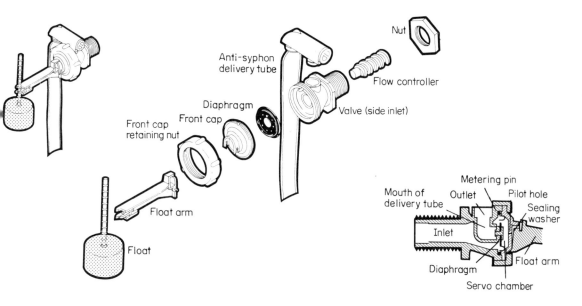

The valve has a wide nozzle aperture, permitting rapid filling. A flow controller is provided for use where the valve is connected directly to a mains supply.

The Torbeck diaphragm/equilibrium valve embodies some of the features of the diaphragm valve and some of the conventional equilibrium valve. Water pressure is used to open and close the valve. It has been found to be efficient and silent in action.

Faults in ball valves

1. Leaking valve—becomes apparent as a steady drip, or possibly a stream of water, from the cistern overflow pipe

With a Portsmouth ball valve the most probable cause is failure of the washer.

To renew the washer cut off the water supply to the ball valve. Withdraw the split pin on which the float arm pivots and remove the float arm. Insert the blade of a screw-driver into the opening from which the float arm has been withdrawn and push the plug, with its washer, out of the end of the valve body.

The plug is in two parts; though this may not be apparent on inspection. It should be possible to remove the washer retaining cap by slipping the blade of a screw-driver through the slot in the plug and then by turning the cap with a pair of pliers.

This can be extremely difficult. Don't risk damaging the plug in your efforts. If the cap cannot be unscrewed, pick out the old washer with the point of a penknife blade and force the new one under the flange of the cap. Make sure that it lies flat on its seating.

Before reassembling the valve, clean the plug with a piece of fine abrasive paper. Wrap a piece of abrasive paper round a pencil and clean the inside of the valve body in the same way. Apply a thin film of petroleum jelly to the plug to act as a lubricant and reassemble.

Other possible causes of a leaky valve are:

A leaking ball float. Renewal of the float is the answer but a temporary repair can be made by enlarging the leak and draining the water out of the ball. Replace on float arm and slip over it a small plastic bag. Secure the neck of the bag around the float arm with a piece of string.

Ball-valve wrongly adjusted for water level. Garston and Torbeck valves are provided with simple means of raising or lowering the float. To adjust the level of water in a cistern served by a Portsmouth valve, unscrew and remove the ball float. Take the float arm gently but firmly in both hands and bend the float end upwards to raise the water level; downwards to lower it.

Low pressure valve connected directly to high pressure main. Remedy is to replace with high pressure valve or, if nozzle inlet is detachable, with high pressure nozzle. Alternatively fit an equilibrium ball valve.

2. Slow refilling after water has been flushed or drawn from cistern

Possible causes of this trouble are:

High pressure valve connected to a water supply from a storage cistern. Replace with a low pressure or full-way valve or, if nozzle is detachable, with a low pressure nozzle. Alternatively fit an equilibrium ball valve.

Hard water scale impeding plug of Portsmouth valve. Dismantle valve. Clean and lubricate plug and interior of valve body as suggested above after rewashering.

Debris from main or supply pipe impeding flow through diaphragm valve. Trouble from this cause is likely to have a sudden onset. Dismantle diaphragm valve and remove debris. To dismantle a diaphragm valve turn off the water supply to the valve. It should be possible to unscrew the large knurled head that retains the valve mechanism by hand. When reassembling, screw up hand-tight only.

3. Ball valve noise

The sound of rushing water is only one, and perhaps the least disturbing, of the noises for which a ball valve may be responsible.

Other noises may include the heavy knocking of water hammer as the valve—or even the tap over the kitchen sink—closes; a roar that I have heard described as being similar to an express train entering a tunnel; or a relatively gentle humming noise that goes on and on—and on!

Water hammer results from the valve bouncing on its seating as pressure from the main attempts to force it open and the buoyancy of the float endeavours to keep it closed. Replacement with one or other of the equilibrium valves that have been described is the answer.

The other noises result from ripple formation on the surface of the water in the cistern as water flows in. These ripples shake the float up and down and to and fro. This movement is transmitted to the valve and thence to the water supply pipe which—especially if it is of copper—acts as a sounding board, to produce a noise out of all proportion to its original cause.

A stabiliser—a plastic disc or even a plastic flower pot—fixed to the float arm so as to be suspended in the water an inch or so below the float, will help. Fitting a modern Garston pattern or Torbeck valve should cure the trouble.

Another point to watch, especially when replacing a metal cold water storage cistern with a plastic one (see chapter on 'Cold Water Services and Cisterns'), is that the cold water supply pipe to the storage cistern is securely fixed to the roof timbers.

Chapter 26
The lavatory

The lavatory, by whichever name you prefer to call it—the loo, the toilet, the w.c.—may be the smallest room in the house, but it is by no means the least important. It is a room that even your least exacting guest will expect to be readily available, silent, unobtrusive and 100% efficient.

In a modern home one would expect to find two lavatories. One might be near the back door, perhaps even approached externally, readily available to the children of the household when playing in the garden. The other will be adjacent to, or perhaps within, the bathroom.

Lavatory suites are often classified loosely as 'high level' or 'low level' but there are a great many more variations.

Let us take the flushing cistern first. British cisterns are constructed to give a two gallon flush. In the building trade they are often called 'water waste preventers' or WWPs for short. There are, at the present time, two different kinds of flushing cistern in common use.

Cast iron cisterns

The older pattern is the traditional high level cistern, sometimes known as the 'bell' or 'pull and let go' type. Rapidly becoming obsolete, it is still to be found, particularly in outside lavatories, in older houses.

This kind of cistern is usually made of cast iron. It has a well in its base in which stands a heavy iron 'bell'. A stand-pipe outlet to the flush pipe rises from the base of the cistern, inside the bell, to terminate open-ended an inch or so above normal water level.

The cistern is flushed by raising the bell, usually by pulling a chain, and then releasing it. The bell's conical shape forces the water within it upwards and over the rim of the stand-pipe as it descends. The falling water mixes with air in the flush-pipe, creating a partial vacuum and thereby starting the siphonic action that empties the cistern.

The bell has metal lugs on its base that permit water to pass under the rim and up to the stand-pipe outlet, once the siphonic action has started.

Strong, hard wearing and reliable as these cisterns usually are, they have a number of disadvantages. They are noisy in action. Noise results from the clank of the bell as it descends, the rush of water from high level and, since they are usually found connected direct to the main, the incoming rush of water as the cistern refills. At their best they are hardly objects of beauty. All too often they are to be found dripping with condensation, with flaking paint and large patches of rust.

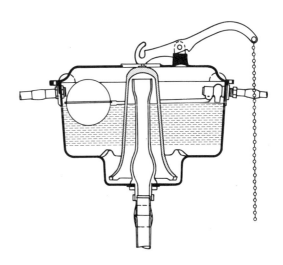

A bell or Burlington pattern flushing cistern operates as a result of the bell, when descending, forcing water over the lip of the standpipe into the flush pipe. Descending water mixes with air in the flush pipe to create the partial vacuum on which siphonic action depends.

Plastic cisterns

These objections are, to a greater or less extent—depending upon the particular appliance—overcome by the more modern 'direct action' cistern. These are sometimes described as low level cisterns though they can be, and frequently are, installed at high level.

This type of cistern is usually made either of ceramic or plastic material. Most have a flat base, though some well-bottomed models are manufactured to facilitate the replacement of old bell cisterns. The flushing mechanism consists of a stand-pipe rising to above water level and then bending over and opening out to form an open-based dome. When the flushing lever is operated a disc is raised within this dome to throw water over the inverted U at the top of the siphon into the flush pipe, thus starting the siphonic action.

The disc has a hole, or holes in it to permit water to pass through freely once the siphonic action has begun. As the

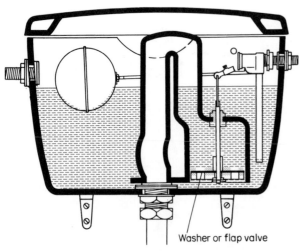

Washer or flap valve

Operating the lever of a direct action flushing cistern raises a plate within the dome of the siphon. This throws water over the inverted U of the siphoning mechanism to start the flushing action. The plate has holes in it to permit water to pass through freely during the flush. These holes are closed when the plate is raised by means of a flap valve or diaphragm.

disc is raised these holes are closed by a valve—usually nowadays a simple plastic flap.

The slim-line cistern

A recent development, of considerable interest to the d.i.y enthusiast, has been the advent of the slim-line flushing cistern or 'flush panel'. Space saving in a new bathroom or lavatory, it also simplifies the conversion of a high level to a low level suite.

The lavatory pan of a conventional low level suite is situated a couple of inches or so further from the wall than that of a high level suite. This is to accommodate the flushing cistern and to enable the seat to be raised when required.

In the past, the conversion of a high level to a low level suite has meant moving the lavatory pan forward and extending the branch drain or branch soil-pipe to which it is connected—a somewhat daunting task. The slim line cistern or flush-panel has changed all that. It is usually possible, using one of these cisterns, to convert from high level to low level without the need to change the position of the pan.

Another new development, likely to become more widely known as the need for water conservation increases, is the dual flush cistern. On a great many occasions a full two gallon flush is not needed after the use of the lavatory. If the operating handle of a dual-flush cistern is depressed and immediately released, the cistern gives a one gallon flush only. For a full flush the lever must be held down for a few moments

Types of pan

There are three basic designs of modern lavatory pan: the wash-down, the single

A wash-down low level lavatory suite depends upon the weight and momentum of the 2 gal flush to cleanse the pan. A conventional suite of this kind has the pan several inches further from the wall than does the equivalent high level suite. This is to permit the flushing cistern to be accommodated. (Courtesy Fordham Pressings Ltd)

The use of a slim-line flushing cistern such as the Fordham flush panel usually makes it possible to convert a high level lavatory suite to low level operation without moving the position of the pan. (Courtesy Fordham Pressings Ltd)

trap siphonic and the double-trap siphonic pan.

The **wash-down pan** is the basic lavatory pan with which everyone is familiar. Cleaning of the pan and its recharging with water depend upon the weight and momentum of the two-gallon flush entering at the back of the pan and via the flushing rim.

The other two types of pan depend, at least partially, on the weight of the atmosphere, upon siphonic action, for their effectiveness. They permit the use of 'close coupled' lavatory suites in which pan and cistern comprise one unit, without even the short flush pipe of a low level suite.

Single-trap siphonic pans are so designed, either by means of a constriction or a bend in the outlet, to ensure that the outlet pipe fills with water as the pan is flushed. This

results in the escaping water pushing the air in the pipe in front of it and producing a partial vacuum—and siphonic action. With these appliances, water level will rise slightly in the pan as the flush first operates and will then empty rapidly, perhaps with a gurgle as the siphon is broken.

Double-trap siphonic suites operate on an ingenious principle that ensures exceptionally silent and effective action. As the first flow of water passes from the cistern to the pan, air is aspirated—by means of a pressure reducing device—from the space between the two traps. The partial vacuum produced ensures that atmospheric pressure pushes out the contents of the pan. The flushing water is required only to set this process in motion and to recharge the pan.

With a properly designed and installed

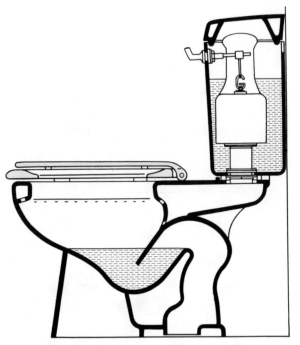

Siphonic lavatory suites can be 'close coupled' — no visual flush pipe is needed. At the start of the flush of a single trap siphonic suite, such as the Twyfords suite illustrated, water rises in the pan. It then rapidly discharges over the outlet of the trap completely filling the constricted part of the outlet. This creates a strong siphonic action.

double trap siphonic suite the water level in the pan should fall visibly *before* water descends from the flushing rim.

Siphonic suites, particularly double-trap siphonic suites, are silent in operation, permit neat close-coupled construction and a large water area. They are especially to be recommended where, as in a lavatory opening from an entrance lobby, silent unobtrusive operation is of first importance.

The only disadvantage of this kind of suite arises from possible misuse. A foreign body, such as a plastic toy or a small cleaning brush, flushed from a siphonic suite can create a blockage that is particularly difficult to clear.

When contemplating the replacement of a washdown suite with a double trap siphonic type, remember that the latter will project further from the wall.

Replacing a cracked pan

Renewing a cracked or leaking wash-down lavatory pan is a job that has been successfully undertaken by many d.i.y enthusiasts Removing the old pan is likely to present the greatest difficulty.

This is easy enough where the lavatory is an upstairs one and has a wooden boarded floor. The pan, in this case, will be screwed to the wooden floor and connected to the branch soil-pipe by means of a mastic or a patent push-on plastic joint. The flush-pipe connection must be disconnected and the floor screws removed. The pan can then be pulled forward and disposed of.

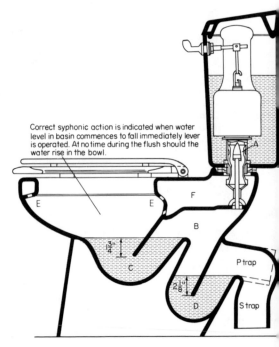

Correct syphonic action is indicated when water level in basin commences to fall immediately lever is operated. At no time during the flush should the water rise in the bowl.

Double-trap siphonic lavatory suites are particularly silent and effective in action. In the Twyfords model illustrated, water flowing from the flushing cistern passes over the pressure reducing fitment A. This aspirates air from the chamber B and siphonic action draws the contents of the pan through the sealed traps C and D. The sides of the pan are thoroughly washed and cleansed by streams of water from the perforated rim E. After flushing, the pan is filled and the traps resealed by the emptying of afterflush chamber F.

Correct siphonic action is indicated by water level in the pan falling immediately the flushing lever is operated — before water appears from the flushing rim.

Greater difficulty arises where the pan is on a solid ground floor and is connected to the branch underground drain by means of a cement joint.

Tackle its removal this way:

Disconnect the flush pipe. Deliberately break the outlet from the old pan with a hammer, just behind the trap. Remove the retaining screws, if any, and pull the front part of the pan forward. If, as is likely, it is cemented to the floor, you will need a cold chisel to prise it away from its base.

You will now be left with the broken outlet of the lavatory pan protruding from the drain socket. Stuff a wad of newspaper into the drain socket to prevent pieces of broken pipe and cement falling into the drain. Then tackle the outlet with a cold chisel and hammer.

Work carefully and systematically, keeping the blade of the chisel pointing towards the centre of the pipe. Try to break down the lavatory outlet to the base of the socket at one point. You will then find that the remainder comes out fairly easily. Clear away the jointing material in the same way.

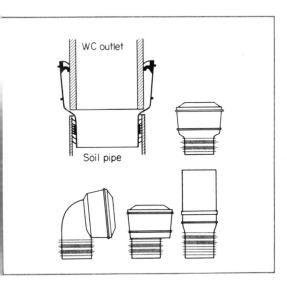

WC outlet

Soil pipe

Push-on plastic w.c. connectors make the connection of the lavatory pan to the branch drain or soil pipe a simple task.

Try not to break the drain socket but, if you accidentally do so, don't despair. Modern plastic push-on drain connectors can be used, without a socket, directly into the drain pipe.

Do *not* set the new lavatory pan on a base of wet cement. It has been established that setting cement can set up tensions that can lead to early pan damage.

Place the pan in position and mark through the screw-holes with a ball point pen refill on to the floor. Remove the pan. Drill and plug the points that you have marked. Replace the pan and screw down - not too hard - using lead washers to protect the pan from the screw heads.

I have suggested using a plastic push-on connector for the drain connection. An alternative is to bind a couple of turns of waterproof building tape round the pan outlet and caulk down hard into the drain socket. Fill in the space between outlet and socket with a non-setting mastic filler and complete the joint with another couple of turns of waterproof tape.

Don't forget to remove the wad of paper from the drain pipe before placing the pan in position!

Faults in lavatory installations

1. Failure to flush when lever is operated
This is a common and embarrassing fault. Check that the water level in the cistern is correct: about ½ in below the overflow pipe.

If the water level is correct then the fault is almost certainly due to the failure of the flap valve that closes the holes in the disc within the siphon when this disc is raised.

You must remove the siphon to renew this valve. Tie up the ball-valve to prevent water flowing in and flush cistern to empty. Disconnect the flush pipe. The siphon can then usually be withdrawn after unscrewing the large nut immediately beneath the cistern.

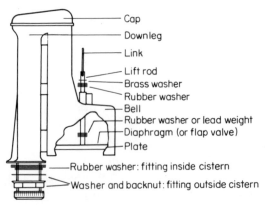

- Cap
- Downleg
- Link
- Lift rod
- Brass washer
- Rubber washer
- Bell
- Rubber washer or lead weight
- Diaphragm (or flap valve)
- Plate
- Rubber washer: fitting inside cistern
- Washer and backnut: fitting outside cistern

A view of the siphon removed from the flushing cistern.

Have a new valve ready for replacement. These plastic 'flap-valves' or 'siphon washers' can be obtained from any builders' merchant. You should get a valve large enough to cover the disc and touch the sides of the siphon dome.

2. Cistern fills too slowly

After flushing, the cistern should be ready for use again within two minutes. If it is not, it is probable that a high pressure ball valve has been fitted to a low pressure water supply. Alternatively the valve may be clogged with scale or, with a Garston pattern valve, debris from the main or main storage tank may be clogging the nozzle outlet (see 'Faults in Ball Valves in Chapter 25).

3. Cistern flushes but fails to cleanse pan

Check that the flush pipe connects to the pan inlet squarely and that the inlet is unobstructed. Check, with the fingers or a mirror, that the flushing rim is clear. Check, with a spirit level, that the pan is set dead level.

When flushed, water should run equally round each side of the flushing rim to meet at the centre. There should be, no whirl-pool effect.

4. Double-trap siphonic suite fails to siphon out when flush is operated

This is usually due to obstruction of the pressure reducing device with jointing material or debris from the cistern.

5. Leakage from joint between lavatory pan outlet and soil-pipe or drain socket

Renew this joint as suggested in instructions for renewing a defective lavatory pan.

6. Condensation on flushing cistern—perhaps giving the impression that the cistern has become porous

The real answer to this problem lies in better ventilation and the provision of a radiant heat source. Where the lavatory is in the bathroom avoid drip-drying clothes over the bath. Always run an inch or so of cold water into the bath before turning on the hot tap.

Intractable cases may be improved by lining the inside of the cistern with strips of expanded polystyrene—as used for insulation under wall paper. Dry the cistern thoroughly and use an epoxy resin adhesive. Do not refill the cistern until the adhesive is thoroughly set.

7. Noise from the lavatory suite

For noise in filling see 'Faults in Ball Valves' Chapter 25. The most probable cause is failure of the ball valve washer. For noise when in use, bear in mind that a low level suite is quieter than a high level one and that the quietest of all is the close coupled double trap siphonic suite. Make sure that there is a mastic, not a cement, joint between the pan outlet and the branch drain or soil pipe.

Noise from an upstairs lavatory may be reduced by raising a floor board and running fine sand or vermiculate chips on to the ceiling of the room below.

Chapter 27
Baths and showers

Baths come in all shapes and sizes these days. Some appear to have been specially designed to meet the suggestion made, in the interests of economy, by a Government Minister a few years ago that married couples should, 'share a bath'. Others seem to be much too splendid examples of domestic architecture to be relegated to the bathroom!

You can be quite confident that, whether you live in a cottage, a suburban semi or a mansion, you will find in the showrooms and the manufacturers' glossy catalogues, the size and shape of bath that you need. The price, which will depend to a large extent upon the material of which the bath is made, may be another matter.

The traditional material is enamelled cast iron. Enamelled cast iron baths are strong, tough, hard wearing and extremely heavy and expensive! As cast iron is a good conductor of heat they have the added disadvantage of robbing the bath water of its warmth. This is of greater importance nowadays than it was in the past when unlimited supplies of hot water could be cheaply obtained.

Enamelled pressed steel baths are made of material similar to that used in modern slim-line pressed steel hot water radiators. They are considerably cheaper than cast iron baths and, once installed, can be relied upon to give years of trouble-free service. They are, however, much more liable to accidental damage in storage, delivery and installation.

My choice nowadays, whether for d.i.y or professional installation, would be one of the modern acrylic plastic baths. These are tough, but extremely light and easily handled. They can therefore be installed by one man working alone. They are available in a variety of colours. Slight surface scratches can be polished out and, of course, surface damage will not lead to the corrosion to which the other kinds of bath are prone.

Acrylic plastic material is a poor conductor of heat. Consequently baths of this material tend to retain the heat of the water and to be comfortable in use.

They can be damaged by excessive heat however. A burning cigarette rested, even briefly, on the edge of the bath can do irreversible damage. For the same reason,

(a) A metal cradle, which speeds and simplifies installation whilst affording a base for fixing side and end panels is a standard extra of all Cleopatra range acrylic baths.
1. *The universal wallfixing bracket can be used under, at the side of, or over the lip of the bath.*
2. *Simple screw adjustments at five points compensate for irregular floor levels.*

(b) Details of the cradle for Armitage acrylic baths.

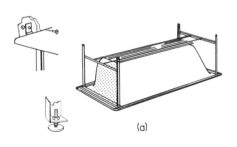

(a)

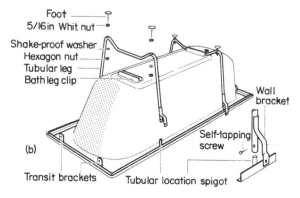

Foot
5/16in Whit. nut
Shake-proof washer
Hexagon nut
Tubular leg
Bath leg clip
Wall bracket
Self-tapping screw
(b)
Transit brackets
Tubular location spigot

keep the flame of any blow torch that you may be using for pipe jointing, well away from the plastic material.

There was another snag about some of the earlier pioneer models. Being less rigid than metal baths, they tended to sag and creak as they were filled with water and, even more disconcertingly, as the bather stepped in.

This drawback has been overome by the manufacturers providing substantial metal or wood cradles and means of securing them to the bathroom wall. Since these baths are as new to many professional plumbers as they are to the d.i.y man, full and detailed instructions are provided with each bath sold. These instructions should be followed exactly.

The space behind the bath will be very limited and difficult to work in. As much as possible should be done before the bath is moved into position. Fix the taps or mixer as described in Chapter 25. Have the hot and cold water pipe lines in position ready to be connected to the tails of the taps by means of a compression joint incorporating a tap connector (see Chapter 32).

The trap should also be connected to the waste pipe in advance and the waste outlet of the bath bedded into the hole provided for it in a non-setting mastic such as 'Plumbers Mait'. All that will then need to be done when the bath is moved into position is to tighten up the nut connecting the waste outlet to the trap and to connect the taps and overflow pipe. Be sure to do the final operations in logical order. Connect up the further tap first, then the overflow and finally the nearer tap.

With plastic baths it is wise to use a plastic trap and waste pipe. The plastic material of the bath will move slightly as a result of expansion when filled with hot water. A rigidly fixed metal trap and waste could damage the bath plastic.

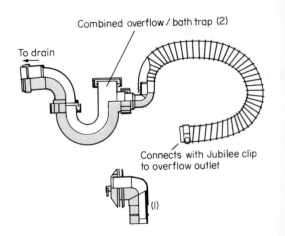

The bent bath overflow outlet 1 connects by means of a jubilee clip to the flexible overflow pipe of the combined overflow/bath trap 2

Finally, of course, you must seal off the gap between the edge of the bath and the wall. Again, a non-setting mastic is best for this purpose. There are a number of these on the market.

Faults in baths

1. Blocked waste outlet—water fails to run away when waste plug is pulled out.

Use a 'force cup' or 'sink waste plunger' to clear blockage in the trap or waste pipe. This consists of a hemisphere of rubber or plastic mounted on a wooden handle. It is a basic plumbing tool that every householder should possess.

Place the rubber hemisphere over the waste outlet. With the other hand hold a damp cloth firmly against the overflow outlet. Plunge down sharply several times with the wooden handle.

Since water cannot be compressed, the force of the plunger action will be transmitted to the obstruction to dislodge it. The overflow outlet must be blocked to prevent this force from being dissipated up the overflow pipe.

A very slow flow of water from the waste outlet indicates a partial blockage.

Check that the waste outlet grid is not obstructed with hair or other debris. If the trouble persists after this has been cleared use one of the proprietary chemical drain cleaners that you can buy at any household store.

These drain cleaners have a caustic soda base and are potentially very dangerous. Read the makers' instructions and follow them carefully. Keep the tin well away from children.

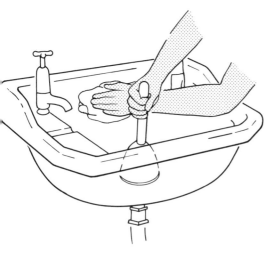

To clear a blockage in a sink, basin or bath waste hold a dampened cloth firmly over the overflow outlet while plunging the waste outlet with a force cup or plunger.

2. Stains in bath below bath taps.

Proprietary bath cleaners such as Jenolite are usually very effective in removing these. An old fashioned remedy, that I have known to succeed where modern ones have failed, is to mix up a paste with hydrogen peroxide and cream of tartar. Apply to the stains. Leave overnight and wipe off in the morning.

Stains of this kind indicate a dripping tap. Change washer as suggested in a previous chapter.

3. Enamel of cast iron or pressed steel bath worn and in poor condition

Bath renovating preparations of various kinds are advertised in all do-it-yourself publications.

An essential prerequisite of success with these preparations is thorough cleansing of the bath surfaces. Wash with a very dilute solution of hydrochloric acid and rinse. Apply a fine abrasive to the whole

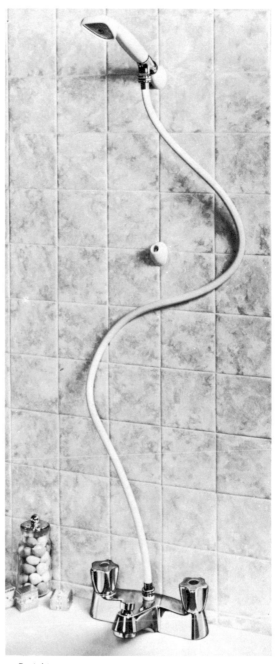

Bath/shower mixer made by Barking Brassware Company. This permits the mixed hot and cold water to be diverted upwards to the shower sprinkler at the flick of a switch.

bath surface. Wash again in very dilute hydrochloric acid and rinse with a solution of washing soda. Rinse again with plain water and dry thoroughly.

A shower cabinet may be installed on a bathroom, in a bedroom, on a landing or even in the cupboard under the stairs. (Courtesy Twyfords Ltd).

Showers

There's a great deal to be said for a shower. A shower uses less water and takes less time than a sit-down bath. It has been estimated that five or six satisfying showers can be obtained for the same amount of hot water that would be needed for one bath. Even with quite a small family a morning sit-down bath for each member would be a physical, as well as an economic, impossibility in most homes. It is by no means impossible where a shower is installed.

Showers are more hygienic—the bather is not sitting in his own dirty water—and mean less work for the housewife cleaning up afterwards. Elderly people, who may be incapable or afraid of getting into a sit-down bath, can step into a shower cubicle without trouble or anxiety.

Showers can be installed as an adjunct to a conventional bath or as a separate amenity in their own shower cabinet. They are particularly useful where older properties are being brought up to date and there is not space for a bathroom. A shower cubicle can be accommodated on a landing, in a bedroom or even in the cupboard under the stairs.

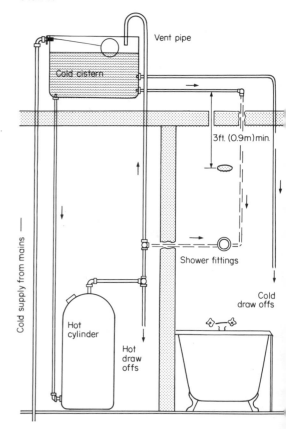

The essential design requirements for a conventional shower are:
1. *Hot and cold water supplies under equal pressure from a storage cistern.*
2. *A minimum head of 3ft but 5ft is to be preferred.*
3. *A cold water supply taken direct from the cold water storage cistern.*

There are certain minimum plumbing design requirements that must be met if a shower is to be both effective and safe.

The hot and cold water supplies to the shower must be under equal pressure. Where hot water supply is from a cylinder storage system, water pressure on the hot side of the shower will derive from the cold water storage cistern. The cold supply must therefore also be taken from this cistern. It is both illegal and impracticable to take the cold supply to a shower installation of this kind direct from the main.

Then again, pressure must be adequate. Pressure at the shower sprinkler depends upon the vertical distance between the sprinkler and the surface of the water in the cold water storage cistern. The absolute minimum vertical distance or 'head' is 3 ft. This will give an effective shower only if the pipe runs are very short and free of bends. Best results will be obtained if the 'head' between shower sprinkler and cistern base is 5 ft or more.

It should be noted that the level of the hot water cylinder relative to the shower is

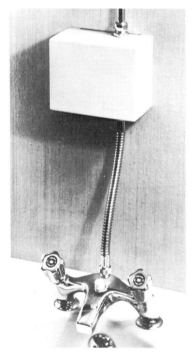

The Flomatic shower booster pump operates on a flow switch and permits shower installation even where the vertical distance between the shower sprinkler and the surface of the water in the storage cistern is no more than 200 mm (8 in) (Barking Brassware Co.)

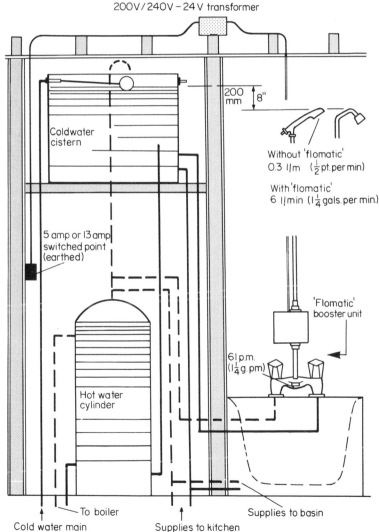

immaterial. It can be above, below or on the same level as the shower. It is the level of the *cold water storage cistern* that matters.

Another important design point is that the cold water supply to the shower should be taken direct from the storage cistern. It should not be a branch taken from a pipe-line supplying other draw-off points.

This is a safety measure. If the cold supply were taken from such a branch pipe-line then the flushing of a lavatory or the turning on of a cold basin tap would reduce cold water flow to the shower. Dangerous scalding could result from the sudden rise in water temperature.

For a similar reason it is best to take the hot water supply in a separate pipe-line from the hot water storage cylinder. This is however a little less important A sudden drop in temperature may cause discomfort, but is hardly likely to be dangerous, to the bather.

If your plumbing system is so designed that it just is not possible for you to meet the minimum requirements that I have set out, it may still be possible for you to install a shower.

There are, nowadays, flow-operated electric shower pumps on the market that can be used to boost pressure where the minimum 3 ft head is not available. These add to the cost of installation but they can be very useful in a flat or maisonette where the level of the storage cistern cannot be raised.

Some manufacturers of multipoint gas instantaneous heaters provide the means of supplying a shower from their appliances. As these water heaters are usually fed direct from the main, cold water from the main may be permitted to mix with hot water from the appliance. A patent anti-scald valve is an essential feature of instal-lations of this kind.

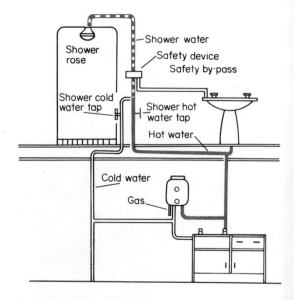

A shower can sometimes be connected directly to an instantaneous gas hot water system without the need for a cold water storage cistern.

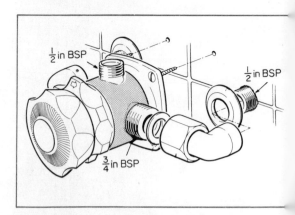

A Bourner's manual mixing valve can be fixed as shown

There are also a number of electrically heated instantaneous showers on the market. These need only connecting to the rising main and to a suitable elec-tricity supply. The simplicity with which these appliances can be installed in prac-tically any situation has made them increasingly popular in recent years. It should be said however that their rate of delivery of warm water is considerably less than that from a conventional shower.

Mixing valves

All conventional showers are provided with some kind of mixing valve to enable the user to vary the temperature of the water at will. The simplest kind of mixing valve consists of the two bath taps. Rubber push-on connectors can be used to join these taps to a shower attachment above the bath. Water temperature and flow are adjusted by opening the taps until the shower water is at the required temperature.

An improvement on this arrangement is to be found in the combined bath mixer/shower from which water at the required temperature can flow into the bath from the spout of the mixer or, at the flick of a control knob, be diverted up to the shower fitting.

Most independent showers have a single manual mixing valve which can be turned to vary the temperature and, in some instances, the flow of the water.

Yet another refinement is the thermostatic mixing valve. A thermostatic valve will maintain water temperature at a constant level despite fluctuating pressures in either the hot or the cold supply. It can therefore cancel the otherwise essential requirement that every shower must have its own independent cold water supply.

It is important that the limitations of thermostatic valves should be appreciated. They cannot *increase* pressure in either the hot or the cold water supply. They will simply reduce the pressure on one side of the valve to match that on the other. If, for instance, cold water pressure should drop in the thermostatic mixing valve of a shower already operating on minimum head, then the shower would simply dry up until pressure was restored.

Both bath and independent showers must be provided with plastic curtains or a glass or plastic screen to prevent spillage. Independent showers have a foot tray which may be made of ceramic, enamelled steel or plastic material. The waste outlet from a shower tray is connected to the waste pipe in the same way as the outlet from a bath.

Faults in shower installations

1. Impossibility of obtaining a shower at a comfortable temperature. Shower runs cold and then, after adjustment of the taps or valve, suddenly hot
This is usually the result of having the hot supply under pressure from a storage cistern and the cold supply direct from the main. The remedy is to take the cold supply from the cistern supplying the hot water cylinder.

2. Water descends from sprinkler in a feeble stream instead of a shower
This results from insufficient water pressure. The cheapest remedy is to raise the level of the cold water storage cistern, if necessary building a platform for it within the roof space. If this cannot be done consider the possibility of providing an electric shower pump.

3. Distributing holes in shower sprinkler blocked, giving reduced flow
This usually results from scale formation within the shower head. Dismantle and clean out. Consider the possibility of installing a mains water softener (see Chapter 30).

Chapter 28
Sinks, basins and bidets

Sinks, basins and bidets, despite their very different uses, present similar plumbing problems and can conveniently be considered together.

Sinks

In the '30s and '40s, the glazed ceramic Belfast sink with its wooden draining board, was regarded as the epitome of surburban luxury. It was certainly a tremendous improvement on the shallow 'London pattern' sink that had preceded it.

There are still plenty of Belfast sinks about. They are usually supported by strong brackets built into the wall. They have a weir overflow and are usually supplied with water from bib-taps projecting from the glazed tiles of the wall behind them. Their hard, unyielding base spells certain destruction to any item of crockery accidentally dropped into them.

Nowadays they are being replaced by sink units incorporating a pressed enamelled steel or—more probably—a stainless steel sink and drainer. Units of this kind are the standard fitting in new homes.

Enamelled steel sinks are obtainable in a number of attractive colours to match the kitchen decor but they have the disadvantage that the enamel can be chipped, and the sink permanently ruined, by accidental damage. Unless a plastic can be produced capable of standing up to the very heavy use—and misuse—to which sinks are subjected, it seems likely that stainless steel will remain the most popular kitchen sink material for years to come.

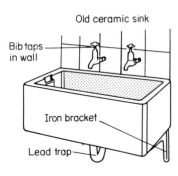

Old ceramic sink

Bib taps in wall

Iron bracket

Lead trap

(a)

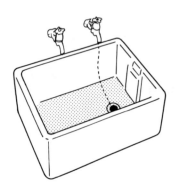

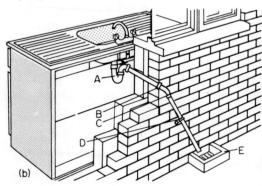

(a)Ceramic 'Belfast' pattern sinks are often fixed to the kitchen wall with strong cantilever brackets which must be removed or cut back flush with the wall when replacing with a modern sink unit. Water supply is usually from bib taps protruding from the tiled wall above the sink.
(b) A modern sink unit with 'pillar type' sink mixer.

A   waste trap
B   waste pipe passing through wall
C   elbow connector joints two straight lengths of waste pipe
D   pipe clip supporting waste pipe
E   gulley

(b)

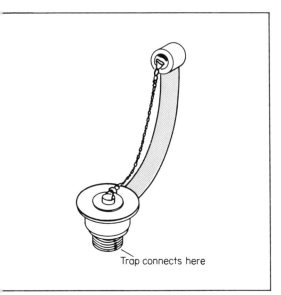

Trap connects here

The combined waste and overflow of a modern stainless steel sink resembles that of a bath.

Stainless steel sinks may be provided with double or single drainers. Some are made with double sinks to facilitate washing up and hot rinsing or, alternatively, to permit washing up and food preparation to proceed at the same time. Most are of the traditional rectangular shape but recently smaller round sinks have become popular. These make it possible to dispense with the washing up bowl.

Water supply is provided by pillar taps, or by a sink mixer, fitted into holes provided at the rear of the sink (see Chapter 25). Some stainless steel sinks are provided with a built-in overflow but the tendency nowadays is to manufacture them with an over-

flow outlet only. This is connected to the waste outlet by means of a flexible pipe similar to that used for bath overflows.

All sinks must have a trapped outlet; either the traditional U bend or the more attractive looking bottle trap. The trap seal may be 50 mm (2 in) if discharging over a drain gully or connected to a two-pipe drainage system. If the waste outlet is connected to a single stack drainage system (see Chapter 29) it must have a seal of 75 mm (3 in).

The waste disposal unit

Another labour saving device (or status symbol) that can be attached to the modern sink is the sink waste disposal unit; known as a garbage grinder in the USA. Operated by an electric motor the disposal unit will grind soft household and kitchen waste, vegetable peelings, food scraps, dead flowers and so on, to a slurry that can then be flushed away by running the cold tap.

To take a disposal unit the sink must have a 87.5 mm (3½ in) waste hole instead of the more usual 38 mm (1½ in) outlet. The outlets of stainless steel—but not enamelled—sinks, can be enlarged to the required size with a tool that can usually be obtained from the supplier of the disposal unit.

Waste disposal units are fitted by placing a rubber or plastic washer round the outlet hole and inserting the flange of the unit. The unit is then connected beneath the sink by a snap fastening. The outlet is to a trap in the normal way.

Traps come in all shapes and sizes. Their purpose is to prevent smells — and draughts — from the waste pipe entering the bathroom or kitchen.

To branch waste pipe

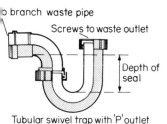

Screws to waste outlet

Depth of seal

Tubular swivel trap with 'P' outlet

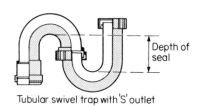

Depth of seal

Tubular swivel trap with 'S' outlet

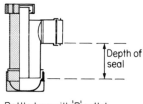

Depth of seal

Bottle trap with 'P' outlet

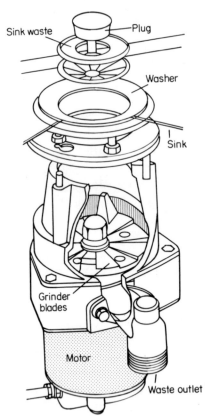

Sink waste — Plug

Washer

Sink

Grinder blades

Motor

Waste outlet

A sink waste disposal unit ('garbage grinder') is easy to fit, provided that your sink has the right size outlet, but an electrician should attend to any new wiring needed.

Replacing a sink

A d.i.y. plumbing job that many house-holders may wish to undertake is the replacement of an old Belfast sink with a modern sink unit. As with so many jobs of this kind, removing the old appliance is likely to prove far more difficult than fitting the new one!

Disconnect the waste pipe. Lift the old sink off its brackets and remove it. It will be **very** heavy. Don't attempt it without assistance.

The cantilever brackets must now be dug out of, or cut flush with, the wall behind the sink.

You will want to fit new pillar taps, or perhaps a sink mixer, into the new sink. Turn off the main stop-cock to cut off the supply to the cold tap and drain the supply pipe to the hot tap as suggested in Chapter 25.

Unscrew and remove the old taps and pull forward the water supply pipes. These may be chased into the wall.

Fix the new taps and the sink waste and overflow before moving the unit into position. The new taps should be fitted with a plastic flat washer above the sink and a spacer or top hat washer below. Bed the waste outlet into the hole provided in a non-setting mastic.

Place the sink unit in position. Cut the supply pipes to the correct length and connect them to the tails of the taps or mixer using cap and lining joints.

You **may** be able to use the old trap and waste pipe. If not, replace the trap with a plastic or metal bottle trap with an adjustable outlet that will enable you to connect up to the old waste pipe.

Faults in sinks

1. Blocked waste pipe

Sinks, because of the nature of their use are more likely to develop a choked waste pipe than any other plumbing fitting.

Try plunging with a force cup as suggested in Chapter 26 to clear bath wastes. If this proves to be ineffective the trouble is probably due to a solid object jammed in the trap.

All traps have some means of access. Straightforward U traps have screw-in caps at their base. The entire lower part of a bottle trap can be unscrewed and removed.

Place a bucket under the trap before attempting this. The sink will still be full of dirty water! Unscrew the access cap on the base of the bottle trap and probe inside with a piece of flexible wire. The chances are that you will dislodge, amid a flood of water, a hair grip, a match stick or even—if you have young and inquisitive children—a discarded ball-point pen refill

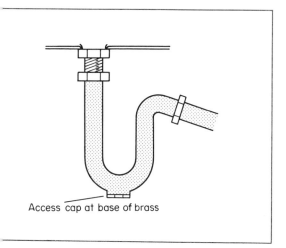

Access cap at base of brass

*he traditional U-bend trap has an access cap at the base
that can be unscrewed to enable you to clear a blockage.*

Wash basins

Vash basins—known as 'lavatory basins' or
even as 'lavatories' in the trade—like baths,
come these days in all shapes, sizes and
materials.

The traditional bathroom basin is likely
to be made of glazed vitreous china and will
be either a pedestal or a wall-hung basin.
Pedestal basins conceal the plumbing connections and the pedestal provides additional support. It should not be the *sole*
support however. Modern pedestal basins
are provided with concealed brackets or
hangers which are screwed into plugs fixed
in the wall behind.

Wall-hung basins are cheaper and are useful where floor space is limited. Before
fixing one, make sure that the wall behind
is capable of supporting the weight of the
basin and, perhaps, an adult leaning upon
it. Brick walls are safe enough but internal
breeze walls can provide a somewhat
dubious support.

Basins have a built-in overflow which
connects to an overflow slot in the metal
basin waste. When bedding this waste
outlet down into the outlet hole make
sure that the slot coincides with the outlet
of the built-in overflow.

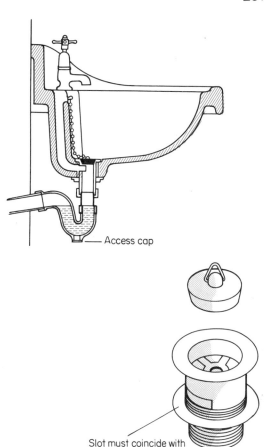

Access cap

Slot must coincide with
built in overflow of basin

*When fitting a ceramic basin of this kind it is essential
to make sure that the overflow slot in the basin waste
coincides with the built-in overflow of the basin.*

When fitting a new basin insert the taps
into their holes before placing the basin
into position. The taps are fitted in the
same way as those of baths and sinks but,
with relatively thick ceramic material, you
can use a flat, instead of a top-hat, washer
underneath. Do not overtighten the back
nuts. It is very easy to damage a ceramic
basin.

A vanity unit—the modern equivalent
of the Edwardian 'wash stand'—is a piece
of furniture, perhaps complete with drawers
for toiletry, into the surface of which is
inset a wash basin. The basin is usually of
enamelled steel or of plastic though there
are ceramic versions.

Vanity units are most often found in bedrooms where they are the 20th century equivalent of the Edwardian 'wash stand'. They can however also be an attractive and useful piece of furniture.

Occasionally found in very modern bathrooms, the Vanity Unit is particularly useful as a piece of bedroom furniture where it can do a lot towards removing the 8 o'clock queue at the bathroom door.

A vanity unit is fitted in exactly the same way as a sink unit except, of course, that the cold water supply will normally come from a storage cistern and not from the main.

A basin mixer can, in fact, only be fitte if the cold water supply is from a storag cistern. Unlike sink mixers, they do nc have separate channels for the hot an cold streams of water. These mix withi the body of the fitting and the same rule apply as for a shower mixer.

Some modern basin mixers incorporat 'pop up' waste plugs which eliminate th need for the traditional plug and chain. A control knob, between the hot and col water controls, can be operated to mak the waste plug 'pop up' and allow th basin to empty.

In addition to its use in the bathroor and bedroom the wash basin has a vita role in the lavatory or, as an estate agen would prefer to put it, where there is 'bathroom and separate toilet'. No civilisec person would question the importance o hand washing after visiting this room. Thi cannot conveniently be done unless ther is a basin with hot and cold water installed

In the past, considerations of space ma have made the provision of a basin in th lavatory all but impossible. This is not s today. There are available corner basins built in basins and basins of every degre of miniaturisation that can be fitted int even the smallest 'smallest room'.

Cold water supply cannot present problem; it must be available there for th flushing cistern. Where a separate lavatory is remote from the general hot wate supply system of the house, a small instant aneous gas or electric water heater car prove invaluable to provide hot water fo washing when it is required.

Bidets

Until quite recently the bidet was regardec as an exotic piece of Continental decadence—certainly not a desirable fitting for a re spectable British home.

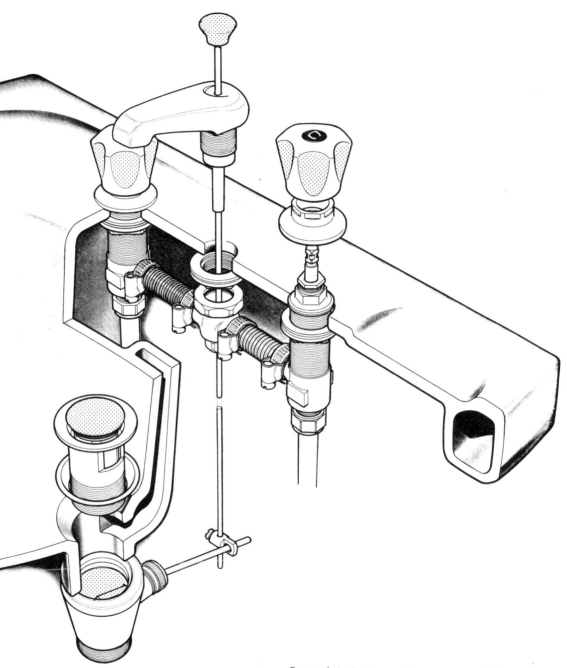

Bourner's basin mixer with pop-up waste looks extremely
complicated — until its component parts are revealed.
The pop-up waste eliminates the unsightly chain and
stopper and permits the basin to be emptied without
wetting the hands.

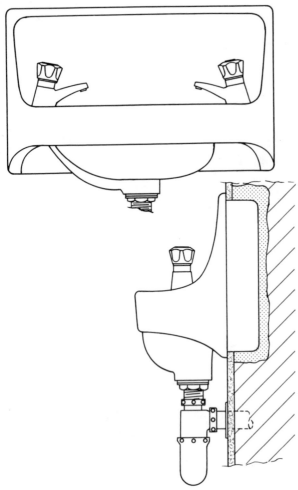

Twyford's built-in wash basin can be fitted into even the smallest lavatory compartment. To fix, cut out brickwork slightly deeper than built-in portion of basin. Line cavity with a weak cement. Place basin in position making allowance for final wall finish. Support basin until cement has set and, finally, apply wall finish. Alternatively a good quality modern adhesive can be used to fix the basin into the wall.

Old habits of thought die hard but these extremely useful pieces of sanitary equipment are gradually gaining acceptance in this country. Certainly, they figure prominently in builders merchants' showrooms and in the glossy catalogues of sanitary ware manufacturers. They are to be found too in growing numbers of British bathrooms.

The bidet is best considered as a specially designed low level wash basin on which the user can sit to wash the lower parts of the body. It can also—as anyone who has spent a walking holiday on the Continent will know—perform a useful secondary function as a foot bath.

There are two kinds of bidet and the differences between them are of considerable importance to the installer.

The simpler kind is, so far as plumbing in is concerned, indistinguishable from a wash basin. Usually described in the catalogue as having an 'over rim water supply', it has two pillar taps, or a mixer, mounted above the fitting at one end. It may have a pop-up or ordinary chain waste stopper and the usual waste outlet and trap.

It can be plumbed into an existing bathroom in exactly the same way as a new wash basin. The hot and cold supply pipes to the bath and basin can be cut, tee junctions inserted, and branch supply pipes taken to the hot and cold taps. It presents no special problems.

The more sophisticated type of bidet is usually referred to as 'rim supply with ascending spray' and special precautions are needed with regard to its installation.

Water enters this kind of bidet in two ways—via a rim, not unlike the flushing rim of a lavatory pan, and via an ascending spray. Warm water passing round the rim warms it and makes it comfortable for use. The ascending spray is directed towards those parts of the body that are to be cleansed.

With any kind of submerged inlet appliance there is a risk of contamination of the water supply by back siphonage.

To avoid this, the hot and cold supplies to the bidet must be taken direct from the hot water storage cylinder and the cold water storage cistern. They must not be taken as branches from pipelines supplying any other fittings. Furthermore the base of the cold water storage cistern must be at least 2.75 m (9 ft) above the inlet to the bidet.

From the point of view of drainage, bidets are regarded as being 'waste', not 'soil' fittings. Where the two-pipe system of above ground drainage is provided (see next chapter) the waste pipe from a bidet should discharge over a gully in the same way as that of a bath, basin or sink. It should not, like the outlet of a lavatory pan, be connected directly to the drain or soil pipe.

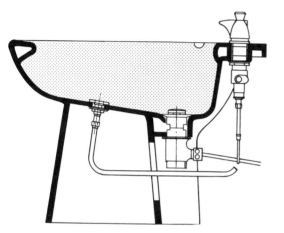

A rim supply, or ascending spray, bidet has a flushing rim round which water passes to fill the bidet and warm the seat for the user and an ascending spray directed towards the parts of the body to be cleansed. To prevent contamination of water supplies special design precautions are necessary in the installation of this kind of bidet.

An over-rim supply bidet is essentially a low level wash basin and presents no special plumbing problems.

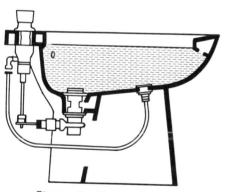

Rim supply with ascending spray

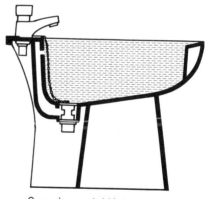

Over-rim supply bidet

Chapter 29
The drains

There have been tremendous changes both in design and materials in domestic drainage during the past two decades. These changes have been particularly revolutionary in the part of the drainage system that is above ground level.

If your home was built before the early 1960s it will almost certainly have a two-pipe drainage system. This system drew a distinction between 'soil fittings' (lavatory suites and urinals) and 'waste fittings' (sinks, baths, basins and bidets). The outlets from soil fittings were connected directly to the drainage system. The outlets from waste fittings were disconnected from the drainage system and entered it only via an external yard gulley.

A heavy cast iron or asbestos cement soil pipe would rise, to above eaves level, against an external wall of the house. This would be open ended to provide a high level ventilator to the drain. Into it would be connected the branch soil-pipe from any upstairs lavatory suite. The outlets of ground floor lavatories were connected directly to the underground drainage system by a branch drain joining the main drain at the nearest inspection chamber or drain man-hole.

The outlets from ground floor baths, sinks or basins protruded through the wall of the house to discharge over a yard gully which would, in its turn, be connected to the main drainage system via a branch drain.

Upstairs waste fittings (baths, basins and bidets) presented special problems. In the provinces it was usual for them to discharge in the open air, over a rain water hopper head. This would take the wastes to ground level through a length of waste or rain-water pipe to discharge, like the sink waste, over a yard gully.

Hopper heads were, and are, smelly, insanitary fittings. Soapy water discharged from bath and basin waste pipes dries and decomposes on their internal surfaces, producing unpleasant smells in the immediate vicinity of bedroom windows. Draughts, whistling up the open-ended main waste pipe, discharge smells from the gully in the same vicinity.

In some towns, notably London, the insanitary nature of these fittings was recognised and they were banned by local drainage bye-laws. In these areas the main waste pipe, like the soil pipe, had to extend to above eaves level. Branch waste pipes were connected into it but, as with the hopper-head arrangement, the bottom end of the waste pipe still discharged into the open air above a yard gully.

The Building Regulations of the mid-1960s, by requiring that all soil and waste pipes should be contained within the fabric of the building, hastened the almost universal adoption of the 'single stack' system for all above-ground drainage work. In the single stack system the distinction between 'soil' and 'waste' fittings is discarded and waste outlets from all sanitary appliances discharge into one main soil and waste stack, connected directly to the underground drain. Apart from the open end of this stack, protruding through the roof, the whole of the drainage is contained within the walls of the building.

Take a look at a house built in the last few years and note the difference from one built fifteen years or more ago. Gone is the hopper head, the waste pipe and the soil pipe climbing, as someone once said 'like petrified worms', up the wall of the house. Apart from the rain water gutters and down-pipes the only evidence of a drainage

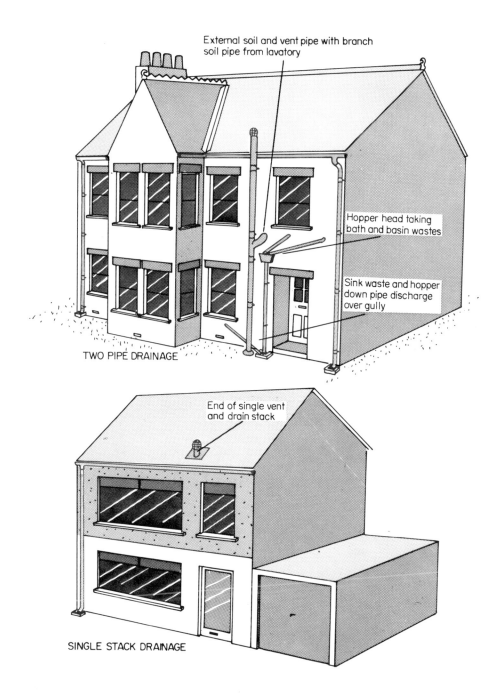

External soil and vent pipe with branch soil pipe from lavatory

Hopper head taking bath and basin wastes

Sink waste and hopper down pipe discharge over gully

TWO PIPE DRAINAGE

End of single vent and drain stack

SINGLE STACK DRAINAGE

The elevation of a house built before the mid-'60s will probably look like the top diagram. A branch soil pipe from an upstairs w.c. connects to a main external soil and vent pipe rising, open ended, to above eaves level. A hopper head collects wastes from an upstairs bath and basin and discharges them over the grid of a yard gully. A ground floor sink waste discharges over the same gully.

Apart from rain water guttering and down pipes, all that is likely to be visible of the plumbing of a modern house (shown in the lower diagram) is a few inches of PVC vent and drain stack protruding from the roof. The main stack, within the fabric of the building, may take w.c., bath, basin and sink wastes.

system that you will see will be a few inches of capped PVC tubing protruding from the roof above the bathroom.

When first introduced into this country, from the other side of the Atlantic, the single stack drainage system was regarded with suspicion by plumbers and public health engineers alike.

I well recall—at Battersea Polytechnic in 1947—earning the lecturer's unstinted praise for an essay in which I unequivocally condemned the single stack drainage system. It would, I said, undo all the progress made in sanitary science during the previous half century and would inevitably result in drain smells pervading domestic bathrooms and kitchens.

I pointed out the dangers of loss of seal in sink and basin traps from self-siphonage and induced siphonage. Basin traps had always had a tendency to self-siphonage. They were shallow (often with only a 1 in or 1½ in seal) and the discharge of the basin into a small diameter branch waste pipe often produced the partial vacuum that is a prerequisite of siphonic action. With the two-pipe system temporary loss of seal was of no great importance. Only smells from the short branch waste could enter the room. With a single stack system such loss of seal would—so I said—have catastrophic results.

Then again, siphonage of basin traps would be induced by bath wastes discharging past the connection of the basin waste to the main stack and aspirating the air from between the trap and the waste connection.

I pointed out too, that any blockage at the foot of the main soil and waste stack would make itself known by sewage flowing into the ground floor kitchen sink. If the single stack drainage system served a block of flats, residents on the upper floors would carry on using the drainage system oblivious of the havoc that they were creating in the flat of their ground floor neighbour.

The points that I made in that essay, that earned me full marks in 1947 (and would earn a student none today!), were valid enough. The introduction of the single stack system could have produced all the disasters that I so confidently predicted.

The dangers of siphonage, compression and blockage are real ones but they can be—and have been—overcome by careful planning and design.

Design of the waste system

For really successful single stack drainage the house needs to be designed round the plumbing system. Waste pipes from all appliances should be kept as short as possible. They should be laid with minimal falls. All fittings should be provided with 75 mm (3 in) deep seal traps. The connections to the stack pipe should be carefully planned to prevent any risk of the discharges from the lavatory suite outlet fouling and possibly blocking the outlets from other appliances.

The connection between the vertical waste stack and the underground drain must be made with an easy bend and the lowest connection to the stack pipe should be at least 760 mm (2 ft 6 in) above the level of the underground drain.

The design of the waste from the wash basin is particularly critical. These waste pipes are of small diameter (1¼ in or 30 mm) and are likely to be filled with water when the basin is emptied. There is therefore a considerable risk of the water in the trap being siphoned out.

To prevent this the basin waste must be laid with a very slight fall and should be no more than 1.68 m (5 ft 6 in) in length. Where circumstances compel a longer basin waste

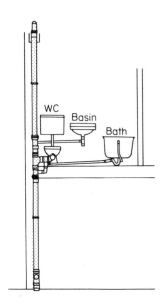

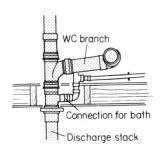

Connection for bath

Discharge stack

In order to avoid the danger of the outlet from the bath becoming fouled with discharges from the w.c. the bath waste — in a conventional single stack system — must be offset and taken into the main drainage stack at a point below the w.c. connection.

pipe, a larger diameter pipe may be used or, alternatively, a small ventilating pipe may be taken from behind the basin trap to connect to the main stack at least 1 m (3 ft) above the highest waste connection.

Prevention of the fouling of waste pipe outlets by lavatory suite discharges presents problems so far as the bath waste is concerned. One way to get over the difficulty is to offset the pipework through the floor so that it enters the main stack in the ceiling space or below it.

This is by no means a convenient arrangement and an alternative solution is to use the Marley collar boss which permits the bath waste to enter the stack immediately below the lavatory suite waste via a collar that protects it from any possibility of fouling or blockage.

Polyvinyl chloride (PVC or vinyl for short) is used almost universally for domestic single-stack above ground drainage. It may be joined by solvent welding or by ring-seal joints (see Chapter 32). Because this material expands as hot water passes through it, special expansion joints should be fitted where any straight run of waste pipe exceeds 1.8 m (6 ft) in length.

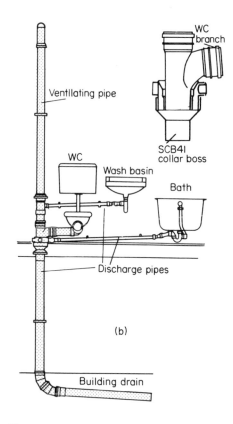

The Marley collar boss avoids the necessity of offsetting the bath waste pipe while affording it absolute protection from w.c. discharge.

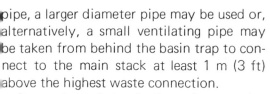

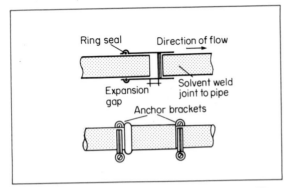

PVC tubing expands as hot water runs through it. The introduction of an expansion joint into a long run of tubing accommodates this expansion.

Although the waste pipe from a ground floor sink may be, and frequently is, connected to the main drainage stack, there is something to be said for taking it to an external gulley in the traditional way. The risk of a blockage at the base of a properly designed stack system may be remote. It is not, however, altogether impossible and the thought of sewage backing up into the kitchen sink is one that lacks appeal.

Furthermore, if the sink waste pipe discharges over a gully, it may be possible to lay the underground drain at a shallower depth—and depth means money where drainage is concerned!

If the sink waste pipe is taken to a gully it should enter it above water level but below the grid. This makes sure that the full force of the sink discharge is available to flush and cleanse the gully. It also ensures that autumn leaves blowing on to the grid cannot result in a flooded yard.

Underground drains

So far as underground drainage is concerned the changes that have taken place in recent years have related to materials rather than to design. Underground drains must still be laid in straight lines at a regular self-cleansing gradient. There must still be means of access for rodding every part of the drain.

Branch drains must still connect to the main drain, in the direction of flow, at inspection chambers or other access points.

If your home was built more than about twenty-five years ago the underground drains will consist of salt-glazed stoneware drain pipes, 2 ft long and connected with cement joints. They will be laid on a 6 in deep concrete bed and concrete will be haunched over them to protect them and to give the entire drainage structure some stability to reduce the risk of damage in the event of ground settlement.

They will, almost certainly, be laid to a fall of 1 in 40 (3 in in 10 ft). At each change of direction and wherever branch drains connect to the main drain there will be a brick built inspection chamber or manhole with an iron cover.

The drain passes through the inspection chamber in a half-channel with concrete benching on either side to prevent the walls of the chamber being fouled. The brick walls of the chamber *may* be rendered with cement and sand to make them watertight. This is now recognised as bad practice. The rendering is all too liable to flake off and block the drain. If concrete rendering is necessary it should be on the external walls of the chamber, between the walls and the surrounding earth.

The inspection chamber

Just inside your front gate will probably be a final inspection chamber containing an 'intercepting' or 'disconnecting' trap. The object of this trap, almost universally discarded in modern drainage systems, was to prevent gases, and perhaps rats, from the sewer entering the house drains.

The intercepting trap, where it exists, is undoubtedly the commonest site of drain blockage. Its disadvantages are very real and its benefits largely illusory. There should not *be* rats in a modern well-maintained

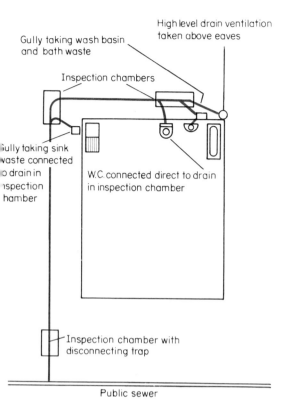

A plan of a traditional drainage system shows bath, basin and sink wastes disconnected from the drain by means of gullies. Inspection chambers are provided at junctions and changes of direction and an inspection chamber with an intercepting trap disconnects the house drainage from the public sewer.

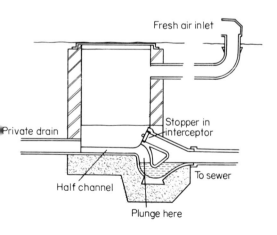

Intercepting or disconnecting traps are now regarded as obsolete. Their purpose was to prevent sewer gases or rats entering the house drains. They were a frequent site of blockage and the fresh air inlets associated with them were a common source of 'drain smells'.

sewer and, if the sewer is ventilated through the soil and vent stacks of every house connected to it, the sewer should be free of offensive gases.

The intercepting trap incorporates a rodding arm, closed by a stoneware stopper, through which it is possible to rod the drain right through to the sewer. It should perhaps be emphasised at this point that the householder's responsibility for his drain does not end at the boundary of his property. He is responsible for any blockage or defect that may occur in the drain right up to the point at which it connects to the public sewer.

If your final inspection chamber has an intercepting trap it will also probably have a 'fresh air inlet'. This is a metal box with a grille at the front against which is hinged a mica flap. You will find this near the trap.

The idea was that air could enter the drain at this point, flush through it, and escape via the soil and vent pipe. It rarely worked quite like that. Fresh air inlets are particularly susceptible to accidental damage. A stroll down any suburban street developed between the '30s and '50s will reveal a dozen fresh air inlets with their metal boxes broken or their mica flaps jammed. Many will have been simply sealed off by their owners as being a source of smells and performing no useful purpose.

Layout of underground drains

Modern underground drains are likely to be of PVC or pitch fibre with simple push-on ring seal joints. They are not laid on a concrete base though preparation of the bed on which they lie remains important. Where the sub-soil consists of heavy clay or chalk it may be necessary to prepare an imported bed of gravel to form a base.

Gradients are a good deal less than they were with the many-jointed stoneware drains. Too steep a drain gradient is as likely to create a blockage as a too shallow one; the liquid will run on, leaving solid matter deposited in the pipe. Falls of 1 in 60 to 1 in 70 are quite usual.

There will still be inspection chambers at junctions and changes of direction. These may well be built of brickwork and have stoneware half-channels. They may, on the other hand, be prefabricated in fibre-glass reinforced plastic or constructed on site from concrete sections. Marley Extrusions have produced a sealed drain access system which bears a close resemblance to the sealed iron drainage systems sometimes provided in very high class building work in the pre-war years.

It must be emphasised that although, in a sense, drainage work is 'easier' than it was with the old methods and materials, there is much less margin for error in design and installation; particularly where above ground work is concerned. Taking a waste pipe from an additional wash basin or a newly

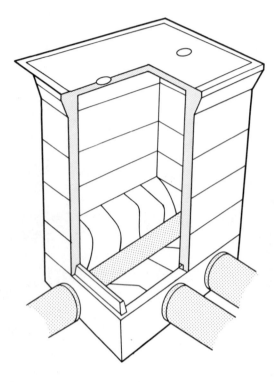

Sectional concrete inspection chambers can be quickly installed by an inexperienced worker.

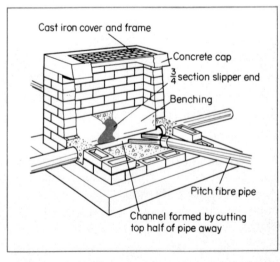

A conventional brick-built inspection chamber with a pitch fibre drain running through it. Note the concrete benching beside the half channel in the middle of the chamber and the fact that branches join the main drain 'in the direction of the flow'.

Cast iron cover and frame
Concrete cap
$\frac{3}{4}$ section slipper end
Benching
Pitch fibre pipe
Channel formed by cutting top half of pipe away

installed shower cabinet to an existing gully or hopper head could not possibly have any adverse effect upon a traditional two-pipe drainage system. Making such a connection wrongly into a single stack system could have very serious results.

All new drainage work—even that involved in the provision of an extra wash basin—must comply with the Building Regulations that are enforced by your local District or Borough Council.

Before embarking upon any project of this kind and, above all, before committing yourself to any expense, have an informal chat with the Council officer responsible for enforcing the Building Regulations relating to drainage. It could be the Environmental Health Officer or the Building Control Officer that you will need to see. He will tell you what the Council's requirements will be and may well be prepared to give you some useful on-the-spot advice.

Do not believe all that you may read in the national press about 'Town Hall bureaucrats'. They are there to help—not to try to 'catch you out'!

Gutters and down-pipes

Collection and disposal of rain water falling on the roof is an important aspect of domestic drainage. You will find that the material of which the gutters and downpipes are made give a pretty good indication of the age of a house.

Pre-war, and immediately post-war, houses always had cast iron gutters and down pipes. These are strong, hard wearing and give plenty of support to ladders propped against them.

Their only real disadvantage, and it is a major one, is their liability to corrode unless protected by paint. As well as painting externally they must be cleaned out and treated internally with bituminous paint at regular intervals. This is a vital chore that adds time, and money, to house maintenance.

Shortly after the war there was a brief vogue for asbestos cement gutters and down pipes. These do not rust and need no decoration. They are rather thick, heavy and clumsy in appearance though and can break all too easily if a ladder is dropped against them. Similarly, the downpipes can easily shatter on accidental contact with, for instance, a wheel barrow or a lawn mower.

Most newly-built houses nowadays have PVC gutters and downpipes and rainwater goods of this material are increasingly used for replacement work. PVC is lightweight, easily fitted—for a replacement job you're likely to find removing the old gutters far more difficult than fitting the new ones—attractive in appearance, cannot corrode and needs no decoration.

It is not however strong enough to support a ladder. If you need to get to the roof, rest your ladder against either the wall or the fascia board. The Marley PVC rain water system is illustrated on the next page.

How many down pipes? For most houses one at the back and one at the front of the house is ample. An arrangement of this kind will be adequate for a total roof area of 2800—1400 sq ft front and 1400 sq ft back.

Fall should be minimal. For domestic roof drainage a fall of 1 in in 50 ft is sufficient. If the fall is noticeable from ground level it will spoil the appearance of the house.

The ultimate destination of the rainwater will depend upon the policy of the local sewerage authority (prior to 1 April 1974 the District or Borough Council, since that date the local Water Authority). In some areas rainwater gullies are allowed to be connected directly to the household's main drain.

Other areas, in order to reduce the cost of sewage treatment and to guard against surcharging of the foul sewer during periods of heavy rain, either provide a separate surface water sewerage system or require the provision of a soakaway for the disposal of water draining from roofs.

Faults with drainage systems

1. Blockages

Blockages in traps and waste pipes have already been dealt with. A blockage in the underground drain may make itself known by water flooding from a yard gully or from under the rim of a drain inspection cover. Another common first symptom is for a lavatory suite, when flushed, to fill almost to the rim of the pan and for the water then—very slowly—to subside.

If flooding from a yard gully is the first

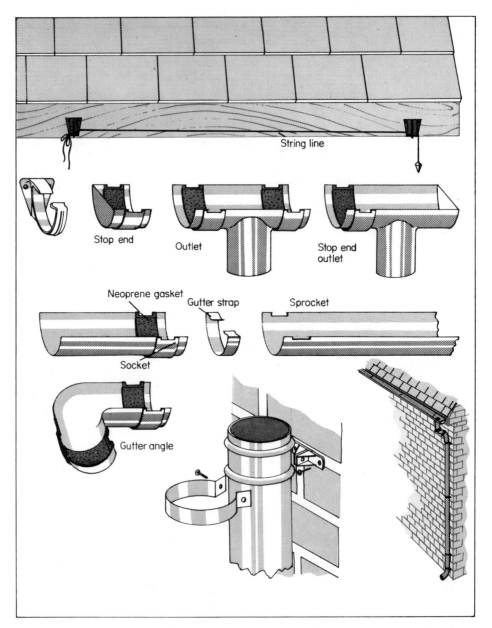

String line

Stop end

Outlet

Stop end outlet

Neoprene gasket

Gutter strap

Sprocket

Socket

Gutter angle

PVC rain water gutters and down pipes are light, easily fixed and need no decoration. The Marley system is illustrated.

sign, check first of all that the trouble isn't due to the grid being choked with leaves or similar debris.

Next, raise the covers of the drain inspection chambers, beginning with the one furthest from the sewer. If this chamber is flooded but the next one is empty then the blockage must obviously lie between the two chambers.

You will need a set of drain rods or sweeps rods to clear it. Screw two or three rods together and lower the end into the flooded chamber. Feel for the half-channel at the base and push into the drain towards the blockage. Screw more rods on to the end and thrust along the drain until the obstruction is reached and dislodged.

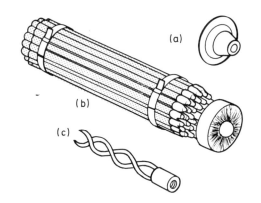

A useful kit for drain clearance comprises a set of drain rods with a 4 in drain plunger (a), a drain cleaning brush (b), and a screw for removing difficult obstructions (c)

If your drain has an intercepting trap the chances are that it is here that the blockage will be located. To clear it you will need a drain plunger—a 4 in diameter rubber disc—screwed on to the end of a couple of drain rods.

Lower the plunger into the inspection chamber. Feel for the half channel and push the plunger along until you can feel the drop into the trap. Plunge down sharply two or three times and, almost certainly, there will be a gurgle and the water level in the inspection chambers will fall as the sewage runs away.

A blockage between the intercepting trap and the sewer is, fortunately, relatively rare. To clear it you need to knock the stopper out of the intercepting trap rodding arm and rod through to the sewer.

When using drain rods there is one important point to remember. Twisting them clockwise will help them along the drain and will also help you to withdraw them when the blockage has been cleared. *Never twist anti-clockwise.* If you do you will unscrew the rods and leave some of them in the drain.

2. Drain smells

If the smell is in the house check on nearby yard gullies or rain water hopper heads. They may take only soapy water from baths and basins—but this can have an objectionable smell as it dries and decomposes. Cleanse with hot soda water.

Consider the possibility that a trap—of a wash basin perhaps—connected to a single stack system, may have siphoned out. You should be able to see the surface of the water seal below the grid of the waste. If this is the cause of the trouble you may have to consider ventilating the waste pipe to prevent self siphonage. Seek the advice of the Council's Environmental Health Officer.

Remember too that the overflow of a wash basin can be very difficult to clean and may smell from a build-up of soapy water.

A smell of drains in the garden is usually an indication of a choked, or partially choked, drain.

A very common form of partial blockage occurs when the stopper falls out of the rodding arm of an interceptor trap. This may occur as a result of pressure building up within the sewer during a heavy rainstorm.

The stopper falls into the intercepting trap and produces a blockage—but it is not a blockage that becomes immediately apparent. Water level rises in the intercepting trap inspection chamber but the sewage can escape by flowing down the now open rodding arm.

This may take place over a period of several weeks during which time the lower part of the intercepting chamber becomes a minature cesspool, the sewage in it becomes fouler and fouler as a result of decomposition.

Eventually the blockage makes itself all too apparent by the offensive smell that welcomes visitors near the front gate!

When this trouble occurs it is a good idea to remove the stopper altogether. Replace it in the inlet to the rodding arm with a disc of glass or slate, cut to size and lightly cemented into position. On the rare occasions that it is necessary to rod through to the sewer this disc can be broken with a crowbar and afterwards replaced.

Don't overlook the possibility that an offensive smell may *not* emanate from the drains or the sewer. A leaking gas main could be a cause. Dead bushes or shrubs in a hedge or shrubbery under which the main passes can give an indication of this.

There used to be manufactured a particular kind of plastic used for electric fittings which exuded an exceptionally unpleasant 'fishy' smell when it became hot. I discovered this the hard way after spending hours trying to find which tenant in a block of flats always 'cooked up cat food' just at dusk—after the electric lights had been switched on!

These fittings are happily obsolete but I would be surprised if there are not some still in use.

3. Leaky drains

If a persistent patch of dampness on a path or on a basement wall leads you to suspect that the drains may be leaking, always seek the advice of the Council's Environmental Health Officer. He can check this by smoke testing or colour testing.

4. Water overflowing from rain water gutters or leaking from joints in down-pipes

Check on the fall of the gutters and check that they are unobstructed. An astonishing amount of silt—not to mention children's balls and similar objects—can accumulate in rain water gutters during the course of a year.

A flow of water, during heavy rain, from joints in downpipes could indicate a blocked rain water drain. It is more likely though, to be a sign of a silted up soakaway.

Soakaways usually consist of a pit, about 5 ft deep and 4 ft square in plan, filled to within about 1 ft of the surface with brick rubble and with the surface soil made good on top.

After a period of use the spaces between the rubble become clogged with silt and the soakaway needs to be dug out and remade. There are concrete sectional soakaways on the market, with holes in the side through which water can soak into the surrounding soil. These have manhole covers to give access for digging out when necessary.

It should be added that soakaways are unlikely to be very successful where the soil is heavy and the level of subsoil water is high. In prolonged periods of heavy rain any soakaway may prove to be incapable of coping with the volume of water flowing into it.

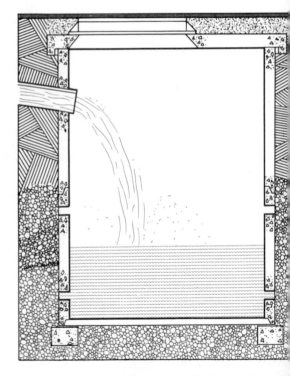

A precast concrete soakaway can easily be opened up and dug out when it becomes choked with silt. Like any soakaway it will be effective only where the subsoil is light and absorbent.

Chapter 30
Hard water problems

Pure water'—the hydrogen oxide (H_2O), with which every schoolboy is familiar—is unknown in nature. The reason for this is that water is *the* great solvent. There are few gases or solids that it cannot take into solution to some extent.

Rainwater is distilled by nature, it leaves the clouds free of impurities. Yet in its brief passage from raincloud to earth it dissolves measurable amounts of carbon dioxide and sulphur dioxide gas. Despite smoke-free zones it may still, over industrial towns, bring down with it several tons of soot, grit and dust per square mile every year.

The water that we draw from our taps fell originally as rain. Yet before it reached the water authority's reservoir it had flowed in a river or stream, or had soaked into the ground through layers of rock, to be pumped up again from deep, natural underground reservoirs. All the surfaces and gases with which it came into contact added their contribution and can be found in solution.

In the reservoirs of the water authority, more chemicals may be added. Some are to destroy the germs of disease with which the water may have become contaminated. Other chemicals, in certain areas, are added to reduce the risk of dental decay.

Some chemicals produce the condition in water known as hardness. Hard water is wasteful with soap, turning it into an insoluble curd. It can ruin woollens washed in it by matting the wool with undissolved soap. It can make a misery of hair washing. It furs up kettles and hot water systems.

It is wasteful too with fuel. A mere 1/8 in of scale inside a gas, oil fired or solid fuel boiler can raise the cost of using the appliance by as much as one third. I have already mentioned, in Chapter 23, how scale can result in boiler damage as a result of the scale insulating the metal of the boiler from the cooling effect of the circulating water.

Hardness is the result of water, in its journey from rain-cloud to reservoir, taking into solution the bicarbonates and sulphates of calcium and magnesium. Water from deep wells and from rivers with a chalky bed is most likely to be hard. This applies to most public supplies in the southern and eastern areas of Britain. Water from mountain catchment areas and from upland reservoirs—the holiday areas of the north and west—is likely to be soft.

Kettle fur and boiler scale

When hard water is heated to temperatures above about 140°F (60°C), carbon dioxide is given off and the dissolved bicarbonates of calcium and magnesium are changed into insoluble carbonates. These are deposited to form kettle fur or boiler scale.

This kind of hardness, which can be removed by boiling, is called temporary hardness. The hardness caused by the sulphates of calcium and magnesium cannot be removed in this way. This is called permanent hardness.

A chemical analysis of a public water supply is likely to quote a figure for temporary hardness, permanent hardness and, the sum of the two, total hardness.

Means of preventing the formation of boiler scale - temperature control, the use of an indirect hot water system, the use of chemical scale inhibitors - have been discussed in Chapters 23 and 24.

A more radical solution to this, and to all other hard water problems, is to install a modern base exchange or ion exchange mains water softener. This will ensure that every drop of water that flows into your home is as soft as—or even softer than—the water that you enjoyed during your last holiday in Cornwall or the Western Highlands.

Water softeners

The principle on which these water softeners operate was discovered from the observation that when hard water flowed through natural zeolite sand, the chemicals causing hardness, 'exchanged bases' with chemicals in the sand. Sodium zeolite would, for instance, become calcium zeolite and the calcium bicarbonate in the water would be changed into sodium bicarbonate which does not cause hardness.

Modern water softeners use a synthetic resin instead of a natural zeolite sand, but the way in which they operate remains the same.

Typically, a mains water softener consists of a cylinder made either of plastic, reinforced with glass fibre, or of metal protected against corrosion, connected to the water main and with a soft water outlet. Hard water flows in from the main and is softened as it passes through the resin bed.

Eventually the resin bed needs regeneration if it is to continue the softening process. This is done quite simply by running through it a strong solution of sodium chloride (common salt).

When the base exchange, or ion exchange, material in a water softener becomes exhausted it can be regenerated. First, a back wash to loosen the material and to remove any grit or debris that has collected on its surface. Next, salt is added and flushed through the softening material. This regenerates the softener which can then be brought back into use.

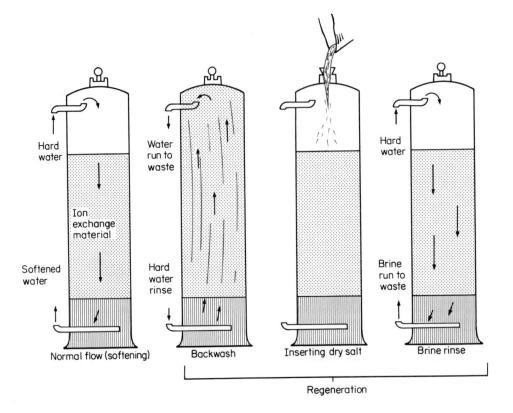

Normal flow (softening)   Backwash   Inserting dry salt   Brine rinse

Regeneration

Recharging water softeners

Recharging the water softener with salt, usually weekly or fortnightly, used to be a somewhat tedious chore. The filter had to be back-washed to remove any debris that the resin had filtered out. Salt was then poured into a salt-space at the top of the appliance and the valves of the softener opened to allow water to flush the salt through the resin bed and then flow to waste. When all taste of salt had gone, the waste valve was closed and the normal softened water supply to the house resumed.

Nowadays, automatic controls make life easier for the water softener owner. A modern water softener is likely to incorporate a salt reservoir capable of containing sufficient salt for anything between 15 and 30 or more regenerations. An electric time control prompts the softener to regenerate itself automatically at a preset interval. The householder has only to recharge the salt reservoir—possibly no more often than once every eight or nine months.

Those who live in a rural area and have their own septic tank sewage treatment plant should make sure that the salty flush from regeneration does not flow into the household drains. Salt is a disinfectant which does not distinguish between benevolent and harmful bacteria. Septic tank sewage treatment is a bacterial process. Regular flushing with a strong salt solution could seriously affect its action.

For those who cannot afford a mains water softener there are less expensive ways of obtaining limited quantities of softened water.

Most manufacturers of water softeners, make small portable softeners as well as their big mains models.

A typical portable softener, the Permutit Water Midge, is only 18 in high with a maximum diameter of 7 in. It has a flexible hose suitable for connections to ½ in or ¾ in taps and, with a water supply of average (18°) hardness, will soften about 150 gallons of water between regenerations. Regeneration is carried out by unscrewing and removing the screw cap, pouring salt into the salt space at the top of the appliance, and flushing through.

Water softening powder

An even simpler way to obtain small quantities of softened water for washing up, hair washing and baths, is to add a water softening powder such as Albright & Wilson's Calgon, to the water after it has been run into the bath, basin or washing machine. Calgon works by combining with the chemicals causing hardness and preventing them from having their unpleasant effects.

It should be remembered however that a hard water supply is not all loss, nor is soft water without its disadvantages.

If a plumbing system is of iron—rare nowadays but used very commonly between the wars—a hard water supply will

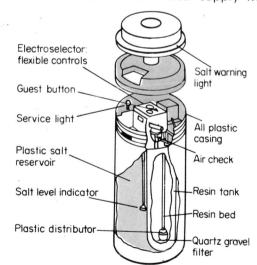

Electroselector: flexible controls

Guest button

Service light

Plastic salt reservoir

Salt level indicator

Plastic distributor

Salt warning light

All plastic casing

Air check

Resin tank

Resin bed

Quartz gravel filter

A modern automatic water softener such as the Sofnol Saturn has a large salt reservoir and automatically carries out the cycle of regeneration at regular intervals. Occasional replenishment of the salt reservoir is all that is required.

line the iron pipes with an eggshell layer of scale that will protect them against corrosion.

Danger to health

It has been suggested that, in certain circumstances, a soft drinking water supply can present a health hazard. As long ago as April 1969 the 'Lancet' (Britain's leading medical journal) published an article which claimed that deaths from cardio-vascular diseases were consistently higher in areas with a soft drinking water supply then in those with a hard supply.

Later studies have confirmed this claim. No one is quite sure of the reason. It could be that the chemicals causing hardness are needed as part of the defence mechanism of the human body. I think it more likely though that the explanation lies in the fact that soft water is a better solvent than hard, and more likely to pick up metallic contaminants, such as lead, from the pipes through which it passes.

Lead values greatly in excess of the accepted safety levels have been found in water from consumers' taps in soft water areas, particularly where the water had been standing in a lead pipe overnight or longer.

None of this need deter a householder from installing a water softener. Iron and lead pipes are not used in modern plumbing. Where they have been installed (in a hard water area where a softener is likely to be required) they will already have acquired an internal coating of eggshell scale.

To feel *absolutely* safe it might be wise to install the softener in the water supply pipe line *after* the branch taking the cold water supply to the kitchen sink. This will mean that you will still have hard water for drinking, cooking and the preparation of food. Soft water will be available for baths, washing and—from the hot tap over the kitchen sink—for washing up.

If you live in an area where the water supply is naturally soft, a sensible health precaution is to run off a few pints of water from the cold tap over the kitchen sink first thing in the morning before you fill the kettle for the pre-breakfast cup of tea.

Remember too, that hot water is a far more efficient solvent than cold. *Never* let late rising tempt you to fill the morning kettle from the hot water tap.

Chapter 31
Coping with frost

In the previous chapter we discussed the disconcerting property of water of taking into solution some part of practically any substance with which it comes into contact.

An even more significant characteristic of water is the fact that although, like everything else in nature, it expands when heated and contracts when cooled, it expands again when its temperature approaches 32°F (0°C) and it becomes ice.

From a world viewpoint this is extremely providential. If water *contracted* on freezing, then ice would sink to the bottom of rivers, lakes and oceans. Fish and other marine life could not survive. Since the sun's rays could never penetrate to the depths of the ocean to thaw the ice, any intelligent creatures that could survive in such a world would be familiar with water principally in its solid form.

From the rather narrower point of view of the householder, or the plumber, in earth's temperate zones, this property of water is a mixed blessing. Unless counter-measures are taken, the expansion of water into ice during a cold spell will stop the flow of water through pipes and cause them to burst.

The folk-myth that pipes 'burst with the thaw' dies hard. It is, of course, quite untrue. Pipes burst as the water within them expands and freezes. The burst becomes evident as the ice thaws and water starts to flow again.

The United Kingdom has had, at the time of writing, a succession of extremely mild winters. Vigilance will have relaxed.

It is a safe bet that when the next prolonged cold spell comes (as it undoubtedly will) thousands of householders will find their plumbing systems frozen solid. With the thaw will come the remorseless drip of water through a thousand bedroom ceilings!

I hope that no readers of this book will be among those affected. Every householder should check his frost defences in the autumn; *before* the temperature drops to zero and icy north easters begin to whistle round the roof tops.

The external supply

Design safeguards against frost have already been referred to in Chapters 22 and 23. The external water supply pipe should be at least 0.82 m (2 ft 6 in) below the surface of the ground throughout its length and should be protected as it rises to the surface within the house. The rising main should rise to the cold water storage cistern against an internal wall. Boiler, hot water storage cylinder and cold water storage cistern should, as far as is possible, form a vertical column so that the vulnerable cistern may get the benefit of the ascending warm air.

Where pipe runs must, of necessity, be taken against an external wall they should be thoroughly lagged. An inorganic lagging such as fibreglass or foam plastic lagging units, is to be preferred. Make sure that the lagging extends behind the pipe. It is worse than useless to protect the pipe from the warm air within the house and leave it exposed to the cold wall!

The roof space

The roof space is a particularly dangerous area. If you have, in the interests of national fuel economy and your own rocketing fuel bills, insulated the spaces between the ceiling joists, you will have made your home warmer—and the roof space colder!

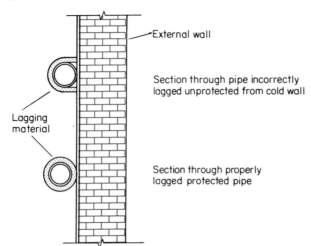

External wall

Section through pipe incorrectly lagged unprotected from cold wall

Lagging material

Section through properly lagged protected pipe

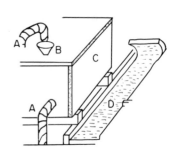

Always make sure that lagging extends behind the pipe that is to be protected. It is worse than useless to insulate the pipe from the warm air of the room and to leave it exposed to a cold external wall.

In the roof space all water pipes should be thoroughly lagged. A. The storage cistern should have a dust-proof cover into which is set a funnel to accept any water from the vent pipe B. The walls, but not the base, of the cistern should be lagged C, and the fibreglass mat laid between the rafters to conserve the house warmth should be omitted from immediately below the cistern D.

Pipe runs within the roof space should be as short as possible and should be thoroughly lagged. Don't forget to extend the lagging material to cover the tail of the ball-valve and all but the handles of any stop-valves.

The sides, but not the base, of the cold water storage cistern should be well lagged and the cistern provided with an insulating cover. Do not insulate the bedroom ceiling immediately below this cistern. There is something to be said for draping a 'curtain' of insulating material from the base of the cistern to the uninsulated ceiling below. This will funnel the slightly warmer air up to the base of the cistern.

The overflow or warning pipe from the cistern could permit icy draughts to penetrate the roof space. At one time it was the practice to provide a hinged copper flat at the external end of this pipe. This closed when the wind blew against it.

If you have this kind of protection apply a drop of oil to the hinge to make sure that it doesn't jam either open or closed.

Nowadays it is more usual to bend the internal end of this pipe inside the cistern so that it extends for an inch or so below the surface of the water. A water seal is thus provided that effectively prevents the entry of draughts. There are gadgets (such as the plastic Shire's Frostguard) that can be screwed on to the ends of existing overflow pipes to provide this protection.

Outdoor lavatories

Outdoor lavatories are very vulnerable in frosty weather. There are electro-thermal pipe lagging cables on the market which, plugged in to a power socket and switched on throughout frosty nights, will protect the supply pipe.

Provided that the lavatory is more or less draught proof, a 60 watt electric light bulb, switched on and suspended a few inches below the ball valve inlet (outside the cistern of course!) will supply sufficient warmth to protect against several degrees of frost.

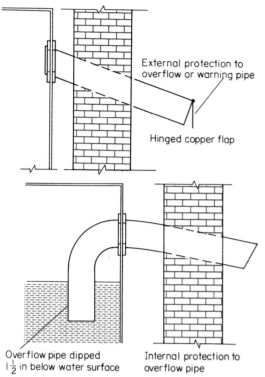

External protection to overflow or warning pipe

Hinged copper flap

Overflow pipe dipped $1\frac{1}{2}$ in below water surface

Internal protection to overflow pipe

Icy draughts can be prevented from whistling up the overflow pipe into the roof space either by providing an external hinged copper flap or by dipping the internal end of the overflow pipe about 36 mm (1½ in) below the surface of the water to provide a trap. The latter method is to be preferred. Copper flaps are liable to jam open or closed.

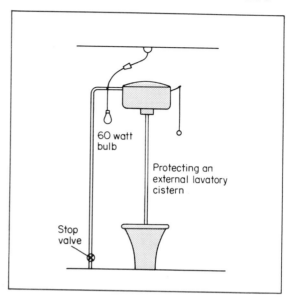

60 watt bulb

Protecting an external lavatory cistern

Stop valve

An external w.c. cistern can be protected from frost by suspending a 60-watt lamp bulb outside the cistern but below the inlet pipe. If this is switched on in icy weather it will, provided that the compartment is more or less draught-proof, give adequate protection.

Leaving the house unoccupied

It is important to appreciate that no amount of lagging (other than electro-thermal protection) will *add* heat to a plumbing system. All that it can hope to do is to conserve warmth already there. This point is particularly important as winter holidays become increasingly popular and many homes are left empty for two or three weeks at a time during the winter months.

For so long as a house is occupied, efficient lagging will protect against frost throughout a prolonged cold spell. Water flows into the plumbing system from the main at a temperature a few degrees above freezing point. Lagging reduces the rate of heat loss and the constant draw off and replacement of water in the pipes and storage cistern ensure that the domestic water supply remains above freezing point.

If the house is unoccupied during a prolonged spell of freezing weather even the most efficient lagging will only delay the eventual freeze-up. The fabric of the house chills off. Water stagnates in the supply pipes and becomes colder and colder. At last a plug of ice forms somewhere in a pipe-line—and quickly spreads throughout the system.

If you have a *reliable*, automatic central heating system, turn it on at low level if you are going away for more than a few days at a time in the winter. Leave internal doors open so that warm air can circulate and remove the trap-door to the roof to allow some warm air to penetrate up there too.

Draining the system

The only other safe means of protecting your plumbing system, if you are absent from home for any length of time during which a cold spell might be expected, is to drain it completely.

Turn off the main stop-cock and drain from the drain-cock immediately above it. Open all hot and cold taps and leave open. Connect one end of a length of hose to the drain-cock beside the boiler (or at the base of the cylinder if you haven't a boiler) and take the other end to an outside gully. Open up the drain-cock and leave until no more water flows.

Human memory is fallible. Having done this write PLUMBING SYSTEM DRAINED —DO NOT LIGHT BOILER UNTIL REFILLED on a card and prop it on the boiler.

Incidentally, when refilling, you can reduce the risk of air-locks forming by connecting one end of your hose to the cold tap over the kitchen sink and the other end to the boiler drain-cock. Open both up and the system will fill *upwards*, driving air in front of it.

Boiler explosions

Many people, particularly the elderly, worry unnecessarily about the risk of a boiler explosion during icy weather. This may lead them to let their boiler fires out at night which is the worst possible course of action.

Boiler explosions are, in fact, extremely rare but, when they do occur, their effects are so catastrophic that it is not surprising that they should be a source of anxiety.

Domestic hot water systems form a kind of extended U-tube with the vent pipe and the cold water storage cistern as the two open ends. Provided this U-tube remains unobstructed there is no risk of

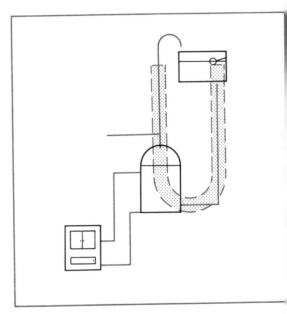

The open ended U-tube formed by a cylinder storage hot water system is the first, and strongest, defence against the possibility of a boiler explosion.

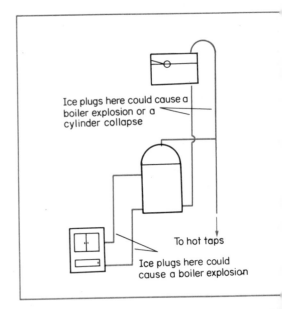

Ice plugs here could cause a boiler explosion or a cylinder collapse

To hot taps

Ice plugs here could cause a boiler explosion

A boiler explosion can occur if the boiler fire is lit after ice plugs have blocked the U-tube at the points indicated

an explosion. The safety valve usually situated by the boiler provides a final line of defence against the possibility of an obstruction occurring.

Typically, boiler explosions occur when a family returns from a winter holiday without having taken the precautions suggested in this chapter. During their absence, plugs of ice have formed in the vent pipe and in the supply pipe from the cold water storage cistern to the hot water cylinder. There could even be ice plugs in the flow and return pipes between cylinder and boiler.

The boiler fire is lit and the water in the boiler heats up. It cannot circulate and quickly overheats, rapidly reaching a temperature well above boiling point. It cannot however boil and turn to steam because it is confined to the limited space of the boiler and perhaps a few feet of circulating pipe.

Pressure within the boiler builds up and, eventually, something gives—releasing the internal pressure. Instantly, the super-heated water turns to steam—with many thousand times the volume of the water from which it was produced—and the boiler explodes like a bomb, usually with equally lethal results.

Cylinder *implosion*, or collapse, during icy weather is a rather more common phenomenon.

This can happen when a boiler fire, kept alight all day, is let out at night. Ice plugs form in the upper part of the vent pipe and the cold water supply to the cylinder, blocking the U-tube. In the meantime the water in the system begins to cool and also contract.

Copper hot water storage cylinders are manufactured to withstand considerable internal, but very little external, pressure. Collapse, like a paper bag, often occurs first thing in the morning when the house-holder attempts to draw off some hot water—the final straw that breaks the camel's back!

Sometimes, when the ice-plugs thaw and water flows back into the cylinder again, the resumed internal pressure will restore the cylinder undamaged to its former shape; but I wouldn't guarantee this.

How to tackle a freeze-up

Supposing, despite all your precautions, you still get a freeze-up. You will know about it because water will cease to flow from one or more of the taps.

Take immediate action. Find the ice-plug and thaw it out before it has a chance to spread through the system. If water is still running from the cold tap over the sink but is not reaching the cold water storage cistern, then the ice-plug must be in the rising main between the sink supply branch and the ball-valve feeding the cistern.

Strip off the lagging and apply heat to the pipe; cloths soaked in hot water and then wrung out are a good way to do this. Don't use a blow torch among the dry timbers of the roof space. An electric hair-dryer, or even a vacuum cleaner operating in reverse, provide means of directing a stream of warm air to inaccessible lengths of pipe.

If the freeze-up is tackled quickly it will be cleared easily. The copper of which modern water supply pipes are made is a good conductor of heat. Heat applied to the pipe will be conducted along it to clear an ice plug that might be several feet away.

Repairing a burst pipe

And supposing you get a burst pipe? The first indication is likely to be water dripping from a ceiling.

Once again, immediate action is called for. Turn off the main stop-cock and open up all the taps to limit the amount of damage. Only then should you look for the site of the burst.

If you have copper tubing joined by non-manipulative compression fittings or by soldered capillary joints, the chances are that expansion of the ice will have simply forced the joints open. The joint can be remade (see Chapter 32).

A lead pipe will, quite probably, have split under pressure from the ice.

The orthodox method of repairing a burst lead pipe is to cut out a length of pipe extending 9 in to 1 ft on each side of the burst, and to insert a new length, joining to the old pipe with wiped soldered joints.

This is, in my opinion, strictly a job for a professional plumber.

However the householder can make a 'temporary' repair (which may last as long as a permanent one!) using one of the epoxy resin repair kits (Isopon, Plastic Padding, Holts Fibreglass repair kit and so on) that are available from all d.i.y. shops.

Make sure that the pipe is clean and dry and knock the edges of any split together. Rub down with coarse abrasive paper to form a key. Mix up the epoxy resin filler and hardener according to the makers' instructions and 'butter' over the area of the leak and for a few inches on either side. While the filler is still plastic, bind a fibreglass bandage round the buttered area and, finally, apply another coating of resin filler.

A repair of this kind, which will permit you to have the pipe in use again within a few hours, may not meet with the approval of your local water authority. I think though that even they would agree that it is preferable to letting the water leak and waste away until you could obtain the services of a professional plumber.

Chapter 32 Plumbing techniques for the householder

This chapter, which may well be of most interest to the d.i.y enthusiast, has been deliberately placed at the end of this section. Before attempting any plumbing operation it is essential that the householder should have a thorough grasp of the principles involved.

No-one who has read the preceding chapters would make such elementary—and serious—errors as, for instance, taking the cold supply to a conventional shower direct from the main, connecting a rim supply bidet to existing bathroom hot and cold water supplies or disconnecting the flow and return pipes from a hot water storage cylinder without having drained the system *from the drain-cock beside the boiler.*

In this chapter I shall deal with plumbing techniques—joining and bending lengths of pipe and connecting them to taps and other fittings—which, in my opinion, are well within the scope of the determined home owner. Making wiped soldered joints between lengths of lead pipe, bronze welding, lead and zinc roof work are important aspects of the professional plumber's skill but are not tasks for the inexperienced.

The development of copper, stainless steel and plastic tubing has provided the amateur with materials that he can handle safely and effectively.

Copper tubing

Copper tubing is undoubtedly the most common plumbing material used in post-war homes. Its development, and almost universal adoption, has probably been the biggest single factor in bringing home plumbing within the scope of the home handyman.

The sizes of copper tubing most likely to be used in domestic plumbing are 15 mm, 22 mm and 28 mm. The Imperial equivalents of these sizes are ½ in, ¾ in and 1 in respectively.

A check with a rule will reveal that these are not literal translations from metric to Imperial measurements. The reason for the apparent discrepancy is that Imperial sizes are the measurements of the internal diameter of the tube. This means that all tubes of equal capacity, no matter of what material they are made, are of the same Imperial size. The metric measurement is of the *external* diameter; Don't ask me why!

Joining copper tubing

Copper tubing may be joined by means of non-manipulative (Type A) manipulative (Type B) compression joints and fittings or by means of soldered capillary joints.

Non-manipulative compression joints are the easiest means of joining copper tubing for the amateur with no previous experience and a minimal tool kit. The only essential tools are a hacksaw, a rasp, a spanner of the appropriate size and a wrench. If, however, you have a fairly large plumbing project in hand, a tube cutter incorporating a reamer is a good investment.

Non-manipulative compression joints have three essential features; the joint body, a soft copper ring or 'olive' and a cap nut. To make the joint, the tube end must be cut absolutely square and all internal and external burr removed. This is where the tube cutter with reamer comes in useful.

Loosen the cap nut of the compression fitting (with most makes there is no need to remove it) and thrust the tube end in as far as the tube stop. Hold the body of the joint firmly with the wrench and tighten the cap nut with the spanner. This action compresses the soft metal ring against the outside surface of the tube to provide a secure and watertight joint.

Provided that you use a spanner, and not a wrench, to tighten the cap nut, it is practically impossible to overtighten. Many plumbers add a smear of boss white or similar jointing material to the tube end and to the inside of the compression fitting. It should not be necessary to do this but it does ensure a watertight joint first go.

Any builders' merchant will let you browse through his illustrated catalogues of compression joints and fittings. You will find there fittings for every conceivable purpose—straight couplings, reducing couplings, bends, tees and so on.

Connecting new metric tubing to existing imperial tubing presents no serious problem with this kind of joint. 15 mm and 28 mm compression fittings are exactly interchangeable with ½ in and 1 in fittings respectively. Thus, you can, for instance, fit a 15 mm compression tee joint into a run of ½ in tubing to take a new 15 mm branch supply to a wash basin or lavatory cistern.

22 mm fittings are not *exactly* interchangeable with ¾ in fittings. The body of a 22 mm joint can be used with ¾ in tubing but a special copper ring and cap nut are needed to ensure a watertight joint. Your supplier should be able to fix you up with these.

The home plumber isn't really very likely to need to use manipulative (Type B) compression fittings. Many Water Authorities however require this kind of fitting for use underground.

With a manipulative compression fitting the cap nut must first be unscrewed from

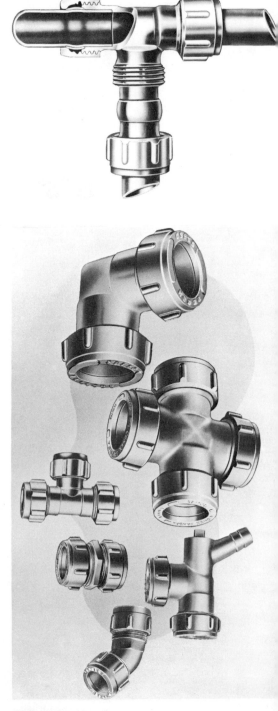

When the cap-nut of a compression joint is tightened the soft copper ring or olive in compressed against the outer wall of the copper or stainless steel tube to provide a watertight joint. Compression fittings, like those illustrated, can be used for a variety of plumbing jobs (Courtesy of Conex-Sambra Ltd)

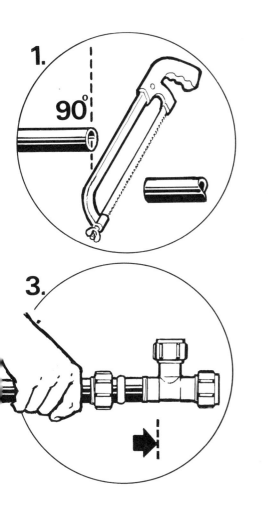

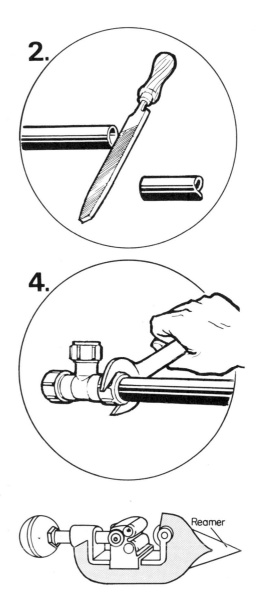

To make a compression joint cut the tube end square (1). A tube cutter will make it easier to be certain of a square end . Remove internal and external burr (2). Insert tube end into fitting (3) and tighten with a spanner (4) (Courtesy of Conex-Sanbra Ltd)

A tube cutter with reamer is shown on the right

the fitting and slipped over the end of the pipe. The tube end is then 'manipulated'. This is usually done by hammering a steel 'drift' into the tube end to bell it out, though with one make of Type 'B' joint a swage or ridge is made round the end of the tube with a special swaging tool. The body of the joint is then placed into the tube end and the cap-nut tightened up hard. With this kind of joint the use of boss white or some other waterproofing compound is recommended.

It can be seen that a Type 'B' fitting cannot be dismantled in the same way that a Type 'A' fitting can—and it cannot be pulled open by expansion due to frost.

Straight connector
(copper to copper)

Tee junction

Slow bend

Cap and lining

Bent tap or ball-valve
connector

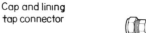

Tail of bit tap
screws in here

Wall plate elbow for
outside tap

Cap and lining
tap connector

Connection to
storage cistern

Copper to lead joint

Compression fittings are made for all purposes. Here is a small selection from the Prestex range:

A straight connector for joining two lengths of copper or stainless steel tubing.

A tee junction for taking a branch water supply from a main supply pipe.

A slow bend.

A tap connector with compression joint at one end and cap and lining for connection to the tail of a tap at the other.

A bent tap or ball-valve connector. This is very useful for connecting the ball valve to a cold water storage cistern. The rising main is taken up the outside of the cistern vertically and the bent connector fitted onto its end with the cap and lining joint in position to connect to the threaded tail of the ball valve.

A connection to a storage cistern.

A wall plate elbow designed to take a bib-tap for a garden water supply. PTFE thread sealing tape should be bound round the tail of the tap before screwing it home into the female thread of the wall plate elbow.

A copper to lead joint. The 'lead end' of this joint must be connected to the lead pipe by means of a soldered joint.

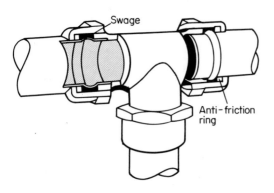

Manipulative, Type B, compression joints are used for underground water supply pipes. The cap nut is slipped over the tube end which is then 'manipulated' either by

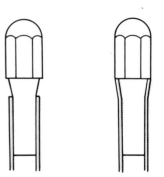

A steel drift opens up the tube end

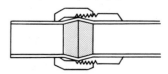

opening the end with a steel drift or, as in the Kingley coupling, by forming a swage with a swaging tool. Manipulating joints cannot pull apart and cannot, of course, be readily dismantled for re-use.

Making a soldered joint

Soldered capillary joints and fittings are smaller, neater (and cheaper) than compression fittings. Using them is well within the scope of the determined handyman. Their effectiveness depends upon capillary action—the force which makes liquids (in this case liquid solder) flow into any confined space between two smooth, solid surfaces.

As with compression joints there are two kinds of capillary fitting; the integral ring and the end-feed fitting. Integral ring fittings, often called 'Yorkshire fittings' (though this is the name of just one well-known brand), have a ring of solder, sufficient to make the joint, incorporated in the fitting itself. With end-feed fittings solder to make the joint has to be added with solder wire.

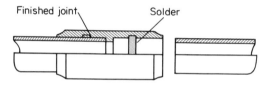

Integral ring soldered capillary joints incorporate a ring of solder sufficient to make the joint.

End-feed fittings are identical except that they do not incorporate a solder ring. After heating, solder is fed into the mouth of the joint from solder wire.

Making an integral ring 'Yorkshire' soldered capillary joint.

Absolute cleanliness is the key to success in making any kind of capillary soldered joint.

As with a compression joint the tube ends must be cut square and all trace of internal and external burr removed. Clean the tube end and the internal bore of the fitting thoroughly with steel wool and smear an approved flux onto the tube end and internal bore.

Insert the tube into the fitting to the tube stop. All that now has to be done with an integral ring fitting is to apply the flame of a blow-torch—a butane torch is perfectly satisfactory for this purpose—first to the tube and then to the fitting. The joint is made when the solder melts and appears as a ring all round the mouth of the fitting.

End-feed fittings are, naturally, cheaper and are not a great deal more difficult to use. The tube end and the fitting are prepared and fluxed as with an integral ring joint. Bend over a length of solder wire—about ½ in for a 15 mm fitting, ¾ in for a 22 mm fitting, and so on—and, after preliminarily heating the tube and fitting, feed the bent-over length of solder into the end of the joint. Once again, the joint is complete when all the bent-over length of solder has been melted and drawn into the joint and a bright ring of solder is apparent all round the mouth of the fitting.

1. clean end of tube and bore of fitting with steel wool

2. flux bore of fitting and tube end. With phosphoric acid flux use a brush!

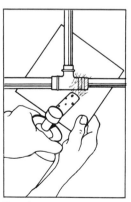

3. apply heat with blow torch (note asbestos sheet behind fitting)

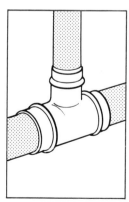

4. leave completed joint to cool

Once the joint is made do not disturb until the solder has set and the fitting is cool enough to touch. Where—and this is usually the case—more than one joint is to be made with one capillary fitting, (for instance, the two ends of a straight coupling or the three ends of a tee junction) it is best to make all the joints at the same time. If this cannot be arranged, a piece of damp cloth should be wrapped round any joint already made to prevent the solder from melting.

Always bear in mind the fire risk involved when using a blow torch to make capillary joints. It is all too easy to become so engrossed in making a first class joint that the smouldering timber behind the pipework goes unnoticed until too late! Interpose a sheet of asbestos between the pipe on which you are working and the skirting behind it. Be particularly careful when working amid the bone-dry timbers of the roof space.

Unlike compression joints, 15 mm, 22 mm and 28 mm capillary joints *cannot* be used with ½ in, ¾ in and 1 in tubing. Capillary action requires a more critical fit than does a compression joint.

Imperial to metric couplings and tee joints are manufactured but a simple way out is to use a compression fitting for the actual connection between old Imperial and new metric tubing and then to carry on using metric capillary joints.

Making a watertight joint

Every manufacturer supplies compression and capillary fittings with threaded ends (either male or female) for connection to galvanised steel tubing, cylinder tappings or to take the back-nuts securing pipework to storage cisterns. Screwed joints may be made watertight by binding PTFE plastic thread sealing tape round the male thread.

PTFE is sold in rolls, rather like the familiar rolls of surgical tape. Tear off an appropriate length, bind round the thread and screw home.

Although there are no technical difficulties involved in connecting new lengths of copper tubing to an existing galvanised steel plumbing system, the risk of electrolytic corrosion (see Chapter 22) should be borne in mind. It is always unwise to use copper and galvanised steel in the same plumbing system; particularly for hot water services. Where additions are to be made to a galvanised steel plumbing system it is safer to use the stainless steel tubing referred to later in this chapter.

Connecting taps and ball-valves

Taps and ball-valves are normally connected to copper (or any other) tubing by means of swivel tap connectors or 'cap and lining' joints.

These useful little fittings are inserted into the tail of the tap or valve and the nut is tightened up on to the thread of the tail. They are normally supplied with a fibre washer that makes the use of PTFE tape unnecessary.

Connecting new copper tube to lead pipes

One of the most difficult tasks likely to confront the amateur plumber is the connection of new copper tubing to an existing lead pipe. Typically a householder wants to replace a leaky and out-of-date lead plumbing system with a copper one—and he has to begin by making a connection to the lead rising main protruding from the kitchen floor.

All manufacturers of compression and capillary fittings include lead-to-copper joints among their range. Unfortunately the lead end of this fitting has to be connected to the lead pipe with some kind of soldered joint.

The conventional, approved and professional method of doing this is with a wiped soldered joint. Few amateurs are likely to make a success of such a joint at their first, or even their second, attempt and the vertical position in which the joint is likely to have to be made makes the task even more difficult.

I would strongly advise the amateur to seek professional help for this part of the job at least. Once the lead-to-copper connection has been made he will have no difficulty in continuing with his plumbing project.

There are two lead-to-copper joints which are within the capacity of the householder but there are snags about both of them. The first, the Staern or soldered spigot joint, provides a kind of *in situ* capillary joint. It is little used in the trade nowadays and the home plumber may find difficulty in getting hold of the necessary tools.

The method of making the joint is shown in the diagram. A special cutting tool is inserted into the end of the lead pipe and rotated to produce a chamfered lip. The mouth of the pipe is then opened with a mandrel and a hollow hardwood cone is tapped down over the opened out pipe end to shape the sides inwards.

Next clean and rasp the end of the brass or gunmetal lead-to-copper joint and 'tin' the surface with solder. Smear the tinned end of the fitting with flux and insert into the end of the lead pipe. Apply a blow-torch flame to the brass fitting and bring down to heat *gently* the end of the lead pipe. Feed solder into the lip of the lead pipe from whence it will flow, by capillarity, into the space between the spigot of the brass fitting and the lead socket.

As with a conventional capillary joint a ring of bright solder will appear round the mouth of the joint. Continue heating gently until bubbles of flux cease to rise. Wipe off surplus solder while still plastic to give a neat finish.

The other joint, the cup and cone joint, is easily made but is unlikely to meet with the approval of the local Water Authority, certainly not for a pipe carrying water under mains pressure.

To make this joint the end of the lead pipe is opened out with a hardwood cone until the spigot of the brass fitting can be

The Staern joint provides — if you can obtain the tools required — a straightforward means of connecting lead tubing to the brass end of a lead-to-copper compression joint.
a A cutting tool is used to chamfer the mouth of the lead pipe.
b The end of the lead pipe is opened out with a mandrel.
c The end of the lead pipe is then shaped inwards with a coning tool.
d The brass tail is then tinned and inserted after being fluxed. The result might be described as an 'in situ' soldered capillary joint.

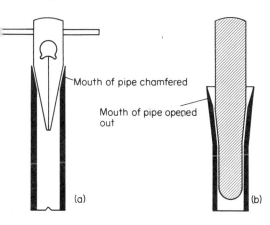

Mouth of pipe chamfered

Mouth of pipe opened out

(a)

(b)

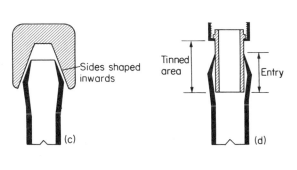

Sides shaped inwards

(c)

Tinned area

Entry

(d)

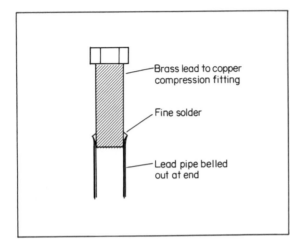

The cup and cone joint illustrated is an easy method of joining brass to lead. There is no reason why a joint of this kind should not be used for a waste pipe, which does not carry water under pressure, but it will not meet Water Authority approval for a water supply pipe.

accommodated to a depth equal to half its diameter—¼ in for a 15 mm fitting. Rasp, tin and flux the spigot end of the fitting. Insert into the belled out end of the lead pipe and run fine solder into the space between the belled end and the brass spigot.

As well as being able to join lengths of pipework the amateur plumber needs to know how to negotiate bends. All makers of compression and capillary joints include a variety of bends in their ranges.

However, copper tubing can, with the aid of bending springs, be bent by hand to easy bends and, for a major plumbing job, the use of this technique can save a good deal of money.

Pipes of up to 28 mm (1 in) *can* be bent cold by hand but the amateur would be wise to limit himself to easy bends in 15 mm (½ in) and 22 mm (¾ in) tubing. The purpose of the bending spring is to support the walls of the pipe which would otherwise collapse as the bend is made.

This is the method: Use a spring of the correct size, grease to facilitate easy withdrawal, and insert into the tube to the point

at which the bend is to be made. Bend over the knee. Best results will be obtained by slightly overbending at first and then bringing back to the required curve.

To withdraw the spring insert a tommy bar through the metal loop at the end turn clockwise to reduce the diameter of the spring, and pull. *Never* be tempted to 'dress', hammer or otherwise interfere with the tube until the spring has been withdrawn. If you do you will find it to be irretrievably jammed within the tube

Stainless steel tubing

It has been a source of surprise to me that stainless steel tubing, which has been available in this country for some ten years, has not proved to be more popular than it has. It offers many advantages both to the professional and to the amateur plumber.

As a home produced product it has a relatively stable price which has been consistently below that of copper tubing.

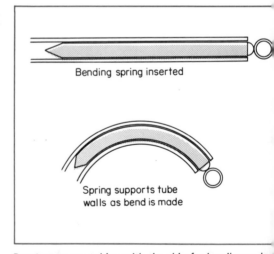

Bending spring inserted

Spring supports tube walls as bend is made

Bending copper tubing with the aid of a bending spring. The spring is greased and inserted (above) to the point at which the bend is to be made. The tube is then bent over the knee (below), first overbending and then bringing back to the curve required. To remove the spring insert a tommy bar into the loop at the end. Twist clockwise to reduce the diameter of the spring — and pull.

It has an attractive appearance and needs no decoration. Above all, it can be used in conjunction with galvanised steel tubing (provided that this is not already rusting) or copper tubing, without risk of electrolytic corrosion.

It is no more difficult to use than copper tubing and the same methods of jointing and manipulation can be adopted.

Joining stainless steel tubes

Stainless steel tubing can be joined by means of either Type A or Type B compression fittings or by means of either integral ring or end-feed capillary fittings. There are however one or two points of technique that must be borne in mind.

Preparation of the tube ends for any kind of jointing is the same as with copper tubing. Stainless steel tube can be cut with a tube cutter or with a hacksaw but, with stainless steel, a hacksaw—ideally a high speed steel hacksaw blade with 32 teeth per inch—is to be preferred. This is particularly important if Type B (manipulative) compression fittings are to be used. The use of a tube cutter work-hardens the tube ends and there would be a tendency for the end to split when opened out with a drift.

Apart from this, both types of compression joint are used with stainless steel exactly as with copper. Since stainless steel is a harder material a little more pressure needs to be applied when tightening the cap nut in order to ensure a watertight joint.

When joining stainless steel tubing with either integral ring or end-feed capillary fittings it is important that a flux based on *phosphoric acid* should be used. The suppliers of the stainless steel tubing should be able to recommend a suitable flux. *On no account should you use a chloride based flux.*

In making a capillary joint with stainless steel a gentle flame from your blow-torch should be applied to the fitting itself—*not* to the tube.

Many manufacturers provide a, possibly limited, range of chromium plated compression and capillary joints and fittings intended for use with stainless steel tubing.

Stainless steel tubing is harder than copper tubing and is consequently more difficult to bend. The amateur might be well advised to use compression or capillary bends for all changes of direction but it is possible to make easy bends in 15 mm (½ in) stainless steel tubing using the bending spring technique already described.

Other pipe materials that may be used, or encountered, by the home plumber are plastics (polythene, polyvinyl chloride—PVC or vinyl for short—and polypropylene) and pitch fibre.

Polythene tubing

Black polythene tubing enjoyed quite a vogue with amateur plumbers a few years ago because of the long lengths in which it was obtainable, the ease with which it could be connected to copper tubing and its built-in resistance to frost.

It has disadvantages however. It cannot be used for hot water supply; though it is satisfactory for waste pipes which do not carry hot water under pressure. It has a rather thick, clumsy appearance and its tendency to sag necessitates continuous support on horizontal runs.

A very important use of polythene is as a material for underground supply pipes; perhaps taking a supply to a garage or to a stand-tap at the bottom of a large garden. Neither its appearance, nor its need for support, present problems when used in this way. The long lengths in which it is obtainable, eliminating underground joints, and its in-built insulation give it very real advantages.

Polythene tubing is joined with non-manipulative compression fittings similar to those used with copper tubing. Polythene has not, at the time of writing, been metricated and is still sold as ½ in, ¾ in or 1 in internal diameter. When ordering compression fittings for polythene tubing it is wise to take a short length along to the builders merchant to make sure that you get the right size fittings.

Because polythene is a relatively soft material a metal insert, provided by the manufacturer of the compression fittings, must be inserted into the tube end as the joint is made.

The correct procedure is to unscrew the cap nut of the compression joint and slip it, followed by the copper ring or olive, over the end of the tube. Push the metal insert into the end of the tube. Insert the tube end into the body of the fitting as far as the stop and tighten up the cap nut. Tighten as far as possible with the fingers and then give one and a half to two turns with a spanner.

Easy bends can be made cold with polythene tubing provided that the bend is then firmly secured. For making permanent bends the tubing must first be heated. A professional plumber would probably do this by *very* gently playing a blow-lamp flame over the length to be bent. An amateur might be better advised to immerse the length for ten minutes in water that is kept boiling for that period.

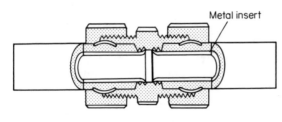
Metal insert

Polythene tubing may be joined by means of Type A non-manipulative compression joints but a metal insert is required in the end of the polythene tubing to protect it from collapse when the cap-nut is tightened.

Polyvinyl chloride (PVC o. Vinyl) tubing

PVC is nowadays very widely used for abov and underground drainage and for roo drainage. It may also be used for col water supply and provides a cheap an quickly assembled means of providing a domestic cold water services.

PVC cannot be used for hot water unde pressure. Because of this there are two nominally cold water supply pipes whic should never be of PVC. These are the col water supply pipe from the cold wate storage cistern to the hot water storag cylinder and the cold water supply pip from the feed and expansion tank of a indirect hot water system. Metal pipe should always be used in these position as the water in these pipes can becom very hot at times.

PVC tubing can be joined either b solvent welding or by ring seal jointing

Solvent welding must be used for col water supply pipes. For waste and drainag pipes a mixture of the two methods is ofte used—solvent welding for small diamete waste branches and ring seal jointing fo the larger diameter stack and drain pipes

To make a solvent welded joint the tub end must be cut off squarely with a hacksav and all swarf and burr removed fron internal and external surfaces.

With a file or fine toothed rasp chamfe the outer edge of the pipe end to a angle of 15° or 20°. Insert into the socke and mark with a pencil the extent to whicl the pipe end enters the socket. Roughen th pipe end and the interior surface of th socket with fine abrasive paper or cloth an degrease these surfaces using a cleanin fluid approved by the manufacturers an clean absorbent paper.

Using a brush, apply an even coat o solvent cement to both pipe end an fitting in lengthwise strokes. The pipe en

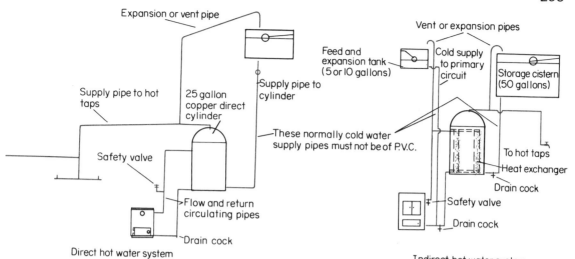

Direct hot water system

Indirect hot water system

PVC tubing may be used for all cold water supply pipes but should not be used for nominally cold pipes which may, in fact, sometimes get very hot. PVC should not be used for the cold water supply to the hot water cylinder of a direct hot water system (top left). It should not be used for the cold water supply to the cylinder or the cold water supply to the primary circuit in an indirect system (top right).

should have a thicker coating than the socket surfaces.

Immediately push the socket on to the pipe without turning, hold in position for about fifteen seconds and then remove surplus cement. The joint should not be disturbed for approximately five minutes and should not be put into use for twenty-four hours.

Preparation for ring seal jointing is similar. Use a fine tooth woodsaw or a hacksaw to cut the—usually—larger diameter pipe. A useful tip, to ensure an absolutely square cut, is to place a sheet of newspaper over the pipe and to bring the edges together beneath it.

Draw a line round the cut end of the pipe 10 mm from the end and chamfer back to this line with a rasp or other shaping tool. Insert the pipe end into the socket and mark the insertion depth, making an allowance for expansion of 10 mm between the end of the pipe and the bottom of the socket. In other words,

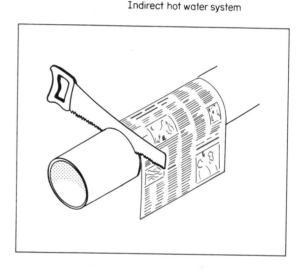

To ensure a square cut with large diameter PVC or pitch fibre pipes a sheet of newspaper may be laid over the pipe and its edges brought together underneath. This then acts as a guide. When sawing through pitch fibre pipe lubricating the saw blade with water will prevent it from sticking.

draw a pencil line round the pipe at the socket edge, then withdraw 10 mm and draw a further line. The second line will be the one to which the pipe end is finally inserted.

Clean the recess within the pipe socket and insert the ring joint. Lubricate the pipe end with a small amount of petroleum jelly (vaseline) and push the end firmly home into the socket through the joint ring. Adjust the pipe position so that

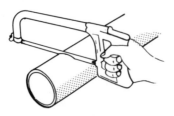

1. Cut tube squarely with fine tooth saw

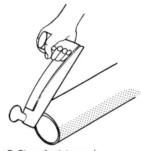

2. Chamfer tube end

3. Mark depth of tube in socket

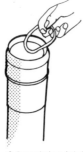

4. Insert ring joint in socket

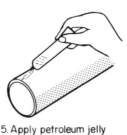

5. Apply petroleum jelly to tube end

Ring seal in specially shaped recess

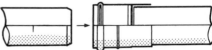

Socket solvent welded to pipe in factory on standard socket and spigot pipe length

6. Align tube end to socket and push home

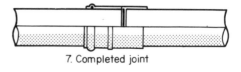

7. Completed joint

Ring seal joints are easily made as shown above and, unlike solvent welded joints, can accommodate the expansion and contraction of the pipework. Ring seal joints may be used with PVC waste and drainage systems and must be used with polypropylene systems.

the insertion depth mark is level with the edge of the socket.

A variety of means are provided by the manufacturers for connection of PVC water, waste and drain pipes to taps and ball-valves, copper or galvanised steel tubing and stoneware or iron drainage goods.

Polypropylene tubing

Polypropylene waste and above-ground drainage systems are used mainly for high temperature and chemical wastes from factories, laundries and other commercial premises.

They are not therefore very likely to be encountered by the home plumber. *The* important difference between polypropylene and PVC is that the former material cannot be solvent welded. Only ring seal joints may be used with this material

Pitch fibre pipes

Although pitch fibre pipes are sometimes used for above ground waste and soil stacks their most common use is for underground drainage work.

There are several methods of jointing but the simplest is undoubtedly the snap ring joint. The snap ring is placed over the end of the pipe, care being taken to ensure

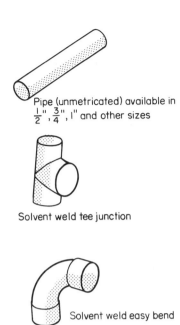

Pipe (unmetricated) available in
$\frac{1}{2}$", $\frac{3}{4}$", 1" and other sizes

Solvent weld tee junction

Solvent weld easy bend

Solvent weld elbow bend

Cistern connector for PVC pipe

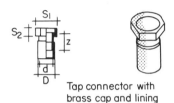

Tap connector with
brass cap and lining

PVC cold water supply pipe and some of the solvent weld fitting available.

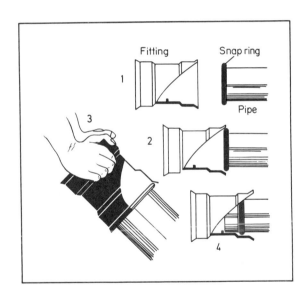

Making a snap-ring joint with pitch fibre pipe.
1   The snap ring is placed on the pipe end.
2   The joint is aligned with the tube end.
3   The joint is pressed firmly home.
4   The complete joint.

that the ring is square to the axis of the pipe and that its flat surface is in contact with the pipe. The coupling is then pushed home over the ring and pipe end so as to force the ring to roll along the pipe.

Due to the shape of the section of the ring it is compressed and jumps into its final position. This can be distinctly felt and is an indication of a sound joint.

As with PVC waste and drain pipes a variety of means are provided for the connection of pitch fibre drain pipes to pipes of other materials.

The astute reader will have noted that, in discussing PVC and pitch fibre underground drain pipes, I have omitted to give the diameters of the pipes.

This must be blamed on to the progress of metrication. Domestic drainage, in the old 'imperial' days, was always carried out in 4 in pipe. It is still carried out in the equivalent of 4 in pipe. However the makers of pitch fibre pipes described theirs as being 100 mm (the internal diameter of the pipe) while the makers of PVC pipes describe theirs as being 110mm (the external diameter of the pipe).

Chapter 33
Some rural plumbing problems

A cottage in the country, remote both from the city's smoke and bustle and the soul-destroying monotony of suburbia, is every townsman's dream. Some realise it, either for retirement or for commuting to the office, only to find that what had appeared to be a dream was, in fact, a nightmare!

Rural life has its problems too; very different from those of the town. Foremost among them is likely to be the question of drainage. Town dwellers are so accustomed to pulling the plugs out of their baths, sinks and wash basins and operating the flush of their lavatories, that they tend to forget these facilities are possible only because a comprehensive system of street sewerage, culminating in a large-scale sewage treatment works, has been provided.

Many villages and rural communities nowadays have their own sewerage systems and sewage treatment plant. There are however still many isolated properties which have no access to a public sewer.

It does not necessarily follow that, because a village has an up to date sewerage system, every property in the village is connected to it. Local authorities' power to compel existing properties to connect to a newly laid sewer is far more limited than many people imagine.

Far too many townsmen, when buying a rural property, accept the house agent's breezy, 'There's cesspool (or septic tank) drainage of course', with only the vaguest idea of what this may mean. After a few months' residence they may be only too well aware of its implications!

Cesspools

It is not uncommon for the descriptions 'cesspool' and 'septic tank' to be used as though they meant the same thing. In fact they are vastly different. A cesspool (known in some parts of the country as a 'cesspit' or a 'dead well') is simply an underground watertight tank designed to hold sewage *temporarily*. It must be emptied regularly and frequently.

A country cottage built between the wars or earlier might well have a cesspool of the size and type illustrated. It is 6 ft in diameter and has an effective depth of 6 ft below the level of the inlet. Its capacity in cubic feet can be obtained from the formula ($\pi r^2 h$) that you learned at school to calculate the volume of a cylinder. Multiply the square of the radius by 3.14 and multiply the result by the effective depth. In the example given the calculation would work out like this: $3^2 \times 3.14 \times 6 = 169.56$ cu.ft.

Cubic feet can be converted to gallons by multiplying by 6.25. The cesspool therefore has a capacity of $169.56 \times 6.25 =$ about 1 000 gal. This sounds like quite a lot of sewage. How long would the cesspool take to fill?

Waterworks authorities allow something like 45 to 50 gal of water per head of the population per day. This includes street washing and industrial purposes so it is probable that for domestic use only (including baths, clothes washing, flushing and so on) between 20 gal and 25 gal per day should be allowed for each individual. All of this water will find its way, in one form or another, into the cesspool.

Taking the lower figure of 20 gal per day, it will be obvious that a family consisting of a husband and wife only would fill

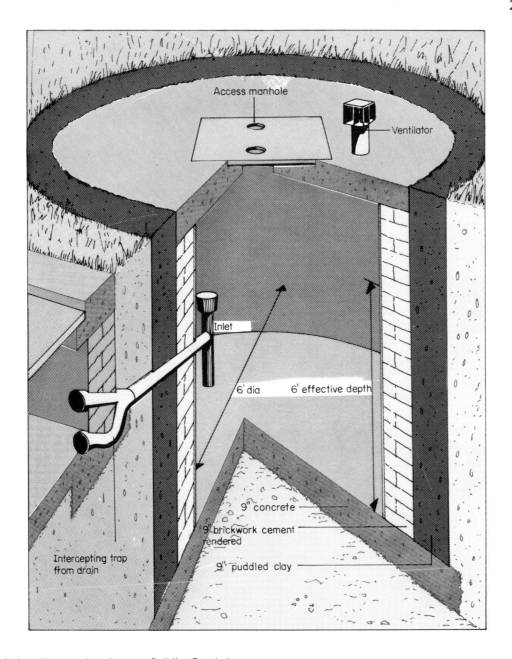

A typical small cesspool serving a pre-Building Regulation cottage. Never buy a cottage with drainage in this kind in ignorance of the cost and availability of the cesspool emptying service. You will need it very regularly!

the cesspool in just under a month. If they had two children it would be full in less than a fortnight!

The need for continual emptying—a smelly, unpleasant business under the best of circumstances—is the big snag about cesspool drainage.

Before even considering the purchase of a house with cesspool drainage check the capacity of the cesspool and work out how often it will need to be emptied. Check with the local district council about the cesspool emptying charges. Most local councils in rural areas operate a cesspool emptying service. If they don't, they will certainly be able to put you onto a private contractor who undertakes this work.

Find out about the charges for the cesspool emptying service and about its *availability.* If your cesspool is overflowing and the drains are backing up it is little comfort to be assured by even the most sympathetic voice on the phone at the council offices that, 'your cesspool will be emptied within a week or ten days, sir'.

Some local authorities offer a free cesspool emptying service though this may be limited to a fixed number of emptyings per year. Others operate a subsidised service and yet others expect cesspool owners to pay the full economic cost of emptying. Charging the full cost to the owner of a cesspool drained house within a sewered area is one way in which local councils may encourage connection to the sewer.

The basis on which the charge is made may also vary considerably from area to area. It may be a flat rate of so much per cesspool or so much per load on the cesspool emptier. It may, on the other hand, be an hourly charge based on the time between the cesspool emptying vehicle leaving its depot and its return there after completing the job and discharging the cesspool contents.

Prospective house purchasers, raising the question of cesspool emptying with an estate agent or owner, are sometimes answered with a knowing wink and the assurance; 'There's no need to worry about emptying *this* cesspool sir. There's a hole in the bottom. It'll never need emptying'.

Discount such assurances. Quite apart from the illegality—and potential danger to health—of a leaky cesspool, a moment's reflection will make it obvious that, if the contents can leak out, subsoil water can leak in. In many parts of the country, where the subsoil water level is high, this is a far more probable occurrence.

I have seen subsoil water pouring through the walls of a leaky cesspool like a miniature Niagara as its contents have been sucked out by the cesspool emptier. In a wet season such a cesspool can be filled again to overflowing before the emptier has reached its depot.

The Building Regulations recognised that the overwhelming majority of existing cesspools were far too small. They require that the minimum capacity of new cesspools must be 4 000 gal; almost four times that of the pre-Building Regulations cesspool that we discussed earlier in this chapter.

Don't forget though that this new minimum applies only to cesspools constructed after the Building Regulations came into force in the mid-'60s. For many years to come most cesspools in this country will be far smaller than that.

The new large capacity cesspool should need emptying far less frequently than its predecessor. With a family of two it should need emptying only some three times a year.

The large capacity has snags however. Older and smaller cesspools could usually be emptied with one load of the cesspool emptier. The vehicle may have to make several expensive visits to empty 4 000 gal.

Then, of course, a large cesspool is much more expensive. to build, and much more difficult to make watertight, than a smaller one. A cesspool with a capacity of 4 000 gal must have a cubic capacity, below the drain inlet, of 644 cu. ft; this could be obtained with a cesspool 12 ft deep and with an area of 54 sq. ft.

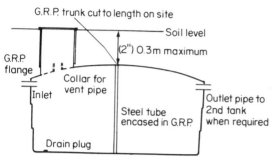

G.R.P. trunk cut to length on site

Soil level

(2") 0.3m maximum

G.R.P. flange

Collar for vent pipe

Inlet

Steel tube encased in G.R.P.

Outlet pipe to 2nd tank when required

Drain plug

This 2,000 gal capacity plastic/glass fibre cesspool made by Rokcrete Ltd. will be watertight and need less frequent emptying. Remember though, that all forms of cesspool drainage only postpone disposal of the sewage.

It should be added that some local authorities will modify the requirements of the Building Regulations under certain special circumstances. They may, for example, accept a 2 000 gal capacity cesspool in an area expected to be sewered within, say a year.

Recognising the difficulty of constructing an absolutely watertight large capacity cesspool an Essex firm has produced a glass fibre reinforced plastic cesspool of 2 000 gal capacity which, being made in one piece, can be guaranteed to be watertight.

Two of these can be linked together to give a capacity of 4 000 gal. They have been successfully installed in rural areas of north-east Essex, even where there has been an exceptionally high water table in conjunction with wet running sand.

Septic tanks

So much for cesspools. A septic tank is, or should be, a different matter entirely. At its best, a septic tank system is a small, private sewage treatment plant which will function satisfactorily, with the minimum of attention, for years.

The septic tank itself is an underground chamber designed to retain sewage for at least 24 hours. During this period the sewage is liquefied by the action of bacteria. A thick scum forms on the surface of the liquid in the tank and sludge forms at the base. The liquid in the middle is drained off from beneath the scum.

A typical small septic tank system, designed by Burn Bros. (London) Ltd, is illustrated. Sewage enters, without disturbing the surface of the liquid already in the tank, by means of a dip-pipe inlet. It leaves

A septic tank and filter installation designed by Burn Bros. Ltd. A properly designed septic tank installation can provide a satisfactory sewage treatment home for a single house or small group of houses. Always check with the District or Borough Council before committing yourself to any expense in connection with the installation of such a plant.

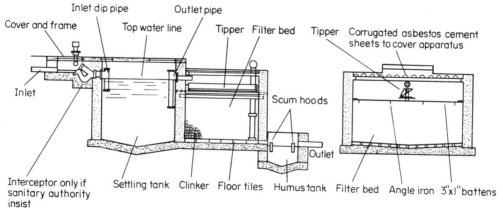

Inlet dip pipe *Outlet pipe*

Cover and frame *Top water line* *Tipper Filter bed* *Tipper Corrugated asbestos cement sheets to cover apparatus*

Inlet

Scum hoods

Outlet

Interceptor only if sanitary authority insist *Settling tank Clinker Floor tiles Humus tank Filter bed Angle iron 3"x1" battens*

by a similar dip-pipe at the other end of the tank.

Septic tanks do not purify sewage. They simply liquefy it. Before it can be discharged into a ditch or stream it is necessary to aerate it by allowing it to percolate slowly through a 3 ft to 4 ft deep bed of stone or clinker.

Aeration, like septic tank action, is a bacterial process. The effect of septic tank treatment and aeration is to speed up and control the natural processes of decomposition. The complicated chemical constituents of untreated sewage are broken down by bacterial action into harmless and inoffensive nitrites and nitrates dissolved in the final effluent.

The bed of stones or clinker through which the effluent from the septic tank passes is usually referred to as a filter bed. It must be stressed however that its function is aeration and *not* filtration.

On no account should what is sometimes known as a 'submerged filter' be constructed. This kind of filter is sometimes encountered on a level site where there is not sufficient fall for the construction of a proper filter bed. It has its inlet and outlet at the same level. The filtering medium is therefore constantly submerged and is consequently quite unable to perform its sole function— that of aeration.

If there is insufficient fall for a conventional filter bed with a gravity outfall, then a collecting pit should be constructed below the level of the filter outlet. This should be provided with a float operated electric pump to raise the treated final effluent to its outfall level.

It will be seen that the septic tank and filter system illustrated has an automatic tipper which ensures that the effluent from the septic tank is distributed first over one side of the filter medium and then over the other. This ensures even distribution and allows each side of the filter bed to have a 'recovery period'.

The manufacturers of the plastic/glass fibre cesspool have also produced a ready made 700 gal capacity septic tank unit in the same material. This can be installed as quickly and easily as the cesspool but

(a) Ready made plastic/glass fibre septic tank manufactured by Rokcrete Ltd. The effluent will need further treatment either by aeration through a 'filter bed' or by subsoil irrigation.

(b) Precast concrete septic tank and filter manufactured in sections by Ingol Precast Ltd. This amounts to a compact 'packaged' sewage treatment plant. Septic action takes place in the inner chamber and the effluent overflows from the drip edge to percolate through an aerating filter.

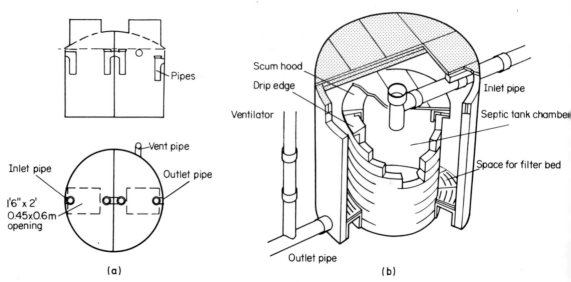

(a)   (b)

it will, of course, normally need the provision of a filter.

'Packaged sewage works'

A 'packaged sewage works' incorporating both septic tank and filter is made by Ingol (Precast) Ltd. of Preston, Lancs. The cutaway diagram shows the method of construction and principle of operation.

Sewage enters via the inlet pipe and discharges into the circular septic tank through the central dip pipe. The scumhood prevents the scum which forms on the surface from washing out on to the filter medium.

The effluent flows under the scum hood and on to the surface of the circular filter bed from the drip edge. After passing through the filter the effluent is collected at the base and passes out of the system to its outfall.

Drainage

Under very favourable circumstances—an absorbent subsoil, no sources of water in the vicinity and a sufficient area of land—it may sometimes be found possible to dispense with the filter or aerator and to dispose of the effluent from the septic tank by subsoil irrigation.

Land drains for this purpose should be laid flat, or almost flat, on a 1 ft deep bed of clinker or brick-bats. There should be a further 1 ft of this material on each side of the pipeline. Perforated pitch fibre land drain pipes are the best for this purpose.

Some 100 ft to 150 ft length of pipe will be necessary in average soil. Depth will depend upon the depth of the outlet from the septic tank but it should be kept as shallow as possible. The soil near the surface is generally the more absorbent.

With a system of this kind it is usual for the effluent from the septic tank to flow directly into the land drainage system. A disadvantage of this is that the soil in the

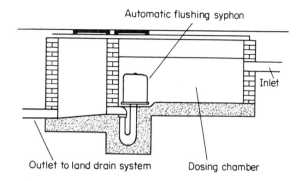

Where it is possible to dispose of septic tank effluent by subsoil irrigation the provision of a dosing chamber and automatic flushing siphon will ensure that the effluent is distributed evenly throughout the system and that the subsoil has an opportunity to 'recover' from each dosing.

immediate vicinity of the septic tank outlet becomes very heavily charged with sewage while for many weeks or months no effluent will reach the far end of the pipe line.

To avoid this, it is a good idea to construct a final dosing chamber at the point where the effluent is discharged from the septic tank and to equip it with an automatic flushing siphon. With this arrangement the level of effluent will rise in the dosing chamber until it reaches the point at which the automatic flushing siphon comes into operation, All the liquid in the dosing chamber will then be released in one flush throughout the land drainage system.

This ensures that the effluent is distributed evenly through the system and that the soil in the immediate vicinity of the septic tank is not overloaded and soured. It also ensures that, after each flush, there is a period of time in which the soil can absorb, and the soil bacteria act upon, the released effluent.

Maintenance

A properly designed system of this kind should need little maintenance beyond a periodic clearance of sludge from the bottom of the tank.

Rain water should always be excluded both from cesspools and from septic tanks. Discharge rain water drains directly into a ditch or construct a soakaway.

Since septic action is bacterial action, those who have a septic tank system should not use strong disinfectants excessively. No harm will result from using a household disinfectant or drain cleanser on the gullies and lavatories once a week.

Excessive use of detergents is also unwise. Some housewives do tend to be over-generous in their use of these materials. If overused, synthetic detergents can emulsify the fats naturally present in sewage. Instead of a scum forming on the top of the septic tank and a sludge at the bottom with a relatively clear fluid between, a liquid of soup-like consistency will fill the tank. This will wash through the outlet to clog the filter or land drainage system.

Taking precautions

If you are thinking of purchasing a rural cottage which is not connected to a sewerage system examine its drains and their outfall in the light of this chapter. If there is a cesspool, check its capacity and the cost and availability of the cesspool empty-ing service. If there is a septic tank system check on its eventual outfall; into a ditch or stream perhaps. If it is black and evil smelling you can be fairly certain that the time is not far distant when the council will require that state of affairs to be remedied.

It may be that your rural home has not any drainage system at all. Waste water is thrown on to the garden and there is an old fashioned pail closet. Part of your modern-isation scheme will be to provide a compre-hensive drainage system, bath, sink, toilet and all the trappings of modern civilisation.

In this event you should call at the district council offices and have a chat with the building control officer, or the environ-mental health officer, before committing

yourself in any way. It may be that some kind of septic tank installation is possible. Here you must take the advice of the local official, A basic septic tank system that could be perfectly satisfactory for a remote moorland cottage could be a serious threat to health on the outskirts of a populous village.

Think twice, and then again, about the provision of a cesspool. Remember the responsibilities that it entails and the fact that it only **postpones** the problem of dis-posing of the household's sewage. I person-ally can imagine no circumstances in which I would be prepared to buy a home with a cesspool or one where it was necessary to construct one.

Find out if, or when, a public sewer is likely to be constructed near your pro-posed new home and make your plans accordingly, If this is likely to be within say, a year, you might well be wise to postpone the installation of your drainage system.

The idea of a chemical closet may lack appeal to the townsman for permanent use. Yet modern chemical closets (Elsan, Racasan and Perdisan) are very different from the old pail or earth closet. To my mind they are infinitely preferable to having a modern flush lavatory that one is afraid to use because the cesspool is already overflowing—and with no hope of its being emptied for days!

Water from a well

Water supply is less likely than drainage to be a problem to the seeker after rural solitude. Local authorities have, in the past, always inclined to provide mains water services in advance of any sewerage system and there is no reason to suppose that the Area Water Authorities, who are now responsible for both these services, will adopt any different policy.

There are, of course, still many rural cottages supplied with water from a well. The prospective purchaser would be wise to regard them with suspicion; particularly if the well is of the picturesque brick type beloved by the producers of picture postcards.

The 'olde worlde' thatched cottage of these postcards traditionally had two holes in the back garden: the well and the cesspool. Not even the most fanatical conservationist is likely to feel too much enthusiasm for the kind of 'recycling' produced by this arrangement.

Discount assurances that the previous inhabitant of the cottage was the healthiest man in the village and that he was accidentally killed while hunting at the age of 104. He may well have had fifteen children, all of whom died in infancy from typhoid fever!

Never rely on a water supply of this kind without first asking the Environmental Health Officer of the local District Council to sample the water for bacteriological analysis. It would take several negative samples taken over a considerable period of time before I felt happy about it.

If you have, or there is the possibility of your having, a young baby, it would be wise to arrange for the well to be sampled for chemical as well as bacteriological analysis. Water that is bacteriologically satisfactory may contain excessive nitrites which, if used in a baby's feed, can extract the oxygen from his blood to produce the 'blue baby' condition.

Local Councils normally take routine chemical samples from wells serving homes in which there is an expectant mother. If the water has excessive nitrites they will make arrangements for an alternative water supply for use until the child is old enough to be able to cope with them.

There are, in fact, two kinds of well: deep and shallow. *Actual* depth, from ground level to water line or from ground level to the base of the well, is not the deciding factor in classification.

A 'shallow well' is one that depends for its water supply upon subsoil water—water that is found *above* the first impermeable rock stratum beneath the soil. On a good building site, beneath a layer of top-soil 1 ft to 1 ft 6 in deep, there may be a 15 ft depth of gravel lying on a 20 ft thick bed of impermeable clay.

A well, dug on such a site, drawing water from above the clay would be a shallow well. If, on the other hand, the well were dug deeper—through the clay stratum to a water-bearing stratum, perhaps chalk, underneath it would be described as a deep well.

A shallow well taps subsoil water held above the first impervious stratum. Water from such a well is suspect. A deep, and generally safe, well taps water held below the first impervious stratum. The actual depth of the well has no bearing on the classification.

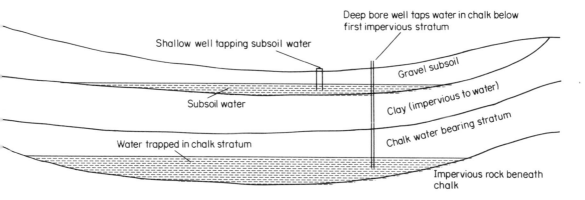

Water from a deep well is much more likely to be satisfactory for drinking purposes because of the additional layers of rock through which the water has filtered to its underground reservoir.

Dug, brick-lined wells are generally shallow ones. Deep wells are usually bored and are often referred to as 'bore wells'.

A bore well of this kind will probably provide you with a safe and wholesome water supply. It is still worth while though to arrange for the Environmental Health Officer to check it for you.

If you have a water supply of this kind you will probably have a float activated electric pump to pump it up to the main storage cistern in the roof space.

Don't overlook the fact that this will mean that *all* your domestic water, including that used for cooking and drinking, will come from the roof storage cistern. This makes it imperative that the cistern should be kept clean and that it should have a cover capable of excluding the mice, birds (and possibly, bats) that may find themselves in a rural roof space.

Section 4

Home Electrics

Acknowledgements

The author of this section and the publishers would like to thank the following firms for their help in supplying information and illustrations relating to their products.

AMF-Venner Ltd.
Ashley Accessories Ltd.
Belling & Co Ltd.
BSR (Housewares) Ltd.
BICC Ltd.
E. Chidlow & Co Ltd.
Concord Lighting International Ltd.
J. A. Crabtree & Co Ltd.
Creda Electric Ltd.
Crownette Water Heaters Ltd.
Duraplug.
Egatube Ltd.
Electrical Association for Women.
Electricity Council.
Fotherby Willis Electronics Ltd.
Home Automation Ltd.
Humex Ltd.
Lewdon Metal Products Ltd.
Maclamp Co Ltd.
M.E.M. Ltd.
MK Electric Ltd.
Nettle Accessories Ltd.
Osram-GEC Ltd.
Ottermill Switchgear Ltd.
Philips Electrical Ltd.
Rock Electrical Accessories Ltd.
Santon Ltd.
George H. Scholes & Co Ltd.
Superswitch Electrical Appliances Ltd.
Thermair Electrical Appliances Ltd.
Thorn Lighting Ltd.

Introduction to Section 4

Home electrical work whether it is mending a fuse, fitting a plug, adding a light or socket outlet or even completely rewiring a house is within the capabilities of the keen mechanically minded d.i.y man (or woman).

Electricity, because it flows along wires instead of through pipes, cannot be seen or heard nor produces any smell, is often regarded with great mystery. This is really a fallacy since the actual wiring, fixing accessories and other associated work is very much a practical and down to earth exercise requiring no physics degree nor a college diploma. Most of the work is non-electrical and consists of lifting floorboards, drilling holes and fixing cables and boxes.

Since an electrician is paid the same rate for the job, whether he is lifting floorboards or connecting up a consumer unit, you can save a lot of money by doing the work yourself, your only outlay being materials. Prices charged by contractors vary considerably but you can take it that in general the cost of materials represent only a fraction of the total.

Safety is an important aspect. Before you start any electrical work on the house, switch off at the mains. If repairing an appliance pull out the plug. Follow the instructions given in this section implicitly, using the correct materials and the correct sizes and types of cables and you are unlikely to go wrong.

Chapter 34
Your electrical installation

The home electrical installation is in two parts. One part belongs to the electricity board. The other part which is termed 'the consumer's installation' belongs to the house owner.

The components of the electricity board's installation consist of the incoming cable known as 'the service cable' which runs in from the street, usually underground but overhead in rural areas; the mains box con-taining the service fuse and a neutral link; the meter, and a time switch for off-peak heating. This apparatus is connected to-gether by cables and is sealed to prevent unauthorised persons tampering with the supply.

The householder is not concerned with the board's apparatus unless the service fuse blows and the board has to be called in to replace it. The consumer can however be held responsible for any damage to the board's equipment.

All apparatus on the house side of the meter is the responsibility of the consumer. This consists of a consumer unit or, in older houses which may not have been rewired, a number of main switch and fuse units and fuseboards.

Mains layout and equipment showing how the consumer unit is connected to the mains via the electricity meter; the earthing connections are also shown

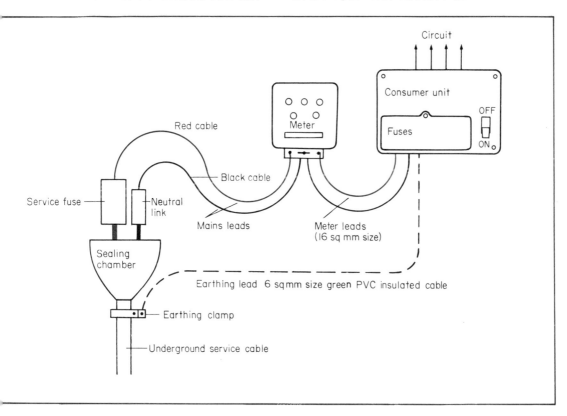

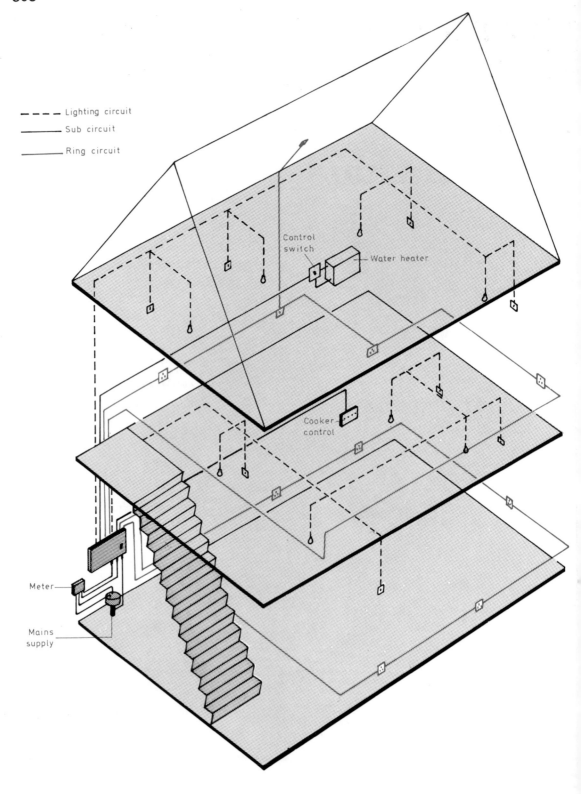

Lighting circuit
Sub circuit
Ring circuit

Control switch
Water heater
Cooker control
Meter
Mains supply

Earthing

As will be mentioned in later sections an installation and most of the appliances have to be connected to earth. Earthing is the responsibility of the consumer and not the electricity board.

Nevertheless, the electricity board, where possible, provides earthing facilities by means of an earthing terminal situated near the meter and connected by the board to its system. This earthing is usually the metal sheathing of the underground service cable. Where the electricity board is unable to provide earthing facilities the consumer must do so. Almost invariably this will necessitate fitting an earth leakage circuit breaker to be used in conjunction with some form of earth electrode, such as an earth rod driven into the ground outside the house.

Three separate main switch and fuse units connected to the mains via a terminal distribution box, and used instead of a single consumer unit, are shown on the right

Two consumer units are shown below. One is for general use, the other for night storage heating connected to a dual-rate (white) meter

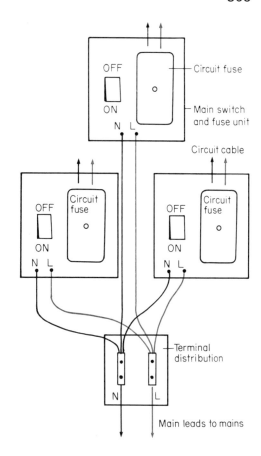

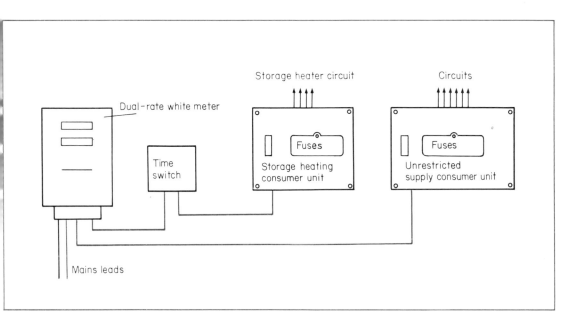

Earthing to a water pipe

Many installations are earthed to the mains water pipe by means of an earth clamp secured to the pipe on the street side of the house stop cock. Nowadays water authorities are using plastic mains pipes which means the water pipe may no longer be used as the sole means of earthing. If in doubt, it is essential to check with the electricity board whether it is advisable to use the existing water pipe earthing arrangement. When an existing water pipe can no longer be used, the electricity board requires the provision of alternative facilities which invariably means the installation of an earth leakage circuit breaker (ELCB).

Crossbonding of services

Another recent requirement is that the mains water and the mains gas services must be crossbonded to earth. This is also the responsibility of the consumer when installing new wiring or rewiring an existing installation.

To crossbond, an earthing clamp is secured to the mains water pipe on the street side of the house stop cock and to a clamp secured to the main gas pipe on the house side of the gas meter. The two clamps are connected to the installation earthing system by 6 mm² green PVC insulated cable. *(Note. At a date not later than 31 December 1977, the colour of the earth conductors and leads run independently and that of PVC sleeving to enclose the ends of bare earth conductors will be green/yellow instead of green).*

How an earth leakage circuit breaker (ELCB) operates

An ELCB is a form of main switch (actually a circuit breaker) having a tripping coil which, when energised by an earth-fault current flowing through the system, trips, opens the circuit breaker, and cuts off the power supply to the faulty circuit. It can be regarded as a main switch having an automatic switching off device. (See also Miniature Circuit Breakers).

There are two principal types of ELCB; one current operated and one voltage operated. The choice of type depends on the soil conditions and other factors. These are known to the electricity board whose advice should be sought.

The current-operated ELCB

The operation of the current-operated ELCB depends on detecting out-of-balance current in the two poles caused by the flow of earth-fault current which energises the tripping mechanism. This method has certain advantages in that it is unaffected by other ELCB's or earthing arrangements but as it requires either 1A or ½A to operate it, it cannot be used where the soil resistance around the earth rod is more than normal. From the illustration on page 311 you can see that neither the installation earth conductor nor the earthing lead running to the earth rod is connected to this type of ELCB.

The voltage-operated ELCB

This is a simple unit where the fault current from the installation flows directly through the tripping coil to operate the tripping mechanism. Only a small current is needed to operate it but unlike the current operated type it can be influenced by auxiliary and even spurious earthing arrangements. For example, it has been known for a fault in one house to operate the voltage earth leakage circuit breaker in another.

Two or more voltage-operated ELCBs should not be used in one installation unless the installation metal-work associated with one ELCB can be isolated from that associated with the other ELCB (or ELCBs).

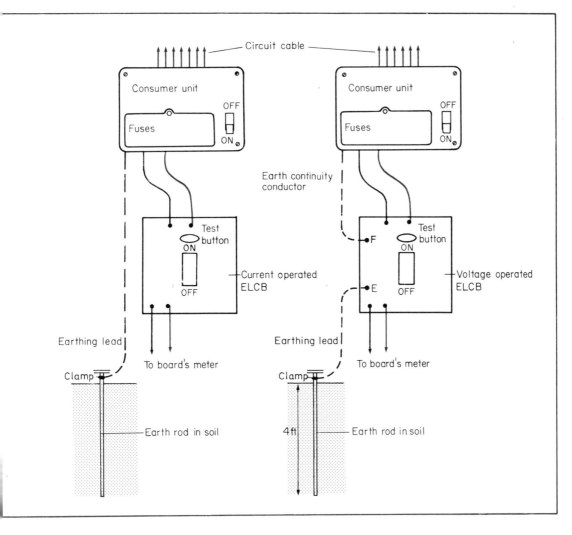

The connections at the mains for a current operated earth leakage circuit breaker and a voltage-operated earth leakage circuit breaker

The earth electrodes (earth rods) must be separated and be preferably at least 2.4 m (8ft) from other earth metal-work.

The high sensitivity ELCB

A high sensitivity ELCB is a current-operated type which operates in a fraction of a second when only a tiny current (under 30 mA) flows through the tripping coil system. This will prevent a person who comes into contact with a live wire from being electrocuted because the amount of current and the time taken for the ELCB to operate, is less than that usually required to electrocute a person.

Due to their extreme sensitivity this type of ELCB is subject to 'nuisance' tripping and is not suitable for *controlling* the whole installation, though some versions are suitable for *protecting* the complete installation. The more sensitive types which provide personal protection are used in circuits supplying power tools and similar hand-operated appliances where there is a high shock risk. Portable versions for plugging into individual socket outlets are available for use with power tools etc.

In order to be effective, the installation system has to be sound and connected to an effective means of earthing, such as an earth clamp or an earth rod.

Lighting circuits

The principal circuits of the home installation are the lighting and the power circuits.

Lighting circuits are confined principally to supplying the lighting but are sometimes used for supplying electric clock points, electric shaver sockets and small (2 A) sockets used for small appliances as well as for table lamps and floor standards.

In the two-storey house it is usual to have two lighting circuits one for each floor. In a bungalow the two circuits are, or should be, fairly evenly divided between the lighting points. In major rooms in a bungalow, the circuits could to advantage overlap so that the lighting in such rooms is supplied from more than one circuit.

Wall spot lighting

Where wall lighting and/or spot lighting is installed this can be supplied from a separate circuit. This has the advantage that the current can function when necessary as auxiliary lighting, if the fuse 'blows' in the main lighting circuit.

Power circuits

Power circuits are usually defined as circuits supplying socket outlets used for portable heaters and other appliances. The term, though not strictly accurate, stems from the days when electricity authorities charged a high rate for lighting and a lower rate for power (power meaning 15 A socket outlets), with special (low) rates for cooking and water heating.

Ring and radial circuits

Modern power circuits are chiefly wired in the form of a ring and as such are called ring circuits. Other power circuits are termed radial power circuits which supply two, or in some circumstances a maximum of six, 13 A socket outlets (power points) from the one circuit.

A ring circuit is limited to supplying socket outlets and fixed appliances over an area of 100 m² (1080 ft²). Where a floor area exceeds this, two (or more) ring circuits are necessary. For the average two-storey house even having a total floor area under 100 m², it is usual and desirable to install two ring circuits one for each floor.

Radial power circuits are installed in situations where a number of socket outlets are required but it is not worth installing a ring circuit.

Other house circuits

Other circuits which may be installed in the home include; cooker circuits, water heater circuits, outside circuits (e.g. garage), and storage heating circuits.

Current rating of circuits

Each circuit is given a specific current rating. This current rating determines the size of cable in which the circuit is wired, the maximum load (watts) which a circuit can carry at any one time, and the current rating (size) of fuse that is to protect that circuit. It is a requirement of the regulations that the current rating of a circuit fuse must not be greater than the current rating of the smallest conductor (wire or cable) in that circuit. Current ratings of circuits in the home which range from 5A for lighting to 45 A for large cookers are given in Table 1a at the end of this chapter.

Circuit cables

It has already been explained that sizes of cables vary with the particular circuit. These circuit cables are those used for the fixed wiring and should not be confused with flexible cords. The latter are used to connect lights to fixed wiring via ceiling roses, electrical appliances to fixed wiring via socket outlets, fused connection units or other outlet points. In most houses and bungalows the type of cable used for fixed wiring is 2-core and earth PVC sheathed. Blocks of flats and some houses are wired in insulated cable run in metal or plastic conduit. This is a professional job outside the scope of the d.i.y. man, but the cable sizes are the same as with PVC sheathed.

It will be seen from Table 1b that fixed wiring cable sizes range from 1.0 mm² used for a lighting circuit to 10 mm² used in some cooker circuits. When you have a wiring job to do, whether an extension or a complete circuit, you must select the appropriate cable size.

Metric and Imperial sizes

Cables in Britain have been made in metric sizes for some years and have replaced imperial sizes entirely. However, as most installations were wired with imperial size cables it is necessary to know the equivalents, especially when extending a circuit. These are shown in Table 1a.

Circuit fuses

Every circuit must be protected by a fuse or similar device which will operate on excessive overload, short circuits and—where earthing conditions are good—on line-to-earth faults. Where earthing conditions are not good, ELCBs must be used.

Fuses are made in four principal current ratings—5, 15, 20, and 30 A. A fifth size, having a 45 A current rating, has been recently introduced. Table 2 gives the current rating of fuses for circuits and 13 A plugs. The fuses are usually arranged in a consumer unit or a fuseboard but can be in individual switch fuse units.

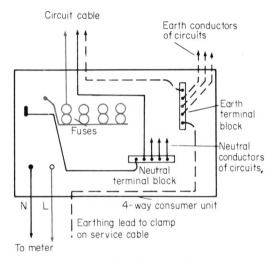

The internal connections of a typical 4-way consumer unit with one circuit connected to the fuseway, the other three circuits still to be wired

Consumer units (and modern fuseboards) are designed to allow fuse units of any of the four current ratings (5-30 A) to be inserted in any of the fuseways and in any order. A consumer unit will therefore have fuses of mixed ratings according to the circuits supplied, but preferably ranged in the order of the fuse of highest current rating to be adjacent to the main switch and the lowest rated fuse at the extreme end.

Where a consumer unit has spare fuseways and the function and current ratings of future circuits are not known, it is usual to blank these off using blanking plates supplied.

Types of fuse

There are two types of fuses: rewirable and cartridge. The majority of fuses installed in dwellings are of the rewirable type. The cartridge fuse is superior to the rewirable, but must be replaced by a new cartridge; it cannot be mended.

The fuse unit comprises a fuse holder, a fuse element, and a base or shield. The fuse holder is either of plastic or ceramic, and has two knife contacts one at each end for inserting into corresponding contacts in the consumer unit.

The fuse element of the rewirable fuse is tinned copper fuse wire which is secured in the fuse holder by terminal screws. The fuse element of cartridge fuses is totally enclosed in the cartridge and cannot be rewired. The cartridge is secured in its holder by spring contacts or is a close-fit in a tubular contact.

Fuse holders and fuse shields, where fitted, are colour coded according to their current rating as in Table 2. The knife contacts of fuse holders are usually of different physical dimensions according to their current rating so that a fuse of a given rating, say 30 A, is not inserted in one of lower current rating. Cartridges are also of different physical dimensions making it impossible to load say a 5 A fuse holder with a 15 A, 20 A or 30 A cartridge.

Although rewirable fuse holders are of different dimensions according to their current rating it is possible to rewire a fuse with heavier fuse wire than the fuse rating. This is undesirable as it creates a potentially dangerous situation.

Miniature circuit breakers (MCBs)

The miniature circuit breaker is fitted into some consumer units in place of fuses. It is a single-pole automatic switch which trips when the circuit is being subjected to serious overload or a fault occurs in the circuit.

The MCBs are available in similar current ratings to circuit fuses, and, where intended to be used in the same consumer's units, carry the same colour markings. The MCB is superior to a fuse, is more reliable and acts with greater speed and with a smaller overload current. Although the initial cost is more than that of a fuse, once fitted MCBs save the trouble and cost of renewing fuses.

An MCB cannot be closed (switched on) against a fault and cannot be abused, as can be done with a fuse by fitting a larger diameter of fuse wire. Another advantage is that individual circuits can be switched off or left on as required. For example, a circuit supplying a refrigerator or freezer can be left on when all other circuits are switched off because the house is being left unoccupied for a period, e.g. holidays.

Cable colours

The 2-core and earth PVC sheathed cable used in home wiring has two insulated cores (wires) and one uninsulated wire. One insulated wire is coloured black, the other red. The red wire is always used in the live pole. The black is used in the neutral pole of a circuit but is sometimes used in the live pole. For example, the 2-core and earth cables running to a switch are used for the live and the switch return wire respectively which means that one is black; this is usually the switch return wire. To avoid confusion the ends of the switch return wire should be enclosed in red PVC sleeving though this is not always done.

The uninsulated wire running through a cable between the two insulated wires is the earth continuity conductor (ecc). Where the sheath of the cable is removed, i.e. at a switch, ceiling rose, socket outlet, joint box, consumer unit or any other termination, the end of the wire is enclosed in green PVC sleeving.

In some sections of a lighting circuit, 3-core and earth PVC sheathed cable is used. This is in 2-way switching circuits

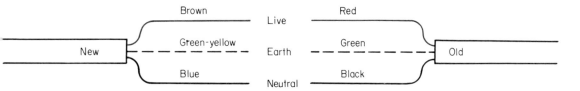

		New	Brown	Live	Red		Old	
			Green-yellow	Earth	Green			
			Blue	Neutral	Black			

When connecting 'old' and 'new' 3-core flex the cable colours must be connected as shown. The same applies when replacing old flex with new flex

and where two lights are controlled by a 2-gang switch, with a 3-core and earth cable running from a joint box to the switch unit.

The 3-core and earth cable has three insulated wires and an uninsulated earth wire. The core colours are red, yellow, and blue. These colours have no significance in domestic wiring, as the cable is made for 3-phase power circuits in non-domestic installations. The colours are useful for identification but the ends should be enclosed at switch circuits in red PVC sleeving.

Eventually the colours of the cores of fixed wiring cables will be changed as they have been for flexible cords. The colours are under discussion by the various authorities representing the electrical installation industry but have not yet been finalised. This is because each country has its own national colour coding for cables so it must not be assumed that the colours adopted will be the same as for flexible cords. The new colours are expected to be introduced in the 1980's.

Table 1a HOUSE WIRING CABLES (PVC sheathed)

Metric Size of conductor mm²	Imperial size (old) No. and diam. of wires	Current rating (nominal)* (A)
1.0	1/.044	12
1.5	3/.029	15
2.5	7/.029	21
4	7/.036	27
6	7/.044	35
10	7/.064	48
16	19/.044	64

*These ratings are for circuits protected by rewirable fuses
For cartridge fuses and MCBs a one-third higher current rating is applied

Table 1b CIRCUIT CABLES AND FUSES

Circuit	Cable used (mm²)	Circuit fuse (A)
Lighting	1.0 or 1.5	5
Immersion heater or other 15 A circuits	1.5	15
Immersion heater (alternative) storage heaters and 20 A radial circuits and instantaneous water heaters to 5 kW rating	2.5	20
Ring circuit and spurs	2.5	30
Small family size cookers Instantaneous water heaters to 7 kW Radial circuits (30 A)	4.0	30*
Large size cookers	6.0	45
Meter tails from consumer unit	10 or 16	Service fuse (electricity board)

*Cartridge fuse or MCB; otherwise use 6 mm² cable

Table 2 CAPACITY OF FUSES

Current rating (A)	Colour	Fuse wire size, diam. (mm)	Current rating (A)	Colour
CIRCUIT FUSES			13 A PLUG FUSES	
5	White	0.20	13	Brown
15	Blue	0.50	3	Red (or blue)
20	Yellow	0.60	10	Black*
30	Red	0.85	5	Black*
45	Green	1.25	2	Black*

*These fuses are used for special purposes

Chapter 35
Rewiring

The rewiring of a house may become necessary for a variety of reasons, e.g.

(i) The cables are old and their insulation is perished.
(ii) Equipment and accessories are out of date and lights, switches and socket outlets are needed in new positions.
(iii) The original wiring has been extended indiscriminately with too many lights on one circuit and various types and sizes of cable have been used. This type of installation can be generally regarded as unsatisfactory and possibly potentially dangerous.

Rewiring usually means replacing all cables and most wiring accessories such as ceiling roses, switches and socket outlets. It may not be necessary to rewire all the circuits but, where there are any doubts, it is as well to make a 'clean sweep' and rewire the whole installation.

Which circuits need rewiring?

The lighting circuit is the principal circuit which is likely to need rewiring for it is usually the oldest circuit in the house. The older type of power circuit, which is described elsewhere, will also need rewiring.

Circuits which will not require rewiring are as follows.

Ring circuits

If a ring circuit has been installed during the last 20 years and the cables are PVC sheathed (or PVC insulated if an all-conduit installation) or in MICC (mineral insulated copper covered) cable, they should not need rewiring. The opportunity should be taken, however, to bring the circuits up to date and to add more socket outlets.

Cooker circuit

A cooker circuit should not need rewiring unless the cable is very old and is not PVC sheathed (or PVC insulated if run in conduit). The cable used for a cooker circuit is of comparatively large size and expensive so there is no point in rewiring the circuit unless essential.

Water heater circuits

If an immersion heater circuit, or a circuit for a shower unit, or for any other electric water heater has been installed in recent years, it should not need rewiring.

Lighting circuit extensions

Where a lighting circuit has been extended using new cables and modern wiring accessories the new sections should not need rewiring with the main lighting circuits. These extensions can form part of the new wiring.

Outdoor electrical extensions

A cable running to a detached garage, greenhouse or shed, if installed correctly and using proper cable to conform with the IEE Wiring Regulations need not be disturbed. Otherwise it should be disconnected from the mains until it has either been rewired or modified to bring it into line with the regulations.

Under no circumstances may a detached garage or other outside building be supplied from a flexible cord connected to a socket outlet or other outlet in the house.

Inspecting an installation for rewiring

It is usually obvious when a house needs rewiring but as the installation will probably continue to give good service it is as well to conduct a methodical inspection and where possible to carry out tests.

Tests using instruments

Instruments are available for testing an installation and are used by electrical contractors and electricity boards. These test the insulation of cables, the continuity of the earthing and whether the earthing system is effective under fault conditions.

All-insulated wiring systems

An all-insulated wiring system, wired in TRS (tough rubber sheathed) cable or PVC sheathed cable, will usually show good results from an insulation test. This is the case even though the wiring may be in a poor state and the insulation perished, but dry. If part of the wiring, especially where the cable is jointed at switches and ceiling roses, is damp the test result will be poor, even if the remainder of the wiring is in good condition. Also an insulation test may not give an accurate result. This applies particularly to a lighting circuit having no earth conductor.

'Breaks' in metal conduit are quite common in houses and destroy the continuity of the earthing system. Most likely spots where 'breaks' occur are shown

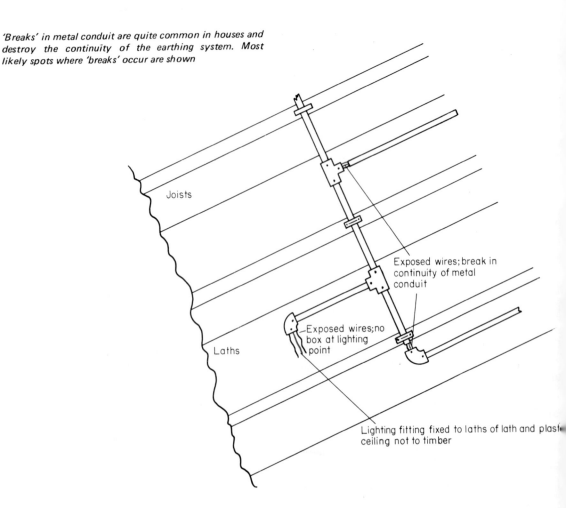

Joists

Exposed wires; break in continuity of metal conduit

Exposed wires; no box at lighting point

Laths

Lighting fitting fixed to laths of lath and plaster ceiling not to timber

Metal sheathed systems

If an installation, or parts of it, are wired in lead sheathed cable (as are many older installations), or it is an all-metal conduit installation with the lead sheath or metal conduit earthed, an insulation test will usually give an accurate result. Insulation tests can be inconclusive, if not misleading, and a physical examination of the wiring is essential to ascertain whether a rewire is required.

Tests using proper instruments will be carried out by the electricity board on request. This service is often free of charge and the board will also present a report on the installation. A similar service is also provided by registered electrical contractors.

Examining wiring and accessories

The first preliminary to rewiring is to make a thorough examination of the wires and accessories, in the loft, under the floor-boards, in the meter cupboard and wherever there are cables and wiring accessories.

An inspection in the roof space or loft gives a good indication of the general quality and condition of the wiring throughout the house. If it is a conduit installation, check that the conduit is secured to joists and other fixings by saddles or clips. The conduit should be continuous and secured in the Tees, elbows, conduit boxes and other conduit fittings.

Where a metal conduit has come adrift from a conduit fitting, the earth continuity of the conduit is broken. If the conduit is the earth continuity conductor the earthing of the circuit will also be broken. The wires may also be exposed at these breaks and create a potentially dangerous situation. Also check whether any lengths of conduit have been damaged; one of the most likely places is in the vicinity of the cold water storage tank. Damage can often be caused here after the ball valve mechanism in the tank has been repaired.

Check whether any wires are exposed at the ends of conduit terminating at lighting points. The conduit should terminate in a conduit box but these boxes are often omitted leaving the wires exposed.

Inspecting sheathed cable installations

In the roof space one can usually tell at a glance whether the cables are neatly run over and between joists and securely clipped in position. All too often they are loose and have become tangled over the years. If there are joint boxes, check that these are secured to timber supports and that no un-sheathed ends of the cables are outside joint boxes.

If lead-sheathed cable is used, the sheath must be electrically continuous and earthed. If the sheath has become detached from the metal clamping plate of a lead-sheathed cable joint box the earth continuity will be broken.

Cables at switch drops

Sheathed cables dropping down the walls to switches are usually enclosed in conduit, the top end of the conduit terminating correctly below the tops of joists. Check whether the conduit is damaged, and whether it has a rubber bush on the end to protect the cable sheath. If there is no rubber bush or it is damaged, check whether the cable sheath is also damaged. A second bush should be fitted at the lower end of the conduit but this can be checked only when the switch is removed.

The switch drop conduit of conduit installations is part of the earth continuity system and should be secured to the main conduit at an elbow or Tee fitting.

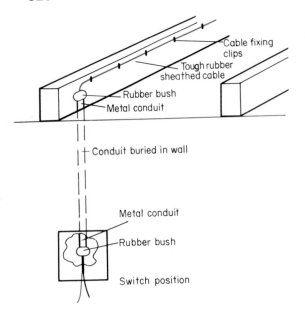

Sheathed cables in the loft or roof space are clipped to the sides of joists and PVC (or rubber) bushes are placed on the ends of metal conduits at switch drops

Cables under floorboards

A similar inspection should be made of cables under the floorboards. These are less likely to have been damaged than those in the roof space, unless the floorboards have been lifted for installing central heating or for any other major alterations.

However, since the cables are out of sight once the floorboards are relaid, this wiring is often subject to bad workmanship, especially when extensions are made to an original installation. Special attention should be paid to joint boxes. Check also whether too many cables have been inserted in the joint boxes preventing the covers being screwed on properly.

It is not practicable to check more than a portion of cables under the floorboards. If you lift one or two boards which have obviously been raised before, a good indication of the state of the wiring can be gained.

Inspection at switch and light positions

It is here that cables usually show the first signs of deterioration and whether the insulation has perished. The same goes for the cables at socket-outlets of power circuits.

The principal reasons for deterioration are:

(i) Excess temperatures occur because of poor contacts at switches; heat transfer from the lamps of close ceiling fittings and batten lampholders; overloading and/or poor contact between a plug and its socket.

(ii) Insulation may have been damaged when replacing or changing switches, lighting fittings and socket-outlets, especially when the insulation is already perished.

To check the cable at a switch, first turn off the electricity at the mains, and remove the switch. Carefully examine the insulation of the wires and note whether it is brittle or perished. Repeat the process at a number of switch points.

Where the switch is the old round, tumbler action type mounted on a hardwood block it is as well to remove the block as well as the switch. Then the cables, if they are buried, can be examined right up to the point where they come out of the wall, and up to the conduit or sheath if they are fixed to the wall surface.

If the switches are the modern 'square' rocker or dolly action type they will be mounted on either plastic surface boxes or in metal boxes sunk into the wall. The sheath of a sheathed cable should extend into the box (or the conduit fixed to the box) allowing the wires to be properly examined. If the boxes (and switches) have been fitted in recent years to moderıise the installation it may be necessary to emove the box in order to examine the nsulation at the end of the sheathing.

The insulation on old TRS cables will lmost certainly have hardened or perished nd will pull off the conductor. These ables must be replaced by rewiring.

Replacing switches

Vhen a switch has been removed to examine he cables and, in so doing the insulation as come off leaving the conductor bare nd uninsulated, the switch can be re-laced temporarily until rewiring. However, t is necessary to enclose the bare wires in VC sleeving and wrap PVC adhesive in-ulation tape over the sleeving to ensure hat it is properly electrically insulated.

Inspecting wiring to ighting points

To inspect the ends of cables at lighting ittings it is usually necessary to remove he ceiling rose or ceiling fitting plate. The nsulation of the wires is examined as for he switches and, where necessary, the nsulation should be fortified with PVC leeving and PVC insulation tape.

Where a ceiling rose or a lighting fitting as more than two terminals and therefore nore than two bunches of wires take care ıot to separate jointed wires otherwise you vill have difficulty in identifying wires to estore the current throughout the circuit or to get the light to operate normally.

Inspection at socket-outlets

Having turned off the power supplying hese circuits, select the socket-outlets vhich can be removed for inspection of the ables. If the socket-outlets are known to e wired on the old radial system the circuits will have to be rewired so there will be no advantage in removing the sockets to examine the condition of the cables.

If wired on the ring circuit system, you

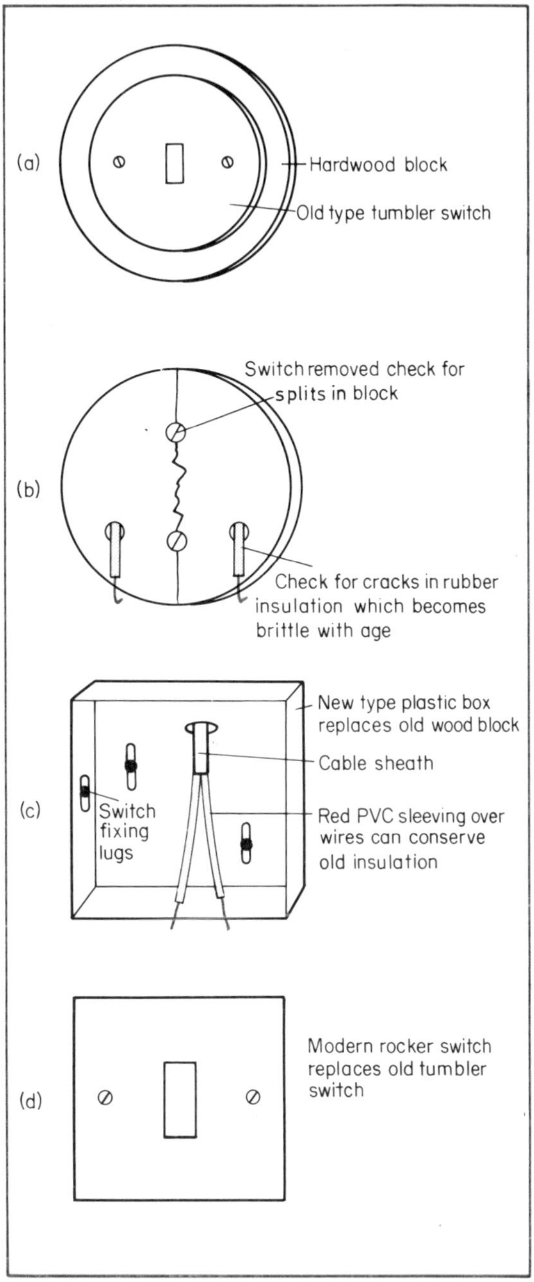

Replacing an obsolete tumbler switch with a modern plate switch. (a) and (b) show the existing switch and blocks, (c) is the new switch mounting box and (d) plate-switch connected and fixed

322

can check whether TRS cable or PVC cable has been used. If the wiring is TRS the cables should be replaced as the insulation is likely to be perished.

The fact that the socket-outlets are the modern 13 A type with flat pin fused plugs does not mean that a ring circuit is used or that the cables are fairly new. The sockets may have replaced the old roundpin type and connected to the old wiring. If they are replacements, it is as well to check that the circuit contains an earth conductor and is connected to the earth terminals of the sockets.

When checking sockets it is better to select those fixed to the skirting or to a wood surface to save replugging the wall to refix sockets or the mounting boxes.

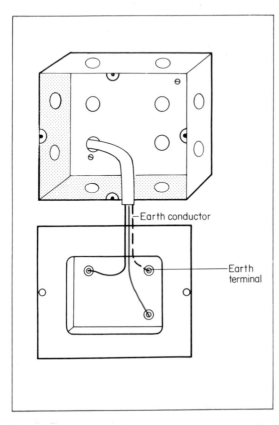

Every 3-pin socket must have an earth conductor connected to the earth terminal of the socket. The earth conductor is within the sheathed cable

Inspecting consumer units

An installation having a number of main switch and fuse units instead of one composite unit supplying all circuits is a good indication that it is old and in need of an early rewire.

If you inherit such an installation it will be as well to examine the switchgear for cracked or broken covers and also that the main switches actually work and switch off when the handle is operated. Also open the switch covers — these are or should be interlocked with the operating handles so that the switch is turned off before the cover can be opened.

Having opened the cover of a main switch and fuse unit, check the fuseholders. Check whether the porcelain is broken exposing the live contacts and the fuse wires are of the current rating given in Table 2 on page 316. It is also important to check whether the fuse wire is of the correct current rating for the circuit. Also check whether single- or double-pole fusing. Double-pole fusing should not now be used. The fuseholder in the neutral pole should contain a larger wire than the size of fuse wire in the live pole. It should be a wire, and not a fuse wire.

Earthing too is important. Old switch units usually have a metal casing which must be earthed by means of an earth conductor connected to an earth terminal on the outside of the casing. The earth conductor is almost certain to be uninsulated since an insulated earth cable only became essential about a decade ago. If the uninsulated earth cable is green with corrosion it must be renewed prior to rewiring if the installation is connected to the electricity supply and therefore in current use.

The modern consumer unit was not introduced into domestic installations until the late 1940's but since then it has been fitted to a number of old installations without those installations being rewired

The existence of a modern consumer unit does not necessarily mean that the circuit cables are in a good condition.

Checking a modernised installation

Where a new consumer unit has been fitted to an old installation to replace obsolete switchgear, there are usually obvious signs of this.

An examination of the cables may show that some are TRS or VRI in conduit, or lead-sheathed. Some cables will probably be PVC sheathed running into, and connected to, the new consumer unit. These may be entirely new circuits, such as ring circuits, but some may be a new final length of cable which has replaced a length of old cable too short to be connected to the new consumer unit. Do not therefore be surprised to find old cables at the switches and lighting fittings, and in the roof space and under the floorboards, with new cables at the consumer unit. These new lengths of cables may be used as the first sections of circuits when rewiring.

Checking an old earthing system

An old installation due for rewiring is unlikely to have effective earthing throughout, apart from the lighting circuits which were normally not earthed. Also, it is most likely that the installation will be earthed to the mains water pipe, whereas nowadays the mains water pipe may no longer be used as the sole means of earthing. This is because the water authorities are using plastic pipes in their mains systems. The effectiveness of the earthing will be checked when conducting the earth continuity tests and earth loop impedance tests.

Deciding on rewiring

When you have decided that a rewire is necessary you will have to make the following decisions:

1. Time of year to do the work.
2. Whether the whole installation should be rewired at the one time.
3. Whether all the existing wiring needs to be rewired.
4. If 'YES' to (2), which sections and which circuits will be wired first.
5. Whether, and for how long, you can manage without electricity. It is an advantage to rewire during the summer with its long days and little need for electric heating.
6. Whether you can have a temporary supply of electricity, if only for lighting in the roof space.

The time of year is a personal choice, bearing in mind the advantages of doing the work during the lighter days.

It is not essential to wire all the circuits or sections at one time, nor is it necessary to pull out all the old wiring before starting on the new. Old wiring is usually best pulled out as the rewiring progresses.

If more convenient, you may rewire one circuit at a time, for example, the upstairs lighting circuit in the spring. This will leave another lighting circuit until, say, the autumn.

Programme for rewiring

You can start rewiring at any point, but, in a 2-storey house, it is usually best to rewire the upper floor first. Most of the wiring is in the roof space and by tackling this circuit first you can have portable lighting plugged into socket outlets of the ring circuit, or other circuit if you have yet to instal ring circuits.

Next, rewire the ground floor lighting as most of these cables are laid under the floorboards of the first floor rooms. To raise the necessary floorboards you will have to shift heavy furniture and lift floor coverings which may include linoleum and wall-to-wall fitted carpets.

You will not want to move furniture and lift floor coverings more than once. Any other circuits to be rewired, or new circuits to be installed, should be done at the same time where the cables run under the floorboards of the same rooms. These other circuits are likely to be the ring circuit supplying socket-outlets and fixed appliances in the first floor rooms, landing and other service areas; circuits supplying immersion heaters and/or water heaters; and the cooker circuit in cases where this cable cannot be laid under the ground floor because the floor is solid or has a floor covering such as adhesive tiles preventing access to floorboards.

The last circuit to rewire or to instal as an entirely new circuit is the ring circuit feeding socket-outlets in the ground floor rooms. The cables of this circuit are run under the floor. If the floor is solid, then the cable may be run behind the skirting or, where this is not practicable, you will have to run the cable under the floorboards of the upstairs rooms and down the walls to the socket-outlets in the rooms below.

Availability of electricity

Plan the work so that you have mains electricity available until the very last stages of the job. It is not necessary to remove the old main switch and fuse units until you are ready to fix the new consumer unit.

To rewire a circuit, remove the cable from the fuse unit and when the rewired circuit is completed and all accessories connected and fixed, connect it temporarily to the old switch and fuse unit. Then, when all circuits are rewired arrangements can be made for the electricity board to disconnect the supply temporarily. They will do this by withdrawing the service fuse and disconnecting the cables from the meter.

The old switchgear can then be removed and the new consumer unit fixed. Connect the circuit cables to the consumer unit and arrange with the Board to have the supply reconnected. This last job should not take more than a few hours so if you arrange for the Board to disconnect the supply early one morning and reconnect it later the same day you need not be without electricity overnight.

A typical consumer unit suitable for use when re-wiring. The cover is removed showing connections of the circuit cable and mains cables. The fuse units (or mcbs) are yet to be fitted

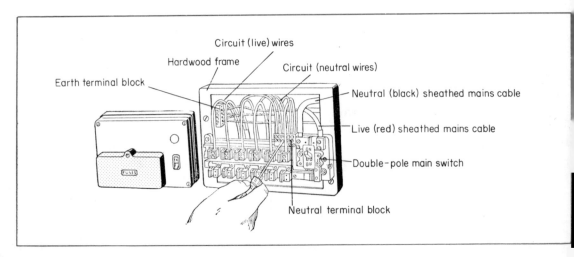

Although the job will normally take only a few hours to complete, snags sometimes arise and you may not finish in one day. When this is likely allow more time for the work.

Alternatively, you can sometimes fix the consumer unit at the start of the job and have the unit connected to the mains at the same time as the old units are disconnected. You can then temporarily connect them to the new consumer unit yourself. When the rewiring is completed you request the Board to come and test the installation and connect it permanently to the mains. This is requested by completing a consumer's application form.

Utilising an existing consumer unit

Where a modern consumer unit is already installed you have no need to contact the electricity board until the rewiring is completed. The rewired circuits can be connected to the appropriate fuseways, having earlier disconnected the old circuit wires.

Permission to rewire

If you own the house, bungalow or flat you do not have to seek permission from any person or organisation to rewire it or to carry out any electrical work on the consumer side of the installation. However, if you are a tenant you must inform the landlord of your intentions. In either case you do not have to ask the electricity board or the local council for permission to rewire.

Tips on rewiring

The procedure and method of rewiring adopted depends upon many factors and the following tips apply to most, if not all, circumstances.

1. Decide on the positions of each light, switch, socket outlet and other points including fixed appliances.
2. Determine the circuits and draw up a schedule (see Table 3).
3. Where the positions of lighting points are to be different from those they are to replace, mark the new positions on walls and ceilings etc.
4. Decide on the routes for the cable runs and which existing runs can be utilised to save cutting away more woodwork and brickwork in the house structure.
5. So far as possible make use of existing conduits dropping down to switches.
6. When existing metal conduits are used, fit a PVC or rubber bush at each end of the conduit.
7. Cable and conduit buried in walls and fixed in inaccessable places can be abandoned but seal the ends of cables where there is a possibility during rewiring that the conductors are live when switching on the power.
8. Where there is no existing buried conduit at a switch drop for enclosing the cable and the wall is not being repapered, fix the cables to the surface of the wall and sink them later when redecorating.
9. When you bury sheathed PVC cable in walls no conduit or other protection against mechanical damage is normally required.
10. When raising floorboards look out for boards which have been previously raised. When raising T and G (tongued and grooved) floorboards which have not been raised before you may need a rip saw to remove the tongues. Before raising boards take care not to cut cables and pipes which are beneath them.
11. Cables crossing joists under floorboards have to be threaded through holes drilled in the joists at least 50 mm (2 in) from the tops.

Electric bells, buzzers and chimes

These operate at elv (extra low voltages) between 3 and 12 V. The single bell, buzzer and many models of chimes are powered by dry batteries but the more powerful chimes and intricate bell systems have to operate from mains transformers. Usually a transformer is preferable for any bell or chimes. Where an illuminated bell push is used a mains transformer is essential as the lamp of the push would exhaust a battery in a day or so.

The purpose-made bell transformer is double wound and the secondary winding is connected to earth so that should a fault occur in the transformer, the low voltage apparatus and wiring would not be subjected to mains voltage. The transformer is supplied from a 5 A circuit or from a fused connection unit (with 3 A fuse) served by the ring circuit, using 1.0 mm² 2-core and earth PVC sheathed cable.

This cable is connected to the 240 V mains or primary terminals of the transformer and the elv bell wire is connected to two of the three elv output or secondary terminals of the transformer. The three terminals give a choice of 3, 5, and 8 V with most transformers. Some chimes require a higher voltage and for these, mains transformers are available with terminals giving 4, 8 and 12 V.

Burglar alarms

These are bought in kit form for connection to a battery. For this purpose batteries are more reliable than the mains supply and remain permanently in operation, provided the batteries are replaced when necessary.

Materials required for rewiring

Draw up a list of materials needed. For a 3-bedroom house (wired as the schedule in Table 3) the following materials would be needed.

Table 3 TYPICAL SCHEDULE OF POINTS FOR REWIRING

Location	Lights	Switches	Socket outlets	Other outlets
Living room	1 pendant 3 wall lights	1 rocker 1 rocker	4 doubles 2 singles	—
Dining room	1 pendant	1 rocker	4 doubles	—
Kitchen	1 pendant	1 rocker	4 doubles	Cooker
Hall	1 pendant	1 rocker	1 single	Door chimes
Porch	1 porch fitting	1 rocker (in hall)	—	—
W.C. (outside)	1 batten lampholder	1 rocker	—	—
Bedroom No 1	2 pendants	1 rocker 1 cord operated	4 doubles	
Bedroom No 2	1 pendant	1 rocker	3 doubles	—
Bedroom No 3	1 pendant	1 rocker	3 doubles	—
Bathroom	1 close ceiling fitting	1 cord operated	None	—
W.C.	1 batten lampholder	1 rocker	None	—
Landing	1 pendant	2 2-way (1 in hall)	{ 1 double { Immersion heater in tank cupboard	
Garage	2 (1 fluorescent)	2	2 doubles	—

Lighting circuit

Up to 100 m of 1.0 mm² 2-core and earth PVC sheathed cable.

5 m (approx.) of 1.0 mm² 3-core and earth PVC sheathed cable.

10 m (approx.) green PVC insulated cable (2.5 mm²) for earthing and bonding.*

3 m (approx.) green PVC sleeving.*

One box of plastic cable fixing clips.

Three 4-terminal plastic joint boxes.

Nine loop-in ceiling roses, lampholders and flexible cord. If special pendants are to be bought, one fewer ceiling rose and lampholder will be required for each.

Two batten lampholders.

Eight one-way rocker switches.

Two 2-gang rocker switches.

One 2-way rocker switch.

Thirteen switch mounting boxes, plaster depth metal for flush mounting and slim plastic for surface mounting.

Two cord operated ceiling switches.

Three wall lights.

Three mounting boxes for wall lights complete with cable protection grommets.

Assorted screws, nails, etc.

From 31 December 1977 colour is green/yellow as in flex.

Ring circuit

50 m (approx.) of 2.5 mm² 2-core and earth PVC sheathed cable.

One box of cable fixing clips.

Three single switched (or unswitched if preferred) 13 A socket-outlets

Three one-gang surface or flush mounting boxes.

Twenty-five double 13 A socket-outlets (switched or unswitched).

Twenty-five 2-gang surface or flush mounting boxes.

Assorted wood screws, etc.

Immersion heater circuit

One length of 2-core and earth 2.5 mm² PVC sheathed cable, sufficient to run from the consumer unit.

One 20 A double-pole water heater switch or other controls (according to the type of immersion heater and the method of control required).

1 m (approx.) 2.5 mm² 3-core heat resisting flex.

Fixing screws, cable fixing clips and other small items as needed.

Cooker circuit

One length of 6 mm² 2-core and earth PVC sheathed cable; to run from consumer unit to cooker control unit fixed near the cooker about 1.5 m above floor level. An additional length of this cable (preferably with white sheath) to run from control unit to cooker.

A quantity of cable fixing clips.

One cooker control unit, with or without 13 A kettle socket and with or without pilot lights (neon indicators).

One surface mounting box or flush box for the control unit.

One cable terminal box or cable outlet box (optional) for connecting the final cable to the cooker.

Chimes or bell circuit

One door chimes or bell (or buzzer).

One mains transformer for the chimes.

One bell push.

A quantity of bell wire and insulated staples.

Main switchgear

One 8-way consumer unit fitted with two 5 A, three 30 A, one 20 A fuses or mcbs and two blanking plates for the spare fuseways.

Chapter 36
The lighting system

The home lighting system consists mainly of lighting circuits devoted to supplying fixed lighting only. Other lighting is sometimes termed auxiliary lighting, but in some rooms this may, in fact, constitute the main lighting.

Auxiliary lighting comprises spot lights, pelmet lighting and other special lighting and effects. This lighting can often be more conveniently supplied from the ring circuit via a special fused outlet (see ring circuits, Chapter 38). Table lamps and floor standards are also supplied from a ring circuit via plugs and socket-outlets. An advantage of supplying this type of lighting from a ring circuit, apart from convenience in wiring, is that room and other area lighting is supplied from two circuits, so that in the event of a fuse blowing the room is not blacked out.

Lighting circuits

A lighting circuit consists of a number of lighting points individually controlled by switches. These are usually fixed to the wall near the access door but in some instances, such as in the bathroom, the lighting control is from a cord-operated switch fixed to the ceiling.

Some lights, especially the landing light, and the general light in a bedroom, are controlled by two switches. For the landing light, one switch is on the landing, the other in the hall. In the bedroom, the second switch is usually at the bedhead. Two-switch control of a light is known as '2-way switching' which is a special switching cir-

cuit. These circuits are dealt with later in this chapter.

A light can also be controlled by three or more switches located in different positions. This is termed 'intermediate switching' and is a development of the 2-way switching circuit by the insertion of special switches in intermediate positions. The switches are termed intermediate switches.

Maximum lights for a circuit

A lighting circuit has a current rating of 5 A which is the maximum current that the circuit may carry at any given time. As lights on a circuit are switched on and off when required and the wattage of the bulbs inserted in the lampholders of lighting fittings varies with the situation and the requirements of the household, a method of current assessment has been worked out to ensure that a lighting circuit is unlikely to be overloaded. Assessment is made on the basis of the number of lampholders. For instance, a plain pendant has one lampholder whereas a multi-light fitting has two, three or more lampholders.

Each lampholder is then assessed at 100 W where the bulb in the lampholder is no more than of 100 W rating. Where larger bulbs are fitted, the actual wattage is used in the calculation. The total effective wattage of a 5 A lighting circuit is 1200 W. This is obtained by multiplying the current rating of the circuit (5 A) by the voltage of the supply, which in the UK is 240 volts, giving:

$$240 \times 5 = 1200 \text{ W}.$$

If no lampholder has a bulb larger than 100 W a lighting circuit may have 12 lampholders.

Number of lighting points and lighting circuits

To allow for a number of multi-light fittings and perhaps a couple of 150 W bulbs, the number of lighting points to a circuit in the home should not exceed eight but preferably no more than six. The fewer lights on a circuit the less the inconvenience should a fuse blow. Also, by having only six lights on a circuit when originally wired there is greater scope for the addition of extra lighting points.

The lighting in the home should be divided fairly evenly over two circuits which for the average 2-storey house means a circuit for each floor. In a bungalow or flat the lighting can be divided over two circuits as desired with the main living rooms being supplied from both circuits where they have more than one light.

Wiring a lighting circuit

There are two principal methods of wiring a lighting circuit, the loop-in system and the joint box system. In practice a circuit is often a mixture of both methods, the principal sections being loop-in with some lighting points being wired in conjunction with joint boxes to save cable and to facilitate the wiring. For both methods twin-core and earth PVC sheathed cable is used.

The joint box method of wiring a lighting circuit showing the connections at the joint boxes and ceiling roses. Additional joint boxes are connected in the same manner

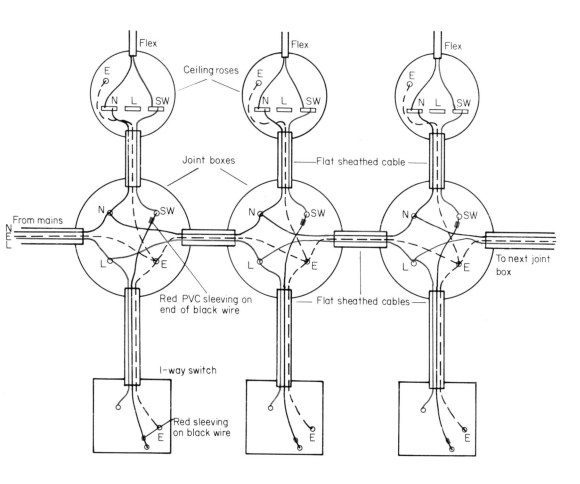

The loop-in system

In the loop-in system, ceiling roses combine the functions of ceiling rose and joint box as the circuit wires are jointed at the ceiling rose terminals. The flexible cord of the pendant is connected to the rose terminals.

When wiring the circuit, the twin and earth cable is run from the consumer unit to each of the lighting points in turn and terminates at the last. The cable is therefore looped in and out of the ceiling rose, hence its name. From each ceiling rose a length of

The loop-in method of wiring three lighting points. Additional ceiling roses are added as needed to complete the circuit. The lower diagram shows how the connections within the ceiling rose are made

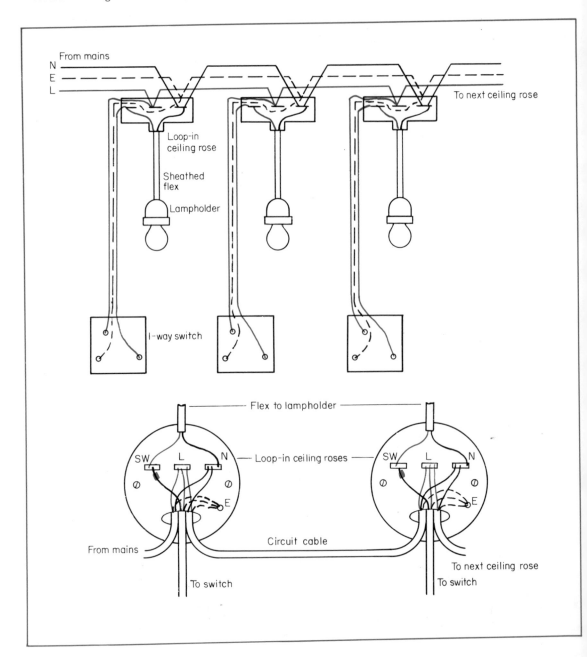

the same cable is run to the switch. The connections at the ceiling rose are shown in the illustration. Lighting points do not necessarily have to be wired in-line along the cable. Some may branch off from ceiling roses at any point but there is a limit to the number of cables a ceiling rose will comfortably accommodate.

The joint box system

With the joint box system the cable from the consumer unit runs to a series of joint boxes instead of to loop-in ceiling roses.

The joint box is often a 4-terminal type, one box being needed for each light and its switch and situated about midway between them. From the joint box, one length of twin and earth PVC sheathed cable is run to the light and another length to the switch.

Where two lights are in close proximity, and/or two switches form the one 2-gang assembly, or there are three switches in an assembly, 5- and 6-terminal joint boxes are used instead of using two (or more) joint boxes. This can be seen from the illustration.

Combined loop-in and joint box circuits

A joint box is employed instead of a loop-in ceiling rose where the cable is run on the surface and also in situations where it would be difficult to loop a cable. Using a joint box simply means looping a cable out of a ceiling rose and running it to a joint box instead of direct to a lighting point. In normal situations the loop-in system is preferred because joint boxes are eliminated, they do not have to be fixed nor is time spent in making the joints.

The combined loop-in and joint box method of wiring a lighting circuit which is useful in many situations. The connections at joint boxes and ceiling roses are shown

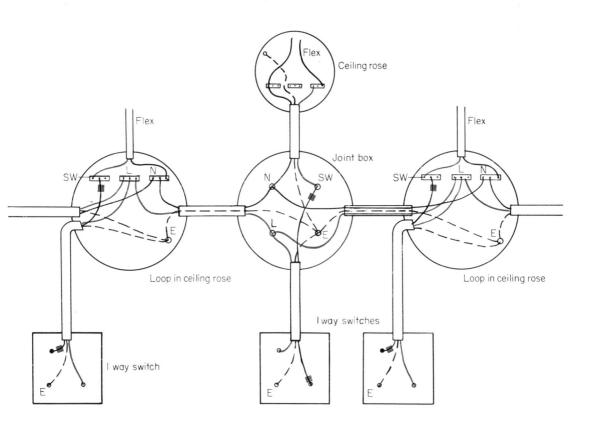

With the loop-in system all circuit joints are readily accessible at the ceiling rose, and also have the advantage that they are in the same room as the light and switch and not tucked out of the way under floorboards and floor coverings. This is of particular importance if a fault occurs and the circuit has to be tested and wires separated at the various joints.

Looping-in on lighting fittings

Where lighting fittings, other than plain pendants using a ceiling rose, are installed provision has to be made for the jointed live loop-in wires not attached to one of the flex cores. These live wires are jointed at an insulated connector which is either accommodated in the ceiling plate together with the connector joining the circuit wires to the flex of the fitting or, more likely, have to be housed in a box fixed into the ceiling above the ceiling plate of the fitting. For this a **BESA** circular box is used and has screw lugs for fixing the lighting fitting.

Wall light wiring

The loop-in system applies equally to wall light wiring. As the lights are fixed to the wall, it becomes difficult and costly to run two cables to each fitting, one looping in, the other looping out. Instead it is usually better to fix a joint box in the void above the ceiling of the room and from it run a twin and earth cable to each wall light point.

See under 'Fixing wall lights'.

Fixing joint boxes

Where a joint box is situated in the void between floorboards and ceiling or in the roof space it should be fixed to a piece of timber secured between two joists. This can be done as follows.

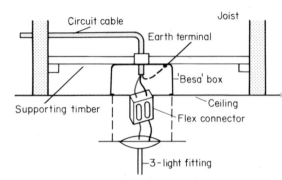

When a lighting fitting has a ceiling plate instead of a ceiling rose it is usually necessary to fit a conduit box into the ceiling to house the connections and to support the fitting

Measure between the span of the joists and cut a piece of 100 mm × 20 mm timber of the appropriate length. Secure this between the two selected joists about half way from the tops. Fix the joint box to the timber using wood screws, and check that the joint box will clear the floorboard when laid.

Fixing wall lights

A wall light is fixed by its baseplate either to a box sunk into the wall or it is fixed direct to the wall. The box, termed **'BESA'** box, is a termination box to contain the ends of the circuit wires from which the sheath is removed, and a flex connector which joints the wires to the flex of the fitting.

Only wall lights having a baseplate with 50 mm (2 in) fixing centres to match the lugs in the box can be mounted on this circular box. Most wall lights have other types of baseplate of which there are many shapes and sizes. These generally will not cover the circular box nor can they be fixed to it. As a box is essential to contain the ends of cables and wires and the flex connector, another type of box is used. This is a narrow metal box designed for use with architrave switches. The baseplate covers the box, which is sunk in the wall and the wall light is fixed to the wall itself in plugged holes.

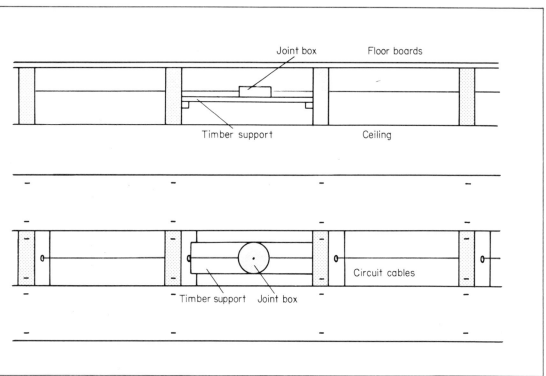

*A joint box in the void between the ceiling and floor-
boards is mounted on a piece of timber fixed between the
joists as shown*

Wall lights

From mains

N
E
L

Joint box

1-way switch

*Circuit for a number of wall lights controlled from one
switch. The joint box saves running more than one cable
to any wall light*

Slide-on wall lights

One lighting fitting maker produces a range of wall lights which have a special base-plate in two sections. One section is a backplate with socket terminal connections for the circuit wires and is fixed to the wall. The other section forms the base-plate of the fitting and contains two contact pins which plug into the socket tubes of the backplate.

The fitting slides on to the fixed backplate and can be detached at any time (for cleaning) by sliding it off.

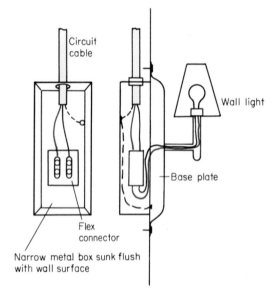

Wall lights have baseplates of various shapes and sizes and require a narrow architrave switch mounting box sunk into the wall to house the wires and connector

Switching a light from two positions

To switch a light from two different positions a 2-way switching circuit is installed. There are a number of ways of doing this but the most simple is to wire the light as for one way switching. Connect the cable to the first switch and from this switch run 3-core and earth cable to the second switch position. At each position fit a 2-way switch.

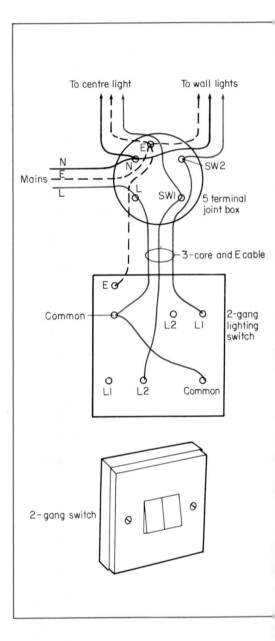

The circuit wiring where two lights or two sets of lights such as wall lighting and ceiling lighting are to be controlled separately from a 2-gang switch

With this method two cables run down the wall to the switch. One is the 2-core and earth sheathed cable, the other is the 3-core and earth sheathed cable. Both cables are run side by side in the one chase cut into the wall and are plastered over using plaster filler.

Two lights switched at one position

Where two lights are switched from one position, for example the ceiling light and wall lights to be switched from the entrance door, the two switches can be a 2-gang assembly mounted on a one gang box and supplied by a 3-core and earth PVC sheathed cable. Where both switches of a 2-gang unit are 2-way switches but both are used as one way switches, only two of the three terminals of each switch are used.

In the hall where the 2-way switch for the landing shares the same assembly with the hall light one-way switch, one is used for 2-way operation and the other for one way operation. With this arrangement, two 2-core (and earth) cables are needed because of the extra wire for the 2-way switch.

With this arrangement it is essential that the hall light and the landing light are supplied from the same circuit.

A 2-way switching circuit (a) the conventional circuit now used only in all-conduit installations; (b) the method used in sheathed cable installations in the home

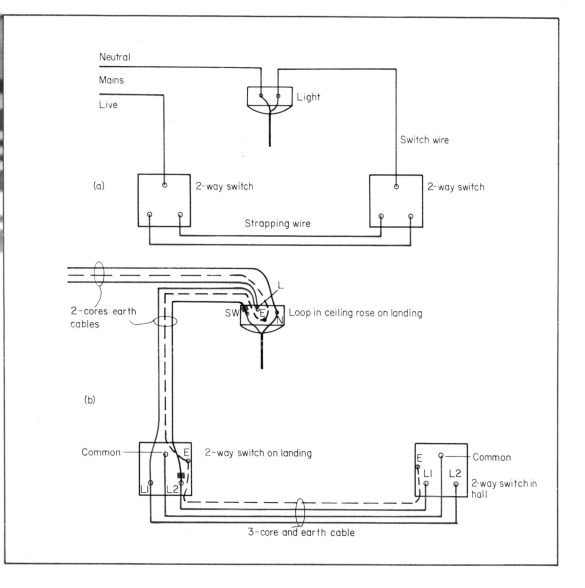

Switching a light from three (or more) positions

A light can be switched from three positions by fitting a special 4-terminal switch in a 2-way switching circuit. The switch, termed an intermediate switch, is connected at any point in the cable linking the 2-way switches as shown in the diagram.

Further switch positions can be made by adding more intermediate switches, one for each additional switch position.

When one of the switches of a three-switch circuit is to be a cord operated ceiling switch, the ceiling switch must be one of the two 2-way switches. This is because there are no intermediate ceiling switches. In practice the ceiling switch is usually the last switch in the circuit, as in the diagram, and connected to the one cable.

An intermediate switching circuit for controlling a light (or lights) from three positions. For control from four (or more) positions additional intermediate switches are inserted into the circuit

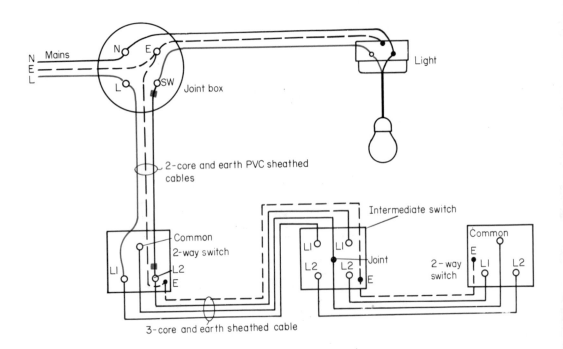

Chapter 37
Lamps

The amount of light given out or produced by an electric lamp — bulb, striplight or fluorescent tube — depends on the type of lamp and its wattage. The light produced is measured in lumens and a bulb or tube of a given wattage produces an average output of so many lumens. This will continue throughout most of its life.

Equally important is the number of lumens produced for each watt consumed, so it is usual to say, when comparing types, that a bulb or tube produces so many lumens per watt. The more the lumens per watt, the higher the efficiency of the lamp.

Comparison of lamp efficiencies

The electric light bulb operates at a fairly low efficiency whereas the fluorescent tube operates at a much higher efficiency at least three times that of the bulb. It is because of the inherent low efficiency of the bulb that there has been so much scope for improvement.

The efficiency of an electric light bulb is in the region of 25 %; the remainder of the power consumed being emitted in heat. A bulb is really an illuminous heater and is often used as such. On the other hand, a fluorescent tube is cool in comparison; though the coolness of the glass is partly due to the fact that there is more glass in a bulb of given wattage and the heat is distributed over a wider surface area.

The luminous output of a fluorescent tube also varies with its 'colour'; the 'white' tube having a light output double that of the 'artificial daylight' tube for the same watts consumption. However, provided a tube of a given wattage produces sufficient light of the right colour in a room, variation in lumens output of the different colours is of little concern. This is not so with bulbs, where you may need to have one of higher wattage to get adequate light for the purpose, and therefore consume more electricity.

Types of electric light bulb

The ordinary electric light bulb is made in two principal types and in a wide range of wattages. The two types are single-coil and coiled-coil. The coiled-coil produces more light than a single-coil for a given wattage. Where possible it is therefore wise to choose a coiled-coil type.

Single-coil bulbs

These are made in about a dozen sizes ranging from 15 W to 1500 W though in the home the 150 W bulb is the largest normally used. This latter is also the largest type made with a bayonet cap to enable it to fit an ordinary lampholder (see Table 5a). Some variants are plain, pearl and pink pearl, conventional bulb shape and mushroom shape.

Coiled-coil bulbs

The coiled-coil type is limited to five wattages: 40 W, 60 W, 75 W, 100 W and 150 W, and is available in plain and pearl versions for all four sizes. It is not made in mushroom shape nor in pink pearl 'colour'. If, therefore, you require sizes other than those listed above you must buy single-coil lamps.

Coloured bulbs

Coloured bulbs of conventional size and shape are made in the colours: amber, blue,

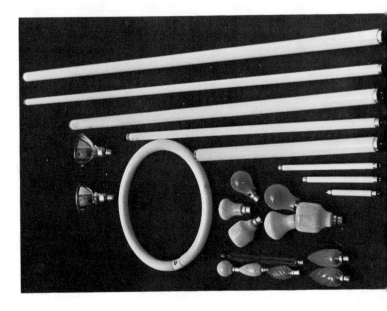

Selection of Osram bulbs and fluorescent tubes

green, pink, white, yellow and red, and in 15 W, 25 W, 40 W, 60 W, 100 W and 150 W sizes. The 15 W and 25 W types are suitable for outdoor use, but other sizes must be enclosed for protection against the rain. Most, but not all the colours, are available in the larger wattages.

Round bulbs of 15 W and 25 W, in various colours, are available for festive purposes together with other shapes.

Candle lamps

Plain and twisted candle lamps are made in 25 W, 40 W and 60 W sizes and in pearl, plain, amber and silvered colours. They are made in bc (bayonet cap) and sbc (small bayonet cap) versions.

These are used for wall lights and for period pendant fittings.

Tubular lamps (strip lights)

These are sometimes called 'strip lights' and are non-fluorescent, being tungsten filament lamps. There are two versions, one type is commonly used for applications in the home, and the second type is known as 'architectural lamps'.

The first type is available in double or single cap versions and used with special reflector type fittings as bedhead lights, mirror lights, etc. They are available in 30 W and 60 W sizes and may be clear, opal or amber.

Architectural lamps are made in two versions, straight and circular. The straight type is available in various wattages in opal finish and the curved version is made in eighth, quarter and half circle sizes in 60 W with opal finish.

Architectural lamps have peg type lamp caps and can be fixed to walls and ceilings without any fitting other than the two lampholders.

Sealed beam reflector lamps

These lamps made in 100 W and 150 W sizes are used as spot and floodlights and suitable for both outdoors and indoors. For outdoor use, special waterproof lamp holders are required for attachment to wall and other structures or with spikes for insertion in the lawn or border soil. The lamps are available in clear type and various other colours.

Long life lamps

The ordinary electric light bulb has an average expected life of 1000 light hours when used in normal situations. This is the longest life possible with the optimum efficiency. Increase in light output will mean a reduction in the expected life.

Any increase in life means a corresponding drop in efficiency and therefore of lumens output per watt consumed. To obtain the equivalent wattage of the conventional bulb, means higher consumption of electricity. Some longer life bulbs are made which have an average expected life of 2000 hours; twice that of the ordinary bulb.

It is a personal choice as to whether it is better to have your bulbs last longer or to use less electricity for the same light output. You should have regard to the current price of electricity when compared with the cost of replacing bulbs and, in some situations, the inconvenience of replacing a bulb.

The fluorescent tube

The fluorescent tube is made in a large number of straight versions of various lengths and wattage, in four sizes of circular tube and one of 'U' shape.

The lengths of straight tubes range from 450 mm (18 in) of 15 W rating to 2400 mm (8 ft) of 125 W rating. There are also miniature fluorescent tubes of small diameter in four lengths and wattages ranging from 150 mm (6 in) of 4 W to 530 mm (21 in) of 13 W.

How a fluorescent tube works

A fluorescent lamp consists of a glass tube filled with mercury vapour and coated with fluorescent powder on its inside surface. At each end of the tube is an electrode consisting of a tungsten wire or braided filament coated with electron emitting material. The ends of the electrode are connected to a bi-pin lamp cap, or in the 5 ft 80 W version, to a bc conventional lamp cap and now available in a bi-pin version as an alternative.

When the lamp is operating, electrons flow along the tube from one electrode to the other. These electrons bombard the fluorescent powder on the tube surface causing it to produce light in a similar manner to a picture appearing on a television screen.

To start the flow of electrons a very high voltage is required, this being produced by a canister starter switch in conjunction with a choke. The starter switch has a make-and-break device which, when opened, creates a surge of very high voltage. This discharges between the electrodes in a manner similar to a motor car engine at the sparking plugs. Once started the flow of electrons continues, the current being restricted by the choke which now functions as a ballast.

The starter switch has another function — to pre-heat the electrodes by sustaining a current flow until the points open. This is the reason for the short delay on switching on a fluorescent light and the tube 'striking'.

Quick start tubes

Some fluorescent fittings have no starter switch(s) for the tubes. Instead there is a transformer to provide the prewarming and the tube itself has a metal stripe running throughout its length from one lamp cap to the other. The lamp caps are earthed at the lampholders.

This assists in the starting of the electron flow and, as there is no starter to operate, the lamp strikes without the characteristic delay of the switch-start type.

Fluorescent lighting circuit. (a) the switch-start circuit which includes a replaceable canister starter. (b) the quick-start circuit which needs no separate starter. (c) a twin-tube circuit

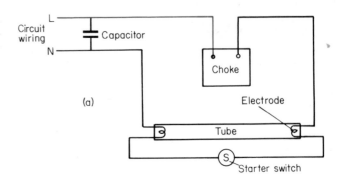

(a)

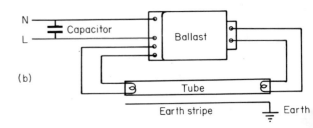

(b)

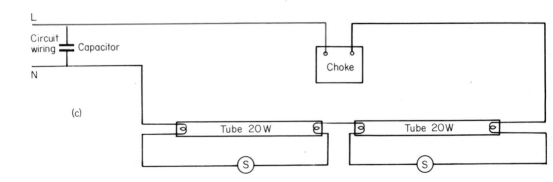

(c)

Tube life

A fluorescent tube has an expected life of 5000 to 7000 light hours or up to seven times that of an electric light bulb. The actual life of a tube is shortened by frequent switching on and off because each time the tube is switched on some of the coating on the electrodes is eroded, but with such a long life — about ten years — with average use any shortening of the life of a tube is hardly noticed.

A quick-start tube on a starterless circuit has a shorter life than a switch-start tube because more active material is eroded from the electrodes, but the life is still in the 7000-hour region.

Choosing the correct tube

The length of tube chosen depends to a large extent on the fitting chosen. The 4 ft 40 W type in either single- or double-tube version is a useful size for the kitchen. One 40 W tube gives a light output in excess of that from a 100 W bulb and with less than half the electricity consumption.

For reception rooms, hall, bathroom and other areas the smaller tubes are usually adequate and preference is often shown for the circular tube contained in an attractive fitting. For pelmet lighting, and other lighting where the tubes are hidden, the 5 ft 65 W or 80 W tube should be considered. For a long pelmet the 8 ft 125 W tube may be the better choice.

In the garage one or more 5 ft 80 W tubes of a high light output 'colour' will give the best light for car repairs. Mini-tubes are suitable as strip lights but usually come with the fittings, for example a shaving mirror light.

Colour range of fluorescent tubes

Fluorescent tubes are available in an extensive range of 'colours' but only a few of these are acceptable in the home for which warmer colours are recommended. Colour rendering is also important so that the colours of objects and materials are not too distorted. The most popular colour is de-luxe Warm White and this is chosen for living rooms in conjunction with filament lamps.

Where maximum light output is required, such as in a kitchen, White or Warm White should be chosen but with the sacrifice of some colour rendering. There is also available a colour which is used where a warmer colour than from filament lamps is required. These are sold under various trade names and, in addition to giving a warm colour, have good colour rendering qualities.

For decorative lighting giving a very warm effect, you can choose a pink tube and accept its poor colour rendering. For the garage you can have White or Warm White but where accurate colour matching may be required you should choose Artificial Daylight, or Daylight, to blend with natural daylight.

Circular tubes are made in Warm White

only. This is generally considered to be the best all round colour for the home.

Fluorescent lighting circuits

The fluorescent fitting is connected to the same wiring as any other lighting fitting except that an earth is essential with the starter-less type. Modern lighting circuits have an earth conductor at each lighting point. An earth conductor should also be installed at every lighting point where the fitting is of metal. Where there is no earth at a point it is necessary to run a 1.5 mm² green insulated cable from the point to the earthing terminal at the consumer unit (refer to the notes on earthing in Chapter 34).

The internal wiring of the fluorescent fitting depends on the type of tube and whether it has one or two tubes. The three principal circuits are: switch-start circuits; quick-start circuits and twin-tube circuits.

Switches for fluorescent lighting

The normal wall switch one-way on/off and two-way are used with fluorescent lights but, because of the surge on starting, the switch must be capable of handling the current, otherwise the contacts of the switch will burn out.

The standard plate switch of good quality available from all leading makes is adequate for fluorescent lighting. There should be no problem except, possibly, with low quality switches.

Fluorescent tube faults and remedies

Unlike a bulb which burns out completely at the end of its useful life a fluorescent tube lingers on and behaves in a strange,

Table 4 FLUORESCENT TUBE FAULTS AND SYMPTOMS

Tube behaviour	Possible cause	Remedy
Tube appears to be completely dead	Blown fuse; faulty lampholder; broken tube electrode	Mend fuse; or check lampholder or fit new tube
Electrodes glow but tube makes no attempt to start	If white glow, faulty starter If red glow, tube end of life Earth connection of quick-start tube ineffective	Change starter Fit new tube Check earthing
Tube glows one end and makes attempts to start	Lampholder at dead end short-circuited or disconnected from wires or not making contact with lamp; or broken tube electrode	Check lampholder and connections or fit new tube
Tube makes repeated attempts to start	Faulty starter Low mains voltage Tube at end of useful life (especially when it has a shimmering light effect)	Fit new starter Try again later when mains voltage is normal Fit new tube
Tube lights at half normal brilliance	Tube at end of useful life	Fit new tube
New tube lights with shimmering effect	Tube not likely to be faulty	Wait for the effect to settle down and behave normally

Table 5a LIGHT OUTPUT OF LAMPS

Wattage	Single-coil light output (lumens)	Coiled-coil light output (lumens)
15	110	—
25	200	—
40	325	390
60	575	665
75	780	880
100	1160	1260
150	1960	2040

Table 5b LIGHT OUTPUT OF FLUORESCENT LAMPS

Wattage	Length mm	ft	Lumens White	de luxe Warm White
80	1500	5	4875	3730
65	1500	5	4425	2400
40	1200	4	2700	1500
30	900	3	2000	1450
20	600	2	1050	780
15	450	18 in	700	500
MINIATURE TUBES				Warm White
13	525	21	730	730
8	300	12	340	360
6	225	9	225	245
4	150	6	150	150

though characteristic, manner. A new tube sometimes behaves similarly when first switched on but this ceases after a while.

A faulty starter, or other faults in the fitting, also cause a tube to behave strangely.

The most common faults and their remedy are given in Table 4, so you will know what to expect and what to do.

Chapter 38 Power circuits

As mentioned in Chapter 34 the ring circuit is a domestic power circuit supplying a number of 13 A socket-outlets and fixed appliances situated within a floor area of 100 m² (1080 ft²). Cable used for this circuit is 2.5 mm² twin-core and earth PVC sheathed. The cable starts at a 30 A fuseway in the consumer unit, runs to the first socket-outlet, loops out of this to the next socket-outlet then to subsequent socket-outlets until it reaches the last. Here the cable is looped out and returns to the same 30 A fuseway in the consumer unit, thus completing a loop or ring.

Connections at the consumer unit

The two cables are connected at the fuse-way to the same terminals, i.e. red and red together, black and black together. The two earth conductors are connected to a terminal on the earthing strip, but being bare wires are first enclosed in green PVC sleeving to insulate and identify them.

Wiring remote socket-outlets

Socket-outlets situated off the main route of the cable do not have to be connected to the actual ring cable. Instead they are usually supplied from spur cables branching off the ring. These spurs are wired in the same size cable as that used for the ring.

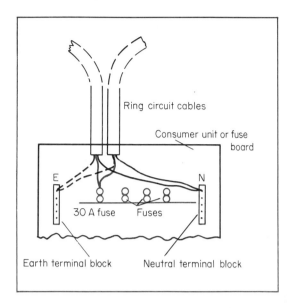

Connections of the outward and return cables of a ring circuit. Both red wires go to the fuse terminal, the two blacks go to the neutral terminal block and the two earth conductors go to the earth terminal block

Connecting fixed appliances

Fixed appliances which may be connected to a ring circuit include skirting heaters, wall heaters, small water heaters and any non-portable electrical appliances having individual loadings of not more than 3000 W (13 A approx.).

Storage heaters for these are connected to separate time controlled circuits as described in Chapter 41. An immersion heater must not be supplied from a ring circuit, even though the loading is no more than 3000 W. The reason is that an immersion heater is classed as a continuous load and as such would reduce the effective capacity of the ring circuit; the primary function of the latter is to supply numerous appliances in use at various times during the day and night.

Connections of fixed appliances

A fixed appliance may be connected by its flexible cord to a fused plug and socket-

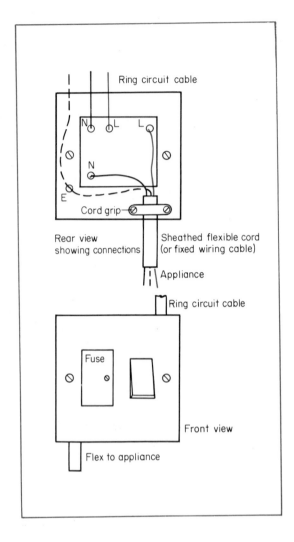

Ring circuit cable

N   L   L

N

E

Cord grip

Rear view showing connections

Sheathed flexible cord (or fixed wiring cable)

Appliance

Ring circuit cable

Fuse

Front view

Flex to appliance

Cable and flexible cord connections at a switched fused connection unit are shown in the diagram on the left. The red and black circuit wires go to the L and N terminals marked 'mains'. The brown and blue wires go to the remaining L and N terminals and the green sleeved circuit earth conductor and the green/yellow flex core go to the E terminals of the unit

(Below) Connecting spur cables to the ring circuit. (a) to the terminals of a 30 A 3-terminal joint box inserted into the ring cable and (b) to the terminals of an existing 13 A socket outlet

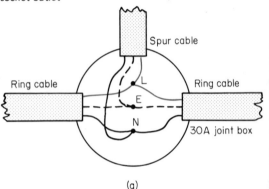

Spur cable

Ring cable   L   Ring cable

E

N

30A joint box

(a)

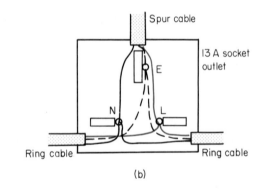

Spur cable

13 A socket outlet

E

N   L

Ring cable   Ring cable

(b)

outlet but often it is more conveniently connected to a special fused outlet known as a fused connection unit. This used to be known as a fused spur unit.

The advantage of a fused connection unit is that the flex of the appliance is connected permanently. to the unit, whereas when connected to a plug and socket-outlet someone might pull out the plug and use the socket for a portable appliance. Fused connection units are available with and without a switch and are available, if required, with a neon indicator.

Connecting spurs

A spur cable branching off a ring circuit may supply either one or two 13 A single socket-outlets, or one double socket-outlet, or one fixed appliance. Spurs from any one ring circuit are limited in number to the number of 13 A socket-outlets and fixed appliances actually wired into the ring cable.

If, therefore, there are eight socket-outlets wired into a ring circuit there may be up to a total of eight spurs branching

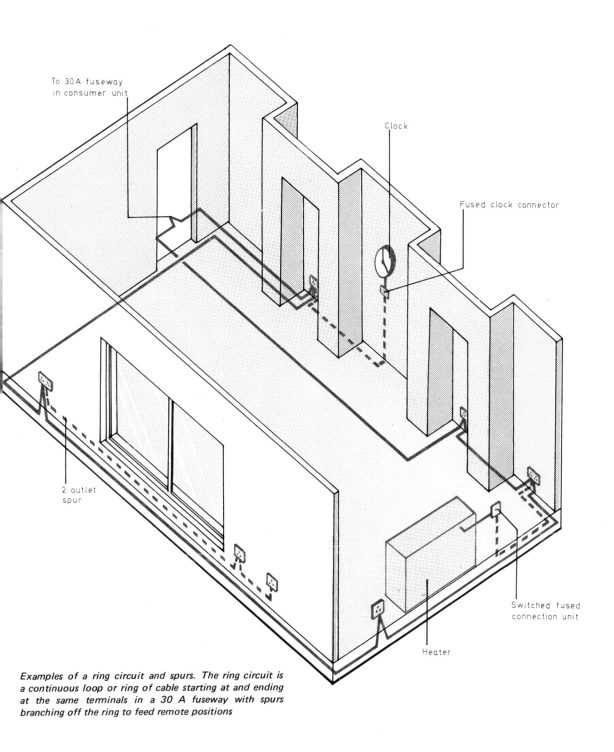

To 30 A fuseway
in consumer unit

Clock

Fused clock connector

2 outlet
spur

Switched fused
connection unit

Heater

Examples of a ring circuit and spurs. The ring circuit is a continuous loop or ring of cable starting at and ending at the same terminals in a 30 A fuseway with spurs branching off the ring to feed remote positions off the ring. As each spur may supply two socket-outlets twice as many socket-outlets may be fed from spurs, as are connected to the ring cable itself. Where some of the spurs feed fixed appliances with only one on a spur, the number of spur fed socket-outlets will be less.

A spur cable may be connected to the ring cable either at the terminals of a ring socket or at a joint box wired into the ring cable at a convenient point. When adding spurs to a ring circuit it is usually better to insert a joint box into the cable under the floor rather than to break into an existing socket-outlet box. Also the terminals of a socket-outlet will not accommodate more than three cables — two for the looping ring cable and one for one spur.

Joint boxes used to connect spurs are of the 3-terminal 30 A type.

Fused spurs

A fused spur is a cable branching off a ring circuit similar to that of a conventional spur, except that the connection to the ring cable is at a fused connection unit (fused spur unit) instead of being solidly connected to the cable at a joint box or at the terminals of a ring socket-outlet. A fused spur can supply one or more socket-outlets, but as the total current demand of the points served by a fused spur must not exceed 13 A, only one 13 A socket-outlet can be supplied from a fused spur.

A number of sockets of lower rating may be connected to supply portable lights and small appliances. For instance, two 5 A 3-pin or six 2 A 3-pin sockets.

Electric clocks

Mains electric clocks may be supplied from a ring circuit. The connection to the clock must be made at a special fused connection unit called a clock connector.

The clock connector is in two portions, one being fixed and connected to the circuit wires and the other being a form of fused plug. This is connected to the flex of the clock and secured in the fixed portion by a captive screw to prevent anyone accidentally pulling it out and stopping the clock. The fuse is usually 3 A, but sometimes a 2 A fuse is fitted.

Clock points can be supplied from spurs. Where there is more than one clock point, a fused spur is preferred and the fused connection unit at the ring cable would be a non-switched version. Clock connectors can be flush or surface mounted. The flush type can be fixed behind a wall-mounted clock.

Height of fused connection units

There is no regulation height for fused connection units. The best position is close to the appliance it serves so that the flex is as short as possible.

Some appliances are connected to the fused connection unit by fixed wiring. This should be only a short length so that anyone working on the appliance is within reach of the switch of the connection unit.

Height of socket-outlets

The recommended height of a socket-outlet is not less than 150 mm (6 in) above the floor or above a working surface such as in a kitchen or above a sideboard in the dining room. Low mounted sockets in a room fitted with deep skirting boards should not be mounted on the skirting even if the skirting is more than 150 mm deep. In this position they have less protection from cleaning tools or from heavy furniture when being moved.

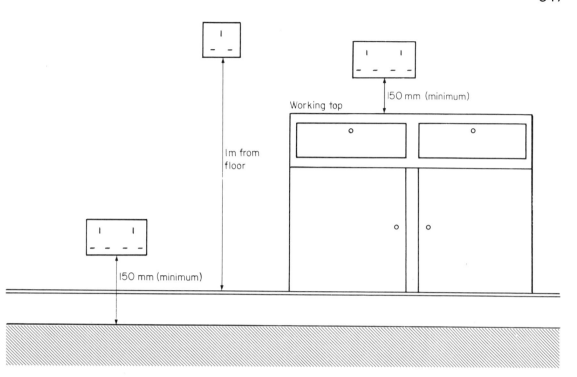

Socket outlets should be fixed at least 150 mm above the floor level and above a working surface such as in a kitchen. Where there are invalids and elderly persons a height of 1 m above floor level is recommended

Where a room is occupied by elderly people or invalids a height of 1 m (3 ft) for the socket-outlets is recommended. This means that one does not have to bend down to switch a socket on and off or to insert or withdraw a plug.

Bathroom shaver sockets

The shaver supply unit may be connected direct to the ring cable or from a spur cable without the need for a fuse in the spur. It may be installed in any position in the bathroom for although the unit may embody a switch, regulations permit it to be installed within reach of a person using a the bath or shower. This is the only switch where this applies.

Normally the unit will be fitted in the most convenient position for shaving which will be adjacent to the bathroom mirror. In many instances the unit will be out of reach of the bath but the regulations take into account that this is not always possible in the small bathroom of the average house.

Shaver sockets are also available for rooms other than the bathroom. As these have no isolating transformer they sell at a much lower price but must not on any account be fitted in a bathroom. (see page 383).

Garage and outdoor socket-outlets

Socket-outlets installed in the garage can be the same as installed in the house. Where there is a risk that they may be damaged, a metalclad version should be installed. The socket-outlets may be connected to the house ring circuit only if the garage is

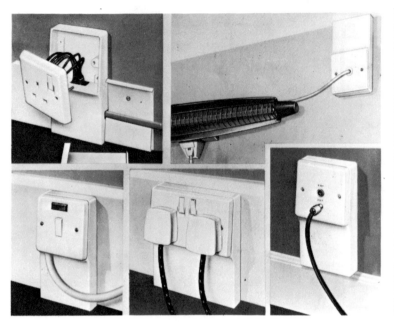

The various mounting boxes for socket outlets, fused connection units in 1- and 2-gang versions and for 20 A double pole switches, clock connectors and flexible cord outlets and other 'square-plate' accessories

attached to the house or is an integral construction. A detached garage needs a separate electricity supply, see Chapter 42.

Outdoor socket-outlets may be required for mowers, hedge-trimmers and other garden power-operated tools. These socket-outlets may be fixed to the outside wall of the house or on posts or other structures in the garden. They are normally of weatherproof pattern but there is now available a weatherproof cover which fits over the conventional socket-outlet to enable these to be used outdoors.

Radial power circuits

A radial power circuit is the name given to a circuit supplying a number of 13 A socket-outlets and fixed appliances using one cable which is not wired in the form of a ring but terminates at the last outlet.

The permitted number of socket-outlets (and fixed appliances) depends on the current rating of the circuit which can be either 20 A, wired in 2.5 mm² cable, or 30 A wired in 4 mm² cable. The number of socket-outlets and fixed appliances which can be served by a 20 A radial circuit depends also on the location of the circuit and whether the outlets are confined to one room.

Types of radial power circuit

There are, in effect, three types of radial power circuit. A 20 A circuit supplying more than one room; a 20 A circuit supplying one room only and a 30 A radial circuit supplying one or more rooms.

Two-room 20 A radial circuit

This circuit can have a maximum of two 13 A socket-outlets (or fixed appliances) each in a different room, hall, landing or other service area. It is wired in 2.5 mm² 2-core and earth cable starting at a 20 A fuseway used solely for that circuit.

One-room 20 A radial circuit

This circuit is also wired in 2.5 mm² cable from a 20 A circuit fuseway and may supply up to a maximum of six 13 A socket-outlets and fixed appliances. This is provided they are all in the one room of an area not exceeding 30 m² (300 ft²) and that the room is not a kitchen and none of the appliances is a fixed water heater.

(a) a 20 A radial circuit for two singles or one double 13A socket outlets. (b) a 30 A radial circuit which may supply up to six 13 A socket outlets and fixed appliances

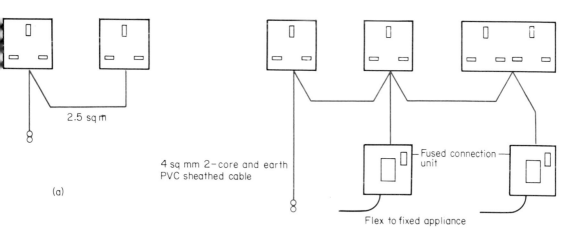

2.5 sq m

4 sq mm 2-core and earth PVC sheathed cable

(a)

Fused connection unit

Flex to fixed appliance

(b)

30 A radial circuit

This is wired in 4 mm² 2-core and earth PVC sheathed cable from a 30 A fuseway. It may supply up to a maximum of six 13 A socket-outlets and fixed appliances but without the restrictions applying to a 20 A radial circuit. The socket-outlets and fixed appliances (if any) may be installed in any rooms and service areas and the fixed appliances may be of any type having individual loadings not in excess of 3 kW. This circuit is excellent as a supplementary to a ring circuit and particularly suitable for a fully equipped kitchen to lighten the load on the ring circuit; especially where the kitchen is also used as the home laundry.

The 15 A power plug system

Before the advent of the ring circuit and its associated 13 A fused plugs and socket-outlets, the 'power system' consisted of 15 A round-pin plugs and socket-outlets, each wired from a separate circuit. A multi-way power fuseboard or splitter main switch and fuse unit containing 15 A fuses supplied these circuits. The system was open to abuse as it was usual to extend the circuits by adding 15 A socket-outlets resulting in two, three or more socket-outlets to a circuit.

Originally the plugs and sockets were all 2-pin and many of these still exist in some installations. This means that appliances connected to them are not earthed. Subsequently, the 3-pin plug and socket-outlet was introduced and these replaced existing 2-pin sockets but with no attempt to provide earthing. These also still exist in some installations and only when they are replaced by the modern 13 A socket-outlet is it noticed that they are not earthed.

The 5 A socket-outlet

The 5 A round pin plug and socket-outlet was also used extensively in dwellings, these too being in 2-pin and 3-pin versions. They were intended mainly for small appliances of up to 1000 W.

One 5 A socket-outlet was supplied from a 5 A circuit, two from a 10 A and three from a 15 A circuit but, in many instances, more than one 5 A socket-outlet was supplied from a 5 A circuit. The 2 A plug and socket-outlet was installed especially for table lamps, floor standards and other portable lighting and are still installed for this type of lighting.

As each socket has an assumed maximum load of ½ A (equivalent to 120 W on 240 V supplies) up to a maximum of ten 2 A socket-outlets may be connected to a 5 A circuit exclusively used for the socket-outlets. The 2 A socket-outlet is also supplied from a lighting circuit, but it must be assessed at 120 W when adding up the lighting load.

Round-pin plug adaptors

Because of the scarcity of 15 A sockets on the old radial wiring system, plug adaptors were used extensively on these circuits. Principally they were to enable 5 A and 2 A plugs to be used from the 15 A sockets but the adaptors also enabled two 15 A plugs to be used from one 15 A socket-outlet.

The use of multi-plug adaptors is bad practice as, apart from a risk of overloading a socket-outlet, long flexes have to be used which are themselves a hazard.

The radial system

The numerous 15 A circuits radiating from a central fuseboard are known collectively as the radial system. This system is now superceded by the ring circuit. It has no connection with the modern radial power circuit.

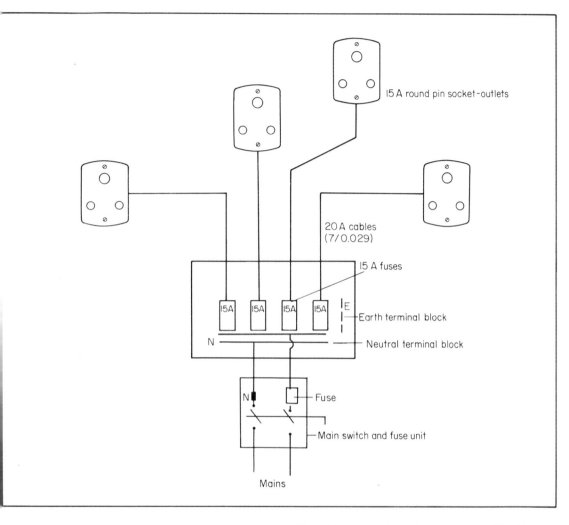

15 A round pin socket-outlets

20 A cables
(7/0.029)

15 A fuses

E
Earth terminal block

N — Neutral terminal block

N — Fuse

Main switch and fuse unit

Mains

Circuits for conversion

The old radial system of wiring power (15 A) socket outlets where a separate circuit from a fuse unit is required for each 15 A outlet

Where only one 15 A socket-outlet is on a circuit this may be replaced by a 13 A type. Two may be replaced provided the circuit cable is 7-strand and that the fuse can be uprated to 20 A.

If there are more than two 15 A socket-outlets on a circuit, conversion is not permitted and the circuit should be scrapped. Because of the old wiring, attempts to change the sockets will almost certainly result in the insulation breaking off the conductor. The only satisfactory solution is to rewire by installing a ring circuit.

Conversion to 13 A socket-outlets

Most 15 A socket-outlets can be replaced by the modern 13 A socket-outlet. When replacing a 15 A socket-outlet by a 13 A type, check that there is an earth wire at the outlet. If not, it is necessary to run an earth conductor from the socket-outlets to the consumer unit using 2.5 mm² green PVC insulated cable. The 15 A 2-pin and 3-pin socket-outlets often will not have an earth.

Chapter 39
Circuit for electric cookers

Small table cookers and other portable appliances having individual loadings not in excess of 3 kW are run off 13 A fused plugs and socket-outlets. They require no special wiring though extra socket-outlets may be needed in the kitchen when additional electrical cooking appliances are bought. These additional socket-outlets may be served from the ring circuit and spurs.

Family-size cookers, whether free-standing or built-in split-level, need an exclusive circuit from a fuseway of appropriate current rating.

A table cooker of up to 3000 W rating may be supplied from a 13 A socket outlet on the ring circuit or from a 15 A socket outlet of an old radial circuit

Current ratings of circuits

Most electric cookers have a total loading of about 12 kW or less and are supplied by a 30 A circuit, wired in 6 mm² cable (or, sometimes 4 mm² cable) from a 30 A fuseway. The cable terminates at a cooker control unit or switch of 50 A current rating.

Large-size family cookers, usually with loadings in excess of 12 kW are supplied from a 45 A circuit wired in 6 mm², or 10 mm² cable from a 45 A fuseway but terminated at the same 50 A cooker control unit or switch as the 30 A circuit cable. This is because the switchgear makers have designed the control units for the higher current demand.

Cooker control units

The conventional cooker control unit consists of a double-pole switch and a switched socket-outlet for an electric kettle. Some units have a neon indicator for the cooker switch and also for the kettle. The unit can be either flush- or surface-mounted.

An alternative to a combined unit is a

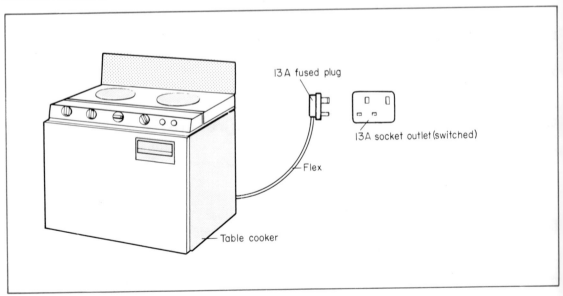

13 A fused plug

13 A socket outlet (switched)

Flex

Table cooker

cooker control double-pole switch (with or without neon indicator) but which does not incorporate a kettle socket-outlet.

Cooker current demand

If the total current of a 12 kW electrical appliance used on 240 V is calculated by dividing 12,000 by 240, then the result will be 50 A. If you add to this figure, 12 A for a 3 kW electric kettle plugged into the socket-outlet of a cooker control unit, you get a total of 62 A which is the total current rating of a 12 kW family size cooker and kettle.

A cooker of the above rating is, in fact, supplied from a 30 A circuit which at first sight does not make sense though complying with the regulations. The reason for the apparent discrepancy is that the regulations have assumed a current demand based on the known fact that not all boiling plates, grill and oven of a cooker, and also the kettle are in use at the same time.

Even on those rare occasions, such as cooking the Christmas dinner, when everything may be switched on for a time, the thermostat of the oven and the variable controls of boiling plates and the grill reduce the actual current demand. The regulations have therefore introduced a diversity factor for calculation assessed or assumed demand for domestic electric cookers.

Calculating cooker diversity

The assumed demand for an electric cooker is based on 100 % of the first 10 A, plus 30 % of the remaining current, plus 5 A for an electric kettle socket-outlet if incorporated in the control unit. For a 12 kW cooker plus kettle the assumed demand is as follows:

Total current of cooker: 50 A	
100 % of first 10 A	10
30 % of remaining 40 A	12
Kettle socket	5
Total assumed current	27

The current rating for the circuit supplying the cooker is therefore 30 A.

Circuit cable route

The cable running from the circuit fuse to the cooker control unit takes the shortest possible path. This is usually under the floorboards and up the wall to the control unit.

If the floor is solid, as in many kitchens, the cable is taken up the wall through the ceiling into the void beneath the boards (or roof space if a bungalow) and down the wall to the control unit. The cable may be run on the surface or be buried in the plaster. If run on the surface, cable with white sheathing is usually chosen.

The cooker control unit is normally situated at a height of about 1.5 m (5 ft) from the floor and preferably to one side of the cooker. It must be within 2 m (6 ft) of the cooker it controls.

Types of control unit

Of the two principal types of cooker control unit, the type incorporating a kettle socket-outlet is the more popular. Since, however, it is important that the kettle is not used on the cooker hob where its flex would trail over a switched-on boiling plate it is better to have the unit without a socket where it has to be fixed immediately above the cooker.

Cooker control units incorporating a kettle socket-outlet were introduced before the days of the ring circuit when one other 'power plug' was the 'Norm' in a kitchen.

354

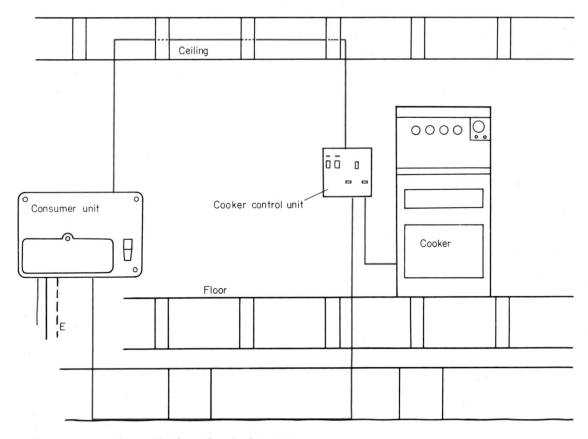

Ceiling

Consumer unit

Cooker control unit

Cooker

Floor

E

Alternative routes for a cable of a cooker circuit running
from the fuseway in the consumer unit to the control
switch adjacent to the cooker. If the kitchen floor is solid
the cable can usually be run in the void above the ceiling

New houses are usually wired to include a cooker circuit
and a 13 A socket outlet is fixed in place of the cooker
control unit. To convert this back to a cooker circuit the
socket outlet is replaced by a cooker control switch as
shown

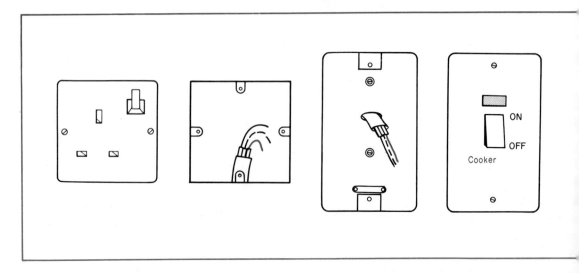

ON

OFF

Cooker

Replacing a socket-outlet with a control unit

Where a socket-outlet has been fixed at the end of a cooker circuit and a change to electric cooking is being made it is simply a question of replacing the socket-outlet by a cooker control switch. As mentioned above, if the socket-outlet is immediately above the cooker another socket-outlet above a working surface will be needed for the kettle.

Connecting a cooker to the control unit

The same type and size of cable is used both from the control unit to the cooker and for the circuit. For a free-standing cooker this cable drops down the wall to the cooker with a free droop at the end to allow the cooker to be pulled away from the wall for cleaning. The cable end in the control unit or switch is well anchored though the upper section of the cable drop can be fixed to the wall with cable clips.

There is now available a terminal box which is fixed to the wall behind a free-standing cooker and breaks the cable from the control unit to the cooker. The section from the control unit to the terminal box is fixed and can be buried in the plaster and the final cable connecting the cooker to the terminal box remains free.

If the cooker is removed for repairs, or changed for a new model, the cooker section of the cable is disconnected from the box and the moulded plastic cover replaced.

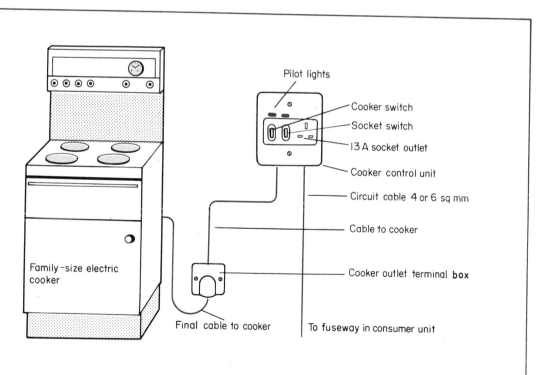

Pilot lights
Cooker switch
Socket switch
13 A socket outlet
Cooker control unit
Circuit cable 4 or 6 sq mm
Cable to cooker
Cooker outlet terminal box
Family-size electric cooker
Final cable to cooker
To fuseway in consumer unit

Instead of having a cable trailing down the wall loosely from cooker control unit to the cooker you can fit an outlet box which can be a terminal box as shown and bury the top section of cable in the wall

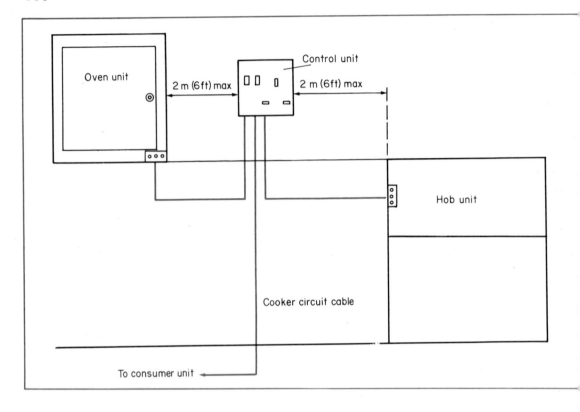

Reconnecting the cooker or connecting a new cooker takes only a few minutes.

An alternative is a cable outlet box which has no terminals. The cable is not cut but the section down the wall can be buried in the plaster.

Split-level cookers

A single circuit is used to supply the two sections of a split-level cooker and one cooker unit or control switch can be used for both provided neither is more than 2 m (6 ft) from the control. Usually both oven and hob sections are close together. If the sections are well apart and the control unit is situated midway, the sections can be up to 4 m (12 ft) apart and still be within the regulations. The control unit can be with or without a socket-outlet as desired.

The same type and size of cable is used between the control unit and the cooker sections as for the cooker circuit and the current demand is assessed as for a free standing cooker. Each section can be supplied by a separate cable which means two cables from the control unit, one to the oven section, the other to the hob. Alternatively, one cable can be run from the control unit to the nearest section and from the terminals of this section another cable of the same size and type is run to the second section.

It is important that the same size of cable is used throughout as this is governed by the circuit fuse as well as by the actual current a section will need to carry. In other words, splitting a cooker into two sections does not permit any reduction in cable size.

Chapter 40
Electric water heaters

Electric heating of water can be carried out in a variety of ways. These include small capacity heaters fitted above the sink, instantaneous sink heaters or immersion heaters in the hot water tank.

The selection and plumbing-in of electric water heaters is dealt with in Section 3 (Home Plumbing).

Small storage water heaters

Small storage water heaters fitted over the sink or washbasin having capacities of up to about 3 gallons and electrical loadings of 1 to 3 kW are usually supplied from the ring circuit by means of a spur. Except in a bathroom, the outlet can be a fused plug and switched socket-outlet, preferably with neon indicator.

The connection from plug to the water heater is heat-resisting 3-core flexible cord. In the bathroom, where no socket-outlets are permitted other than an approved shaver socket, a switched fused connection unit is used as the outlet. This should also have a neon indicator and be connected to the water heater by 3-core flexible cord.

The switch of the connection unit, as other wall switches, must be out of reach of a person using the bath or shower. Where this is impracticable a cord-operated ceiling switch is necessary and the outlet to the water heater should be a cord outlet unit. As there must be a fuse in the circuit, a non-switched fused connection unit can be fixed outside the bathroom at the point where the spur cable is connected to the ring circuit.

A small storage water heater having a loading not exceeding 3000 W may be supplied from a 13 A plug and socket outlet or fused connection unit connected to a spur from the ring circuit

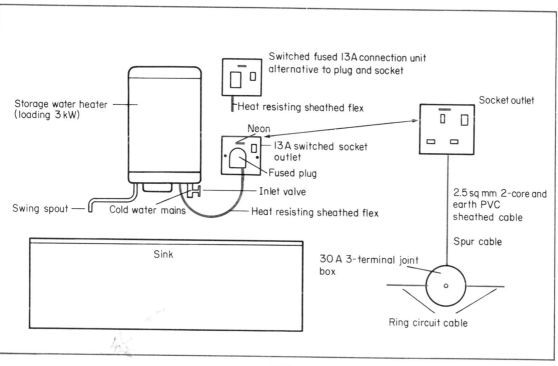

Switched fused 13A connection unit alternative to plug and socket

Storage water heater (loading 3 kW)

Heat resisting sheathed flex

Neon

13A switched socket outlet

Fused plug

Inlet valve

Swing spout

Cold water mains

Heat resisting sheathed flex

Sink

Socket outlet

2.5 sq mm 2-core and earth PVC sheathed cable

Spur cable

30 A 3-terminal joint box

Ring circuit cable

Immersion heaters

An immersion heater is classed as a continuous load and as such should not be supplied from a ring circuit since its 3 kW loading would deprive the ring circuit of nearly half of its 7.2 kW load capacity. Instead a separate circuit is used for the immersion heater which can be wired in 1.5 mm² PVC sheathed cable from a 15 A circuit fuse, or preferably in 2.5 mm² cable from a 20 A circuit fuse.

An essential requirement for an immersion heater circuit is a double-pole isolating switch which should be fixed within reach of the immersion heater so that anyone adjusting the thermostat with the terminal cover off has access to the isolator. For a single-element immersion heater this switch is a standard 20 A double-pole plate switch available with or without neon indicator and flex outlet facilities. Where required, the plate can be engraved **WATER HEATER**.

A 13 A fused plug and switched socket-outlet is sometimes used instead of a double-pole switch. Isolation is effected by pulling out the plug, but with a sustained 3 kW loading, a plug and socket tends to overheat especially in the vicinity of a hot water tank and even more so when enclosed in a tank cupboard. Where, as is often the case, a tank cupboard opens into the bathroom, a socket-outlet is prohibited as it could be misused by plugging in a portable appliance.

Although the water heater switch should be within reach of the immersion heater, it is essential that it cannot be reached by a person using the bath or shower. In these circumstances, either the switch must be fixed outside the bathroom or a cord operated ceiling switch is necessary.

A circuit feeding a single element immersion heater terminates at an on/off double pole 20 A switch and from this 3-core heat resisting flex runs to the immersion heater

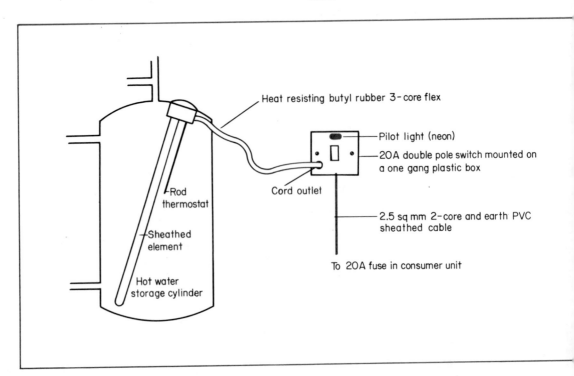

Heat resisting butyl rubber 3-core flex

Pilot light (neon)

20A double pole switch mounted on a one gang plastic box

Cord outlet

Rod thermostat

Sheathed element

Hot water storage cylinder

2.5 sq mm 2-core and earth PVC sheathed cable

To 20A fuse in consumer unit

Dual immersion heater

A dual immersion heater is designed for fitting into the top of a hot water storage cylinder and consists of two elements, one short and one long. The short element is for heating a small quantity of water for normal daily use, the long element is for heating the full contents of the tank when large amounts of hot water are required for a bath or other purposes.

Some models have an integral change-over switch mounted on the heater head to switch over from one element to the other. Immersion heaters without this integral switch require an external change-over switch wired into the circuit. The switch used for this is a combined 20 A double-pole switch and change-over switch fixed in the place of the ordinary isolating switch and connected to the immersion heater by heat-resisting flex. As an extra wire is required for the second element and 4-core flex is not generally available, it is usual to have two 3-core flexible cords as though for two separate elements but connected as shown in the diagram.

Remote control of immersion heater

When an immersion heater is switched on and off as hot water is needed and not in continuous operation, it is useful to have a remote control operated from the kitchen.

A special 2-point control is available for this arrangement, consisting of two double-pole switches, each with a neon indicator. One switch (the master switch) incorporates an isolator and is fitted at the immersion heater end; the other (auxiliary switch) is fitted in the kitchen. The immersion heater can be switched on and off by either

An immersion heater can be controlled from the kitchen as well as from the tank cupboard by installing a 2-point control system. The switch at the immersion heater end contains an isolator

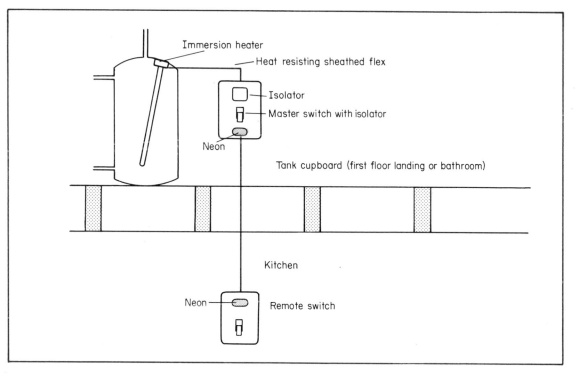

Immersion heater

Heat resisting sheathed flex

Isolator

Master switch with isolator

Neon

Tank cupboard (first floor landing or bathroom)

Kitchen

Neon

Remote switch

switch, both neon indicators going on and off when one switch is operated.

This arrangement is intended mainly for single-element immersion heater installations but can be used with dual immersion heaters with the changeover switch wired in between the master switch and the immersion heater. Another arrangement is to have a remote switch to control the long element only of a dual immersion heater so that, when extra hot water is needed, the long element can be switched into circuit from the kitchen.

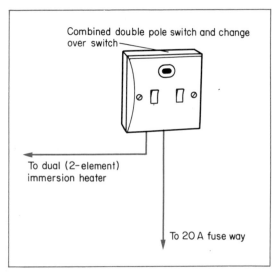

The two elements of a dual immersion heater are controlled by a change-over switch and double-pole isolating switch in a combined unit

Two-immersion heater installations

Where the hot water storage tank is rectangular or there is insufficient headroom to insert a top-entry immersion heater into a cylinder, side-entry immersion heaters are fitted.

An immersion heater fitted a few inches from the base heats the full contents of the tank but where only small quantities are normally run off during the day a second immersion heater is fitted. This is a few inches from the top of the tank, according

to the dimensions of the tank and the amount of water to be heated. The top immersion heater will be fitted lower down from the top of a small-diameter cylinder than for a large rectangular tank.

Two immersion heaters operate similarly to one dual immersion heater and, if both have 3 kW loading, a change-over switch is used to change over from one to the other.

Off-peak operation

Where the white meter tariff is in operation it can be an advantage to heat the full contents of a tank overnight when the cheaper rate for electricity is in force and switch on the short element when additional hot water is needed.

This normally requires two circuits for the immersion heater installation. One circuit is used for the night rate supply, when time controlled in conjunction with night storage heaters, this supplying the long element of a dual immersion heater or the lower immersion heater of a two-immersion heater arrangement. The other circuit is from the unrestricted supply and, as it will be only for intermittent use, the circuit can be a spur of a ring circuit. For two immersion heaters, each is controlled separately but for a dual immersion heater a twin double-pole isolating switch is needed.

Automatic control

An immersion heater can be switched on and off automatically by means of a timeswitch. A timeswitch (e.g. the 'Imerset') has been designed especially for this purpose and gives a choice of two switch-on and switch-off periods each 24 hours. These can be programmed to suit the family's requirements but a common arrangement is to switch off the heater late at night, on early in the morning, off after breakfast as the

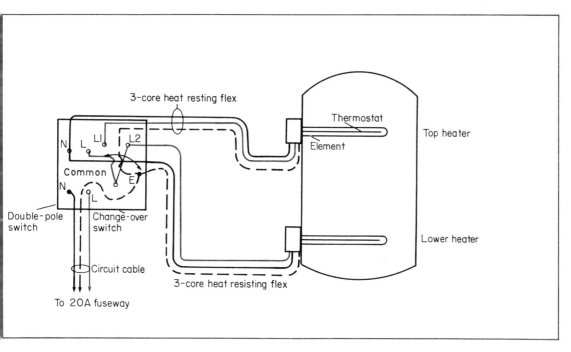

3-core heat resting flex

Thermostat

Top heater

Element

N L L1 L2

Common

N L

E

Double-pole switch

Change-over switch

Circuit cable

3-core heat resisting flex

Lower heater

To 20A fuseway

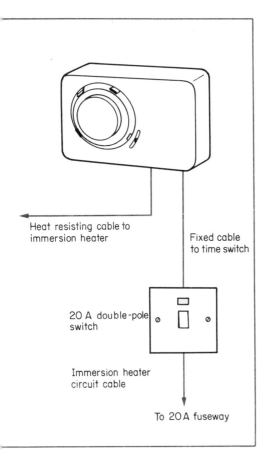

Heat resisting cable to immersion heater

Fixed cable to time switch

20 A double-pole switch

Immersion heater circuit cable

To 20A fuseway

(Above) Two immersion heaters fitted into the one tank are controlled by a combined on/off double pole switch and a change over switch. A separate 3-core heat resisting flexible cord goes to each heater

The illustration on the left shows a special time switch inserted between the double pole switch and the immersion heater to provide switch-on periods to suit the family

family leaves for work, and on again just before the first member of the family returns home. Other manufacturers also have available similar timeswitches which are equally suitable. The purpose of the timeswitch is to save electricity by not keeping a tank of water hot when none is being drawn off.

Some timeswitches have an over-ride switch to enable current to be provided to the immersion heater out of programmed hours, such as over weekends. If the time-switch has no over-ride switch a 20 A double-pole switch can be fitted and connected to the timeswitch to bridge the open switch contacts of the timeswitch to obtain hot water out of hours.

The live pole of the double-pole switch bridges the single-pole contacts of the timeswitch and also supplies current to the neon indicator. The neutral pole merely supplies the neon indicator which needs both live and neutral poles to energise the neon.

The use of a timeswitch to cut off the current to an immersion heater overnight, and at other times, does not eliminate the need for lagging the tank. The lagging, which should be at least 100 mm (4 in) thick, reduces heat losses and conserves the hot water whether the heater is 'On' or 'Off'.

Instantaneous water heaters

Washbasins

Instantaneous water heaters having loadings of 3 kW fitted over the washbasin for hand washing can be supplied from a ring circuit spur. The connection at the water heater should be either a 13 A fused plug and socket-outlet or, as in a bathroom, a switched fused connection unit with the switch out of reach of a person using the bath.

Shower units

Instantaneous water heaters used as shower units have electrical loadings of 5 kW and 6 kW. These need separate 30 A circuits from 30 A fuseways in consumer units, the circuits being wired in 4 mm² 2-core and earth PVC sheathed cable. An isolating switch is needed with these water heater units and should be fixed within reach of the heater unit.

Where the shower unit is installed in the bathroom, there is usually difficulty in siting the switch out of reach of the fixed bath and out of reach of the person using the shower. To meet this situation a 30 A

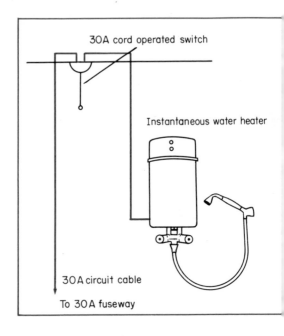

An instantaneous water heater of a shower unit is fed from a 30 A circuit and needs an isolating switch within reach, if possible, of the heater unit. To meet regulations this should be a 30 A cord operated ceiling switch as shown

double-pole cord-operated switch has been introduced. The circuit cable, therefore, runs from the fuseway in the consumer unit to the ceiling switch and from this to the water heater unit.

Sink water heaters

For the sink, a 5 kW version of the shower instantaneous water heater is available. The circuit is the same as for a shower unit but need be only of 20 A current rating using 2.5 mm² cable and a 20 A double-pole switch fitted near the water heater.

One version of this heater, having a loading of 7 kW can be used to supply two outlets — the shower and the sink or the shower and a washbasin — a special 2-way faucet tap being fitted for the purpose, since each outlet must be of the open type.

Chapter 41
Night storage heaters

Night storage heaters operate on the principle of thermal storage blocks being charged with heat during an overnight period when electricity is supplied at a lower price and releases the heat during the day when electricity is more expensive. Heat is stored during an 8-hour period starting at about 11 p.m. and ending at 7 a.m. the following morning. The times vary slightly between areas and some electricity boards have a 10-hour period starting at 9 p.m. An 8-hour period is sufficient to fully charge a heater.

Types of storage heating

The greatest proportion of night storage heating consists of individual storage heaters installed in the various rooms, though usually limited to the ground floor of a 2-storey dwelling.

Other forms of storage heating are:

(i)   Floor warming where warming wires are embedded into the concrete of the floor, the concrete acting as the storage medium; and

(ii)   A central heating system consisting of a large size storage heater situated in a central position and supplying the various rooms by warm air flowing through a duct system, or by a central boiler supplying hot water to a conventional radiator system. The warm air system is termed Electricaire; the hot water method is called Centrelec.

The individual night storage electric heaters are made in two principal types: storage radiators and storage fan heaters.

The electric storage radiator consists of a thermal storage block enclosed in a metal casing but separated from it by thermal insulation. Heat is emitted from the casing into the room by radiation, the rate of heat output being controlled by the thickness and quality of the thermal insulation determined at the design stage of the heater. An internal thermostat prevents excessive heat being stored and therefore determines the amount of heat stored during an overnight charge period. An input controller operated by the householder can reduce the amount charged.

Rate of heat output

The rate of heat output in kilowatts depends on the size of the heater. The larger the storage block, the more heat stored and therefore the greater the heat output the next day. Apart from varying the input of heat, the user has no control over the rate of heat output.

Makers of storage radiators reckon that a constant heat output is maintained for the first 10 hours after which the heat output tapers off. To counteract this tapering off some storage radiators incorporate booster devices which push out the remainder of the heat stored.

Sizes of storage radiator

Storage radiators have kilowatt loadings ranging from about 1¼ kW to about 3¼ kW, but these loadings do not represent the rate of heat output as do the loadings of direct acting heaters. The higher the loading the greater the storage capacity and the greater the amount of heat stored which in turn increases the rate of heat output.

This means that the kW loading serves as

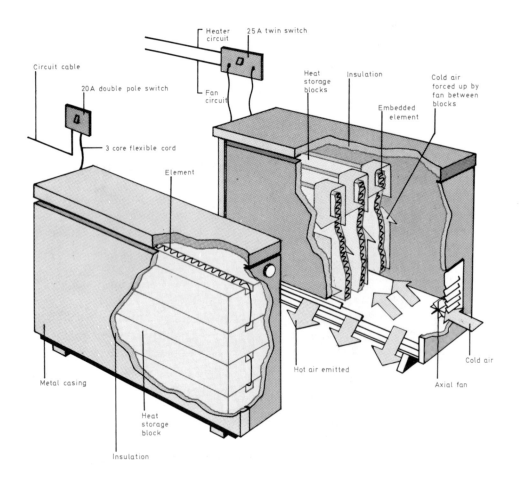

Circuit cable

20 A double pole switch

Heater circuit

25 A twin switch

Fan circuit

3 core flexible cord

Element

Metal casing

Heat storage block

Insulation

Heat storage blocks

Insulation

Cold air forced up by fan between blocks

Embedded element

Hot air emitted

Cold air

Axial fan

The picture on the left shows an interior view of an electric storage radiator. Storage radiators are usually supplied by separate 20 A circuits each of which terminates at a 20 A double-pole switch having a cord outlet for the 3-core flex to the heater

An interior view of a storage fan heater is shown in the illustration on the right. These are supplied from two circuits, one on the cheap night rate under time switch control for the heater, the other from the unrestricted supply for the fan

a guide which, together with the makers' data, enables you to choose the sizes best suited to your individual requirements.

Storage fan heaters

The storage fan heater is similar to the storage radiator, but incorporates a fan system which blows cold air over the heated storage block and expels the heated air through a grille into the room.

To reduce the radiated heat to almost nothing, the fan storage heater has much more thermal insulation. In effect, therefore, heat is emitted only when the fan is switched on, thus giving the user control of the output of the heat. Although the elements are switched on for the 8-hour overnight period only, the fan can be switched on at any time during the 24 hours because it is supplied from an ordinary unrestricted circuit.

By an arrangement of stub ducts and grilles, one storage fan heater can be sited to supply two or more adjoining rooms.

Circuit wiring for four storage radiators. Each circuit originates at a 20 A fuseway in the 4-way consumer unit under the control of the night-rate time switch

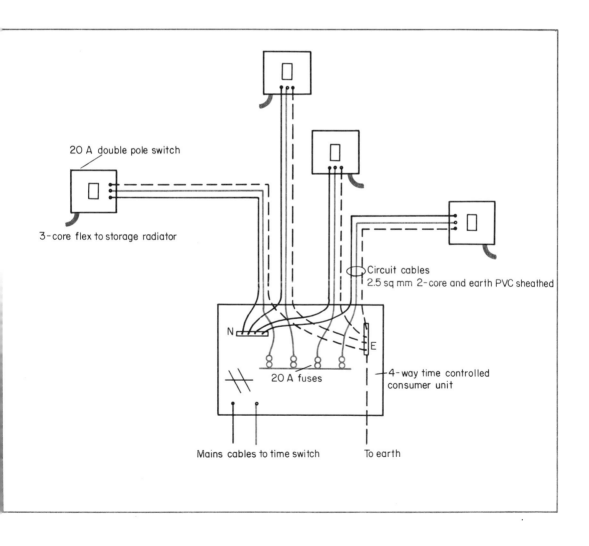

Storage heater circuits

Storage heaters require a separate circuit for each heater. This is because, unlike direct acting heaters which are switched on and off as required, storage heaters are all switched on together during the 8-hour period. They cannot therefore be supplied from a ring circuit which is based on diversity of use of various appliances; each heater must have its own circuit.

The circuit for a storage radiator consists of 2.5 mm² 2-core and earth PVC sheathed cable. The cable starts at a 20 A fuseway in the time-controlled consumer unit and terminates at a 20 A double-pole switch fixed next to the storage radiator and connected to it with 3-core flexible cord via the cord outlet of the 20 A switch.

There are circumstances where two storage heaters are supplied from a single 30 A circuit. Each heater must then be supplied through a fused outlet which is a switched 13 A fused connection unit. Such an arrangement would be limited to two heaters

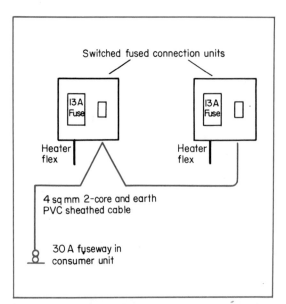

Two electric storage radiators, each having a loading not in excess of 3000 W may be supplied from one 30 A circuit each heater being supplied via a fused connection unit

having loadings of not more than 3 kW to prevent possible overheating of the fused connection unit.

Storage fan heater circuits

The circuits supplying the heater will be the same as those supplying storage radiators, but it is also necessary to provide a circuit for the fan.

As a fan takes very little current, small size cable as used for lighting circuits is suitable. The fan can, in fact, be supplied from a lighting circuit but rather than introduce a lighting circuit into a heating circuit it is better to feed the fan from a fused spur cable off the ring circuit (see Chapter 38). Where there is more than one storage fan heater all fans can be served by the one fused spur.

Switched outlet at heater

Both the heater and the fan require an isolating switch fixed near the heater to terminate the circuit cables and as a flex connection for the heater unit. As this heater will be supplied by two circuits, regulations require that the two switches are mechanically linked so that one cannot be switched off without the other.

To meet these requirements there is available a 25 A twin switch with or without pilot lights and with two cord outlets; one marked 'Fan' the other marked 'Heater'.

Automatic control

Heat output of a fan heater can be automatically controlled by introducing a room thermostat and/or timeswitch into the fan circuit, but generally it is sufficient to control the fan manually.

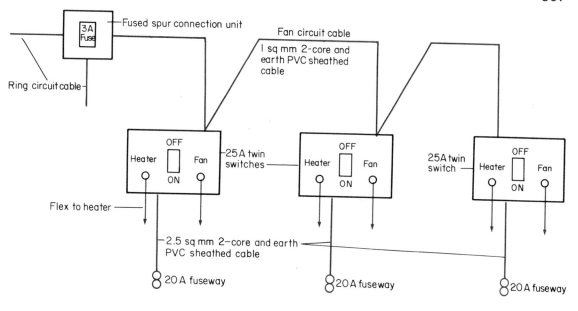

The two circuits (heater and fan) needed for storage fan heaters. A separate circuit is supplying each heater but one circuit supplies all the fans

The two circuits of a storage fan heater terminate at a 25 A twin switch so that the supply to both is cut off simultaneously. Each has a separate 3-core flexible cord

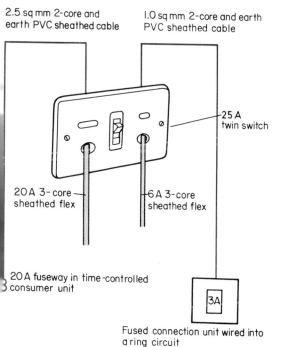

Fused connection unit wired into a ring circuit

Floor warming

Electrically warmed floors are applicable only to new houses, bungalows and flats during construction. If you move into a dwelling where this type of heating is installed, seek advice from the electricity board particularly regarding off-peak tariffs and running costs.

Electricaire heating

This is a system which directs warm air through a ducts system. It must be installed as a house is being built or being reconstructed under a home improvement scheme. The system needs a 45 A circuit from a 45 A fuseway to a control unit fixed near the unit.

Centrelec

This system is comparatively new. Before embarking on an installation it is advisable to discuss the project with the electricity board.

Chapter 42 Outdoor electrical extensions

Lighting and power to a detached garage, greenhouse or shed has to be a separate circuit running from the mains switchgear and not as an extension from one of the circuits in the house. Preferably, it is controlled by a separate main switch in the house which can be fed from the main consumer unit via an appropriate fuseway.

Flexible cord extensions

All too often a light in the shed or other outhouse is supplied from a flexible cord plugged into a socket-outlet in the kitchen and left as a 'permanent' extension, where it is likely to become damaged and be a shock hazard.

There are strict regulations concerning outdoor cables and wiring and the only recognised temporary supply is an extension lead. This may be with or without a reel and supplying a portable power tool, a portable light or a gardening tool, such as mower or hedgetrimmer, *only* during the time the appliance is actually being used.

The outdoor cable

The cable running from the house to the detached building, whether a mere shed or a fully-automatic greenhouse, can either be run overhead, buried in the ground, or run along a wall. Under no circumstances may it be fixed to a garden fence — for obvious reasons.

Overhead method

Ordinary PVC sheathed house wiring cable can be used as an outdoor overhead cable but it must be fixed at a height of at least 3.5 m (12 ft) above ground level. If the span between the house and outbuilding exceeds 3.5 m the cable must be supported by a catenary wire. This is a galvanised steel wire or cable secured by eyehooks to take the weight of a cable attached to it by clips or slings.

Provided you can get the height at the shed or garage, overhead wiring is satisfactory for short spans where, for instance, the shed (or garage) is at the side or back of the house within a few feet of the house. An alternative is an unjointed length of heavy gauge galvanised steel conduit or rigid conduit which will not fracture at low temperatures (below −5°C) this having the advantage that it may be at a height of 3 m (10 ft).

For long spans, which may require intermediate supporting poles an overhead cable is not an attractive proposition. It is often unsightly and is exposed to strong winds and other hazards.

Burying the cable underground

The underground method has the advantage that once installed it is permanent, out of sight and protected from the weather. To instal the cable, means digging a trench from the point where the cable enters the house to a corresponding point at the outbuilding. The trench has to be at least 500 mm (18 in) deep and if it is to go through a vegetable plot where deep digging is likely, the depth should be increased in this section.

The route for the cable must be carefully selected. Concrete paths and terraces should be avoided and diversions made around obstacles. A good route for the cable is at

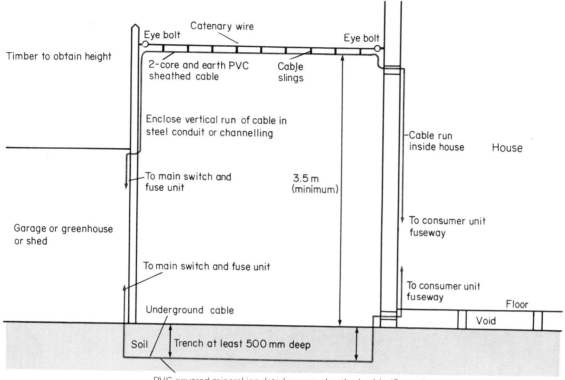

Timber to obtain height

Eye bolt

Catenary wire

Eye bolt

2-core and earth PVC sheathed cable

Cable slings

Enclose vertical run of cable in steel conduit or channelling

Cable run inside house   House

To main switch and fuse unit

3.5 m (minimum)

To consumer unit fuseway

Garage or greenhouse or shed

To main switch and fuse unit

To consumer unit fuseway

Floor

Underground cable

Void

Soil   Trench at least 500 mm deep

PVC covered mineral insulated copper sheathed cable (2-core)
armoured PVC insulated and sheathed cable (2–core)
The outdoor cable supplying an outbuilding may be run overhead or underground. Both methods are shown here together with the cable routes

the edge of a border or lawn where the ground is least likely to be disturbed and digging the trench is usually easier. It is best to avoid taking the trench across a lawn for, unless the lawn is being renovated, the trench scar will remain.

Cables for outdoor use

Two types of cable are especially suited to running underground. One is PVC covered 2-core mineral-insulated copper-sheathed which is often referred to as MICC. The second type is PVC-covered armoured PVC-insulated and sheathed 2-core cable.

Ordinary PVC sheathed house wiring 2-core and earth cable can be run underground provided it is enclosed in heavy gauge galvanised steel conduit or rigid plastic conduit.

Fixing MICC cables

This cable with its distinctive orange PVC covering (also available in white PVC for indoor situations) is of small cross-sectional area — about that of a pencil — and can readily be continued in the section above ground. This type of cable can even be passed through an air vent into the void below the suspended floor of a dwelling or through a hole drilled in the wall above skirting level where the floor is solid or there is no access under the floor. Being very robust, the cable can be passed through a hole drilled in the door frame or sill, if it is not possible to drill a hole through the outside wall.

One possible snag with MICC cable is that the mineral insulation is hygroscopic and the prepared ends, as the sheath is stripped off, must be immediately fitted with seals to exclude moisture. The seals are fairly easy to fit, but instead of buying the special tools and materials needed for sealing, it is better to buy the cable with the seals fitted. In this case it is important that the required length has been accurately measured as a joint cannot be made in the buried section.

For some switchgear with screwed conduit entry holes, it is also necessary to have screwed glands on the ends of the MICC cable. These glands are fitted at the same time as the seals and are specified when buying the cable.

Earthing with MICC cable

The copper sheath of MICC cable is used as the earth-continuity conductor and because of this the junctions at the ends of the cable must be electrically sound so that continuity is maintained.

This continuity is provided by the screwed gland, or if there is no gland, by the seal which must be secured in the junction box fitted with MICC outlets. Seals are also available fitted with an earth screw for an earth conductor.

Fixing armoured PVC cable

This cable has much larger cross-sectional area than the MICC type, and as PVC insulation is not moisture absorbing the ends do not require seals. However, a gland is fitted to each end of this type of cable for screwing into a box or switchgear and to provide earth continuity; the wire armour being the earth conductor.

Glands are of the compression type and are similar to those of tees and elbows fitted to copper water pipes. They are easy to fit and need only a wrench and pliers.

Fixing the house section of cable

The outdoor cable whether MICC or armoured PVC can be run through the house in the conventional manner to the main switch position near the meter. Alternatively the outdoor cable can be terminated at a junction box fixed to timber under the floor in close proximity to the point where the cable enters the house. From this box ordinary PVC sheathed cable runs to the main switch.

When PVC sheathed cable is used in the outdoor section, either overhead or underground in conduit, it is continued (without conduit) to the mains without the necessity of a junction box.

Outbuildings

The whole of an installation in an outbuilding has to be under the control of an isolating double-pole switch so that the installation can be isolated from the mains at the turn of a switch when necessary. This switch is usually part of a switch fuse unit or the main switch of a consumer unit where there is more than one circuit.

In the outbuilding, the main switch whether a switch fuse unit or a consumer unit, is usually fixed in close proximity to the point where the incoming cable enters. This will reduce the length of run of the special cable.

The cable trench

Digging a trench for the cable is about the hardest part of the project. Before laying the cable, remove sharp stones and flints from the bottom of the trench and from the soil as it is replaced. If this is not done the PVC covering of the cable will be damaged and the copper sheath or wire armour become corroded.

Intermediate junction box

When fitting a junction box inside the house to join the MICC (or armoured) cable to the PVC sheathed cable running to the main switchgear this can be fixed to or between joists under the floorboards.

Where the floor is solid and the outside cable passes into the house above skirting level, fit the junction box to the inside wall. If preferred, the box can be sunk into the wall and have a moulded plastic cover to match the plate switches and socket-outlets in the room.

Connections to the switchfuse

Fix the switchfuse unit next to the main consumer unit and connect the incoming cable to the load terminals of the unit. If there is a spare fuseway connect a cable (of the same size as the outdoor circuit cable)

The outdoor special cable may be terminated in the house at a junction box and from this box ordinary PVC sheathed cable is run to the main switch and fuse unit

to the mains terminals of the switchfuse unit, and the other end to the fuseway of the consumer unit.

The fuse unit for the spare fuseway will be of the same rating as the circuit which is either 20 A or 30 A.

If there is no spare fuseway, the switchfuse unit is connected to the mains by the electricity board. A pair of sheathed cables must be connected to the main terminals of the unit for the Board to connect to the meter.

Wiring in outbuildings or greenhouses

First connect the incoming cable to the switchfuse unit mounted on the wall at the appropriate height — 600 mm (2 ft) or more above the floor. This cable is connected to the mains terminals of the switchfuse unit.

The circuit wiring is connected to the 'Load' terminals of this unit.

The wiring and the number of lights and socket-outlets in the outbuilding will depend

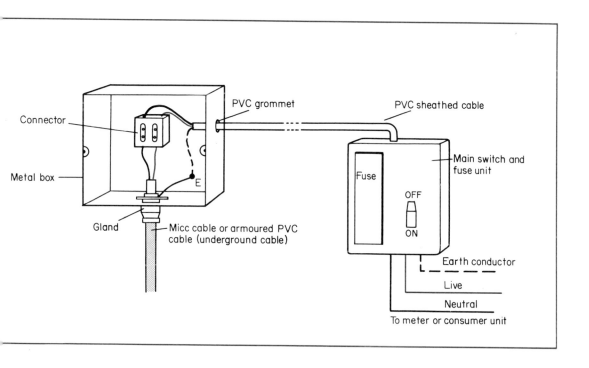

Connector — Metal box — Gland — PVC grommet — Micc cable or armoured PVC cable (underground cable) — PVC sheathed cable — Main switch and fuse unit — Fuse — OFF — ON — Earth conductor — Live — Neutral — To meter or consumer unit

372

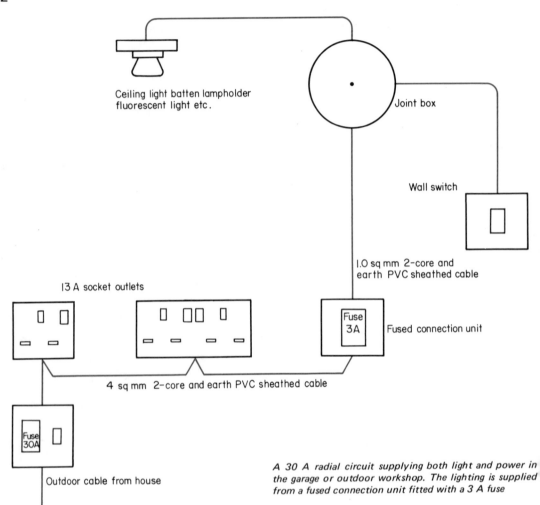

Ceiling light batten lampholder
fluorescent light etc.

Joint box

Wall switch

1.0 sq mm 2-core and
earth PVC sheathed cable

13 A socket outlets

Fuse
3A   Fused connection unit

4 sq mm 2-core and earth PVC sheathed cable

Fuse
30A

Outdoor cable from house

A 30 A radial circuit supplying both light and power in the garage or outdoor workshop. The lighting is supplied from a fused connection unit fitted with a 3 A fuse

on individual requirements, these depending on the function of the building. A shed may need only one light, but if used as a workshop it will need socket-outlets as well. A garage or greenhouse will need more socket-outlets which again will depend on the equipment used or installed.

For a greenhouse a number of socket-outlets, in addition to lighting, will be needed. These socket-outlets are usually mounted on a special distribution panel along with fused connection units and a main switch or a circuit breaker. As it is essential that heating is not switched off inadvertently, the socket-outlets and fused connection units should have neon indica-

tors. The fused connection units supply fixed heating, soil warming and can also supply the fixed lighting.

Wiring accessories and lighting fittings

Switches, socket-outlets and other accessories in the shed, garage or greenhouse can be of moulded plastic which is the same type as installed in the home. Where there is any risk of damaging them, metalclad switches and socket-outlets are installed. In the greenhouse, protection from water spray is desirable.

Batten lampholders, close ceiling fittings

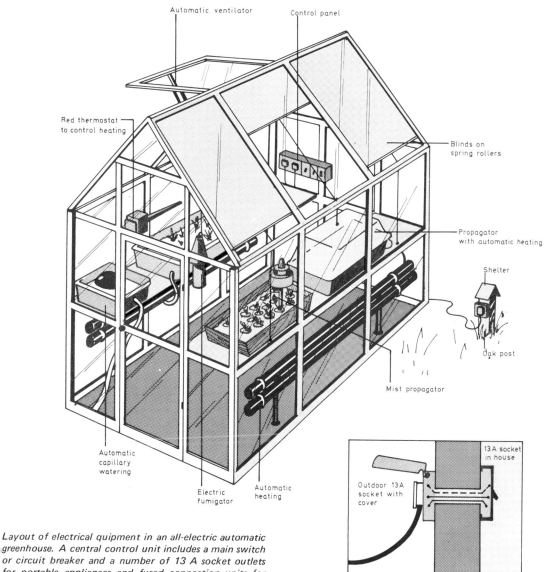

Automatic ventilator

Control panel

Red thermostat
to control heating

Blinds on
spring rollers

Propagator
with automatic heating

Shelter

Oak post

Mist propagator

Automatic
capillary
watering

Electric
fumigator

Automatic
heating

13A socket
in house

Outdoor 13A
socket with
cover

Layout of electrical quipment in an all-electric automatic greenhouse. A central control unit includes a main switch or circuit breaker and a number of 13 A socket outlets for portable appliances and fused connection units for fixed wiring
Socket outlets installed outdoors can either be fixed to the house wall or to posts protected by weatherproof covers. Ordinary socket outlets can be fitted with weatherproof covers as shown

and other non-pendant lighting fittings, including fluorescent, are used in these situations. If a fitting is to be installed out of doors it must be of the weatherproof type.

Weatherproof lighting fittings are available in an extensive range of attractive designs giving a wide choice to the householder. These include bulkhead totally-enclosed all-insulated fittings for fluorescent or tungsten lamps.

Number of circuits

Only rarely will more than one circuit be needed in an outbuilding. For most outbuildings, this can be a 30 A radial circuit which may serve up to a total of five 13 A socket-outlets plus a fused connection unit for the fixed lighting. Portable lights can be run off a plug and socket.

The fused connection unit is fitted with a 3 A fuse and the lighting section of the circuit can then be wired in the small-size cable used for lighting circuits. This is 1.0 mm² 2-core and earth PVC sheathed. Where only one 13 A socket and lighting is required, such as in the small workshop, the circuit can be 20 A wired in 2.5 mm² cable instead of 4 mm² cable used in a 30 A circuit.

Mains cable rating

The cable from the house must be of 30 A rating (4 mm²) where the internal circuit is 30 A. Where the circuit in the outbuilding is only 20 A, the cable from the house need be only of 20 A rating (2.5 mm²).

Running a cable underground out-of-doors is a difficult job and it is always as well to use the 4 mm² cable to allow for future extensions. The larger size costs very little more than 2.5 mm².

Outdoor socket-outlets

There are many occasions when outdoor socket-outlets come in useful, for example, for supplying an electric mower, a hedge-cutter, a power tool and other electric tools. Socket-outlets are also necessary for pool lighting, a garden fountain operated by an electric pump and garden lighting. These latter can be from either mains voltage or low voltage via a transformer.

Outdoor socket-outlets are of the weatherproof type or are fitted with weatherproof covers. They are best supplied by MICC cable buried in the ground in the same way as a cable feeding an outbuilding. Socket-outlets can be fixed to posts in the garden or to a garden wall. They should be served by a separate circuit from the house consumer unit with a switch installed in a convenient position for switching off from the house. This switch can be a high sensitivity earth-leakage circuit-breaker to give a person using the garden tools and equipment additional protection from electric shock. (See Chapter 34 for information on earth-leakage circuit-breakers).

In wet weather it is possible that the earth-leakage circuit-breaker will trip. This will happen if a hedgecutter is used when the hedge is wet and for this reason, it is a good protection. A high-sensitivity earth-leakage circuit-breaker should not be installed in a greenhouse, where there is a risk of it tripping. This may ruin the growing crops in soil warming beds and propagators.

Chapter 43
Electrical hardware

The 'hardware' of home wiring includes switches, ceiling roses, lampholders, socket-outlets, fused connection units (fused spur units); joint boxes; consumer units, fuse-boards and main switch and fuse units or switchfuse units.

These are mainly of moulded plastic in white (of various tones), brown, or in various colours. Some accessories may be made of metal instead of moulded plastic.

Styling and quality

With the possible exception of joint boxes, all this hardware is exposed to view and, because of this, styling has been an important factor in the design. An important factor of home decor is the question of matching accessories. Switches, socket-outlets and fused connection units are available in patterns to match as well as in colour tone. The colour may also extend to ceiling roses, lampholders, batten lampholders and ceiling switches which also have the overall matching appearance. Joint boxes are often under the floorboards or in the roof space but these have good styling which can be an asset where surface-mounted and exposed to view.

Quality of hardware is generally high, but low quality accessories are also available — not necessarily at low prices.

The various accessories are dealt with in the respective sections of this book. In this section they are covered in more detail so that the reader may have some guidance as to the correct type to select for a specific purpose.

Current rating of switches

Switches used in the home are: 5 A lighting switches, 20 A switches for controlling storage heaters, water heaters and other appliances; and 30-60 A switches for controlling cookers and other heavy current consuming appliances.

A selection of switches for lighting and power are shown below and on the following page. These are all double pole switches of 20 A and above

20 A double-pole switch with neon indicator

20 A double-pole switch with flex outlet

30-50 A double-pole switch

Metal clad 20 A double-pole switch with neon indicator

Lighting switches

The one-way switch

The conventional modern lighting switch is the single-pole one-way on/off plate switch. This is a small-gap (not quite micro-gap though often referred to as such) switch mounted behind a moulded plastic 'square' faceplate. The switch has a rocker or a dolly to operate it; the dolly now largely superseded by the rocker switch. The switch can be mounted on either a surface plastic box, or on a flush metal box as desired.

The 2-way switch

The 2-way plateswitch is identical in size and appearance to the one-way switch but has a 2-way action and has three terminals instead of two, which are necessary for the circuit wiring. Its function is to enable a light to be switched on and off from two positions.

The intermediate switch

The intermediate plateswitch is also of identical size and appearance to the one-way switch. It has double action like the 2-way switch and has four terminals. Its function is to enable a light to be switched on or off from three (or more according to the number of intermediate switches in the circuit) positions in conjunction with two 2-way switches.

Multi-gang switches

A multi-gang switch consists of two or more switches on the one switchplate. A square faceplate similar to a one-way switch is made in 2- and 3-gang versions. Where 4- to 6-gang switch units are needed; these are incorporated on a rectangular (double) switchplate.

The two (or three) switches of a multi-gang square plate assembly, and often installed in the home, are all 2-way switches; though, in fact, one or more are used for the one-way control of the lights. The reason for this is a production one. When used as a one-way switch, only two of the terminals of each switch are used, the third remaining blank. In fact, any 2-way switch can be used either as a 1-way or a 2-way switch.

Intermediate switches are made only in single/switch assemblies.

Round switches

Until the introduction of the plateswitch, the lighting switch was a circular switch and had a tumbler action instead of the small gap contact action. These switches are still in service in very many houses. They are mainly surface mounted, either on hardwood blocks or more latterly on plastic pattresses.

Tumbler switches are also made in a flush mounting version. This is a coverless switch fixed inside a hardwood box and covered by a metal plate, secured to the switch by a centrally positioned screwed ring. Plastic plate versions are also available.

The 20 A switch

The 20 A switch is a double-pole unit for the remote switching or isolating of fixed electrical appliances. It should be situated near the appliance and connected to it with either flexible cord or fixed cable.

The switch is made in switchplate form having the same size square plate as the lighting switch. As the switch unit is larger, it requires a deeper box than the plaster depth or shallow box used for a lighting plateswitch. It is available with or without neon indicator, and with or without cord outlet. For immersion heaters and water heaters switches are available with the plate engraved in red — WATER HEATER.

As a plateswitch it can be mounted on a surface plastic box or a metal flush box. Alternative versions are designed as surface-mounted units, either with a composite box or for mounting on a pattress.

The 30-60 A switch

This switch is a plateswitch for either surface or flush mounting. It is available with or without a neon indicator and is made in a number of current ratings: 30 A; 45-50 A and 60 A.

The 30 A size is used largely as an isolation switch for instantaneous water heaters, and the two larger sizes are used as cooker control switches in place of the conventional cooker control unit incorporating a socket-outlet for an electric kettle (see Chapter 39).

The cooker control versions are available with the word COOKER engraved in red letters.

A cord operated ceiling switch. These are used mainly in bathrooms and as an extra switch in the bedroom above the bedhead. The ceiling switch illustrated has an integral backplate and matches the modern loop in ceiling rose of the same make.

Cord-operated switches

The cord-operated switch is used principally as a ceiling-mounted switch for installation in bathrooms in place of the conventional wall switch, where the wall switch would be within reach of a person using the bath or shower. As a lighting switch it is also used as a bedhead switch either in conjunction with the wall switch on a 2-way circuit, or to switch the bedhead light on and off. One version of the switch is suitable for wall as well as for ceiling mounting.

Cord-operated ceiling switches for controlling heaters and other appliances are available in 15 A current rating, in a number of versions: single-pole, double-pole, and double-pole with pilot light.

The 30 A ceiling switch

The 30 A double-pole cord-operated ceiling switch is of recent introduction. It has been designed for controlling a 5-7 kW instantaneous water heater supplying shower units installed in bathrooms or in other positions where a wall switch would be within reach of a person using the shower (or bath).

Ceiling roses

The modern ceiling rose is a plastic backplate containing three terminal blocks situated in-line, an earthing terminal and an optional strain terminal for the connection of a strain cable in the flex which supports a heavy shade. The backplate has 'knockout' facilities for sheathed cables and a screw-on cover with an outlet for the pendant flexible cord.

A built-in safety feature of this ceiling rose is the shielding of the live conductor terminal block. This is now a regulation requirement designed to prevent a person, when re-flexing a pendant fitting and not

Ceiling roses. The top photograph shows the cover removed and the lower picture shows a plug-in ceiling rose which makes connecting the cord simple

having taken the elementary precaution of switching off at the mains, accidentally touching the live terminal and receiving a fatal shock. In the latest designs the other two terminal blocks (the neutral and switch return wire terminal block) are also shielded, although this is not a regulation requirement.

Loop-in facilities

The central live terminal block and one end terminal block are the live and neutral terminal blocks for the looping in terminal connections of the mains cable. Because of this the ceiling rose is called a loop-in ceiling rose.

As shown in the illustration, the loop-in ceiling rose also functions as a joint box so obviating the need for joint boxes in the circuit. With its integral backplate the ceiling rose is fixed direct to the ceiling; no intervening pattress or block being required.

Old type ceiling roses

The old type ceiling rose, either of porcelain or plastic, is still in service in many homes. It is usually mounted on either a hardwood block or a plastic pattress. There are two principal versions: the 2-plate type, which is a ceiling rose having two terminals; and the 3-plate type which has three terminals, the third being for looping in the live feed of the circuits. This latter terminal has the same purpose as the live terminal of the modern loop-in ceiling rose but, in this case, the terminal is unshielded and not marked as 'live'.

Pattresses on which ceiling roses are mounted, sometimes include a terminal where the earth conductor can be connected. Another pattern has two terminals, one of which can be for the live loop-in with a 2-plate ceiling rose.

When re-flexing these old ceiling roses or, when intending to replace them with up-to-date patterns, a careful examination of the connections is advised.

Plug-in ceiling roses

These are special ceiling roses having socket connections for the circuit wires and a small plug to which the pendant flex is attached and plugged into the socket section. A screw cover encloses the socket and plug and the unit resembles a conventional ceiling rose.

It has the advantage that it can be detached for cleaning or interchanged with other plain pendants without disturbing the fixed wiring.

Detachable ceiling plate

This unit is of metal in two sections, one fixed and containing the circuit wire terminals, the other attached to the pendant is detachable from the fixed base by a sliding action. The pendant can be a flex, a rod fitting, or a hook and chain pendant.

Multi-light pendants and other special pendant fittings have a conventional fixed ceiling plate in a variety of shapes and diameters.

Lampholders

The majority of pendant lampholders are of moulded plastic and of BC (Bayonet Cap) pattern for use with the ordinary electric light bulb. These lampholders have cord grips for use with flexible cord plain pendants but are threaded for fixing direct to wall lights and pendant fittings (other than plain pendants).

A switched version is used in table lamps and floor standards.

Another version is the SBC (small bayonet cap) lampholder used with SBC candle lamps of the plain and twisted patterns.

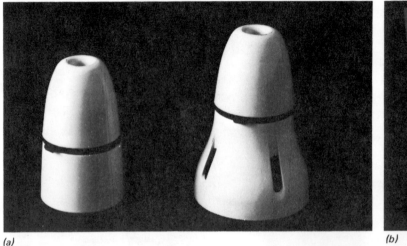

(a)

(b)

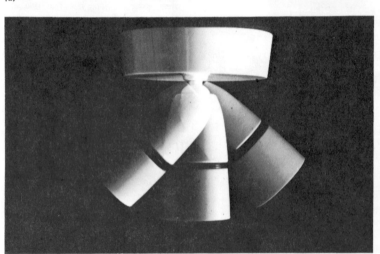

(c)

(d)

(a) Short and deep skirt lampholders. (b) Deep skirt lampholder

(c) Angle batten lampholder. (d) Table lamp dimmer

Earthed lampholders

Metal lampholders have to be earthed as do some heat-resisting lampholders where the metal lamp cap holder is separated from the plastic. 3-core flex is used with these lampholders.

ES lampholders

The ES lampholder has a large size thread to accept the Edison Screw (ES) lamp cap of continental and American bulbs. It also has a centre contact corresponding with the centre contact of the ES bulb. When wiring these lampholders, it is essential that the neutral wire is connected to the lamp cap terminal and that the live wire is connected to the centre contact terminal.

GES lampholders

These GES (Goliath Edison Screw) lampholders are used for jumbo size bulbs which are rarely used in the home. In contrast the MES (Miniature Edison Screw) bulb is the common torch bulb and the lamp cap of fairy light bulbs.

Joint boxes
(a) 4-terminal joint box used for lighting circuits

(b) 30 A ring circuit joint box having separate terminals for single-strand cables

(c) Universal joint box

SBC lampholders

The SBC (Small Bayonet Cap) lampholder is fitted to wall lights and to multi-light pendants for candle lamps and other special bulbs having an SBC cap.

Batten lampholders

Originally designed for light battens on the theatre stage, these are really low-priced complete lighting fittings for use where there is limited headroom and in other confined spaces. They are also installed in bathrooms, WC's and in kitchens as an alternative to a pendant fitting.

Skirted batten lampholders

When fitted in the bathroom and in similar situations, the batten lampholder (or any lampholder) should have a deep HO (Home Office) pattern skirt. This is to prevent a person, when changing a bulb, touching the metal clamp while the bulb is making contact with the live pins of the lampholder.

Modern designs of batten lampholders have loop-in facilities and are versions of the loop-in ceiling roses. Heat-resisting types are available which, in many situations, are essential to prevent overheating of the lampholder and wiring.

Joint boxes

Joint boxes are usually circular and form part of the circuit wiring. They are fixed permanently to the house structure and used principally in lighting circuits. Joint boxes are available in 4- 5- and 6-terminal versions.

A 3-terminal joint box of 30 A current rating is used for ring circuits to connect spur cables to the ring cable, as shown in the illustration.

Socket-outlets

The socket-outlet is the fixed portion of a plug and socket arrangement and the termination point of circuit wiring to provide a ready means of connecting portable appliances to the fixed mains wiring.

The 13 A socket-outlet for use with the flat-pin fused plug is the standard socket in Britain for domestic installations. It is made in many variants: single switched socket, single non-switched socket; double socket, switched and non-switched, and switched with neon indicator. All these versions are available in the plate type for mounting on surface and flush boxes.

The single socket is mounted on a 1-gang box; the double on a 2-gang box, and two singles may be mounted side by side on a dual box. This dual box is slightly wider than the double or 2-gang box and has extra screw lugs for the separate sockets.

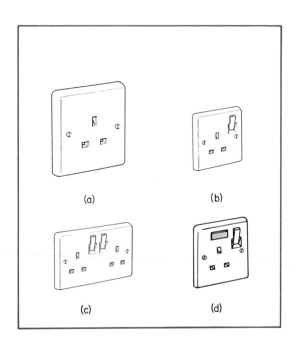

13 A socket-outlets. (a) Unswitched 13 A socket-outlet (b) Switched 13 A socket-outlet (c) Switched double 13 A socket-outlet (d) Switched 13 A socket-outlet with neon indicator

Surface pattern socket-outlets are designed only for surface mounting and are usually mounted on a pattress.

Fused round pin plugs

Although the fused plug is associated with the 13 A flat pin plug and socket of the ring circuit, fused round pin plugs are made to the appropriate British Standard (BS 546) and may be found in some homes. The fuses are of the cartridge type but slightly smaller than the 13 A plug fuse. The ratings and colours are: 5 A (red); 2 A (yellow) and 1 A (green), made to BS 646.

These fuses are fitted in some clock connectors, so if the clock connector has either a 2 A or a 1 A fuse, check whether it is stamped BS 642. If it is, buy the same size replacements and not a 2 A (black) or 3 A (red) which are for 13 A plugs.

Fused connection units

A fused connection unit (originally known as a fused spur box) provides a fused outlet in a ring circuit as an alternative to a fused plug and socket-outlet (see Chapter 38). It is used to supply fixed appliances and remotely positioned fixed lighting.

The fuses are cartridge fuses of the same size, colours and current ratings as used with the 13 A fused plug.

Proposed 16 A plug

An entirely new plug and socket outlet having a current rating of 16 A is being developed world-wide and will replace all existing plugs and sockets including the 13 A fused plug and the round pin plugs used in the UK. It is unlikely to be in production before 1980 and it will be many years after this before existing plugs and sockets are entirely obsolete.

It is also expected that the 13 A ring circuit sockets will be able to be replaced without modification to existing wiring.

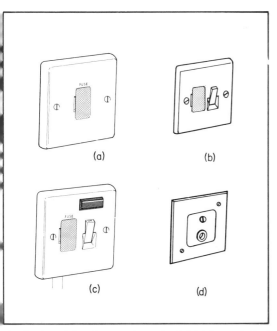

A selection of fused connection units. (a) 13 A unswitched fused connection unit (b) 13 A switched fused connection unit (c) 13 A switched fused connection unit with neon indicator and flex outlet (d) Fused clock connector

The sockets will probably be twin units for mounting on a one-gang box, but for the ring circuit the twin unit will consist of one socket and a fused unit.

Fused clock connectors

A fused clock connector is a small non-switched fused outlet designed expressly for supplying a mains electric clock.

The unit is in two sections: a fixed base which is connected to the fixed circuit wiring, and another section in the form of a flat pin plug which plugs into sockets in the base. The plug section carries the flex of the clock and contains the fuse. The plug is secured in the base by a retaining screw. This prevents the plug being pulled out accidentally and stopping the clock.

Fused clock connectors are sometimes used for other appliances, such as extractor fans.

Full details on wiring electric clocks are given in Chapter 38.

Shaver supply units and shaver sockets

The shaver supply unit is designed especially for shavers used in the bathroom. It has a 2-pin socket which accepts British, Continental and American standard 2-pin round and flat pin plugs.

The unit contains a transformer to isolate the socket from the earthed mains supply to provide greater safety in the bathroom. The voltage at the socket is 240 V, but a dual version provides an alternative voltage of 110 V for American shavers.

A thermal cut-out in the unit prevents any mains voltage portable appliance (or portable lamp) other than a shaver being plugged into the unit and used in the bathroom.

A shaver socket is a socket which accepts the 2-pin plugs of shavers but does not contain a transformer. It is therefore cheaper and may be installed in any room except a bathroom. Some models are fitted with thermal cut-out.

Some striplights intended for shaving mirror lighting are fitted with a shaver socket. Some have an isolating transformer and may be installed in the bathroom. Others are simply shaver sockets with no transformer. These may be installed anywhere except in the bathroom.

Cord outlet units

A cord outlet is simply a moulded plastic 'square' plate containing three terminals and a cord grip behind the plate and a flexible cord entry hole in the centre. It is mounted on the standard flush or surface socket outlet box.

The function of the unit is to provide a connection of an appliance to the circuit wiring other than by socket-outlet or fused connection unit. It is installed in situations, such as in a bathroom, to connect the flex of towel rails and other heaters where the switched outlet must be out of reach of a person using the bathroom. In these situations the switch is usually a cord-operated ceiling switch.

Socket multi-adaptors

These are also known as plug adaptors. They are inserted into socket-outlets to enable more than one plug to be used from any one socket-outlet. The two outlet 13 A unit is commonplace, since it enables an extra plug to be used from a 13 A socket-outlet.

Other versions have mixed ratings for 5 A and 2 A plugs; the adaptor in these containing a fuse to protect the smaller outlets. Some makes have no fuse, although designed for plugs of various current ratings. These adaptors are unauthorised and should not be used in the home. Also available are shaver socket adaptors enabling a shaver to be used from a 13 A socket-outlet.

Outdoor wiring accessories

Socket-outlets, switches and other wiring accessories exposed to rain and snow outside the house must be weatherproof. These are either metalclad or are unbreakable types in plastic or rubber. Accessories which are installed outside, but under cover, can be of the plastic-moulded type.

Accessories installed in the garage, garden shed or greenhouse are normally of the plastic-moulded type.

Consumer units and switchgear

Consumer units situated at the mains for supplying have already been covered in Chapters 36 and 38. As previously explained these replace the old-fashioned main switch and fuse units and have also largely replaced the fuseboard with its separate main switch and fuse unit.

Shaver sockets. The top illustration shows a shaver supply unit for installation in bathrooms and the bottom picture illustrates a shaver socket for use in rooms other than bathrooms. A shaver mirror light with shaver socket suitable for installation in bathrooms is shown on the right

Chapter 44
Electrical repairs about the home

There are many electrical repair jobs which the householder can do himself, such as mending fuses, replacing flex, fitting a new plug, etc.

It is essential to have a card of the different sizes of fuse wire and/or spare cartridge fuses for each of the current ratings of the circuit fuses.

What to do when a fuse blows

First find out which fuse has blown. Is it a lighting circuit, a ring circuit, water heater circuit or any other circuit?

If you have a modern consumer unit (or fuseboard) having fuses which are colour coded you will know that for a lighting circuit you will have to check the white fuses and, if a ring circuit fuse, or a cooker circuit fuse, it will be red. If the immersion heater circuit fuse has blown the fuse colour will be either blue or yellow, see Table 2 on page 316.

Details of the circuits should be available at the consumer unit or fuseboard. The consumer unit usually has a sticker on the fuse cover where circuit details are listed. This enables you to know which fuse has blown. Check the circuit number with the list and withdraw the appropriate fuse holder.

If the consumer unit has no circuit list, or there is a number of main switch and fuse units, self-adhesive labels can be used. These should not be stuck to the actual fuse holder, for if you remove more than one fuse holder of the same current rating, you may mix them up.

In general, a ground floor lighting circuit will include the lighting points on the ground floor and the first floor circuit will serve the lighting points on the first floor. However, there are sometimes a number of lights which do not follow this rule and some may be fed from the ring circuits. The same can apply to the ring circuits with some socket-outlets on the ground floor being connected to the first floor ring circuit and some may possibly be served by one or more radial circuits, see Chapter 38. It is an advantage to check all lights and socket-outlets and list them, so that when a fuse blows you will know exactly what are affected.

Turning off the main switch

It is always good practice to turn off the main switch when mending fuses. This is true even in the case of the modern consumer unit where the fuses have a separate cover and no live parts are exposed when taking off the cover or when removing a fuse.

Even if you don't switch off the main switch before taking out the fuse, you should switch off before you replace it in case there is a fault which will cause the fuse to blow immediately. In this case the fuse will 'blow' with a bang which can be frightening, but this is not dangerous with modern fuse holders which shield the fusewire.

A disadvantage of turning off the main switch is that all lights and power go off and mains electric clocks have to be reset after restoring the power. Always have a torch handy near the fuseboard or consumer unit.

Before mending a fuse try and find out why it blew. If it blew as you switched on a light it is probably the bulb. Some bulbs contain a fuse to prevent the circuit fuse blowing when the bulb fails. Examine the bulb and if this appears in good condition examine the light flex.

If a lighting circuit fuse blows apparently without warning, it is probable that the fuse wire has deteriorated. However, if the fuse is of the cartridge type, which does not deteriorate, the trouble is more serious. A ring circuit fuse blows if there is a fault in the circuit. It is rarely due to a faulty appliance, since in this case, the plug fuse blows leaving the circuit intact.

Mending a fuse

Remove the fuse cover from the consumer unit. Locate the blown fuse and withdraw the fuse holder. Examine the fuse element — fuse wire — and it will be obvious if it has blown. If the fuse is of the cartridge type this has to be removed for testing as it is not possible to tell by visual inspection whether it has blown.

Rewirable fuses are mended as follows

(i)   Having removed the fuse holder from the consumer unit or fuse board, loosen the two screws and take out the bits of fuse wire remaining.

(ii) Clean off any melted blobs of copper and clean off any burn marks.

(iii) Select the fuse wire of correct current rating on the fuse wire card.

(iv) Pass the end of the wire through the ceramic or asbestos tube and connect it to the terminal.

(v)   Cut the wire to length and connect this end to the other terminal. If a clamp type terminal, place the wire end under the washer clockwise and when tightening the screw take care not to stretch the fuse wire. If stretched, its current rating will drop and overheating may result.

Mending a rewirable fuse

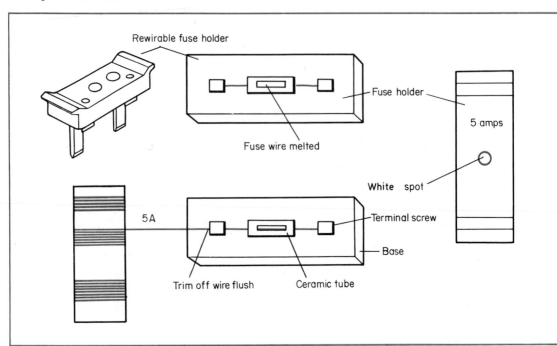

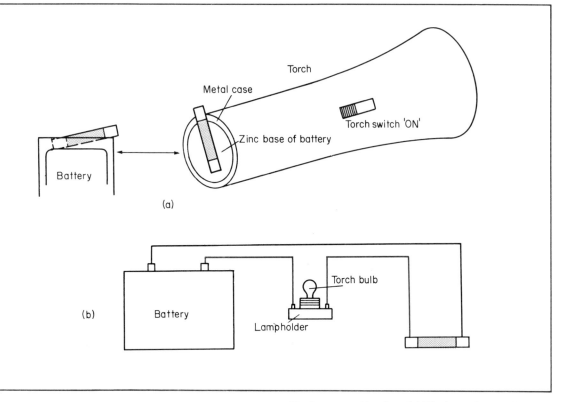

Torch

Metal case

Torch switch 'ON'

Zinc base of battery

Battery

(a)

Torch bulb

Battery

Lampholder

(b)

Testing a cartridge fuse. (a) The base of a metal torch is unscrewed and the fuse placed inside with one contact on the case, the other on the zinc base of the battery. If the torch lights when switched on the fuse is OK. (b) A bulb and battery as an alternative method

(vi) Trim off the ends of wire.

(vii) Turn off the main switch (if not already turned off) and insert the holder in the fuseway.

(viii) Turn on the main switch. If there is an immediate 'bang' the fuse has blown again indicating a serious fault. It is advisable in this case to have an electrician to locate the fault.

(ix) If the fuse is OK, test the lights. If you suspect the flex of a lighting fitting caused the fuse to blow, attend to this before turning on the room switch.

(x)   Finally replace the fuse cover.

The procedure for 'mending' a cartridge fuse is simple. It is replaced by another.

Remove the cartridge from its holder and lay it aside for testing. Select a fuse of the same current rating (and therefore the same colour and the same physical dimensions) fit it into the fuse holder and replace the fuse holder into the consumer unit. Switch on and, as with rewirable fuses, if the fuse immediately blows the fault is serious.

Miniature circuit breakers

If the consumer unit contains MCB's (miniature circuit breakers) instead of fuses the procedure when the lights fail is simple. Take a torch to the consumer unit and note which MCB is switched off; this is the faulty

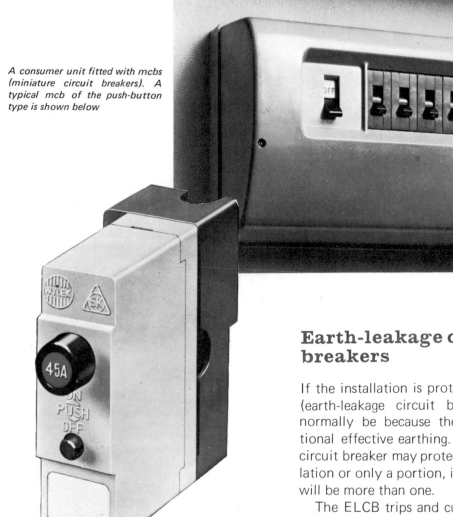

A consumer unit fitted with mcbs (miniature circuit breakers). A typical mcb of the push-button type is shown below

Earth-leakage circuit breakers

If the installation is protected by an ELC (earth-leakage circuit breaker) this wi normally be because there is no conver tional effective earthing. The earth-leakag circuit breaker may protect the whole insta lation or only a portion, in which case ther will be more than one.

The ELCB trips and cuts off the curren when a live wire or connection comes int contact with earthed metal. Where there i conventional earthing the fuse will blov when this fault occurs, but where there i an ELCB instead, the fuse will not blow.

Before the current can be restored (th ELCB switched on) it is necessary to locat and repair the fault for, as with the MCB an ELCB will not close when a fault re mains. In this case a current flows throug the earth conductor and the tripping coil o the circuit breaker. If you cannot rectif the fault immediately try and isolate th faulty section; this is easy if you suspect a appliance as you simply pull out the plug.

A disadvantage of having only a singl

circuit. Unless you think a flex is faulty or some other fault has caused the MCB to trip, you simply restore the switch to its 'ON' position. If it trips immediately, or you cannot switch it on, there is a circuit fault because it is not possible to close a circuit breaker against a fault.

There are various types of circuit breaker switch. Some are press-button, where the button pops out when the circuit breaker operates. With other types, the switch trips to a central position between ON and OFF so that it is obvious that it has tripped and was not switched off.

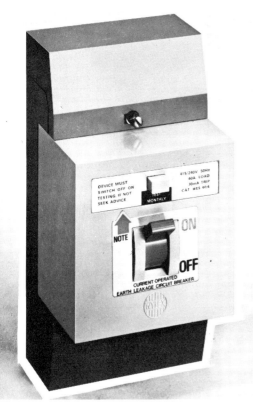

An example of a current operated ELCB (earth leakage circuit breaker) which is made in high sensitivity versions to provide personal protection

ELCB on an installation is that a single fault will cut off the current to the entire installation. It is therefore an advantage to have more than one ELCB but this is possible only where there is either more than one consumer unit or where individual circuits, such as the cooker circuit, are supplied from a separate main switch and fuse unit.

Renewing flexes

When a flexible cord shows signs of wear, or damage, it must be replaced without delay. You need a new length of flex of the same type and size, see Table 6 on page 403.

The flex of a plain pendant is traditionally twisted twin, but circular sheathed flex is now used extensively. Where the existing flex is twisted twin, you should replace it with circular sheathed at an early opportunity. This may also mean replacing the ceiling roses and lampholders, for many of the older types will not accept circular sheathed flex as the cord grips are designed for twisted twin flex.

The flex can be changed as follows:

(i) Remove the old flex and cut the new flex to the same length.
(ii) Prepare the ends of the circular sheathed by stripping off about 100 mm (4 in) for the ceiling rose end and about 50 mm (2 in) of sheath for a lampholder.

You can now connect the flex to the ceiling rose but, if you have cut the new flex to the correct length, fit the lampholder first. This should be done on a bench or table instead of from the top of steps.

Wiring the lampholder and ceiling rose

The flex is connected to the lampholder as follows:

(i) Unscrew the lampholder cap.
(ii) Strip about 12 mm (½ in) of insulation from the two wires.

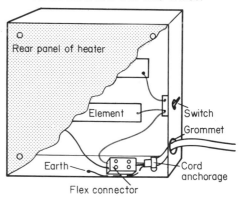

Connecting 3-core flex to an electric fire. Connect the brown wire of the flex to the L terminal, the blue to the N terminal and the green/yellow to the earth terminal. Make sure the sheath is secure under the anchorage and replace the access panel

(iii) Bend the bared ends double to provide a better grip in the terminals.

(iv) Loosen the terminal screws and insert the wires.

(v) Tighten the screws.

(vi) Thread on the lampholder cap and screw it on to the lampholder.

(vii) Check that the unsheathed portion does not protrude from the lampholder, if it does, disconnect the flex, shorten the wires and repeat the process.

Where a lampholder has an earth screw you use 3-core flex. The third core (green-yellow) is secured to this terminal which is usually of the clamp type. Do not double the end of this wire but place it under the clamp screw washer clockwise and tighten the screw.

To connect flex to the ceiling rose, first thread on the ceiling rose cover. This is often forgotten. Modern ceiling roses have post terminals, so prepare the ends of the two wires as for lampholder and insert them in the appropriate terminal holes and tighten the screws. When loosening the screws to do this, take care not to screw them out or you will have difficulty in replacing them from the top of a pair of steps. Place the insulated portion of the wires over the anchorage and screw on the cover.

Check that the unsheathed portion of the wires is contained within the ceiling rose. If not you will have to disconnect the flex, shorten the ends and repeat the process. If you are reflexing more than one pendant, and all ceiling roses and lampholders are identical, carefully measure the trimmed ends of the first and use this as a guide for the remainder.

If you are wiring the ceiling rose with 3-core flex because the lampholder has to be earthed, you connect the earth core to the earth terminal of the ceiling rose. Otherwise the flex is not connected to the earth terminal; this being used only for the earth conductors of the circuit wiring.

Where you have the old-type ceiling rose and are not replacing them by the modern type, you will find that the method of connecting and anchoring the flex differs. Many ceiling roses have clamp-type terminals, but some have tunnel type. In some types, wires are anchored to slots or holes in the ceiling rose base, usually enabling sheathed flex to be used, but with others the flex is gripped by tightening the cover which will only accommodate twisted twin flex, or the insulated ends of sheathed flex from which the sheath is removed. The solution here is to fit modern ceiling roses.

Rewiring multi-light fittings

When it becomes necessary to renew the flex of a multi-light pendant fitting, or a single-light pendant, other than a plain pendant, it is rewired using the same type of flex, usually parallel twin flex. First remove the screws securing the ceiling plate to its box or pattress. Carefully lower the pendant a few inches to give you access to a porcelain or plastic block connector which joins the fitting wires to the circuit cable.

Loosen the screws securing the circuit wires so that you can remove the fitting with the connector attached to its flex, but make sure you don't disturb any jointed circuit wires. As a precaution you can bind them with adhesive tape, provided someone else can take the weight of the fitting while you bind the tape.

A multi-light fitting will have a flex to each lampholder, one core of all flexes being joined in one terminal of the connector, the other core of all flexes being joined in the other terminal. Rewire the fitting in this manner and you can then connect it to the circuit wires and refix the pendant in the reverse order from taking it down.

A single light special fitting will have only one flex so it is best to leave the connector secured to the circuit wires with no risk of disturbing jointed conductors.

Earthing metal lighting fittings

An electric light fitting having exposed metalwork has to be earthed. To do this you connect a short length of green PVC insulated earth cable from the earth terminal of the pattress box to an earth terminal on the fitting, so obviating 3-core flex when wiring the fitting.

If, as is usual in an old installation, there is no earth at the lighting point and probably no earth terminal on the fitting, to earth the fitting means running an earth wire from the consumer unit especially for the fitting and then fixing a terminal screw to the fitting.

Reflexing portable appliances

When a portable appliance requires a new flex the most difficult job is usually locating the terminals to which the flex is connected. In many instances this means partly dismantling the appliance. In others it means simply removing a terminal cover, an example being the steam or dry thermostatically controlled electric iron. Other appliances, such as electric kettles, some coffee percolators, non-automatic irons and similar small appliances containing heating elements, incorporate a removable flex adaptor. Renewing a flex in these cases means fitting it to the adaptor and sometimes in replacing the adaptor by a new one.

Radiant electric fires, convectors, fan heaters and practically every electric heater has its flex passing through a grommet into a terminal block situated within the casing. To get to the terminal block usually means removing a back or side panel or, in some cases, removing the panel under the base of the heater. With other models of heater, the whole of the front panel complete with the elements and reflectors, is removed to obtain access to the terminal block.

Having located the terminals you can disconnect the old flex, taking careful note of the polarity of the terminals. These may be marked for live and neutral or have splashes of red and black paint. If not, note very carefully the terminals with the red (or brown) wire and the black (or blue) wire. The earth terminal will be obvious as it is fixed to the metal frame of the heater. Before you can pull the disconnected flex out through the grommet you will have to release the cord anchorage, so note how this is effected for the new flex anchorage.

The new flex will normally be of the same type, size and length as the old but if you have any doubt that it is not the original flex and not the correct type make sure the new flex is correct. If the insulation of the wires within the heater has obviously been affected by the heat, the new flex must be heat resisting. The length of a portable heater flex should not be in excess of 2 m (6 ft) or 3 m (9 ft) including connections.

Pass the end of the new flex through the grommet and pull through sufficient flex for the connection at the terminal block and earth terminal. Strip off enough sheath to make the connection — no more. If braided flex, remove the braid to the required length and slip on a rubber sleeve to contain the ends of the braid and fillers. Strip sufficient insulation from the ends of the conductors for making the connection in the terminals. Tighten the terminal screws and secure the flex in the anchorage.

Replace the panel or panels or terminal

cover as necessary. Fit the plug on the other end of the flex (see wiring a plug, later in this chapter) and test the heater by inserting the plug into its socket-outlet.

The procedure for fitting a flex to other appliances is similar, except for those appliances incorporating a flex adaptor (see below). The important thing to remember is to fit the right type and the right size of flex.

Fitting flex to a connector

A flex connector such as that fitted to an electric kettle is made in two principal forms though with many variants. The older pattern of connector which is still widely used is made in two halves which are split apart to connect the flex and brought together when wired. The other type has its terminals at the rear and accessible by removing an end cap. Both are available in 2- and 3-pin versions.

Split connector

Remove the two bolts securing the two halves together. Split open and disconnect the flex wires from the terminals of the socket tubes. Lift off the grommet and pull out the old flex. Thread in the end of the

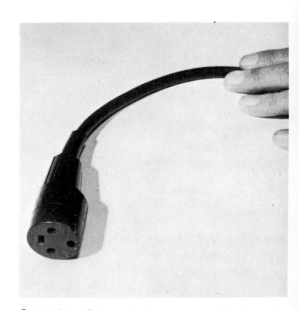

Connecting a flex to a kettle connector. This is a 3-pin kettle connector. The three cores of the flex are connected to the appropriate terminals as shown in the top illustration. In the lower picture the terminal cover has been replaced and the connector is now ready for use

new flex and strip off the sheath for a few inches using the old flex as a guide. Bare the ends and connect them to the respective terminals. Lay the wires in the slots of the halves. Place the other half on top of the one containing the wires and secure the two halves together with the two screws and nuts.

With some patterns of split connector, the earth core is passed through a hole in one half of the moulding and secured under an earth contact strip. This is one of two contact strips which make a rubbing contact with the metal shroud of the kettle to earth the kettle body.

One-piece connector

To wire this type of kettle connector, remove the screws securing the end cover, loosen the terminal screws and pull out the old flex. Then thread in the new flex, strip the ends and connect the wires to the respective terminals. Replace the end cover and fit the plug on the other end of the flex.

Fitting a new connector

If the existing kettle flex connector is in a poor state of repair you should also buy a new connector. The flex is connected by one of the methods described above, but it is best to buy a connector with the flex already fitted.

When fitting a new element to a kettle it is likely that you will also have to get a new connector (and flex) because the existing connector will not fit the element.

Fitting plugs

Most plugs in use in the home today are of the 13 A fused variety having flat pins. There are also many round pin plugs still in use. These are of various current rating and have different sizes of pins, some with three pins, some with only two pins.

The construction of the plugs is fairly standard with the flex entering the plug at the side, though some round-pin plugs have end entry flexes.

Wiring 13 A fused plugs

To wire a 13 A plug, remove the screw securing the cover to the plug base and lift off the cover. Loosen, or remove the screws of the cord grip and loosen the terminal screws. Place the end of the flex on to the plug base and estimate the length of sheath to remove for the wires to be inserted into the terminals; the wires should lie loosely in the grooves and the end of the sheathing to be clamped under the cord grip.

In some versions of plug, the wires may have to be of different lengths, the earth wire usually being the longest so allow for the longest wire. In other versions, the wires can be all of the same length. Now strip off the required length of sheathing and if necessary cut each wire to length.

Connecting a flex. (1) Cable ends cut to the same length. The insulation is stripped back $^9/_{16}$ th of an inch (15 mm) ready for inserting into the MK Safetyplug

(2) Removing the fuse, prior to insertion of the cables

(3) Pressing cables down into the cord grip prior to placing cable ends in position

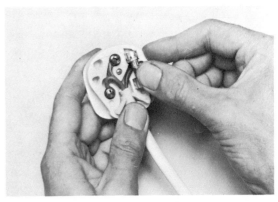

(6) Replacing the fuse into the fully wired Safetyplug. Correct fuse should always be used

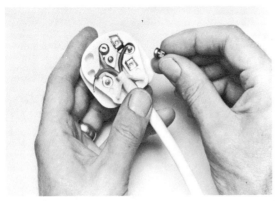

(4) Green/yellow cable (centre) fixed to earth; brown cable (right) being fixed to live; blue cable (left) ready to be connected to neutral

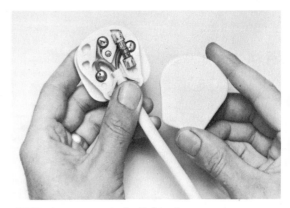

(7) Placing cover on to the Safetyplug

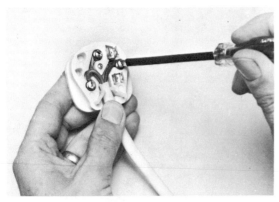

(5) Final check on the terminal screw. The cord grip helps to prevent cable being pulled out of plug which can cause shorting at the ends of the terminals

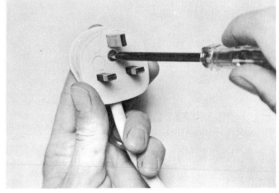

(8) Securing the cover screw. The plug is now ready for use

These photographs are the copyright of MK Electric Ltd, and are reproduced here by permission

Strip off about 15 mm of insulation from the end of each wire. Connect the green/yellow wire first, this to the earth pin terminal, then the brown wire to the live (L) terminal, and finally the blue wire to the neutral (N) terminal. Position the sheath under the cord grip and tighten the screws. Then place the wires into the slots, replace the fuse and the plug cover and tighten the cover screw. Some patterns of plug have two screws but these are now no longer available.

Wiring round pin plugs

Round pin plugs are generally of the same pattern as 13 A flat pin plugs except they do not contain a fuse. The flex is side entry and the cord grip is similar. Some patterns have end entry holes for the flex and are sometimes more difficult to wire depending on the type of flex and its overall size.

The different current ratings of the plugs — 2 A, 5 A and 15 A — are used for the different appliances. The 2 A plugs are used mainly for table lamps and floor standards. The 2-pin plug and the 2-pin socket are largely obsolete but the 2 A plug is suitable for all-insulated and double insulated lamps and appliances fitted with 2-core flex.

In no circumstances may a 2-pin plug be connected to 3-core flex as this would mean leaving the essential earth wire unconnected.

Plugs with double-insulated appliances

A double-insulated appliance, stamped with a double-insulated double hollow square, is fitted with 2-core flex by the makers and has no facilities for earthing.

A flex renewal must also be 2-core. When connecting the 2-core flex to a 13 A fused plug the earth terminal of the plug is left blank.

Screwless cord clamps

The sheath of the flex must always be secured to the cord clamp of the plug as shown in the illustration.

One pattern of plug (made by MK) has no screws to the clamp. Instead the sheath is pressed into the nylon clamp which grips the cord. This design has the advantage that the greater the strain placed on the flex the tighter the grip of the clamp.

Connectors for flexible cords

Generally flexible cords should not be jointed. A flex should be as short as practicable and where an extra length is required temporarily a proper extension lead consisting of the flex, trailing socket and mains plug should be used. Ideally this should be a reel of flex with the socket mounted on the reel.

There are however occasions where a flex needs to be lengthened. In this case a purpose-made connector must be used which is electrically sound and mechanically strong with cord grips to prevent the flex being pulled out of its terminals when under strain.

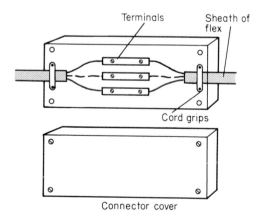

Method of joining two pieces of flex using a flex connector

There are three forms of flex connector for jointing: (i) single-piece connector; (ii) two-section connector; and (iii) line-cord switch. These are described below.

Single-piece connector

This is a line-cord joint box comprising a base containing either two or three terminals, cord grips and a cover secured by screws. The 2-terminal version is for joining two lengths of 2-core flex, the 3-terminal for jointing two lengths of 3-core flex.

Two-section connector

This is a line-cord 3-pin plug and socket with the centre pin (the earth connection) offset to conserve polarity and so preventing reversal. This is essential so that the live wire is connected to the switch of an appliance. The socket section is marked 'mains' and must be connected to the mains length of flex. The plug section must be connected to the appliance flex.

Line-cord switch

The principal purpose of a line-cord switch is to enable a table lamp or an appliance, such as an electric mower, to be switched off and on when in use. It is also a suitable flex connector where a flex is to be extended permanently.

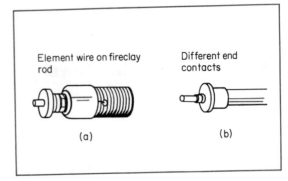

Electric heater elements are made in a variety of lengths, wattages and having different end caps. These are examples of a pencil rod element and a silica enclosed rod element

Line cord switch used as a flex connector. Similar switches are available for 3-core flex

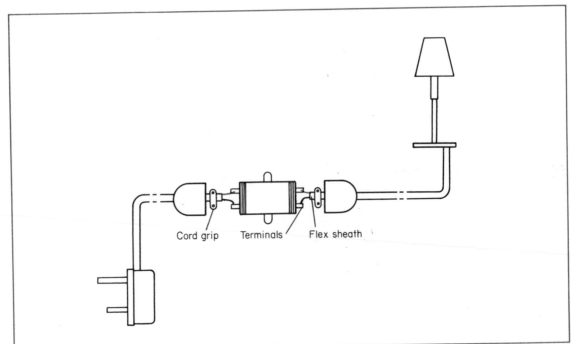

The pear-shaped type used for table lamps and bedhead lamps is a single-pole switch and also has terminals for the through neutral wire. The version used for other appliances is usually a double-pole switch.

Jointing old and new flexes

When an extension flex is to be jointed to the flex of an existing appliance, the flex of the existing appliance will usually have the old code colours of red (live); black (neutral) and green (earth). New flex will have the colours brown (live); blue (neutral) and green/yellow (earth). It is most important to ensure that the green is connected to the green/yellow, the red to the brown and the black to the blue.

This is simple to remember with the fixed connector and the line-cord switch, but is not so simple with the 2-section connector where the terminals are marked L, N and E.

Appliance repairs

In addition to renewing flexible cords there are other repairs within the capability of the householder. These include replacing faulty elements.

Before carrying out any repairs to an appliance first pull out the plug, or in the case of a fixed appliance supplied from a fused connection unit, remove the fuse. If the appliance is not supplied through a fused outlet, turn off the power at the mains.

Repairs to electric fires

Radiant electric heaters have either rod elements or flat bar elements. Convectors and other heaters operating at 'black heat' have special elements which are either open wire spiral elements, sheathed elements, or are totally enclosed.

Rod elements

Conventional electric reflector fires have pencil elements consisting of a wire wound ceramic rod and exposed to touch. 'Infra-red' radiant reflector fires have spiral wire elements enclosed in a silica tube. Each type is made in a variety of lengths, watts loading and with a variety of end contacts. A replacement element must be identical to the original and designed for the make and model of heater. A rod element is attached to the heater either by spring clips or is secured by milled or hexagon nuts.

To remove a pencil type element, it is usually only necessary to release the dress guard, and detach the element from its contacts. If this is of the screw type contact, you loosen the milled or hexagon nut. If the end contacts are enclosed in shields, the shields have to be removed before the element can be taken out.

Silica-enclosed elements

The end contacts of silica-enclosed rod elements are enclosed in shields which have to be released before you can check the type of end contact and measure the length of the element for replacement. Normally the complete element is replaced, though if the silica tube is in good condition, this can be rewired with a new spiral.

Cleaning the reflector

Before fitting a new rod element clean and polish the reflector so that it will operate at maximum efficiency. The reflector is cleaned with soap and water; if chrome, you can use a chrome polisher, subject to the advice of the manufacturer.

A dirty reflector does not reduce the heat output of the fire. It reduces the reflected heat causing the casing to run hot; this heat being emitted by other means including convected heat which could be lost via the flue of a heater standing in a fireplace.

Fire bar elements

Sometimes termed brick elements, these consist of a spiral wire element laid in parabolic grooves of a 'brick-shape' former. If not fractured, the former can be rewound but the replacement spiral must be of the same length and the same watts loading of the original.

Removing a bar element usually means taking off a rear panel of the heater though, on some models, there is access from the front after the dress guard is released.

Before removing the securing nuts of the bar, it is necessary to disconnect the current carrying wires. These wires are usually either asbestos covered or are stiff uninsulated wires. Some have ceramic beads so take care not to lose some of the beads when disconnecting the wires. Also make a note of the connections.

Check the insulation of the flex within the heater. If damaged by heat, fit a new flex of the heat resisting type.

Replacing convector elements

Partial dismantling of the heater may be necessary to gain access to the elements. Do not buy a replacement until you have removed the faulty element, as designs change and identical replacements must be fitted.

Pilot lights and fuel effect spinners

A pilot light, whether simply an illuminating device or part of a fuel effect unit, is usually removed from a heater by means of a detachable panel. With some types, the fuel effect unit has to be lifted to gain access to the lamp.

Lamps may be either clear or coloured but most types have ordinary bayonet caps (BC). These types are readily available but some models use lights with bi-pin caps which may have to be ordered for the particular model of heater.

When a fuel effect spinner ceases to function the cause is either that the spinner is out of alignment or that the bearing is corroded. Remove the spinner assembly, clean and adjust the bearing.

Safety aspects of illuminating devices

The purpose of a pilot light is to indicate that the heater is in circuit and current carrying parts are live at mains voltage. It is also a visual indication that a heater operating at 'black heat' is consuming electricity.

From the safety aspect, replace a faulty pilot light as soon as possible as, if an element has burnt out, the contacts though 'cold' will be live with the added risk of an electric shock. Single-element radiant heaters have no integral switch on the heater, unless the heater is of the fuel effect type. This element serves as a visual indicator and, if it fails, the heater should be taken out of service.

For the same reason one element of a multi-element radiant heater without fuel effect is not switched at the heater but glows when the plug is inserted or the socket-outlet switched on. This element is usually the first to fail as it is the one that is most used. This should also be replaced as soon as it fails.

Radiant fires manufactured subsequent to 1975 are required by statute to be fitted with an isolating switch, so that all live parts can be made 'dead' before handling the elements or when attending to the dress guard.

Switch failures

When a switch on the heater fails it is necessary to order a new one that is identical to the original. If any difficulty arises the heater should be taken to an electrical repair shop.

Electric kettle elements

The immersion heater of an electric kettle is made in a variety of shapes and electrical loadings. The flange of the element also varies with the make and model, some being 3-pin, others 2-pin with spring contacts for earthing the kettle body.

When an electric kettle element fails, the replacement element must be one which will fit that kettle. When buying the new element, either take the old element or the complete kettle. With the replacement element are two flange washers, one rubber and one fibre. You may also need a new flex connector and possibly a new flex. These come in various kits with or without connector and flex.

If your kettle is of the high-speed type having a high loading element then the replacement element must be of this type. If it is a standard (low loading) kettle, you may be able to buy a high speed element to fit it should you so wish.

An automatic kettle has an element which switches off as the water boils. If not attended to, it will switch on and off at intervals with no risk of the kettle boiling dry.

Most standard electric kettles will accept an automatic replacement element so when your element fails you may be able to take the opportunity of converting your kettle to an automatic.

Take your kettle to the local electrical shop so that you can check whether there is a suitable automatic element to replace the old element.

Replacing an element

Proceed as follows:

(i) Unscrew the flex connector shroud, taking care not to damage it if chromium plated, or fracturing it if moulded plastic.

(ii) Push the flange and pin assembly into the kettle body. If you live in a hard water district it may be necessary to remove the scale around the element before you can ease it into the body.

(iii) Lift the element out through the top of the kettle body.

(iv) Scrape off the scale around the flange hole, inside and outside the body and finish it using fine emery cloth, or glass paper.

(v) Fit the new rubber washer over the flange of the new element.

(vi) Pass the element into the kettle body, the correct way up, flange first and pass the flange through the flange hole.

(vii) Fit the fibre washer on to the flange and replace the connector shield.

(viii) Tighten the connector but do not use a wrench which would damage the shroud.

(ix) If you have bought a new connector but not wired to a new flex, connect this to the flex and also the plug.

(x) Fill the kettle, plug in and check for any leaks at the flange. If leaking, tighten the shroud until the leaking stops.

Electric irons

When the element of an electric iron fails, the iron has to be dismantled to fit the new element. This is sandwiched between a pressure plate and the sole plate. Some

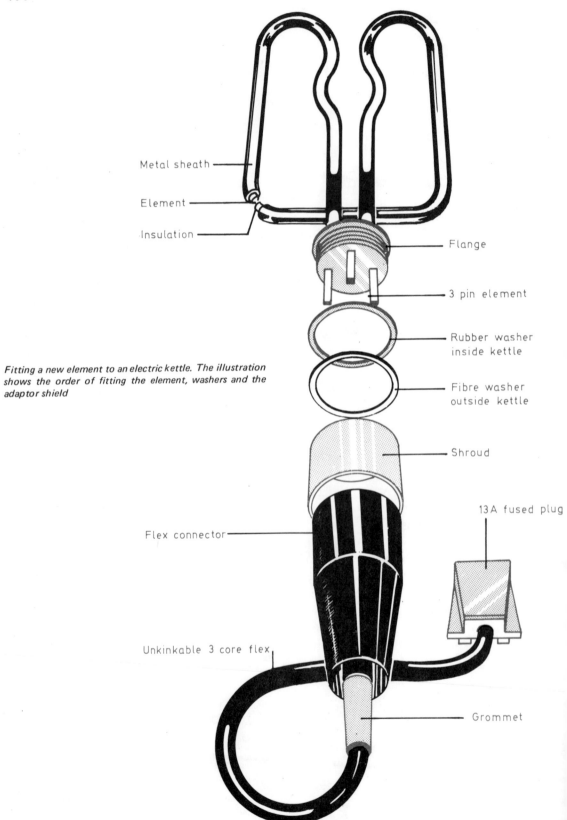

Metal sheath

Element

Insulation

Flange

3 pin element

Rubber washer
inside kettle

Fibre washer
outside kettle

*Fitting a new element to an electric kettle. The illustration
shows the order of fitting the element, washers and the
adaptor shield*

Shroud

13A fused plug

Flex connector

Unkinkable 3 core flex

Grommet

models have the element embedded in the sole plate. When these fail the soleplate is replaced as a unit.

Dismantling a dry or a steam iron should not be attempted without following the manufacturers instructions. If these are not available then the repair should be carried out by the manufacturers.

If the iron overheats, or the sole plate temperature does not correspond to the setting on the dial, the thermostat needs adjusting or replacing. This, too, is a job for the trained mechanic.

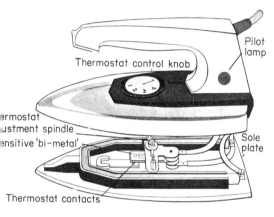

Exploded view of a thermostatically controlled electric iron, showing the sole plate with element and the thermostat contacts and adjusting device to provide variable control of the sole plate temperature

Electric toasters

An automatic (pop-up) toaster has a complicated mechanism. If the toast does not brown correctly the pop-up mechanism needs adjusting. If one side only browns either or both slices of toast, an element has failed. If the toaster does not heat, the fault is usually in the cut-out provided the flex is in order and the plug fuse has not blown.

Check the fuse and the flex, if these are not faulty have the toaster tested at the electrical shop. It is not advisable to attempt to repair the toaster yourself.

Small cooking appliances

Apart from fitting a new flex, small cooking appliances are not easy to repair without the aid of the makers' servicing manuals. If you are unable to obtain these, the appliances should be returned to the electrical shop from which they were bought.

Powered appliances

When the motor of a powered electrical appliance, having a brush-type motor, fails the trouble may be in the brushes.

If the brushes have worn down to less than about 6 mm (¼ in) they need replacing. Replacements are readily obtainable for most appliances but they must be identical replacements. If the fault is not due to the brushes or the motor is of the induction type (having no carbon brushes or commutator) one or more windings or coils may have burnt out. This can usually be detected by a smell of burning. It is best to take the complete machine to the dealers rather than attempt to remove or dismantle the power unit.

Vacuum cleaners

Apart from the flex, the most usual failure of an upright machine is belt breakage or the belt coming off the spindle. If the motor runs erratically accompanied by sparking inspect the carbon brushes and, if worn down to 6 mm, replace them.

Loss of suction is usually traced to the dust bag, or in the hose connections of the horizontal machines. When the motor of a vacuum cleaner produces an unusual noise, other than that of increased speed when a belt slips off or breaks, it should be examined by a qualified repairer.

Power tools

These have a similar motor to the vacuum cleaner; the most common fault being brush wear. Burning out of the windings is also fairly frequent and is usually caused by overloading due to misuse.

Electric mower faults

The popular low-priced rotary mowers are usually powered by a brush motor similar to that of an electric drill (power tool). Carbon brushes need replacing when they wear but the component which is likely to give the greatest concern is the thermal cut-out usually situated in the handle. The function of this is to cut off the current to the motor when there is a risk of overload when cutting very long grass.

The cut-out trips and stops the motor, but will not start again until the motor cools which may be a few minutes. If the cut-out fails then either the cut-out or motor (or both) will burn out and the machine should be taken to the dealer for repair.

If the switch fails you can usually buy a replacement. Dismantle the handle, disconnect and remove the faulty switch. If you sever the flex, either fit a new flex or join it using a proper connector designed for outdoor use.

Large electrical appliances

When major electrical appliances such as washing machines, refrigerators, freezers and cookers break down or fail it is advisable to contact the manufacturers or dealer. It is not advisable to attempt to repair these other than fitting a new flex or replacing a plug fuse.

To replace components, other than those mentioned above, usually means partly dismantling the machine. This requires special tools and the makers' servicing manual which is not made available by the majority of manufacturers.

Know your flexible cords

Flexible cords are made in a variety of types for the various appliances and situations and for lighting fittings. When rewiring a pendant or replacing a worn flex on an appliance you should choose the correct type and size. The types used in the home are listed below and the sizes are given in Table 6 on page 403.

(i) Parallel twin flexible cord

PVC insulated cores of the same colour usually of opaque white but with distinguishing ribbing or a colour stripe for one core when used with an appliance having a single-pole switch or thermostat which must be connected to the live pole. Applications include small all-insulated and double-insulated appliances such as electric clocks and also lighting fittings.

(ii) Flat twin PVC sheathed flex

PVC insulated cores, one brown, one blue enclosed in PVC sheathing of flat cross section. Is fitted to some double-insulated appliances in place of circular sheathed flex.

(iii) Circular braided flex

Vulcanised rubber-insulated cores plus cotton fillers to provide circular cross section enclosed in two-colour cotton braiding. Is fitted to many domestic appliances including, heaters, irons and kettles.

(iv) Unkinkable circular sheathed flex

Rubber-insulated cores and cotton filler enclosed in a light covering of vulcanised rubber and an overall two-colour braiding. Available in 3-core only and is fitted to electric kettles, percolators, irons and similar appliances.

(v) Circular rubber sheathed flex

Rubber-insulated cores together with fillers enclosed in black or grey vulcanised rubber sheathing. Is fitted to a wide range of appliances especially in situations subjected to fairly wide temperature variations.

(vi) Circular PVC sheathed flex

PVC insulated cores (2- and 3-core) enclosed in moulded PVC in circular cross-section but, being moulded, requires no fillers. It is very robust for indoor and outdoor use and will withstand fairly rough treatment and much flexing without kinking. Is fitted to a large range of indoor appliances in place of circular braided and circular rubber flexes, and also in lighting pendants.

Sheath colours are grey, black, white, orange and safety yellow; these last two are used with mowers and hedge trimmers.

(vii) Heat-resisting flex

A 3-core flex having butyl or EP rubber compound heat-resisting insulation. Is fitted to immersion heaters, water heaters, space heaters and to some lighting pendants.

Table 6 FLEX SIZES AND USES

Core size mm²	Current rating, A	Application
0.5	3	Lighting fittings
0.75	6	Lighting fittings; small appliances
1.0	10	Appliances up to 2000 W
1.25	13	Appliances up to 3000 W
1.5	15	Appliances up to 3500 W
2.5	20	Appliances 4500 W (max)
4.0	25	Appliances 6000 W (max)

Chapter 45
Tools

Many of the tools required for electrical work and repairs are usually those to be found in the home toolbox. Some special tools are needed as also are some instruments for testing.

Small tools for repair work

Tools required for small repairs are as follows:

    Small screwdriver.

    Medium size screwdriver.

    Pair of pliers.

    Pair of round nose pliers.

    Phillips screwdrivers for Phillips and Posidrive screws.

    Wire stripper.

    Sharp knife.

    One torch.

Tools for house wiring

Saws:

    Tenon saw for cutting floorboards.

    Rip saw for cutting tongues from T and G floorboards.

    Pad saw and blades.

    Hacksaw and blades.

Rawlplug tool and bits.

Power tool and drills (optional).

Carpenter's ratchet brace and bits.

Electrician's ratchet brace (optional) for drilling cable holes in joists.

Hammers:

A 2 lb ball pein hammer for general use.

    Medium weight hammer.

    Pin hammer for fixing cable clips.

Wood chisels:

    One 1 in chisel.

    One ½ in chisel.

Cold chisels:

    One small diameter 6 in chisel.

    Two 12 in chisels for lifting floorboards.

    Two electricians's bolster chisels for floorboard lifting, cutting chases in walls for cables and flush boxes for switched socket-outlets and other wall mounting wiring accessories.

One bradawl for piercing holes.

One pair of pipe grips for tightening cable glands.

One pair of gas pliers for tightening brass bushes in conduit boxes.

One steel tape.

One ruler.

A straight edge — this could be a straight length of timber — for marking cable runs.

One chalk line and plumb line weight for marking cable runs.

One small spirit level.

One small trowel for making good breaks in plaster.

Instruments required for testing

For testing you basically need only a neon screwdriver, a test lamp and a continuity tester.

Neon screwdriver

A neon screwdriver has a small neon lamp in the handle. When the tip of the blade comes into contact with a live terminal or wire, the neon light glows. This tells you that the terminal or wire is in the live pole of the circuit. It will also indicate that the unearthed metal frame of an electrical appliance is live to touch.

Test lamp

A test lamp is simply an electric light bulb in a lampholder with two leads connected to the lampholder terminals. It should be fitted with a wire guard. This is used to test whether there is electric current at a ceiling rose, socket-outlet or joint box.

Continuity tester

A continuity tester tests whether a fuse has blown, whether a wire has a break in it and the electrical continuity of the earth wire and earthing. The tester can be a sophisticated instrument or it can be constructed with a battery, torch bulb and bulb holder.

Chapter 46
A guide to lighting fittings

Although the primary purpose of a lighting fitting is to provide light, a fitting is exposed to view throughout the hours of daylight and it is, therefore, equally important that it is pleasing to look at when not alight. Before buying a fitting decide whether you would prefer a ceiling fitting or wall lights. If you decide on a ceiling fitting choose between a pendant or a close-mounted ceiling fitting.

Also, decide on the position of the fitting as this will also affect the choice. When choosing in the shop or department store try and visualise how a fitting would appear in your home. This is not easy when the shop has a forest of fittings, some alight and others unlit.

Planning a lighting scheme

If planning a lighting scheme from scratch you should still plan it on a room basis and in conjunction with the furnishing scheme. Remember too that panel lighting, alcove lighting, table lamps and floor standards all contribute to the quantity of lighting and will influence your choice of fittings.

Spotlights, too, have become increasingly popular but do not overdo it. Choose these later if they are to be supplementary to the main lighting to illuminate fabrics or features in a room. Also consider fluorescent lighting, but be careful with the colour rendering of different tubes or you could ruin your decorative scheme during the hours when the lights are switched on.

Types of fitting

Lighting fittings cover a vast range of types and styles with new fittings being added almost continually. The choice is therefore wide.

Lighting fittings cover five main types: Pendants; close-mounted ceiling fittings; wall lights; spotlights and bulkhead fittings.

Pendant fittings

The simplest and most commonplace pendant is the plain pendant, which is just a ceiling rose and a lampholder suspended by a flexible cord. It covers a majority of lighting fittings in the home and is made in various styles, all of which are basically similar.

Plug-in ceiling rose

A break from the conventional, is the 'plug-in' ceiling rose which has 3-pin socket as a base and a 3-pin plug for the flex connection. This assembly is contained in a moulded plastic ceiling rose cover resembling that of a conventional ceiling rose. Its function is to simplify wiring the flex and allows the pendant to be detached for cleaning.

Detachable ceiling plate

Another but similar type, is a metal plate carrying the flex which slides into the fixed portion. In addition to the cord grip type, versions are available having either a chain hook for a heavy-weight fitting or fitted with a rod for rod suspension. The function of this type is to facilitate cleaning and maintenance of the lighting fitting.

Wall mounted spotlight

3 light pendant

Pinup spotlight with cord switch

Spotlights on lighting track

Lighting fittings for a living room

Single light pendants

Apart from plain pendants, single light pendants are made in various styles and types with flex, chain or rod suspension and a variety of shades and diffusers.

Rise and fall pendants

Of more unusual interest is a rise and fall pendant enabling the height of the light, suspended by the sheathed flex, to be adjusted as required. One application is in the dining room over the dining table. As the light unit is raised the flex winds into the rise and fall unit in the ceiling plate. Matching fixed-height pendants are also available. The rise and fall principle is a development of the old rise and fall pendant operated with a system of pulleys and ballast weights.

Accent lights

This is a term applied to a range of low-level long-flex single-light pendant fittings in various colours containing a reflector lamp. These produce pools of light to put a fresh accent on coffee tables and on individual room features. They are available in a fixed version as well as the rise and fall version, with matching wall light versions.

Multi-light pendants

The main choice here covers 2- 3- and 4-light fittings as well as fittings having large numbers of small powered lamps including candle lamps. Conventional bulbs burn in the 'cap-up' or the 'cap-down' position and some have both 'cap-up' and 'cap-down' burning bulbs.

Switch control

Any multi-light fitting can be switched by more than one switch. This means that when choosing a multi-light pendant you are not committed to having all bulbs in use when you switch on the light.

Close-mounted ceiling fittings

A close-mounted ceiling fitting is necessary in situations where restricted headroom does not permit a pendant. It is also fitted in the bathroom where a flexible cord is not approved and it must not be possible for a person using the bath to be able to touch a lighting fitting.

Batten lampholder

The batten lampholder is the simplest and cheapest close-mounted fitting. It can be used with or without a shade, but in bathrooms or W.C.s and similar situations, the lampholder should be fitted with a deep HO (Home Office) pattern skirt. This prevents a person changing a bulb making contact with the metal lamp cap while the lamp is in contact with the lampholder pins. In addition to the straight batten lampholder, there are angle lampholders for fixing in situations with very little headroom or where the lamp projection is to be at a minimum. More recent developments are a swivel batten lampholder and an adjustable angle lampholder (see page 380).

Enclosed fittings

Totally-enclosed close-ceiling fittings have either a glass or a plastic light diffuser and are intended mainly for bathrooms, kitchens and similar situations including a weatherproof version for fixing out of doors. There is also a decorative range for living rooms including a range having crystal glass diffusers and also circular fluorescent fittings with the circular tube enclosed in attractive diffusers of various patterns and colours.

Some circular fluorescent fittings have an external tube with the diffuser inside the circle and mounted flush with the tube.

Downlighters

Downlighters are ceiling fittings of tubular shape alloy containing reflector bulbs or spotlights to produce pools of light on the table and floor against a dark ceiling background. They can be mounted as close-ceiling fittings but there are also versions for sinking flush with the ceiling and some are semi-recessed. The flush version, and to a lesser extent the semi-recessed version require a deep void above the ceiling.

Wallwashers

These fittings are also mounted flush with the ceiling but instead of producing pools of light on the horizontal plane, produce them on walls as part of a lighting scheme. Colour lamps and coloured walls produce the required effect.

Wall lights

Wall lights are made in single lamp and in multi-lamp versions and are available as matching accessories to the main lighting fittings.

Wall lights are available with and without integral press-button or cord-operated switches. Those having integral switches are chosen where it is desired to be able to switch individual lights on and off as required. These should be master switched by a circuit switch, as must the switchless type.

Slide-on wall lights

A range of wall lights from one manufacturer has a novel backplate enabling the fitting to be detached from the fixed backplate by sliding action. The connection between the circuit wires and the wires of the fitting is by a plug and socket arrangement.

Spotlights

A spotlight, and its associated floodlight is a special lamp or bulb having an internal reflector and mounted on a swivel bracket fitting. The fitting housing the lampholder is in various styles and colours to match the decor or to provide a pleasing effect. The lamps are made in various wattages and colours.

Sealed beam spotlights and floodlights, termed PAR 38 lamps, are intended principally for outdoor use in waterproof lampholders. These allow immersion in the garden pool but they are also being used increasingly inside the home either as supplementary or as main lighting for a room and also for discos.

Although it is basically a lighting system rather than fittings, trunking is used to provide a flexible lighting system using mainly spotlights.

Porch light fittings

The lighting fitting for the porch can be a close mounted ceiling fitting, a pendant fitting or a wall mounted light.

Close mounted fittings are mainly enclosed diffuser fittings which can also be mounted on the wall. Pendant fittings are chiefly lanterns suspended by a chain but there are many styles of pendant which can be installed in the porch where not exposed to the rain.

Wall lights are also available in lantern form; a popular unit being an imitation coach lamp.

Front porch fittings are available bearing the number or name of the house in various styles of letters or figures.

Weatherproof fittings

Outside lighting fittings exposed to rain and snow are of weatherproof construction. These are mainly bulkhead fittings or totally enclosed fittings mounted on brackets including angle brackets for corner mounting.

Chapter 47
Control of lighting and heating

Lighting in the home is controlled mainly by conventional switches fixed to the wall and operated by a dolly or a rocker which switches the light on and off. Some lights such as those in bathrooms, over the bed-head and in similar situations are controlled by cord-operated ceiling switches.

Both wall and ceiling switches are of the one-way type for single switch control, two-way for controlling a light from two different positions, and intermediate switching for controlling a light from three or more positions. The circuits for these switching arrangements are described in Chapter 3.

Two other forms of control are dimmer switches and time-lag switches.

Dimmer switches

A dimmer switch enables the light from an ordinary electric light bulb to be varied from full brilliance down to a mere glow. It is an electronic device consisting of a thyristor (or triac, which is a kind of transistor), a printed circuit and associated components. Unlike a wire wound resistor, it consumes an insignificant quantity of electricity and represents a saving in electricity even though a bulb operates at a lower efficiency at lower brilliance. By turning down the light less electricity is used though saving electricity is not the primary purpose of installing dimmer switches.

Types of dimmer switch. The top illustrations show a conventional dimmer switch giving easy control of room lighting. The centre picture shows a combined dimmer and on/off switch. A two-gang dimmer switch for controlling two lights independently from one position is shown in the lower picture

The dimmer switch is styled to match the ordinary electric light switch and as it has a standard-size faceplate it will fit the standard switch mounting box in both flush and surface versions. The dimmer can therefore replace the modern plate switch without changing the mounting box or modifying the wiring.

The dimmer switch is made in various patterns depending on the make. The majority have a rotary knob, but some have a milled edge control, whilst others have a slide control. The dimmer switch is suitable for controlling any home lighting using filament lamps, i.e. the main lighting in the living room; wall lighting; bedroom main lighting or bedhead fixed lighting; the light on the landing or in the hall. It can also be used as a night-light when required in a child's bedroom.

A dimmer switch has a maximum rated wattage, usually 200 W, 300 W or 500 W. Versions are available having ratings up to 5000 W. The 500 W version is commonly used in the home enabling multi-light fittings and groups of lights to be controlled by the one dimmer without risk of damaging it by overload.

Dimmers usually have a minimum watts rating below which they will not operate. This is usually 40 W which means that you would not use it to control a single 15 W or 25 W bulb. Where you have a light containing a small bulb you wish to control by a dimmer you can fit a higher wattage bulb.

Dimmers for 2-way switching

A more recent introduction is a dimmer switch for replacing a 2-way switch. Formerly it was necessary to fit a dimmer in addition to the conventional 2-way switch in a 2-way switching circuit.

This dimmer switch has an on/off switch housed in the same assembly as the dimmer and mounted on the same faceplate. The combination is usually a rocker switch and the dimmer control knob or slide situated side-by-side. Some makes have a single knob which provides on/off control by press-button action and rotating the knob provides the dimmer control.

The combined dimmer and on/off switch is also used for one-way control. The on/off switch enables the light to be switched on and off without disturbing the setting of the dimmer.

Combined dimming and fixed intensity switching

The combined dimmer and on/off switch has yet another function. The dimmer is used to control some of the lighting in a room and the switch is used to control lighting at fixed intensity. From the one switch, therefore, you can have a centre light under dimmer control and wall lights in the same room switched on and off at fixed intensity entirely independent of the centre light, or vice versa.

In a large lounge having a dining recess, you can have the lounge section of the lighting, centre light, or wall lights, under the control of the dimmer and a rise and fall light over the dining table switched at fixed intensity.

Multi-gang dimmers

Dimmer switches are also made in multi-gang assemblies, similar to those of conventional switches. A 2-gang unit is mounted on a one-gang plate for mounting on a one-gang box and will cover most home requirements.

Assemblies of 3-gang and more are mounted on larger plates and require larger mounting boxes. These are mainly used in applications other than the home.

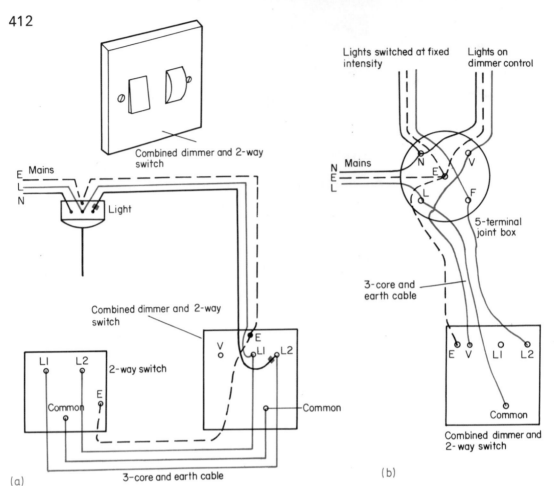

Combined dimmer and 2-way switch

Circuit wiring for (a) a combined dimmer and on/off switch and (b) when used to control dimmed lighting and fixed intensity lighting independently

Dimming portable lighting

Table lamps, floor standards, bedside lights and other portable lights can have dimmer control using any one of three methods. One method is a dimmer socket adaptor which plugs into the standard 13 A socket-outlet. This unit has two 2-pin sockets and is especially suitable for controlling two bedside lamps in a twin-bedded or a double-bedded room. The control knob on the adaptor dims both lamps at the same light intensity; they cannot be controlled independently.

Another method uses a line-cord dimmer which is wired into the flex of the lamp. The dimmer can be a standard wall type

mounted on a plastic box and placed on the arm of the chair, table, desk, or any other chosen position. Alternatively, it can be a mini-dimmer switch resembling a torpedo table lamp switch. This type is especially suitable for the individual control of bedside lamps.

The third method uses lampholder dimmer which fits most patterns of table lamps and floor standards. With this type of dimmer you 'turn down' the light as one turns down the wick of the old oil lamp.

Yet another method uses the plug-in 'Mood-setter' dimmer as produced by MK Electric Ltd.

Dimming fluorescent lighting

The ordinary dimmer switch is designed for controlling tungsten filament lighting only—electric light bulb, spotlights, architectural tubes, filament striplights, candle lamps and all other forms of filament lighting. Under no circumstances must this type of dimmer be wired into a fluorescent lighting circuit. To do so would damage the dimmer switch beyond repair.

For dimming fluorescent lighting, a purpose-made dimmer is required, as well as a special choke in the fluorescent fitting. An extra wire has to be run from the dimmer to the lighting fitting. Dimming is rarely applied to fluorescent lighting in the home. It is usually better to have auxiliary tungsten lighting in the same room and to control this by a dimmer.

Dimming striplights and spotlights

Tungsten-filament striplights are treated for the purpose of dimming exactly the same as wall lights, using the wall mounted dimmer as a master switch irrespective of whether or not the strip lights have integral switches.

Where spotlights are fitted with flexible cord for connection to a plug and socket-outlet and are to be controlled by a dimmer you can use the socket adaptor type of dimmer. It is essential to make sure that the total wattage of the spotlights does not exceed the watts rating of the dimmer. If one spotlight is supplied from one socket-outlet, there is no risk of overload.

Spotlights, which are expensive to replace, will last much longer when operated at lower output from a dimmer switch but do not sacrifice effect merely to save on lamp replacement.

Dimmer control of track lighting

Lighting tracks consisting of an alloy track which will accommodate a number of spotlights. Track lighting is being increasingly used in the home and is usually connected to the fixed wiring. When ceiling mounted, this type can be fitted with a cord-operated switch.

If dimming is required, a wall type dimmer of adequate watts rating is used.

Time delay switching

There are a number of situations in the home where it is useful to be able to control a light by a time lag switch, which will switch off a light automatically after a given interval. Examples include: the hall light, the landing light, outside the back door, in the front porch and similar situations.

A simple time lag switch is a vacuum-operated press-button device which fits the standard plate switch mounting box and will therefore replace any switch without changing the box or altering the wiring. The button is pressed to switch on the light and, after a period ranging from a few seconds to several minutes, the button pops out and the light switches off.

The period of delay is preset by means of an adjusting screw located behind the plate and cannot be tampered with without removing the switch from its box.

The time lag setting, within the limits of the model, should be fixed to suit the situation, bearing in mind that a light will switch off virtually without warning, which could be inconvenient and in some circumstances dangerous. For example, if the light suddenly went out when someone was descending the stairs an accident could result. A time lag switch suitably adjusted is excellent for providing a light in the

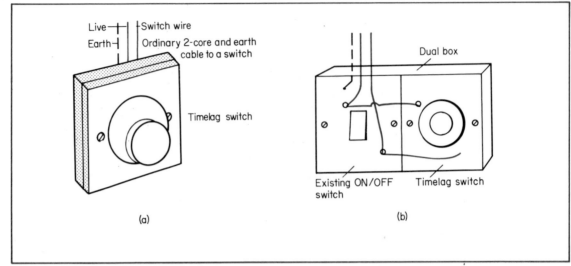

A time lag switch. (a) replaces a conventional 1-way switch. (b) wires in parallel with an existing 1-way switch and both mounted on a dual box

porch as you leave the house, go to the car or lock up for the night and in many similar circumstances. Timers providing random switching periods are also available.

Control of heating

Portable electric heaters and many fixed electric heaters are controlled by a switch or switches mounted on the frame of the heater. In addition, the heater is switched at a switched socket-outlet or switched fused connection unit or is connected to a non-switched socket-outlet which means pulling out the plug to switch off the heater.

Integral thermostat

Wall panel heaters, oil filled radiators, convectors and other heaters operating at 'black heat' have an integral thermostat which is set to the required room temperature.

Room thermostats

Where a heater has no integral thermostat, thermostatic control can be arranged by wiring a room thermostat into the circuit. Where the heater is supplied from a socket-outlet, such an arrangement is not practicable. Instead a plug-in thermostat is used, (see below).

If a fixed heater is supplied from a fused connection unit, even when supplied from the ring circuit, a room thermostat can be wired into the heater circuit as shown in the illustration. If, therefore, you have a fixed heater supplied from a socket-outlet on the ring circuit you can control it by a room thermostat by replacing the socket-outlet with a fused connection unit.

Plug-in thermostat

A plug-in thermostat is a very convenient means of providing automatic control for an electric heater. It can be used at any socket-outlet and, like the heater, can be taken from room to room, it not being

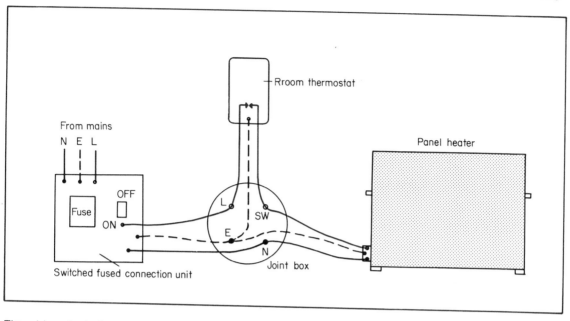

The wiring circuit for a panel heater supplied from a switched fused connection unit wired into the ring circuit and controlled by a room thermostat

A plug-in time switch used for individual control of a heater and a matching plug in thermostat also for the individual control of any one heater. By plugging one unit into both, facilities are provided at one socket outlet

necessary to have one for each room. There are a number of models available all of which have an integral socket-outlet for plugging in the heater.

It is not recommended that radiant electric fires are controlled by a thermostat. Apart from being unsatisfactory, the sudden switching on of a radiant portable fire is potentially dangerous.

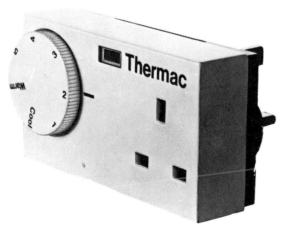

Time switches

A time switch is another form of control for electric heaters. It can be used as the sole means of control or it can be used in conjunction with a thermostat. One time switch of adequate capacity wired into a heater circuit can supply a number of electric heaters enabling a whole system of background heating to be switched on and off automatically as required. Alternatively, single heaters can be supplied from time switches each wired into the circuit.

Plug-in time switches

There are also available plug-in time switches, which like plug-in thermostats, can be used to control portable electric heaters. These too should be restricted to convectors and other heaters operating at 'black heat'. It is not advisable to control radiant electric fires from time switches.

Setting the time switch

Most time switches are provided with two switch ON periods and two switch OFF periods per 24 hours; these times being set by the user. There is also a time switch having facilities for three switch ON and OFF periods each 24 hours.

A useful arrangement of switching for background heating is as follows. First switch ON about an hour before the family get up in the morning and then switch OFF as the family leaves for work. The second switch ON about an hour before the first of the family returns home and the final switch OFF during late evening.

Over-ride switch

An over-ride switch is usually incorporated into the time switch to enable the heater,

A single wall mounted panel heater supplied from a switched fused connection unit and controlled by a wall mounted time switch

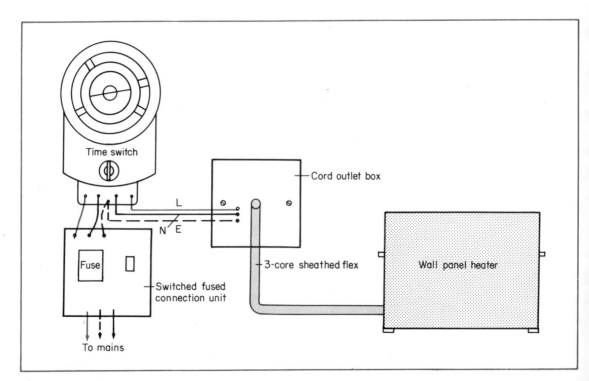

Time switch

Cord outlet box

L

N E

Fuse

Switched fused connection unit

3-core sheathed flex

Wall panel heater

To mains

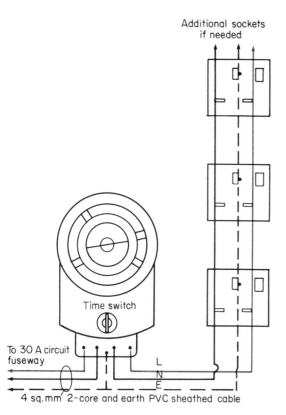

Additional sockets
if needed

Time switch

To 30 A circuit
fuseway

L
N
E

4 sq.mm 2-core and earth PVC sheathed cable

*A radial power circuit providing time switch control of
a number of panel heaters used for background heating.
Switched fused connection units may be used instead of
socket outlets*

or heaters to be used out of programmed
hours without upsetting the time switch
setting. When the time switch has no over-
ride switch, a suitable switch of the correct
current rating can be wired into the circuit.
This switch can be of 20 A, 30 A, or 45 A
and should have a pilot light as a warning
that the heating is under manual control
with the time switch temporarily inoperative
until the over-ride switch is turned off.

Combined thermostat and time switch control

The principal function of a room thermostat is to maintain a given temperature in a
room or rooms. This can be costly, for the
heating is running virtually 'flat out'. To
conserve energy and reduce one's electricity
bills a time switch can be wired into the
circuit as well. A portable thermostat and
a portable time switch can be plugged into
each other to produce the same result.

The time switch restricts the hours of
switch ON and the thermostat prevents the
temperature rising above a predetermined
level.

Non-storage electric central heating

An electric heating system comprising a
number of non-storage panel heaters and/or
oil filled radiators is available from a number
of makers as a complete package. The heaters (or radiators) are controlled from a
central control panel to restrict the heat
output though providing adequate warmth
in the various rooms.

The most recent development is a combined storage and non-storage heater. The
main heating is from the storage block,
charged at the overnight cheaper rate. But
when this is exhausted during the latter
part of the day, the direct acting non-
storage heater in the same heating unit is
switched on automatically at the control
panel.

Zone control

Packaged electric central heating systems
which includes zone controllers are also
available. These zone controllers provide
different switching periods for bedroom
and daytime rooms.

A typical zone controller has two time
switches. One is used for the bedroom
heating to switch on during the night time.
The other switches on the heating in
living rooms.

Chapter 48
Hints on safety

Most, if not all, people know that mains electricity in the home is lethal. This means that if you come into contact with a live terminal, live wire or metalwork, which because of a fault is charged with electricity, you will receive an electric shock which could be fatal.

Electricity at the mains voltage of 240 V is present at every ceiling rose, lampholder, switch, socket outlet and other outlets. It is also present at every electrical appliance connected to the mains when plugged into a socket outlet and the switched socket is 'ON'.

Every cable and wire of an installation, except the earth conductors, carries electric current at mains voltage, so should you accidentally sever a cable or damage its insulated sheath you are likely to make contact with a live conductor and receive an electric shock. With more than 15 million homes in Britain receiving a supply of electricity from the mains and these having an estimated average of 25 appliances each it may seem surprising that the number of deaths due to electrical accidents per year is usually below 80. Although these are tragic and bring much distress to the families concerned, they are but a tiny portion of the 8000 deaths arising from all accidents in the home each year. This figure usually exceeds the number killed in road accidents. In the main electrical accidents can be regarded as avoidable and are often due to carelessness.

The relatively few deaths from electrocution are due principally to the high quality of cables and wiring accessories which are made to rigid British Standards designed to prevent wires and contacts being exposed to touch when properly installed. As we have seen in the relevant sections of this book, modern switches and other accessories have high quality moulded plastic faceplates whereas older switches have easily removable screw-on covers which expose the terminals.

Socket-outlets and ceiling roses were usually of porcelain which readily fractured and exposed the live terminals. Flexible cords are now sheathed instead of being merely insulated, wiring cables have a tough PVC sheath. Modern mounting boxes, which have replaced the old wood blocks, ensure that the unsheathed ends of cables are totally enclosed in non-combustible material as are the contacts and terminals of the accessories connected to the cables.

Danger from fire

Although deaths from electrocution are relatively rare, the same cannot be said about fire. Many fires in the home have been traced to bad or overloaded wiring, though these do not necessarily result in deaths. In fact many of the fires reported as electrical are caused by fats and oils igniting in cooking utensils left unattended on the cooker. Such fires also occur on gas cookers and although this does not excuse accidents from electric cookers it is necessary to get the right perspective. There are however many fires caused by electricity, which being small and extinguished by householders, have not been reported and do not appear in official reports.

Causes of fire and shock

The principal causes of fire and shock from electrical installations are faulty wiring the misuse of appliances and using appliances which are no longer safe.

Faults on appliances can usually be eliminated by periodic inspection but the misuse of appliances is within the hands of the householder and his family. Faulty wiring is more complicated but this too can be rectified by periodic inspections.

DIY wiring and safety

The do-it-yourself enthusiast has, in the past, often been blamed for fires and electric shock accidents due to faulty wiring installations and to incorrect procedures being followed.

Although there is some justification for this and the facts have been substantiated by official reports, there is evidence to show that most amateurs are responsible people and take great care when dealing with electricity. It cannot be disputed that the householder carrying out his own work, whether electrical or other forms of home improvement, is likely to be extremely conscientious. The householder having good mechanical aptitude, experienced in doing jobs about the house, using good quality cables and wiring accessories and carrying out the work in accordance with the information in this book, need have no fear that the finished job will be safe and can be expected to pass any inspections and tests carried out by the electricity board when connecting the wiring to the mains supply.

Never add more lights or socket-outlets to circuits or to parts of a circuit than those specified or you will risk overloading a circuit.

In the interests of safety, though with some repetition from the previous chapters the following summarises the principal points which should be observed when carrying out electrical installation work.

Bathrooms

Take particular care in the bathroom where special regulations apply.

Do not install a socket-outlet in the bathroom other than an approved shaver supply unit for a mains voltage shaver.

Do not make provision for using a mains voltage portable appliance. For example do not run a portable electric heater from a socket-outlet situated outside the bathroom i.e. on the landing or in an adjacent bedroom. If the tank cupboard opens into the bathroom and the tank has an immersion heater do not supply it from a socket-outlet (not a good method in any case) which could be used for plugging in a portable appliance.

Do not have open lampholders in the bathroom where the bulb could be removed and a hair dryer or other appliance plugged in.

Ensure that all switches in bathrooms and washrooms are of the cord-operated type (except, of course, a shaver supply unit). Where this is not practicable, ensure such a switch is out of reach of a person using the bath or shower; this may mean fixing the switch outside the bathroom door.

Do not have a lighting fitting situated over the bath where it could be reached by a person attempting to replace a faulty bulb, standing in the bath.

Make sure that lampholders, even when in an enclosed fitting, have a deep (HO) skirt so that it is not possible to touch the metal lamp cap while the lamp is still making contact with live pins.

Pay particular attention to striplights such as are fixed over a shaving mirror. These designed for bathrooms have shielded lampholders so that the lamp caps cannot be touched when replacing a lamp. Flexible cord pendants must not be fixed in a bathroom.

Where appropriate, bond to earth any extraneous metalwork.

Flexible cords

Flexible cords which are the means for connecting portable appliances and lights to fixed wiring are among the most likely source of accidents.

When renewing flexible cords on appliances make certain that the flex used in each instance is of the correct size and type. If too small (conductor size) it will be overloaded and could result in a fire. If of the wrong type there may be a risk of mechanical damage or in high ambient temperatures the insulations may be damaged.

Do not use twisted twin non-sheathed flex for appliances ana wherever possible use sheathed flex on lighting pendant fittings. Do not 'repair' frayed flex with insulation tape but replace the flex when showing signs of damage or wear.

Do not run flexible cord under carpets or other floor coverings.

Under no circumstances use flexible cord for fixed wiring.

Do not connect 3-core flex to a 2-pin plug. The latter is used only with all-insulated and double insulated appliances having no earthing facilities.

Use 2-core flex only for double insulated and all-insulated appliances and for appropriate lighting fittings. Where 2-core flex is connected to a 3-pin plug make sure that the two cores (brown and blue or red and black) are connected respectively to the live and neutral pins of the plug, leaving the earth pin without a connection.

Keep flexes as short as possible when connected to domestic appliances and avoid using multi-plug adaptors. These usually result in long trailing flexes, which apart from risk of damage to the sheathing, are a hazard especially to the elderly and the very young.

Do not have the flex of an electric iron, or even of a kettle too short. This will resul in undue strain on the flex.

When connecting flex to its plug or t the appliance, ensure that the sheath is wel secured under the clamp so that any strai on the flex will not pull the flex from it anchorage and sever the conductors at th terminals.

Take care that a flex does not droo over a radiant electric fire or that a kettl flex does not come into contact with cooker hot-plate or gas ring.

Handle with care the flex of your vacuur cleaner and do not drag the cleaner alon by its flex.

Take care that the washing machine doe not run over its flex when moving it abour in the kitchen.

Do not extend the flex of your powe tool; the plug should always be withi reach when using the tool. When you neec a longer flex use an extension flex on drum fitted with a socket-outlet.

Take particular care of the flex whe using an electric mower or hedge trimmer These flexes are usually either orange o safety yellow in colour to reduce th possibility of the mower running over th flex or the hedge trimmer cutting it. Th flex tends to get dragged through ros bushes and shrubs and other obstacles whicl will damage the sheath. You should there fore inspect the sheathing at the end o each mowing or hedgecutting session or i you suspect damage when using thes garden tools.

Repairing damaged long flexible cords

If the sheath of these long flexes is damaged it is practically impossible to effect a satis factory repair. Unless the damage is nea one end you will not wish to sacrifice an of the flex by cutting off a portion. Yo can obviate this by using a weatherproof fixed connector. This needs to be water resistant where it is likely to be drawn through wet grass. The connector will form an obstacle and will need more care when using the mower or hedge cutter.

Lamps and lighting

Do not fit a high wattage bulb into a shade or fitting designed for bulbs of lower ratings. Some shades give the maximum wattage but if there is no indication, restrict the wattage to 60 W or preferably 40 W. Otherwise overheating may occur and the shade material either melt or ignite. Damage can also be done to the fixed wiring by transference of heat through the lamp-holders; this is particularly the case if it is a close ceiling fitting. Damage can also be done to the flex, if pendant and the flex is not of the heat-resisting type.

Take particular care when replacing a bulb in a wall light if the light is not independently switched. If the light has only an integral cord switch or a press button switch, there is usually no means of knowing whether the switch is ON or OFF when the bulb has failed.

Do not leave lampholders empty for this represents a shock risk. If you have no spare bulb, leave the old bulb in the lampholder.

Do not add flex extensions to a ceiling rose designed for only one flexible cord.

Do not use twin lampholder adaptors for running an appliance from the light. Apart from putting undue strain on the pendant flex the appliance is likely to over-load the lighting circuit.

Electric heaters

Scorching and fire are the principal hazards associated with electric heaters, particularly radiant heaters and all portable electric heaters.

The first rule of safety is to ensure that a radiant heater is fitted with a correct dress guard. Modern heaters are fitted with the approved guard to prevent a person poking a finger through the mesh as well as to prevent fabrics falling on or brushing the elements and catching fire. Radiant heaters not fitted with approved pattern dress guards should be scrapped.

Periodically check that the fixtures securing the guard have not loosened and that none of the wires of the mesh are broken or have become distorted.

Never stand a portable radiant heater, when switched off, against furniture or fabric or place it facing a wall even when the plug is out of the socket. There is always a risk of someone inserting the plug by mistake and causing scorching and possibly a fire.

Replace a broken element without delay for, not only may stray ends or parts of the rod touch the reflector, but a child may insert a metal object or be able to touch the broken end with a finger and receive a fatal shock.

Do not use a radiant fire with an element missing because the live contacts become a potential hazard when the switch is on without the hot element acting as a warning.

Replace a 'dud' lamp of a fuel effect fire as soon as it fails for this also serves as the necessary pilot light and a warning that the flex is live when the plug is in the socket.

Do not attempt to replace an element or remove a dress guard of a fixed heater without first turning off the main switch if the heater is not supplied from a plug and socket enabling the plug to be withdrawn.

Never place clothing or other materials to dry over the grille of a convector heater, fan heater or storage heater.

Do not let fabrics fall on to tubular and skirting heaters for this would cause a build up of temperature resulting in scorching and possibly a fire. Also do not let curtains come into contact with this type of heater.

Take particular care in the choice and positioning of heaters in a nursery. Babies are likely to throw clothes on to a free standing convector and can be burned by radiant fires even when these are mounted on the wall at high level but easily reached from a displaced cot.

Cookers

Always switch off the control before cleaning a cooker even if it is not being dismantled.

Do not let metal cooking foil come into contact with spiral type elements.

Take care if the cooker is mounted on wheels and likely to be interfered with by youngsters.

Never leave fat in a pan unattended on a hotplate and take care with the position of handles of vessels containing boiling liquid in the presence of children.

Do not attempt to remove pieces of broken toast from a toaster using a knife or other metal object. Pull out the plug before releasing the obstruction.

Kettles

Do not stand a switched-on electric kettle on the cooker where the flex is likely to drape over a hotplate.

Always switch off at the socket when filling the kettle and do not leave the flex plugged in with the exposed kettle connector removed from the kettle and lying on the work top or table.

Do not leave a non-automatic kettle switched on when answering a call at the door or the telephone or when 'popping upstairs for a second'.

If you replace a slow standard element by a high-speed element, wait until the kettle boils before leaving the kitchen as you may under-estimate the speed of boiling. All kettles have thermal cutouts but if yours fails to operate, a serious fire could result if unattended.

Electric blankets

Buy only a blanket having the British Standard Kitemark. It is now an offence for anyone in Britain to sell a blanket not bearing this symbol.

Follow the makers instructions on fitting and using a new blanket and have every blanket inspected by the makers every three years at least.

Get rid of old blankets and cut off the flex so they are unable to be used again.

Never switch on a mains voltage under blanket when the bed is occupied. An over blanket may be switched on when the bed is occupied but it must not be used as an under blanket.

Repairs to appliances

Always pull out the plug before repairing or making adjustments to any electrical appliance and where there is no socket outlet, switch off at the mains. Do not attempt any repairs beyond your capabilities and then only in conjunction with makers servicing instructions for other than simple appliances.

Periodically check the cover securing screw of each plug; if the cover comes off as you pull out the plug (or inserted it) you are likely to touch the live terminals

Section 5

Home Decorating

Introduction to Section 5

There is nothing new in the desire to decorate our homes. It dates back to our cave-man ancestors and their very descriptive wall paintings. What is relatively new is the vast industry that has grown up to supply tools and materials to the home owner. This has made decorating easier, faster and more attractive.

There are really two main reasons for decorating. One is to make the place look nice and the other is the need to preserve the fabric and prevent deterioration by the elements. The second reason is the more important as, given a chance, damp in many forms will cause endless trouble. So, whatever you plan to do, bear in mind that one needs to preserve as well as beautify.

This section assumes that your home is in a reasonable state of repair. If it is not, you will need to study Section 1.

Choice of decor is a very personal

Accurate records and advance planning will bring a sense of order to your decorating programme

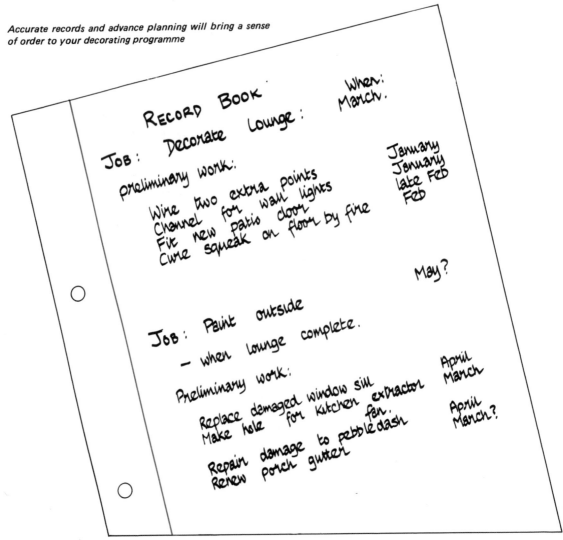

RECORD BOOK

JOB: Decorate Lounge: When: March.

Preliminary work:

Wire two extra points — January
Channel for wall lights — January
Fit new patio door — late Feb
Cure squeak on floor by fire — Feb

JOB: Paint outside   May?
— when lounge complete.

Preliminary work:

Replace damaged window sill — April March
Make hole for kitchen extractor fan. — March
Repair damage to pebbledash — April March?
Renew porch gutter

matter, and we are in the main far too cautious. Do not be afraid to experiment with new colours, textures, patterns and materials. It is useful to find a showroom where room sets incorporate these new materials. It always pays to experiment in a small way first, so that you can gauge what the overall effect will look like. In this way you will not spend a lot of money on something that you may not enjoy living with.

Modern materials make change far easier than in earlier times, so one can think of redecorating a room such as the lounge after two or three years. For example, easy-strip vinyls enable you to strip a whole room in a matter of minutes, and you are ready to hang a pre-pasted alternative, or give the remaining lining paper a couple of coats of quick drying water-based paint. The job is easier, far quicker, and a lot less messy than it was in the past.

Whatever you intend doing, work to a plan. A record book is invaluable, for in it you can set out what has to be done, with a rough working timetable. Your schedule can of course be varied as necessary, but at least you have something to work to. Big jobs, like decorating the outside, need holiday periods if the work is to be completed in reasonable time. Small jobs, like decorating the spare bedroom can be fitted into odd days and evenings without causing too much disruption. Kitchens and bathrooms need a short concerted effort, or the family routine will grind to a very strained halt!

Painting window frames means the windows must be left open while the paint hardens. Paint dries far faster in the late spring and summer but, when painting the exteriors remember that mid-summer is also the time of dust and flying insects. Late spring and early autumn offer less problems.

These points are made only to illustrate the kind of factors which can influence your timetable. Having decided what to do—roll up our sleeves and make a start!

The photographs used in this section are by courtesy of Crown Decorative Products

Chapter 49 Colour and pattern

Choice of colour is of course a very personal matter, but even so there is a psychological significance which affects us all whatever our taste. It is certainly worth keeping some basic ideas in mind when choosing colour schemes.

Grey is a very much neglected colour, but it can give a feeling of spaciousness, and it is a very good foil for splashes of brighter colours. As it is neutral, it makes a good background for colour changes as it blends with most colours. It is also a very practical colour where grubby fingers are involved, and it goes well with very modern furniture with chrome frames and black seats.

Blue is looked upon as a cool colour, and again it has the ability to make small spaces look larger. It is restful and relaxing and will have the effect of calming down busy living areas. Dark blue can look most effective, though, like most bold colours, it is best used in small areas—such as one wall dark blue and three white.

Green, and particularly the warmer greens, is a very satisfying summery colour conjuring up pictures of the countryside. A lime green has far more sharpness to it and goes well with a modern lifestyle. It is a restful colour too and is ideal as a base colour for the lounge.

Orange is a lively colour, and is one of those colours which close in a room rather than extend it. It is not particularly restful on its own, but it combines well with browns and rusts. This is the colour that will brighten a north facing bedroom, or add warmth to a cold basement area.

Yellow can be cool or warm, according to the tone chosen, and those colours nearer the orange end will bring sunshine into the colder north facing rooms. It combines well with the rusts, browns and green to give a feeling of security and warmth.

Pink and red. Pink is a pretty colour which will warm a cheerless area, and which is unbeatable as a base colour in a girl's bedroom. Reds are far from restful, but which can, in small quantities, add zest to the decorating. Red will go well in the nursery—but not as the main colour in the kitchen where it can become overpowering when considerable time is spent looking at it. Red will also make the larger room look smaller. or lower a high ceiling.

Mauve and lilac. These are gracious, elegant colours and give an air of spaciousness which goes well with traditional furniture and furnishings. Add a little vibrant colour, if you wish to wake the place up.

Patterns

Apart from colour, pattern has its effect too. Heavy bold stripes may look good in a pattern book, but they may give you a restless feeling in large quantities. Then there is the practical problem in that if walls are out of true, stripes will quickly highlight the trouble. Watch out for patterns which, in small areas, seem to have no stripe, but when a whole wall is covered, a definite stripe pattern is clearly seen.

Vertical stripes will make a room look taller, and tend to shorten it. Horizontal stripes have the reverse effect. Bold patterns with very large designs are best kept for large rooms. In a small area they can be stifling, making the walls close in on you. They can also be quite wasteful if a very large repeat is involved. If you are looking

426

for something restful avoid large patterns with a sense of movement. Sailing ships on a very rough sea, for example, are not necessarily ideal at breakfast-time in the dining room!

At the other extreme, examine fine detail bright patterns at a distance. What may appear at close quarters as a bright pattern of summer flowers can appear as a khaki mess at a range of 5 m (16 ft).

First, decide how you will allocate pattern, for you can over-do things. A floral paper may call for a plain carpet; or you may prefer floral curtains and carpet and a very plain paper. Bear in mind the colour of the furniture covers; for best effect it is worth making up a very simple model out of an old shoe box, painting in the colours and patterns, to see how it all goes together. There are few of us who can really visualise what a complete room will look like unless it is presented to us in some visual form.

Do not forget to include smallish items like cushions and lampshades. These can add a wonderful splash of colour to an otherwise lifeless room.

Textures have a part to play too, particularly where a plain colour is required. It can be plain yet attractively textured, and if wall lights or spotlights are used carefully, the whole surface can be made to live.

Finally, as you plan, keep your lighting in mind. For example, darkish shades of brown and rust may be very restful, but they absorb light very readily. So, for those occasions when one may wish to read, write or do hobbies, you will need perhaps more light available in the form of standard lamp, table lamps and wall lights. At the other end of the scale, a particularly pale colour scheme with lots of pastels and whites do not need masses of light overall or it will look like a hospital operating theatre. It needs areas of lighting which can be subdued—perhaps by dimmer switches—for those occasions when a restful atmosphere is required. (Lighting is covered in Section 4.)

Chapter 50
Tools

The quality of your decorating will be influenced by three main factors. The right tools; the time you give to preparation of surfaces, and the use of good quality materials.

In this chapter we will deal with the tools, then devote separate chapters to materials and preparation.

The gathering together of a first class

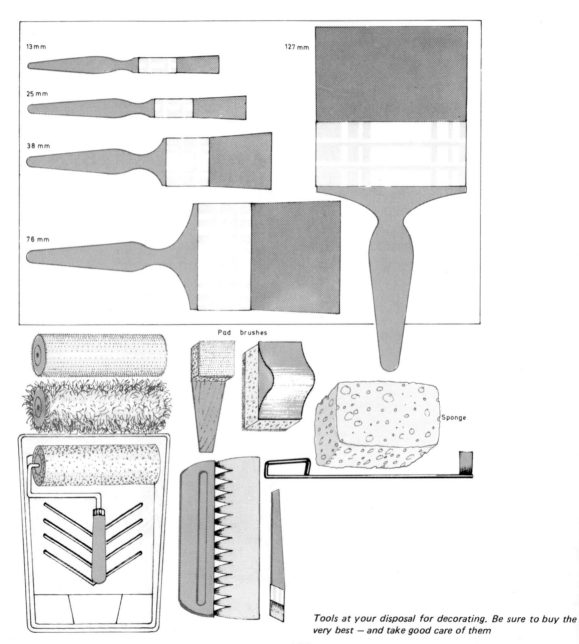

13 mm

25 mm

38 mm

76 mm

127 mm

Pad brushes

Sponge

Tools at your disposal for decorating. Be sure to buy the very best — and take good care of them

kit of tools is always a problem for the couple just making a start, and there is a temptation to buy cheap so you can get more things. Avoid this at all costs and buy the very best—even if in the meantime you have to borrow certain items from members of your family. Poor quality tools produce poor finishes, and it does not take long to recognise the difference.

For example, a cheap brush will contain a minimum of bristle, it will be poorly shaped, and the bristle may be poorly anchored so that as you use it bristles are pulled out and deposited on your work. Some brushes will be bulked with artificial fibres which have not the qualities of a natural bristle, so the holding power of the brush is impaired. On some brushes the metal ferrule may be a poor fit on the handle. All these faults add up to a poor finish.

A good brush, properly cared for, will give almost endless service. Even when its bristles have worn short, it will still serve for applying primers and, perhaps finally, as your favourite dusting brush.

Some of the tools you will need for decorating are as follows.

Brushes

There is a wide size range of brushes, but for most jobs a 13 mm (½ in), 25 mm (1 in) and 38 mm (1½ in) will do for frames. For larger areas like flush doors, use at least a 50 mm (2 in) and preferably a 76 mm (3 in), brush so that you cover quickly. A smaller brush will lead to ugly dry edges which are impossible to disguise. For wall surfaces use a 100 mm (4 in) or 127 mm (5 in) brush so that you cover quickly.

You also need a dusting brush for removing dust after rubbing down. This can either be brought specially, or an old

well worn brush can be kept just for this job. Never use a dusting brush for painting!

For smoothing paper in place you need a smoothing brush, which needs to be kept dry and clean; for modern vinyls, a sponge is better than a brush. For applying paste to wallcoverings you will need a pasting brush, and here again, it is wise to keep a brush just for this use.

Obviously it is wise to have more than one of each type of brush. For example, when painting, use a newish brush for priming and undercoating so that if it sheds a few bristles they can be rubbed off. After a few careful uses, the brush can be promoted to finishing coats.

Paint pads

Although the pad has been available for very many years, it has had very slow acceptance, perhaps because of its unusual design. Basically the paint pad consists of a fine mohair pad mounted on a layer of foam, which in turn is stuck to a handle. Only the mohair is loaded with paint, which is then applied to the surface to be painted.

Paint pads are best for large areas of work and will quickly coat walls and ceilings, whether textured or plain. A wide range of sizes is available. Small pads on short handles for frames, and larger ones on longer handles for walls and ceilings. Some have a hollow handle which will take a broom handle to extend your reach. With all pad work it is wise to have a small paintbrush handy to touch in small areas where the pad does not reach properly.

Pads should be kept for use only with water-based paint materials—emulsions, acrylic gloss and water-based vinyls. This means the pads can be cleaned in water. Oil-based materials involving the use of chemical cleaners can mean damage to the

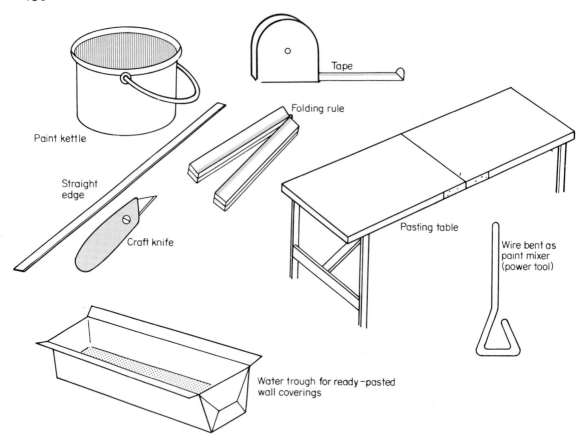

Paint kettle

Straight edge

Craft knife

Tape

Folding rule

Pasting table

Wire bent as paint mixer (power tool)

Water trough for ready–pasted wall coverings

Tools you will need. A pasting table is not necessary when using pre-pasted wallcoverings

adhesive bond between pad and foam or foam and handle, causing the pad to curl away. In other words, they will handle gloss paints very well—but the resultant cleaning of the pad brush is hard.

With the pads will come a tray in which to hold paint; though a flat baking tin is a good substitute. Some pads come with a deep trough, used as a reservoir, and a plastic drum which picks paint from the trough and transfers it to the roller. This gives an accurate measure of paint, ensuring the pad does not pick up too much.

It is unwise to leave pads loaded with paint after use. The mohair is so fine that it soon hardens. Make a habit of washing out your pads after each session; this saves a great deal of trouble subsequently.

Paint rollers

The paint roller is now a well established tool in the field, and incidentally developed especially for it. There are three basic types available.

Foam. Among the cheaper tools, the foam roller gives a reasonable finish, though it does tend to spatter due to its cellular structure. It is better for emulsions than for use with oil-based paints. Because the sleeve slips off the central core, cleaning is easy, and replacement of a worn sleeve equally simple.

Mohair. This type of roller has a hard central core with a fine mohair pile stuck to it. This makes it ideal for applying thin coats to flat surfaces, and it will give a good finish to gloss coats. It is not much use on textured surfaces, as the short pile will not reach into hollows. The pile is not easy to clean as the sleeve cannot be removed; because of the delicate nature of the pile, never leave a mohair roller loaded with paint. Clean the roller as soon as work stops.

Lambswool or nylon pile. This is the most popular type of roller, and it comes in a number of varieties. A short pile will give a good finish on plain or textured surfaces, but from a cleaning point of view it is best to keep it to water-based paints. A long, shaggy, pile roller is ideal for highly textured surfaces such as pebbledash or textured ceiling finishes, though it will not give such a smooth coating. If you need a roller for outdoor use, buy one designed for this purpose; it will have a tougher, more durable pile.

Paint trays are usually supplied with a roller kit. The tray is designed to combine a paint well with a sloping area where the roller can be run to spread the paint and discard any surplus. The thinner the paint, the easier it is to transfer to the roller.

Apart from standard decorating rollers, special thin versions are available for getting at awkward spots, such as behind pipes and radiators. These may only be stocked by the larger decorator's suppliers.

Aerosol paints

These are classed as tools, as you really buy a miniature paint sprayer along with your paint. The aerosol is best suited to small, intricate jobs such as painting a wicker chair or a wrought iron gate.

The can has a limited capacity, and the paint has to be extra-thin to come out of the very fine nozzle, so it is not suited to larger areas such as doors. (see also paint spray guns later in this chapter).

Scrapers

These fall into two main categories. There is the very sharp bladed variety designed for rapid paint stripping without the use of chemical stripper. It can be rather harsh, but on surfaces like banister rails it is very effective if care is taken not to tear the wood. It certainly saves on chemical stripper and it avoids the possible scorching by blowtorch. Replaceable blades are available, but be careful when checking whether a blade is sharp! Do not use your fingers!

The second type of scraper has a flexible blade designed to ease wallpaper from the wall after softening. It can also be used for scraping cellulose filler smooth once set, and for removing scraps of paper remaining on the wall after stripping. Do not sharpen the blade; a square edge is preferable.

The shave-hook is really of the same family, though it is not flexible. Two main types are available; pear shaped, for tackling mouldings, and triangular for flat surfaces. Again, a sharp square edge is preferable to a sharpened edge.

Filling knife

This is really a thin bladed scraper, designed to flex well. It is made for spreading and levelling filler used for hiding cracks and gaps in wood and plaster.

Plumb bob

This is merely a weight fixed to the end of a length of twine, it is designed to give a true vertical when marking to hang the first length of wallcovering. Types vary from a simple pear-shaped bob to one fitted with scriber or pencil.

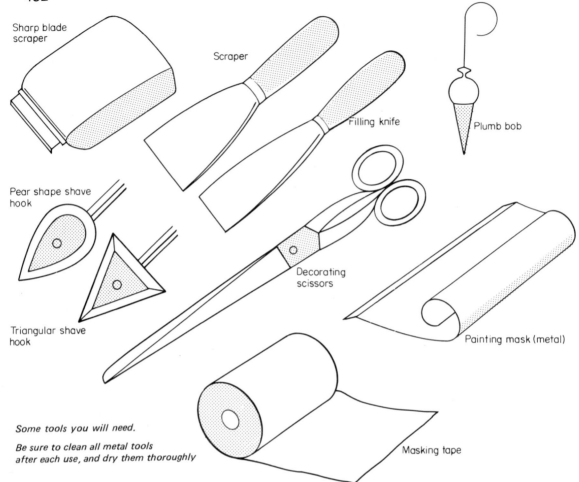

Sharp blade scraper

Scraper

Filling knife

Plumb bob

Pear shape shave hook

Decorating scissors

Triangular shave hook

Painting mask (metal)

Some tools you will need.

Be sure to clean all metal tools after each use, and dry them thoroughly

Masking tape

Scissors

A good pair of decorators' scissors is essential when papering. They are used for pre-cutting to length and trimming after hanging. One of the principal uses was for removing the selvedge. or protective edge, from rolls of wallpaper, but now, almost without exception, this selvedge is already cut off. Even so, a good pair of scissors ensures a neat finish.

A smaller pair of scissors may be added to deal with the small fiddling jobs, such as cutting around ceiling roses and light switches. Decorating scissors should not be used for any other cutting jobs, or their edges will soon become dulled and they will tear rather than cut—especially when paper is wet.

Painting mask

This is useful for keeping paint where it belongs, the mask being laid on the area not to be painted. A typical use is on the glass of a window while the frame is painted—allowing just a few millimetres of paint on the glass to seal the gap between glass and putty.

Special masking tape is also available for masking long runs, such as between a cove cornice and a wall being painted. The adhesive used is a special quick release one which will not pull a decorative surface, or leave adhesive behind. Transparent adhesive tape should never be used for masking. It will probably pull off paint—or in some cases leave it's adhesive behind.

Tack or tacky rag

This is a special duster impregnated with resin, making the rag tacky but not sticky. It is ideal to use when fine finishing, to pick up traces of dust and dirt prior to painting.

However the rag should only be used after dusting with a dusting brush, or it will clog up too quickly.

Glasspaper

You will need a selection of grades of glasspaper, ranging from coarse to very fine, or flour grade. For fine finishing you can get a waterproof type which, if used with a little water, will give a very smooth surface without creating a lot of dust. Known as 'wet or dry', it is often found in shops supplying materials for car body repair.

You will need a sanding block around which to wrap the glasspaper; a cork block is ideal and there are also blocks available which grip the paper.

Power tools

Power tools can be used for sanding, and you will encounter three basic methods.

Disc sander. A simple rubber disc designed to hold a sheet of abrasive. It is suitable for rubbing down timber where appearance does not matter too much for, however used, it tends to scratch across the wood grain. When used on painted surfaces the disc will very quickly clog, as the friction produces heat, which in turn melts the paint. There are variations on the disc but the same basic problems remain.

Orbital sander. An attachment which holds an abrasive pad, but which works with a very fine reciprocal movement. It produces a fine finish with scratches of such fine proportions as to be invisible in normal use. It is designed for fine finishing, and it is not intended for removal of material in quantity. It is not ideal for paint removal.

Drum sander. As the name applies, it is based upon a foam plastic drum to which is fitted a belt of abrasive, held in place by a heat-melted wax. A variety of grades of abrasive are available, and because of the direction of rotation the drum can be directed along the grain of the wood so that no scratches are visible. With a coarse abrasive, it will remove paint, where, because of the drum size, the abrasive is not overheated. So, it does not clog like the disc. This is by far the best tool for smoothing.

Paint kettle

This is a good old traditional tool, but with a very sensible use. It is merely a container with carrying handle, for a quantity of paint for immediate application. It makes carrying easy especially when working from a ladder, and it ensures that should anything contaminate the paint—masonry dust or falling leaves—it only affects the paint in use.

If you only have one paint kettle and you plan to change colours, lining the kettle with foil will make it easy to clean. In fact no cleaning should be necessary.

The traditional kettle was metal, but a plastic one is perfectly acceptable.

Rags

These are hardly a tool, but plenty of clean, lint-free rag is necessary when painting—particularly for wiping up splashes as they occur. Wet paint is easily removed; dry paint is not.

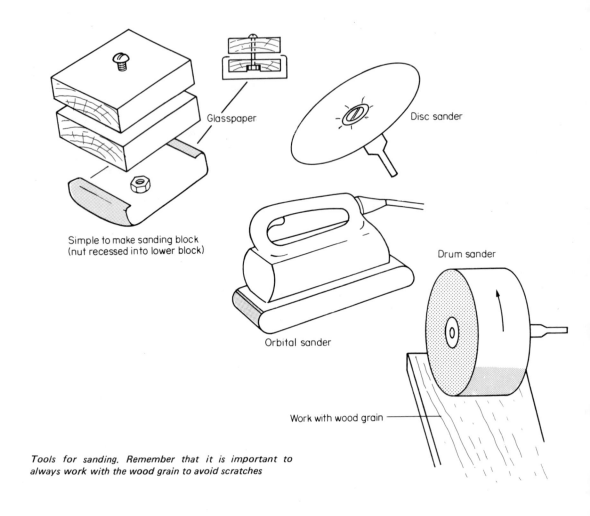

Glasspaper

Disc sander

Simple to make sanding block
(nut recessed into lower block)

Drum sander

Orbital sander

Work with wood grain

Tools for sanding. Remember that it is important to
always work with the wood grain to avoid scratches

Chalk line

You can buy a chalk line stored in a special container, but for home use a simple length of string rubbed with a piece of coloured chalk is usually adequate.

It is used for snapping a mark on a ceiling to indicate where the first length goes, or similarly on a floor to mark a centre line for floor tiles.

You need a tack one end to hold the line to a measured mark or marks on the ceiling; pull it taut with one hand, and snap it smartly with the other.

Tape measure

For decorating, choose the longest measure you can get. It saves double or treble measurements, when error can creep in. Use metal or reinforced plastic tape—not the cotton tape type measure used for dressmaking.

A folding boxwood rule will also be useful for measuring shorter distances, such as marking measurements on a piece of wallcovering. If you have to use a tape, one with a little lock on it which stops the tape retracting will make work easier.

Pasting table

Some form of table is essential if you are using the traditional papering system. Good folding tables are available which makes storage easier when the table is not required. If one is not available, a flush door with the door furniture removed and rested over a couple of stout boxes is a good alternative.

Paint stirrers

It is vital that paint is thoroughly mixed before use, especially if it has been standing for any length of time. You can buy paint stirring rods, but a flat piece of stick, or an old long-bladed knife will do. For small tins use lolly sticks, washed and dried, rescued from the children.

A power tool may be used for stirring, in which case you need to buy a stirring rod, or you can bend a piece of stiff wire to shape. Always ensure the rod is in the paint before the tool is started, and make sure it comes to rest before the stirrer is withdrawn!

The exception to the above is with thixotropic, or jelly paints; these need no mixing before use. If in doubt, read the directions on the can.

Paint strainer

Certain hardware or painters' supply shops will supply paint strainers for removing skin and bits from paint, but for normal home use, a piece of well washed nylon stocking stretched over a tin will do.

Alternatively, make the piece big enough to push down into the paint, then secure around the tin with elastic bands. You can then pick up paint from within the piece of stocking.

Do not strain your paint until it has been thoroughly mixed. Often, oils gather under a paint skin—and this oil is a necessary ingredient.

Safety goggles

For jobs like wire brushing rusted areas, rubbing down walls, or applying chemicals like paint strippers, it pays to wear protective glasses. These can be purchased from tool shops in two types. A small variety which fit close to the eyes, and larger models designed to go over existing glasses if you happen to wear them.

Do not rely on ordinary glasses for jobs like cutting paving slabs. Flying pieces can badly chip glass, even if they do not actually break it. For jobs such as applying chemicals, motorcycling goggles could be used.

Dust sheets

Often it is not possible to remove all furniture from a room when decorating. In this case cover the remaining items with dust sheets. The best type is the cotton sheet as it is absorbent enough to hold light splashing.

Polythene sheets are available, but remember water will run down and gather on the sheet, and wet polythene is very slippery. Dust sheets can also be used to protect tiles on porches, or flower borders, when working on the exterior.

Blowlamps/blowtorches

The standard blowlamp which burns paraffin and needs regular refilling, has gone out of favour in recent years, though it still offers an economical method of paint stripping. Its main problem was getting it lit after filling—especially in cold, windy conditions. Nowadays the bottled gas blowtorch is favoured, though one has to pay for the privilege of extra convenience.

The simplest type is lit by a match or gas lighter, but the latest types have a built-in crystal igniter operated by a simple trigger.

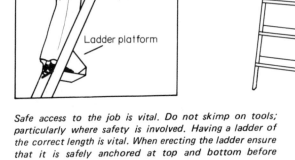

Traditional blowlamp

Blowtorch

Choose a ladder which extends
3 rungs above gutter level

This ladder has rubber suction
cups to prevent slipping

Step ladder with
hand rail

Combined ladder/steps

Ladder platform

*Safe access to the job is vital. Do not skimp on tools;
particularly where safety is involved. Having a ladder of
the correct length is vital. When erecting the ladder ensure
that it is safely anchored at top and bottom before
venturing on to it.*

This makes the tool ideal for outside use,
on ladder or scaffold. The torch can be
lit, then switched off as soon as necessary,
with no problem of re-ignition when
required.

When buying blowtorches, check which
types of refills will fit as the different
makes are rarely interchangeable.

Paint spray gun

While ideal for car re-sprays and large
areas like a garage door, there are few
other jobs of a decorating nature where
the spray gun will help. It can be used
for painting window and door frames,
but the time spent in masking surrounding
areas to avoid over-spray can soon out-
weigh the advantages.

For small jobs, such as wickerwork,
wrought iron and small whitewood items,
an aerosol paint can will prove adequate.

Sponge

This is the ideal accessory for smoothing vinyl wallcoverings in place and is better than a smoothing brush.

It is necessary to have at least two sponges. One sponge for general mopping up and washing down and one kept specially as a smoother for wallcoverings.

Water trough

This item is fairly new on the decorating scene, for it comes with rolls of pre-pasted wallcoverings.

It is supplied flat but pre-creased and is made of waxed card. It is merely folded into shape, the flaps tucked in, and you have a waterproof trough.

Craft knife

A stout knife with interchangeable blades will be needed for cutting stouter decorating materials, such as vinyl floorcovering or carpet. Special blades are available—hooked for carpet cutting, and shaped for laminate scoring.

A steel straight-edge is useful when using the knife. Be sure at all times to keep your hand behind the direction of cut. These knives are very sharp!

Ladders

For exterior work, a sound ladder which will extend at least three rungs above the highest point you wish to reach is essential. It can be of timber or alloy and, with the price of timber having climbed, there is now little to choose as far as price is concerned. Timber feels warmer in cold weather but alloy is far lighter making the ladder easier to move and position.

A two-extension ladder is usually adequate. If you go for the three-extension,

bear in mind it is that much harder to raise on your own.

Choose a ladder with wide treads which give reasonable support for your feet. Working from a ladder can be very tiring. Ladder platforms are available which, if fitted at the height you wish to work, will give a bigger platform on which to stand. For hints on ladder safety see Chapter 11.

Steps

For interior decorating, you will need at least one pair of wide tread steps, preferably with a hand rail to grip when working high or overhead. Two pairs are even better, for by using a strong scaffold board between them, you have a safe working platform.

One pair of steps and a strong timber box is an alternative arrangement as a board support, but you are stuck for height by the size of the box. Never work from kitchen stools or an old chair.

If you live in a bungalow, ladders are now available which very simply convert from ladder to wide base steps. 'Three ladders in one' if you also look upon such an arrangement as also offering access to the loft.

Roof ladder

Most homes do not need to invest in a roof ladder as it is not required that often. If you do buy one, see that it is designed for the job. Wheels make it easy to move up the roof tiles, and a large specially shaped section is designed to hook over the ridge.

The roof ladder must be used in conjunction with a well-anchored extension ladder so you can move from one to the other easily. If you feel unsafe at roof height, call in expert help. Never take risks!

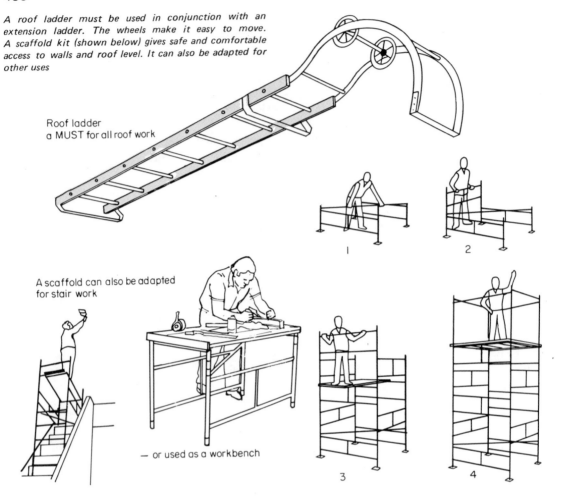

A roof ladder must be used in conjunction with an extension ladder. The wheels make it easy to move. A scaffold kit (shown below) gives safe and comfortable access to walls and roof level. It can also be adapted for other uses

Roof ladder
a MUST for all roof work

A scaffold can also be adapted for stair work

— or used as a workbench

1

2

3

4

Hiring equipment

There are many jobs about the house where a piece of specialist equipment would make the work much easier. In the past, such equipment has been for the professional, but with the introduction of chains of specialist hire shops, many items are now available to the home owner.

Obviously it does not pay to buy specialised items, but being able to hire these either by the day or week has completely transformed the situation.

It is not only large items which can be hired. If you need to decorate before you have tools of your own, then most decorat-

ing tools are available but, of course, you must pay for the privilege.

Collecting and returning items yourself will help reduce charges, while careful planning can reduce the period of hire. For example, a floor sander will make short work of a dirty parquet floor. If you remove furniture, check for nails and other possible obstructions that could damage a sanding belt prior to hiring the sander, you can then put it to use as soon as you get it home.

Before tackling decorating, get hold of a current catalogue of a local hire firm and check to see what they stock. There may be something there which could save you at lot of unpleasant work as well as hours of your time.

Two examples are given below.

Steam wallpaper stripping machine. If you encounter a really tough paper that is bonded to the wall, days can be wasted in cleaning it off. The steam stripper will do the job in hours.

Water in a special container is heated by bottled gas or electricity until it becomes steam and this is fed to a special plate which is held against the wall.

The effect of the combined heat and water is to dissolve the adhesive, allowing the paper to be pulled away by the sheet.

Ladders. Perhaps your own ladder will not reach a particular spot such as a chimney stack. The hire of a longer ladder can solve the problem. Alternatively you may wish to add another ladder to the one you already have, then add a pair of cripples to form a platform for scaffold boards. The boards and cripples can also be hired from your local hire shop.

A roof ladder will give you safe access to the loose tiles or missing ridge tile, and a scaffold kit of the type designed for handyman use can give you comfortable working platforms when painting large wall areas.

Chapter 51
Materials

There is a wide selection of materials available today, to the point that it can be very confusing when trying to choose. This is particularly true of the paint field, where technology has encouraged the introduction of many new additives. Modern paints tend to get fancy names which help very little when it comes to choosing what you need, so the first job is to establish which family the paint belongs to, and whether it is designed for interior use, exterior use, or perhaps both.

When choosing paint, ask at the same time just what materials back it up. Is there a special primer or undercoat? Is the material oil-based, needing special thinners and brush cleaners? Is it water-based, where brushes can be rinsed under the tap?

Choosing your colour can be equally confusing as the colour mixing machine is being extensively used. The machine has base colours into which a practically limitless variation of tints and combinations of tints can be added. If you are choosing a colour scheme, it will pay to take any samples you have—pieces of carpet, curtain, wallcovering—so that you can match the colour.

Alternatively ask for a detailed colour card, or for colour chips which can be taken home and examined at leisure. Bear in mind that small samples give a very false picture of what a large area of colour will look like. A large area will tend to look darker than the small sample.

As a general rule, pastels can be chosen from a mixing machine, though it is wise to buy as much as you require right away in case of slight variations in any further mix. Strong, bold colours are best chosen from a ready-mixed range of paints.

Now let us look at some of the materials currently available, starting with paints.

Alkyd resin paint

There is nothing new about alkyd resin gloss paint, it has been around for many years and is the standard good quality gloss which replaced the old lead-based paints. Materials painted need to be primed to seal the surface, undercoated to give body and obliterate any under-colour, then top coated. Alkyd paint is mainly used for high gloss work, though sheen and matt finishes are also available.

Up to now, the British market has always demanded a high gloss, but many countries accept a sheen or semi-gloss for surfaces such as doors and woodwork. While semi-gloss paint may collect dust or dirt more readily out of doors, for interior work it is much kinder where blemishes or irregular surfaces are encountered.

Acrylic paint

This is a material of the same family as the emulsion paints we have been using for years—though with more sheen. It is water-based, which makes it very easy to handle. It has virtually no smell; a boon to those who suffer from chest complaints or who just dislike the lingering smell of drying paint. In addition, the painting tools can be rinsed out in water.

Remember to protect water-based paints from frost, and not to store them in containers which could rust from the effect of the water content. Drying time is much faster than with oil-based materials, so if you are willing to accept less gloss on your work, the acrylic paint is ideal for a quick re-paint.

Stemming from the acrylics, come a whole range of water-based materials with additives such as vinyl and polyurethane to give a more durable finish and change the surface reflection. Some are soluble in water, while others need the addition of some form of solvent, such as washing up liquid, added to the water. As these products cannot possibly be classified, it is advisable to check carefully when choosing to see just what you are buying.

Emulsion paint

This water-based material has been well established for many years now, and fortunately the characteristics of peeling and flaking which gave the early emulsions such a bad name have gone forever. Distemper has now been replaced by emulsion paint but can still give considerable trouble in older homes, where its chalky, unstable surface must be either completely removed or sealed with a special sealing material before anything new is put over the top.

Emulsion paint, being water-based, makes the ideal material for large wall surfaces. It is quick drying, leaves no brush marks, and it has no unpleasant smell. It is best not applied direct to bare wood, as the water content will raise the wood grain. Brushes can be rinsed with water.

Thixotropic paints

Here again, another advance in paint technology has made it possible to produce a jelly-like paint which thins only when stirred or spread. The principle has been adapted for both emulsion and gloss paints, producing paints well suited to the beginner. They can be applied thicker without sagging; do not drip easily, and the paint stays on the brush. In the main these 'jelly' paints do not appeal to the experienced painter as they cannot be brushed out to a very fine finish.

Because of the extra thickness which can be applied, a new one-coat paint system was introduced with these paints, where the undercoat is incorporated in the top coat. On new work this system can be adequate, but where a change of colour is necessary, often there is insufficient pigment to obliterate an under-colour without applying two coats. A standard undercoat and top coat would be more effective. The one-coat system best suits the beginner. It has not replaced the standard painting system but rather has supplemented it.

Polyurethane paint

This has all the characteristics of a high gloss paint, but with an exceptional toughness built in. The coating is hard and is perhaps a little more prone to chipping than standard gloss, but it is able to withstand abrasion in a way not found in most other paints.

It is ideal for painting metal surfaces, such as garage doors, where it will give good protection. Because of its hardness, the instructions concerning applying second coats should be read very carefully. If too long is left in between coats, the under-coat will be so hard that the top one will not adhere well.

Enamels

These are high quality paints where the ingredients are ground very fine to give a dense, high gloss. Drying time can be controlled during manufacture according to use; the fastest drying enamels are those supplied for car body touch-up work.

As far as decorating is concerned, enamels are best suited to smaller jobs such as small items of whitewood furniture in nurseries, coathangers, door knobs and toys.

When used on such surfaces, as long as the wood is smooth, no primer or undercoat is necessary.

Aerosol paints

With aerosols the paint has to be ejected through a very fine nozzle under pressure. It has to be an extremely thinned-down material, and this is the main problem. The very thinnest of coats is applied, so a new technique must be adopted.

The surface must be covered by applying one thin coat upon another until the required density is achieved, allowing each coat to dry. As drying time is measured in minutes, this is no real hardship. Applying too thick a coat at one go merely results in drips and runs.

Aerosols are not cheap because of the sophisticated packaging and, as the paint is inside a sealed container, it is difficult to gauge easily how much paint you have. The aerosol is best used on smallish difficult surfaces such as wrought ironwork, perforated materials such as pegboard, and woven materials such as wicker furniture. Aerosols are not really suitable for large areas such as doors. One aerosol may not cover, and the next can may differ very slightly in colour, particularly if the can comes from a different batch. You will find a batch number on the base.

Masking is essential to avoid spray getting on other surfaces. Never use an aerosol out of doors where the wind could carry spray on to the surfaces such as your neighbour's car! If you work out of doors you need to make a spray booth from hardboard or cardboard.

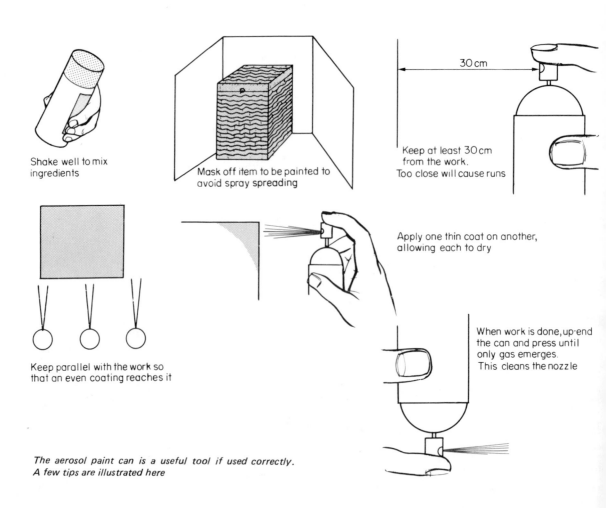

Shake well to mix ingredients

Mask off item to be painted to avoid spray spreading

30 cm

Keep at least 30 cm from the work. Too close will cause runs

Keep parallel with the work so that an even coating reaches it

Apply one thin coat on another, allowing each to dry

When work is done, up-end the can and press until only gas emerges. This cleans the nozzle

The aerosol paint can is a useful tool if used correctly. A few tips are illustrated here

Anti-condensation paint

This is an emulsion specially developed for use in areas where condensation is a problem. It has the ability to absorb a certain amount of moisture, which can evaporate when conditions are dry. This paint contains a fungicide which discourages the growth of mould. It is a very useful material in bathrooms and kitchens.

Fire retardant paint

Such materials have been widely used industrially for many years, but they are finding their way into the d-i-y market as people become more aware of the danger of fire in the home.

The paint looks very similar to a normal emulsion, but when exposed to severe heat it expands to form an insulating crust. It can be used on timbers, and also on expanded polystyrene tiles for kitchens.

Texture coatings

These should be classed as compounds, for they are supplied, in the main, as ready-mixed coatings in tubes and are far thicker than a paint. Their main advantage is their ability to hide irregular surfaces, so they have been widely used for ceilings where there are joins to hide or nail heads to lose.

Once applied by brush or roller, the material is textured by patterning or pulling up the compound, after which it sets hard. Once dry, it is painted, using a shaggy lambswool or nylon roller.

This material can also be used for wall coating, and again it has the ability to disguise poor wall surfaces. The main point to bear in mind is that it is designed as a permanent decoration, and it is hard to remove. You cannot paper over it.

Masonry paints

Basically, these are paints with durable ingredients or additives, well able to withstand external weathering. They can be cement-based, stone-based or emulsion-based, to which bulk may be added in the form of nylon fibre or silica.

A material like nylon is a very efficient binding agent, and it acts as a filler, hiding minor hair cracks and gaps.

When purchasing, ask about back-up products such as stabilising solutions to prepare a surface for painting, and fungicides to kill off any mould growth on the external walls.

Materials for preparation

The paints and compounds we have looked at so far are classified as decorative coatings. There is, however, a whole range of materials which are necessary in the preparation of surfaces. Some of these materials are described in the following paragraphs and include products used for knot sealing, primers, fillers, mastics, pastes, paint strippers, brush cleaners, etc.

Knotting

Knotting-compound is a shellac-based material designed to seal off knots in wood. This is most important on external work for knots may bleed resin, which will ruin any decoration.

The compound will prevent resin escaping, and it need only be applied to the actual knot area.

Primers

A priming paint is designed to seal off the material being painted from the decorative coating, and it is important to see you use the correct one.

There are metal primers, plaster primers and wood primers, in the main, sold as separate items. Multi-purpose primers can be bought which are suitable for a number of materials.

Fillers

While a primer has the ability to seal off a surface, it cannot seal holes, cracks and gaps. This is the job of a fillers. Various types are available as follows.

Cellulose filler. This will tackle cracks and holes in plaster and any timberwork which is not exposed to damp. It may be supplied by the packet to be mixed with water, or in a tub ready-mixed. Where large areas are involved, a material such as Keene's cement will be more economical. Deep cracks should be built up layer by layer, keying each by scratching the surface before it sets.

Fine surface fillers. This is a further development of the cellulose filler. It comes ready-mixed, has adhesive properties and will not be affected by damp. It should be worked well into the surface with a flexible filling knife and rubbed smooth when hard.

Wood stopping. A very well established form of adhesive filler which is ideal for timberwork. Supplied as a fine paste, it is worked well into the wood and allowed to set hard before rubbing smooth. It is available in a number of wood colours so that clear varnish finishes can be used after filling. Two grades are supplied: internal and external. The external grade should be used wherever damp conditions are likely to be encountered.

Epoxy resin based filler. This is supplied as a grey paste in a large tube. The material is activated by the addition of a hardener supplied in a smaller tube. Once mixed, setting is by chemical action, and nothing will stop it. This type of material is ideal for repairs to gutters and downpipes where cracks and gaps in metalwork need to be filled. Once set it can be filed or sanded smooth.

Mastics

A mastic differs from a filler in that it is designed to remain flexible even though it hardens on the surface. So you would use a mastic to fill any gap where there is likely to be movement, either through shrinkage of timber or through temperature variations. This makes mastics particularly suitable for outdoor work, especially window frames and other areas where cracks need filling.

Mastic is available either in strip form, rather like rolled out Plasticine, or in tubes with a special dispenser nozzle, or in cartridges to be fitted in a mastic gun. The strips are adequate for most small jobs, whereas a gun would be ideal if, say, all the window frames of the house were to be treated.

For gutter work and for sealing gaps in surfaces, such as flat roofs, there is a bituminous mastic available in tins. This would be applied by a small trowel. To strengthen an area, such as a tear in roofing felt, the mastic can be reinforced by using jute scrim or glass fibre bandage.

Keene's cement

A plaster-like material which is more economical to use for larger filling jobs. Pinkish in colour, it is fast drying, so no more should be mixed than can be used in about five minutes. For deep holes, build it up coat on coat, keying the previous one by scratching it with a trowel point before it sets.

Perhaps it should be mentioned here that plaster of paris is not really suitable for repair work. It sets far too quickly to be manageable. The most it could be used for is filling a deep hole to within 25 mm of the surface, then finishing with a standard filler. To give a stronger key, tap galvanised clout nails into the first coat, going well below the plaster surface.

Wallcovering pastes

There are several types of pastes and the correct one should be chosen according to the job in hand.

Cellulose paste. Ideal for lightweight wallpapers where there is a chance of staining. It has high water content, so makes a wallcovering very wet. A heavy duty cellulose is available for heavier materials.

Cold water paste. A traditional flour paste which is very full bodied, making it ideal for heavier materials such as ceiling papers and Anaglyptas. Because it has less water content, it has less tendency to expand heavier papers than a cellulose paste. It would be used in conjunction with a glue size, which is applied to the wall prior to decorating.

The size adds 'slip', making a paper easier to position, and it increases the adhesion of the paste. It shouldn't be applied too thickly or there may be a chance of surplus size coming up through joints when papering.

Vinyl wallcovering paste. This is a special paste to which is added a fungicide, because the vinyl film is impervious and will not allow moisture to evaporate off. Always use the paste recommended by the manufacturer when hanging vinyls.

Fungicide

When mould growth is encountered on walls or paintwork, it must be killed off with a fungicide prior to redecorating. This is available in bottles or in 'one use' sachets.

The fungicide cannot be applied over wallcoverings. You must strip off the decoration, then apply the fungicide to the clean wall. Household bleach is often used to kill mould growths, but experience shows it has no lasting effect. It is far better to use a proprietary fungicide. However, keep it away from children!

Chemical stripper

This is a thick liquid designed to attack and break down a paint film so that it can be removed with shave hooks and scrapers. Types vary considerably, so the instructions on the container should be followed very carefully, both with regard to application and neutralising after use.

Eyes and hands should be protected when using these materials. Most strippers will also soften hard paintbrushes if the brushes are suspended in the material until soft.

Brush cleaners

Proprietary materials designed for the easy cleaning of brushes after use with oil-based paints. An alternative is to use paraffin in a jar to loosen and remove the paint, then thoroughly rinse the brush with soap and water to remove the paraffin. This is a cheaper process than using a brush cleaner, but it does take longer.

To conserve proprietary brush cleaner, let it settle after use, then pour off the still useable material into another container, only throwing away the dregs. An economical way of using cleaner is to pour a little into a polythene bag, insert the brush, seal the bag with an elastic band and work the brush bristles through the plastic.

Damp sealers

These are special liquids designed to form a thin skin of the surface of a wall to prevent damp coming through.

While they can be effective, they are best used after the cause of the damp has been treated. If the damp is persistent, it will tend to move elsewhere and come through in a new place which has not been sealed.

Silicone water repellant

This is a transparent liquid designed to coat brickwork or rendering so that water cannot penetrate. The seal does not stop the wall 'breathing' so vapour in the wall surface can still get out.

Stains and varnishes

These are described in Chapter 10 'Wood-finishing'.

Wallpapers

These fall into four main categories: plain where a pattern is printed on to a roll of paper; duplex, where two papers are bonded together during manufacture, adding texture and strength; wipable, where superficial marks can be wiped away without spoiling the surface, and washable, where a protective film is added over the pattern so that it can be cleaned.

As a general rule, the heavier the paper, the easier it is to handle. It is false economy to start with a very cheap paper, for in inexpert hands it will tear and mark very easily.

Also, the heavier the material, the longer it should be given to soak, prior to hanging, to avoid bubbling. The continued expansion while on the wall can cause bubbles, and very often the paste will get a grip before the paper has dried out—so the bubbles remain.

Wall coverings

These include wallpapers in various categories and comprise vinyls, heavily-embossed paper-backed coverings (for instance, Lincrusta), hessians and grass cloths. All these are described in the following paragraphs.

Vinyls

Printing on plastics and the texturing of sheet plastics has improved tremendously in recent years, making the vinyl wall-covering a most attractive proposition. True they still cost more than papers, but they have many advantages. Vinyls are easy to cut and handle; the surface is unaffected by water, paste and fingermarks.

Apart from the standard one, you can now buy pre-pasted vinyls, where the adhesive on the back merely needs activating by dipping the vinyl in a water trough. There is ample adhesive for any surface, and in some cases a surplus may squeeze out at the joints. This is quite normal, and the surplus can be wiped away. The only difficulty you may encounter is at points where vinyl overlaps vinyl. The joints need special treatment and this subject is dealt with in Chapter 53.

Another advantage of most vinyls is that they are easy to strip. Lift a corner and pull the whole vinyl sheet away from the backing paper. The paper is left in place and is used as a lining paper for the next vinyl. This is a great advance on the old methods of wallpaper stripping.

Anaglypta, Supaglypta and Vynaglypta

These are heavy embossed materials adding a pleasant texture to a wall surface. A whole range of patterns is available, from simple plaster swirl effects through to basket weaves and contemporary designs.

They are ideal for use on ceilings and walls where the surfaces are not really smooth, for the textured surface will hide defects very well. The material can be emulsion coated to form an attractive and tough wallcovering.

Lincrusta

This is a traditional wallcovering material very much resembling putty stuck to a paper backing. It is available in very many effects, from coiled rope designs through to imitation panelling, and it gives a very deep pattern.

A special adhesive must be used to apply it, and the material should be looked upon as permanent.

Woodchip paper

In this case a plain paper is coated with wood chips, then covered by another sheet of paper so that the chips are sealed in. The effect is a pleasing texture which, when painted, produces a very durable wall-covering.

Too much of this material tends to cheapen the effect, so it looks at its best as a feature wall or in alcoves. It is not ideal for children's rooms because it feels rough if you fall against it.

A similar effect is probably available in Anaglypta which is much smoother to the touch.

Cork-faced wallcovering

This rather luxurious finish consists of a paper backing with a paint finish, to which is stuck very thin veneers of natural cork so the colour shows through.

It gives a very warm, luxurious effect and, because of its structure, it does tend to be expensive.

Hessians

These have become popular in recent years, despite the fact they are at the dearer end of the market. Those for d-i-y use are paper backed, and are stuck to the wall by means of a special heavy adhesive.

As they are merely woven panels, no matching between pieces is possible. You must accept that you will see every join quite clearly.

An interesting range of colours is available.

Grass cloths

These were primarily designed as a feature material. The wallcovering is woven from natural grasses, giving a very pleasant texture.

It is best kept for feature walls and alcoves where it will not be subject to wear and tear. Again, as it is a natural product, no matching of panels is possible.

Imitation effects

Apart from the normal run of decoration, you will now find a steadily growing range of imitation effects for your walls. These range from special effect papers first used in photographic studios, through to panels of imitation stone, brick and timber panelling.

The masonry and stone wall effects look most realistic. Panelling tends to look a bit like wallpaper through obvious repetitions of grain patterns and knots.

Wall panelling

Moving away from thinner sheet materials, real wall panelling has become very popular. It comes in various forms, the cheapest being sheets of thin plywood scored to represent panelling and perhaps faced with a thin veneer of high quality wood. At the other end of the scale are timber strips which are designed to be fixed individually. These look most effective, but are expensive.

An alternative is to use tongued and grooved boarding, choosing the boards for their grain pattern and knots. These may be stained and sealed to suit any décor.

Fixing is by means of special adhesive, or by battening the walls and pinning the timber to the battens. Obviously the adhesive offers the simplest way, and it cuts out the cost of battening.

Colour should be borne in mind when choosing panelling. A dark colour may look fine in a big old study, but it can be very overpowering and make the room feel enclosed in our smaller homes. Perhaps a dark feature wall may be sufficient, or it may be better to choose a light colour, like pine, if a room is on the small side. Once sealed correctly, panelling is very easy to maintain.

For those who want the real thing, brick, stone and slate are available in very thin sheets to use rather like tiles. Stuck in place, these can give very pleasing effects, especially where a period effect is required. Very often a feature wall is all that is needed, or perhaps a chimney breast incorporating a ledge and seat.

Floor and ceiling coverings

For details of floor and ceiling materials, see Chapters 56 and 57.

Chapter 52
Preparation

With any decorating job, adequate preparation is 90 per cent of the battle. Practically all faults and failures which are blamed on materials can be traced back to the fact that the surface upon which the material was placed had been poorly prepared. Let us take just one example which highlights the problem. A ceiling which has been distempered.

If all the old material is not removed or neutralised, any subsequent coating, say an emulsion paint, is not in contact with the ceiling at all. It is resting on what for all intents and purposes is a layer of chalk. Is it surprising that before long the emulsion will pull away?

So we must face the fact that a lot of groundwork has to be done before any new materials are applied—however much we hate waiting to see what the finished effect will be!

Planning the job

The very first stage is planning. Work out how much time you have at your disposal. Will it be a number of evenings? Weekends? Or perhaps a week's holiday? Will it be winter, when night comes on quickly and there are no evenings; when the cold weather will prevent drying of damp surfaces and wet paint. Or will there be long summer evenings with dry weather and faster drying times for materials?

Having decided how much time you have, work out how best to divide the work up to fit it. Out of doors, you should plan so that at the end of a day no timber or metal is ever left without the protection of at least a priming coat. This may mean doing only one frame at a time. You may decide that the weekend will only allow one face of the house to be treated, in which case plan to do just one face of the house at a time, completing all the work on that face before moving round.

Having decided on a plan of campaign, measure up for materials. Assuming you have chosen the type of paint you require, the colour card will detail coverage. I have found the simplest way for windows is to treat the window as if it were a flat area equal to window height times width. This would be for a timber frame with a fair amount of mouldings. Obviously, a modern picture window with metal frame would need considerably less.

Simple scale plans of the various elevations will help in calculating wall areas where perhaps a masonry paint is needed. Check to see whether two full coats are recommended, or whether the first is a thinned coat. Are you covering an existing colour? If so you may need an extra undercoat to obliterate the under-colour. Remember that top coat has .not the obliterative power of undercoat. It is merely decorative and protective.

Try to order paint in the biggest batches possible, and see that batch numbers are the same, especially where colours are used. With wallcoverings, it pays to order an extra roll or two if there is any doubt as to how much you really need. Most stores will take back an unopened roll, but few can guarantee to order one more roll with the same batch number! If you have to accept different batches, open the rolls and check for colour and shading. If you find variations you will have to plan to lose the discrepancy in a corner or behind furniture.

Ordering materials

Order your materials well in advance if they are not in stock. We are all very prone to ordering on a Friday, telling the poor shopkeeper we hope to use it next day!

If materials are delivered, check them through before signing the vanman's docket. If it says you have received the materials ordered in good condition and you sign to that effect, you cannot expect the shopkeeper to be sympathetic when you discover that some items are missing.

Apart from the obvious materials like paint and paper, check through your stocks of items like brush cleaner, filler, refills for the blowtorch. These are so often the kind of thing which bring everything to a grinding halt on Saturday evening when all the shops are shut. This is where your record book mentioned earlier would come in useful. A list of tools and materials for any given job would be invaluable. When it is written down you will be amazed just how many items are needed for even the most simple task.

First of the preparatory jobs may involve tackling projects which are best done when it does not matter if you spoil the decoration in the process. Thinking of new windows? It would be that much less of a worry if the room were empty. New doors? A change of decoration could well include a new door. Perhaps a nice panelled front door, or a glass door to the kitchen to let in more light, or a stable-type back door so that the top could be opened during the summer months. Perhaps just pulling off that hardboard panel which covers an attractive panelled interior door. It is not as hard to paint panelled doors as it used to be!

There may also be floor repairs. Damaged or worn boards to turn or replace. Damp or rot to treat, uneven boards to sand smooth. Perhaps you have to re-wire and this can involve lifting floorboards to route new cable. Central heating also involves lifting boards to run pipes under the floor. Perhaps you would like the picture rail down to make the walls look higher. This is a messy job (see Chapter 53).

How about a hatch between kitchen and dining area? This involves bashing a hole through the wall—never a clean job at the best of times. Or perhaps you want to put up cove-cornice, which has to be fixed to wall plaster, not wallpaper.

Then again you may be planning to fit wall lights. This will involve channelling the walls, with the resultant mess. Perhaps you have plans to put in a new fireplace; build one in stone, or merely resurrect the existing one now that fuel prices have gone so high. You may like to fit a back boiler to utilise heat from a fire that is in use—or replace an open fire with an enclosed stove. All these jobs may involve more than just moving a new unit in place. There can be cutting, widening and altering, the fitting of a flue liner or the relining of a flue.

Badly damaged ceilings may need cutting away; walls may have loose areas of plaster; there may be structural damp to treat, or cold walls to insulate.

When you really sit down to think about it, actual decorating may seem light years away! But it is far better than seeing someone cutting away the decorations you have just completed.

Preparing the room

Now what sort of work is involved in preparation? let us look at the interior first.

Assuming a room has to be completely decorated, it first needs emptying of furniture as far as is possible. Lift rugs and carpets, underlays and carpet holding strips.

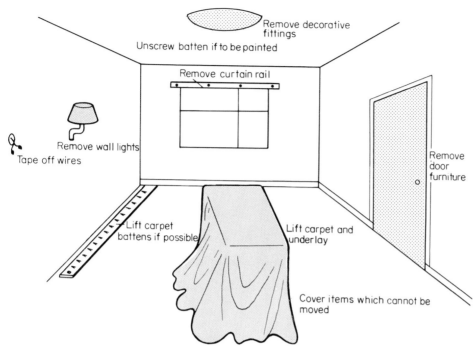

Preparing the room. The more a room can be cleared, the easier will be the job of decorating it

Take down light fittings; disconnect wall lights if possible (having cut off the power at the fuse box or consumer unit first!) Take down curtain rails and remove door furniture. If any furniture has to stay in the room, place it in the centre and cover with dust sheets.

The ceiling

Now have a look at the ceiling. If there is work to be done, cover the floor with newspaper to prevent the floorboards getting dirty and the gaps between them filling with dust.

If the ceiling paper is sound but just dirty and you plan to paint, merely wash the ceiling using warm water to which sugar soap has been added. A roughish cloth, such as an old towel, will do ideally. Rinse with clean water. Check to see that the paper hasn't bubbled up through being wet. If it has, see if it dries out. If not, slit any

bubbles, tear the paper back, paste and press back. Such treatment rarely shows when re-painted.

If there were signs of bubbling; when you apply emulsion paint see that the room is not heated. If the emulsion dries faster than the paper contracts, you can end up with permanent blisters.

If the paper is in poor shape and is pulling away, soak it with water and pull it off. A scraper may be needed to remove stubborn areas, but be careful not to dig the ceiling plaster. Check the ceiling by rubbing wet fingers over the plaster. If your fingers come away white, there is distemper on the ceiling and this probably caused the paper to lose its grip. Use a coarse cloth and plenty of water to rub it off.

If the distemper is really thick, never tackle it dry. It will make a dreadful mess. Wet it thoroughly, then use a scraper to remove it. Hold a dustpan under the scraper to collect the distemper as it falls away. This will save a lot of mess on the floor. Then finish off with your coarse rag and plenty of warm water.

Where a ceiling is paint on plaster, washing down should be sufficient. If it is flaking away, suspect distemper underneath, and treat as already described for the removal of distemper. Where paint is sound, you can apply new paint, or, if you wish, paper over the old paint. Before papering, it is wise to roughen the surface to afford a better key.

It is quite in order to redecorate the ceiling before removing wallpaper from the walls. Dirty splashes or paint splashed on to the walls will come off when the paper is stripped.

The only ceiling decorating job that can be left until later is perhaps tiling. If tiles are left until the room has been decorated,

be sure to paint them before putting them up! Apart from being the simplest method, it will ensure that paint is not splashed on new decoration.

Stripping wallcovering

The wallcovering can come next. Assuming it is to be stripped, soften it with warm water to which has been added some washing-up liquid. This acts as a wetting agent, and it will speed up the stripping process. On thicker papers, the addition of a handful of cellulose wallpaper paste to the stripping water will help. The paste keeps water on the wall where normally it would just run down.

With varnished papers, wipables and washables, you will have to break down the surface so the water can get through. Use a wire brush or an abrasive pad, but

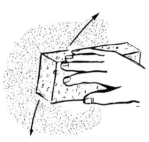
Collect thick distemper in a dustpan

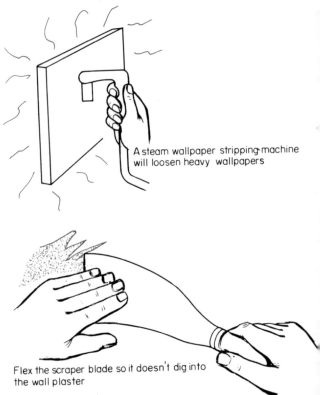
A steam wallpaper stripping machine will loosen heavy wallpapers

Break down the surface of washable papers to let water soak in

Flex the scraper blade so it doesn't dig into the wall plaster

Some ways of removing wall finishes. Remember that dampened surfaces make far less dust than dry surfaces

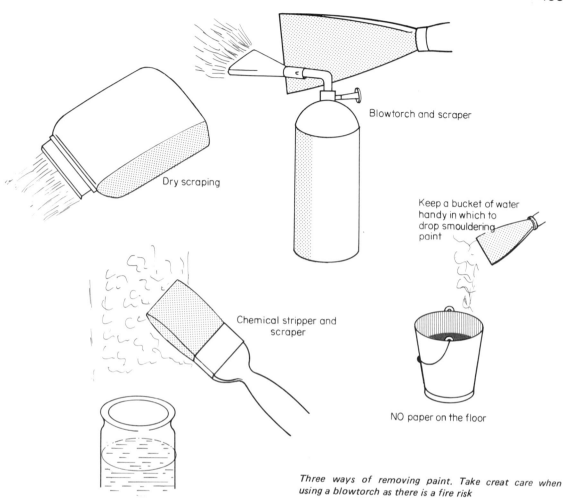

Dry scraping

Blowtorch and scraper

Keep a bucket of water handy in which to drop smouldering paint

Chemical stripper and scraper

NO paper on the floor

Three ways of removing paint. Take creat care when using a blowtorch as there is a fire risk

take care not to damage the plaster beneath.

If you encounter a really tough paper, or layers of paper, it is worth hiring a steam wallpaper stripper. This will speed up the job considerably, and paper can be pulled from the wall by the sheet. This process is also ideal where surface plaster is weak and would pull away with the paper. The only snag with a steam stripper is that unless you are very careful you will strip the ceiling as well!

If you are fortunate to find a room where a relatively new wallcovering has been used, you may be lucky. It could be one of the easy-to-strip range. Peel back a corner of one length and see if the patterned surface

will pull away. If it is an easy strip, the whole piece will pull from its backing, leaving a lining sheet behind. This need not be removed as you can decorate over it. Obviously, such papers save an enormous amount of time when it somes to redecorating.

Woodwork

Next, examine the woodwork. If paint is in good condition it may only be necessary to rub it down and re-paint. There is no point in stripping off a good coating, unless it is so thick that it is interfering with the opening of doors or windows. Full details of repainting are given in Chapter 53.

Removing old paint

If the paint is damaged in places, perhaps through items having been knocked against it, you may be able to rub down these areas with fine glasspaper, and dust clean. If there is quite a deep hole, apply undercoat with a fine camel hair brush, keeping it within the confines of the damage. When this is dry, you can apply top coat to bring the surface level with the surrounding area.

Once the repairs are really hard, say after a week, you can flat down the whole area with a pumice stripping block to remove surface gloss; wipe clean and re-paint.

If the damage goes right through to bare wood, it will be necessary to apply primer to the bare patches prior to putting on the undercoat. This seals the wood pores.

Where paint is badly worn, or is flaking away, it will need to be stripped to bare wood. There are three ways you can do this.

Paint scraper. A special sharp bladed scraper will pull paint away from many areas, though care should be taken not to dig into the wood. It is a help when you encounter several coats of paint for, by pulling most of the paint away dry, you will save a little on cost of fuel or chemical stripper. You would be wise to protect your eyes when doing this job as pieces fly off in all directions.

Blowlamp or blowtorch. This is a quick way of removing paint, but it does need a little practice before you can coordinate one hand holding the torch and the other wielding a scraper. The torch must be kept on the move to avoid scorching the wood and the heat should be withdrawn as soon as the paint blisters up. It should not catch fire intentionally. Be sure to hold your scraper at an angle so that very hot paint doesn't drop on to your hand.

A blowtorch and scraper offers an economical way of stripping paint

If you use a chemical stripper, allow ample time for it to soften the paint before scraping

A shave hook will get into the awkward areas like mouldings and decorative beadings

Use patent knotting to seal knots before applying a coat of wood primer

It is a wise precaution to have a bucket of water nearby into which you can drop any burning paint. Never let the paint drop on the floor and never have newspapers down when burning off. Good ventilation is wise too, or the smell of burned paint will hang in the house for days.

When burning off on window frames, never work with curtains in place (and people have!) and do not play the lamp on the glass. You may crack it, and add another job to your list. Be particularly careful when working in sunlight as it makes a bottled gas flame invisible where it is hottest.

Chemical strippers. If you are at all worried about using a blowtorch, a chemical stripper can be used instead. This is designed to break down the paint structure, making it blister and crack. You need to be patient, for where a number of coats of paint are involved, it can take time and will need

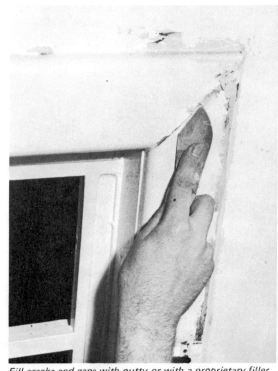

Fill cracks and gaps with putty or with a proprietary filler. Rub smooth when set

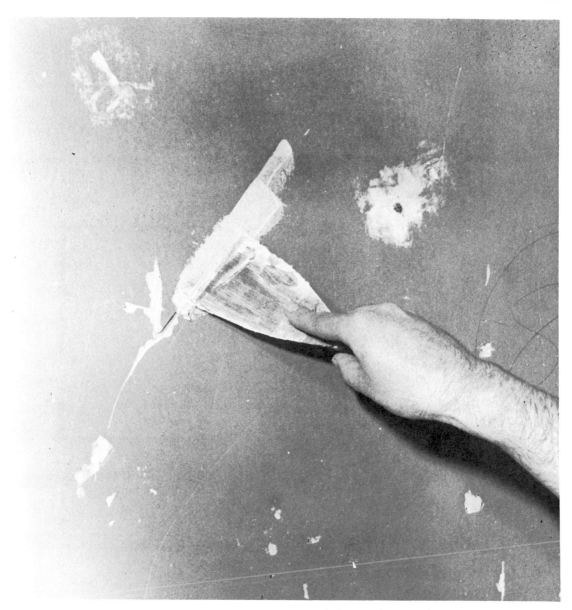

Fill wall cracks with cellulose filler. Take proud of the surface then rub smooth when hard

more than one coat to really soften the paint. Do not try to strip the paint until it is soft enough to be scraped away. You will merely waste the stripper.

Once soft, use a shave hook and scraper to remove the paint down to bare wood. For difficult areas, wear a rubber glove and use wire wool to rub the area, always working with the wood grain. When applying stripper with a brush, it is also wise to wear protective glasses. If you should get stripper in your eye, wash it with plenty of water as soon as possible.

The instructions on the container will give advice on neutralising any stripper left on the wood after stripping. In some cases it may mean a rinse with clean water, after which the wood is left to dry. Then it can be rubbed smooth with fine glasspaper working with the wood grain, and the surface is ready for filling and priming.

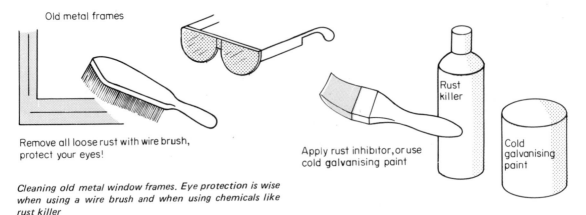

Old metal frames

Remove all loose rust with wire brush, protect your eyes!

Apply rust inhibitor, or use cold galvanising paint

Rust killer

Cold galvanising paint

Cleaning old metal window frames. Eye protection is wise when using a wire brush and when using chemicals like rust killer

Cracks in woodwork

Cracks and gaps in timber must be filled prior to painting, for paint cannot be expected to hide them. While ordinary cellulose filler can be used, it is far better to use a more durable material such as fine surface filler or wood stopping. This must be pressed well into cracks, left to set, then rubbed smooth. Where damp may be encountered, such as on a window sill where condensation may gather, fill with a waterproof wood stopping. Ordinary cellulose filler would dissolve in moisture.

Where knots are encountered, coat them with patent knotting to seal the resin in the knot. If this is not done the knot may bleed at some later date, and the resin

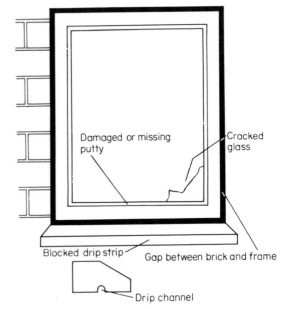

Damaged or missing putty

Cracked glass

Blocked drip strip

Gap between brick and frame

Drip channel

Points where damp may get in around a window frame. Use mastic for sealing gaps as in previous illustration

Mastics for gaps and cracks

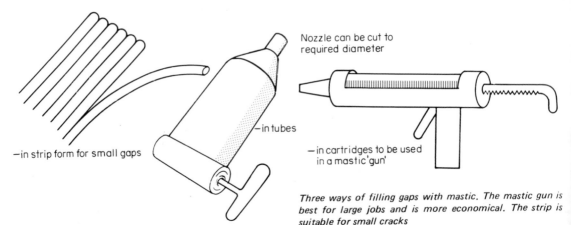

Nozzle can be cut to required diameter

—in tubes

—in strip form for small gaps

—in cartridges to be used in a mastic 'gun'

Three ways of filling gaps with mastic. The mastic gun is best for large jobs and is more economical. The strip is suitable for small cracks

will push its way through your paint coating. This applies particularly to areas of paintwork exposed to the heat of the sun.

If you encounter soft areas of wood (the effects of wet rot) you need to cut out the damaged wood then build up with new wood. If the area is only small, a repair filler may be used. Take the filler a little proud of the surrounding area, then sand it to shape when hard.

Metal window frames

With old metal window frames, look for signs of rust. Rusted areas must be rubbed free of all loose scale then treated with a rust killing liquid prior to repainting. Make sure that *all* rust is removed, even if it means scraping off an area of seemingly sound paint. Hidden rust may well start up a new attack.

Modern metal frames will be heavily galvanised and should not rust, In my opinion, however, galvanising is very often not a very stable base for paint, and you may find paint peeling away from it. All flaking paint must be stripped to bare frame, then you need to prime and under-coat the galvanised surface.

Where paint is sound on metal frames, leave it there. Merely use the pumice block to remove the gloss from the paint, and re-paint.

Window furniture often looks a mess, mainly because most people try to paint this in place. For best results, remove window stays and handles and decorate them separately. With many metal frames, it is not possible to remove handles—in which case you need to mask the surrounding area while you do the best you can. Leave the window furniture as long as possible before closing windows, or you will find all your new paint has been rubbed away by friction against the frame.

Smoothing-down plaster walls

Plaster walls need to be examined for flaws. Bulging areas which give a hollow sound may need to be cut away and re-plastered. The same goes for areas of crumbling plaster. Cellulose filler can be used to fill minor gaps and cracks, but for larger areas, a material such as Keene's cement is more economical. It is fairly fast drying, so do not mix too much at a time. If holes are quite deep, build layer upon layer, scratching the surface of each layer to afford a key for the next. If you try to fill in one go, you will find the filler slumps out of the hole.

Remember not to fill plugged holes if that is where fittings go! It is a good idea to push a matchstick in such holes so that when you re-paper, the matchstick will push through the paper. Otherwise you may find it very difficult to find the holes again.

Full details of repair work to plaster walls, including relining walls with plasterboard, is dealt with in Section 1 (Home Repair and Maintenance).

Exterior preparation

Now let us move to the exterior of the house. Obviously we will be looking for similar problems on exterior joinery as were encountered indoors, but the exterior is more prone to damage due to exposure to the weather.

Where paintwork is sound, leave it alone and merely rub down with a stripping block to remove grime and to take the gloss from the paint surface. If you are keeping to the same colour, you could apply two coats of new exterior gloss over the prepared old coat, but if you are changing colour, always use an undercoat to obliterate the old colour. A top coat is relatively thin and it has little obliterative power.

Where paintwork is chipped, the treatment described for interior paintwork can be carried out. Make sure to prime any bare patches of wood prior to undercoating.

Badly damaged paint must be stripped away to bare wood, and cracks and gaps in the wood filled with waterproof stopping or fine surface filler. Sills made of oak present a particular problem, for the open grain of oak makes it hard to fill. Air trapped in the wood grain tends to expand in the heat of the sun, and this will push off a paint coating however well applied the paint may be. Some people overcome this by leaving the oak unpainted and treating it with a clear or pigmented preservative. Alternatively you can paint it with a clear exterior grade varnish.

If you really wish to paint the oak to match the rest of the house, strip it clean, then rub fine surface filler deep into the grain with a piece of lint-free rag. Rub over the whole wood surface, then when set, rub it smooth with fine glasspaper, working only with the wood grain. You can then prime and undercoat as normal.

Outside windows and doors

Metal frames need the same kind of examination as we gave internally, paying particular attention to areas of rust. If this creeps under the glass, the pressure is sufficient to crack a pane of glass. This is very often the explanation for mysterious cracks which seem to appear without reason.

Look for loose or cracking putty on frames, and be ruthless. Dig it out; clean the area and prime the bare wood before putting in new putty. Make sure there is a seal between glass and putty, for this is where water creeps in, rotting the frame beneath. On metal frames damaged putty must be replaced by special metal casement putty. Ordinary putty does not set, as the oil cannot soak in as with timber frames.

The same examination applies to glazed doors, for a bad seal between glass and putty or beadings will allow water into the door, causing wet rot. If it is not checked, you will soon need a new door, or some pretty extensive repairs. If the glass in the door is fluted or otherwise textured, make sure that the flutes are on the inside. If they are outside, this may result in a bad seal between glass and door.

Look for cracks around window and door frames. This is quite a common fault due to slight shrinkage of timber frames. These cracks should be filled with a flexible mastic; never use putty or cement mortar. The latter set hard and you soon have a new crack appear. A mastic remains flexible throughout its life, even if it does dry on the surface.

Pipes and gutters

Check the rainwater gutters for signs of damage. Down pipes give little trouble as they do not hold water, but gutters can rust and rot away if neglected. An accumulation of debris in the gutter may trap water, adding to the problem, so the first job is to clean out gutters, flush through with water, then examine for damage. Dead leaves are particularly troublesome if left.

Rusted areas should be wirebrushed to remove scale, then treated with a rust killer. Holes can be filled with bituminous mastic applied with a trowel, or with one of the epoxy repair materials. Be sure to make the inside of the gutter smooth, otherwise the projection may trap debris.

Where gutters are in poor shape, it may be wise to remove them and replace with plastic ones. You will need help to lift down the metal ones, but you may be able to manage the lightweight plastic gutters on your own.

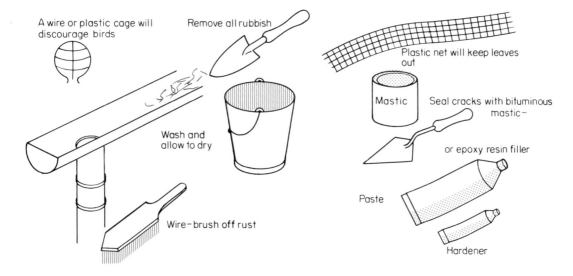

A wire or plastic cage will discourage birds

Remove all rubbish

Wash and allow to dry

Wire-brush off rust

Plastic net will keep leaves out

Mastic

Seal cracks with bituminous mastic –

or epoxy resin filler

Paste

Hardener

Cleaning gutters. Regular maintenance of gutters, to remove rubbish and treat rust, is advisable. It is sensible to do this job after the leaves have fallen

Outside walls

Walls need examining for faults prior to decorating. The most a decorative brick needs is a thorough wash with clean water. Do not be tempted to add chemicals or detergents to the water as you may end up with a whitish residue which is difficult to remove. If the bricks are grubby, find a piece of brick of the same type and colour, and use this as a pumice block. A brisk rub, plus an application of clean water can do wonders.

Examine the pointing between bricks. If it is loose and crumbling, dig it out to a depth of 12 mm (½ in) and re-point with a dryish mortar mix. A wet mix will slop on to your brickwork and then be very hard to clean off.

To make decorative bricks stand out, you can use white cement for the pointing mortar. This merely adds more contrast in colour between pointing and brickwork.

Walls rendered with cement will need a thorough wash down to remove grime, plus a rub with a coarse floor scrubbing brush to loosen persistent dirt. Areas of mould should be treated with a fungicide, for if the mould is not killed off, it could discolour any new paint you apply. Holes and cracks should be filled with a mortar mix. Do not rely on a new coat of paint to hide cracks, masonry paint will cover fine hair cracks, but no more.

Pebble dash and spar dash can present problems if the surface is crumbling or if areas are bulging away from the wall. Loose material is best brushed away with a stiff brush, and hollow areas need cutting out and rebuilding, using a mortar mix to which some pva adhesive has been added to improve adhesion. Keep the stones that are taken off, as these will give the best match when doing repairs.

If you have to buy new stones, try to mix in some darker ones so the repaired areas are not too obvious. Stones are best thrown on to a wet mortar surface, using a coal shovel. You need sacking or polythene sheeting at the base to catch any stones which do not stick first time.

Painted walls may need a thorough wash down to remove grime, using a scrubbing brush to loosen obstinate dirt. Once clean, cracks can be filled with mortar mix.

Cladding

Many homes now have an area of cladding as part of the exterior decoration. This may be of timber, either painted or treated with preservative, or it may be of plastic and, in a few cases, aluminium. Timber needs examining and treating as for any other timber surface, filling cracks and gaps with a waterproof stopping. If the wood is stained and sealed, choose a stopping which matches in colour. For painted work, any colour will 'of course' do.

Plastic cladding needs little attention apart from a thorough wash with water and detergent or household cleaner. Do not use abrasive materials, or let dirty water run down the decorative brickwork. This leaves the whitish stains mentioned earlier.

Exterior repairs

Obviously, this is also the time for effecting any exterior repairs which need attention. In fact any of those jobs which, if left until later, could spoil new decorations.

Amongst the jobs may be replacing damaged slates or tiles, dealing with faulty damp proof courses, fitting an extractor fan through the wall, cleaning glass or plastic roofing to outhouses or extensions, removing damaged trellis, cutting back climbing plants, or building a porch to the back door.

Chapter 53
Paintwork

Having looked at the tools, materials and general preparation necessary for decorating, let us consider the more exciting aspect —actually applying our new finishes. We will start indoors.

There is no general rule as to which comes first, walls or woodwork. The author's preference is that if walls are to be papered, do all the paintwork first, taking the paint just on to the walls so that if there are any slight gaps where paper does not meet wood, no wall will show through. If walls are to be painted, it may be preferable to do these first followed by the woodwork, having primed all the wood prior to painting walls. The reason is that it is harder to control large brushes than small, so there is more chance of wall paint straying on to woodwork.

Painting walls

So, let us start with the walls. Assuming they are clean, dry and filled where necessary—is the plaster smooth enough to take a coat of paint? If there are irregularities, the paint could highlight them, making the job look very cheap.

Assuming the wall plaster is good, what paint should we use? An oil-based gloss paint can be used, but it must be preceded by a plaster primer and preferably an undercoat. Once applied, it would be durable, but a high gloss does tend to highlight faults in the surface, and as the paint is an impervious coating, it can encourage condensation if walls are on the cold side.

Then there is the problem of brush or roller cleaning, using some form of proprietary cleaner. As I mentioned earlier, some cleaners affect pads and some others may affect paint rollers.

There are enough discouragements here to rule out the use of gloss paints in favour of one of the more easy to handle emulsion coatings. Apart from the standard emulsion paint with which we are all familiar, you could use a water-based acrylic gloss if you wanted more sheen, or a vinyl for real durability. No special undercoat is required, and painting tools can be cleaned in water. Check to see whether you use plain water or whether detergent needs to be added to the cleaning water. This information should appear on the can.

If the wall is bare plaster, make up a dilute coat of emulsion, half paint and half water, and prime the wall with this. If it has been previously painted, the priming is not necessary.

Now to choice of tools. A wide paint brush, preferably 127 mm, (5 in) is the traditional tool, and it gives a good finish once you have mastered its use. Only dip a third of the depth of bristle in the paint; do not overload the brush or it will drip. Starting at the top of one wall, nearest the corner, apply paint in vertical strokes, then brush out horizontally, and finally stroke off vertically again, spreading the paint as far as it will go without skimping. Try not to cover too large an area, imagine the wall divided into squares, and do one at a time.

Work down the wall, but if there are signs that the paint is drying quickly, extend your work a little sideways as well so that you keep all edges 'wet'. This is to avoid join marks between sections. For ease of working, keep the room temperature low so that drying is prolonged. You will still find your first coat is touch-dry in about 20 minutes. If you find it hard to work a large brush into corners, keep a smaller brush handy for touching in.

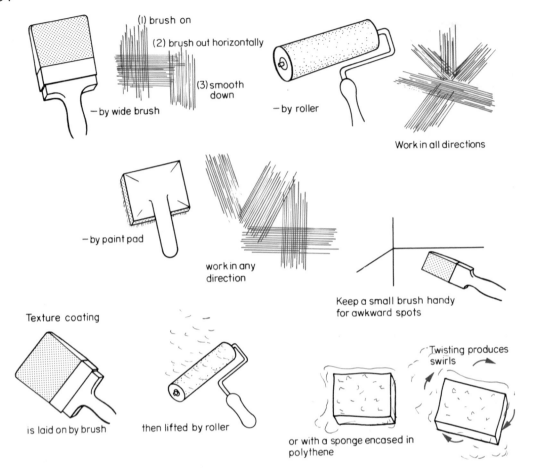

(1) brush on

(2) brush out horizontally

(3) smooth down

— by wide brush

— by roller

Work in all directions

— by paint pad

work in any direction

Keep a small brush handy for awkward spots

Texture coating

is laid on by brush

then lifted by roller

or with a sponge encased in polythene

Twisting produces swirls

If you are not happy with a brush, you can use a roller. For a plaster wall it is preferable to choose a short pile lambswool or nylon roller, but you could use a foam one.

Roller technique is entirely different from using a brush. You merely work out from a point, and it does not matter much in which direction you roll as long as you cover every part of the wall. Again it is important to keep edges wet so that no joins show, but as working with a roller is faster than brush work, this is not such a problem. Make sure you do not over-charge the roller, and do not spin it too rapidly or paint will be thrown off.

If your paint does not cover well in one coat, do not try to put the paint on thicker. Be content to apply a thinner coat, then

The three basic tools for wall painting are seen here. Brush, paint roller and paint pad. Note especially the different painting methods for brush and roller application

put another over the top when the first is dry.

Alternatively, you may care to experiment with a paint pad, which I have used almost exclusively for walls over very many years. Again the technique is different. The direction of stroke really does not matter as long as all your sections overlap. Using a large pad, you can work quite fast, with little fear of drips or splashes. Do not overcharge a pad, or paint may squeeze out of the foam backing. You may find it easier to finish in corners with a small paintbrush, but a little experimenting will soon show you how best to work.

When the first coat is dry, check to see there are no bits of dust spoiling the surface, and check also that you have not missed any patches of wall. If you paint at night, it pays to save the second coat until daylight. You will be amazed what so often shows up.

Dealing with rough walls

So far we have dealt with a smooth wall, but what if the surface is rather irregular—perhaps due to rather poor plastering? Unfortunately a coat of paint tends to highlight such faults, so it would be wise to disguise the fault by adding a new texture. The Anaglypta range of papers has some interesting effects, ranging from a simple plaster daub through to quite intricate basket weave patterns. You can read how to hang this material in Chapter 54.

With an Anaglypta paper in place, you can emulsion coat as for a plaster wall, using any of the tools already mentioned. A couple of coats of paint is advisable, however well it seems to cover, to ensure that you get into all the surface texture.

Some of the patterned effects are also available as coloured wallpaper, so it is possible to combine paper and paint to good effect.

In a cottage setting, you may prefer to amplify an irregular wall surface to make a real feature of it. In which case there is a special texturing compound which is applied to the wall as a thick plastic coating. It may then be patterned by running a roller over it or by pulling up the surface with a sponge covered in polythene. With a little practice, some interesting daub patterns can be reproduced, after which the material sets hard.

The best tool to paint such a surface is a long pile lambswool or nylon roller. A foam roller would be damaged, and pads will not get into the deep texture. The brush could be used if handled with a dabbing motion rather than the usual painting strokes.

Painting woodwork

Now let us look at the woodwork. Assuming that it is in a good state of repair, and that all cracks and gaps have been filled as recommended in Chapter 52, work to be painted should be given a final smoothing over with fine glasspaper. Dust off carefully and apply your tack rag to gather up any remaining bits.

Bare wood must be primed with primer, and this should be worked well into the wood grain. A thick coating is not necessary as long as the wood is completely covered. This clogs the pores of the wood so that subsequent coats do not soak into the surface. It also acts as a key for the undercoat.

When the primer is dry, check to see if there are any nibs in the surface. If there are, give only the lightest rub with fine glasspaper, rub too hard, and you will be back to bare wood! Dust off, and the surface is ready for undercoat.

The purpose of the undercoat is to add body to the surface and to obliterate any under-colour. If a medium coat of undercoat does not hide an under-colour, you must apply another when the first is dry. Do not rely on a top coat to hide anything.

A top coat is purely protective, and most gloss paints are quite thin, with little real covering power. Before it is applied, give the undercoat a light rub over to remove any nibs, dust off, use the tack rag, then the surface is ready for its next coat.

The tool most likely to be used here is the standard paint-brush, and you should choose a width to suit the job in hand. For frame work, the 12 mm (½ in) will get more use, backed by the 25 mm (1 in) for wider sections. Switch to the 50 mm (2 in)

466

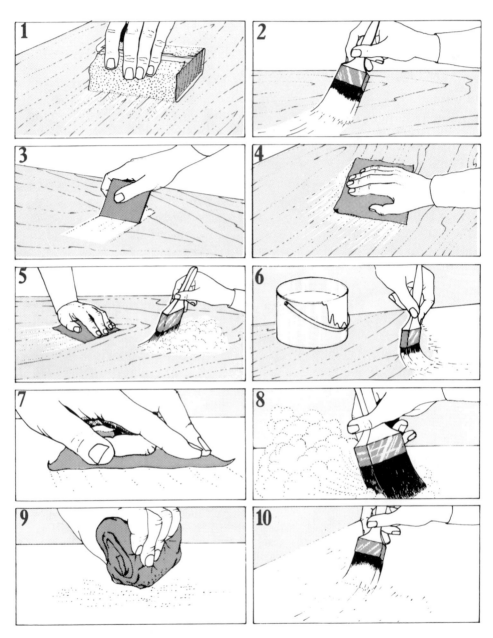

for window ledges, and back to the 12 mm (½ in) for edges. As a general rule, work with brush strokes in the direction of the wood grain, or along the length of the wood. Try to ensure that an adequate layer of paint is deposited on edges where, unless you watch it, the brush tends to wipe paint off.

Steps in painting a timber surface: 1, rub smooth, working with the wood grain. 2, apply patent knotting to wood knots. 3, work filler into cracks and gaps. 4, when set, rub smooth. 5, then dust off with a dusting brush or lint-free rag. 6, apply wood primer, then undercoat. 7, lightly sand to remove any nibs. 8, use the dusting brush to clean the surface. 9, then pick up any remaining dust on a tacky rag. 10, apply your top coat

Avoid overloading your brush, particularly when dealing with mouldings. Paint may gather and run down to form tears which will spoil the general appearance of your work. The same rule applies for larger panels, for too much paint may form sags and runs. It is far better to apply two thin coats than one heavy one.

The only exception to this rule is when using the thixotropic or jelly paints. Often referred to as 'one-coat paints', these combine undercoat and top coat in a jelly-like consistency which should not be over-stirred. The effect of dipping in the brush is to liquefy the paint, after which it starts to 'gel' again. When applied to the wood, it is laid on rather than brushed out, so you get a much thicker coating than with standard paint. Despite the name 'one-coat', when changing colour, particularly from dark to light, you may well need two coats to cover adequately.

The order of painting window frames and doors is purely a matter of convenience and common sense. While the illustrations show suggested orders, do not feel bound by regulations!

Gloss paint is still widely used for internal woodwork, but there is a trend towards using acrylic gloss finishes as an alternative. True you do not get a very high gloss—but is it really necessary anyway? A high gloss will highlight any faults in joinery and it can make a job look cheap.

A nice sheen makes an attractive alternative, and you have the benefits of fast drying and ease of brush cleaning. For those who suffer from chest troubles, there is the added bonus that you do not get the smell as with gloss paints. In other words, you are using glossy emulsion paint.

A suggested order for painting doors and windows. Always brush out along the length of each panel

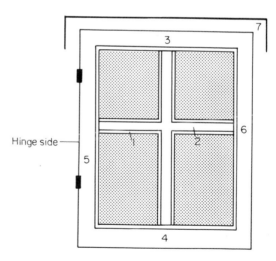

The handle side of the door and window is done last

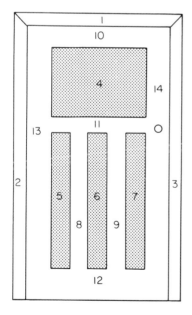

Painting a panelled door

Painting metalwork

Painting metal differs little from timber once the preparation is done except, perhaps, that you have no grain to follow. Edges are even more important on metal frames as they will be thinner and that much harder to paint. Again, be careful not to overload a surface or you will end up with runs.

Radiators present little problem. Most come ready-primed, and once you have removed any grease from plumbing work, plus the inevitable grubby finger marks using turps substitute, you can apply gloss coat. If you have chosen a strong colour, then an undercoat may be advisable just to give depth to the colour.

Copper pipes can be painted without priming as long as they are free from grease and dirt. It is not wise to paint over compression fitting nuts as it makes them hard to undo should it be necessary to remove the radiator.

Cove cornice

If you have put up new gypsum cove cornice as part of the redecorating, seal the surface with plaster primer prior to painting. The choice is yours as to whether the cove is painted to match the walls or the ceiling.

Gutters and pipes

Moving outside, the same basic principles apply as for interior painting, except that more care is needed to ensure that all surfaces exposed to the elements are well protected. One unfilled crack may be all that is needed for damp to get behind your defences and push protective coatings off from behind, so careful preparation is essential.

For exterior painting, start at gutter level, and work down. To reach this level you need a ladder which will take you three rungs above gutter level. This is so that there is always a hand-hold when working from the ladder. It is highly dangerous to adjust the ladder below the gutter then reach up, for the gutter should never be used as a support. This is particularly so with plastic guttering.

Make sure the ladder is standing on a secure base, and place a sandbag over the feet of the ladder to prevent slipping. Alternatively lash a rope around any nearby downpipe to the base of the ladder. To prevent sliding at the top, it is wise to anchor the top by means of a ring bolt in the fascia board through which nylon cord can be passed, then secured to the ladder. This is even more advisable with plastic guttering as its surface is very smooth. Do not worry about a ladder resting on plastic guttering, the plastic is quite able to take the strain.

The gutter brackets are normally screwed into a fascia board, and this needs to be painted. Ideally, remove the guttering so you can get at it. This is easy with plastic units, but with heavy cast iron sections, you will have to do the best you can. As with all timber, bare patches must be primed before undercoating and top coating. Two top coats are advisable. Try not to overload your brushes or you will get drips on to the brickwork.

Holding your paint at this height is always a problem, and a paint kettle will prove useful if used in conjunction with an S-hook looped over a suitable rung. Alternatively you can buy a simple ladder tray which, when hooked over the rungs of the ladder, forms a platform for paint and spare brushes. It is never advisable to hold a can of paint in your hand while painting with the other. Always keep one hand for the ladder!

With the gutter cleaned and repaired, make sure it is dry inside before painting. At this level you have the opportunity to

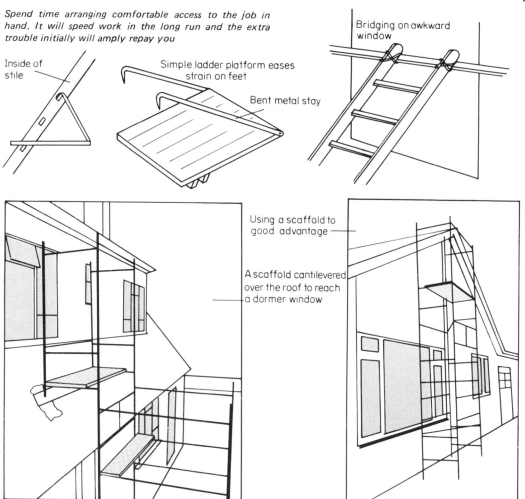

Spend time arranging comfortable access to the job in hand. It will speed work in the long run and the extra trouble initially will amply repay you

Inside of stile

Simple ladder platform eases strain on feet

Bent metal stay

Bridging on awkward window

Using a scaffold to good advantage

A scaffold cantilevered over the roof to reach a dormer window

use up any left-overs of good quality exterior gloss paint for the inside of the gutter. No one will see it up there—except the birds. If a heavy bituminous paint has been used previously, use the same again. Unfortunately bitumen will bleed through other paint coatings unless it is isolated by an aluminium sealer.

When changing colour, remember it is the undercoat which must hide the under-colour. Two or more coats if necessary. Finish with two coats of gloss.

Down-pipes get similar treatment. It is wise to hold a piece of card behind the pipe you are painting so you do not get paint on the brickwork.

Window frames

Next on the list are the upstairs windows. Here the problem is to use a ladder without resting it on the glass. It is often possible to lash a piece of wood across the top of the ladder so the wood rests either side of the frame, holding the ladder clear. Better still is to use two ladders with supports called 'cripples', on to which a stout scaffold board can be rested. This gives you a working platform along which you can move as necessary. If you are unused to working at heights, a scaffold pole fixed as a rail will discourage you from stepping back to admire your work!

An even better arrangement is a scaffold tower of the type developed for home use. This is easily erected from tubular sections, and it provides a safe working platform with safety rail all round. What you need is a hard, level area upon which to erect the scaffold; a wide path or patio would be suitable. If the tower can be moved along on wheels as supplied on some types so much the better.

Such a tower is fairly expensive, but often a group of neighbours will share the cost. If you prefer, you can hire one from a local hire shop. In this case plan your work so that you do not keep it longer than you need. Incidentally the tubular units can be utilised for interior work too, such as on stairs or to reach a high ceiling. You can make up a temporary bench, pasting table or trestle, while one outfit converts into a car port or garden shed by the addition of roof pieces and a stout plastic cover.

The actual painting of window frames is the same as for internal painting. If you wish to close your windows at the end of the day, start by painting those surfaces which have to meet when the windows are shut. If there is some doubt as to how dry the paint is, sandwich clean polythene between window and frame, and do not shut windows tight. Take your paint on to the putty of the window frames, extending it just fractionally on to the glass. This is to seal any fine gap between putty and glass where driving rain so often gets in. Paint the underside of the sills, and the ends. Ensure that there is a clear drip strip under the sill. This is usually a groove cut in the underside of the sill, and it is designed to force water to drip off rather than be carried over to the brickwork.

If the groove is clogged by too many old coats of paint, scrape it clean, prime and re-paint.

Never leave any bare wood or metal unprotected at the end of a day. At the very least put on a good priming coat to keep out damp. Do not be tempted to paint over damp wood; to seal the damp in will only encourage rot. If you must paint, a blowtorch will speed things up, but you must keep it on the move all the time to avoid scorching the wood.

Downstairs windows get the same basic treatment, except that a pair of well splayed steps will be far easier to work from than even a small section of ladder. Spend time establishing a firm, level base for the steps. Never take chances. If you are not happy even at these heights, it pays to invest in steps which have an extended hand rail so there is always something to grip. As with a ladder, never lean over to reach your work, always move the steps.

Door and door frames

Door frames are treated as for window frames. Treat the door as a separate unit, and paint it well. A suggested sequence for painting is shown in the illustration.

Timber garage doors can receive similar treatment, but metal doors are best painted with a polyurethane-based paint which is much tougher than normal paint. Because it dries hard, check the instructions on the can as to the time lapse between coats. If it is left too long to harden, subsequent coats will not bond to the undercoat.

Types of paint

One final word. At the time of writing, acrylic gloss has not been widely tried for exterior use, though at least one company markets it for this purpose. It has the advantage of quick drying; a real asset during winter months.

For full details of wall painting, including other types of paint suitable for exterior use, see Chapter 55.

Chapter 54 Interior walls

Careful preparation of the walls is necessary, as detailed in Chapter 52, before any form of new decoration is applied. It is assumed that any defects causing damp will have been dealt with. Painting of walls is described in detail in Chapter 53, so in this chapter we will deal principally with other forms of wall decoration.

Before the walls are tackled, all paintwork adjoining the walls—such as door frames, picture rails and skirting boards and window frames will have been done.

Insulation

The next consideration is whether a cold wall needs some insulation to reduce the risk of condensation. Only the external walls need be worried about, for internal partitions will not normally get very cold.

If you plan to treat a wall, measure up and buy sufficient expanded polystyrene wall veneer to cover it. At the same time, buy the special adhesive needed to fix it; preferably a rubberised or pva adhesive. You will see that the veneer is of different width to a standard roll of wallcovering so you will not get any matching of seams.

Apply adhesive to the wall surface, cut your veneer slightly oversize and press it on to the adhesive. A paint roller is a useful tool for pressing it in place. Note that if you apply too much hand pressure you will compress the veneer. Now paste the next wall area and apply a further length of

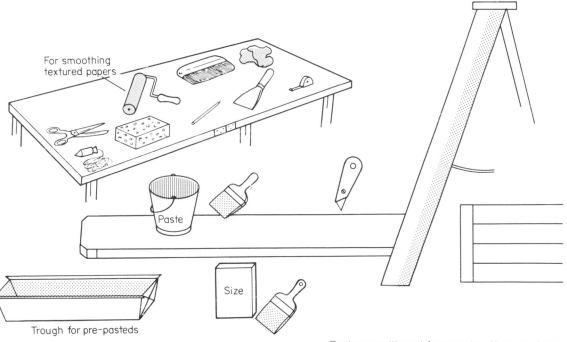

For smoothing textured papers

Paste

Trough for pre-pasteds

Tools for papering

Size

Tools you will need for papering. No paste, brush or pasting table needed with pre-pasted wall-coverings

472

veneer. If the edges of the wall veneer are true you can merely butt one piece of veneer to the next. If you encounter irregularities, it pays to overlap the second piece a fraction over the first, then cut through both with a sharp craft knife, using a straight-edge. Peel away the surplus pieces, and you will have a neat butt joint between both pieces.

Carry on until the whole wall has been covered, making sure all edges are well down. Trim off any surplus top and bottom, and the wall is ready for decorating. The remaining walls should be sized.

Wallpapering

Let us look at standard wallpapering first. For this you will need your pasting table and all the tools illustrated.

Assuming you choose a good medium weight paper, you need a paste with plenty of body and not too much water content. Bear in mind that you need to allow time for the paper to expand before you hang it. Once you become a little experienced at handling the paste brush, you will find you can paste one length of paper, fold it, put it aside and paste a further piece while the first is soaking. This way you will avoid bubbles.

Start work at a window wall, and measure the width of your paper less about 12 mm (½ in) and make a mark on the wall. This will force 12 mm of paper around the corner, and the idea of this is to allow for any inaccuracy in the corner. Now hold your bob so that it hangs over the pencil mark you made on the wall, and make a further pencil mark. This ensures that you will be hanging the first piece to a true vertical. Never rely on the corner being true, for any error encountered here would by duplicated all along the run of the wall.

Now hold your paper to the wall and

decide where you want the pattern to start. Make a fine mark and allow 40 mm (1¾ in) or so extra for trimming. Now measure your length and allow a further 40 mm at the base for trimming. Cut the length with scissors.

Lay the piece on the pasting table with the top to your right and pattern down. The top of the piece will at this point be on the floor. Apply paste, herringbone fashion, working from the centre out, making sure you cover every spot.

When all the paper on the table has been coated, pull the paper to the left and make a fold, pasted surface to pasted surface, then allow the fold to move to the left until all the unpasted paper is on the table. Finish pasting the length and allow it to soak. You can fold the top in at this stage and move the paper while you clean your table ready for the next piece. Never allow the paste to dry on the table.

Now move to the wall, release the top fold, and offer your right hand to the wall so that paper edge lines up with the pencil marks. Press the paper lightly to the wall with your right hand—still holding the left hand well away from the wall, then use your right hand to ensure the paper lines up with the pencil marks. Allow your left hand to take the rest of the paper to the wall, then use the smoothing brush down the centre of the paper to press the paper to the wall.

Work outwards from this point, then press the top against the picture rail and the bottom against the skirting board. Use your closed scissors to press the paper into the angle, pull the paper away and trim it top and bottom, allowing 3 mm (⅛ in) beyond the crease so that paper just turns. This will hide any crack there may be at rail or skirting level.

Push the paper back to the wall, and ease the surplus round to the adjoining wall. Press it into the corner with the brush.

The plumb bob and line ensures that the first piece on the wall is truly vertical

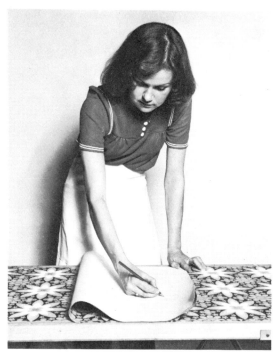

If it is not clear from the pattern, mark which is the top of the length

With one piece cut to length, match and cut two or three more lengths, again marking the tops

Paste from the centre out, herringbone fashion, making sure you do not miss any patches

Check to see the edges are down and that you have no bubbles, and that the first piece is in place.

Offer the roll to the first hung piece and note where the pattern match comes. If you are going to waste a fair piece of paper in matching, put that roll down and try some of the others. By using different rolls, it is often possible to cut waste quite dramatically which, in the long term, may save cutting into a new roll of paper. Hold your match in place, then mark top and bottom, with the spare 40 mm (1¾ in), top and bottom for trimming. Cut your length, paste, fold and allow to soak.

Obviously, if the pattern fits well into the room height, it may be possible to cut three or four pieces at a time. But if you have any problems with matching, it is still best to match one at a time, working from whichever rolls offer the best economy.

Carry your new piece to the wall, but

Fold the pasted area in, paste to paste, wipe the table and pull the remaining paper in place

Fold in again and leave the length to soak. When hanging, the smaller fold will be released

Position the paper and smooth out from the centre, just enough to hold the length in place. Release the lower fold

Use a brush to smooth the length in place, making sure no air is trapped underneath

Crease the paper into the skirting board and picture rail and trim off with scissors. Wipe off excess paste

this time it is the left hand which contacts the wall first, matching the pattern to the previous piece and easing the paper close to the first. With the paper in place, run the brush down the centre and out towards the far edge of the paper. Make sure that the seams match without pressing too tight, and if there are problems, pull the length away and try again. Do not try to force the paper into place, for at best you will stretch it and at worst tear it.

With the length in place, trim as before and wipe away any surplus paste. It is far harder to remove once it becomes dry.

Papering continues in this manner until some obstruction is encountered. If it is a further window, you need to do some careful measuring so that you can cut out any surplus piece, allowing at least 25 mm (1 in) over-size for trimming. Pasting will not be quite so easy as for a whole sheet, and you must be sure to wipe surplus

Slide the next piece in place so the pattern matches perfectly before pressing the paper down

A seam roller will ensure edges are pressed down. Don't press too hard on textured papers

Mark around obstructions with a light pencil mark. Don't press too hard

Cut out surplus allowing a few mm to turn on to the painted surface

paste from the table before pulling new paper into place.

When the piece is in place, press surplus paper into the edges of the frame as you did for the rail and skirting, and trim as before, allowing for a 3 mm (1/8) turn.

Light switches present another hazard which you will soon learn to deal with. Paste the paper as normal, hang it as for a flat wall, but do not press it tight down. Find the centre of the switch plate and, using your fine scissors, make a cut from the centre out. If the switch is a modern square one, cut towards each corner, but stop just short of the corner. If you encounter an older round switch plate, make star cuts all the way round as illustrated on page 493.

With a square plate, cut away surplus paper to within 6 mm (¼ in) of the edges of the plate, then loosen the holding screws enough to allow the surplus of

Wipe off surplus paste, then press the piece into place. Ensure no air is trapped

Finally smooth into place with the brush. Ensure all paste is removed from paintwork

paper to go behind the plate. Finish pressing down the paper, then use a lolly stick to ease the paper behind. A knife blade is unwise unless you have the power switched off!

With the round plate, you will have to press the edges of your star against the plate, make a crease, then trim off the surplus paper less a 3 mm (1/8 in) turn on to the plate. It sounds a complicated business, but once you have done one, it comes quite easily on any others you encounter.

Should you meet any bulges or other irregularities which prevent the paper laying properly, tear the paper over the difficult area, then press it back in place. This sounds drastic, but it gives a far more disguised repair than cutting with scissors. Never try to cut wet paper with a knife, however sharp; you will inevitably tear the paper.

On internal corners, it may be simplest to go right into the corner to cover the paper turn off the adjoining wall. The only exception is where the corner is really true and you can get a perfect match. Wherever you encounter external corners, it is wise to cut your paper width so that it turns about 25 mm (1 in) then join on the cut piece once you are round the corner. If angles are perfect, you may get a whole width to turn, but where there are inaccuracies in the plastering, you can end up with big problems where even tearing may not help much.

Ready-pasteds

One great advance in decorating in recent years has been the introduction of pre-pasted wallcoverings, where the adhesive comes as a dry layer on the back of the covering. With the rolls you get a special waxed trough, supplied as a flat sheet, but pre-creased so that it very easily converts into a strong water container.

The great advantage here, of course, is that no pasting table, bucket of paste or brush is required. The trough is filled about three-quarters full of cold water, then the wallcovering is cut as normal with spare at each end for final trimming. Roll the length loosely from the bottom with the pattern inwards. To activate the paste, press the loose-rolled length down into the water ensuring the back of the paper is completely wetted. Then slowly pull the length from the trough, allowing surplus water to drain back into the container. The trough should be positioned close to the wall, immediately below the area to be covered.

You may find a surplus of paste on the back of the piece, for the problem the manufacturers have is to supply sufficient paste for any situation. On a highly porous plaster you need far more paste than on a previously painted wall. The surplus is no real problem. Merely ease it out of the joints and wipe it clear with a sponge. The covering is positioned as for any other system, then smoothed down with a sponge.

The only trouble you may encounter is if you have to overlap a piece of vinyl wallcovering over another length. The paste supplied does not grip very well on vinyl and the surfaces may curl away from each other. In this case, let the vinyl dry, then put down the seams using a latex adhesive. This is clean to use, it will not stain, and any surplus can be rubbed off.

Specialist coverings

When buying special materials, like grass cloths, ask if there are any special points to watch. Are special adhesives required? Are the lengths and widths of rolls the same as for papers? Do pieces have to be trimmed? Will they match? A few tips are given below.

Flocks. These are now available in vinyl wallcoverings, and this makes them far easier to keep clean. Try to avoid getting paste on the flock pile, but if you do, wipe the flock clean with a damp sponge. Allow the paper to soak for about 15 minutes before hanging. Never press the paper down with your fingers when hanging, you may depress the flock pattern. Use the flat of your hand or a clean paint roller.

Cork decorated papers. It is best to line a wall which is to be covered with this material. Although hung in the same way as wallpaper, it does need trimming before hanging, using a long steel straight-edge and sharp trimming knife. Let the material become really supple before hanging, and keep paste off the cork face.

Grass cloths. Walls are best lined before a grass cloth is applied. Again the material needs trimming with a steel straight-edge and sharp knife. Use a prepared paste and allow the material to become supple before hanging. Do not turn the material at internal angles. Butt it into the corner. Turn about 50 mm (2 in) on external corners.

Hessian. Unless you have experience of this material, choose a hessian with a paper backing. This makes it much easier to handle. Backed types are pasted as for normal wallpaper, but if you choose an unbacked material, paste the wall then press the hessian on to the paste. Use a clean paint roller to press the material to the wall. Do not overlap the joints.

Silks. It is best to line walls first. Use a prepared paste and ensure that it does not get on the silk face. Fold the material only in pleats. Do not crease it or roll it or you will get marks you cannot lose, Keep your fingers off the delicate surface as much as possible, and do not overlap at the joints.

Murals. Special instructions are supplied with these. It is important to get the first piece truly vertical and to spend time getting a good join between sections. A prepared paste is usually advised, but

thinned down. It is important to work from the centre with a roller to ease out all air bubbles. Avoid folding or creasing the paper.

Wall tiling

The use of ceramic tiles increased tremendously with the introduction of the thin tile designed to be stuck in place with adhesive instead of the traditional bedding in cement mortar. The d-i-y tile was introduced in the size 5/32 in thick by 4¼ in square and at the time of writing it is still sold to these dimensions despite metrication.

As long as a surface is clean and dry, and is stable enough to support tiles, it may be covered. This includes old tiled surfaces where, perhaps, a rather ugly 6 in tile was used in the past. To remove these tiles is a terrible job, but tiling over is simple. The biggest problem is hiding a fair sized ledge formed where a wall was half-tiled, but this may be done with a hardwood edging strip, holding the top edge of both old and new tiling.

Tiles are available in plains and textures, and while plain tiles had a very good run there is an increasing interest in patterns and textures, despite the fact they cost more.

In some cases a combination of both may be the answer. An area of plain tiling relieved by the occasional patterned tile. Apart from simple patterns, picture tiles are available to enhance an area such as a splashback. Reproductions of vegetables, fish or plants. Then there are special tiles incorporating hooks, toilet roll holders and soap trays for use in the bathroom.

Leaflets are supplied with tiles explaining the method of applying, but here are the general rules.

Measure up one tile height from the floor or skirting board, and fix a straight-

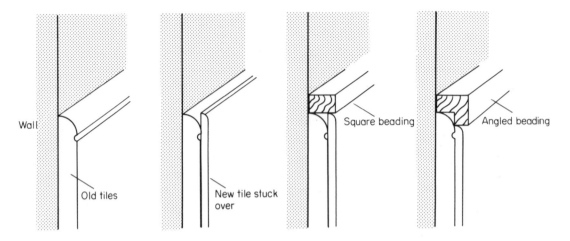

You can tile over old tiles. Here is how to finish off at the top of a half-tiled area

Wall
Old tiles
New tile stuck over
Square beading
Angled beading

Tips on wall tiling. The most vital point is to ensure that you start dead level. You cannot lose irregularities!

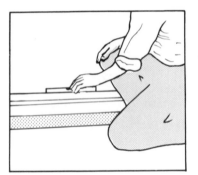

Fix a starting batten check with a level

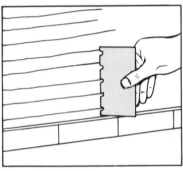

Spread adhesive with a special comb

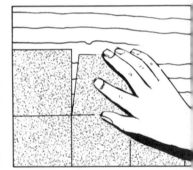

Ease tiles in place, don't slide

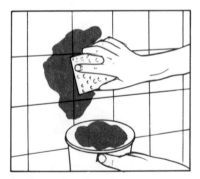

Apply grouting to gaps

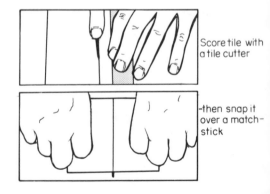

Score tile with a tile cutter

—then snap it over a match-stick

edge at this point with nails not driven right home. You will need a spirit level to get the board truly horizontal. If you find certain points are now wider than a tile width, due to floor irregularities, lower the batten a shade. It will be easier to nibble away a small portion from one or two tiles than cut slivers to insert into gaps.

Use the straight-edge as your base for the first row of tiles. Apply tile adhesive to the wall and spread it with the special serrated comb supplied. The comb ensures an even and not too liberal spread of adhesive. Press each tile into the adhesive, lowering it but not sliding it into place. If you slide the tile, you will force adhesive up between the joints. Wipe away any surplus adhesive before it sets.

Many tiles have built-in spacing nibs to ensure correct spacing between tiles, but if you encounter ones which have not, use thin strip of card as spacers, removing the strips once the tiles have set. Don't remove the batten too soon or the weight of the tiles may cause them to drop slightly.

Special tiles are available in certain ranges for finishing off edges. This must be borne in mind when ordering. These have one or two rounded edges without nibs.

Cutting tiles. This is quite simple, because only the top glaze is really hard. The 'biscuit' underneath snaps quite easily. Use a straight-edge and sharp tile cutter to score the tile on the glazed face, then lay the tile pattern up over a couple of matchsticks. Press either side of the line of cut, and the tile will break clean. Alternatively use a pliers-type cutter which has special jaws. If you grip the tile in the jaws in the correct manner and apply pressure, the tile will snap clean along the score mark.

For cutting shapes, such as where a pipe must pass through a hole cut in a tile, there is a special tile cutting blade which fits in a miniature hacksaw frame. It is also very useful for removing a very thin sliver from a tile where it would be hard to score and snap.

Grouting. Once tiling is complete, the gaps are filled with a special grouting powder mixed with water. It can be worked into the gaps with a small piece of sponge, then when dry, the surplus polished away with a ball of newspaper. This is a very good tile cleaner; more effectice than a rag. The illustration shows how hardwood beading can be used to cover the edge of a half-tiled wall.

Plastic tiles

Apart from ceramic tiles, you can also get dense polystyrene wall tiles and decorative aluminium or stainless steel ones.

These are designed for fixing by adhesive, and they can look most attractive. They are much lighter than ceramic tiles, but it must also be said that they have not the tough surface of the ceramic tile. Plastic tiles can be scratched by abrasive cleaners, they are affected by heat such as from a cigarette, and certain cleaners, like brush cleaning liquids, can affect the surface.

Wall panelling

Here again, detailed instructions are supplied; the details vary according to type. The most common way of fixing wall panelling is to first batten the walls at regular intervals, as recommended by the supplier, then secure the panelling to the battens with panel pins. Fixing is usually through a section of a panel which is hidden when the adjoining panel is pushed into place.

One problem is that the battens add to the thickness of the wall so that the ledge at skirting board level disappears. There is also the problem of the depth of door frames, and repositioning light switches and wall lights. On the credit side this is the ideal time to plan extra wiring for items like wall lights as the new cable can be hidden behind the panelling without having to channel the walls.

An alternative to battening, which is becoming more popular as the price of timber has increased dramatically, is the use of a special panel adhesive so that wall panelling is stuck direct to the wall. Obviously, walls must be flat, clean and dry, but assuming this is the case, the total depth to worry about is now only the thickness of the actual panel material, which is considerably less than panel plus wall battens.

Apart from timber effects, panels imitating brick or stone are now popular for adding character to a wall area. Before buying, check how points like brick joints are dealt with on the panels. Do they actually interlock, or do they match in such a way as to appear to interlock? Very often an effect can be ruined by obvious joints between panels, which you would not get with the real thing.

Removing a picture rail

There may be occasions where a picture rail may get in the way of a new panel covering, or you may wish to take your decoration right up to the ceiling to increase the apparent height of the room. Removal of the rail is possible, but it does call for a little caution if you do not wish to make too much of a mess.

A picture rail is usually secured by means of cut nails, and these are often reluctant to leave the wall; they may have rusted in. Try to lever the rail away with a claw hammer resting on a thin block of wood. If the nails will not move, do not use force or you will pull away a large chunk of plaster. Locate the nail positions and use a

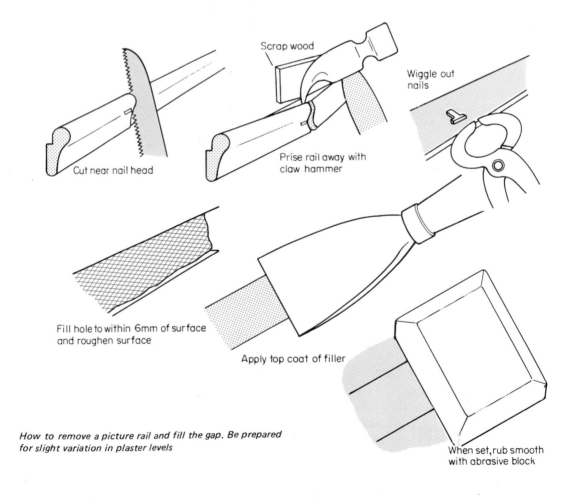

Cut near nail head

Scrap wood

Prise rail away with claw hammer

Wiggle out nails

Fill hole to within 6mm of surface and roughen surface

Apply top coat of filler

When set, rub smooth with abrasive block

How to remove a picture rail and fill the gap. Be prepared for slight variation in plaster levels

multi-purpose sheet saw to cut through the rail, as near the nail as possible, down to plaster level. Now use the claw hammer to rip the wood away from the nails.

With the wood out of the way, you can wiggle the nails out with pliers or a wrench. If you measure up, you may find you have problems with plaster levels, for the final coat may have been skimmed on after rail fixing. Clean out the gap, damp and fill with a compound such as Keene's cement, using two layers if the hole is deep.

Take the filler just above surface level, then use a permanent abrasive pad, which has particles of abrasive bonded into a metal sheet, to take down the plaster surface until it is level. If there is a difference in levels, you may have to compromise a little. Normally this does not show; the

only exception being if that wall surface is lit by a wall light and the light source is close to the wall.

Applying a textured wall coating

This is really neither paint nor paper, for it is a way of using a thick compound to give a relief surface to a wall. It should be looked upon as a permanent finish which, once applied, cannot be papered in future.

Accepting this fact, the textured coating offers a very simple way of adding character to a plain wall, and of hiding the defects in a rather poor wall surface.

Further details of actually applying the finish are given in Chapter 56 dealing with ceilings.

Chapter 55 Exterior walls

Before any decisions are made as to how the external walls should be decorated, you should consider very carefully the reasons behind decorating the areas involved.

First, how will your ideas fit in with the surrounding area? Will what you plan to do enhance the road you live in, or will your place stand out like a sore thumb? Of course, we are all individualists at heart, but too much can be a bad thing. This is particularly true if you live in a semi-detached house. Does your neighbour plan to come into the scheme with you, or will his place look completely run down when your decorating is finished? Ideally, both should be treated together as if it were one detached house, but if this is not possible, some form of compromise is advisable.

How best should the walls be treated? The desire may be to hide the old red bricks, but a straight coat of paint on top of the bricks could make the place look cheap and nasty. It would be better to consider a coat of tyrolean finish (see later) over which you can paint, for in this way the wall has in fact been rendered before painting.

Never paint over a good facing brick to give the place a fresh look. As stated above, painted brickwork, in the main, looks cheap and nasty and once paint has been applied to the bricks, you will never be able to remove it.

Are the walls very cold? Perhaps you have solid walls which are therefore harder to insulate. Obviously, applying coats of paint may make the wall drier, but it will add

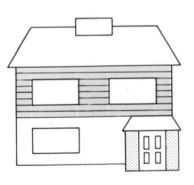

Dark timbering and white base walls

White plastic cladding and pastel lower walls

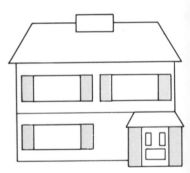

All white walls and contrasting timber shutters

Natural brick walls and contrasting shutters and window boxes

Cedar shingles and white lower walls

Variations on a theme. Choice of materials can transform the exterior of your home

little to the insulative effect. It may be worth considering at least part timber cladding, shingles, plastic weatherboard or perhaps vertical tiling which, if used correctly, and in conjunction with insulation materials, could vastly improve the insulation of the wall.

In view of the need for higher insulation standards, there are specialist companies who are considering ways of applying external insulation, then applying a coat of wall texture over the top. This is not a job for the handyman.

Where decorative brickwork is involved, if the walls are in any way porous, this will in itself lead to a colder house. In this case, the application of a clear silicone water repellent to the walls will help.

Ladders and scaffolds

When you have in mind just what needs doing, access to the job is the next important consideration. Working from an individual ladder can be very tiring, and because the ladder has to slope, different parts of the wall surface will be nearer or further from you. There is also the dangerous tendency to lean off the ladder to reach areas which would otherwise involve moving the ladder along. Far better make some form of safe working platform upon which you can stand.

A scaffold kit, supplied in knock-down form as a number of tubular sections, is ideal. It can be erected on any hard, flat surface, and it will provide a safe working platform at any height, with plenty of storage space for all the gear you need. It pays to add a safety rail to prevent your stepping off.

True, kits are expensive, but they can be hired for any given period and, if the work is planned correctly, hiring could prove well worthwhile. Wheels can be added to make the platform more mobile and sec-

tions of the kit can be used to form a workbench or a simple low platform for jobs nearer the ground. If this is not possible, you can use two ladders with items called builders' cripples to form a strong support for a stout scaffold board. Again this would be far more comfortable than standing on an individual ladder.

As mentioned earlier, never take chances with work above ground level. Safety must be the number one priority. Assuming you now have safe access, let us look at some of the surfaces we have to decorate.

Plain brick walls

As already mentioned, a thorough wash down with plain water and a scrubbing brush may be all that is needed.

Really grubby areas can be scrubbed with a piece of matching brick, or you may remove the grime with a wire brush, but remember to be sure to protect your eyes. Seal the surface with a silicone water repellent to keep out rain and also to discourage the settlement of dirt on the wall surface.

Renewing pointing

It often improves the appearance of the wall if the pointing looks attractive. Rake out the mortar with a tool made from a piece of steel sharpened to a point and bent to form a small rake. Go in at least 12 mm (½ in), brush out all loose material, then re-point using a mortar mix. This is available by the bag and all you need do is add water. Add a minimum amount so the mortar does not drip on to the brickwork. It should be dry enough to leave no marks. Shape the face of the mortar to match the surrounding brickwork.

For a hollow joint you will need a piece of mild steel rod bent to a curve. For a more traditional weathered joint, you can achieve this with a small pointing trowel.

Tyrolean finish

If yours is an older house with rather poor quality brick walls, it may pay to consider hiding the brick. A machine called a tyrolean projector can be hired from many hire shops, and this is designed to throw a wet mortar mix on to the wall to give a very attractive dash effect. This hides the brickword completely, including joints.

This system offers an excellent alternative to the more traditional spar dash or pebble-dash finish which really calls for more expertise. It is quite a lengthy job and is really best left to a contractor who specialises in this kind of work. Once the tyrolean finish has set, it can be painted to suit.

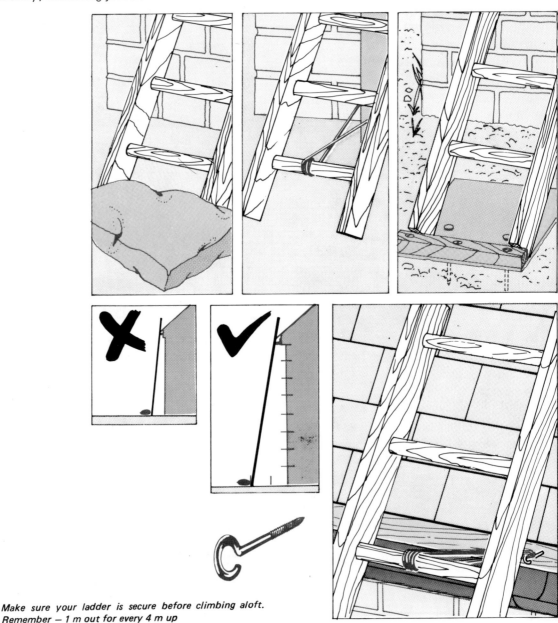

Make sure your ladder is secure before climbing aloft.
Remember — 1 m out for every 4 m up

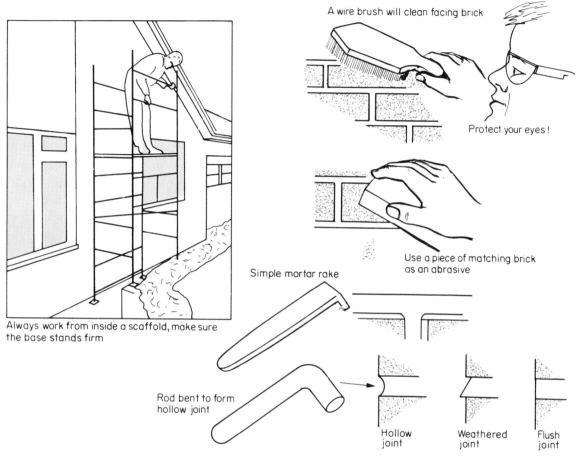

A wire brush will clean facing brick

Protect your eyes!

Use a piece of matching brick as an abrasive

Simple mortar rake

Always work from inside a scaffold, make sure the base stands firm

Rod bent to form hollow joint

Hollow joint

Weathered joint

Flush joint

Re-pointing an area of good facing brick can transform its appearance. Never add chemicals to any washing water

Rendered walls

Assuming the wall has been prepared as discussed in Chapter 52, a rendered wall can be painted with any one of a number of masonry paints. Exterior grade emulsion paint is fine as long as it does not have to fill hair-line cracks, for it has no bulking out like some of the paints. A coat thinned to 50% with water will do as a priming coat, then followed with two top coats. The emulsion can be applied by brush, at least 127 mm wide or, alternatively exterior grade paint roller.

The advantage of a good emulsion is that with age it 'chalks' on the surface, which means that just enough of the surface finish breaks down to bring off dirt and grime when it rains.

This makes it fairly self-cleaning, an important point in industrial areas.

Alternatively, you can use a cement-based paint, supplied as a powder and mixed with water as required. It can be applied by brush; a dustpan brush is very useful for any masonry paint. It is easy to hold and gives good coverage quickly.

A stone-based paint is more durable than a cement paint, and the next step up in durability and coverage is a masonry paint to which an additive such as mica or nylon fibre has been added. This combines decoration with extra strength, and the paint will hide minor blemishes and fill hairline cracks.

Be sure to wipe up any spills as you progress. All these rendering materials are far

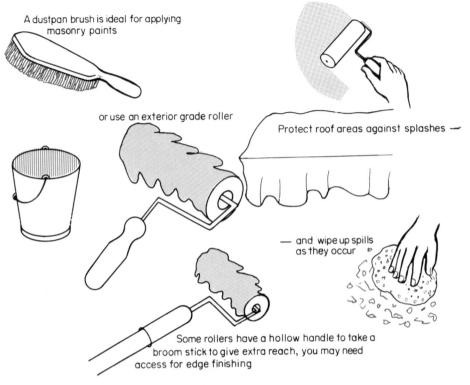

A dustpan brush is ideal for applying masonry paints

or use an exterior grade roller

Protect roof areas against splashes →

— and wipe up spills as they occur

Some rollers have a hollow handle to take a broom stick to give extra reach, you may need access for edge finishing

If you choose a roller for exterior work, be sure it is designed for the job. Foam and mohair are not suitable for this work

Work masonry paint into a surface and go gently so as not to damage dash surfaces

easier to remove when wet than when set hard. It also pays to protect surfaces like porch roofs, paths and flower beds, which are far easier to protect than to clean up afterwards.

To apply masonry paint, stipple pebbledash with a paint brush

or use a shaggy pile roller

Pebbledash

Pebbledash is always more difficult to decorate because of its deep textured surface. Assuming it is in good shape, a hose down with the jet on not too fierce a spray will remove loose dirt.

After drying, a masonry paint can be applied. Paint can be worked in by stippling with a well-loaded brush, or you can use a shaggy exterior grade paint roller. It is best to have a smaller brush handy for areas around windows and doors. As the

Scrub vertical tiling using clean water, detergent leave stains brush will be contaminated with a certain amount of grit, it is wise to keep it for this kind of work and not transfer it to gloss work. The same basic treatment applies to a spar dash finish. Do not be too rough on older surfaces or you will dislodge stone chippings.

As soon as painting is finished, be sure to clean up all rollers and brushes used for masonry finishes. It is not wise to leave them soaking.

Tiles

Vertical tiling will usually respond to a scrub down with clean water. Do not be tempted to add detergents to the water as this often leaves whitish streaks which are impossible to remove when the tiles are dry.

If the tiles look very jaded, there are tile-coloured floor paints based upon rubber which will give a very good finish. The secret is to select one which really does not make the tiles look as if they have been painted. Keep the colour muted and preferably of the same colour as the tiles. Apply a thin coat well rubbed into the surface of the tiles so you get no brush marks.

Tile polish of the kind used for steps is an alternative, but it has not such a long life as a paint.

Shingles

Cedar shingles can look rather jaded on a house front once the warm colour of new cedar bleaches out and you are left with an uninteresting grey tone. The colour can be restored by using a preservative designed for red cedar which contains a stain. This is able to impart some of the warmth of the original wood while at the same time preserving it.

A coat of varnish over the timber will further preserve it against the weather, though you must bear in mind that the varnish would have to be removed should you wish to apply another coat of stain preservative. Obviously this is designed to soak into the wood, not sit on the surface.

Timber cladding also needs treatment, and this is mentioned in Chapter 10 'Wood-finishing'.

Plastic cladding

Plastic cladding is really designed to be self-cleaning as it has a smooth surface. To remove grime, all it should need is a wash with water containing a household detergent. It is not wise to use an abrasive material, as this will provide a rough surface to which dirt will adhere. It is far better to use something like a metal polish wadding to remove obstinate marks, as this will improve the gloss, not remove it.

Plastic cladding can be painted as long as it is clean and dry. Only a top coat is necessary unless you plan a change of colour. Be prepared to keep painting it in the future, as paint would not be easy to remove. Obviously a blowtorch is out of the question, and many chemical strippers will attack the surface of the plastic. In the main, it is best to leave it in its natural colour.

Stone facings

Natural stone facings are popular today, and these too need care when decorating. Again, only clean water should be used, in conjunction with a stiff scrubbing brush. If you need to rub the stone, find a piece of matching stone and use this as a pumice block, keeping it constantly wetted with water.

A stone facing may be painted, but again once done you will have to continue painting in the future. Probably the best finish is a stone-based masonry paint applied sparingly with a brush and worked well into the stone. But be warned, it can make your natural stone look like an artificial finish. Far better stick to the natural thing if at all possible.

Drives and paths

Although this is really another aspect of decorating, when thinking about exterior walls it is wise to consider paths and driveways.

These may not be decorated in the strict sense of the word, but you may consider coating paths with a cold macadam finish. This is available in black and a few warm colours, and it is supplied by the bag ready for spreading and rolling out. A special primer is supplied to bond the macadam to the path, and once it has started to harden, loose chippings of a contrasting colour are available to sprinkle on and relieve the solid colour a little.

Converting the paths from a normal concrete colour to perhaps black can contrast well with walls painted white.

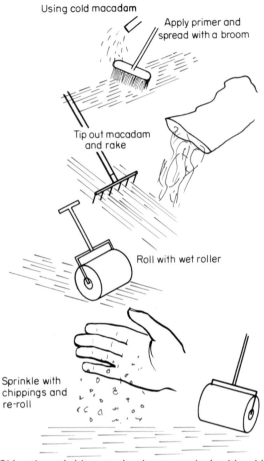

Using cold macadam

Apply primer and spread with a broom

Tip out macadam and rake

Roll with wet roller

Sprinkle with chippings and re-roll

Old paths and drives can be given a new look with cold macadam. Few tools are required

Chapter 56 Ceilings

As mentioned in an earlier chapter, the ceiling is best tackled before other decorating, and even before old wallpaper is stripped off the wall. In this way, any splashes will be removed with the old wall covering. It is at this stage you decide whether to add a cove cornice.

Fixing a cove cornice

The cove cornice bridges the gap between wall and ceiling, and adds a very neat finish to a room. This join between wall and ceiling is always a weak spot in house construction, and any slight movement in the fabric may appear as a crack which it is impossible to seal. As it cannot be sealed, the coving effectively hides it.

The simplest type of coving is made of expanded polystyrene lengths around 1 metre (or 1 yd) long, and apart from straight runs, internal and external corners are available. Fixing is very simple and is done by special adhesive. Do not be tempted to use any adhesive as some of the rubberised ones have solvents which dissolve expanded polystyrene. While very simple and light to handle, the main snag is that joints between pieces are very difficult, if not impossible, to hide because of the nature of the material. It is best just to accept the joints will be visible.

A better effect is gained by using a gypsum plaster coving covered in a stiffish paper. This is also available in short lengths, but joints can be hidden as long as the ceiling is not too irregular. If you can, it is better to get the longest lengths so that it is possible to do most room lengths or widths

in one piece. Obviously this will look far neater than any other treatment.

The coving has to be stuck in place with a special adhesive and despite the considerable weight of a length of coving, the adhesive holds it firm without any other support. The adhesive must go on to bare wall and ceiling, so existing wallcoverings must be cut back to the recommended width, and the same on the ceiling.

The trickiest job is cutting mitres on the ends of the pieces, and while a templet is supplied, it pays to experiment on a spare piece of coving to ensure that you cut it correctly. Slight inaccuracies do not matter too much as the gap can be filled quite easily, but mis-use of the templet can result in a large oval hole!

Once in place, the coving is primed with a plaster primer, and is then ready for decorating along with the rest of the room. Coving offers a nice deep ledge up to which ceiling and wall coverings can come.

Painting the ceiling

Assuming that the ceiling has been cleaned and prepared, if the plaster is in really good shape, you can paint straight on to it, but any slight irregularities at joints may show up.

In the main, a ceiling always looks more attractive if it is first papered then painted; though of course there is nothing to stop you papering it to match the walls if you wish.

The paper may be smooth, rather like a good lining paper, or you can choose one of the Anaglypta range of textured finishes, offering anything from a simple pebbledash design through to some very pleasing plaster daub effects. These look even better when room lighting is near the ceiling, as the light picks up the texture.

Papering the ceiling

The operation for ceiling papering is similar to dealing with the walls, except that lengths involved are usually greater. So folding prior to papering has to be given more thought.

The first essential prior to papering is to arrange a working platform so your head is about 75 mm (3 in) from the ceiling. You can do this with a pair of steps and a suitable box, between which you support a scaffold board. Alternatively two pairs of steps will do. Do not try to work from one pair of steps; it just will not work!

Start papering at a window wall, parallel with the window and working away from it. The reason is that, should one piece overlap at some point, the overlap will be highlighted by light from the window. If you worked in the reverse direction, a similar overlap would appear as a dark shadow. Measure out from the window wall and subtract about 6 mm (¼ in) so that the paper will turn on to the wall by this amount. If you are working to a cove cornice, this turn need not be allowed for, as there will be no crack to hide between wall and ceiling.

How to fix a cove cornice. Experiment with scrap material first so you can make good internal and external joints

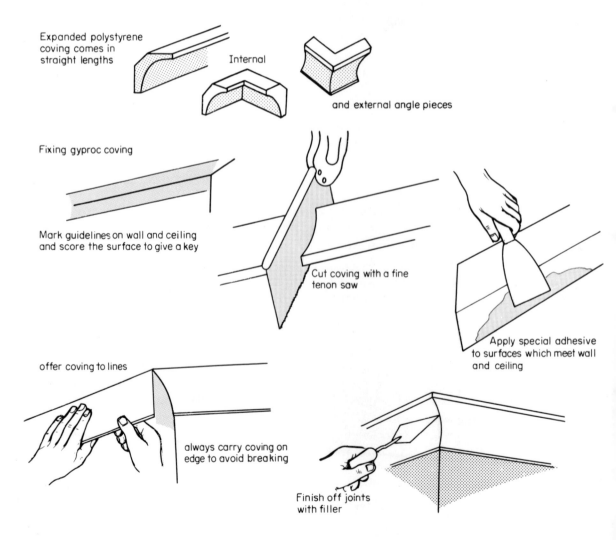

Expanded polystyrene coving comes in straight lengths

Internal

and external angle pieces

Fixing gyproc coving

Mark guidelines on wall and ceiling and score the surface to give a key

Cut coving with a fine tenon saw

Apply special adhesive to surfaces which meet wall and ceiling

offer coving to lines

always carry coving on edge to avoid breaking

Finish off joints with filler

Cut star shaped slits to fit around the ceiling rose, trim as for a wall switch

A broom will keep a heavy paper in place

Until you are experienced, get help with ceiling paper hanging — especially when dealing with heavy papers

Make two marks, then snap a chalk line right across the ceiling. This is the line to which the first piece of paper will be hung. You can buy quite elaborate chalk lines contained in a special case which holds the chalk, but for just occasional use it is sufficient to rub a length of coarse string with a coloured chalk. Secure one end of the string to a pin tapped into the ceiling. Hold the other end so the string is taut, then snap the string so that it leaves a mark.

Place the first cut piece of paper to the right of the pasting table with paper on the table ready to paste. Work from the centre out, herringbone fashion so you do not push paste under the length. As pasting is complete, fold the pasted part, concertina fashion, on to itself until the whole length is ready. If the paper is a fairly heavy one, allow it to soak before hanging.

Prior to papering, it is advisable to size the ceiling with a special glue size. This adds considerably to the adhesion of any paste used, and it also adds 'slip' to the paper, making it far easier to slide into place. This is important when you are working in a very awkward position with your hand above your head!

Now support the folded paper over a spare roll of paper as illustrated and use this as a carrier. Climb your scaffold, and offer the end to the ceiling, allowing the first fold to drop out. Position the paper to the line, ignoring the wall side at this stage, then slowly move along the scaffold board, letting out the folds. With a heavy paper it may help to have another pair of hands with a broom. They merely need to use the broom head to stop the hung piece pulling away from the ceiling, which it may try to do. You really appreciate the force of gravity when doing this job!

Once the length has been positioned along the line, use the smoothing brush to brush it down, making sure all wrinkles and any trapped air are eliminated. The ends are creased with scissors as with wallpaper, the paper pulled away and the surplus trimmed off. Allow a slight turn if the paper adjoins the wall. If a coving is involved, trim the paper accurately with no turn.

Now proceed with the next length, matching it to the edge of the previous length. You may well encounter an obstruction fairly soon in the form of a ceiling rose. If you do, it pays to do some accurate measuring and mark the position on the dry piece of paper. Make a number of star cuts in the paper, then paste the whole piece in the normal way.

When you get near the ceiling rose, merely feed the flex through the hole, and ease the paper around the rose. Press the cut pieces to the rose base, then trim off with small scissors. Again you can allow a slight turn on to the rose so no gap is visible. Be sure to wipe paste off the rose, before it hardens.

If you work with a textured Anaglypta, avoid the temptation to press the paper hard to the ceiling. This will flatten out the pattern to the extent that when you see the completed ceiling you will have tramlines of flattened pattern. Apply just enough pressure to make sure the paper is down. As with any heavy material, allow an Anaglypta plenty of time to soak before hanging. If it bubbles on the ceiling, allow more soaking time on subsequent pieces.

Fixing expanded polystyrene

An alternative to paper is sheet expanded polystyrene supplied by the roll. This is available in a number of patterns and the idea is that it is hung rather like ceiling paper, butting each piece to the next.

There is quite a difference in technique of hanging this. The adhesive is a special one which is applied to the ceiling and not the sheet. The polystyrene cannot be bent or folded, so it must be cut quite accurately to length. An obstruction, such as a ceiling rose, needs very careful marking out as it will have to fit exactly. It pays to cut the hole on the small size, then once the flex has been fed through and you have established the hole is in the right place, you can enlarge the hole with a craft knife.

Do not press hard on the sheet or you will indent it and it may not recover. Fill any slight gaps with a cellulose filler rubbed in with a rag. Gaps are easy to lose.

Once all these materials are in place the ceiling can be painted, using either brush, roller or pad brushes. It pays to apply at least two coats, one of which should be done in daylight so you can see if you have missed anything.

Ceiling tiles

Where a ceiling is sound, but looks pretty poor, ceiling tiles can transform it. There are a number of types of tiles, but the most used for d-i-y work are made of expanded polystyrene. They come in two main sizes, 300 mm² and 600 mm² approx. There are many patterns and textures available. For a large room, obviously the larger tiles are ideal as you need less, and each covers a larger area. They are not so convenient in a smaller room where cutting may be involved.

If you intend to paint your tiles, it pays to do so before putting them up. It is much easier, particularly as far as edges are concerned, and it is certainly less tiring on the arms.

Be sure to apply tile adhesive over the whole ceiling area and not by the old five blob method. A tile stuck overall is not a fire risk, even when not made of self-extinguishing grade expanded polystyrene. It is a fire risk if stuck by the blob method, as it has been shown that flaming pieces tend to drop away from the blobs of adhesive.

It is also essential that emulsion paint or a fire-retardant paint is used for decoration. Never use gloss paint as this has been shown to add considerably to the fire risk.

If you have to trim tiles, use a razor blade and straight-edge, or a very sharp knife. A blunt blade will rip at the plastic, causing it to crumble rather than cut.

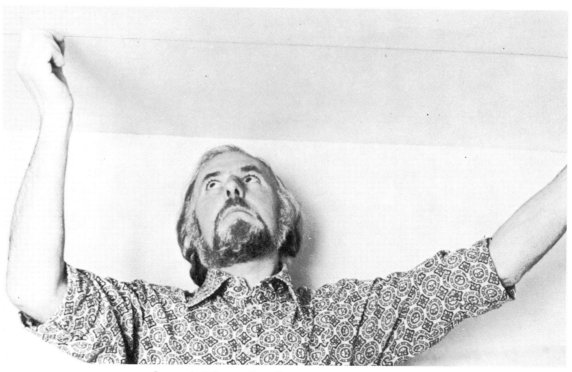

Snap a chalk line on the ceiling to give you a starting point

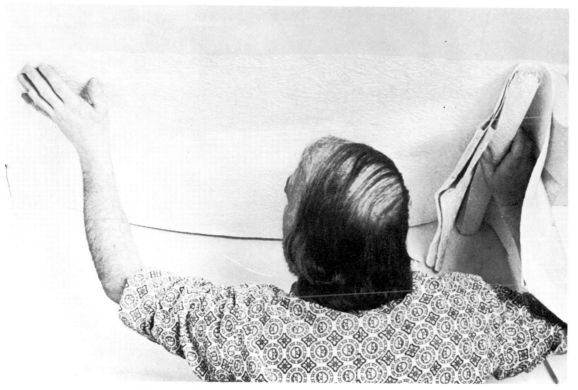

Align your first length with the chalk mark, sliding the paper to the line

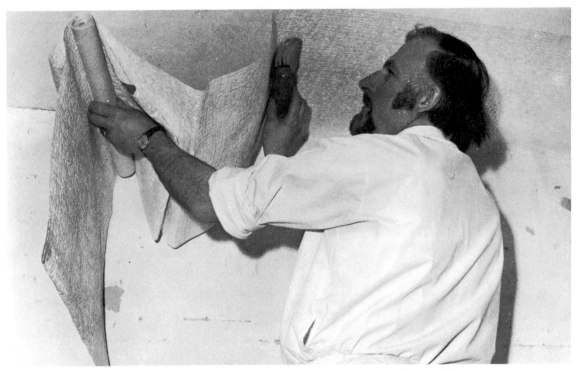

Use a spare roll of paper to support the pasted paper, releasing the folds one by one

Mark the surplus paper with a fine pencil line. Don't press too hard

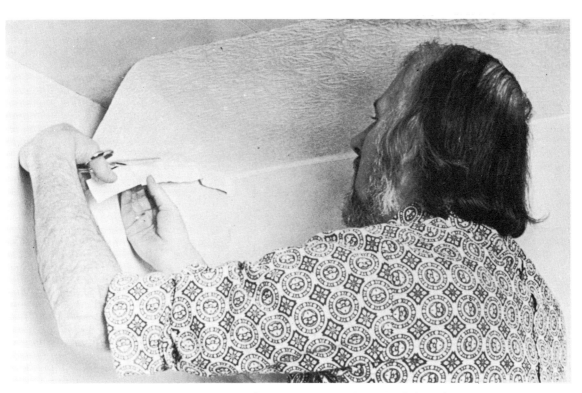

Trim surplus so you leave a few mm to turn on to the walls to hide cracks

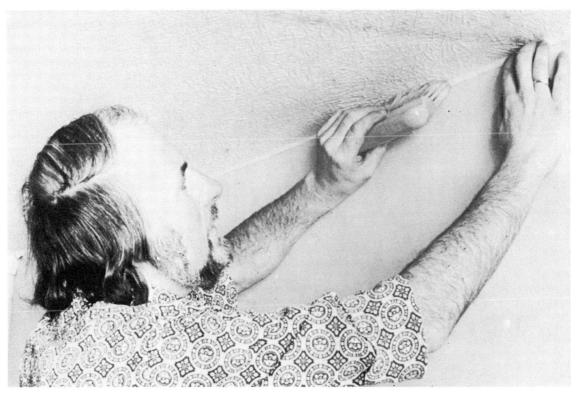

Press paper firmly in place using the smoothing brush. Check seams are down

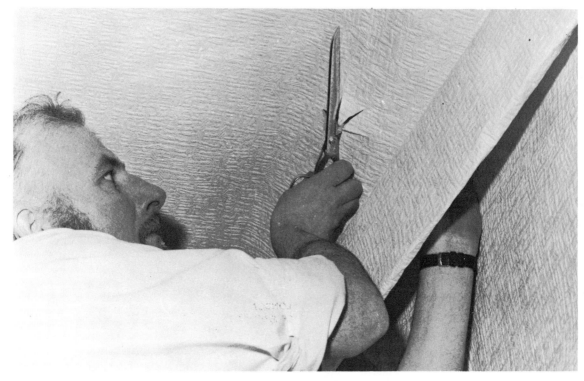

Make a star-shaped cut to pass light rose through

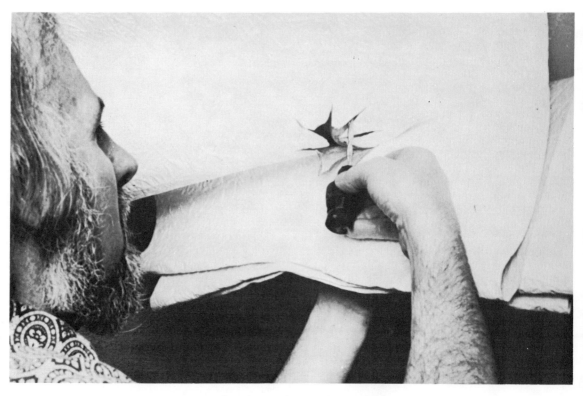

Ease the rose through the hole

Press paper around the fitting and mark lightly with a pencil

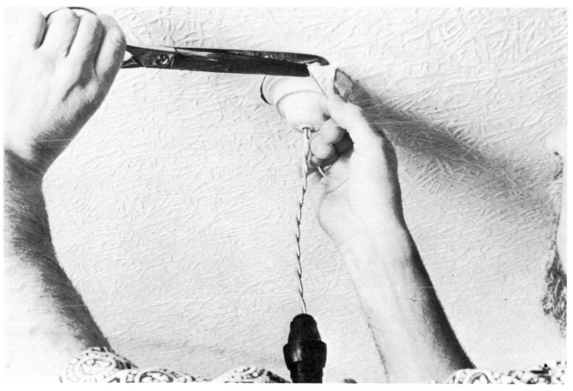

Trim off surplus paper, press paper down and wipe paste from the fitting

500

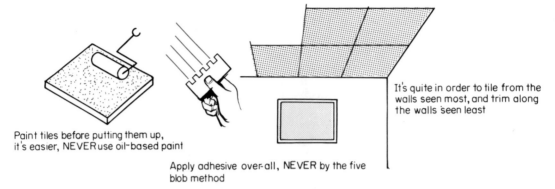

Paint tiles before putting them up,
it's easier, NEVER use oil-based paint

Apply adhesive over-all, NEVER by the five
blob method

It's quite in order to tile from the
walls seen most, and trim along
the walls seen least

Fixing ceiling tiles. As a fire precaution always apply tile adhesive over the whole ceiling. Tiles would melt but not drop away. The old method of applying a blob of adhesive to each corner of the tile should never be used

Opinions vary, but I do not consider it necessary to start in the centre of a ceiling and work out with tiles. Work from the two walls seen most as you enter the room, towards the walls noticed least—at these walls you can do your trimming. This method looks neater than perhaps having to trim all around the room.

Decorative finishes

Where a ceiling is not too well covered—perhaps with plasterboard where the joins are still visible—you can improve the appearance with a decorative compound. This comes in tubs, and you spread it thickly on the ceiling, using a wide brush.

Do not brush it out like ordinary paint. Cover an area no more than about ½ metre by 1½ metres (2·5ft approx), then start to texture the surface. A sponge inserted into a plastic bag, then pressed on the material and eased away produces a simple stipple. Twisting the sponge before pulling away produces a swirl. A plastic roller run lightly over the surface produces a bark effect and, of course, there are many variations on a theme. It pays to experiment on a piece of board before you start, so you know just what effect you want.

With one area done, continue, area by area, matching each into the pattern. The material sets in about 2 hours in a cool room. It pays not have the room too warm, or the material will dry out too fast.

Be sure to clean up as you go, as the material is not easy to remove once it has set. Do bear in mind that once you have a textured ceiling it is very hard to remove. You cannot paper over it.

Timbered ceilings

For something completely different, a timbered ceiling can look very attractive. Where old plaster is in a very bad state it may pay to pull the whole lot down so that the joists are exposed, but bear in mind that this is a very dusty, dirty operation.

If everything is holding up but just looks bad, it is better to leave the plaster in place, but probe the plaster with a fine drill or sharp awl and mark the exact position of the ceiling joists. Then, if you run your timber at right angles to the joints, you know exactly the location of your fixing points.

Tongued and grooved boarding as used for floors is quite adequate. Select it for grain pattern and firm knots. Fixing can be by fine panel pins angled through the tongue so that the next groove hides the

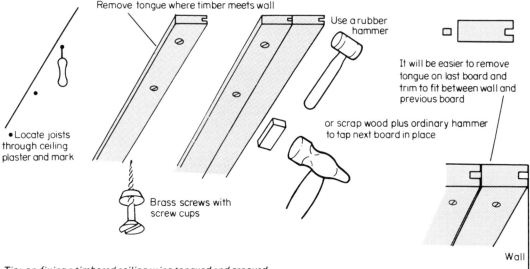

Remove tongue where timber meets wall

Use a rubber hammer

It will be easier to remove tongue on last board and trim to fit between wall and previous board

• Locate joists through ceiling plaster and mark

or scrap wood plus ordinary hammer to tap next board in place

Brass screws with screw cups

Wall

Tips on fixing a timbered ceiling using tongued and grooved boards. Quite a lot of weight is involved, so firm anchoring is essential

nails, or you could make a decorative feature of fixing and use brass screws. Countersink holes at set joist intervals in the boards, tap each in place with a rubber hammer, then drill a start hole and screw the board in place. Line up all the screw slots as you would with boat-building. It makes for a very neat finish. Brass screw cups may be used to further enhance the decorative effect. These go in place in the countersunk hole before the screw is put in.

A polyurethane seal can be used on the boards, or you could use one of the very attractive wood stains which gives a matt finish. As mentioned for ceiling tiles, the simplest way to finish the boards is before they are put up. It makes for much easier working.

False ceilings

Yet another approach to ceiling decoration where a high ceiling is involved is to lower the ceiling by making up a lightweight panel and suspending it from the main ceiling. The panel can be around 300 mm (12 in) smaller all round than the room size, then the space above used to house lighting. In this way the room can be lit indirectly, boosting the light with table lamps and standard lamp.

Alternatively, a package illuminated ceiling can be purchased which fits the whole room. Translucent panels fit in a special grid, and illumination is from above. Lighting can be plain, for areas such as a kitchen, or coloured to give mood lighting in a lounge.

Chapter 57
Floors

Floorcoverings have by far the heaviest wear of all the decorative surfaces in our homes. The first thing to remember is that the life you get from a floorcovering bears a direct relationship to the state of the floor upon which it is laid. To give a simple example, if you lay sheet vinyl on to a rough concrete floor, it will only be a matter of weeks before it shows signs of wear. If that same vinyl were bonded to a sheet of new chipboard, it would last for many years with no sign of wear at all.

So the first essential is to ensure that the floor, whether timber or solid, is in good condition. A very rough concrete floor may need a screed spread over it to provide a brand new surface. A badly worn timber floor may need resurfacing with a sanding machine, or perhaps have sheet hardboard laid over the whole lot to provide a new surface. All irregularities in the surface must be dealt with. Sharp nibs of concrete, or projecting nail heads. Anything which would damage the new floorcovering.

Faults like woodworm and rot damage, structural weaknesses, damp and very badly worn areas are dealt with in Section 1 (Home Repair and Maintenance). For the sake of decorating, we will assume the floors are in good shape.

The next important factor is what kind of floorcovering is to be laid. This may be a matter of preference or of pocket, but there are practical considerations too. We will now consider a few of these.

Choosing floorcovering

There are many grades of carpet very closely linked with the price you are asked to pay, and before you choose, ask at your local showroom for details of the gradings. These will range from the cheaper materials with very little body, where you can see the backing just by moving the tufts, through to a really expensive, dense pile. One may be adequate in the spare bedroom where there is little wear, but it would be hopeless on, say the main staircase. While the expensive one would be ideal for a well used lounge, it would be a waste of money in the spare bedroom.

Certain carpeting with artificial fibres is perfectly usable in the bathroom, if used in conjunction with a bath mat. It will make the room far more cosy, and the carpet will not be affected by damp conditions. On the other hand, the kitchen is not the ideal place for carpeting; with the likelihood of spills, it could soon look a mess. Cork or cushioned vinyl would be a better bet; this is easy to keep clean, yet warm to the feet. It is best to avoid a hard, smooth vinyl in the kitchen, for though it will wear well and be easy to clean, water spilled on it will make it extremely slippery.

If you are just starting a home and money is scarce, do not despise simple materials to start with. Oil-tempered hardboard can make a very attractive surround to a carpet Square. Treat it with a polyurethane seal and it will gleam—until such a time as you can afford a fitted carpet.

Think carefully before deciding whether to use tiles or sheet materials. The tile serves a very useful purpose in that it is very easy to lay, but you must accept pattern limitations. If you want the best of patterns, you will find these in the sheet materials. One problem we used to have with sheet vinyl was that, in most rooms, you needed two pieces to cover a floor; involving a seam.

However, with the introduction of much wider sheets, it is now possible to cover most rooms, such as kitchens and dining areas, in one piece. In addition, there is a far greater flexibility of material, so some cushioned vinyls can be folded like a carpet. This means that sheet materials are not so hard to lay as they used to be.

Above all, with carpeting, do not skimp on underlay. This too has a very real bearing on the feel and the wear of the carpet. Buy the very best you can afford.

Hardboard

This can be used to resurface a rather worn timber floor, but before putting it down, consider whether you need access at any point. It is made more difficult when the floor is covered by a sheet material. To prevent movement it can be spot bonded to the floor with a flooring adhesive. Tiles or sheet materials can then be laid over the top.

Sealing off a floor like this does not add to the risk of floor rot through damp. It is assumed the underfloor is well ventilated, and this is all that matters. The hardboard will eliminate draughts between boards, which is a good thing in these days of heat conservation.

Apart from using it as an underlay, hardboard can be laid as a decorative sheet material, as already suggested.

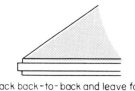

Stack back-to-back and leave for 24 hours in the room to condition. This will avoid buckling

Before laying hardboard, sprinkle board backs with water

Hardboard can be used to completely cover a worn floor. Be sure to condition the hardboard before use, or it will buckle

Parquet

For a touch of elegance in hall, dining room or lounge, parquet is still a favourite, and this includes strip flooring.

To cater for the d-i-y market much thinner sections have been introduced which offer more than adequate wear for the average home and, of course, this brings the price down. There are two main systems offered; the first where thin sections are stuck down on to a hardboard base. The parquet is ready-prepared in squares and these are merely butted together to give the desired effect.

The second method involves prepared squares which have tongues and grooves built into the edges, and the floor is built up by tapping the squares together so the tongues and grooves mate. By this method, no adhesive is necessary, and it would be possible for the floor to be lifted; though it is not always easy to separate the units.

Strip flooring is also produced for the d.i.y market, and this also is available with interlocking edges, where the interlock is invisible when the units are pressed together. Full laying details of all these materials are supplied at the time of purchase.

Hard tiles

While the old quarry tile, so often seen in country homes, has lost favour, floor tiling has again become popular in recent years. This may well be influenced by holidays abroad in countries with hot summers, where the decorative floor tile is much in favour.

A very wide pattern and texture range is now available, and tiles can look very good in areas such as the bathroom, downstairs cloakroom and dining area. A few years back they would have been considered cold to the feet, but with full central heating, this argument no longer applies.

The tiles are, of course, far heavier than the ceramic tiles for walls, and they need more care in cutting. Special adhesives are also available and, for areas where damp may be encountered, waterproof grouting is available.

Sheet vinyl

As already suggested, vinyl floorcoverings have seen some dramatic changes in recent years. The main change has been the introduction of foamed backings, making the material far warmer to the touch, and enabling the manufacturers to build in texture to the pattern. This textured vinyl is the most popular today.

Also, there is less tendency for the sheet to shrink after laying, though this is a characteristic of vinyl which should be kept in mind. The old linoleums used to stretch as they bedded down; vinyl will try to shrink. So final cutting is best delayed until you are sure what is happening.

The latest vinyls are extremely pliable and it is possible to buy a floorcovering which is as supple as carpet, and can be folded and carried like a carpet. When spread out, all wrinkles will disappear. With the older vinyls, a crease could well remain and be impossible to lose. This new material is obviously easier to lay; particularly in a small room, where the sheet will have to be folded while fitting.

Sheet vinyl can be loose laid and then merely held by an adhesive or a double sided carpet tape just around the edges.

For really hard wear, it can be stuck over-all but this obviously adds problems if you have to lift it. This is particularly the case with foamed backings, as the foam tends to tear away.

Try to avoid joins in foam-backed materials in traffic lanes. The join edges are more prominent because the foam backing flexes.

Carpet

This falls into three main categories for the handyman. The traditional Axminsters and Wiltons with their woven backings, used with a traditional jute or foam underlay. These are available as squares for loose laying, or off the roll for close-carpeting where the carpet must be pulled really tight if it is to look good and wear well.

There is a new family of carpets with a built-in foam underlay where the foam is bonded to the carpet. They offer a new approach to close carpeting as they do not need the same amount of tensioning as the traditional carpeting, and the quality range is greater. There are some very poor carpets produced with the minimum of tufts bonded into a poor backing and, in this field, it is a case of you get what you pay for.

Perhaps it should be added, that carpet laying is quite a skilled job, and if you are buying an expensive carpet where expert free fitting is offered as an incentive to buy, take advantage of the offer. The company will then be responsible for careful measuring and cutting.

Carpet tiles

Another interesting development has been the introducion of carpet tiles. These simplify laying and certainly make cutting and fitting that much easier. There is also the consideration that a room does not need to be completely cleared. Tiles can be laid in one half of the room; furniture moved over, then covering completed in the cleared area.

Obviously the pattern range must be limited, but patterns are available in carpet tiles. At the other end of the scale are the plain tiles with a definite direction of pile. By alternating the pile direction, an interesting squared pattern can be built up.

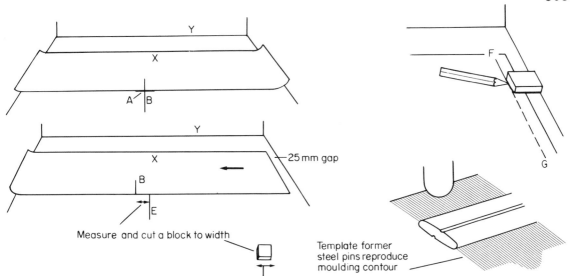

Measure and cut a block to width

How to cut sheet vinyl to fit your floor. The text describes the procedure which should be followed

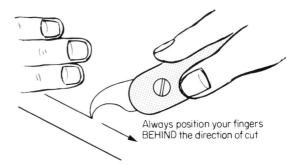

Template former steel pins reproduce moulding contour

Some tiles need to be fixed with tape, but others rely on the pressure of being pushed together to hold them in place, and, with the really shaggy piles, it is impossible to see that the floor consists of tiles. Another bonus of the tiled floor is that should one tile become worn or damaged, it can be lifted and replaced. The great problem inherent in the fitted carpet is that it cannot be moved when areas start to wear.

Always position your fingers BEHIND the direction of cut

Take extreme care when cutting sheet floorcoverings

Laying sheet vinyl

If you can cover the whole floor with one piece of vinyl, do so, for it makes a much more attractive covering. If two pieces are needed, consider carefully where the join will be. If possible, keep the join out of the main traffic areas. Check also to see that the pattern matches correctly and how big the repeat is. Will the pattern still match if a small piece has to be run the other way to fill a space? All these points will influence how much floorcovering you buy.

It is always wise to get the vinyl really warm before starting work. It will be that much easier to handle. Should you encounter a stubborn fold, play the warmth of a hairdryer on the vinyl to further soften it. Do not let anyone walk over folded vinyl, or you may get creases and marks that you cannot do anything about. As mentioned earlier, this does not apply with the new flexible materials.

Fitting sheet material calls for care; particularly in measuring. Remember the old adage—measure twice, cut once. There is nothing more infuriating than cutting a sheet too small.

Use a sharp craft knife and steel straightedge to cut the vinyl about 25 mm (1 in) longer at each end than the required length. This will allow for trimming. Take great care with the knife, always cutting with your hands behind the direction of cut. Never, never cut towards your fingers!

Lay the sheet in place with the extra 25 mm curling up each end wall, as in the illustration. Make sure the edge X is neatly in line with wall Y. Assuming you are working with more than one length, mark the edge of the sheet on the floor at A, then draw a line at right angles to the edge mark, as at B, marking both sheet and floor.

Pull the sheet away from the wall at C so the sheet clears the wall by 25 mm, making sure the sheet still lines up with line A. Now measure the distance between line B on the sheet and the bit of line it left behind at E. Cut a simple block of wood with its width equal to this distance, and use it as a guide to scribe a line FG along the edge of the floor covering. Keep the block in touch with the wall, and it will faithfully reproduce on the vinyl any slight irregularity in the wall. Trim your vinyl to this line, and you will see it now fits neatly to the wall at that end.

Now move to the other end and repeat the process, and the sheet will fit perfectly. Use the same technique for further pieces.

If you are working with a whole sheet, covering the whole floor, you will have to modify the system by marking line B on the far wall instead of on the floor, and it will be harder to ensure you pull the floor-covering back by 25 mm. Be sure to keep edge X against wall Y. Once you have fitted the sheet in one direction, the trimming in the other direction will be easier.

Of course, there will be odd shapes to cut—perhaps around door mouldings or a projecting cupboard. To ensure an accurate fit, make a simple cardboard templet which fits exactly, then transfer this to the vinyl.

For intricate mouldings, there is a useful little tool called a template former. This is a frame, housing dozens of steel pins free to move within the frame. By pressing the pins on to a moulding, it will faithfully reproduce the shape, which can then be drawn on to the floorcovering. When cutting to awkward shapes, always err on the safe side and take off a little less than may be necessary. It is easy to trim a little more off—but impossible to stick a bit back on!

With the covering fitted, secure joints with double-sided carpet tape, or use a latex adhesive.

Laying carpet

Obviously, laying carpet squares is not a problem, but securing a fitted carpet calls for some expertise. The simplest way of fixing is to use special carpet fixing battens which incorporate a series of spikes upon which the carpet can be held. The length of spike varies according to the type of carpet you have to fix, so this is a point to check when buying. The battens will come with instructions as to how far from the wall the batten must be fixed, and how much surplus carpet can be tucked down behind the batten.

The battens are nailed, screwed or glued to the floor according to type, with the teeth projecting towards the wall. Then the underlay is fitted up to, but not over, the battens. It is wise to stretch and anchor the underlay to the floor so it cannot wrinkle. On timber floors, simply pull the underlay taut and tack it down, keeping the tacks about 100 mm (4 in) away from the battens. On concrete floors, use a latex adhesive to hold the underlay in place. Trim any surplus underlay away from the battens so nothing sticks up.

There is a definite technique in hooking carpet on to the pins, and this will be

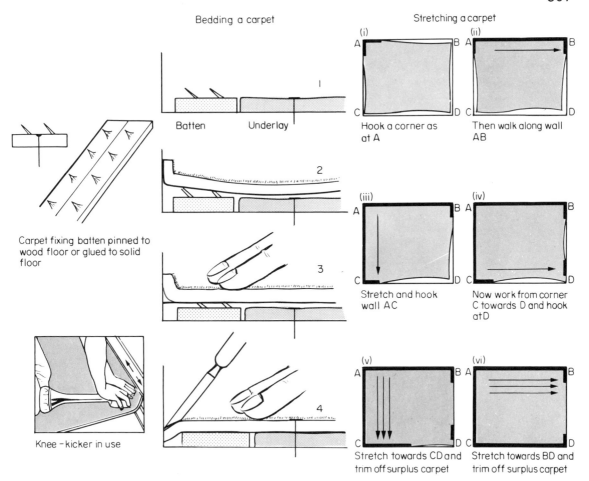

Bedding a carpet

Batten   Underlay

Carpet fixing batten pinned to wood floor or glued to solid floor

Knee-kicker in use

Stretching a carpet

(i) Hook a corner as at A

(ii) Then walk along wall AB

(iii) Stretch and hook wall AC

(iv) Now work from corner C towards D and hook at D

(v) Stretch towards CD and trim off surplus carpet

(vi) Stretch towards BD and trim off surplus carpet

Tips on fitting carpet. However inconvenient, it is wise to lift fitted carpets before decorating. This can be done very easily if the batten method of fitting the carpet has been used

explained in the instructions with the battens, but in the main, the carpet must be eased up the wall about 9 mm (3/8 in), then use your fingers to press the carpet on to the batten. As the spikes start to grip, press the carpet down with an old blunt chisel blade, easing the surplus carpet down behind the batten, but not pressing it right down, or you will find this releases the carpet from the pins at this stage.

Use the same technique to hold the carpet, as illustrated, first at one corner, then along one wall. From this point on, you need the help of a special tool called a knee kicker. This has a spiked pad which grips the carpet, and a padded end which you can push with your knee to apply pressure while leaving both hands free to manipulate the carpet.

This tool applies the necessary pressure to stretch the carpet while you ease the edge over the pins as before—except that this time you will have the natural stretch of the carpet helping you get the carpet on to the pins.

As work progresses, a surplus of carpet will be forced up at least two walls, and once the carpet is correctly stretched, the surplus can be trimmed with a sharp knife, and the remaining edges eased down behind the battens to give a very neat finish.

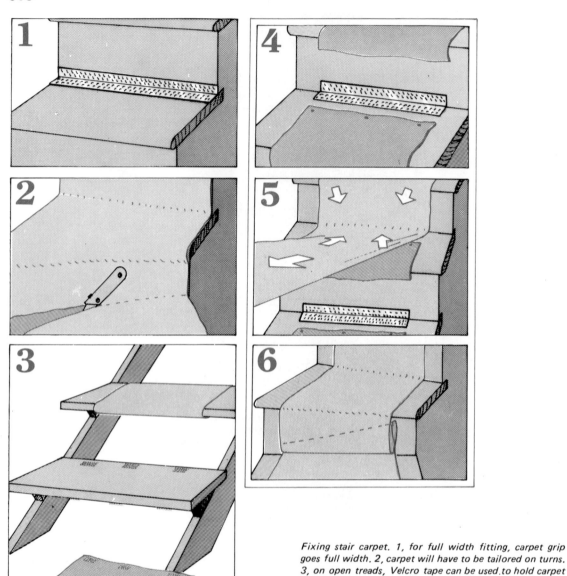

Fixing stair carpet. 1, for full width fitting, carpet grip goes full width. 2, carpet will have to be tailored on turns. 3, on open treads, Velcro tape can be used to hold carpet pads in place. 4, on narrower carpet make sure that the grip strips and underfelt will not show. 5, this is how to press the carpet on to the grip teeth. 6, on turns, carpet can be folded as shown and tucked under at the riser

To make a neat finish at doorways, special edging bars are available. These can be single bars for just hiding the carpet edge, or they may be in the form of a double bar to match up with an adjoining carpet. There are also edging bars which will combine carpet and vinyl floorcovering.

Laying staircarpets

The same kind of spiked grip offers an ideal way of holding stair carpet, though for stairs the grip has a different shape. It incorporates an angled bar with teeth facing into the angle. The bars are screwed in place in the angle of each tread, each being just a fraction short of the carpet

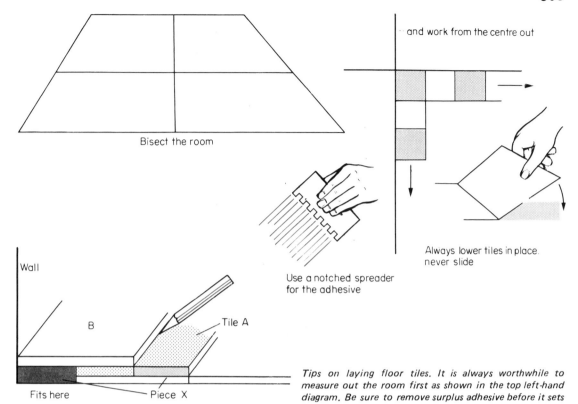

Bisect the room

and work from the centre out

Use a notched spreader
for the adhesive

Always lower tiles in place.
never slide

Wall

B

Tile A

Fits here   Piece X

*Tips on laying floor tiles. It is always worthwhile to
measure out the room first as shown in the top left-hand
diagram. Be sure to remove surplus adhesive before it sets*

width. Then the stair treads should be
pinned in place using carpet tacks. You
need only tack at the edge nearest the grip.
Allow the other edge to lay free over the
stair nosing.

Now lay the carpet down the stairs
with the correct amount left at the top,
then ease the carpet into the first grip.
Keep the carpet taut and ease it into the
next grip—and so on down the stairs. At
the turn, the carpet can be folded and
tacked as shown to lose the surplus. This
assumes that one day you will want to lift
the carpet and re-position it to spread the
wear. Similarly, any surplus at the bottom
can be folded and pinned to the last stair
riser.

With the tendency for full width fitted
carpet on stairs, it is common practice to
cut the carpet and tailor each piece to fit.
This certainly gives a very neat result, but

it does mean that carpet cannot be re-
positioned as it starts to wear.

The open tread staircase presents yet
another problem—that of holding a pad
neatly, yet firmly in place. There are two
main methods you can use. First, special
carpet press studs which are designed to
screw into the treads for one half, while
the other half is sewn to the underside of
the carpet. The second method makes use
of a special tape called Velcro. This consists
of two tapes, one of which is covered with
thousands of tiny hooks, while the other
has thousands of loops. When pressed
together the hooks engage the loops, and
the two tapes will not part unless ripped
apart.

One half of the tape is glued to the stair
tread, while its mating tape is stuck to the
underside of the carpet. This results in a
very neat job which does not involve
drilling into the treads.

Floor tiles

As has already been suggested, laying tiles does not present so many hazards as laying sheet materials. The first job is to find the centre of the room by measuring then using the chalk line to snap marks on the floor. You can then work from the intersection of the lines outwards.

Most tile companies supply a useful squared paper on which you can mark the size of your room, and the proposed pattern. From this you can calculate just how many tiles of each design you need. It will also act as a guide when you lay the tiles. Many plain tiles have a grain pattern added, and it is best to run the grain of each tile at right angles to its neighbours.

Apply adhesive to a small area of floor and press the tiles on to the adhesive. Do not slide them in place or you will force adhesive up between the tiles. If any comes on to the surface of the tiles, wipe it off while wet. Laying is simple until you reach the borders of the room, when it will be necessary to trim tiles to fit. The diagram on page 509 shows an accurate way of doing this.

To cut a perfect fit, lay tile A on top of one of the last full row of tiles. Then slide B over A until it comes into contact with the wall. Now mark the edge of tile B on tile A. Cut tile A, and you will find piece X fits the gap perfectly. Continue cutting until the border is complete.

Most floor tiling can be done in this way, but there is an exception with loose laid floor tiles. These are laid from a wall surface out so that tiles can be placed under pressure. This will be explained on the pack, and it applies in the main to certain types of carpet tile, particularly in the upper price bracket.

When cutting tiles to fit around mouldings or other projections, the same technique is used as for sheet materials, and again the tool mentioned earlier, called a template former, is useful.

Chapter 58
Wood-finishing

We have talked a great deal about decorative finishes which involve a covering-up process, but there are cases where the natural beauty of an item, such as a timber door, needs to be seen and not hidden. This involves different decorating techniques.

These techniques are gaining more popularity as it is realised that natural finishing joinery calls for less work initially and far less maintenance in the future. What is needed, however, is good quality work in the first place, for poor joints and bad cracks cannot be hidden beneath a dense coat of paint. They will be on show for all to see.

Preparing the timber

Before any timber surface can be finished, it must be stripped back to bare wood, removing all old primer and surface filler. If the wood is discoloured, it may be possible to start again by using a wood bleach. These are still available from companies which specialise in woodfinishing products. Then, when clean, the timber should be rubbed smooth with a fine glasspaper, working with the wood grain to prevent surface scratches.

Any holes and gaps are filled with a wood stopping of similar colour. If the wood is to be stained, it is essential that the filler you use will in fact take the stain too. For example, filling a crack in whitewood with putty would give a well hidden repair until a dark stain were applied. Then, the stain would soak in the timber but be rejected by the oily putty, leaving a whitish mark.

Creosote and other stains

For external use, there is a wide range of stains, most of which are incorporated in preservatives. Creosote is probably the best known one, and this is still widely used for fencing of all kinds, and for sheds and other timber buildings. Its only disadvantages are that during its drying it can stain clothing, and it can burn plants with which it may come into contact.

Also, there is little colour variety, whereas in other proprietary ranges a colour card can be offered, giving good imitations of a whole range of wood colours from pine to mahogany.

Other stains offer a pigmented range which have yet to really catch on in this country. Yellows, and oranges through to black can be offered, all of which colour and preserve at the same time.

For staining joinery there are three main types available. Water-based, methylated-spirit-based and oil-based. The water and spirit stains are usually sold as crystals, and they have the disadvantage that they cause the grain of the wood to swell. This means more rubbing down after the stain is dry. The water-based stain is popular with beginners because if too dark a colour is used, it can be lightened by rubbing with a damp rag. The most popular types of stain are the oil-based ones. They have good penetration, are quick drying and do not raise the wood grain.

Apart from normal stains, a whole range of polyurethane finishes incorporating stains is available. These colour and decorate in one process, and they have become very popular in recent years for whitewood furniture. These finishes are also available in large aerosol cans.

For Western red cedar, there are special stain preservatives which restore something of the natural colour of the wood. The warm glow of new cedar can soon be changed to grey with weathering.

Wood finishes

Now a brief word on finishes available.

French polish is still available in simplified form for amateur use, but it is seldom used by furniture manufacturers. It has the advantage that drying time is quick but you do need a fair bit of practice to produce a good finish. It is also easily marked by heat, solvents and abrasion, and it does not like damp. It is better to use one of the products mentioned below.

Polyurethanes

These come in three main types; two-pack, moisture cured and air drying. The first is not widely used by amateurs, but is quite widely used in the furniture trade because of its durability. The moisture-cured types give a good durable surface, but drying time can vary considerably, as this depends on the moisture content of the air.

The most popular is the air-drying type, available as a high gloss, satin or matt finish. This gives a hard finish with good resistance to water, solvents and abrasion, but does not produce a mirror-like gloss expected by the professional furniture maker.

Two-part cold cure lacquers

This is a resin-based material to which a hardener is added as the material is required. It produces a very hard non-yellowing finish which is ideal for surfaces like table tops, which must be able to withstand hard wear.

Linseed oil

This material, like distemper, is best omitted from the range you plan to use —even though it has always been looked upon as a traditional finish for items like natural timber doors. Raw linseed oil takes days to dry, gathering dust in the process, and boiled linseed oil, while drying faster, goes gummy and dark with age.

It is far better to use one of the proprietary teak oils as these are reinforced with resins and other oils to give a more effective and durable finish to timber. If you encounter a nice door coated linseed oil, strip it back to bare wood before redecorating.

Waxes

With the wide range of materials available today, it is best not to use wax as a decorative finish. Once applied to bare wood, few materials will take over the top. Also, as the film is soft, it tends to pick up dust and dirt. Its best use is as a final polish over a surface decorated with a polyurethane seal.

Choice of finish

Many of the products referred to above may have interior and exterior grades available. So if you have a particular job in mind, check to see whether your choice is suitable. For example, weatherboarding would need a really good exterior grade polyurethane— or perhaps better still a good oil varnish. Yacht varnish still needs a lot of beating when it comes to durability.

With all exterior work, it is vital to see that all surfaces of the timber are protected with finish—and particularly the end grain. If water can find a way behind your protective coating, it will often push the new finish off. Damp wood expands, and the expansion alone can break down the toughest of finishes.

Chapter 59
Wrinkles and tips

These are the ideas which may be picked up through experience—either your own or those you come into contact with. Add your own to the list! Some of these tips have been mentioned previously but have been brought together here for convenience.

If paint has to be stored, cut a circle of foil and float it on the surface of the paint before closing the tin. This will keep the air away from the paint.

With small quantities of paint left in large tins, transfer the paint to a screw top jar which it fills, and mark the jar. Never, never turn a tin upside down. You merely end up with a skin on the bottom instead of the top.

To strain paint, use clean nylon stocking (or tights). Fix a piece around the can lid and push the stocking into the paint. You can then pick up strained paint from inside the stocking.

For applying very messy adhesives to small areas, make up a simple brush from coarse string pushed through a short piece of copper piping. The frayed string acts as bristles which can be cut off as they are spoiled.

If you use a paintbrush for dusting off, be sure to mark it for that purpose. Do not use it to paint.

Before you start papering, write on the wall the number of rolls you had to use and how much of other materials the room used. (you can adjust your figures before the last piece goes up if necessary) This will be useful when next the room is decorated.

If you have to patch wallpaper, always tear the patch—do not cut it out with scissors as this produces a hard edge. Learn to tear so you get a feathered edge under the pattern of the paper.

Wherever paper creases through a fault in the wall surface, tear the paper—do not cut it. This way you can disguise the remedy.

Always wipe wet paste from rails and skirtings as you work. It saves time spent afterwards trying to soften dry paste.

Store brushes overnight in cooking foil. Load the brush with paint then wrap it up tightly. It will be ready for use next day. While storing in water does omit air, it can cause swelling of the brush and rusting of the ferrule.

After using brush cleaner, let the sediment settle then drain off the remaining cleaner. This can be used again.

Soften old brushes by suspending them in paint stripper. You may need to work the brush a number of times to allow the stripper to get right into the bristles.

In order to economise on brush cleaner, pour a little in a sound plastic bag. Insert the brush head, secure the mouth of the bag with an elastic band, then work the bristles through the bag.

When suspending a brush in cleaner, drill a hole through the handle and push a piece

514

of wire through. Rest the wire on the jar. Never rest the bristles on the base of the jar. It deforms them.

When painting inside a pipe (not often necessary) wrap a heavy stone in old towelling, tie it to a length of string, and mould the towel to the internal diameter of the pipe. Pour some paint on the towelling and work it up and down in the pipe.

Do not seal the joins between lengths of down-pipe. These joints act as tell-tales if the pipe gets blocked. You can tell at which point the blockage has occurred. If you block them there is no way of telling.

Always secure a ladder base so that it cannot slip when you climb up. If possible anchor it at the top. Never lean off a ladder, and beware of plastic guttering. It is strong enough to take a ladder but is far more slippery than cast iron.

When moving cast iron guttering, get help. Rope the guttering so it can be lowered easily. The weight can very easily throw you off balance.

Never stand a ladder on soft soil. Stand it on a board, and weight the ladder so it can't move off the board.

Clean up paint splashes on tiles and paths as you go. It comes off so much easier than dry paint. Protect border plants and flowers from splashes—especially from masonry paints.

Take care with blowtorches—especially out of doors. The flame can be invisible in bright sunlight. Keep it out of eaves where there may be nests. Avoid open windows, and always take down curtains.

Protect your eyes when working with wire brushes, grinding wheels or chemicals such as paint stripper. Also, when cutting or dressing stone.

Always have adequate ventilation when using materials such as flooring adhesives which produce fumes. Ventilate all clothing used, and avoid naked lights and pilot lights.

Do not have paper on the floor when using a blowtorch for paint stripping. Have a bucket handy in which you can drop burning paint.

Be sure to shake aerosols well before use to mix in any sediment which could clog the valve. Always up-end the can after use and press until only solvent appears. This cleans the jet. Never puncture old aerosols, and do not throw them on a bonfire.

Never use sheet or tile vinyls straight in from the cold. Let them warm up and become pliable. They will be so much easier to handle.

Never have rooms over-warm when decorating. It can speed up drying times of adhesives and paints to the point where you get problems.

When drilling holes in tiles, use your slowest drill speed. A piece of adhesive tape stuck on the tile will help the drill tip make a start without wandering.

Do not try to chip concrete from surfaces like brick or tile. You will probably damage them. Get the solution that builders use for dissolving concrete on tools. It will remove the concrete without affecting the under-surface.

To lift old vinyl tiles, lay a piece of cooking foil over the tile and apply a hot iron. The heat with soften the vinyl and probably the adhesive below, allowing you to pull the tile away. Use a hot scraper to remove any residue of adhesive from the floor.

Remove scuff marks from vinyl floor-coverings and parquet with a very fine wire wool dipped in turps substitute. Rub lightly until the marks disappear. On parquet, only work with the wood grain to avoid scratches.

CHART FOR ESTIMATING WALLCOVERING

Measurement round walls, including doors and windows. The figures in the columns below give the number of rolls required

(ft)	28	32	36	40	44	48	52	56	60	64	68	72	76	80	84	88	92	96	100
Ceiling height(m)	8·53	9·75	10·97	12·19	13·41	14·63	15·85	17·07	18·29	19·51	20·73	21·95	23·16	24·28	25·60	26·82	18·04	29·26	30·48
2·13—2·29 m	4	4	5	5	6	6	7	7	8	8	9	9	9	10	10	11	11	12	12
2·30—2·44	4	4	5	5	6	6	7	8	8	9	9	10	10	11	11	12	12	13	13
2·45—2·59	4	5	5	6	6	7	7	8	8	9	9	10	10	11	12	13	13	13	14
2·60—2·74	4	5	5	6	6	7	7	8	9	9	10	11	11	12	12	13	13	14	14
2·75—2·90	4	5	6	6	7	7	8	9	9	10	10	11	12	13	13	14	14	15	15
2·91—3·05	5	5	6	7	7	8	9	9	10	10	11	12	12	13	14	14	15	15	16
3·06—3·20	5	5	6	7	8	8	9	10	10	11	12	12	13	14	14	18	16	16	17
3·21—3·35	5	6	7	7	8	9	9	10	11	11	12	13	13	14	15	16	16	17	18
3·36—3·50	5	6	7	8	8	9	10	10	11	12	13	13	14	15	16	16	17	18	18

CHART FOR ESTIMATING ROLLS REQUIRED FOR CEILINGS

Ceilings	Measurement in metres round room	Number of rolls	Measurement in metres round room	Number of rolls	Measurement in metres round room	Number of rolls	Measurement in metres round room	Number of rolls
	11.0	2	16.0	4	21.0	6	26.0	9
	12.0	2	17.0	4	22.0	7	27.0	10
	13.0	3	18.0	5	23.0	7	28.0	10
	14.0	3	19.0	5	24.0	8	29.0	11
	15.0	4	20.0	5	25.0	8	30.0	11

FOR YOUR REFERENCE

A great deal of decorating time can be saved if you have at your fingertips information concerning the quantities of materials you will need. It will also ensure that you order just what you require—not too much or too little.

Use the following pages to keep an accurate account of the materials used in various locations, and details of room, window and door sizes.

Apart from the obvious details required, space has been left for any particular points you may wish to record: cables buried in walls for wall lights, boards which lift to reveal cable runs or gas points, location of stop taps, drain cocks, junction boxes, fuse boxes. In fact any reference which may be needed at some future date.

Do not be bound by the headings given; add your own extra ones as needed—and use the squared paper to mark out areas, choosing a scale to suit your rooms. For most rooms, one square can represent 1 ft or 30 cm.

HOUSE EXTERIOR

Gutter lengths:			amount of paint:		
Downpipe lengths: Window sizes: types (metal/wood/casement/sash)			amount of paint:		
Door sizes: Patio door size: Wall areas for each wall face (N.S.E.W) amount of paint required per coat					

Garage size:
    window sizes:
    door sizes and type (make)
 	
Details of fuse boxes in garage
    fuse ratings:
    consumer unit fuse ratings:
 	
Number of socket outlets:					

LOUNGE AND DINING ROOM

Floor area: 　floorcovering type:			amount needed:		
Wall area (total) 　wallcovering type: 　amount of wall paint:			no. of rolls: (bear in mind pattern repeat and pattern size)		
Ceiling area: 　amount of paint: 　number of ceiling tiles: 　amount of ceiling paper used: Radiator types: Socket outlets: (single):	size: number: (double):		sizes:		
Window sizes: 　curtain track lengths: 　amount of curtain material: 　no. of curtains made: 　net curtain sizes:			type of track:		
Lighting: 　wattage of lamps required Problem areas, special points to note:					

KITCHEN

Floor area: 　floorcovering type:			amount needed:		
Wall area (total) 　wallcovering type: 　amount of wall paint:			no. of rolls: (bear in mind pattern repeat and pattern size)		
Ceiling area: 　amount of paint: 　number of ceiling tiles: 　amount of ceiling paper used: Radiator types:	sizes: number:	sizes:			
Socket outlets: (single):	(double):				
Window sizes: 　curtain track lengths: 　amount of curtain material: 　no. of curtains made: 　net curtain sizes: Lighting: 　wattage of lamps required:			type of track:		
Appliances: (a) (b) (c) (d) (e) Boiler type:	ref. number:		guarantee number service period:		
Problem areas, special points to note:					

BATHROOM, CLOAKROOM

Floor area: floorcovering type:			amount needed:		

Wall area (total)
   wallcovering type:
   amount of wall paint:
			no. of rolls:
			(bear in mind pattern repeat
			and pattern size)		

Ceiling area:
   amount of paint:
   number of ceiling tiles:
   amount of ceiling paper used:
	sizes:				

Radiator types: Socket outlets:	number: (single):	sizes: (double):			

Window sizes:
   curtain track lengths:
   amount of curtain material:
   no. of curtains made:
   net curtain sizes:
			type of track:		

Lighting: wattage of lamps required: Problem areas, special points to note:					

HALL AND STAIRWAY

Floor area:
  floorcovering type: amount needed:

Wall area (total)
  wallcovering type: no. of rolls:
  amount of wall paint: (bear in mind pattern repeat
                                         and pattern size)

Ceiling area:
  amount of paint:
  number of ceiling tiles: sizes:
  amount of ceiling paper used:

Radiator types: number: sizes:

Socket outlets: (single):   (double):

Window sizes:
  curtain track lengths: type of track:
  amount of curtain material:
  no. of curtains made:
  net curtain sizes:

Lighting:
  wattage of lamps required:

Number of stairs: length of stair carpet:
Hall carpet size:
Landing carpet size:
Thermostat setting:
Problem areas, special points to note:

BEDROOMS

Main bedroom: Floor area: floorcovering type:			amount needed:		

Wall area (total)
  wallcovering type:
    amount of wall paint:
			no. of rolls:
			(bear in mind pattern repeat
			and pattern size)		

Ceiling area:
   amount of paint:
   number of ceiling tiles:
   amount of ceiling paper used:
 	
Radiator types:
	sizes:
	
	number:
		sizes:			

Socket outlets:
 	
Window sizes:
   curtain track lengths:
   amount of curtain material:
   no. of curtains made:
   net curtain sizes:
 	
Lighting:
   wattage of lamps required:
	(single):	(double):
		
		type of track:			

Problem areas, special points to note: Use of following squared page(s) to provide similar details for other bedrooms, extensions or loft rooms.					

OTHER BEDROOMS

Index